Organizing editor

Robin Keeley

Consulting editors

The Rev. Dr. Donald English	Chairman, World Methodist Council
Dr. Gabriel Fackre	Abbot Professor of Christian Theology, Andover Newton Theological School, Massachusetts, USA
Dr. Dick France	Principal, Wycliffe Hall Theological College, Oxford, England
Bishop David M. Gitari	Bishop of Kirinyaga, Kenya
The Rev. J. Andrew Kirk	Dean of Mission, Selly Oak Colleges, Birmingham, England
Dr. Bruce J. Nicholls	formerly Presbyter, Church of North India, New Delhi
The Rev. Dr. James I. Packer	Professor of Historical and Systematic Theology, Regent College, Vancouver, Canada
Dr. C. Rene Padilla	General Secretary, Latin American Theological Fraternity, Buenos Aires, Argentina

Exploring the Christian Faith

Includes Contributions from

J. I. PACKER • GRANT R. OSBORN
COLIN BROWN AND MANY OTHERS

THOMAS NELSON PUBLISHERS
Nashville • Atlanta • London • Vancouver

First North American edition published in 1996 by Thomas Nelson Publishers, Nashville, Tennessee.

Library of Congress Cataloging-in-Publication Data

Exploring the Christian faith.
Introduction to the Christian faith / includes contributions from J. I. Packer, Colin Brown, Grant R. Osborne, and many others.
p. cm. — (Nelson's Christian cornerstone series)
Originally published: An introduction the Christian faith. Oxford, England : Lynx, 1992.
Includes index.
ISBN 0-7852-1150-0 (pbk.)
1. Theology. Doctrinal—Popular works. 2. Apologetics. I. Packer, J. I. (James Innell) II. Brown, Colin, 1932- . III. Osborne, Grant R. IV. Title. V. Series.
BT77.I57 1996
230—dc20 95-47100
CIP

Printed and bound in the United States of America
1 2 3 4 5 — 00 99 98 97 96

Preface

Christianity is faith in Jesus Christ. In every generation since Jesus' time, people have based their lives on certain beliefs about him. Today, millions of people from every continent are motivated by the same faith.

So what is this faith? What do Christians believe? This book gives a clear and comprehensive account of Christian belief. It is not a systematic theology. It is an introduction, geared to help the reader see the whole sweep of the faith. Its particular aim is as a textbook for students, at home or at college—all who want to understand the Christian faith more deeply and fully.

The sequence of the themes in this textbook follows the order in which people commonly come to them. After a short introductory section on the points at which Christianity touches our lives, we start straight in with Jesus Christ: who he was and what he taught. This is many people's starting-point; they are attracted to Jesus and want to follow him. Then we backtrack to God, whom Jesus called Father. From there we move to God's creation of the universe and of humanity in it. Law, society, culture, science, the arts, the environment . . . so much depends on our understanding of God's good creation.

But this world is also fallen. Its harmony is marred, its potential spoiled. So God came in Jesus to make a new creation, to reconcile people to himself and renew them by his Spirit. The last part looks at this good news and all that follows from it—a new life, a new community and a restored hope.

There is also a supplementary section on the key thinkers and movements who have shaped Christian belief over the centuries, together with a glossary and a full index.

Christian belief is a complete structure, to be seen as a whole. Each belief depends on the others. This is why studying one particular doctrine without knowing the whole pattern can bring a danger of distortion, and hence the need for a complete introduction like this, to cover the whole range of beliefs.

For this new edition of what was originally entitled *The Lion Handbook of Christian Belief*, lists of Bible references have been added at the end of main chapters, together with questions for further thinking. Margin quotations also add to the interest.

The articles have been written by an international team of contributors drawn from twenty countries. They have aimed to describe each belief simply and accurately, showing how it has developed over the centuries. The articles explain different viewpoints but focus on mainstream Christianity, true to the Bible.

No one lives without beliefs. We all believe something, have some view of what life means. And what we believe affects us deeply; in a real sense we are what we believe. So 'doctrine' and belief are not something to be left to the theorists or the experts. Our understanding of Christianity, and our response to it, will be the most crucial thing in our whole lives.

Contents

Contributors

Dr Tokunboh Adeyemo, General Secretary, Association of Evangelicals of Africa and Madagascar, Nairobi, Kenya.

Sir Norman Anderson, formerly Professor of Oriental Laws and Director of the Institute of Advanced Legal Studies, University of London, England.

The Rev. Dr David Atkinson, Fellow and Chaplain, Corpus Christi College, Oxford, England.

Professor James Atkinson, formerly Professor of Biblical Studies, University of Sheffield, England.

Dr Robert Banks, Homer L. Goddard Professor of the Ministry of the Laity, Fuller Theological Seminary, Pasadena, California, United States.

Jerram Barrs, Associate Professor of Christianity and Contemporary Culture, Covenant Theological Seminary, St Louis, Unite States.

Professor Marguerite Baude, Teacher of Philosophy, Lycée Marcel Pagnol, Marseille, France.

The Rev. Dr Paul Beasley-Murray, Principal, Spurgeons College, London, England.

The late Professor E.M. Blaiklock, formerly Emeritus Professor of Classics, University of Auckland, New Zealand.

Professor Henri Blocher, Head of the Department of Systematic Theology, Faculty of Evangelical Theology, Vaux-sur-Seine, France.

Dr Gerald Bray, Lecturer in Historical Theology, Oak Hill Theological College, London, England.

The Rev. Dr Colin Brown, Professor of Systematic Theology, Fuller Theological Seminary, Pasadena, California, USA.

The Right Rev. Colin Buchanan, Vicar, St Mark, Gillingham, England.

The Rev. Chris Byworth, Rector, Fazakerley, Liverpool, England.

The Right Rev. Dr George Carey, Archbishop of Canterbury, England.

Dr D. A. Carson, Professor of New Testament, Trinity Evangelical Divinity School, Deerfield, Illinois, USA.

Michael Cassidy, Team Leader, Africa Enterprise, Pietermaritzburg, South Africa.

The Rev. P. T. Chandapilla, formerly General Secretary, Federation of Evangelical Churches of India, Madras, India.

The Rev. Colin Chapman, Principal, Crowther Hall, Selly Oak, Birmingham, England.

The Rev. Canon Julian Charley, Vicar, Malvern Priory, England.

Myra Chave-Jones, formerly Director, Care and Counsel, London, England.

Paul Clowney, Director, Project Development Services Ltd, London, England.

Dr Peter Cotterell, Principal, London Bible College, Northwood, England.

The Rev. R. E. Davies, Senior Tutor, All Nations Christian College, Ware, England.

Dr John Drane, Lecturer in Religious Studies, University of Stirling, Scotland.

Joni Eareckson-Tada, Artist and writer, California, United States.

Professor Jacques Ellul, formerly Professor of Law, University of Bordeaux, France.

The Rev. Robert G. England, Assistant Master, Regent House Grammar School, Newtownards, Northern Ireland.

The Rev. Dr Donald English, Chairman, World Methodist Council.

Samuel Escobar, Professor of Mission, Eastern Baptist Seminary, Philadelphia, United States.

Ruth Etchells, formerly Principal, St John's College with Cranmer Hall,

University of Durham, England.

Dr Dick France, Principal, Wycliffe Hall Theological College, Oxford, England.

The Rev. R. F. R. Gardner, formerly Senior Consultant Obstetrician and Gynaecologist, Sunderland District General Hospital, England.

The Rev David Gillet, Principal, Trinity College, Bristol, England.

Bishop David M. Gitari, Bishop of Kirinyaga, Kenya.

The Very Rev. John Gladwin, Provost of Sheffield, England.

Martin Goldsmith, Lecturer in Christian Mission, All Nations Christian College, Ware, England.

The Rev. Patrick J. Goodland, Minister, Gorsley Baptist Church, Ross-on-Wye, England.

The Rev. Dr D. A. Hagner, Associate Professor of New Testament, Fuller Theological Seminary, Pasadena, California, USa.

Paul Helm, Senior Lecturer in Philosophy, University of Liverpool, England

The Rev. Dr Alasdair Heron, Professor of Reformed Theology, University of Erlangen, Germany.

Dr. James Houston, Professor of Spiritual Theology, Regent College, Vancouver, Canada.

Dr B. N. Kaye, Chancellor, New College, Sydney, Australia.

The Rev. Derek Kidner, formerly Warden of Tyndale House Centre for Biblical Research, Cambridge, England.

The Rev. J. Andrew Kirk, Dean of Mission, Selly Oak Colleges, Birmingham, England.

Dr Peter Kuzmic, Director, Biblical Theology Institute, Osijek, Croatia.

Tony Lane, Lecturer in Historical Theology, London Bible College, Northwood, England.

Anne C. Long, Christian counsellor, England.

Dr David Lyon, Professor of Sociology, Queens University, Kingston, Ontario, Canada.

John McInnes, Industrial Chaplain, Wellington, New Zealand.

Vishal Mangalwadi, General Secretary, TRACEE, New Delhi, India.

Professor I. Howard Marshall, Professor of New Testament Exegesis, University of Aberdeen, Scotland.

Alistair F. Mason, Lecturer in Theology, Leeds University, England.

Professor A. J. Meadows, Dean of Science, of Science, University of Loughborough, England.

The Rev. Dr R. W. L. Moberly, Reader in Biblical Studies, University of Durham, England.

Professor Gabriel Mützenberg, Professor of History, College Rousseau, Geneva, Switzerland.

The Right Rev. Michael Nazir-Ali, General Secretary, Church Missionary Society, England.

The late Bishop Stephen Neill, formerly writer and teacher in Christian Missions, Oxford, England.

Bishop Lesslie Newbigin, Convenor of Gospel and our Culture Group, Selly Oak, Birmingham, England.

Dr Bruce J. Nicholls, formerly Presbyter, Church of North India, New Delhi.

Dr Agne Nordlander, Principal, Johannelunds Theological Seminary, Senior Lecturer in Theology, Uppsala University, Sweden.

Dr Grant R. Osborne, Associate Professor of New Testament, Trinity Evangelical Divinity School, Deerfield, Illinois, United States.

Deaconess June Osborne, St Mark, Old Ford, London, England.

The Rev. Gottfried Osei-Mensah, formerly Executive Secretary, Lausanne Committee for World Evangelization, London, England.

The Rev. Dr James I. Packer, Professor of Historical and Systematic Theology, Regent College, Vancouver, Canada.

Dr C. Rene Padilla, General Secretary, Latin American Theological Fraternity, Buenos Aires, Argentina.

The late Rev. Jim Punton, formerly

Education and Training Officer, Frontier Youth Trust, London, England.

The Right Rev. Gavin Reid, Bishop of Maidstone, England.

Dr Klaas Runia, Professor of Practical Theology, Theological Seminary of the Reformed Churches, Kampen, Netherlands.

Robert Sabath, Member of the Sojourners Fellowship, Washington, DC, United States.

The Rev. Vinay Samuel, Executive Secretary, International Fellowship of Mission Theologians, Bangalore, India.

The Rev. Dr Joh. Heinrich Schmid, Lecturer in Systematic Theology, University of Bern, Switzerland.

The Rev. Dr David Seccombe, Rector, St Matthew's Church, Shenton Park, Western Australia.

Professor Ronald Sider, Associate Professor of Theology, Eastern Baptist Theological Seminary, Philadelphia, United States.

The late Rev. Hugh Silvester, formerly Rector, Holy Trinity Church, Platt, Manchester, England.

The Rev. Thomas A. Smail, Rector, Sanderstead, England.

Howard A. Snyder, Author, Chicago, Illinois, United States.

The late Canon J. Stafford Wright, formerly Principal, Tyndale Hall, Bristol, England.

Morris Stuart, Pastor/Teacher, Truth and Liberation Concern, Melbourne, Australia.

The Rev. Chris Sugden, Director, Oxford Centre for Mission Studies, England.

The Right Rev. S. W. Sykes, Bishop of Ely, England.

The Rev. Professor Anthony Thiselton, Professor of Biblical Studies, University of Nottingham, England.

The Rev. Tite Tienou, Professor of Theology and Missiology, Alliance Theological Seminary, Nyack, New York, United States.

The Rev. Dr Peter Toon, William Adams Professor of Theology, Neshotah House Episcopal Seminary, Neshotah, Wisconsin, United States.

Professor James B. Torrance, formerly Professor of Systematic Theology, King's College, University of Aberdeen, Scotland.

The Rev. Julian W. Ward, Lecturer, Elim Bible College, Nantwich, England.

The Rev. John Wenham, formerly Warden, Latimer House Centre for Theological Research, Oxford, England.

Dr R. A. Whitacre, Director of Greek Studies, Gordon-Conwell Theological Seminary, Massachusetts, United States.

The Rev. Dr B. R. White, Principal, Regent's Park College, Oxford, England.

The Rev. Dr Christopher J. H. Wright, Director of Studies, All Nations Christian College, England.

David F. Wright, Senior Lecturer in Ecclesiastical History, New College, University of Edinburgh, Scotland.

How Can We Know?

PART

CHAPTER 1

COLIN CHAPMAN

Where Do We Start?

> There will be no major solution to the suffering of mankind until we reach some understanding of who we are, what the purpose of creation was, what happens after death. Until these questions are resolved we are caught.
>
> *Woody Allen*

There are at least five possible starting-points for our study of Christian belief. The particular point at which we choose to begin will depend on what we already believe or how we think about any kind of religious beliefs.

If we start with **the Christian world-view**, this means considering the most basic beliefs about God, humankind and the universe, since they provide the framework within which all other Christian beliefs need to be understood.

If we start with **the Jesus of history**, we come face to face with the person Christians believe was both man and God.

If we start with **the Bible**, we are looking at the source from which all Christian beliefs are derived, and the final authority which determines what a Christian believes.

If we start with the **creeds of the churches**, we are dealing with short statements which have stood the test of time. They summarize the essential beliefs of all Christians, both past and present.

If we start with **reason**, we need to decide what part it should play in Christian belief.

The Christian world-view

Each of us, whether we are aware of it or not, has a world-view—that is, a particular way of looking at the world.

The most basic things about the Christian world-view can be summed up in the following way:

- The universe has not always existed, and it will not exist for ever in its present form.
- The universe has not come into being by chance; it was created by a personal God and is continually held in being by him.
- People have much in common with the animals, but are unique because they have been created to enjoy a special relationship with their Creator.

These beliefs were accepted without question by the vast majority of people in the Western world for many centuries. In the last 200 years, however, they have either been quietly ignored and forgotten, or openly challenged and rejected. This means that for most people in the West, the Creator-God of traditional Christian belief has become more and more remote, and the Christian way of looking at the universe can no longer be taken for granted.

Many Western readers may therefore have to begin by studying Christian beliefs about God, humankind and the universe, since without this essential framework other Christian beliefs, such as those about Jesus Christ, may not be understood. Many Eastern readers may need to begin at this point, too, though for different reasons. Hindus, for example, find it almost impossible to make a sharp distinction between 'God' and the universe. They link 'God' so closely with the universe that they cannot think of him as a personal Being who created it all. The Buddhist seems to say in one breath 'there is no personal God', but in the next breath 'we cannot possibly know'. Both the Hindu and the Buddhist, therefore, will find it hard to appreciate the claims that Christians make for Jesus Christ unless they have understood the basic Christian conviction that we live in a created universe in which something has gone seriously wrong. If this is your best starting-point, try the section on *Creation: humanity and the world.*

The Jesus of history

Here is a man who lived only to the age of about thirty-four or thirty-eight. He was born in a small provincial town in Palestine, and never travelled more than a hundred miles from the place where he was born. He did not write any books. He spent most of his working life as a carpenter. During his last three years he travelled round the country, doing good and teaching. He was betrayed by one of his inner circle of students. After being condemned as a heretic and a potential political activist, he was tortured to death.

Yet one of his followers was making

TONY LANE

The Place of Tradition

'Tradition' comes from a word meaning 'to hand over'. Whenever the Christian faith is passed on from one person to another, there is tradition in action. A sermon in church, a book read at home, notes used for help in Bible reading, sharing one's faith with a friend—all of these are tradition in action. Tradition can also happen without words. The way Christians live is one means by which they pass on their faith.

Tradition and the Bible

In the very earliest church, before the New Testament was gathered together, the Christian message was conveyed solely by tradition. But in due course the Christian Scriptures were collected together and seen as the 'New Testament', which posed the question, how did they relate to tradition? In the first few centuries it was simply assumed that the New Testament and the tradition handed down from the apostles were in perfect agreement. By and large this was true.

In the Middle Ages, however, the practice arose of using 'tradition' to justify beliefs not found in the Bible—about the Virgin Mary, for example. This brought a strong reaction from the Reformers—in fact one of the main Reformation teachings was that all tradition must be tested by the Bible. They were far from despising tradition; on the contrary they had a high regard for the early church fathers and for the creeds of the church. But all such authorities, however venerable, were to be measured by the yardstick of God's word in the Bible. The Roman Catholic Church, on the other hand, continued to maintain the authority of traditions which they claimed were handed down from the apostles. But the majority of these supposedly apostolic traditions were manifestly later in origin, and in practice traditions were only accepted if they accorded with Roman Catholic beliefs.

This resulted in a tendency, in and after the Reformation debates, to think of 'traditions' as a number of specific beliefs and practices over and above what the Bible teaches. But in recent years there has been a return by both Protestants and Roman Catholics to the all-embracing concept of tradition as the whole Christian faith passed down.

Can we do without tradition?

It is impossible for any group, however informal, to exist for a period of time without tradition; nor is it desirable. The apostle Paul taught Timothy to teach and to pass on the Christian faith that had been delivered to him. The Christian faith normally spreads from person to person by being passed on, in other words, by tradition. Most of our grasp of the faith reaches us in this way.

As has been rightly said, the Christian attitude to tradition is summed up in the fifth commandment: honour your father and mother. Tradition is the Christian faith handed down to us by our spiritual forebears. They deserve our honour and respect. To despise them and imagine that we can start again as if they never existed is arrogant and foolish. But to honour parents is not always to obey them. We listen humbly and respectfully to the voice of tradition, but we are subject only to the word of God. There are times when we must say to tradition, 'We must obey God rather than men.'

startling claims about him within a few years of his death. A modern reader will no doubt want to ask many questions about claims as far-reaching as these:

- Can we be sure about the story of his life, death and resurrection? Can we believe that the Gospel documents give us a reliable account of what actually happened in history?
- Who is this 'God' who was working through Jesus of Nazareth? To what extent is he the same as the 'God' of other religions and world-views?
- Why does humanity need a message of forgiveness from God? What is wrong with us that makes us need what is offered in the name of Jesus?
- If the accounts are true, and if we believe the claims made about Jesus, how will this affect the way we think about God, and the way we look at life and death?

The best way for many people to start considering Christianity is by looking at Jesus Christ. This is why the first major section of this book is about him.

The Bible

This unique book, which consists of sixty-six smaller books written by many different writers over a period of at least 1,400 years, is treated by Christians as one book, because it deals with one single theme—God's great plan for the universe he has made.

Christians therefore see the Bible as a collection of books written by ordinary people who used their own style and expressed the truth in different ways as they understood it. But they believe that God's Spirit was working in the writers in a special way, and that what they wrote was a message which ultimately came from God. This is why the apostle Peter could say, when writing about the Old Testament, '*men* spoke *from God* as they were carried along by the Holy Spirit'.

When we ask how the writings of fallible human beings could come to carry so much weight for Christians, we find that the authority of the Bible is derived from the authority of Jesus. The authority of the New Testament rests on the special mandate which Jesus gave to his disciples (the apostles). Thus the books of the New Testament, which were written either by apostles or by others very close to them, came to be recognized by the church as authoritative documents which summed up the teaching of the apostles.

Similarly, the authority of the Old Testament is based on the claims which Jesus made for it and the way he used it in practice. Since he described it and treated it as 'the word of God', Christians feel bound to accord it the same place in their own lives and thinking.

How then do Christians interpret the Bible today? These are some of the main principles which explain how Christians approach the Bible, as summed up by John Stott:

'We look for the *natural* meaning because we believe that God intended his revelation to be a plain and readily intelligible communication to ordinary human beings.

'We look for the *original* meaning because we believe that God addressed his word to those who first heard it, and that it can be received by subsequent generations only in so far as they understand it historically. Our understanding may be fuller than that of the first hearers (e.g. of the prophecies of Christ); it cannot be substantially different.

'We look for the *general* meaning because we believe that God is self-consistent, and that his revelation is self-consistent also. So our three principles (of simplicity, history and harmony) arise partly from the nature of God and partly from the nature of Scripture as a plain, historical, consistent communication from God to men.'

The creeds of the churches

When we see so many churches in the world, with different beliefs, forms of worship and methods of church government, we naturally want to ask, what do they have in common? Are there any basic beliefs which they *all* accept?

One way to answer this question is to look at the earliest statements of Christian belief which were used in the Christian church. One of the best examples is found in the New Testament itself, and consists of the simple confession: 'Jesus is Lord.' When Christians said these words in a Jewish context,they were declaring their faith that Jesus of Nazareth was to be identified with God—the same God whom the Jews had spoken of as 'the Lord'. In a pagan context, where people believed in many different gods and goddesses, the person who confessed 'Jesus is Lord' was declaring that there is only one true God who has revealed himself in and through Jesus. And at a time when the Roman emperors were claiming to be divine and demanding that all citizens in the Empire should say 'Caesar is Lord', Christians

COLIN BROWN

Revelation and Reason

'Revelation' means what God has revealed; God disclosing truths which could not otherwise be known. Reason is the process of reaching logical conclusions from facts and statements everyone can see to be true.

Are revelation and reason mutually exclusive? From time to time people have thought so. Sometimes the distinction is used against Christian belief, as when people say, 'Since reason gives a completely adequate basis for living, why do we need faith?' Occasionally, however, attempts have been made to prove the existence of God by reason alone.

The outstanding example of this is the Ontological Argument, first put forward by Anselm (1033–1109), which seeks to demonstrate the existence of God from the idea of God. God is defined as the greatest conceivable being. Such a being must exist, for if he did not, he would not be the greatest conceivable being. (For discussion of this argument, see *Can God be proved?*)

In Thomistic thought, following Thomas Aquinas (1225–74), reason is not given quite such a free rein, but a certain distance is still preserved between reason and revelation. We may arrive at some truths about God, such as his existence, as we use our reason to reflect on what we see to be natural causes in the world. If there were no First Cause, the whole train of cause and effect would never have started. Other truths, such as the doctrine of the trinity and the mystery of the incarnation, we could not know other than by revelation.

In Reformed theology, revelation and reason are sometimes set sharply against each other. This is to guard the truth that we know God only as he chooses to reveal himself, as against the all too human efforts of philosophy and the world's religions to make God in the image of humankind. Only God can reveal God. Knowledge of God is a gift from God himself which is not at our disposal. And our reason is not so independent as we sometimes think. It is really only able to work on facts and ideas which are given it from outside itself.

When Christians claim to know God through his revelation, reason is by no means suspended. For without reason we could not discern what God is saying. Without reason we could not identify or interpret anything. Faith needs reason. Otherwise we could never recognize what and whom we believe in. Even those who claim mystical or charismatic experiences use reason to interpret, to themselves and others, what these experiences mean. Christians believe that God is the source of reason, for he himself is supremely rational. By this we do not mean that God may be discovered by pure reasoning, working out our beliefs simply on the basis of ideas. For at best such reasoning would be purely abstract and speculative. But Christians do believe that our ability to reason is a gift from God which has its proper use in all areas of life—not least in our knowledge of God.

openly confessed their allegiance to Jesus as the supreme authority in heaven and on earth by saying 'Jesus is Lord'. This simple confession, therefore, expressed the most fundamental belief which made the Christian faith different from Judaism, from the pagan religions, and from the religion of the Roman state.

Confessions of this kind were often used when a person declared his faith publicly and was baptized. We know, for example, from the writings of Justin Martyr (died AD 165) that converts who wanted to be baptized in the church in Rome were asked to declare their faith by answering the following questions:

'Do you believe in the Father and Lord God of the universe?

'Do you believe in Jesus Christ our Saviour, who was crucified under Pontius Pilate?

'Do you believe in the Holy Spirit, who spoke by the prophets?'

These summaries of Christian beliefs gradually developed into the creeds (from the Latin word *credo*, meaning 'I believe'). The earliest and best known is called the Apostles' Creed, not because it was written by the apostles, but because the early church believed that it summed up the apostles' teaching. The form in which we now have it dates from around AD 600, but it is very similar to earlier creeds which were being used at the end of the second century. It came to be accepted by the whole of the church in the West.

The second main creed is called the Nicene Creed, and dates from the fourth century AD. It shows how the church responded to some of the challenges to its beliefs both from inside and outside its membership. In about AD 300, for example, an Egyptian priest named Arius began teaching that Jesus was not the eternal Son of God, but was merely a heavenly being, created by God before the creation of the universe. After much argument and controversy, an important Council of the church, held at Nicea (in modern Turkey) in AD 325, rejected this teaching as heretical. The so-called Nicene Creed developed as a result of this controversy, and was put into its final form by the end of the fourth century. It included some important sentences about Jesus, in order to make it very clear that Jesus was believed to be both man and God, fully human and fully divine.

This creed became the basic creed of all the Eastern churches, and gradually also came to be adopted by the churches of the West. These two creeds—the Apostles' Creed and the Nicene Creed—are now accepted by Christians all over the world as summaries of essential Christian beliefs, and are recited regularly in many churches in services of worship.

There are at least three reasons why these creeds are important for our study of Christian beliefs:

- They provide a summary of the most basic beliefs which are held by all Christian churches. When Christians recite them, they are identifying themselves with other Christians all over the world and with the Christian church throughout history.
- They restate several vital Christian beliefs which have been challenged in the past and are continually being challenged today, such as the resurrection and the divinity of Jesus.
- The way they are used in the church is a reminder that Christian beliefs are not merely a subject for discussion and academic study. When they are recited in a service of baptism, an individual or family are publicly declaring the faith by which they are going to live and die. When they are recited in a service of worship, Christians are reaffirming their basic convictions as part of their worship of God.

Reason

It is impossible for us to *start* with reason if this means emptying our minds of all preconceived ideas about Christianity and trying to work out Christian beliefs with our own unaided intellect. This approach merely allows us to create a God in our own image, and to believe what we want to believe. Christians claim that certain events actually happened in history, through which God has made himself known. We cannot proceed as if such claims do not exist.

But if we cannot use reason in this way, this does not mean we have to abandon it altogether as we investigate Christian belief. Reason *does* have an important role to play.

Christians have always recognized that there is an element of mystery in the Christian faith; they have never claimed that they can provide a detailed, scientific explanation of everything that they believe. But they have always tried to give reasons for believing, and these reasons have taken different forms at different stages in history.

Certain Christians in the Middle Ages, for example, used some of the methods of logical argument they had learned from Aristotle, the Greek philosopher. They formulated the arguments which came to be known as 'proofs' of the existence of God. Their arguments helped many Christians over several centuries to understand that their faith was not totally irrational or unreasonable. In the last 200 years, however, the limitations of this line of argument have become increasingly apparent. And people today find it a more helpful approach to ask the same kind of questions as are asked in other subjects, such as science, history and philosophy:

- Is it more reasonable to believe that the universe was created by a personal God or that it came into being by itself, by chance? (This is very close to the approach of the *scientist*.)
- Is there convincing evidence for the historical events recorded in the Bible which have become the basis for Christian beliefs about God and about Jesus? For instance, what sort of historical evidence is there for the exodus of the Israelites from Egypt, or the resurrection of Jesus? Have we a firm enough basis to believe that these were real historical events? (This is the kind of question the *historian* asks.)
- Are Christian beliefs consistent with each other, or do they contradict each other? Do they make sense? How can we know if they are true? (This kind of question interests the student of *philosophy*.)

All of these questions are concerned with the search for truth in different areas of knowledge, and they all involve the use of reason.

Christian world-view, Jesus of history, Bible, creeds, reason—are they mutually exclusive? Do we have to choose one of these five approaches to examining Christianity, and reject the others? Not at all. Each of them has its place. This handbook gets involved with all of them as the pattern of Christian belief unfolds.

For further thinking

Five starting-points are given in this chapter for exploring Christian faith: the Christian world-view, the Jesus of history, the Bible, the creeds and reason. Choose one starting-point, and try to describe Christianity purely from that point of view, without introducing another point at all. What are the strengths of this description? What are its weaknesses?

CHAPTER 2

GAVIN REID

The Spiritual Dimension

Never has there been a more secular century than our own. Each generation has tried more whole-heartedly than its predecessors to build a way of life and morality as if there were no God.

This structure of thought has had to be built to a new design. Modern secular thinking has developed from particular ideas in the last two centuries, but no previous age has been so firmly convinced of the idea that this material world is all there is.

Yet religious feeling has been a part of humanity from the beginning. Religion is still alive and well in most continents of the world today. And even in the most secular countries, interest in the spiritual side of life is showing signs of recovery.

The beginnings of religion

Some of the most astonishing archaeological discoveries have been made deep inside cave systems—vivid paintings dating from the Palaeolithic era (50,000 to 10,000 BC). They have been found in parts of France and Spain, and similar pictures as far east as the Ural mountains.

These vivid and realistic paintings show scenes of animals such as deer and bison, many of them riddled with the arrows and lances of hunters. Surprisingly, they have been found deep down inside the caves. In the Niaux and Trois Frères caves in France, their distance from the cave entrances is several hundred metres. In another cave at Caberets, it takes an underground journey of several hours to reach the paintings!

Why are they there? If primitive human beings were artists, why did they bury their art galleries so deep in the earth?

The fact is that no serious archaeologist believes we are looking at art for art's sake in these hunting scenes. Theories vary, of course, and in any case we are in the area of the unprovable, but it is generally agreed that the basic meaning of these pictures is ritualistic or magical. The view held by many experts is that religious ceremonies took place around these pictures before hunters left the caves to go and seek food for themselves and their families. Indeed, painting these pictures was probably in itself a religious or magical act. In the cave at the Trois Frères near Ariège, one of the painted figures appears to be a man with the mask of a bison, playing a flute-like instrument. Does this represent some sort of priest, involved in those primitive rituals?

Whatever else these Stone Age paintings reveal, they make it abundantly clear that the earliest humans were far more than brutes fighting for survival. They had a spiritual dimension.

From even further back in history than the Palaeolithic artists, there is evidence that prehistoric human communities took care how they buried their dead. Why? Why did they use the same red ochre we find in the cave paintings to dust or paint their corpses? Today Australian aboriginals believe that red ochre is a symbol of blood and life. Was that how these primitive races felt? Did they believe that there was life beyond death? Some have argued that the mere fact of ordered burial makes it clear that they did.

Some skeletons from this era appear to have been buried in the sort of position that a baby in the womb would take. It would suggest that this points to beliefs about a new birth into a new life. Prehistoric communities believed that there was more to life than they experienced on earth.

As the centuries passed and the hunters began to take an interest in agriculture (probably through their womenfolk at first!) they faced up to the rhythms of vegetable life. Seed was planted, and when it died new life emerged. Seeds were reproduced and replanted as the developed vegetation died or was eaten. Round this cycle of birth, death and rebirth, myths were developed. People thought religiously about what was going on all round them.

Human beings have never been purely materialist. We have always sensed that the invisible is as real as the visible. We have probably always felt that there is life after death. And, judging by the customs of some of today's very primitive societies where ancient traditions have survived, early communities may well have believed in a High God. A blend of belief in one God, awareness of sin and the use of animal sacrifice to put things right has many echoes in ancient religions.

Organized religion

As people began to organize themselves into cities and agricultural activity provided their food, the spiritual dimension within human nature also began to take a more clearly defined shape. The development of writing furnished a new means of passing on religious ideas and discoveries. The newly organized religions produced their various scriptures. Organized people did not abandon religion, they organized it!

Three areas stand out—the Middle East, India and China. These three areas became the cradles for the great world religions. In Israel the Hebrew prophets were at the centre of Judaism, from which both Christianity and Islam were to develop. In India important Hindu scriptures were being written—today's Hindu is as indebted to those *Upanishads* as the Christian is to the Bible.

From this Indian Hindu tradition emerged the Gautama Buddha, from whose teaching sprang a highly successful missionary religion. Buddhism was to spread to Sri Lanka, Burma, South-east Asia, Tibet, China, Mongolia, Korea and Japan.

What are we to make of the presence in the world of several rival major religions, and an even greater number of lesser ones? There are sceptics who find it hard to believe that Christianity might be right while everything else is wrong. But there is a far more positive way of looking at it. It shows that throughout the entire history of humankind, and throughout the world today, the vast majority of people have sensed that there is more to life than we can see. Someone (or several someones) is 'over' us and our existence is not an accident. People have always suspected that we will have to account for the way we have lived while on earth. They have felt that there is some sort of life after death. Within many of these religions there is the conviction that God (or the gods) makes moral demands which affect the way we should live. Anyone who wishes to take up an atheistic or secularist position must face the fact that right through its history the human race has leant heavily in the other direction.

And, contrary to what is often said, the fact that there are several rival sets of beliefs about God does not mean that all are wrong, or that all are right, or that one cannot be right as opposed to the others. If, as the Christian believes, God has made humanity in his own image and to have fellowship with him, then it is not surprising if people all over the world try to find him.

Paul, the great first-generation Christian missionary, preached on this theme to people in Athens, the cultural and religious centre of the ancient world. He said that since God had created us, people would always 'look for him and perhaps find him as they felt about for him'. But this did not stop Paul pressing home his message about Jesus Christ. He acknowledged that his listeners were 'very religious', but they had not yet made the key discovery. 'That which you worship,' he said, 'even though you do not know it, is what I now proclaim to you.'

The Christian believes that in Jesus Christ God himself has come among men and shown us what he is like and what he wants from us. At the same time, such a view supports the wisdom of the adherents of other religions searching for God and agrees with their conviction that there is someone or

It has been said, 'If we want to make a thing real, we must make it local.' That is precisely what God has done in Jesus Christ: the divine love now has a local habitation and a name.

Norman Pittenger

The central neurosis of our time is emptiness.

Carl Jung

something 'out there' beyond us all.

The rise of secularism

The twentieth century has seen a turning away from spiritual convictions. Agnosticism and secularism have come to hold the stage. It is intellectually fashionable to talk as if we have grown up and out of dependence on the idea of God. Nor is this always an arrogant way of talking. There are many people who take up agnostic positions because, in the light of all the discoveries that have been made in modern times, they genuinely feel increasingly uncertain about any ultimate reality. And in many areas of the world, an atheistic communism firmly claims that humanity's spiritual dimension is out-of-date.

Yet there is increasing evidence that Marxist totalitarian governments have lost the struggle to impose atheism on their people. In China, after years of repression, there have been signs of openness to religious activity. Churches in Eastern European counties were always a long way from dying, even during the decades of official discouragement. Perhaps the biggest irony of all is that the teaching of even Marx himself is not so 'religionless' as is usually supposed. It contains deep echoes of both Jewish and Christian thinking. 'God may have been absent from Marx's view of the world,' writes Ninian Smart, 'but there was something about his teaching that appealed to springs of human hope.' Just as Christians look forward to the fullness of the coming kingdom of God, so Marxists long for the time to come when communism will be implemented universally.

Western materialistic secularism has not led to the collapse of religious belief either, although it has certainly had a sapping effect on organized religion and on the depth of individual commitment. Jesus warned that we cannot serve 'God and money', but the affluent, industrialized societies of the West are often tempted to try to prove him wrong!

Right at the heart of our self-confident secular society lies a revealing disability. Many people find it impossible to cope with the great moments of life—marriage, death, birth—in secular ways. The majority of people sense the appropriateness of some sort of ritual at such occasions. Death in particular confronts the secular mind with a dilemma; as society at large has become less and less 'religious', so it has found death more and more of an embarrassment—something to be kept out of sight and cleared away as quickly as possible.

Western materialistic secularism has failed at just the same point as organized Marxism; it has not convincingly stamped itself on the minds and hearts of people. The evidence for this has become increasingly apparent over the last few years. There is a greater interest in Eastern religions in the West than there has ever been. Cults are mushrooming on all sides. There has been an enormous increase in superstition, a fascination for the occult and the supernatural, a preoccupation with popular astrology in the mass-circulation press, a willingness to believe in anything from UFOs to reincarnation. The spiritual dimension keeps breaking out.

People are what they believe

A person's beliefs (or lack of them) are crucial. It is a mistake to restrict them to being a merely private matter. Our beliefs shape our character.

The dominant beliefs of a society, too, put a stamp on its whole way of life. A country dominated by Islam is very different from one where Buddhism is the major influence. People's attitudes are shaped by what they believe. Legal systems often take religious values as their starting-points.

Christianity, Judaism and Islam produce more activist cultures than Hinduism and Buddhism with their traditions of meditation and passive endurance of adversity. If our picture of God includes righteousness and justice, we will think that what is right and just on earth is important and worth fighting for. If we believe in a God of love, we will care for others, not just seek a mystical spiritual

DAVID LYON

Folk Religion

Black cats, walking under ladders, reading horoscopes, carrying mascots and being concerned about number thirteen are still important to many people in today's advanced industrial society. Life-cycle rituals to do with birth, marriage and death are often thought of as matters where 'religion' should be brought in, even though this may be the only interest shown in God or in church in a person's lifetime. Why is this? Does it mean that modern societies are not as secular as we think?

Folk religion is about superstition (belief in fate or luck), and about rituals and routines which give life meaning or help people cope with crises. Christians should not be surprised if they find alternative religions in the world. Jesus' hearers apparently had no difficulty understanding what he meant by saying 'where your treasure is, there your heart will be also'. People who fail to worship the Creator fix instead on something created. The Bible frequently refers to magic and superstition of various kinds, often linking them directly with the world of evil spirits. The domestication of folk religion in popular magazines and pub-talk in no way reduces its potential for spiritual danger.

Rivals or partners?

For many centuries folk religion has existed, often alongside official or conventional religions such as Judaism or Christianity. Sometimes folk religion may contain aspects of official religion, and vice versa, although official religion may also be hostile towards folk religion. In the time of Israel's King Saul, even though witchcraft was forbidden by Jewish law, the witch of Endor continued to ply her trade. But in medieval Europe many ancient rituals and symbols were incorporated and made acceptable within Christianity. One obvious example is Christmas, a 'Christian' festival superimposed on widespread celebration of the winter solstice, and involving numerous folk traditions quite unrelated to Christianity.

During the nineteenth century, however, the idea emerged that increasing rationality would erode 'irrational' beliefs, which would finally wither away completely when the day of science dawned. Many still hold this view today. But sociologists and anthropologists have found that this has not happened. So-called irrational beliefs and practices persist even in the most technologically sophisticated industrial societies. Especially in times of distress—through sickness, death, natural disasters, war, economic depression—the sacred dimension of life is given new impetus. Secularization is not so easily demonstrated.

Many rituals endure into the modern world, and have to do with civic pride or national loyalty, sport, drinking, art and entertainment. They often exhibit folk-religious characteristics. But among the most significant are those associated with the life cycle, for here official and folk religion meet. Getting christened, married or buried in church is for many a magical means of warding off bad luck and ensuring hope both in this world and the next. Church people still find a dilemma here. Should the church support such folk-religious superstition and make itself available for what is really a display of popular sentiment? Or should it refuse, recognizing the basic inadequacy of such beliefs and offering instead the good news of Jesus Christ which can alone provide genuine comfort, assurance and hope?

state of ecstasy for ourselves.

If the spiritual understandings of a nation have been dominated by atheism or secularism then it will show. Losing the conviction that they are made in the image of God, people will tend to treat each other as animals or machines. People are what they believe.

The Christian believes that God has thrown back the curtain and shown what he is like in Jesus Christ. As a result, Christians are called to follow Jesus, to live a life of loving concern for their neighbours and obedience to their heavenly Father. When there is a strong Christian element within a country, something of the nature of Christ shows through in the prevailing culture. It may be a very flawed and imperfect picture—but it is there all the same.

For further thinking

QUESTION

What would life be like if there were no spiritual dimension at all?

CHAPTER 3

BRUCE NICHOLLS

We All Believe Something

To be human is to hold some sort of system of belief. We may be largely unaware of the beliefs that are at the root of much of our thinking, but they are there just the same. We all believe something.

We know we have convictions on particular issues. Most of us are prepared to say what we think about the great institutions of society, such as marriage, education, law and order. But such views are not held in a vacuum. Each of them is an element in the total pattern of our system of belief: what we hold to be of greatest value, whether we believe that life is basically purposeful or meaningless, and so on.

How do we come to the beliefs we hold? Are they the product of our own individual thinking? Not entirely. Few would deny a real personal factor, but all of us are shaped to a greater or lesser extent by the whole wide context of people and events that surrounds us from birth. These powerful influences include:

- **Heredity**—not so much in the genetic sense as meaning everything that comes down to us from our forebears.
- **Culture**—the system of moral and aesthetic values, developed over centuries in the society we live in.
- **The structures** of the society we live in, and our place in them.
- **Family and national crises**, which make us ponder deep questions alongside our fellows in the wider or narrower community.

These formative factors are soon supplemented by others, secondary but still important: childhood experiences, at school and at home; the person we marry; the people we work with and who live in our neighbourhood—all influence the direction of our belief. We express these beliefs, not just in words and ideas, but in a variety of ways that involve the interaction of our bodies and our minds, our feelings and our wills in varying combinations. These are the gateways through which our inner self expresses its doubts and beliefs.

In this matter of systems of belief, we are all insiders. We all speak from within some pattern or another. This means that we can never be entirely objective, either about our own beliefs or in evaluating other people's. But it does not mean we can never seriously examine our basic assumptions.

In fact coming to realize that we have foundational beliefs may prove an important first step towards just such an examination. The powerful moulding influence of culture and heredity does not mean that everything is relative, that we can never know the truth. But understanding what shapes our beliefs should give us a proper humility about ourselves, and a determination to look at alternatives as clearly as we can.

We may measure these alternatives by several yardsticks: How well do they fit with the world as we experience it? What sort of effect do they have on people who adopt them? How valid a purpose do they offer for our lives? Yet, at the end of the day, Christians believe that it is God who takes the initiative in this question of knowing the truth. In Jesus Christ he comes to us. Jesus speaks for the Christian in his great prayer, the night before he died: 'Now this is eternal life, that they may know you, the only true God, and Jesus Christ, whom you have sent.'

Christians begin with the foundational belief that God as creator gives meaning to life itself. Their beliefs about who Jesus is and why he lived and died will reflect their belief about the trustworthiness of the Bible and how it is to be interpreted for life today. Other religions have different ideas. Some, such as Buddhism, question whether we can know God. Others look for God within the self or even deny his existence. There follows a brief survey of some areas where we all believe something. It may help us identify our own pattern, and perhaps question it.

Beliefs about what life is

The foundation of any religious system is its basic world-view. What is the relationship of ultimate reality to the world of our senses? Many believe that life is without meaning or purpose because there is nothing beyond our experience.

Atheists, who in practice are usually few in number, deny the existence of God. For them the universe is a closed system with no beyond. For the 'logical positivist' philosopher, the term 'god' is meaningless: God's existence cannot be scientifically verified. For some, science alone can give meaning. The science of evolution, which attempts to explain the process of growth in the complexity of life, is turned into a philosophy or ideology which seeks to give meaning to the world without reference to God. At least two thousand years before Darwin the Sankhya-Yoga philosophers of India embarked on the same quest—to give meaning to the universe in evolutionary terms.

The term **agnosticism**, introduced by T. H. Huxley in 1869, denotes the belief that humanity does not know whether God exists, and cannot know. Modern secular people, imbued with the spirit of materialism, are generally agnostic. For them science holds the key to life, religious beliefs are irrelevant. A secular person takes pride in being open-minded on all metaphysical questions. Gautama Buddha, the founder of Buddhism, was silent on such questions: Buddhism is practical agnosticism. An increasingly popular form of agnosticism is the belief that life's meaning is found only in a mystical identification with nature. The harmonization of self with nature, whether along the lines of the novelist D. H. Lawrence or the contemporary Hindu guru Rajneesh, accepts meaninglessness as a basis for living. It attracts a large number of young people in the 'counter-culture', who visit the East in search of inner peace.

In contrast to these humanistic, experience-centred approaches to reality, many throughout history have turned to an impersonal **monism**—the belief that all reality is one and any impression that one sphere of being can be distinguished from another is unreal, or illusion. Absolute monism, in its most severe logical form, was argued by the Indian philosopher Shankara (AD 788–820), drawing together the monistic beliefs of the Hindu *Upanishads*. Dr S. Radhakrishnan, the former President of India, was a modern apologist for monistic thinking. He sought to evaluate the truth-claims of all religions on this basis. The great Bhakti, or devotional, philosopher Ramanuja (AD 1016–1137) modified monism to find a place for plurality within reality. God, the soul and the world are distinct but not separate.

In the West, Plotinus (AD 205–270) was the founder of **neo-platonism**, a modified version of Plato's thought. He attempted to join ideas from Greek philosophy to the mysticism of Eastern monism. Neo-platonism deeply influenced both the medieval Christian mystics and the idealist philosophers of the eighteenth-century European Enlightenment, which shaped much modern Western thinking.

The Christian world-view is grounded in the belief that God is eternally personal and moral. He is the Creator of all things and continues to reign over the universe. Thus the created world is real and not illusion. Further, humanity is God's unique creation, made in his own image with the capacity for fellowship with himself. This personal and moral understanding of God as creator is shared, in different forms, by Jews and Muslims. Belief in the Creator-God becomes the watershed between impersonal and personal views, between meaning and meaninglessness.

Beliefs about suffering and evil

Christians believe that God is the creator of all things and that all truth is in him. He created the world morally good. But in the story of the fall, in Genesis chapter 3, we learn that human beings chose to sin, and as a result the whole human race, even creation itself, has been corrupted. All men and women are subject to sinful desires and actions. And so we are drawn two ways: because we are created in God's image we long for fellowship with God, but because we are sinners we rebel against him. We become idolaters, creating God in our own image. In a nutshell, this seeking-and-rejecting God is the centre of all religions. Every religion offers a way to God and to happiness, which is also a way of escape from the downward pull of evil and suffering.

While everyone believes in the existence of sin and evil, it is not always called by these names. **Hindus** offer many explanations for what causes suffering and evil. They call it ignorance of the true self, or failure rightly to worship Brahman who comes in many forms, or breaking the social rules of caste. They believe in reincarnation, or rebirth, and blame their present sufferings and misfortunes on actions in a previous life. They do not understand sin as rebellion against a just and holy God. Buddha, who reacted against the corrupt priesthood of Hinduism, taught that the desire for possessions, for selfish enjoyment and for separate existence are the root causes of all human suffering. He did not call it sin. To escape from all desire, Buddha offered a noble eightfold path of right attitudes, speech and conduct, and enlightened understanding. Buddhism, as a way of self-improvement, appeals to Western as well as Eastern followers.

The **Muslim** believes that God created all humanity good, to live as his vice-regents on earth. People are not subject to original sin. Their weakness is that they fail to live according to God's law, revealed in the Qur'an. God calls them to submit to him—*Islam* means 'submission'. They are always in danger of being led astray by Satan and his fallen angels.

At the popular level of the ordinary family, the followers of most religions mix their orthodox beliefs with **superstitions and fears** about the 'gods' and evil spirits that surround them. They turn to magical practices, the wearing of charms, rituals—all intended to avoid suffering and to ward off evil powers. A striking example is astrology, which is found in every religious culture, including the secularized West.

Astrologers believe that the stars and the planets can influence the actions of individual people in everyday life, either for good or for evil. On a day in India when there was a rare alignment of the planets, the invariably overcrowded trains were almost empty; people feared a major natural calamity. When faith in the living, personal God weakens or disappears, people turn to the occult for protection against suffering and for answers to problems of daily living. Why is the number thirteen so feared, even by so-called Christians?

The **tribal peoples** of Africa, Asia and the South Pacific believe that their ancestors are alive and their spirits are always near them. Unless honoured or rightly placated, these spirits can do them good or harm. Suffering is never an independent event; it is always part of the life of the ever-present spirit world.

Among those who profess to be **atheists** or **agnostics** are many who look for causes of suffering in the structures of society. This can be eased only by changing powerful economic and social forces, which may involve violent revolution. The Marxist sees injustice and oppression as caused by the continuing class struggle. Religion, for him, is one of the causes of this suffering. It is a kind of opium, which dulls the pain of oppression and reinforces society's inertia against change.

Beliefs about death and beyond

Death is the one inevitable fact of life. To those who fear it, or have no hope of life beyond death, it is very often a forbidden topic of conversation. And yet the majority are conscious of the plain fact that to give meaning to death is to give meaning to life. Many people spend their wealth on elaborate funerals, embalming the body and building grand mausoleums to honour the dead. They are looking to perpetuate earthly happiness or to ward off the terrors of the afterlife. Few people really believe that death is total annihilation, the end of all personal existence. Many atheists have died in fear. The materialistic, pleasure-seeking person tries to ignore death.

To most **traditional religionists of Africa**, death is a completely unnatural event, generally caused by the sorcery of an enemy. The disembodied soul joins the spirit world, waiting to enter another body. The relationship between the living and the living dead is always a present reality.

For other people, death is an escape from the bondage of passion and desire, or from the weary cycle of reincarnation: birth, death and rebirth. **Buddhists** call this *nirvana*, 'extinction of the fire'. It is the cessation of change, a passionless peace. **Hindus** also long for release from the wheel of bodily life, though their emphasis is different. They look for the absorption of the individual soul into the world-soul, the ultimate oneness of reality. They think of this absorption as a drop of water falling into the ocean, or a river flowing into the sea. A single life and death has limited value; it is only one event in an endless cycle. Greek philosophy also gave little value to the body. It was likened to a prison house for the soul.

The **Hebrews** had a wonderful faith in God, but only glimmers of understanding of the fullness of life after death. God's revelation of the meaning of death and life beyond reached its fulfilment in the resurrection of **Jesus Christ** from the dead. His resurrection revealed a genuine continuity with his earthly life and yet also a total transformation, heralding a life beyond the physical creation. He is the foretaste of a new creation, the hope for every believer; his resurrection is the pattern of our resurrection. This hope is closely connected with his promised return to this earth, when, in the apostle John's words, 'we shall be like him for we shall see him as he is'. The Christian's hope of heaven is more than a return to the paradise of Eden, it is a new creation with new depths of personal relationship with God and with one another. This hope is a great comfort in times of physical weakness and bereavement. On the other hand, the pain of hell, of eternal separation from God, is an awesome thing to contemplate. It reflects the holiness and justice of God.

Muslims dimly share with Christians the hopes and fears of life beyond death. But they do not know hope as seen in the resurrection of Jesus Christ. For them heaven is a place of fulfilment for the sensual pleasures of this life and hell a place of torment to which Allah predestines those to whom he is not merciful.

Beliefs about salvation

We all believe something about how to cope with suffering and sin, death and beyond. Traditional **tribal religions** recognize that there is a High God who is Creator and saviour, but he is generally remote and secondary to the gods that are near at hand and the all-pervading spirits of the living dead. **Hindus** believe in many gods and goddesses, but generally the local deity is more important to the people. Their worship, and their prayers for deliverance from sickness and the fear of death, involve acts of sacrifice, observing festivals and pilgrimages to holy places. The higher castes may turn to such practices as yoga and the mystical trance to find release from bondage to the world.

Some **national religions** have turned to emperor worship, as in the Roman Empire at the time of the early church, or in the Shinto worship of the Japanese emperor up to the end of World War II. In such cases religion and politics are interwoven with the national culture and the state controls every part of the lives of the people. This is also true in Islamic states where religion, culture and political life form a unified whole. The five pillars of Islam—reciting the creed, prayer, fasting, almsgiving and pilgrimage—are the basis of the Muslim hope of heaven. If Muslims do have to suffer the fires of hell, it will not be for ever, as it will for the infidel.

The **Christian hope** is grounded in the conviction that Jesus Christ, the incarnate Son of God, died on the cross for our sins and rose again. In his death he paid the penalty for humanity's sin and in his resurrection he overcame the powers of death. If we believe in him, we are identified with his dying and rising again. A person's salvation from sin and evil begins when they repent and trust in Christ for forgiveness. From beginning to end salvation is the work of God's grace through Christ. God the Holy Spirit is the divine agent in this process of salvation, bringing the individual into reconciliation and fellowship with God. But more than this, he creates a new community of God's people, so that they become one family—a unity the churches are struggling to embody. Christians believe in the church as the sign of God's reign in the world. The Muslim emphasizes the Muslim brotherhood, other religions have their communities of monks, or their castes, but belief about the church is unique.

Beliefs about living well

All people have some understanding of the law of good and evil. **Hindus** believe in *Karma*: that a person carries with him into the next life the results of the good and evil he has done. As we sow, so shall we reap. This principle of cause and effect in ethical behaviour is almost universal. Even what we sometimes think of as primitive religions have embedded in their social custom clear ideas about the wrongness of stealing, lying, adultery, murder and so on.

In **biblical history**, Moses was given the Ten Commandments as a guide for the good living of God's people and as a check against evil. Jesus summarized the law in these words: 'Love the Lord your God with all your heart and with all your soul and with all your mind. Love your neighbour as yourself.' In the sermon on the mount, Jesus expounded these laws in a way that exposed the inward attitude of heart lying behind our outward behaviour.

Somewhat parallel ethical principles are found in other religions. The difference lies in how the moral power is to be found to live as we believe. **Christians** believe that without the power of the Holy Spirit no amount of self-effort is enough to keep these laws. Only the love of God in Christ can enable a person to keep on loving his enemies. Living good lives is the fruit of salvation and not its source. In the midst of greed we are called to a simple life-style, in an age of sexual perversion to godly family living, and in a world of violence and oppression to compassionate service to the poor and deprived. What we believe must be matched by what we do.

If man is the highest, is his own creator, then good and evil are created by majority vote.

William Golding

For further thinking

QUESTION

Think of a novelist whose books you have read, or a television drama series you know well. Do these novels or dramas show consistent beliefs about the world and human life? What are these beliefs? How do they affect the way the characters behave?

CHAPTER 4

JERRAM BARRS

Christianity: True to the Way Things Are

People have always asked the same basic question. What is the meaning of the world and our lives in it? Christians claim that the faith of the Bible gives true and satisfying answers to this question and the many that flow from it. Christianity is not just true in what it teaches about God and salvation. It is also true to the way things are.

Some people dislike this approach to Christian faith. It appears to belong to the realm of philosophy, which they see as complicated where Christianity should be simple, abstract where Christianity should be real, and intellectual where Christianity should be spiritual. They quote the apostle Paul, who wrote that 'since in the wisdom of God the world through its wisdom did not know him, God was pleased through the foolishness of what was preached to save those who believe'. But Paul is in no way saying that the gospel is actually foolish; only that it seems foolish in the eyes of people who discount God. In the same passage he goes on to say that it is the non-Christian thinking or philosophy which is in truth foolish, and the Christian message which is the only true wisdom.

Christians, therefore, ought to be prepared to answer the questions that philosophy asks, both because all men and women everywhere ask them in some way and because the Bible itself gives answers to these questions. The biblical faith fits like a glove on the hand of the way things are.

Some of the basic questions are these:

- How do we know about anything?
- How can we understand our world?
- What is human nature?
- What are right and wrong?
- Why is there suffering and evil?
- Is there a purpose to our existence and a meaning to history?
- How should we live?

As we look at each of these questions and see the biblical answer, we will compare it with the views of twentieth-century secular thinkers.

The question of knowledge

How do we know? How can we be sure that what we think we know is accurate?

Western society's pervading philosophy is humanism. Humanism answers this question by appealing to human reason: man starting from himself has to work out all the answers. As eighteenth-century Scots philosopher Hume put it: 'Reason appears in possession of the throne, prescribing laws and imposing maxims, with an absolute sway and authority.' This belief in the power of reason is basic to our whole modern, Western society. And yet Hume himself acknowledged that, if we begin from ourselves alone, we can never demonstrate the value of reason, nor the accuracy of our sense perceptions, nor be sure that we exist, that the material world exists, that cause and effect exist. In a famous passage Hume acknowledged, however, that though his reliance on reason as the basis for all knowledge could not be shown to be adequate, yet he would not despair. In practice he would carry on as if it was.

In the twentieth century this problem that arises from trusting in reason has led many thinkers to a position of complete despair. We have made our reason into a god—but it has become an albatross round our neck, reminding us constantly of the decay of meaning, of the death of value in human existence.

The problem has arisen because we are

finite, we are small, we cannot from our own very limited grasp of reality generate sufficient knowledge to answer all the questions, or understand the whole of reality. Everything seems so big and yet we are so little, how can we be sure that any of our knowledge is dependable?

For the Christian, human finiteness is not a problem. We can freely acknowledge that we are small, and that our understanding is limited. But God exists and his knowledge is complete; everything in the universe is known to him. God has given us his revelation in the Bible (his 'word'), and this word, though it does not tell us everything, tells us truly. We have a sure foundation for knowledge in God's word, and in it God assures us that he has created us in his image to understand the world in which we live; so that our perception of the world is generally accurate. Reason when it stands under God's revelation becomes a servant of great value, which can be used to explore and reflect on the world in which we live. It is only when reason is made master that it becomes a tyrant leading us into the blackest night of ignorance and confusion.

The nature of the world

Modern humanist and secular thought in our society is tied up in a single parcel with the theory of evolution. At its crudest this can be stated as the belief that all of the things we see in the world around us have developed by chance—that there is no God who has created the world, no First Cause that has brought into being the extraordinary diversity of the natural world. This belief requires us to accept that purely chance processes have given rise to the immensely complex and interdependent web of life.

Christianity declares in contrast that the order, the diversity, the intricate interdependence and beauty of the natural world have been created by the living and self-existent God whom the Bible reveals to us. Order, diversity and beauty are the result of God's creative activity, not chance processes and blind natural selection. The Bible sees this truth as self-evident, that it is simply a matter of common sense to look at the world and see that it is the product of a Creator. The Psalmist wrote: 'The heavens declare the glory of God; the skies proclaim the work of his hands.'

When we look at a beautiful painting we ask 'Who painted that?' and we praise its creator. In the same way when we look at the universe we ought to want to know and praise its maker.

'O Lord, our Lord, how majestic is your name in all the earth.'

Human nature

Bertrand Russell sums up the dilemma that confronts non-Christian thought as people try to understand human nature without reference to God. Russell has to acknowledge that humanity is different, that we are unique in this world; our moral character, creativity, love, heroism, thought and devotion to other people set us apart from every other form of life. But Russell has no better explanation for this uniqueness than any other modern, secular philosopher. Thinkers such as Russell admit that humanity is different, but cannot explain why. Others try to deny this uniqueness and insist that the only difference is one of complexity. For them, human beings are complicated pieces of chemistry, physical organisms like the mosquito and the mouse, but so complex as to be comparable to the digital computer.

Perry London, an American psychotherapist, appeals to this totally mechanistic model for human nature, and then acknowledges that this means that we have no more ultimate significance than a computer has. If we are no more than mechanical, we have no responsibility whatsoever for anything we do. In the end our distinctiveness is quite illusory; the things that we experience every day—love, commitment, choice, creativity, rationality—have no meaning at all: they are fleeting shadows on the wall, tricks of sunlight, thrown up by the complicated nature of the brain.

The Christian faith, however, gives an

Man is the product of causes which had no prevision of the end they were achieving... his origin, his growth, his hopes and fears, his loves and his beliefs, are but the outcome of accidental collocations of atoms... no fire, no heroism, no intensity of thought and feeling, can preserve an individual life beyond the grave... and the whole temple of man's achievement must inevitably be buried beneath the debris of a universe in ruins.

Bertrand Russell

explanation for the uniqueness of humanity. Male and female, we are made in the image of God. The infinite person, God, has made other beings, men and women, who are finite and yet are persons like himself. We are reflections of God's nature:

- 'God is love' says the apostle John. We are made to love God and to love one another.
- God is righteous. We are made to distinguish between good and evil and to choose the good.
- God is the Creator. We are like him, made to create life, relationships, beauty, order.
- God is a communicator. We are made to communicate in language with one another and with God.
- God is a God of order and not chaos, sense and not nonsense, reason not absurdity. We are made as rational persons, called to reflect on our life, and the world in which we live.

> There is no final resolution for the tensions of the human soul—all one can do is try to illumine human existence—but this illumination is a tiny flickering light set against the encompassing darkness of the night.
>
> *Karl Jaspers*

All these aspects of our experience which set us apart are characteristics of personality. Rather than lamenting that our experience of personality is an illusion in an impersonal universe, we can rejoice in it, because as persons we are at home in a universe made by the personal God.

Right and wrong

How can we know what is good and evil? If we are mere machines, it is meaningless to speak of good and evil or moral responsibility. We do not accuse computers of criminal behaviour, nor do we bring the animals to stand trial for breaking the law. Taking this view, good and evil and moral responsibility are imaginary, although it is still widely recognized that for some reason we seem to need them to live meaningfully. This mechanistic outlook has led people to suggest ways of programming us all to create a better society, forgetting that the term 'better' is on this basis quite meaningless.

This theory of human nature seems to fly in the face of the belief common to all human societies that good and evil are different from each other, and people are moral agents. In our own day we see the terrible fruit of a philosophy which denies any final distinction between good and evil. We see it in the West, where the frequency of abortion and the increasing pressure for euthanasia are making serious inroads into the value set on human life. And we have seen it in the communist or former communist world, most strikingly in Kampuchea where between a third and a half of the population were killed in the name of a pure Marxist revolution.

Christianity does not suffer from this uncertainty over good and evil. It is not reluctant to admit that real evil can and does exist. God's own character is one of perfect goodness, justice and holiness. His character defines for us what is good and right. All our behaviour must be measured against that yardstick, and also in the light of the final judgment when all our actions, words and thoughts will be seen for what they are.

God's will, revealed in the Bible, expresses his righteousness, and human beings, made to reflect that righteousness, are called to obey God's law and judge their lives against it. Everyone is created with a moral conscience, the law of God written on our hearts, but this can become confused or hardened, either by cultural tradition or by our own sinful choices. But we also have a deeper and indeed an absolute basis for knowing what is good and what is evil, for we can check all our ideas against God's character and law. This means that the Christian has firm ground to stand on when confronted with the immorality of those in power, or with the will of the fifty-one per cent in a Western society where morality changes with the consensus of the day.

And then there is the doctrine of judgment—not an embarrassment but something we should rejoice in as one of the glories of the Christian faith. We all feel in our hearts that some things are right and others wrong, although we may be unable to explain ultimately why this is so or even to give to the notions of good and evil final significance. The Christian can say with confidence that there is a difference and that in the end, at the judgment, all evil will be exposed and found wanting.

The problem of suffering and evil

This point follows on from the last, because if modern philosophy has no final means of discerning between good and evil or of granting moral significance to humanity, then equally it has a hard time understanding suffering, sickness and death. In the end our culture has to say that suffering is normal, a part of reality. There is good and evil, light and darkness, life and death, kindness and cruelty—all are aspects of the whole.

This way of looking at things is quite alien to Christianity. The Christian sees suffering and death as abnormal and unnatural, as in fact every human being feels in his heart, at least sometimes. Until they become hardened, little children are appalled at death and see it as horribly unnatural rather than as simply an aspect of life. The Christian knows that this feeling is true to the way things are, for the Bible tells us that we are living in a fallen world, that sin entered the world through humanity's rebellion against God, and that suffering, sickness, pain and death come in its train. This means that suffering and death are *abnormal*—that the world was originally good, but now it is marred and broken.

Jesus Christ could be sorrowful, compassionate and angry when faced with pain and death, even though he is God. He could be angry and sad because he did not create them, rather they resulted from people's rejection of him and his law. The Christian, too, must follow Jesus Christ in seeing all suffering as abnormality, and rather than consenting to the brutality of the age towards the weak and needy, should reflect God's character of concern for the widow, the orphan, the broken in body and mind, the unborn, the old, the dying.

The purpose of existence

We all feel that life has some purpose and that history must be going somewhere. But when we inspect this feeling, several questions come to mind. Why should life have purpose? What is that purpose? Can we be sure history is going somewhere? And where is it going?

People are not slow to invent all kinds of meanings, both for themselves and for the human race as a whole: a better lot for all, personal affluence, gods and religions of various sorts, peace for the world... But we need to be clear these are secondary goals, not the ultimate purpose of life. Otherwise they can become refuges from facing up to what Bertrand Russell sees as the ultimate reality of history—the death of the individual and the death of the solar system. How can we avoid the consequence that all is meaningless if Russell is right? Neither the individual life nor the history of the human race has any final value on such a view, and Russell is honest enough to acknowledge this. Russell has no real answer to this question, nor can he have once he has denied the existence of God.

The Bible tells us that our longing for purpose and for meaning in history has been placed within us by God, and that this longing can be satisfied only by our turning to him. We have been made to love God, to reflect his character, and enjoy him for ever. We have been made to love, enjoy and serve one another, and to enjoy God's creation and care for it as his stewards. We are living in a fallen and twisted world where sin has brought enmity and brokenness at every level—between ourselves and God, within our own personalities, between ourselves and others, between us and the creation, within creation itself. Everything is touched by sin and death. Yet God in his love has sent his own Son, Jesus Christ, to redeem us and the whole creation from sin and death. Through what Jesus Christ has done, by faith in him, we are restored to fellowship with God. Within that relationship we can begin to find new wholeness as people. We have a calling to bring God's restoration to the whole of life, and to work for the healing of all the brokenness which sin has produced in ourselves and in the world. God promises us that the goal of history is a new creation, in which the brokenness of every aspect of life will be removed and everything made new. Our own individual lives are given eternal significance and history is heading towards a glorious conclusion.

How should we live?

Our age confronts us with several alternatives, none of them satisfactory. The government decides what is right for the people; the majority decides what is right; or individuals decide on the basis of their own feelings of what is good for them. There are no abso-

COLIN BROWN

Relating Philosophy and Theology

The word 'philosophy' literally means love of wisdom. Pythagoras, born around 570 BC and said to have been the first thinker to call himself a philosopher, saw philosophers as being like the spectators at the festal games, rather than the athletes. And philosophers ever since have prided themselves on taking a detached view of things. But they would repudiate the suggestion that philosophy is a mere spectator sport. It is a relentless quest to distinguish reality from appearances. Only by standing back and asking the right questions can we hope to get at the true nature of things.

Understanding the nature of things

All down the ages philosophers have disagreed among themselves as to what the true nature of things might be:

- ☐ **Plato** (427–347 BC)—had a vision of eternal Ideas or Forms which lay behind our changing, decaying physical world. At the head of this hierarchy of forms was the Form of the Good.
- ☐ **Aristotle** (384–322 BC)—saw the world as the product of the interplay of various causes. If we push back far enough, we must presume a First Cause for everything.
- ☐ **Seventeenth-century rationalists**—sought to discover the rational structure of reality, guided by reason alone.
- ☐ **Empiricists**—reason alone is not sufficient: all our knowledge must be based on the information provided by our senses.
- ☐ **Materialists**—there is no reality beyond the physical.
- ☐ **Idealists**—everything physical is the expression of the working of an absolute, spiritual mind.
- ☐ **Agnostics**—such questions cannot be settled one way or the other because of the limitations of human knowledge.
- ☐ **Existentialists**—concerned with what to make of human existence in view of the uncertainties of life and the absence of absolute values in the materialistic world.

Underlying all these philosophies are the repeated questions: What are we to make of the world we live in? What, if anything, lies behind it? What can we know? How do we come to know it? Can we be sure? The variety of answers that have been given depends not least on the basic assumptions and commitments of the philosopher who gives the reply.

The study of God

The term 'theology' basically means discourse about God. But to speak of God raises the question: How do I know that what I am saying about God is true? Hence, the word 'theology' is used for the disciplined study which treats of God, his nature, his attributes, and his relations with the universe and people. Christian theology is based on the belief that God reveals himself in nature, history and human affairs. The God who made himself known in these ways is the one who speaks in the Bible and who became man in Jesus

lutes any more, and we see on every side the resultant confusion and sorrow in people's lives and homes.

God promises us liberty if we obey his law. The law of God, his will for our lives, is a reflection of God's character. We are made to be like God. The law, then, is not a set of arbitrary rules imposed by a dictatorial God, rather it is fitted to human life. In the letter of James we find that 'the man who looks intently into the perfect law, that gives freedom, and continues to do this, not forgetting what he has heard, but doing it—he will be blessed in what he does'. If we obey God's law we shall enjoy life. God's truth sets us free to live. We can see this in any area of life—if we obey God's commandments about marriage, for example, to love, value and be

Christ. Christian theology tries to understand what God has revealed to us and what this revelation means.

From the days of the early church there has been a constant love-hate relationship between theology and philosophy:

- ☐ **Justin Martyr** (Greek apologist, died 165)—saw Greek philosophy as preparing the Gentile world for the coming of Christ in much the same way as the Old Testament prepared the Jewish people.
- ☐ **Tertullian** (Latin apologist, 160–220)—philosophy was of the devil and the root of all heresy.
- ☐ **Origen** (185–254)—freely adapted Platonic thought as an explanation of Christian doctrine.
- ☐ **Thomas Aquinas** (1225–74)—used the recently rediscovered writings of Aristotle as a philosophical basis for theology. In Thomistic thought, based on Aquinas' teaching, *natural theology* (the knowledge of God based on our observation of the world) serves as a basis for *revealed theology*, which depends on special revelation in Christ and the Bible.
- ☐ **The Reformers** —although they did not altogether eliminate Greek and medieval ideas from their schemes of thought, they generally shunned natural theology in favour of the revealed theology contained in the Bible.

Since the seventeenth century philosophers have been increasingly—though not exclusively—hostile to theology. Frequently philosophy has been seen as completely replacing theology—or at least offering a world-view into which theologians have to fit their ideas as best they can.

Even now there is no agreed consensus as to how the two are related. But we need to bear in mind that philosophy is not a subject like (say) chemistry, physics or literature. Each of these has its own subject-matter, but philosophy does not have a province of its own. Strictly speaking, there is no such thing as philosophy.

It is always the *philosophy of* something else—the philosophy of science, the philosophy of history, the philosophy of morals (ethics), the philosophy of knowledge (epistemology), the philosophy of being (metaphysics), the philosophy of language, and the philosophy of religion. It is always this *something else* which provides the raw material for philosophy.

Philosophers of science do not possess some superior knowledge which gives them a short cut to scientific truth, but they are concerned with the kind of knowledge gained by the scientist through hypothesis, observation and controlled experiment. In the same way, philosophers of religion do not have some superior access to their subject-matter which is denied to lesser mortals. But they do perform the important if at times humdrum task of asking questions about the theologians' language and claims to knowledge. This brings us back to Pythagoras and his claim that the philosopher is a detached spectator. To practise philosophy properly we need to stand back and reflect—but also to get involved. A philosopher of science who had no practical experience of modern science would hardly be qualified to make pronouncements on scientific method. What is true in the realm of natural science is no less true for theology.

faithful to each other, then we will enjoy marriage. If we do not obey his commandments, then the resulting chaos and unhappiness in our society are only too obvious. Again Christianity fits.

At point after point, then, the Christian faith makes more sense than secular philosophy. This is because Christianity is the true wisdom revealed by God, and so wiser than any other wisdom. If we look into the Bible, we find it answers the questions that are raised by our life in this world. Christianity is true to the way things are.

For further thinking

QUESTION

Choose one of the basic questions spelt out in the fourth paragraph of this chapter. Imagine a friend asking you this question. How would you answer, in a way true both to biblical Christianity and to the way life really is today?

RENE PADILLA

A People-Centred Faith

CHAPTER 5

People usually come to know and be convinced about Christianity, not by a rational process leading to intellectual conviction, but by contact with caring Christians, people whose lives are a witness to the love and power of Jesus. This should not surprise us, because Christianity is a people-centred faith. The Christian faith does not look on a human being as isolated from other human beings, but rather as made for community. This does not deny, of course, the need for a personal relationship to God through Jesus Christ, but it does deny that such a personal relationship is possible without the people of God. In other words, Christianity is personal but not individualistic. It is both personal and social.

Human nature

We are social beings. According to the Genesis account in the Bible, when God created humanity he did not create a male alone or a female alone; he created human beings, male and female, with the capacity to relate to one another in love. Human life was meant to be lived in society right from the beginning.

One of the effects of humankind's revolt against God—the 'fall'—was that human beings became separated from their neighbours. This comes out clearly at several points in the story:

- Adam blames his own disobedience on his wife.
- Eve is made subject to her husband.
- Cain kills his brother Abel.

Yet even after the fall, people continue to be social beings. Because of the unity of the human race, all men and women are corporately involved in sin. This does not mean that there is no individual responsibility, but it does mean that the Bible sees sin as a social as well as an individual reality.

Sin spoils relationships between people. One of the effects of Jesus Christ's death is to restore them. The apostle Paul makes this clear in a passage in his letter to the Ephesians. His argument is that the enmity between Jews and Gentiles (the most dramatic division affecting humanity in the ancient world) has been removed through the death of Christ. Jews and Gentiles are now included in a new, undivided humanity. And in this new humanity other divisions are equally erased: between those who are slaves and those who are free, between men and women. The social divisions caused by our revolt against God are totally eliminated, at least in principle. The basis is thus provided for new relationships in which people recover their true humanity.

That human beings are designed to live in community has been widely recognized throughout history. The Greek philosopher Aristotle was not alone in believing that 'man is by nature a political or social being'. But modern Western society is built on an individualistic approach to life, and this approach continues to gain force on a global scale as the world becomes increasingly Westernized. Individual freedom and individual rights are regarded as of higher value than social responsibility and human solidarity. One of the results of individualism is that religion becomes a private matter with no social or public consequences. A person may be a 'good Christian' in their private life but totally unable to relate their faith to their business practice and completely unconcerned for the needs of those around them. Unless such a person becomes aware of the social dimensions of the Christian faith, he or she will never attain Christian maturity. Mature Christians so respond to God's grace that they live as 'people for others'. This is

Under his [Christ's] control all the different parts of the body fit together… So when each separate part works as it should, the whole body grows and builds itself up through love.

Paul, in Ephesians 4

how God designed human life to be.

God's purpose

The focus of God's purpose is not simply individual salvation, but the formation of a new humanity and a new creation. Personal salvation is included, of course, but God's purpose is not limited to it. Paul can write to the Galatians, 'this life that I live now, I live by faith in the Son of God, who loved *me* and gave his life for *me*', underlining the meaning of Jesus' death for *himself*. But he can also tell Titus that Christ 'gave himself for us… to make us a pure people who belong to him alone and are eager to do good', throwing into relief the significance of Christ's death for the creation of *a people*, and a people with a social conscience.

Several theologians have claimed that Jesus could not have intended to establish the Christian church, because he thought that the end of the world was about to come. But all the evidence suggests that Jesus looked on the founding of his church as an essential part of his mission. If he was the Messiah announced by the Old Testament prophets, there is nothing strange in saying that he intended to establish a community of those who acknowledged him as such. The Messiah was to be a king, and there is no king without a people who recognize his kingship. And so to cast doubt on Jesus' purpose to found a church which would be distinctively his is also to cast doubt on Jesus' messiahship.

Jesus' historical mission, then, included the founding of the Christian church, in fulfilment of God's purpose to form a new humanity. This means the church is a part of the gospel, since it is one of the results of Christ's work. Paul saw the formation of the church, with the participation of Jews and Gentiles on an equal basis, as God's secret plan revealed by the Spirit to the New Testament apostles and prophets. This plan is 'to bring all creation together, everything in heaven and on of earth, with Christ as head'. The church, created through the gospel, is the foretaste of the plan, yet it also embodies here and now God's intention to bring all creation together under the lordship of Jesus Christ.

God desires not only to save individuals but to form a people. And so no evangelism is biblical unless it leads women and men to become part of a local congregation, where they can experience the reality of fellowship in Jesus. The New Testament knows nothing of solitary Christians; it only knows Christians who, as members the 'body of Christ', *together with others*, grow in Christ.

Christian mission

The Christian mission includes both evangelism and service, word and action. Mission involves both bringing God's love to people where they are, and working for a better world, with social and political structures that reflect God's good will for human life. It begins with God, who in love is always reaching out after the human race, and it returns to God, as that same love draws men and women from all nations to form his own people.

Church and mission are inseparable; there is no church without mission nor mission without the church. The agent of mission is the Holy Spirit, but the Holy Spirit works through the church.

The first thing to notice is that the church fulfils its mission not only by what it *does* but also by what it *is*. We have already seen how people today are more influenced by Christian corporate life than by Christian argument. This was equally so in New Testament times. The early growth of the Jerusalem church had a lot to do with the quality of community life portrayed by Christians.

We are told in the Acts of the Apostles that 'All the believers continued together in close fellowship and shared their belongings with one another. They would sell their property and possessions, and distribute the money among all, according to what each one needed. Day after day they met as a group in the Temple, and they had their meals together in their homes, eating with glad and humble hearts, praising God, and enjoying the good will of all the people. *And every day the Lord added to their group those who were being saved.*' Whenever and wherever this kind of truly corporate life is present in the church, outsiders cannot help being attracted to Jesus Christ, even when they know very little about him.

Because of the close association between the church and its mission, missionary concern included concern for the unity of the church. That mission and unity belong together is made quite clear by Jesus himself in his great prayer: 'I pray that they may all be one. Father! . . . May they be one, so that the world will believe that you sent me.' Accordingly, we cannot give importance to the mission of the church without at the same time giving importance to the unity of the church, into which new believers will be incorporated.

If the unity of the church points to the reconciling power of the gospel, the division of the church puts a question mark against all Jesus Christ achieved. Christianity is a people-centred faith and the oneness of the people of God is a concrete expression of God's purpose—to unify the whole universe under the lordship of Jesus Christ.

The unity of the body of Christ, then, is to be experienced as a concrete reality. The place to begin working at this question is the local congregation. It is there, at the local level, that the people of God can live out that love which Jesus tells us is the distinctive mark of a Christian. This is not to deny the importance of inter-church unity, but it is to emphasize the importance of the local congregation as the place where unity is experienced at the grass-roots level. When the corporate life of the local congregation is characterized by love, reconciliation, forgiveness, mutual acceptance and accountability, and when each member freely uses his or her Spirit-given ministry for the good of the others, the basis is laid for the spontaneous expansion of the gospel.

God's love and power are then not mere words but a spiritual reality affecting people in very practical ways. When this is true, half the work of persuading non-believers of the validity of Christianity is done before the gospel is ever preached!

There is often a contrast between modern Christianity and biblical faith. Modern Christianity has been deeply influenced by Western individualism. Its main thrust is on each person's relationship to God, to the neglect of the social dimensions of sin and the gospel. It is an individual-centred faith. As a result, it tends to make a sharp division between theology and ethics, between belief and practice, between faith and works. Biblical Christianity is a people-centred faith. It views us as social beings, it views God's purpose in terms of the formation of a new humanity and a new creation, and it views the Christian mission as inseparable from the church.

For further thinking

QUESTION 1

Why did you become a Christian? Was it partly because you were drawn to a community of people who follow Jesus?

QUESTION 2

How important to your Christian life are the other members of the church you belong to?

Jesus Christ

PART

2

CHAPTER 6

HOWARD MARSHALL

Who Was Jesus?

If we were to ask a Christian living some time around the year AD 60 'Who was Jesus?' we would probably have been told that we had put the question the wrong way. We should have asked, 'Who *is* Jesus?' and the answer would be something like 'Jesus is the Son of God and the Saviour of mankind'.

This is not a wild guess about the answer. It so happens that an early Christian wrote a book about Jesus somewhere in the second half of the first century—which we know as John's Gospel. He ended it by saying, 'These things have been written in order that you may believe that Jesus is the Messiah, the Son of God'. So John gives us our starting-point in trying to describe what Christians believed in the first century and still believe today.

But of course this raises several questions, and the only way to answer them is to go back to the beginning and ask who Jesus *was*.

Jesus As They Knew Him

What did people make of him, those who knew him at first hand? In what way did his followers continue to know him, even after his death and resurrection?

A real man

If we had asked ordinary Jews or informed pagans, 'Who was Jesus?' they would have understood us perfectly well. 'Jesus' was a common enough Jewish name, but one particular bearer of it had become notorious—the Jesus who came from the town of Nazareth in Galilee. He had been a travelling teacher and preacher who had toured round the land and acquired something of a reputation. Some of his comments were outspoken and he was popularly believed to have performed many remarkable cures. His activities had earned him the hostility of the Jewish authorities. He had been arrested and tried, and then handed over to the Roman governor of Judea, Pontius Pilate, who duly executed him by crucifixion. There were, it is true, some continuing strange rumours about him, and his followers claimed that he had come back to life. But surely no one took these seriously, or did they? The number of his followers seemed to be increasing in Judea and further afield.

The Christians would have denied none of this. They would merely have regarded it as a selective and one-sided account of the facts. And even in this form it has something important to tell us. There *was* a real person called Jesus, who really lived and really died.

People have sometimes tried to claim that Jesus never existed. His name is that of a fictitious character, they say, invented by Christians to explain how their religion came into being. The fatal difficulty with this theory is that it fails to explain how the Christian religion could possibly have arisen without Jesus. Some have suggested that originally the Christians believed in a mythical dying-and-rising god of a type not uncommon in the ancient world, and that they then proceeded to turn this mythical figure into a fictitious person for whom they invented a life story. But this suggestion is completely implausible. The first Christians were Jews, members of a nation whose religion would never have tolerated such pagan ideas. Marxist writers of fifty years ago were prepared to take up this 'Jesus-myth' theory; but their successors today no longer do so when attempting to discredit Christianity.

Jesus, then, existed as a real person, in every way a real member of the human race. His birth took place in the normal way, even though it was in a squalid outhouse of an inn. He grew up through boyhood to manhood, he learned and practised a manual occupation as a carpenter before his brief career as a preacher. He displayed the normal physical and mental characteristics of human beings, such as hunger and tiredness, joy and sorrow. He died a normal death, admittedly a far more cruel and painful death than most people have to suffer, but certainly not an abnormal one in the troubled conditions of first-century Palestine where hundreds of people were put to death by crucifixion by the tough Roman occupation.

Of course there were some common experiences in which Jesus did not share. He was not married and did not have any children. He died young and never experienced middle age or old age. But nobody would claim that a person who lacked these experiences and relationships was not for that reason a real human being. By all normal standards he lived an ordinary human life.

It may be significant that all the information of this kind about Jesus is given quite casually and incidentally by the people who wrote about his life. They were not trying to prove that he was a real human being. There is no need to prove what everybody accepts, and the point was unquestioned, at least in the early days of the Christian church. For various leading Christians it was a matter of some importance. It was fundamental to their faith that Jesus really was a man like any other man who took his place among humankind and as a man achieved certain things on behalf of other people. This makes it all the more striking that they found no need to prove that Jesus really was a man. The manhood of Jesus was not so much something that Christians believed about Jesus, as something they could take for granted with complete confidence.

A unique man

What was it that made this man distinctive?

- **The message that he preached.** Jesus announced the coming of the rule, or kingdom, of God, a sovereign, powerful action of God which would establish righteousness and peace in the world and set people free from the power of evil. His contemporaries compared him with the Jewish teachers of their day (the Rabbis) or with the prophets of a former age who spoke on behalf of God. But his message went a good way beyond what the prophets had said. They often spoke of what God would do in the future, but Jesus made it clear that the time in which he lived was the time of fulfilment; God's promises were already being fulfilled and would come to fruition in the imminent future.
- **The actions of Jesus.** The people regarded him as a worker of miracles. He himself believed that he had unusual powers to heal people of illness and to exorcize those who suffered from demon-possession. The important thing is how he interpreted these actions: not simply as supernatural cures, but rather as signs that God was working in power through him, establishing his rule over evil.
- **The way he summoned his hearers to follow him exclusively.** A teacher might gather a group of pupils or disciples around himself, but Jesus demanded a loyalty from his hearers that went beyond anything known in the Jewish society of his time. He called for a total commitment to himself, coming before any other claims on a person's loyalty and service. He taught that people must obey God, but the new dimension in his teaching was how this obedience was to be put into effect—in people's decision to follow him, God's messenger. Perhaps the most forceful way he expressed this was when he claimed that a person's ultimate destiny depended on their attitude to

Take hold of Jesus as a man and you will discover that he is God.

Martin Luther

him: if anybody acknowledged him, that person would be accepted at the last judgment, and if anybody denied him, they would be condemned.

Who did people think he was? Some were prepared to put him alongside the great prophets of earlier centuries. Others asked whether he was the Messiah, the king who was expected to arise and establish God's kingdom for ever. The difficulty was that a wandering preacher hardly looked like a future king, especially when he rejected the use of violence. He was obviously not interested in leading a war to liberate the Jews from their hated overlords, the Romans.

Those who were closest to Jesus and who shared in his travelling ministry had opportunity to think the matter over more deeply. They became aware of the closeness of Jesus' relationship with God. He was a person who spent much time in prayer, and when he prayed he addressed God as his Father, with a degree of confidence and intimacy greater than anyone else before or since. If a person calls God 'Father', it means he sees himself as in some sense a son of God, and Jesus certainly did so.

The friends of Jesus must have wondered just what all this meant. It is difficult to say how much they came to believe about him during his lifetime. They were certainly prepared to commit themselves to him. They left their homes and family ties to share in his work. One of them, Peter, voiced the belief that Jesus was the Messiah. But how firm was this belief at this stage? The rising opposition to Jesus, particularly from the religious leaders whose hypocrisy Jesus attacked so fiercely, his arrest and trial, and finally his death, all came as a cruel shock to the disciples and dashed their hopes. Luke caught the immediate mood of the friends of Jesus after his death: two of them talk to a stranger about 'Jesus of Nazareth. He was a prophet, powerful in word and deed before God and all the people. The chief priests and our rulers handed him over to be sentenced to death, and they crucified him. But we had hoped that he was the one who was going to redeem Israel.'

Raised from the dead

Then came the events of Easter. The followers of Jesus discovered that the tomb in which he had been buried was empty three days later. Then, on several distinct occasions, he reappeared to many of them, no longer dead but alive.

The effect of all this was electrifying. Certainly Christianity could not have come into being unless Jesus had really existed. Equally certainly, it would never have come into being unless people had believed in his resurrection. And this belief could not have arisen if the resurrection was not itself a historical event. The best evidence for the resurrection is the rise of the Christian church; nothing less could have turned Jesus' despondent and disillusioned followers into a joyful and vigorous church. But that is not the only evidence. Attempts to explain away the testimonies of early Christians to the empty tomb and the appearances of Jesus have been remarkably unsuccessful. The historical resurrection stands on solid ground.

The event had the immediate effect of confirming the teaching of Jesus. God would not raise from the dead a person who had been a false prophet. And, since only God can raise the dead, it followed that Jesus must have been true in what he said and did. Any doubts about whether Jesus was the Messiah disappeared for his followers. But the resurrection was seen to have other implications too:

- After Jesus had appeared to his friends over a period of a few weeks, he left them, and they had no doubt that he had gone to be with God in heaven. They quickly came to the conviction hat he was now 'seated' with God—exalted and honoured by him.

- The early church quickly appreciated the significance of Jesus' resurrection. As Paul wrote: 'Christ Jesus . . . was declared with power to be the Son of God by his resurrection from the dead.'

As a result of the resurrection, the early church came to the conclusion that the Jesus whom they had known as a unique earthly man was indeed the Messiah, the Lord and the Son of God.

Living presence

To those first Christians Jesus was not simply a figure of the past. Though physically absent, he was still alive. And if alive, active. This activity took various forms:

- If Jesus was alive and present with God the Father, he was **someone to whom they could pray**. One can pay honour to the dead and continue to remember them. But they were conscious of Jesus as a living person to whom they could render worship and offer their prayers, and with whom they could have some kind of personal relationship. Each of these elements is involved in prayer.

There is the element of **worship and adoration**, as when they called Jesus 'Lord' and gave him their whole-hearted praise.

There is also the element of **petition**, in which Jesus is specifically asked to do something for the person praying. Prayers like this, however, are not common. Generally the early Christians directed their petitions to God the Father, but did so by invoking the name of Jesus in their prayers. This means that Jesus was not so much the one who answered their prayers as the one who supported their petitions to God the Father. Not that they pictured the Father as unwilling to answer prayers unless persuaded by the Son. But they knew that the Father, whom they had not seen or heard, was like his Son, whom they had seen and heard, and would show the same love to them.

The third element in prayer is **fellowship**. The Christians were brought into a spiritual relationship with Jesus. In these ways, the Christian activity of prayer testified to a belief that Jesus was alive and active as the hearer of prayer.

- The beginning of the church's life as a self-conscious body was the experience of the first disciples as they received **the gift of the Holy Spirit** on the day of Pentecost. The early Christians saw this fundamental experience as given to them by the living Jesus. Although this was the first and most impressive time when the new reality of the Spirit was given to people, the same gift continued to be given to each new convert. In fact the evidence whether a particular person was a Christian was whether they possessed the Spirit. Paul could say: 'If anyone does not have the Spirit of Christ he does not belong to Christ.' What we may call 'being a Christian' is expressed here by Paul as 'belonging to Christ'. But the important fact is that those who belong to Christ have the Spirit, and he is called the Spirit of *Christ*. This is because the Spirit was seen as the gift of Jesus to the church. As Peter put it, 'Exalted to the right hand of God, he has received from the Father the promised Holy Spirit, and has poured out what you now see and hear.' Thus from Jesus came the gift of the Spirit, a spiritual power so closely associated with him as to be called 'the Spirit of Jesus' or 'the Spirit of Christ'.

- Also, they now saw Jesus, whom they had known as a man, to be a **spiritual, universal being**. He was no longer a person confined to one place and time, as he had been during his earthly life. Now he could be with all his people everywhere, entering into a personal relationship with each of them.

Jesus is a God whom we can approach without pride and before whom we can humble ourselves without despair.

Blaise Pascal

The New Testament writers have various ways of expressing this. Sometimes they refer to the Spirit of Christ as the means whereby he has a personal relationship with his people. (The Spirit and Christ are not totally identified with each other, but their activities are spoken of in a very similar way.) At other times Christ himself is said to come into relationship with people. Paul sometimes speaks of the Spirit in the personality of the believer; he can also say, 'I no longer live, but Christ lives in me.' A person of whom this kind of thing is said is clearly of universal significance.

This point is underlined when Christ is spoken of in a way that can be called 'corporate'. Paul talks about Christians being 'in Christ'. Christ is the sphere in which they live. Certainly he uses this phrase with a variety of shades of meaning, but it is central for him that Christians are somehow joined to Christ—their existence determined by his. He speaks of the church as the body of which Christ is the head, and this is very similar to when John uses the image of the vine: 'I am the vine; you are the branches. If a man remains in me, and I in him, he will bear much fruit.' Christ as the stem and his people as the branches are joined to form an integral unity. Or again, Jesus spoke about building a temple, which, says John, was to be his body, and this links in with Paul's view that believers constitute a new temple in which the Spirit of God dwells. Here again there is this universal unity of Jesus with his people.

These three points show us something of how Christians thought of Jesus, risen and exalted. He received their prayer and communion, he was the giver of the Spirit, and he was joined to his people in a spiritual, corporate union. Those early Christians realized that Jesus was far more than a man who had been honoured by God. They are prepared to make staggering affirmations—about one who only recently had died the death of a criminal on the gallows.

After 1900 years, Jesus Christ still counts for more in human life than any other man that ever lived.

Dean Inge

The coming king

The early Christians knew Jesus to be living with them in the present, but they were also concerned with him in the future. He had taught that he would come with the glory of a king, and they confidently expected his return at the end of the world, which they believed was not far distant. They used imaginative language to picture it: the present structure of the universe would come to a cataclysmic end and Jesus would return visibly to gather together his people, whether dead or alive, and bring them to the eternal life of heaven. They saw him triumphing over all the forces of evil and establishing his kingdom, before handing over his authority to God the Father.

The end of the world has not in fact come as quickly as the first Christians hoped and expected. Some people have concluded that their hope is discredited—not only is the timetable mistaken, they say, but the whole concept of the return of Jesus is a false one. But this is a wrong conclusion. Some of the New Testament writers themselves faced up to these problems about timing and recognized that God had never laid down any precise time at which the return of Jesus might be expected; perhaps the coming of Jesus was delayed in God's mercy—to give more time for people to hear and respond to the gospel. Certainly the end of the world would come when it was least expected, and Christians ought to be in a state of readiness all the time. The Christian hope continues to be centred in the coming of Jesus in power and glory, and this expectation was of great importance in shaping the way the first Christians understood him.

Jesus As They Understood Him

The first Christians knew Jesus first as a man in Galilee and Jerusalem, then in his continuing existence alongside God the Father, and finally in their hope of his future coming. How did they understand the person whom they experienced in this way?

The fulfilment of Jewish hopes

There was one tool ready to hand, which the Christians used extensively in their quest to understand Jesus—their Bible, the Old Testament. They had good reason to look at this source, since it is clear that Jesus understood his own mission in the light of various passages in the Old Testament and encouraged his followers to search it for themselves. Several Old Testament themes proved particularly relevant:

- Jesus' message had been concerned with **the coming of the kingdom** or rule of God. In Old Testament times God exercised his rule over the people of Israel through their king, and there grew up the hope of a coming king belonging to the royal line of David, who would rule in righteousness and peace and act as the shepherd of his people. Since it was normal for a king to be appointed to his office in a ceremony of anointing, the Jews came to use the term 'anointed one' for this future king. The Hebrew word meaning 'anointed' has come over into English as 'Messiah', and the corresponding Greek word as 'Christ'. The frequency with which the Greek word appears in the New Testament shows that this concept was of great significance in understanding who Jesus was. He was the appointed king through whom God would exercise his rule.

It is true that during his earthly life Jesus did not adopt the normal style of a ruler. In fact the effect of his ministry was to show the unique character of God's rule, which is not a matter of force and military action, and is not expressed in politics. Jesus set people free from the power of evil, delivered them from illness and from guilt, and called them to follow him. He also 'preached good news to the poor', saying that the kingdom of God belonged to them. This was very different from the Jews' expectation of the Messiah, which was a complex amalgam of spiritual and political elements. It explains why Jesus himself used the word 'Messiah' only very rarely; he did not want people to have false expectations of what he would do.

Nevertheless, it was as a claimant to messiahship that he was crucified ('This is the king of the Jews'), and his followers announced that he was the Messiah of Jewish expectation, though a Messiah of a very different kind. For Paul in particular it was of the utmost importance that Jesus was a crucified Messiah: '... we preach Christ crucified: a stumbling block to Jews and foolishness to Gentiles, but to those whom God has called... Christ, the power of God and the wisdom of God.'

- Another Old Testament theme, which Jesus had used, was Daniel's picture of **the Son of man**, or a figure like a human being. From his use of this phrase the early Christians recognized that Jesus was the one to whom God had given dominion and authority, and they looked forward to his coming in glory at the end of the world.

- A third Old Testament concept used was **the servant of the Lord**, who was destined to suffer for the people. The early church recognized that various passages in the Old Testament, especially what are called the 'servant songs', applied clearly to Jesus. They used them to illumine both his ministry and his sacrificial death on the cross. In his account of the Last Supper, Luke records Jesus' words: 'It is written: "And he was numbered with the transgressors," and I tell you that this must be fulfilled in me.' This is one of several direct quotations from the servant songs. As they began to preach, the apostles included 'servant' among their several titles for Jesus.

In these and other ways, the early church saw that in Jesus the Old Testament promises of a future deliverer and ruler were being fulfilled. In the Old Testament were prophesied both the role of Jesus as Messiah and the outline and some of the details of what he did. A vast amount of early Christian discussion of the significance of Jesus was based on a thorough exploration of all the material in the Old Testament that could possibly refer to him.

The Son of God

But the meaning of Jesus' coming was not the only vital concern of those early Christians. They needed to understand his nature. Who *is* Jesus?

Again the starting-point lay in what he said about himself. **Jesus addressed God as his Father and spoke of himself as his Son.** Was this intended to mean more than the sort of language used of the Israelite kings, or even of ordinary pious Jews? Jesus' relationship with his Father was clearly on a deeper level. The disciples came to understand that he was uniquely the Son of God. This was shown, for instance, by the unusual way in which the heavenly voice addressed Jesus at his baptism and transfiguration: 'You are (this is) my Son, whom I love.' Early Christians remembered these incidents and also thought over the implications of the resurrection. As they did so, they saw that Jesus had a unique relationship with God.

If Jesus was really God's Son, then a number of important things followed:

- **His death on the cross was not a historical accident, but an action planned by God the Father.** On the cross the Father gave his Son to die for sinners. It was an amazing demonstration of the greatness of God's love. God had not spared his Son, but had given him up for the sake of sinners; there could be no love greater than that. The death of Jesus was not simply the result of Jesus' own decision to die. In a very real sense God the Father was involved in his death, and Paul could say that 'God was reconciling the world to himself in Christ'. Not only so, but the whole mission of Jesus to the world was due not to his own initiative but to the action of God in sending him into the world.
- On this understanding, it was inescapable that **the Son of God must have existed and been with God before he was born into the world as Jesus**. 'God sent his own Son,' wrote Paul. 'He came as the son of a human mother.' Jesus was eternally with God. He came into the world to reveal God to humankind, to save people from their sins, and to set up a whole new world order.
- **Jesus shared in the work of God even before the world began.** In fact, the Son was active along with the Father in the creation of the universe. An early Christian form of confession quoted by Paul expressed the point: 'For us there is but one God, the Father, from whom all things come and for whom we live; and there is but one Lord, Jesus Christ, through whom all things came and through whom we live.' This was a staggering affirmation to make about a man who had been put to death as a criminal some twenty or so years previously.

God became man

If Jesus was the pre-existent Son of God, Christians were faced by a pressing question: how was his coming into the world to be explained? Their answer ran along two complementary lines. On the one hand, there was the concept of incarnation (literally 'embodiment'). This is expressed most clearly in the Gospel of John, which begins with a majestic statement about the Word of God. The exposition makes it clear that the Word was not a mere power or utterance of God, but a personal Being who shared his nature and was involved in the task of creation. It was through the Word that God was revealed to the world. John's description of the Word reaches a climax when he writes that 'the Word became a human being' (literally 'became flesh'). Without ceasing to be what it originally was, the Word took on a human form.

The belief that Jesus is the incarnate Son of God finds perhaps its clearest expression in the prologue to John's Gospel. But it is also found in a good deal of New Testament teaching. It clearly lies behind the picture of Jesus in the whole Gospel of John. There Jesus is presented as the Son of God who has come from God and will return to God. He existed before the time of Abraham. In John's first letter the writer emphatically declares that a person who denies the incarnation cannot have God as his own Father.

Paul also thinks of Jesus as the Son whom God sent into the world, the one who exchanged the riches of his pre-existent state for the poverty of a human life. He describes at length how the one who 'had the nature of God gave up all he had, and took the nature of a servant. He became like man and appeared in human likeness.' He can say that 'the full content of divine nature lives in Christ, in his humanity', and can also stress that it was 'by means of the physical death of his Son' that God has reconciled mankind to himself. For Paul it is important *both* that Jesus was God's Son, his personal representative, *and* that he was truly a man made of flesh who shared in the nature of humanity and so could die on our behalf.

A third important New Testament author presents the same picture of Jesus. The writer to the Hebrews paints a majestic picture of Jesus as the Son of God who 'is the exact likeness of God's own being' and yet who shared the human nature of those he came to save.

These passages, which are not exhaustive, show that John, Paul and the writer to the Hebrews all share the same belief in the incarnation of the Son of God. When some people say that the incarnation is an unimportant doctrine found on the margin of the New Testament, they are quite simply wrong; the three main New Testament theologians all teach otherwise.

Born in Bethlehem

As the other complementary line of approach, we have the presentation of the story of Jesus in the Gospels of Matthew and Luke. Both of these writers are clear that Jesus is the Son of God. The question they try to answer is 'How can Jesus be the Son of God?' (This is not quite the same way of putting the question as we find in the three writers above. They were asking 'How did the Son of God come into the world to save us?') The answer given by Matthew and Luke takes the form of an account of the birth of Jesus and the events leading up to it. They tell how Mary received an angelic message that, although still a virgin, she would bear a child; the Holy Spirit would come upon her, and so her child would be the Son of God. When Joseph discovered that his wife-to-be was with child, he too received an angelic message that 'What is conceived in her is from the Holy Spirit'. So the way these writers explain how Jesus could be the Son of God is by going back to his birth and telling what happened.

The stories of the virgin birth need not imply that Jesus was the *pre-existing* Son of God, and some writers have suggested that in fact they contradict the idea of the incarnation. But in fact both John and Paul reveal that they knew Jesus was born of a human mother, and they evidently saw no incompatibility between his incarnation and his human birth. Indeed, we can probably go further and say that the incarnation of the Son of God was bound to involve a different kind of birth from that of an ordinary human being. Since the Holy Spirit is the power through whom God's new creation takes place, it is wholly appropriate that the Spirit should have been the means whereby the Son of God came into the world.

The Lord of creation

We have seen that Jesus was regarded as Messiah and as Son of God. But there is one further dimension to our question 'Who was Jesus?' This was the recognition that **Jesus occupied a position of power and authority comparable with that of God.**

In the same passage in which Paul describes how the Son of God took the form of a servant, he goes on to tell of his ultimate act of self-emptying: 'He was humble and walked the path of obedience all the way to death—his his death on the cross.' But then it goes on: 'For this reason God raised him to the highest place above and gave him the name that is greater than any other name. And so in honour of the name of Jesus all beings in heaven, on earth, and in the world below will fall on their knees, and all will openly proclaim that Jesus Christ is Lord, to the glory of God the Father.' The crucifixion was followed by exaltation to a position of supremacy as Lord.

There could be no higher status. When a person confessed Jesus as Lord it was a fundamental act of loyalty and faith which declared him to be a Christian, one who accepts the authority of Jesus over his own life. But Paul did not think of Jesus as merely the Lord of individuals. He was Lord too of the whole spiritual and social power structure, summed up in the term 'principalities and powers'. One day everything now broken and fragmented would be brought together in Jesus, whose death was for the reconciliation of the whole of creation under his lordship. One day the one through whom the universe was created would receive the homage of all creation.

There is even more to this homage than meets the eye. When Paul talked about people falling on their knees and making open proclamation of Jesus as Lord, his language was inspired by a verse in Isaiah which speaks of homage addressed to God the Father. The same thing happens in various other New Testament passages: verses from the Old Testament that originally referred to God are applied to Jesus. The early Christians ascribed to Jesus the same honour as they gave to God himself. In fact, the term 'Lord' which they gave to Jesus had been used in the Greek translation of the Old Testament to translate the Hebrew name for God ('Yahweh'). The Son of God was given the same honour as God himself and seen to share his nature and functions. Once or twice he is given the actual name of 'God'. But this use is quite rare and largely restricted to the later books of the New Testament, perhaps because it could so easily be misunderstood to suggest that the Father and the Son were identical with one another. Rightly understood it reflects the true extent of the New Testament appraisal of Jesus.

Here, then, we have the answer to both our questions, 'Who was Jesus?' and 'Who is Jesus?' The New Testament writers saw him as having a unique relationship with God the Father. They did not much explore this relationship or work out how it was possible; that step had to wait for the theologians of the following centuries who worked out in great detail the doctrines of the trinity and of the incarnation. But their conclusion is still clear, and once accepted it changes a person's whole life and thinking—Jesus is the Lord, who shares the honour due to God alone.

Is the New Testament Answer True?

So far we have faced the question 'Who did the writers of the New Testament think Jesus was?' We need now to ask whether their answer is true—whether Jesus really was and is who they claimed.

- Can we rely on the reports in the Gospels about **the life, character and teaching of Jesus**? The New Testament writers base their conclusion that Jesus was Messiah, Son of God and Lord on their account of what he said and did. If this is untrue, then of course their interpretation falls to the ground. The evidence in the Gospels has been

DAVID WRIGHT

The Church's Understanding of Christ

Jesus Christ is the heart of the Christian faith. What has the Christian church believed about Jesus down the centuries? Who was, who is Jesus Christ? Man, or God, or both? If he is both, how are his manhood and his 'Godhood', or divinity, related to each other?

These are questions about the *person* of Christ—who he is. As a subject of Christian belief it has traditionally been distinguished from the *work* of Christ—what he did and does for humanity as saviour and Lord. This article traces the development of Christian beliefs about the person of Christ. 'Christology' is the name theologians use for this subject.

New Testament conviction

The first Christians were Jews and therefore firmly believed in the unity of God. They shared the basic faith of the Jews that 'the Lord our God is one Lord'. Yet by the time of the birth of the Christian church at the Pentecost festival in Jerusalem, the apostles had come to honour Jesus also as 'Lord'. We see this, for example, in the way they applied Old Testament statements about 'the Lord (Yahweh)' to Jesus.

The Gospels show clearly that this conviction about Jesus was reached only slowly and uncertainly. But gradually, through his teaching and life and finally through his resurrection, the first followers of Jesus realized that he was 'the Christ (Messiah), the Son of the living God'. The writings of the New Testament illustrate the different ways in which the first Christian preachers expressed this message.

- ☐ Normally they presented Jesus in terms of **Old Testament** figures, such as Messiah, redeemer, saviour, Lord, Son of God.
- ☐ But some of the titles they used, such as Son of God, Lord and Word (Logos) of God, were more easily understood in **the Gentile world**.

The New Testament teaching about the person of Christ builds towards a high point: the proclamation in John's Gospel that Jesus is the Word and Son of God.

One God or two?

Some of the earliest church fathers strongly asserted that Jesus was both human and divine. **Ignatius of Antioch** (died about 115) affirmed that Jesus was a real man of flesh and blood. He was attacking the **Docetists**, who claimed that Jesus only 'appeared' to be human; he was really a divine visitor in human disguise. (Throughout the history of the church ordinary Christians have often been tempted to think of Jesus in this way.) On the other hand, Jewish-Christian groups such as the **Ebionites** saw Jesus as an outstandingly holy man who was 'adopted' as God's Son at his baptism by the gift of divine power. Others with similar views were called **Adoptionists**. Some Jewish Christians regarded Jesus simply as the supreme prophet.

Thus Christian teachers found themselves declaring that Jesus was both true God and true man. But until the fourth century little close attention was paid to the relationship between the divine and the human in Christ. More urgent questions arose about the divinity (or deity) of Jesus Christ. Both pagans and Jews accused Christians of not being real monotheists but of worshipping two Gods—the Father and Christ. A common response to this charge fell into another serious error. This was known as **Monarchianism** and was popular around AD 200. The Monarchians safeguarded the oneness or singleness ('monarchy') of God by making 'Father', 'Son' and 'Spirit' into merely different names for a single person. God used different names at different times for his different roles or 'modes' of life. The names did not refer to persons really distinct from one another.

Three persons, one nature

The church fathers of the second and third centuries grappled with these and other false teachings. Among them **Tertullian** and **Origen** were outstanding. Both used words not found in the Bible to explain their teaching about Christ. Words like 'person', 'substance' and 'nature' came into use as technical terms to help explain it. Against the Monarchians, Tertullian and

Origen stressed that Father, Son (or Word) and Spirit were three 'persons', eternally distinct from each other. Origen also taught that, when Christians spoke of the Son of God, they did not mean that the Son had no existence until he was born from the Father. This way of speaking focused on Jesus Christ's relationship to the Father; the Son was eternally dependent upon the Father.

The question of the person of Christ was on its way to becoming the most critical issue of Christian belief in the early church. It had two main aspects:

- ☐ **The oneness of God:** what was the relation between God the Father and the Son of God (and also the Spirit of God)? This became known as the doctrine of the trinity, and is dealt with elsewhere in this book.
- ☐ **The person of Christ:** how could he be both true man and true God, yet really one person?

Both of these questions involved the divinity of Christ. Christian thinkers of the second and third centuries, especially **Justin Martyr** and other defenders of the faith (known as the **Apologists**), developed the idea of Christ as the Logos (Word or Mind) of God. This presented Christ as the intermediary between God and the world. But it lacked a strong personal flavour, and it seemed to give Christ the status of second-grade divinity. It was not until the fourth century that Christian theology overcame this tendency to make Jesus Christ's divinity somehow inferior to the Father's.

Dangerous denials

Early in the fourth century, **Arius** taught that the Father alone was true God. This denial of Christ's true deity was countered by councils of church leaders at Nicea (325) and Constantinople (381), and by great theologians such as **Athanasius**. The Nicene Creed was the product of these synods. At last the church established that the Son was as fully divine as the Father. Like **Irenaeus** in the second century, Athanasius showed how the hope of salvation depended on Christ's being true God as well as true man. The Christian could confidently trust Jesus Christ for salvation, because he was none other than God himself, 'who became man for us men and for our salvation'. No one less than God could restore us to fellowship with God.

Later in the fourth century a denial of the full manhood of Christ was also condemned. Against **Apollinarius'** teaching, the church made it absolutely clear that Jesus had not only a human body but also a human mind and soul. Apollinarius taught that the divine Son was totally responsible for thought and action in Christ. He felt he could have no confidence in Jesus if he was controlled by a fallible human mind. His opponents argued that if the Son did not take to himself the whole of human nature—soul and mind as well as flesh, then he did not redeem our whole humanity.

Two different approaches

In the fourth and fifth centuries two different approaches to the person of Christ developed in Christian teaching in the great Eastern churches of Antioch and Alexandria. They have often reappeared in the later history of the church, for example among the Protestant Reformers of the sixteenth century.

Theologians of **Antioch** emphasized the importance for our salvation of Christ's life of complete obedience as man, his victory as a fully-human being over temptation and sin. They insisted that Christ's human nature was quite unchanged by being united with the Son of God. The two natures in the incarnate Christ remained distinct and retained their proper character. As a consequence the Antiochenes were not very convincing when they spoke about the unity of Christ's person.

The **Alexandrians'** viewpoint had the greater influence. For them Christ's divine nature was all-important. The incarnation was all about God coming to rescue humanity. At times they seemed to portray Christ as a divine person merely using a human body (which was close to Apollinarius' error). They were able to hold on strongly to the unity of Christ's person, but at the cost of implying a mixture or fusion of his two natures into one. Jesus Christ's human life and experiences were largely neglected. He was generally assumed to be all-knowing and all-powerful.

Two natures, one person

The struggles between these competing viewpoints led to the council of church leaders at Chalcedon (451). It produced a famous statement which has remained basic to the faith of the church ever since. At the time it was enforced by the law of the state! This definition made clear that Jesus Christ was both fully God and fully man. These two 'natures' were united in one 'person' but without being changed or confused. They remained distinct, but they came together in the single person of Christ.

Parts of the Eastern church were unhappy about the words used by the council. They took a strongly Alexandrian view, following **Cyril of Alexandria**. They wanted to use the phrase 'one-nature' (not two) of the incarnate Christ. The difference was largely a battle over words. Nevertheless, within two centuries, separatist churches had broken away in Egypt and Syria. They were known as **Monophysite** ('single-nature') churches. This division occurred despite repeated attempts to find a compromise (which the emperors wanted for political and military reasons).

Chalcedon did not bring an end to discussion among orthodox churchmen about the 'two-natures' doctrine. Even subtler questions were raised. Did Christ also have two wills, and two modes of action ('energies')? Was his human nature 'personal' or not? Could human nature be real without being focused in a human person? On this point **Leontius of Byzantium** (died 543) developed a view that was widely accepted: Christ's humanity 'became personal' in union with the incarnate Son of God. This avoided the danger of dividing Christ into two full persons, and made more sense of the portrait of Jesus in the Gospels.

Medieval concepts of Christ

As the Christian world divided early in the Middle Ages, both East and West inherited the doctrine of Chalcedon about Christ. In the East it was coloured by a strongly Alexandrian viewpoint. Jesus Christ's human life was seen more as the arena in which God worked our salvation than as an active agent in bringing it about. Salvation itself was often spoken of as 'divinization'—the believer coming to share Christ's divine nature. The glorified Christ was the focus of worship; monasticism and mysticism flourished. All these factors contributed to a neglect of Christ's real humanity, which in turn probably contributed to the growth of devotion to other human figures, such as Mary and the martyrs.

For various reasons, Western churchmen in the Middle Ages showed greater interest in the humanity of Jesus. The influence of **Augustine** (died 430) was enormous. He had emphasized that Christ became our saviour through his humility and humiliation as a man. **Anselm** (died 1109) wrote an important book *Why did God become Man?* According to Anselm, Christ paid off humanity's debt to God, a debt that was due because our sin had robbed God of his honour. This theory made Christ's human life essential to the achievement of redemption. **Abelard** (died 1142) even taught that the purpose of Jesus Christ's incarnation was to set forth a perfect example of love in human life.

Influential leaders in Catholic devotion also directed attention to Christ's humanity. **Bernard of Clairvaux**, in the twelfth century, preached and meditated on the love of Christ, particularly in his death on the cross. 'To follow naked the naked Christ' was the aim of **Francis of Assisi**. He highlighted the simplicity of Jesus' life, and his care for lepers and other outcasts. **Thomas à Kempis** in the fifteenth century wrote *The Imitation of Christ*, which has become a widely-read presentation of the love and holiness of Christ.

Yet among the **Schoolmen**, the important church teachers of the late Middle Ages, the significance of Jesus' human experience was overshadowed by clever speculation. Medieval Catholicism as a whole too easily lost sight of the human Christ. Superstitions about the magical power of his body and blood dominated the mass. Reverence for Mary and the saints partly compensated for—and encouraged—this one-sided view of Christ.

Christ in the Lord's Supper

The Protestant Reformers accepted the teaching of the early councils and creeds about Christ, but they restored to the heart of the faith the living and saving Jesus Christ of the New Testament. They related Christ's person more closely to his work as redeemer, and placed a new emphasis on the historical Jesus of the Gospels. This led in time to a fresh distinction between Christ's 'state of humiliation' on earth and his subsequent 'state of exaltation' in glory.

Martin Luther preached a 'theology of the cross'. He identified closely with Jesus' experiences and struggles as a man. Faith in Christ, he held, must hold fast to the lowly, suffering Christ, and not speculate about his heavenly being. As **Melanchthon** once wrote in criticism of the Schoolmen, 'to know Christ is to know his benefits, not to contemplate his natures and the modes of his incarnation.'

But the person of Christ did become a controversial issue among the Reformers, in their disagreement over the way in which Christ was present in the Lord's Supper. Luther believed that Christ's body and blood were really present in the bread and wine of the Supper. This was possible because they shared in Christ's divine nature, which is present everywhere. Luther accepted the Alexandrian view that there took place a sharing or interchange between the powers of Christ's divinity and humanity. **Zwingli** opposed Luther. He held that if Christ's manhood was true manhood, it could only be in one place at a time—now beside the Father's throne in heaven.

John Calvin aimed to hold together Christ's person and work. Jesus Christ was prophet, priest and king—this was his 'threefold office'. In Christ 'God so received what is ours as to transfer to us what is his'. Unlike Luther, Calvin rejected any blurring of the distinction between Christ's two natures. Luther seemed to confuse them, but Calvin contrasted them. Nevertheless they were united in the incarnation. It was through the Spirit that Christ was present in the Lord's Supper. Calvin also taught, like some of the early fathers, that, even during Christ's earthly life, the Son did not cease to be active throughout the universe as the Word of the Father.

In the turmoil of the Reformation, one minor current of Protestant teaching rejected both the trinity and Christ's divinity. This arose chiefly among Italian exiles. It produced Socinianism or **Unitarinism**, which was strong in Poland. Like the error condemned in the early church, it understood Jesus Christ simply and solely as a man empowered by the Holy Spirit. Unitarianism (which like Arianism regards the Father alone as God) has survived to the present day, and has been given a new lease of life by Jehovah's Witnesses.

The quest of the historical Jesus

Modern theology cannot be understood apart from the influence of the movement of thought in the eighteenth century known as the **Enlightenment.** This gave a new authority and freedom to human reason. Since then, the supernatural character of the life and work of Christ has often been rejected or watered down. **Friedrich Schleiermacher** (born 1768) is frequently called 'the father of modern theology'. He thought of Jesus Christ as divine because of his unique consciousness of God. Jesus was first and foremost the perfect example of a life lived in total dependence upon God. Although 'absolutely distinguished from all other men through his essential sinlessness and his absolute perfection', he was no more than a man.

The Enlightenment spread a questioning, sceptical outlook. This influenced the new movement of historical study of the Bible known as 'biblical criticism'. These different pressures came together to produce 'the quest for the historical Jesus'—the simple, human Jesus of the Gospels who had been buried, so it was held, beneath the complicated doctrines of the church. During the nineteenth century numerous lives of Jesus were written. Most of them portrayed Jesus merely as a man. Here was a Jesus who often simply reflected contemporary ideals, the ideals of liberal theology. He was a supreme religious teacher and hero, a religious genius, rather than God's incarnate Son.

Christ's self-limitation

A fresh attempt was also made in the nineteenth century to understand how God could become man without his divinity swamping or squeezing out his human experience. This was the theory of Christ's *kenosis* or 'self-emptying' (from a Greek word Paul used in his letter to the Philippians). In becoming man, it was claimed, the Son of God 'emptied himself' of his glory, his perfect knowledge and power, and his universal presence. He did not give up his divine *nature*, although he may voluntarily have surrendered his consciousness of being divine. So his miracles were signs of the Father's power rather than his own.

But this 'kenotic theory' came under heavy attack. It seemed unreal to split Christ's divine nature from his divine powers. It almost suggested that God was transformed into man, exchanging divinity for humanity. Nevertheless, the theory has had a lot of influence. Some kind of self-limitation was certainly required by the incarnation. The divine glory of the Son was obviously veiled.

A life wholly open to God

Many recent interpretations of the person of Christ have started with the historical figure of Jesus rather than with the eternal Son. They have worked 'from below' rather than 'from above'. The church's traditional doctrine worked 'downwards'; the initiative lay with the Son who entered human life from his eternal pre-existence. This emphasis, which may be called Alexandrian, has been maintained by some outstanding modern theologians, such as **Karl Barth** (died 1968) and **T. F. Torrance** (born 1913). They and others have also taught that it was our *sinful* humanity that Christ shared. Christ's total identification with human life has been a strong point in most modern interpretations of who he is. Barth developed the idea of 'the humanity of God'. God and man, who became one in Christ, were not opposite to each other; the incarnation was not itself a union of two incompatible beings, divine and human. Barth also combined the doctrine of Christ's two natures with that of his two states: both refer to the two sides of what took place in Christ. His *humiliation* was God's becoming man to suffer and die, his *exaltation* was the life of man raised to true human dignity in obedient fellowship with the Father.

Despite powerful presentations like Barth's, the doctrine of Chalcedon has run into heavy criticism, especially for its use of the language and concepts of Greek philosophy. Its key terms, such as 'nature', 'person' and 'substance', are *static*, whereas the New Testament uses chiefly *dynamic* terms. Titles such as 'Christ', 'Lord', 'Son of man', and even 'Son of God' and 'Word' describe what Jesus achieved for our salvation, not who he was in his inner nature. The early fathers were concerned with Christ in his basic being, while the New Testament speaks about what he did and experienced.

So the life of Christ is frequently reinterpreted as a human life lived totally in the service and power of God, not as the unique personal union of God himself with humanity. Jesus was wholly open to the will of God. He lived out to the highest degree what it means to serve God and others in love. In this way he became a revelation of God and the one through whom God reconciled us to himself. But this way of portraying Christ makes him different only in degree from other servants of God.

Jesus of history: Christ of faith

It must not be forgotten that the traditional doctrine of the incarnation remains the official teaching of most branches of the church. It is embodied not only in the early creeds but also in the great church confessions of the century following the Reformation. At its beginning in 1948 the World Council of Churches declared itself to be 'a fellowship of churches which accept the Lord Jesus Christ as God and Saviour'. In 1961 this basis was expanded to '... confess the Lord Jesus Christ as God and Saviour according to the Scriptures and therefore seek to fulfil together their common calling to the glory of the one God, Father, Son and Holy Spirit'. **The Second Vatican Council** (1962–65) clearly assumed the church's traditional teaching 'concerning Christ the Word of God made flesh'. Its own statements dealt chiefly with Christ's historical place in God's dealings with humanity.

Nevertheless many hold today that the belief in Christ's person arrived at by the church in the early centuries is no longer adequate for today. Some claim that it does not even make sense: a human being could not be divine as well *without ceasing to be truly human.* **Rudolf Bultmann** (died 1976) has popularized the theory that the New Testament's statements about Christ are largely 'mythical'. Phrases like 'becoming man', 'sending his Son', 'raised from the dead' and 'at the Father's right hand' must not be taken literally. These 'mythical' statements use a pre-scientific, outdated world-view to express what Jesus Christ meant to the early Christians. Their meaning for human life today can be discovered only by stripping off the mythical form of expression. This meaning, according to Bultmann's view, belongs entirely to this world. There is no 'other world' for the Son of God to 'come from' or 'return to'. Bultmann and his followers wanted to set Christ free from the strange world of first-century Palestine, and to let the gospel be heard by modern men and women in their own language and forms of thought.

In recent years, scholars have argued for a distinction in the Gospels between 'the Jesus of history' and 'the Christ of faith'. It is often claimed that the first Christians were not interested in what Jesus said and did in Nazareth and Galilee, but only in the risen and exalted Lord Christ. Their gospel-message of the risen Christ has strongly coloured the presentation of Jesus in the Gospels, so that it is now difficult to discover what Jesus was really like. Certainly, the Gospels were written to present Christ as Saviour and Lord, but this did not rule out a keen interest in what really happened. Christian faith affirms that the risen Christ we trust and worship is none other than the Jesus who healed and taught and hungered and died.

In modern times theologians have often put forward exaggerated contrasts about the person of Christ—between who he was and what he achieved, between Chalcedon and the New Testament, between the historical Jesus and the Christ of faith. Such exaggerations may help in the long run to produce a more balanced picture of Christ. Theologians must always aim to bridge the gulf between the world of Jesus and our culture, between Nazareth and Jerusalem and Tokyo and Nairobi. Christ is the Saviour and Lord of twentieth-century people too, and must be presented in terms that are full of meaning for them. But we must beware of the temptation to create our own image of Christ. 'The political Christ' has recently become very popular. Attempts have been made to portray him as a liberator, a forerunner of freedom-fighters and the champion of the oppressed. These portrayals have rightly drawn attention to neglected aspects of the Gospels. But the church's beliefs about Christ will outlive, as they have already outlived, attempts to fit him into current fashions, merely contemporary programmes or ideals. Christ is greater than them all.

exhaustively discussed from this point of view. Certainly some scholars have reached a more sceptical verdict than others; particularly over the last hundred years, the Gospels have been subject to the most intense critical analysis. But they have survived the onslaught! The Gospels are based on reliable history. This does not mean that every detail in them can be *proved* to be true—that is an impossible task in the nature of things—nor even that we can assign to every part of the record an equally high degree of probability. But it does mean that there is a sufficient nucleus of historical material to give a starting-point for the sceptic, and to support the view of Jesus advanced in this article.

This is the way a New Testament scholar looks at it. But perhaps we need to step back and ask ourselves 'How does it seem to us?' How does the Gospel picture of Jesus strike us? Could it possibly be an invention? Of course our answer to these questions will stem from a very personal response, but many, many people have found themselves convinced that we are confronted in the Gospels by something that rings true.

■ Can we rely on the New Testament report of **the resurrection of Jesus**? As Paul said, 'If Christ has not been raised from death, then we have nothing to preach and you have nothing to believe.' Paul looked on the resurrection of Jesus as a historical fact on which faith could rest. If it had not happened, faith would be impossible. Modern writers have debated whether the resurrection of Jesus can be proved historically; some would say that it can, others that acceptance of it as historical is ultimately a matter of faith. Whichever view we adopt, no argument has ever been brought forward which would prove that the resurrection did *not* happen. On the contrary, there is good evidence that it did.

The Gospel accounts of the ministry of Jesus and the reports of his resurrection constitute the two foundations for the structure of the New Testament estimate of who Jesus is. In the end we all have to decide for ourselves whether we will accept the testimony of the New Testament to Jesus or not. If it is true, then the same Jesus whose living presence the early Christians continued to experience after his death and resurrection is still the saviour of our world today. They came to know Jesus as a real man and as the Son of God and Lord of the universe. He still invites our faith and commitment today.

For further thinking

QUESTION 1

Jesus' followers came to believe he was unique. In what ways was he completely different from anyone else? Try and think of at least four ways. Isolate an incident in his life or part of his teaching which shows each aspect of Jesus' uniqueness you have highlighted.

QUESTION 2

Read the Gospel of John, chapter 1, verses 1 to 14; this is one of the New Testament's fullest expositions of the incarnation. How has the fact that 'the Word became flesh' affected the human race?

QUESTION 3

Why is belief in the virgin birth important for Christian faith?

QUESTION 4

Some people have held that the Gospels do not give credible information about Jesus. What reasons would you give for maintaining that the Gospel-writers did not make up what they wrote?

BIBLE REFERENCES

Jesus the Messiah

Psalms 72:1–17; 89:3–4; Isaiah 9:6–7; 11:1–5; 53:1–12; 61:1–11; Ezekiel 37:24–25; Micah 4:1–2; 5:2; Zechariah 9:9–10; Matthew 21:1–9; Mark 8:27–30; 14:60–64; Luke 1:32–33; 2:11; 4:16–21; 7:18–23; John 4:25–26; 14:1—15:27; Acts 2:36; 3:18–26; 1 Corinthians 1:23–24; 1 Peter 2:21–25

Jesus the Redeemer

Exodus 6:6; 13:12–16; Leviticus 25:47–55; Job 33:24; Psalms 49:7–8; Mark 10:45; Luke 1:68; John 8:34–36; Acts 8:32–36; Romans 3:24–26; 1 Corinthians 6:19–20; 2 Corinthians 5:14–21; Galatians 3:13; 5:1; Ephesians 1:7; Colossians 1:14; 1 Timothy 2:5–6; 1 Peter 1:18–19; Revelation 5:9–10

Jesus the Word

Genesis 1:1–31; Psalms 33:6–9; Isaiah 55:10–11; John 1:1–18; Hebrews 1:1–3; Revelation 19:13

Incarnation

Matthew 1:20–23; 4:1–11; Mark 13:32; 14:32–36; Luke 2:39–52; 10:21; John 1:10–14; 4:7; 6:38; 12:27–28; Acts 2:22; 10:38–40; 13:23–25; Romans 8:3; Galatians 4:4; Philippians 2:5–11; 1 Timothy 2:5; 3:16; Hebrews 2:17–18; 4:15; 5:7–10; 1 Peter 4:1; 1 John 4:1–3

DICK FRANCE

Jesus' Life and Teaching

CHAPTER 7

Jesus Christ has been more admired but more misunderstood than any other person in history. To some he is an impostor, responsible for the most damaging and enduring deception ever devised. To others he is the ultimate revelation of God's truth to humanity. Some see him as the well-meaning but tragic victim of a cruel world. Others worship him as the divine conqueror of death. Some see him as a teacher of peace and love, others as the scourge of hypocrisy. Some see in him the children's friend, others the fiery champion of the oppressed masses. But all who go beyond a vague approval to a serious study of his life and teaching find that he cannot be so easily explained, that he is 'the man who fits no formula'.

Here we are concerned not so much with what people have thought of Jesus, but with the earliest accounts of his life and teaching in the Gospels. How did Jesus appear to those who saw and heard him in Palestine–suffering under Roman occupation in the days of the Emperor Tiberius? What impression would he have made on us if we had been there?

Preparing the Way

The opening chapters of each of the Gospels set the scene for the time when Jesus began to preach and to heal. They show us, both in Jesus' own experience and in what was happening in his country, how God was preparing the ground for those three world-changing years.

Before Jesus came to public attention his relative John had caused a sensation by his powerful preaching out in the wild country around the Jordan. He declared that God's judgment was about to fall even on his own people, Israel, and called people to 'turn away from your sins . . . and God will forgive your sins'. The many people who responded to his call accepted baptism or 'washing' in the river Jordan as a token of their change of heart. It was the sort of 'revival movement' that would worry the Jewish authorities.

It was at this point that Jesus first began his mission. He went to be baptized by John, declaring his solidarity with the movement John had begun. For some time Jesus and his followers operated a parallel baptizing movement. But when John fell foul of the local government, Jesus moved to Galilee, where his style of ministry changed.

Jesus' baptism

When Jesus was baptized by John, he had an experience which set the pattern for his future mission. 'He saw heaven opening and the Spirit coming down on him like a dove. And a voice came from heaven, "You are my own dear Son. I am pleased with you."' Old Testament prophecy said that the coming deliverer of God's people, the 'Messiah', would be endowed with the Spirit of God. At the river Jordan he joined those who needed deliverance, but now he was marked out as the deliverer himself.

But the voice from heaven went further and called him God's Son. The words sound like a phrase from one of the psalms, where God addresses the king, the Messiah. They also echo a passage from Isaiah where God speaks of his Servant, his chosen one, on whom his Spirit rests, and who is to be his people's deliverer. So here God himself declared who Jesus was—the servant-king sent to set his people free. It is no wonder that this experience took Jesus out of the carpenter's shop and launched him on a new life of public ministry.

Jesus' testing

Immediately after this experience the Gospels tell us of a period Jesus spent alone in the lonely area near the Jordan river. There his newly-declared relationship with God was tested by a series of suggestions from the devil, designed to probe the reality of his trust and confidence in his Father. 'If you are the Son of God ...', the devil began, and suggested that he should use this new-found status to satisfy his own needs, or to test God's promises of supernatural help—even that he should take a short cut to his destiny of ruling the earth by a pact with his Father's greatest enemy. Jesus responded by recalling the experiences and the lessons of the people of Israel in their desert wanderings long ago. He believed himself called to fulfil the mission of Israel, the 'son of God'; to succeed

CHRIS BYWORTH

The Names and Titles of Jesus

Jesus

was a common first name for a Jewish man. Nine others of this name are known at the time. It was the Greek version of three common Hebrew names, Joshua, Jehoshua and Jeshua. This was the name by which Jesus was known in his lifetime, and it occurs nearly 600 times in the Gospels. Its meaning was: 'The Lord (Yahweh) is my help' or 'Yahweh rescues'. Later New Testament writers use the name rarely; only the writer to the Hebrews uses it much. It stresses Jesus' humanity, as the carpenter of Nazareth.

Lord

Outside the Gospels, 'Lord' is Jesus' dominant title. Paul uses it 222 times, and 'Jesus is Lord' was the first creed for non-Jews. It was used in worship too. All ancient gods were called 'Lord'. Even in the Old Testament, 'Lord' was read out instead of 'Yahweh', which was too sacred to say. Although it could also be used simply to mean 'sir', it chiefly expressed Christ's rule over all, a rule that one day the whole world would recognize: 'All will openly proclaim that Jesus Christ is Lord.'

Son of man

is a title found almost exclusively in the Gospels, used by Jesus himself. This was his self-chosen title, which the early church did not take up, since it was not easy to understand or communicate. Its meaning is not so obvious as the other titles. In the Old Testament, it can simply be a way of saying 'a man'. In the book of Ezekiel, 'son of man' comes ninety times and emphasizes Ezekiel's frail humanity. But it was also used of a divine figure breaking in from heaven, whom the Jews increasingly came to expect. In the book of Daniel, the prophet's vision portrays such a figure; but he also sees the 'son of man' as a group, 'the saints of the Most High', who reign only after suffering.

Jesus' sayings include both aspects. He is human: 'the Son of Man has nowhere to lay his head', and in particular he 'must suffer many things'. Yet he is divine too: 'You will see the Son of Man sitting qt the right hand of Power and coming with the clouds of heaven.' Seemingly Jesus took this vague title and gave it his own meaning, stressing that his messiahship would involve rejection and death before resurrection and final return.

It was this note of suffering linked to future glory that differed so much from contemporary expectations. Peter found it hard to accept, and it provoked a sharp argument between them: 'Jesus began to teach ... "The Son of man must suffer much and be rejected ..." Peter ... began to rebuke him ... "Get away from me, Satan."'

I am

At the burning bush, God revealed his personal name to Moses as 'I am who I am', or simply 'I am'. In Hebrew this is 'Yahweh' (or 'Jehovah' in the older, inaccurate spelling).

In the New Testament, particularly in John's Gospel, we find Jesus used this title when speaking of himself. He used the style of deity: 'I am the vine', 'I am the bread of life', and so on. He even used God's personal name of himself at least once: 'Before Abraham was born, "I am".' His Jewish opponents knew very well what he meant. Understandably, they tried to stone him for blasphemy.

where Israel had failed. So his relationship with his Father stood the test, and he was, prepared to begin his mission.

The Kingdom of God Is At Hand

Mark's Gospel summarizes the theme of Jesus' preaching when he returned to Galilee after Herod had thrown John in prison: 'The time is fulfilled, and the kingdom of God is at hand; repent and believe in the gospel.'

This summary gives us three main themes in Jesus' preaching.

■ First there is the theme of

Messiah

was the main title given to Jesus by Jewish Christians. It is a Hebrew word meaning 'anointed', and its Greek equivalent is 'Christ'. At first it was a title, '*the* Christ'. Later it became part of his name: 'Jesus Christ'. Anointing was an act symbolizing that God had chosen and empowered a person, particularly a king. In the Old Testament the longing grew that God would make his people the top nation. Sometimes they thought of God doing this in person. More often, they hoped for another great king, like David, who would be their 'Messiah'. Later such political hopes faded and the longing grew for a divine figure direct from heaven.

Many claimed to be political messiahs in Jesus' day, particularly in Galilee. A Zealot group existed, and Jesus' disciple, Simon, was a member. Many tried to force Jesus into fulfilling this revolutionary role. Even Peter understood him in this way, and Jesus himself felt this temptation, especially since he saw himself as the fulfilment of all the varied strands of Old Testament hopes.

Misunderstanding was such a danger that Jesus preferred to keep his messiahship a secret, unless formally challenged.

Son of God

may well be the title most used but least understood today. It was central to the first Christians in stating their belief in Jesus and expressing their worship of him. In the Old Testament, angels could be called God's sons, as could Israel, and especially Israel's king.

In the New Testament, Christians are God's children. They have the privilege of calling God 'Abba'—the closest family name, almost 'Daddy'. But Jesus is the Son of God. His sonship is different in nature from his followers'. Thus Paul is careful to say that Christians are sons *by adoption*. And John's Gospel records Jesus speaking of God as 'my Father and your Father'.

Jesus was aware from boyhood of this special relationship to God. Its centrality for him stands out at his baptism, temptation, transfiguration, trial and death. His most normal way of addressing God was as 'Father', the one on whom he depended, and whom he obeyed. In John, who expounds the title most, it expresses a uniquely close relationship. In the Son, the Father can be seen with full clarity: 'Whoever has seen me has seen the Father.'

Son of David

God had promised David that his throne would be established for ever. So the longing grew for the coming of 'great David's greater son'. This was the kind of Messiah popularly expected in Jesus' day. In Matthew, Jesus is called 'Son of David' six times, mainly by simple people. But he only accepted it once, and then reinterpreted it. The first Christians claimed that Jesus was indeed the Son of David, born in David's city, Bethlehem.

The lamb

is a title for Jesus little used in the New Testament, but much used by the church since! The lamb was the animal for sacrifice, and especially for Passover, when the blood of a young, pure, male lamb rescued God's people from death. Philip, Peter, Paul, John the Baptist and supremely John the apostle saw Jesus thus, and especially in his death. They particularly saw this in the light of a phrase in one of Isaiah's 'servant songs', describing the servant as 'like a lamb that is taken to be slaughtered'.

The book of Revelation uses a different Greek word and a new set of ideas. Jesus is a lamb of power and authority, to be worshipped and feared.

fulfilment, of the coming of the long-awaited time of God's salvation. For so long the Jews had expected God to step in and bring to pass all that he had promised through his prophets of the Old Testament. The time, said Jesus, had now come. This was the climax of the long time of preparation.

- This fulfilment is summed up in the phrase **the kingdom of God**—Jesus' 'campaign slogan'. It occurs throughout his teaching and he uses it in many different ways. It is impossible to tie it down to a single clear situation or event. It means that God is king, that he is in control, that his will is being worked out—an idea which can have many different practical applications. But it shows us that the aim of Jesus' mission is nothing less than the total achievement of God's purposes, the assertion of his rightful sovereignty in his world.
- Such preaching demands **a**

The Virgin Mary

Mary holds a special place in Christianity. She was the mother of the Messiah. 'My heart praises the Lord; my soul is glad because of God my Saviour, for he has remembered me, his lowly servant! From now on all people will call me happy.' She was special because she was chosen for a unique task, and because she was available for God.

As the Christian centuries progressed, two factors combined to elevate Mary's position:

- ☐ When other-worldliness became the ideal and **virginity highly prized**, some began to argue that Mary was 'ever-virgin';
- ☐ When **the church tried to safeguard belief in Jesus' divinity**, people started to call Mary *theotokos*, 'God-bearer'.

In the Middle Ages, Jesus' divinity was often stressed in such a way as to make him remote from ordinary people. And so Mary became the focus for human needs. Who better than a mother to understand our pain?

As saints and holy people began to be thought of as interceding with God for men and women, Mary became chief of intercessors. In the Middle Ages, statues of the suffering Mary were almost as common as the cross.

The Reformers opposed these developments because they took people's attention away from Jesus as the one Saviour and Messiah. But the Roman Catholic emphasis on Mary continued. Nineteenth- and twentieth-century popular piety led to Popes putting out decrees making official doctrines of the **Immaculate Conception** (1854) and the **Bodily Assumption of the Blessed Virgin Mary into heaven** (1950). This tendency among Roman Catholics to go beyond the New Testament in their beliefs about Mary has led most Protestants to react by ignoring her altogether.

In recent years, since the **Second Vatican Council** (1962-65), Roman Catholic teaching on Mary has become more balanced:

- ☐ **She was a servant**, available for God and an example of God's grace;
- ☐ **She is part of the church**, not part of the godhead;
- ☐ **She is not a mediator**, that is, she plays no part in our salvation.

Many Roman Catholics are now uncomfortable with the dogmas of perpetual sinlessness and bodily assumption. They cannot be found in the Bible or in early Christian thought.

Protestants need to be reminded that Mary is a great example of faith, hope and love. She is full of grace and worthy of honour; as the angel said, 'The Lord is with you and has greatly blessed you.' To hold Mary in high esteem need in no way undermine worship of Jesus.

response. It is good news (which is what 'gospel' means), but only to those who respond personally to the challenge it brings. So Jesus calls people to 'repent' and 'believe'—a complete turnaround which will affect both their relationship with God and their dealings with one another. It is as men and women respond with this decisive repentance and faith that God's will is worked out, in their lives and in the society of which they are part. In other words, that is how the 'kingdom of God' is established.

We can now look in closer detail at these three themes in turn.

The time of fulfilment

The Jews were full of hope. The Old Testament told them in many ways that God had better things in store for his people. It spoke of a coming 'day of the Lord', and it presented a number of figures through whom God would one day fulfil his purpose: a great king of the line of David, a prophet like Moses, a priest like Melchizedek, a humble shepherd, a rejected servant, and many others. By the time of Jesus some of these ideas, but especially that of the king in David's line, were being referred to by the title Messiah, the Lord's anointed. The political circumstances of the first century made it inevitable that most ordinary Jews linked such hopes with Israel's subjection to Rome. They saw the coming of God's Messiah as the means of national restoration and independence.

Jesus hardly ever spoke of himself as the Messiah (or 'Christ'). If he had done so, his hearers would almost certainly have seen his role in a political or nationalistic light, which he was anxious to avoid. Jesus did not back those who favoured armed rebellion against Rome. He frequently discouraged his followers from having political hopes for his mission.

So Jesus could not freely use politically loaded terms such as 'Christ' and 'Son of David'. But he made no secret of his belief that he had come to fulfil the Old Testament's promises of a God-sent deliverer. Bypassing the passages on which political hopes might be based (those which spoke of a king in David's line), he explained his purpose by using some of the less prominent 'messianic' themes. Significantly, they all focus on peace, righteousness, humility—even suffering and death.

The two passages to which he referred most often were:

- The description of the suffering and death of **God's servant** for the sins of his people in Isaiah 53.
- The vision in Daniel 7 of **'a son of man'**. When this figure was vindicated and raised to the throne of God, it would spell salvation for God's holy people.

These two passages, which had never been brought together in this way before, were basic to the way Jesus understood his mission. He was to suffer and die for his people's sins, and then, vindicated and raised to God's presence, receive an everlasting dominion in which his people would share.

It was from Daniel's vision that Jesus drew his own strange name for himself, turning Daniel's 'son of man' (which means simply 'human being') into a specific 'title', 'the Son of man'. It was not a title with which anyone would be already familiar, and so Jesus could use it for his own unique role without fear of misunderstanding.

But Jesus did not see his mission merely in the light of a few selected 'messianic' passages. When John the Baptist questioned whether he really was 'the one who was to come', Jesus pointed out how closely his ministry corresponded to passages from the book of Isaiah. Jesus is quoting two passages here. One talks about the coming of God's anointed servant to preach deliverance, but the other is simply about what *God himself* will do for his people. Often Jesus explained his work in the light of such passages. So not only were the prophecies of a Messiah fulfilled in his mission, but also the whole range of hopes of the 'day of the Lord', when God would finally bring salvation. It is a claim of breath-taking boldness, the more remarkable because as well as spelling it out in his more formal teaching, Jesus almost casually assumed it in many incidental remarks.

If that were not enough, we find another remarkable pattern in Jesus' references to the Old Testament. Sometimes he spoke of himself in ways which suggested that he corresponded in some sense to the great figures of Israel's history, and even to the institutions and events of their national life. We find him speaking of himself as 'something greater than' the temple, Jonah, Solomon. Several times he drew on the experiences of Old Testament prophets to explain his own mission. Sometimes, as we have seen in the episode of his testing, he apparently saw himself in the role of the nation of Israel itself.

So when Luke tells us that Jesus 'interpreted to them in *all* the scriptures the things concerning himself', this is no exaggeration. The whole pattern of the Old Testament, not

JOHN WENHAM

Jesus and the Old Testament

Jesus was a first-century Jew, and like his contemporaries he believed in every jot and tittle of the (Old Testament) Scriptures. This can be seen from the hundreds of Old Testament quotations or allusions which are found in his teaching in the Gospels. He explained passages from all of its three sections—the law of Moses, the prophets and the writings. He referred to many Old Testament stories, treating them as history. Noah's flood, the destruction of Sodom and Gomorrah and Lot's wife who looked back, the manna in the wilderness, the bronze snake for the snake-bitten to look at and be healed—all these and more are called in to illustrate Jesus' teaching. He referred to incidents in the lives of Solomon, Elijah, Elisha, Jonah. The first two chapters of Genesis serve as a basis for his teaching.

To him the Scriptures were authoritative, not only to use in debate with other teachers, but also in his own wrestling with the devil in the wilderness, whom he answered three times with the words 'It is written'. To him Scripture was written by people of former times under the inspiration of the Spirit of God and now 'stands written' as the word of God.

Bible for the new age

But Jesus understood the Old Testament Scriptures in a deeper, more living way than his contemporaries. He stressed how important it is to obey it in spirit as well as in letter. In the Sermon on the Mount he brought the Commandments 'You shall not kill' and 'You shall not commit adultery' to bear on wrong intentions as well as outward acts. He applied 'You shall love your neighbour' to enemies as well as to friends, and made clear that 'An eye for an eye', which is the divine principle of public justice, must not be used as an excuse for personal vengeance.

Above all he showed how Old Testament prophecy was fulfilled in himself. He was the Son of Man in Daniel 7, the suffering servant of Isaiah 53, the smitten shepherd of Zechariah 13. His coming meant the dawning of the new age to which the whole Old Testament looked forward. He claimed both to be its fulfilment and to interpret it as God intended. Although he did not profess to be all-knowing he did clearly assert that all he taught was the truth of God without qualification: 'Anyone who hears these words of mine and obeys them is like a wise man who built his house on rock.' Jesus taught with divine authority in his own right. '*I* say unto you ...' was a teaching-style quite different from the other rabbis. But he also accorded to the Old Testament Scriptures the fullest authority as the word of God.

only a few specific prophecies, pointed forward to a time of fulfilment. That time had now come. In Jesus' mission the 'day of the Lord' had at last arrived.

But if all this suggests there was nothing more to look forward to, we have missed another important aspect of Jesus' teaching. The fulfilment he had brought was not yet complete. It must run its course until the work he began was fully effected. There had to be an intervening time, during which the good news must be preached and people could receive him as Saviour and accept him as Lord. This period, which began with his coming at Bethlehem, would continue until one day he would come again in glory to receive the worship which was so conspicuously lacking in the humble and rejected circumstances of his first coming. How long that time would be he refused to say. Men and women must always be ready for his return, but they could never calculate its time. It is in this interval between the time of fulfilment and its ultimate completion that we still find ourselves today.

The kingdom of God

The Jews had always believed that their God was the king of the earth. He made it: it was his. Yet some people refused to acknowledge his lordship. So they still had to look forward to the day when he would be recognized as king.

When Jesus spoke of the kingdom of God, it was against this background. It is not a place or a group of people, but God's rule, his sovereignty, the situation where he is king and his will is done. Jesus came to bring that situation, and in his ministry this 'kingdom of God' had already come into the world.

But here too there is an uncompleted fulfilment. Jesus' followers must pray: 'Thy kingdom come, thy will be done.' Certainly the kingdom of God is already present; Jesus has made it possible for anyone to enter into that relationship of trusting obedience to God in which, *for them*, God's sovereignty is established and he is lord. But one day everyone will bow to God's will, and then the kingdom of God will be a complete reality. So we find in Jesus' teaching about the kingdom of God an inevitable tension between the 'already' and the 'not yet'—between the rule of God in the lives of those who submit to his lordship now and his ultimate rule when all opposition will be ended and God's purpose finally achieved.

The kingdom of God is, then, a wide-ranging idea. It includes whatever is God's purpose. It cannot be identified with one specific 'thing' such as the church, or heaven, or human brotherhood, or human rights. It includes all these, and more, but cannot be tied down to any of them. It is, above all, the kingdom of *God*, that which *he* brings about, not something for men and women to achieve, though they may indeed seek it and enter into it themselves.

Jesus came to 'make God king'. To see what this meant for him, we must look at some of the ways it worked out in his mission, first in what he did, and then in what he taught. Then we will see how it worked itself out in the experience of those who responded to his call.

The kingdom of God—in action

'If it is by the finger of God that I cast out demons,' said Jesus on one occasion, 'then the kingdom of God has come upon you.'

One of the most obvious features of Jesus' mission was his miracles. On this occasion he had exorcized a demon, and people were amazed. His power was undeniable, so his enemies countered by suggesting he owed it to Satan. No, said Jesus, it was Satan who was in retreat; his miracles were proof that it was God who was now in control.

The Gospels tell us of several exorcisms, and they were a recognized part of Jesus' work. But most of his miracles were physical healings. All sorts of complaints were involved: blindness, deafness, dumbness, paralysis, leprosy, dropsy, fever, haemorrhage, curvature of the spine—even a severed ear. Indeed the Gospels say people came to Jesus with diseases and deformities of every sort, and 'he healed them all'. There are even three cases where he restored people to life who had recently died.

It was not that Jesus went about looking for people to heal. The Gospels do not reflect a deliberate 'healing campaign'. But he had a power over both physical and spiritual evil, and a sympathy for those in need, which naturally moved him to heal those who came to him. And they came in vast numbers.

So there is no doubt that one of the main impressions Jesus made on people was of a man of supernatural power—power which he used to meet human need, whether sickness, hunger, or danger. No wonder people started asking who he could be.

Jesus said, 'Go back and tell John what you hear and see; the blind see again, and the lame walk, lepers are cleansed, and the deaf hear, and the dead are raised to life and the Good News is proclaimed to the poor; and happy is the man who does not lose faith in me.'

Matthew 11

The Gospel of John calls Jesus' miracles 'signs'. Jesus himself refused to provide 'signs' when his opponents asked for them. He was no cheap showman, nor was it his business to force people to accept him. But he did regard his miracles as a proof that 'the kingdom of God has come upon you'. They were a part of God's all-out attack on the powers of evil. Every miraculous healing was another victory for God. And every miracle showed the unique authority of the one in whose acts the kingdom of God was becoming real.

The other main feature of Jesus' work which the outsider would notice was his life-style as an itinerant preacher. From the time when he joined John the Baptist by the Jordan, Jesus seems to have had no settled home life, though for a time he was based in the house of his follower Simon Peter in Capernaum. He went around preaching to crowds, who gathered wherever he went. Sometimes he and his followers found lodging with friends; sometimes they slept in the open. They had no regular source of income, but depended on the gifts of well-wishers; what they had they shared with one another. It was all remarkably different from the respected status of most teachers in Jewish society.

Jesus' failure to respect society's conventions went beyond his own style of living. It was seen particularly in the company he kept. He soon got a name for himself as 'the friend of tax-collectors and sinners'. Tax-collectors were a hated and despised class. They made money for themselves from their fellow-Jews. As servants of Rome, they were politically and religiously unacceptable. They and other 'undesirables' formed an underworld where Jesus found a ready welcome, but in which he moved at the risk of his reputation. He not only mixed with them—he ate in their houses. This was a scandal to orthodox Jewish piety.

Other despised groups also figure prominently among the people with whom Jesus mixed. Women were regarded as inferior to men, and took little part in Jewish public life, but in the stories of Jesus they appear frequently, and are treated with a marked respect and understanding. Nor was social class important to Jesus. He was equally at home at a Pharisee's dinner-party or a village wedding; he mixed with noblemen and lepers, and he gained followers among the highest councils of the land as well as among the outcast of society.

Racial barriers gave way too. Not that Jesus spent much time outside Jewish territory, but even inside it he could welcome a non-Jewish army officer and praise him above his own fellow-countrymen. Indeed his openness to the work of God outside Israel was another cause of scandal. Particularly offensive to orthodox Jews was his willingness to speak and even accept hospitality with Samaritans. His famous story of the Good Samaritan was calculated to wound Jewish racial sensibility.

So Jesus freely ignored the barriers which society had erected between those of different class, sex, race or religion. He showed in all he did that God's love cannot be so restricted. His criterion was not a person's social standing, but his need and his willingness to receive God's blessings. 'Those who are well have no need of a physician,' he said, 'but those who are sick; I came not to call the righteous, but sinners.' And he showed this breadth of love and compassion not just in word, but in deed, as he touched a leper, asked a Samaritan woman for water,

VISHAL MANGALWADI

The Poor

God meant human beings to live in a garden, sin has sent them to the slums. The gospel is the power of God to save us from sin, therefore from poverty as well. Jesus often interpreted his ministry as 'bringing good news to the poor'.

There are three major ways in which sin produces poverty.

- ☐ **Sin separates people from the true God.** But because humanity cannot live without God, we invent false gods. Often people worship creation rather than the creator. Societies that worship creation lose that ability to subdue and manage it which is essential for economic prosperity.
- ☐ **Sin sets brother against brother.** People begin to exploit each other. In previous generations, for example, it was direct exploitation through colonialism which created large-scale poverty. Today it is indirect exploitation, through unjust trade terms, which perpetuates the poverty of the poorer countries.
- ☐ **Sin ultimately blinds people to the truth about their own nature.** We forget that because we are made in the image of a creator, we can find fulfilment only when we engage in creative and productive work. Laziness, as the book of Proverbs tells us, means poverty. There are many other factors–geographical, historical, cultural, moral and ideological–which contribute to poverty or affluence. But generally the societies where poverty has been the norm for centuries are those which have not had the biblical attitudes towards God, the created order, man and work.

Even though poverty is thus the direct consequence of sin, it is not necessarily the result of the sin of the particular person who is poor. A person or a society can make another person or society poor.

God's love for the poor

As well as flowing from human sin, poverty can be God's judgment on societies which turn their back on him. And yet the Bible makes it abundantly clear that the poor are also the object of God's special love. Jesus said, 'Blessed are you who are poor, for yours is the kingdom of God'. God, as Jesus described him, has a soft spot for the poor, because they are helpless victims of forces over which they have little control:

- ☐ **External forces**–such as powerful oppressors or natural calamities (many of which, such as floods caused by deforestation, may be the result of the thoughtlessness and greed of their own ancestors).
- ☐ **Internal attitudes**—such as fear, fatalism and laziness, developing over generations and robbing individuals and societies of the initiative, confidence and thrift which are necessary for economic enterprise.

Abject poverty in the final analysis is the powerlessness of individuals or societies to help themselves. They need a saviour.

The whole Bible witnesses to God's love for the poor and his willingness to save them. But this is an especially strong feature of Jesus' teaching. The prodigal son needs to return to his father when he starves. The father who feeds all the birds of the sky and clothes all the lilies of the fields is able and willing to meet all the poor person's material needs, if he will only seek God's kingdom and righteousness. To those who were looking for bread, Jesus said that if they really wanted a permanent solution to their hunger, they ought to seek him, the true 'bread of life'.

One of Christ's major antidotes to poverty was to create the church. Poverty in part is a product of unjust economic relationships, whereas the church is a community dedicated to promoting just and caring relationships. The New Testament churches met the needs of the poor and worked to eradicate poverty from among their members, not as an occasional programme but as part of their normal routine.

Just as the church cannot lightly tolerate sin among its members, so also it cannot tolerate poverty within itself. And just as Christians spearhead the battle against sin in the world, so must they spearhead the battle against poverty.

Jesus said, 'The most important commandment is this: "Listen, Israel! The Lord our God is the only Lord. Love the Lord your God with all your heart, with all your soul, with all your mind, and with all your strength." The second most important one is this: "Love your neighbour as you love yourself." There is no other commandment more important than these two.'

Mark 12

and went in to eat with tax-collectors and sinners.

Another of his slogans was 'The last will be first, and the first last', and all his sympathies pointed that way. In his involvement with need at the expense of respectability, just as much as in his power over physical and spiritual evil, Jesus showed that God's kingdom had come. And it was a kingdom where human prejudice gives way to God's compassion.

The Kingdom of God—in word

Jesus was no less famous as a teacher than as a healer. It was to hear his teaching that the crowds followed him, and they were not disappointed, 'for he taught them as one who had authority, and not as their scribes'.

The contrast must have been remarkable. The religion of the scribes (teachers of religious law) was primarily a matter of rules and precedents, leading to ever more subtle distinctions and complex regulations, until the ordinary people had little hope of conforming to their leaders' teaching. It was all very careful and scrupulous, but what was lacking was *authority*: the authority which could simply and clearly declare the will of God. It was in teaching with such authority that Jesus brought the kingdom of God into the lives of those who followed him.

It was no wonder Jesus clashed with the official religious teachers. Their approaches were quite different. They insisted on meticulous ritual cleanness for meals, but Jesus said that uncleanness came from people's thoughts and characters, not from their food. They laid down precise regulations for the sabbath day of rest, but Jesus healed people on the sabbath, and taught that the sabbath was made for man's benefit, not to enslave him. They discussed the appropriate grounds for divorce, but Jesus declared that God's purpose was that marriage should not be broken at all. They argued about which oaths were permissible, but Jesus called for a simple truthfulness which made all oaths unnecessary. They assumed that God's command to love your neighbour (fellow-Jew) meant that you need not love anyone else, but Jesus said God's love drew no such boundaries, and neither should theirs—'Love your enemies'.

Jesus was not providing a short cut to godliness by getting rid of all rules and regulations. In fact what he called for was much harder than the legalistic obedience of the scribes. He called for a righteousness that 'exceeds that of the scribes and Pharisees'. It is comparatively easy to keep a set of rules, however complicated. But Jesus went behind the rules to the attitudes and motives God requires. He replaced regulations with principles, and those principles were far-reaching. They demanded not only a change of behaviour but a total reorientation of mind. Jesus was a true radical—he went right to the root of the matter.

Instead of offering new rules of conduct, then, Jesus demanded new attitudes and values—not so much a change of behaviour as a change of heart. An example is his teaching about wealth. He had come to preach 'good news to the poor', but that good news was not a literal end to their poverty. The message was that in their poverty they were actually better off than the rich. To be wealthy was, for Jesus, not so much sinful as dangerous, because wealth can keep a person away from the things that really matter. That is why he proclaimed 'You cannot serve God and mammon (wealth)': God's kingship allows no rival allegiance. When he called his followers to give up their possessions (as he did quite emphatically), it was not so much to achieve an equal society as to set them free to serve God. 'Blessed are you poor,' he said, not because they would become rich, but because 'Yours is the kingdom of God'.

Jesus called for an unselfish love for others. Inevitably those who respond find they cannot overlook the sufferings caused by poverty and exploitation. He summoned people to a reckless generosity, putting the good of others before personal satisfaction. But these were the results of an inward transformation, a new system of values, which must undermine the selfish materialism of the world. Doing good to others was to be the result, not the means, of the conversion he called for. Its heart was a new relationship with God, an acceptance of his kingship, which left no room for the selfish pursuit of wealth.

In this sense, Jesus' mission was one of liberation. He said little about economic exploitation or political oppression. He refused to make common cause with the freedom fighters among his own people, and was clearly opposed to the nationalistic hopes of many Israelites. He set out no programme for the reform of social injustice or the redistribution of wealth. But instead he attacked the deeper enslavement which affects rich and poor, emperor and slave—the greed for possessions and power, the love of self rather than the love of God. He came to set people free by bringing them under the kingship of God.

The people recognized in Jesus one who taught 'with authority'. It was the authority of God the king. The demands he made were total. To follow him was to give up your own life, to renounce all other loyalty, however natural and right in itself. His followers had to leave everything to follow him. But the amazing thing is that they did so. The impact of Jesus was irresistible.

The totality of his demand is seen particularly in his teaching on love. The greatest commandment was one of love. This love for others was to go beyond natural ties, to include even your enemies. There could be no limit to it.

No wonder then that people saw something new and authoritative in what Jesus taught as well as in what he did. The kingdom of God which he proclaimed involved nothing less than a radical reordering of people's lives—as he put it, a 'new birth'.

Responding to the kingdom of God

When Jesus preached the time of fulfilment and the coming of the kingdom of God he did not just explain his teaching and leave it at that. He called for a response: 'Repent, and believe in the gospel.' It was not the sort of message to which you could just give polite approval. Those who 'entered the kingdom of God' would never be the same again.

Those who responded in this way were called Jesus' disciples. Many others followed him for a time to hear his teaching or to be healed, but to be a 'disciple' was a more serious commitment. It often involved giving away or pooling possessions, and for his closest followers it meant sharing his itinerant life-style. Jesus insisted that loyalty to him must take precedence even over loyalty to family. To those who took this step he promised that God would provide for all their needs.

He sent them out to preach and heal as he did. Their message, like his, was the coming of the kingdom of God, and they too showed God's power—in actions as well as words. But the heart of their role was to be learners. Jesus spent a lot of time with them away from the crowds, teaching them and preparing them for the day when they would take over his mission, to Israel and to the world. In particular he explained to them what kind of Messiah he was, and why he must be rejected, suffer and die, so that when it happened they would be able to understand and to tell others what it all meant.

To be a disciple was to be set apart from other people. They were to be clearly different. Jesus called them the 'salt of the earth', the 'light of the world'; the very distinctiveness of their lives and characters would change the society in which they lived. He did not expect society to welcome this distinctiveness. He himself faced constant opposition, and he promised them no better. He taught them to expect persecution and rejection.

What was it, then, that made it worthwhile to be a disciple of Jesus? His famous 'Beatitudes' spell out the unexpected quality of Christian 'blessedness'. The Greek word 'blessed' does not mean simply a happy state of mind but an enviable situation. It refers to someone who is to be congratulated.

This is a portrait of Christian disciples, and it describes their privileges. These relate to their standing with God. ('Theirs is the kingdom of heaven' means 'they are the people in whose lives God is in control'.) As 'sons and daughters of God' they should reflect their Father's character: righteous, merciful, pure, a peacemaker. All these are foreign to the world's way of living. It is these 'unnatural' ethical standards and attitudes which make disciples an object of suspicion and hatred to those who do not share their ideals. Their actions, and their attitudes to other people, turn the world's sense of values upside down—as Jesus did. They are called to be like their Master: generous, loving others without distinction, concerned for God's will rather than human rules and regulations.

And so they will find themselves drawn into a new community, a new family. They may even have lost their earthly family as the price of discipleship, but this new family of all who respond to the kingdom of God will more than compensate for any loss. And the outcome, Jesus taught, will be much more than just a new deal in this life; the ultimate gain, far more than just 'compensation', will be 'eternal life'. A relationship with the eternal God cannot be disrupted by death. The new life of the disciple is for ever.

The people of God

Jesus was the Messiah of Israel, and his mission was carried out almost entirely within his own nation. It was Israel, the Old Testament people of God, whom he called to return to their Lord, and it was on Israel's Scriptures that he based his whole understanding of his mission. All Jesus' first followers were Jews.

Was the kingdom of God, then, a purely Jewish ideal? Was Jesus' aim simply a restored Israel? Certainly it included this. As John the Baptist had called Israel to repentance, so Jesus made the same demand. But it soon became clear that entry into the kingdom of God did not depend on a person's race, but on his attitude to God, an attitude of repentance and faith. Jews who did not share this relationship with God had no part in God's kingdom; and Jesus made it equally clear that faith was not confined to Israel.

When a non-Jewish officer showed he had a real faith, Jesus declared, 'Not even in Israel have I found such faith.' He went on to add, no doubt to murmurs of disapproval from his Jewish hearers, 'Many will come from east and west, and sit at table with Abraham, Isaac and Jacob in the kingdom of heaven, while the sons of the kingdom (the Jews, who thought it was theirs by right) will be thrown into the outer darkness.'

At first, naturally, Jesus' movement was a Jewish one, but he himself made it clear that it was to be extended more widely. The true people of God were no longer a nation, but a community drawn from all nations. To be a member of the people of God would now depend not on your family or your race, but on your own relationship with God.

Jesus' first disciples were the initial basis for this new community, but it did not stop with them. They were sent out to summon others to the kingdom of God, calling them to repent 'and return to God, and to receive the forgiveness of their sins. And so gradually the true people of God was formed, the community of the forgiven, born again into the family of God.

From what we have said so far it might seem that Jesus' role was purely that of a prophet, preaching God's message and summoning people to respond. Many had done this before and his own followers did so after him. But the Messiah had more to do than this. For God's people could not be restored by a mere appeal, The whole Old Testament revelation had made it clear that mankind's rebellion against God cannot be glossed over and forgotten. It must be atoned for.

And so Jesus' explanation of his mission focused on his suffering and death. He did not die because of an unfortunate accident, or simply the hostility he provoked. His death was the culmination of his mission as Messiah. As the suffering servant of God he 'gave his life as a ransom for many'. On the night before his death he gave his disciples bread to eat and wine to drink—'My body, given for you . . . My blood, poured out for many for the forgiveness of sins'. His death was to be their life.

Another section of this book explains more fully why Jesus died for his people, but we need to be clear this was not some later Christian invention; it was central to Jesus' own understanding of what he had come to do. His teaching is full of the theme that he had come to die. Only so could that forgiveness be achieved which was to be the essential foundation of the new community.

Father and Son

So far we have been looking at what Jesus said and did in order to understand what he set out to achieve. We have built up a picture of his mission, and seen that its highlight is Jesus the Messiah, the one sent by God to being his people back to himself.

To say that Jesus was the Messiah helps us to understand what he came to do, but it does not tell us a lot about Jesus himself. For this we need to turn particularly to another frequent theme in his teaching, that of God as Father.

My Father and your Father

To refer to God as the Father of his people would cause no surprise in Jewish circles; it was a theme familiar from the Old Testament. So when Jesus spoke to his disciples, as he often did, of 'your heavenly Father', they would feel on familiar ground.

But some of the implications Jesus drew from this image would be less familiar. For him it conveyed not so much a formal status as a deeply personal and individual relationship. It was because God was their 'Father in heaven' that Jesus taught his disciples to rely utterly on him for all their most basic needs—food and clothing and daily provision. It was because he was their Father too that their conduct and their attitudes must be modelled on his: 'You must be perfect, as your heavenly Father is perfect.' To be a disciple is to live in a close relationship with a Father in heaven, and this will leave no aspect of life unaffected.

It is not surprising, therefore, that the prayer Jesus taught his disciples to say begins 'Our Father', and goes on to deal not only with the coming of the kingdom of God, but also with the disciples' needs, both physical and spiritual.

But the phrase 'our Father' occurs nowhere else in Jesus' teaching, and here it is given only as what *you* are to say. In other words Jesus never linked himself with his disciples in their relation to God as Father. We even find on one occasion the clumsy phrase 'my Father and your Father, where 'our Father' would have been much simpler. So God is the Father of Jesus, and he is the Father of Jesus' disciples, but the two relationships are different.

This is seen clearly in a passage in Matthew, where the relationship of Jesus, '*the* Son', with the Father is stated to be an exclusive one: 'No one knows the Father except the Son and any one to whom the Son chooses to reveal him.' This conviction of a unique relationship with God is in line with God's declaration at Jesus' baptism, 'You are my own dear son.' It finds striking expression in Jesus' parable of the vineyard, in which the owner's one beloved son is contrasted with the servants (the Old Testament prophets) who had been sent before. In the Gospel of John it is frequently expressed, but nowhere more clearly than in Jesus' sublime prayer before his death: '. . . the same glory I had with you before the world was made.'

So any estimate of Jesus as merely the 'elder brother' in the family of God does not do justice to his own sayings and the conviction they reveal. The difference between Jesus and his followers in their relationship to God as Father is not just one of degree; his sonship is unique. It is the family relationship of one divine being with another. He said on one occasion, 'I and the Father are one.' That saying provoked his Jewish hearers to threaten him with stoning, 'because you, being a man, make yourself God'. They fully understood what his language implied. And in doing so, if not in the

MICHAEL NAZIR-ALI

How Muslims See Jesus

All Muslims acknowledge that Jesus (*Isa*) was a prophet and a messenger of God. He is also called *Al-Masih* (the Messiah) in the Qur'an, although most Muslims would only mean by this that he was anointed to preach salvation to the people of Israel. His virgin birth, his miracles, especially his power to raise the dead, and his purity are also generally accepted.

The Qur'an sometimes uses words for Jesus which, to Christians, sound very similar to titles they themselves would use. Jesus is called 'Word of God' and 'a spirit from God'. By 'Word of God', the Qur'an seems to mean that creative command of God which made the universe and which also created the man Jesus in Mary's womb. Again, *Ruh Allah* (Spirit of God) is the typical Muslim title for Jesus.

Traditionally Muslims have tried to minimize such titles and explain them away. They would say, for example, that there is nothing unique about Jesus coming into existence as a result of the divine command—Adam came that way, and so did the universe itself. True, but then neither Adam nor the universe are ever called 'Word of God' in the Qur'an, whereas Jesus certainly is. Again, Muslims would say that to call Jesus a spirit from God is not to make him unique—are not all spirits from God? Here again, they would point to the similarities between the birth of Jesus and the creation of the first man. Just as God breathed his spirit into the clay to create Adam, so also he breathed his spirit into Mary at the conception of Jesus.

Did Jesus really die?

When we move on to Jesus' death, resurrection and ascension, the Qur'an's attitude is ambiguous. In some places the death of Jesus is clearly mentioned and it is even stated that it took place 'according to the definite plan and foreknowledge of God'. However, there is one passage which has been interpreted to mean that Jesus was not crucified but that his enemies were somehow deceived into believing he had been. In fact God raised him up to himself. As far as resurrection and ascension are concerned, the Qur'an uses some expressions which would, naturally speaking, point to a physical resurrection and others which would indicate an ascension into heaven.

The very reluctance of the Qur'an and of Muslims to speak of Jesus' death is significant. The Qur'an quite plainly accuses the Jews of slaying some of the prophets; it is also prepared to discuss the possibility that Muhammad died a natural death. Why then is there such reluctance to admit that Jesus too could have been killed? Does this point towards a special regard for Jesus in the Qur'an?

Some scholars have suggested that it is possible to reconstruct the Qur'an's view of Jesus' crucifixion in such a way that it does not contradict Christianity. Such a reconstruction would look something like this: the Jews thought they had crucified Jesus, but they were wrong. God caused Jesus to die, using the Jews as his instrument. God then raised Jesus from the dead and exalted him in his presence as a reward for obedience.

Among the *Sufis* (Muslim mystics) Jesus' sufferings have often been seen as an example to follow if we want to draw near to God. Again, some sensitive modern Muslims have pointed out that the real centre of both the Bible's and the Qur'an's accounts of the cross is Jesus' *willingness* to suffer rather than the actual suffering itself. If we imitate his willingness, God will accept us. This is a real attempt to relate the cross positively, but it is a long way from the Christian gospel of grace.

Many Muslims believe that Jesus will return to earth before the final judgment, subdue the forces of evil and usher in the reign of God. Jesus' return is not mentioned in the Qur'an and the idea seems to have infiltrated Islam after the Muslim conquest of the Christian countries of the Middle East.

VISHAL MANGALWADI

How Hindus See Jesus

'Two thousand years ago,' wrote Swami Sivananda, 'Divinity incarnated upon this planet to show all humanity the glorious path to everlasting life by actually living the divine life upon this earth. Jesus was ... the divine power and love incarnated...'

This response to Jesus Christ, which would echo the sentiments of millions of Hindus, is the result of two centuries of Christian service in India by the worldwide church. The Hindu mind today accepts the divinity of Christ, but not that he is unique. Jesus is looked on as one of the many incarnations of divinity—by some even as the greatest of them. In other words, Jesus has been reinterpreted from the Hindu standpoint, which believes that all human souls are divine. As Hindus see it, most remain ignorant of their true nature, but some, such as Jesus, transcend the normal illusion and realize their divinity. This acknowledgement of Christ's divinity means at best little more than accommodation to their view of life; at worst it may beguile Christians into accepting Hindu monism or polytheism.

Christians and Hindu reform

How sincere Hindus can acknowledge Jesus' divinity, but not submit to his lordship, is a problem which can best be understood if we see it in historical perspective.

The first great impact Jesus made on the Hindu mind was in the late eighteenth and early nineteenth centuries, when Christian missionaries courageously took the initiative in advocating a number of social reforms to liberate the downtrodden in India from the oppressive Hindu social order. This missionary activity produced three results:

- ☐ Hundreds of thousands of Hindus accepted Jesus Christ as their Saviour and openly became his followers.
- ☐ Great Hindu reformers, such us Rammohan Roy, Chandavarker, Telang, Renade, Keshub Chandra Sen, Jotiba Govinda Phule, Behramji Malabari, who followed the missionary initiative, studied the Bible diligently. Many of them preached from it regularly in an effort to reform their society. These men admitted their indebtedness to Jesus, though they did not become Christians.
- ☐ A few great reformers, such as Swami Dayanand Saraswati, accepted the need to reform Hinduism, but reacted sharply against Jesus. They wrote and preached against him to prevent Hindus from becoming Christians. This reaction, born of insecurity, continues to this day in some quarters, though in a milder form.

When the Hindu reform movement took on a nationalistic character in the twentieth century, the movement passed entirely from Christian hands into Hindu hands. This was because the Christians were not prepared to take the reform movement to its logical end—national independence. At this point, even though Hindu leaders, such as Mahatma Gandhi, continued to study, follow and instruct others in his life and teaching, Jesus ceased to be an issue in the national debate.

After India became independent in 1947, the Indian Church became a defensive and insecure minority. Then the Hindu attitude to Jesus ceased to be hostile or convinced. Instead Hindus either became indifferent to Jesus or saw him simply as a great historical figure with little relevance for today.

Now, however, since independence, nationalism and reform movements have failed to satisfy the Hindu heart. A new search for answers, for a saviour, has begun. In small pockets of India where Christians are fulfilling their mission courageously, Jesus is coming back to the centre of the stage. It is quite conceivable that, by the close of this century, Jesus will once again become the central issue of debate in India and Hindus will once again choose for or against him.

PETER KUZMIC

How Marxists See Jesus

Marxism was born at the time when Protestant theologians were busy in their search for the historical Jesus—a quest very much predetermined by the rationalistic methods and philosophical views of the time. For Karl Marx (1813-83), 'criticism of religion has been essentially completed', and so he shows no interest in the founder of the Christian faith.

Generally speaking, Marxists hate all gods, including the Christian God-man Jesus Christ. They may be occasionally intrigued by the man Jesus, but only after clearly dissociating him from the New Testament and from the subsequent Christian interpretation of him as Son of God and humanity's Saviour.

Frederick Engels (1820-95) had a pietistic upbringing, but became an atheist. The famous 'Jesus-critic' of his day, D. F. Strauss, influenced him in that direction. Later Engels taught that Christianity began in the second century in Egypt and that the idea of Christ the Saviour was a product of wishful thinking by the lower classes of people who yearned for liberation.

The first systematic study of early Christianity from a Marxist point of view was written by Karl Kautsky (1854–1939) under the title, *Foundations of Christianity*. For Kautsky, Jesus was a 'messianic-communist-oriented revolutionary', a leader of the oppressed and exploited masses. Because he presented a threat to the Roman establishment, they removed him by crucifixion. Faith in the redeeming work of Christ developed gradually out of the frustration of the working masses who were unable to change their conditions.

For Lenin (1870–1924), Jesus never existed and was a mythical invention. The official anti-Christian propaganda in the then Soviet Union found Kautsky's portrayal of Jesus as a revolutionary Messiah too positive. Soviet Marxists, in their attack on Christianity, systematically 'eliminated' Jesus from history. This complete abolition of Jesus was insisted on in all Soviet studies dealing with the subject. It was repeated by other dogmatic Marxists in Eastern Europe.

Jesus and the Neo-Marxists

Since the late 1960s, there has been an increased interest in Jesus of Nazareth among a number of open and critical Marxists (often referred to as Neo-Marxists). Among the better known are: Ernst Bloch, Roger Garaudy, Milan Machovec, Leszek Kolakowski, Vizteslav Gardavsky, Lucio Lombardo-Radice and Konrad Farner. They have in common a criticism of Marxism as a closed dogmatic and infallible system and an openness to reinterpret and reapply it.

For Kolakowski, for example, the attempts to erase Jesus from European history and culture are fruitless and ridiculous. Jesus is 'an example of the most sacred human values' and 'an example of the only radical authenticity by which each human individual is able to realize truly his own life values.' Similarly for the French Marxist, Roger Garaudy, Jesus is 'the highest model of freedom and love, an openness for the infinite . . .'

Neo-Marxists are attracted to Jesus as a model for human life and action. He is an authentic man; a man for others; a totally committed man. They are impressed with Jesus' stand for truth and justice, and by his solidarity with the poor, the suffering, the dying. His love is not abstract or sentimental, but practical and concrete. For Neo-Marxists, Jesus is a 'prophet and reformer'. They see him as one who opens up new possibilities and a new future for humanity.

They give us a dynamic picture of the man Jesus, but they point only to the secular fulfilment of humanity. Neo-Marxist views of Jesus are still based on materialistic-atheistic presuppositions. They still reject the God-centred interpretation of Jesus which the New Testament teaches.

conclusions they drew from it, they were right.

Jesus and God

Christianity regards Jesus as both God and man. Behind those words lie long centuries of theological debate. But where did it all begin? In this article we are going behind the later Christian thinking to learn from what Jesus actually said and did. So finally we ask whether in Jesus' life and teaching we find any foundation for this great theological structure which later generations have built. Could someone who walked and talked with Jesus have come to the conclusion that he was not only a real man but also at the same time God?

The first thing we must recognize is that some of them did! The belief in Jesus' divinity is not something which was invented centuries later. The New Testament was written in the lifetime of some who heard Jesus teaching, indeed some of it was written by them. And in that New Testament we find the seeds of belief in Jesus' divinity firmly planted and already growing to maturity.

Even more remarkably, these first Christians were Jews, and Jews were of all men the least likely to accept lightly the idea of a man being divine. It ran counter to all that the Jew had been brought up to believe: 'Hear, O Israel: The Lord our God is one Lord.' It would never occur to a Jew to mix up the human and the divine. It would take the most compelling evidence to make him even think in such terms. And yet within a very short time of Jesus' death on the cross, some of those who had known him best in all his human reality were talking about him as God. Whatever had happened to drive them to such an un-Jewish conclusion?

Of course one of the main factors was Jesus' resurrection. But even before his death there was ample material in the words and deeds of Jesus to point in this direction.

It was not that Jesus went about announcing in so many words that he was God. But, quite apart from the sort of person Jesus was, and the power and compassion displayed in his actions, a listener would have noticed a basic assumption in some of the things he said. Unobtrusively but definitely, he assumed a divine authority. His claim to forgive sins was questioned by the Jewish leaders precisely on the grounds that only God could forgive.

Yet Jesus, far from retracting it, reinforced the claim by a display of divine power. He called people to believe in him, to trust him, to be loyal to him before all other loyalties. He invited them to come to him, and he would give them rest. He declared that in the final judgment they would be judged by their response to him, indeed that he himself would be the judge, pronouncing final sentences on all nations on the basis of the way they had treated him. He claimed that he could give life, because he had life in himself. He spoke not only of God's kingdom but of his own kingdom. He said that to reject or to receive him was to reject or receive God.

Similarly Jesus sometimes used passages from the Old Testament which spoke of God and applied them to himself, not in any argumentative way but as if it were a perfectly natural thing to do.

This sort of language—and there is a lot of it in Jesus' teaching—must have made people stop and think. Taken together with his claim to be in a unique sense the Son of God, it added up to a claim which had to provoke a reaction. Either it had to be vigorously opposed (as the Jewish leaders inevitably opposed it) or it must lead to a radical change in Jewish thinking. Those who followed Jesus found in the end that they had no alternative. Slowly but surely they found themselves coming to the point where they worshipped as God a man with whom they had lived not many years before. It was not an easy option, but it was the only way to make sense of what they had seen and heard.

For further thinking

QUESTION 1

Which of the titles of Jesus mentioned in this chapter means most to you? Why? How would you explain its significance to a friend?

QUESTION 2

Why did Jesus perform miracles?

QUESTION 3

Choose one of Jesus' parables. What does this parable teach about the kingdom of God? What does it teach about God himself? What does it teach about being a disciple?

BIBLE REFERENCES

Jesus the Teacher

Matthew 5:1—7:29; 13:1–52; 16:21–23; 18:1–15; 21:23–27; 22:15–46; 25:1–46; 28:16–20; Mark 1:14–15; 3:13–15; 4:1–20; 11:18; 13:1–37; Luke 2:46–47; 4:16–22; 6:39–40; 9:1–6; 10:25–37; 11:1–13; 15:1–32; 19:47–48; 24:25–27; John 3:1–13; 7:14–18; 13:1–17; 14:1–10; 16:12–14

The Kingdom of God

Exodus 19:6; Psalms 45:6; Daniel 4:37; Matthew 3:1–3; 4:23–25; 6:10; 13:1–52; 16:13–20, 28; 25:1–46; Mark 4:11; 10:23; 14:25; Luke 9:1–2; 17:20–21; 19:11; John 18:36; Acts 1:6; Romans 14:17; 1 Corinthians 4:20; 6:9–10; 15:50; Revelation 1:9

Discipleship

Matthew 28:18–20; Mark 1:16–20; 3:13–15; Luke 9:1–6, 57–62; 14:25–33; John 1:35–51; Galatians 2:20–21; Ephesians 6:10–20; Philippians 3:12–16; 1 Timothy 6:11–16

CHAPTER 8

AGNE NORLANDER

Death . . . And Then

'The Son of man . . . came to serve and to give his life to redeem many people.' These words of Jesus show that he saw his imminent death as the most important part of his life's work. It was not an accident or a tragedy—rather it was the high spot in God's plan of salvation. Jesus understood that he was the central figure in this plan. 'The Son of man *must* suffer much . . . He will be put to death, but three days later he will rise to life.' One of the many ways Jesus was unique in world history is that he was the only one who claimed his purpose in life was to die!

Jesus therefore went up to Jerusalem for his last Passover, to suffer and die. The disciples went too, trembling and questioning. From the Gospel narratives, it would appear that right to the last they were expecting Jesus to establish God's kingdom in a tangible, external way—to win the final victory over all God's enemies. The entry into Jerusalem on Palm Sunday, cheering crowds, loud hosannas, seemed to meet the disciples' expectations. The common people were now waiting for Jesus to drive out the Gentiles from Jerusalem and re-establish the political and religious identity of Israel. There is no doubt Jesus himself arranged this entry to proclaim that he was the promised Messiah. But his route to glory was not to be by the way of political and military struggle. He must tread the way of suffering and humiliation.

Victory feast

The meal we know as the Last Supper was celebrated during Passover time. In this setting Jesus saw it as an anticipation of the great victory feast when God's kingdom would be finally established. God's rule could be achieved only by Jesus sacrificing his body and shedding his blood in death. Jesus here presents his forthcoming execution as an offer of salvation.

Jesus approached his suffering impressively composed and purposeful. But there was agony and turmoil behind this strength, as we can see in his anguished prayer in the Garden of Gethsemane: 'Father, if you will, take this cup of suffering away from me.' Jesus was in extreme suffering. His sweat was like drops of blood. The cup which Jesus would drink would contain more than physical suffering and death. He would be taking all the world's sin and evil on himself.

The traitor Judas, one of Jesus' disciples, was the one who led the soldiers to Jesus in Gethsemane. The Roman commanding officer was evidently expecting armed resistance and the troops were ready for a struggle. Jesus rejected armed resistance, thus, once again, refusing the role of a political Messiah. The disciples ran away. The potential for mass uproar from the crowds of Galilean pilgrims was not realized.

Trial

It is possible to understand Jesus' death from a purely secular, historical point of view. Jesus was brought before two different courts. The council called the Sanhedrin—was the Jew's supreme court. It condemned Jesus to death for *blasphemy*. The death sentence, the culmination of a long and bitter conflict between Jesus and the people's religious leaders, was pronounced on the basis of Jesus' claims to be divine and to be the Messiah. Moses' law decreed death by stoning for such blasphemy.

The Sanhedrin did not have the legal powers to carry out the death sentence. So Jesus was taken to Pilate, the Roman governor, to be tried according to Roman law. The Sanhedrin's biassed attitude towards the accused showed clearly in the way they formulated the charge against Jesus. 'We caught this man misleading our people, telling them not to pay taxes to the Emperor' (an outright lie) 'and claiming that he himself is the Messiah, a king.' Caiaphas, the high priest, avoided mentioning the reason—blasphemy—that the Sanhedrin condemned Jesus. He knew that the Roman authorities would not want to become embroiled in Jewish theological hair-splitting. So Jesus was now accused on political grounds—as an agitator, rabble-rouser and pretender to the throne. Caiaphas' intention was to get Jesus condemned for *high treason*. And he succeeded.

After many attempts to save Jesus, Pilate gave in to the chief priests and passed sentence on the grounds of high treason. He did not even acknowledge the Sanhedrin's sentence, but pronounced judgment on the basis of a completely new judicial procedure; a new sentence was given, based on completely new reasoning, according to Roman justice. This execution would therefore not be by stoning, but by crucifixion, which was the specifically Roman form of punishment for treason. Pilate therefore emerged as the one judicially responsible for Jesus' death, although the Jewish religious leaders—*not* the Jewish people as such—were responsible morally.

■

In accordance with his own plan God had already decided that Jesus would be handed over to you; and you killed him by letting sinful men crucify him. But God raised him from death, setting him free from its power because it was impossible that death should hold him prisoner.

Peter's sermon on the day of Pentecost, Acts 2

A terrible way to die

The symbol of the cross arouses positive feelings in most Christians today. It signifies safety, warmth, salvation, life, hope. For people in the Roman Empire at the time of Jesus, the cross brought out totally different reactions. Origen, one of the church fathers, accurately described crucifixion when he called it *mors turpissima crucis*, the most terrible way to die.

Crucifixion was a common penalty for criminals in classical antiquity, particularly for political and military trouble-makers. Historians believe it was the Persians who introduced this gruesome means of ridding the regime of undesirable characters. Among the Romans, crucifixion was the usual way of execution for slaves, criminals and terrorists.

Crucifixion represented the most barbaric form of execution. First of all, the victim was stripped, then he was scourged with leather straps studded with thorns, bits of bone or just simply lumps of lead. The soldiers had every available opportunity to indulge in sadism and gratuitous vulgarity. Every latent inhuman, bestial and demonic tendency was given free rein during flogging and crucifixion.

After this, the scourged victim was nailed or bound tightly to the horizontal beams of the cross, which he then had to carry to the place of execution. The body and the cross-beams were then lifted up and secured to the vertical pole which was already in place. Finally, the feet were nailed to the cross.

According to the Gospel accounts, Jesus' death on the cross differs in several ways from what we know from other sources about people who were crucified. The customary desperate, frenzied outbursts and curses from the crucified victims were replaced in Jesus' case by the so-called 'seven words from the cross':

- 'Forgive them, Father! They don't know what they are doing.'
- 'He said to his mother, "He is your son." Then he said to the disciple, "She is your mother." '
- 'I promise you that today you will be in Paradise with me.'
- '*Eloi, Eloi, lema sabachthani?* My God, my God, why did you abandon me?'
- 'I am thirsty.'
- 'It is finished!'
- 'Father! In your hands I place my spirit!'

It would appear from these last words that Jesus was fully conscious even in the moment of death, something extremely unusual for a victim of crucifixion.

Roman justice did not allow the burial of someone who had been executed for high treason. The prohibition on relatives being able to organize a decent burial was considered an additional punishment.

From the Jewish point of view, on the other hand, even a criminal had the right of burial. Not to be buried was the same as suffering eternal damnation. The request to Pilate by Joseph of Arimathea, a member of the Jewish Sanhedrin, to be allowed to bury the body of Jesus revealed great courage and indicates that Joseph was a person of some influence. Pilate showed unexpected co-operation. Jesus was buried—not in the criminals' graveyard, but with dignity, in a private tomb.

Jesus' burial was emphasized in a surprising way in the preaching of the early church. They stated that Jesus was really, and not just apparently, dead.

Sensational news

The disciples were not expecting Jesus to rise again. Doubtless they shared the contemporary belief of the Pharisees in the resurrection of the righteous, but they obviously had not paid attention to, understood or believed Jesus' teaching about his own resurrection. Jesus' shameful death completely shattered their belief that he was the Messiah, the one who would establish God's kingdom. The melancholy words of the disciples on the road to Emmaus expressed the prevailing mood of Jesus' first followers: 'And we had hoped that he was the one who was going to redeem Israel.'

And so we can quite understand why the disciples were not the ones who witnessed the burial or who went to the tomb on the first day of the week. Instead, it was the women of Jesus' inner circle, who had followed him from Galilee. Full of love and devotion to their dead friend, they went to the tomb to anoint Jesus' body with aromatic oil. To their great amazement, they discovered that the stone which covered the tomb-entrance was rolled away and that the tomb was empty. They rushed to report this sensational news to the disciples.

Of itself, the empty tomb could not convince the disciples. Someone could have carried the body away and buried it elsewhere. Only John believed immediately, when he saw the empty tomb. Peter and John found the linen burial wrappings, stiff with dried ointment, just as though they still enclosed a body; and the head cloth lay separately. It was as if Jesus had passed through the shroud.

The disciples were really convinced when they personally met with the risen Jesus, and found their hopelessness and despair turned into joyful belief. The lifelike person they met really was Jesus of Nazareth in bodily form. He was neither a ghost nor an apparition. The disciples saw him with their own eyes, touched him, ate with him. At the same time, Jesus' body was different after his resurrection. He went through closed doors. He could appear from nowhere and disappear to nowhere. Paul later called this sort of body a 'spiritual' or 'glorified' body.

Witnesses of the resurrection

The New Testament nowhere describes *how* Jesus was raised to life from the grave. The risen Jesus appeared to a number of people at different times—on one occasion to 500 people at once—but not to everybody. Not even the guards at the tomb saw him risen. What terrified them was seeing angels at the empty tomb.

The Gospel accounts show signs of the disciples' complete surprise at what happened. They describe different parts of an inexplicable course of events. And so they vary from one another—over such things as the names and number of the women who came to the tomb, the number of angels they met. These variations make the resurrection more believable, not less. If Jesus' resurrection were a concocted story, the Gospel writers would have been most anxious to provide us with identical versions.

Modern psychological studies on courtroom witnesses show that eyewitnesses often give different versions of what they saw, particularly if it was completely outside their normal experience. The accounts of the

'Do not hold on to me,' Jesus told Mary Magdalene, 'because I have not yet gone back up to the Father. But go to my brothers and tell them that I am returning to him who is my Father and their Father, my God and their God.'

John's account of the resurrection, John 20

resurrection are all in agreement about the principal features. All tell us that the tomb was empty and that Jesus physically appeared to the disciples.

So why did Jesus not appear to the masses? Would that not have convinced more people and won them over to the new faith?

If we look at Jesus' strategy during his ministry we meet this same phenomenon. He often told people not to speak about the miracles they had seen him perform. It seems that Jesus wanted to prevent people misunderstanding who he was and what he was doing. He wanted them to follow him for the right reasons. So he gave the apostles special

SIR NORMAN ANDERSON

The Resurrection: Fact or Legend?

The claim that God raised Jesus from the grave is so stupendous that no one could be expected to believe it without very strong evidence. Yet without the resurrection there would have been no gospel, no Christian faith, no church and no New Testament. There might, of course, have been a community of people who honoured Jesus of Nazareth and tried to follow his teaching, but that would have been an entirely different thing. So the question is: does such evidence exist?

What kind of evidence should we expect to find? Historians seldom have conclusive proof of events that happened in the past. They have to rely on the testimony of credible witnesses and on circumstantial evidence that things happened. So it is with the resurrection. No one claims to have seen it happen, and in one sense it is an event that reaches out beyond history. But yet the evidence that it did in fact happen is exceedingly strong. There is reliable testimony that the tomb was empty. A large number of witnesses attest that Jesus appeared to them after his death. The lives of the original disciples changed dramatically from that point. The Christian church has borne witness to the same faith all down the centuries. All this evidence builds up piece by piece into an impressive structure.

Credible witnesses

The weightiest single piece of written testimony comes in the apostle Paul's first letter to the Christians at Corinth. No reputable scholar doubts today that this letter was written by Paul in or around AD 55. In chapter 15 we find evidence which takes us back some twenty years earlier, when Paul received the word-of-mouth 'tradition' he later delivered to the Corinthians, and here repeats in written form.

Where and when did he get this tradition about Christ's resurrection? Surely he must have received at least an outline of it from the Christians in Damascus immediately after his conversion—some two to five years after the crucifixion itself. And he must certainly have received it in full, with the list of principal witnesses, when he visited Jerusalem three years later, stayed for two weeks with the apostle Peter, and also saw James, the Lord's brother. So there can be no doubt that Paul had a list of witnesses to facts about the resurrection on which there was general agreement among the apostles. And that this is all based on evidence which goes back to the very beginning.

Paul writes that once when Jesus appeared after his death he was seen by more than five hundred people at the same time. And he makes a point of insisting that most of them were still alive some twenty years later. Now the apostle was no fool, and he was often under attack. So he certainly would not have made this gratuitous remark had he not known that some hundreds of those who claimed to have seen the risen Christ were still available when he wrote, and could have been questioned by anyone who doubted that these appearances really happened.

People often say that Paul knew nothing of the empty tomb. It is true that he does not refer to it explicitly in this letter—he is chiefly interested in the resurrection appearances. But what first-century Jew could possibly

teaching on who he was and what he had come to do. In the same way, the apostles were charged with the task of witnessing both to the truth and to the significance of Jesus' resurrection.

Fundamentals of the faith

From the day of Pentecost onwards, the resurrection became the focal point of the apostles' teaching. 'Then they put him to death by nailing him to a cross. But God raised him from death three days later...' These are the fundamentals of the Christian faith.

It is worth noting the constant reference to Old Testament prophecies in the New Testa-

have stated that Christ 'died for our sins' (physically of course), 'was buried' (again physically) and then 'was raised on the third day', had he not believed that *something* had happened to the body that had been buried?

Circumstantial evidence

Paul's list of witnesses is the weightiest single piece of evidence. But it is confirmed by what the Gospels tell us—about the tomb and the disciples. Some of the Gospel accounts seem at first sight to contradict each other, but to say that they cannot be reconciled is an overstatement. In fact their apparent inconsistencies add considerably to their value as evidence. Any judge will tell you that honest witnesses never tell precisely the same story, and any discrepancies (real or apparent) have to be ironed out in cross-examination. No one would suggest that the witnesses whose testimony is given in the Gospels made any attempt to concoct an agreed account. And what is more, the truth of their testimony is confirmed by circumstantial evidence.

☐ **The tomb** Plainly the tomb was empty. Otherwise the apostles could scarcely have preached about the resurrection in the very city where Christ's body had been laid to rest. Various unsatisfactory attempts have been made to explain *why* it was empty:

—The disciples stole the body: but some of these very disciples were soon to die for the faith that he was raised.

—The authorities took it somewhere else: then why did they not produce it as soon as there was talk of resurrection?

—The women went to the wrong tomb: but that means the body was still available for inspection in the right tomb.

—He was only unconscious, not really dead, and came round in the grave: after a spear thrust in the side? and after being wrapped from head to foot in grave-clothes?

The preaching of the resurrection could not have continued in Jerusalem if any of the first three had been true, and the fourth does not stand up to examination.

☐ **The disciples** The fact that the witnesses to the resurrection really met with the risen Lord is borne out by the way their lives changed from that point on. Cowardice, doubt and despair gave way to joyful testimony. What other explanation is there? They had never expected Jesus to return from the grave. They were too taken up with traditional Jewish expectations of what the promised Messiah would be and do even to take in what Jesus meant when he said he would die. The idea that he would rise was far beyond their thinking. Yet they were totally convinced they had seen the risen Lord.

Jesus was seen after his death over a period of forty days. But even after his ascension he appeared to other disciples. Paul on the Damascus road, and John on the island of Patmos, both had visions of Christ in glory. And down the centuries many ordinary people have encountered him too—sometimes in dramatic ways, but more often by the inward witness of the Holy Spirit. Their lives, too, have been totally changed by that meeting.

All this evidence builds into a coherent picture of something that actually happened. For any alternative explanation to carry weight it has to account for every stage in this evidence. No theory yet put forward begins to do so. The only convincing explanation of the evidence that Jesus was raised is that it is true.

ment. Jesus was crucified, buried, resurrected *according to the Scriptures*. What happened to Jesus of Nazareth happened according to a divine plan. It was not the Sanhedrin nor Pilate nor the demonic powers, but ultimately God himself who directed the drama at Golgotha. 'God... did not even keep back his own Son, but offered him for us all!' God is the one who acted, both in Jesus' crucifixion and in his resurrection from the dead.

At the beginning of the book of Acts, we read that 'for forty days after his death he [Jesus] appeared to them [his disciples]... and he talked with them about the kingdom of God'. Jesus was bodily, visibly present over a period of forty days. Then 'he was taken up to heaven as they watched him, and a cloud hid him from their sight'. Jesus had been 'taken up', a frequently-used phrase in the New Testament.

It would be a mistake to understand Jesus' ascension as a sort of ancient space trip, and heaven as a place beyond the sun, moon and galaxies. The beauty, vastness and splendour of the heavens stretching over the earth

LESSLIE NEWBIGIN

The Centrality of Christ

Before Jesus put to his disciples the question 'Who do you say I am?' he asked them 'Who do people say I am?' and they answered 'One of the prophets'. That is the natural answer. To the Muslim, Jesus is one of God's messengers. To the Hindu he is one of the *jeevanmùktas*, who have realized identity with Brahman in this life. To the average person in Europe or North America, where religion is an optional leisure-time activity, he is 'one of the founders of world religions'. This is the 'natural' answer, for if there is a variety of alleged revelations the natural thing to do is to assume that the truth lies somewhere between or beyond them all. This is natural, because it leaves me free to shape my idea of God as I like.

But if in Jesus God is actually present as part of the human scene then I am in a different situation. I am called to account. I must either reject or else accept, believe and worship. But to do this is beyond my 'natural' intelligence. 'Flesh and blood', as Jesus said to Peter, cannot reveal it. Only God can bring a man or woman to acknowledge Jesus as Lord. It cannot be proved by argument, for the argument would have to rest on something other than Jesus, and that something other would be the ultimate ground of confidence. 'Jesus is Lord' means 'Jesus *alone* is Lord'. This is not an aspect of the Christian faith; it *is* the Christian faith. It is not my insight; it is God's gift.

Salvation apart from Jesus?

To say that 'in Jesus God is actually present' does not mean that God is otherwise absent. On the contrary, Jesus, in John's words, is 'the light that lightens every man'. And Paul tells us that God has never 'left himself without witness'. Every time the Bible is translated into a new language the translators have to find a word for 'God', and this can only be a word which embodies the idea of God which the people concerned have without knowing Jesus. If there was no word for 'God', how would the first missionary begin to preach the gospel? And if there is a word which he can use, it cannot be one which gives a wholly false meaning.

But if, as we must admit, there can be some knowledge of God apart from Jesus, can there be salvation apart from Jesus? Billions of people have lived and died without ever hearing his name. Can a loving God have consigned them all to hell? Surely (many have argued) he must have made some other way by which this multitude could be saved! The argument takes different forms.

Some have said, 'Jesus is the unique final revelation of God *for Christians*; for the others who have lived and died in other cultures he must have provided some other way.'

Others say, 'For devout Hindus or Muslims, their own religion is the ordinary way for them to be saved.'

point beyond themselves to God's heaven, understood as God's dwelling-place, the reality where God's will is done unhindered and everything bears the stamp of his glory. With poetic pictures, symbols and metaphors, the Bible speaks about this reality. What separates us from heaven as God's dwelling-place is not a distance of time or place but rather the fact that our sin and unbelief shuts us out of this sphere of reality. Jesus used this symbolic religious language when he spoke about the Son of man having 'come down' from heaven, and the Son of man 'going up' to heaven: 'come down' and 'go up' are not spatial movements but speak respectively of Jesus' birth and entry into human history, and of his return to a heavenly form of existence.

Luke also indicated that Jesus' ascension was not to be interpreted as some sort of space flight. Unlike the resurrection, it was not a return into the physical world, that could be described literally, in the words of space and time. And so Luke uses symbolic language; he writes that 'a cloud hid him from their sight'. In biblical language, 'sky'

Or 'Just as Copernicus taught us that it is the sun, not the earth, which is the centre of the solar system, so we must learn that it is God, not Christianity, who is the centre.'

But if the first of these options is true, then the human race is for ever divided in its ultimate allegiances; the hope of human unity is gone. If the second is true, God is the saviour of the devout, not of the sinner. The third looks impressive until we ask: 'Whose idea of God is central?' Truly God is the centre. The different religions embody different ideas of God. What is offered here is just one more religion.

The Bible witness

When we turn to the Bible we find, as usual, that it does not simply answer our questions in the way we choose to put them. We must listen to the witness of the Bible, which can perhaps be summarized as follows:

- ☐ **God's purpose is the blessing of the whole human race and the whole creation.** That is made clear in the covenant with Noah. God's love extends to all he has made. The imagery in the book of Revelation pictures an enormous crowd in heaven, 'from every race, tribe, nation and language'.
- ☐ **God's salvation involves judgment.** 'We must all appear before the judgment seat of Christ'—for he alone is Lord. In his most memorable parable of the last judgment, Jesus indicates that it will turn on whether or not we have responded to the needs of the least of his brothers and sisters. Anyone who thinks he can face that judgment with confid-ence in his own record is a fool.
- ☐ **Jesus' words include terrible warnings of the possibility of eternal loss.** But they are primarily directed to those who are confident that they are 'on the inside'—those who say 'Lord, Lord', but do not do his will, the branches of the Vine that do not bear fruit. The judgment day will be a day of surprises. The first will be last and the last first.
- ☐ **We are not encouraged to speculate about the salvation of others.** We are not to judge before the time. God alone is judge. When the disciples ask 'Are there few that be saved?', Jesus answers: 'You try to get in at the narrow door.'

God has not provided the universe with a spectators' gallery from which I can look down on all the beliefs and unbeliefs of humankind and pronounce about their end. I am on the ground floor—along with my Hindu, Muslim, Marxist and just plain, ordinary neighbours. God has made me a witness of Jesus. It is not my doing but God's. I cannot do other than confess him as Lord, for I know no other source of life. 'Necessity is laid upon me. Woe to me if I do not preach the gospel.' But this gives me no authority for judging whether or not my neighbour will be saved. That authority is God's alone. I have only one duty and joy: to look to him with total confidence, based not on myself, nor even my own faith, but on Jesus Christ the only Lord.

or 'cloud' is often used to denote God's presence among humanity, either in grace or judgment. God showed the Israelites the way through the desert by using a pillar of cloud. When Isaiah was called by God to be a prophet, the temple was filled with a cloud of smoke. A cloud overshadowed Jesus on the Mount of Transfiguration. In the description of the ascension, when Jesus passed from one form of existence to another, it happened by means of a cloud taking him away. When Jesus comes again in visible form, he will come 'on the clouds of heaven'.

Sharing God's rule

'He ascended into heaven, and sits on the right hand of God the Father Almighty.' What exactly do these words in the Apostles' Creed mean?

In Eastern or Roman culture, to sit on the right-hand side of the emperor was the same as sharing his political and military power. This role of co-regent was reserved for the eldest son, and his accession to the throne was celebrated as a national festival. By using this picture language the New Testament is saying that, just as God the Father is almighty and present throughout the universe, so is Jesus Christ—the Son shares his Father's throne. The early church could not have stated more clearly and unequivocally that Jesus is God. He is no longer restricted by the limits of time and space as he was while on earth. He can now be everywhere at once. He can be with his people all day every day. So, when we say 'He ascended into heaven', we are not confessing a Jesus who is far distant. Instead, we are proclaiming that he is with us, in all his love and power, in our own individual lives here and now.

Jesus can share God's throne. Through his death he defeated all God's spiritual enemies and became Lord over all heavenly and earthly powers and authorities. Jesus Christ's victory is cosmic in scope.

Jesus has also—by the power of his victory—been made head of the Christian church, its Lord and leader. From now on, Christians will worship him as their Lord. The first thing the disciples did after Jesus had ascended was to worship him. In fact the chief characteristic of Christians is that they call on the name of the Lord Jesus. Paul writes that 'at the name of Jesus every knee shall bow . . . and . . . confess that Jesus Christ is Lord, to the glory of God the Father'.

As the church's leader and head, Jesus equips his people with power to be his witnesses to the ends of the earth. Peter's sermon on the first Day of Pentecost brings out the connection between Jesus' exaltation and the outpouring of the Holy Spirit. After the ascension, Jesus is installed in the position of power, so that he can provide the church with gifts of grace, charismatic gifts, given to every believer to build up the Christian community.

The New Testament uses other pictures, besides those of the king's son and co-regent, to clarify what the ascension means:

- **High Priest** 'We have a great high priest who has gone into the very presence of God—Jesus.' Jesus has entered the heavens to do, in a heavenly temple, what the high priest used to do for sinners in Old Testament times.
- **Defence counsel**—one called to speak on the accused's behalf. Every time our sins accuse us before the heavenly bar (picture language again), Jesus is a reminder before God of his effective sacrifice. Our guilt has been dealt with once and for all. It cannot block our access to God's throne.
- Jesus is also our **brother and intercessor** in God's presence. He who perfectly shows what it means to be human is not ashamed to call us his brothers. He has shared our circumstances and knows the difficulties we face. He brings together in his own person both power and love, compassion for our problems and the power and right to

forgive. And so he can give strength and help every time we need it. When he left the disciples, he lifted his hands to bless them, and his blessing still flows out to us today.

The King, come and coming

'This Jesus, who was taken from you into heaven, will come back in the same way that you saw him go into heaven.' These words give a clear link between Jesus' ascension and what we call his 'second coming' at the end of time. Our use of language is actually at fault here. Jesus has not gone away from us, to come back at a later stage. He is ruling now, the King of love, but in a way our physical eyes cannot see. Paul says that Jesus must rule 'until God defeats all enemies and puts them under his feet'. The resurrection set in motion a chain reaction of hope and life.

The great victory was won by Jesus Christ in his death and resurrection. He is still actively winning the smaller victories. In this struggle the church, ordinary believing Christians, is called to take part. No one is automatically a citizen of God's kingdom. The risen Jesus—through his church—walks through the world, offering everyone the chance to enter this kingdom. And we all have to decide whether that is what we want. This is the spearhead of the church's mission.

Today Christ's rule is largely hidden from sight. But one day the Jesus who is hidden from our physical eyes, though nevertheless present with us, will appear obviously and visibly to everyone. It will be an unexpected coming, but it will signal history's climax, the beginning of a whole new universe. It will be the time of the final judgment. All evil will be done away with once and for all—everything will be made new. Then redeemed humanity will appear in all its glory. The world will be created anew and will share in the new kind of existence of which Jesus' resurrection was the prototype. The new creation will finally have replaced the old.

For further thinking

QUESTION 1

In the Garden of Gethsemane, Jesus prayed, 'If it be possible, let this cup be taken from me.' Evidently he feared the coming physical pain, as anyone would. What else might he have feared, that was to happen over the next twenty-four hours?

QUESTION 2

If someone said to you, 'I don't see how I can believe in Jesus' resurrection', what would be the first point in your reply?

QUESTION 3

The New Testament declares that Jesus remains Lord of all, even though he is now a hidden king, one we cannot see. How can this assertion be squared with a world which shows so few obvious signs of his rule?

BIBLE REFERENCES

The Ascension

Genesis 28:12; Judges 13:20; Psalms 24:3; 68:18; Isaiah 14:13; Matthew 28:16–20; Luke 24:50–52; John 1:51; 3:13; 6:62; Acts 1:9–11; Romans 10:6; Ephesians 4:8–12; Hebrews 9:24; Revelation 7:2

Be on watch, be alert, for you do not know when the time will come.

Mark 13

God

PART 3

CHAPTER 9

JAMES PACKER

God Is

Books spell the word 'God' with a capital 'G'. Why? Because 'God' is to all intents and purposes a name: the proper name of the personal Three-in-one—Holy Father, Holy Son and Holy Spirit—whom Christians worship, love and serve. 'God' was the English name for the Trinity long before books existed in English.

In our day, indeed for more than a century, the word 'God' has been bent to suit particular Christian view-points. Books of essays have appeared with titles like *My idea of God, The God I want*—titles that tell their own story. It has even been claimed that God is dead—which has made some recall Mark Twain's famous cable, 'The reports of my death are greatly exaggerated.'

We are doing God next year. Please send all details and pamphlets.

Letter from a schoolgirl to the Anglican Church Information Office, London

The attention given to these ideas might make it look as if any view of God put forward within the church has as good a claim to be called Christian as any other. But this is not so. There is a mainstream Christian view of God, biblically based, which has been held since New Testament times and from which the other views have arisen by modification or reaction. This article follows that main stream and will deal with deviations from it as they arise.

Belief in God

Belief in God (*theism*) and belief in one God only (*monotheism*) are the generic terms for the Christian view of God. Theism declares the existence of a personal deity who is the source, stay and goal of everything.

It stands opposed both to pantheism, which identifies God with everything, good, bad and indifferent, and to polytheism, which sees God as one god among many.

- **Pantheism** depersonalizes God and destroys the perfection of his moral character, for it calls evil as well as good divine. Pantheism is one side of Hindu thought.
- **Polytheism** devalues God and destroys the basis of his exclusive claim. For if many gods can help or hurt, and not one of them can do everything—which is always the polytheist assumption—then clearly we must spread our worship among them all. Polytheism was the form of ancient Near-Eastern and Graeco-Roman paganism, against which both Old and New Testaments of the Bible testify; it appears today in the spirit- and ancestor-worship of many tribal cultures.

Christians confess (to quote the Nicene Creed) 'one God the Father almighty, maker of heaven and earth, and of all things visible and invisible'. Only the Old Testament faith out of which Christianity came, and the Islamic faith which went off at a tangent from it, match Christian theism here. Neither pantheism nor polytheism has room to think of God as creator and sustainer of all things. Pantheism cannot do so for it draws no final distinction between God and the world. Polytheism cannot do so for even its 'high gods' prove to lack the power which creating (as distinct from shaping what is already there) requires.

Christian theism is Bible-based, and the Bible speaks out strongly against polytheism. The polytheistic way is to treat all supposedly undying more-than-human personal agencies as gods to be worshipped, and to think of monarchs and other top people as moving up the ladder of existence to reach divinity at death if not before. (Hence the quip of the dying Roman emperor Vespasian: 'I think I'm becoming a god.')

Paul, however, sums up the Bible's view

when he writes: 'although there may be so-called gods in heaven or on earth—as indeed there are many "gods" and many "lords"—yet for us there is one God, the Father, from whom are all things and for whom we exist, and one Lord, Jesus Christ, through whom are all things and through whom we exist.'

In line with this, he describes the Thessalonians' conversion as turning 'from idols to serve a living and true God, and to wait for his Son from heaven . . . Jesus who delivers us from the wrath to come'. (Incidentally, both passages show Paul linking Jesus with the one God as an object of trust and worship, with no sense that this presents a threat to God's oneness. This is an example of the New Testament conviction that there is relationship within God—see *The Bible's witness* below.)

Clearly, 'god' as used by polytheists is a word drastically devalued, as well as misapplied. So by Christian standards the question 'Is there a god?' is not well put. It implies that we all know what a god would be like if he existed, and that there might be room for several gods. It is much better to be precise and to ask 'Does God exist?'—a question in which 'God' has its capital letter. Then we know we are talking about God as Christian theists understand him.

The Bible is equally strong against pantheism, which sees everything and everybody as manifestations of an all-inclusive divine spirit. The pantheist position, as William Temple put it, is that God minus the universe equals nought. The Christian position is that, though the entire universe depends on God every moment for its existence, he does not in any way depend on it for his. 'The God who made the world and everything in it,' said Paul at Athens, 'does not live in shrines made by man, nor is he served by human hands, as though he needed anything, since he himself gives to all men life and breath and everything. 'God minus the universe equals God.'

The Language of Belief

Confessing God

All the creeds, confessions of faith and doctrinal bases that have ever gained currency in the church have defined theism along the lines already sketched.

If we say we believe in God, we are saying something about ourselves as well: that we are creatures wholly dependent on God the Creator for our existence, our continuance, our circumstances and our destiny. Some theologians have said that affirmations about God must be 'cashed' simply in terms of the effect such belief has on the believer, since God cannot be known or spoken of directly.

Although such scepticism must seem unjustified to mainstream Christians, who believe that God has openly revealed himself to mankind in creation, in history, in the Bible and above all in Jesus Christ, it is certainly true that faith in God will change the way we think of ourselves. If it is 'God-with-a-capital-G', the God of the Bible, whom we confess, we shall know ourselves not only as creatures but also as sinners, condemned by God's holiness yet called to salvation in and through Jesus Christ.

I maintained that God did not exist. I was also very angry with God for not existing. I was equally angry with him for creating a world.

C. S. Lewis

Finding the words

Christians believe that God is unique. They also believe that he makes mankind in his own image—like him, that is, in such basic ways as being personal, rational, able to form love-relationships. So the language we use of him must be able to express both our likeness and our unlikeness to him. When Christianity moved out of Palestine into the wider Greek-speaking world, thinkers drew on Greek philosophy for words capable of this double job.

Philosophers in the tradition of Plato and Aristotle thought of the world as eternal but depending in some way on a divine principle, immaterial, impassive, immobile, immutable and timeless. Plotinus, who adapted Plato's thought, held that the only true statements that could be made about this divine principle were negative, saying what it was not.

Christians borrowed some of these verbal forms, and some would say that in so doing, they corrupted their own thinking about the gracious personal God, Maker, Redeemer, King and Friend, whom the Bible reveals. But anyone who reads the early fathers will see that, though their language about God could on occasion be abstract, philosophical and fantastic, they never lost sight of the fact that God is personal, all-powerful and very much alive. In finding words to express the doctrine of God the fathers did well on the whole. And the formulations in which they finally came to define belief in the trinity and in the person of Christ are among the great works of the human intellect.

The fathers' ways of thought and speech about God were overhauled and upgraded in the thirteenth century by Thomas Aquinas. There are three basic principles in Thomas's theism:

- God is essentially the **act** of his own existence, pure and simple. God, we might say, is in no respect a passive principle or static essence, but eternally exists as total, inexhaustible, personal energy—a living God, actively forming and ordering everything in his world.
- God is **perfect**; complete both in power and in virtue. He is infinitely and eternally intelligent and competent. He always wills good (that is Thomas's definition of God's love) and so from every point of view he is worthy of praise. All thought about particular acts of God, or what happens under God, must pass through the grid of this fundamental conviction.
- Human knowledge about God, and the language that crystallizes and conveys it, are alike **analogical**. The language of analogy expresses partial but not complete similarity between things or people. No divine quality or activity (knowledge, love, anger, for instance), and no divine relationship (such as father, shepherd, husband) is identical with its human counterpart. For the fact that we are finite and flawed by sin marks our humanity at every point, whereas God's qualities, activities and relationships reveal his perfection.

We must observe that the knowledge of God which we are invited to cultivate is not that which, resting satisfied with empty speculation, only flutters in the brain, but a knowledge which will prove substantial and fruitful whenever it is duly perceived and rooted in the heart.

John Calvin

Yet the difference is not absolute, for though we are finite and flawed we remain rational creatures who bear God's image. So we may rightly use terms taken from the world of people to specify who God is and what he does. When applied to God, these terms are not used in exactly the same sense as when used of people *(univocally)*, nor in a completely different sense *(equivocally)*, but *analogically* (that is, with a certain correspondence of meaning and at the same time a certain contrast).

So, each time we think or speak about one of God's qualities, activities or relationships, we have to remember that he displays it in its perfection, whereas our human experience of it is flawed. God is a perfect Father, for instance, while human fathers are less than perfect. Christians, following the Bible's example, are always careful to divest each particular quality of all human imperfections when they ascribe it to God.

This is to state Thomas's principles in somewhat modern style and from a perspective supplied by mainstream Protestant theology. Thomas himself, and much Roman Catholic theology since, tried to establish these principles as certainties of *natural* theology.

Many Protestants in the tradition of Luther and Calvin see this venture as misconceived and a failure. But Thomas's ideas about God as energy; about divine perfection as expressed in all that God does; and about theological language as 'analogical', were taken into Bible-based Protestant theology with hardly any change. Theologians saw these notions as implied or presupposed by the Bible, and before Reformation theology was a century old they had all taken their place in its way of expressing the character of God.

Confusion

For many centuries 'theism' as we have described it was a relatively stable element in the Christian heritage. But today many different conceptions of God are voiced, and many people are unsure what they should believe about their Maker. What has thrown Christian belief in God into such a state of confusion and uncertainty?

PETER TOON

Putting Faith into Words

When Christians talk to each other about God, they normally understand each other well enough because they speak from within a shared faith, commitment and experience. They believe that their language about God, who he is and what he does, makes good sense.

The problem

But when a thinking person, whether Christian or not, looks at this language carefully, they see a certain oddity about it. This is hardly surprising. If all our knowledge comes to us via our five senses, and if our human languages are designed to work with this knowledge, how can we speak meaningfully of God whom we do not know via the senses? God is eternal, infinite and invisible. Our human languages are not equipped to cope with these categories!

So it is that all language about God is in words whose meaning is fixed by knowledge which relates to the world of our senses. But since God cannot be seen or touched or smelled, then obviously these words cannot mean what they normally mean. When God is called a Father, King, Shepherd or Bridegroom, he cannot be what these words normally signify. Yet there must be some relation between a man as father and God as Father.

Believers are quite sure that language about God does have real and legitimate meaning. And so Christian thinkers have the task of supplying an explanation for the oddity of religious language. And their explanation has to go beyond what happens when Christians talk to each other; it has to allow for real communication with people who are not Christians.

A solution

The oldest and most persuasive explanation of how religious language works is known as the way of analogy. This asks us to begin with the thought that God is Creator of the universe and human beings are made by him. So there is a relationship between God and people. This relationship is deepened by the further thought that we are made 'in the image of God'—a kind of imperfect mirror of the character of our Creator. The way of analogy rests in the foundation of this close relationship between God and people.

'Analogy' is a relation between two things or persons which may be called a likeness. And there are two types.

☐ The first comes in statements such as 'Jean is healthy' and 'Pattaya beach is healthy'. Only Jean is truly healthy; Pattaya is healthy in a derivative sense—its sunshine and beaches make health possible. In a similar way, God possesses love, righteousness and wisdom in their fullness, while a human being (made by God) possesses them in a derived and more restricted sense.

☐ The second is working when people say such things as: 'You have a clever dog' and 'Einstein is very clever'. The dog is clever in a way appropriate for a dog—he carries the newspaper in his mouth; while Einstein is clever in a way appropriate for a top scientist—he stated the theory of relativity. So we may say that God is wise, good and loving in a way appropriate for eternal Spirit, while human beings are wise, good and loving in a way appropriate for created mortals.

- In the churches, **Christians have neglected the study of God**. Other beliefs have been carefully taught, but belief in God is seldom spelt out. So it is no wonder that eccentricities emerge. Failure to cultivate healthy ideas makes it easy for unhealthy ones to grow.

- **Christian views of God have been challenged.** God-shrinkers have long been at work scaling down the deity to fit him into frames provided by the secular thinking current in each age. The sixteenth-century Reformers proclaimed a Creator who is sovereign in history and who speaks through the Bible. But in the seventeenth century, influenced by a certain interpretation of Newton's discoveries in physics, a way of understanding the universe developed which effectively banished the Creator from his world. The idea of God intervening in the physical order was rejected; he became the universe's absentee landlord.

The greatest eighteenth-century philosopher, Immanuel Kant, believed in God but denied that he could communicate with humanity. God was silenced. The Bible could not be his word of instruction, nor Jesus Christ more than a unique man. On this basis nineteenth-century thinkers equated God with people's best thoughts and feelings about him. But the atheist Feuerbach rightly claimed that in thus speaking of God these thinkers were really only talking about man, that is, themselves and their fancies.

As this process continued, leading scientists and historians were making it their principle to leave God out of account and interpret everything on the basis that 'things happen as they always happen'. Theologians went with them, saying that God reveals himself only in the privacy of a person's inner life, not on the public stage of history, as was once thought. But this had a profound effect on their view of Jesus, whom they now saw not as God incarnate but as a man through whom inward illumination is somehow triggered off in some people's hearts.

The God of the Bible has thus been reduced to a shrunken deity few can believe in. It is no wonder that those who still acknowledge the Creator are now utterly confused as to what they should believe about him.

- **Christian belief in God has been undermined by those who deny God altogether.** Marxism sees belief as a product of social conditioning in an economically unhealthy community. Freud saw it as a neurotic projection, an illusion best dispelled by counselling. From Darwin came the view that everything is relative, and since all thoughts of God (or anything else) are stages in an evolutionary process, they cannot be final or definitive for those who come later in the process. Another assault came from positivism: the attitude that only what we can verify by observation is real.

In science this rules out the unique (for example incarnation, miracle, resurrection) as unreal. In history it dismisses testimony to the supernatural as mistaken. And logical positivist philosophy treats all God-talk as meaningless, except as an expression of private feeling. These four world-views have each been highly influential in the development of modern ideas. The intellectual atmosphere they create has led to great uncertainty about God.

- **Some modern theologians have recast the mainstream view of God**, with the aim of making Christian concepts more accessible to the twentieth-century framework of thought. Karl Barth, for instance, stressed God's absolute transcendence and his hiddenness even in his revelation to such an extent that rational justification of faith was not merely impossible but unspiritual, and therefore should not be asked for. By contrast, the 'process' school of theologians (followed to some extent by John Robinson) places such a stress on the immanence of God and his involvement in the cosmic process that he becomes finite and evolving. (Their name for this view is 'panentheism', meaning 'God is in everything'.) These attempts seem to many to have created more problems than they have solved.

'But, bishop,' a mid-twentieth-century lady is said to have protested, 'surely we all believe in a sort of a something...' That, sadly, is about as far as many people get today. The outlines of traditional theism have been chipped and eroded into shapeless vagueness in many minds. It is part of the spiritual tragedy of our time.

Witnesses to God

The Bible's witness

The mainstream Christian view of God, which has been so muddied and pulled out of shape in our time, came from the Bible. How then does the Bible present God?

The God of the Bible is the self-revealing Creator acting as Redeemer. The sixty-six books of the Old and New Testaments find their unity in this common theme. The Bible's history books tell how God is carrying through a great plan for the salvation of a vast international community which the New Testament calls the church.

This plan started with God's promise in Eden that he would rescue mankind, the call of Abraham and the making of a nation out of his family. Now it has issued in the life, death, resurrection, present reign and promised return of Jesus Christ, the Son of God, who was physically descended from Abraham by the royal line of David. Jesus is now eternally alive; the one mediator through whom sinful people may come to God. The whole of the Bible calls us to respond to God, and expresses the response people made to him for what he has done, is doing and will do as lord of the universe and saviour of his people.

Mainstream Christianity has always seen the whole Bible as God-given in a special, normative way which makes it our abiding rule for faith and life, a source and standard for settling what constitutes true belief and obedience.

According to the Bible, the Creator has spoken to people, sometimes directly, sometimes through messengers, to declare who he is, what he wills and plans, and what must be done to please him. In the pages of the Bible, God reveals to his people, not only in words but also in action, what he is like and what he can do.

In the Old Testament, God's way of making himself known, particularly in his special relationship with Israel, is called his 'name'. In the ancient Near East a person's name declared his nature and function. For example, the name Abraham means 'father of a multitude', and Jesus means 'the Lord saves'. To 'know God's name', then, is to worship and trust God as he has shown himself to be.

In the Old Testament God has several specific names, each proclaiming some aspect of what he is:

■ **El, Eloah, Elohim**, 'God', designates him as superhuman and strong.

■ **Elyon,** 'God Most High', means the exalted one.

■ **Adonai,** 'Lord', marks him out as ruler.

■ **El Shaddai**, 'God Almighty', points to his gracious power.

■ **Yahweh,** 'the Lord' (*Jehovah*, as it used to be rendered), God himself explains to Moses as meaning 'I am what I am' or 'I will be what I will

■

Whoever does not love does not know God, for God is love.

1 John 4

be'—'I am' for short. This most significant name, sometimes amplified as 'the Lord *of* (angelic) *hosts*', is evidently meant to declare that God, like the bush which burnt but was not consumed, is eternally self-sustaining and self-sufficient. It also indicates that God is unchangeably committed to his people. He will always keep his covenant promise; he will rescue and redeem his captive people.

Certain key aspects of God's character are constantly celebrated throughout the Old Testament:

- **Love** which freely blesses, patiently endures and gladly forgives the penitent;
- **Faithfulness** to his people and his promises;
- **Anger** that brings just retribution on those who defiantly choose evil and stick to it.

They are illustrated in all the ups and downs of Israel's history—the exodus; captivity and deliverance in the days of the judges; the kings and the divided kingdom; the Babylonian captivity and return. They are also seen in God's dealings with individuals.

The God of the Old Testament is the personal, living Lord who creates, reigns and speaks; who makes promises, and keeps them. He exposes pagan deities ('idols') for the unreal frauds they are. He upholds justice in his world, as prophet after prophet insisted, by bringing retribution on nations

God and Evil

Times of war have often brought people to question the ways of God. Warfare causes such grief and pain that a reaction can come which says: 'If life is as evil as this, how can we believe in a God who both has all power and also wants the best for us?' This perplexity becomes worse when, as in the 1914–18 World War, both sides claim the support of the same God.

Something of the same reaction can come in times of mass epidemic, or great natural disaster. The French sceptic Voltaire wrote a famous piece along such lines after a severe earthquake in Lisbon in the eighteenth century. But personal suffering sometimes causes loss of faith at the more immediate level of family and local community.

There is no glib, simple answer to the problem of suffering. Wars, torture, oppression and so on are caused directly by the evil in human nature. This evil has resulted from God's gift to humanity of freedom to choose. He has not created robots, but independent beings with freedom to follow right or wrong.

Suffering that comes independently of human evil is even harder to reconcile with belief in a loving God. Disease and natural disaster seem to come precisely from the area where God should be unrestrictedly sovereign. The Bible hints that humanity's fall into sin brought a curse on nature, that will be removed only when the renewing work of Jesus is complete.

These shadows of an answer do not fully and finally resolve the age-old problem of suffering. The Bible nowhere claims to provide a solution at the philosophical level. But at the deepest level Christian faith has something totally positive to say: in Jesus Christ, God shared the experience of suffering. When he entered the arena of our human lives, God did not avoid pain. Jesus bore all the failure, the weakness and the agony that men and women can possibly know. There is no suffering we can endure that he has not already experienced.

Why doesn't God do something about suffering, we cry. In Jesus, he has. He has taken the responsibility for it on himself. In the new age, for which he died and rose again, sin and suffering will be no more.

and individuals that oppress and exploit. And he directs world history towards its final destiny. This God deserves our endless praise and worship.

One word—the word *holy*—holds together all these facets of God's self-disclosure. Holiness is the outshining of all that God is. Holiness is all that sets God's eternal and infinite existence apart from ours; all in God that makes us want to worship him as the glorious one who always does right. Holiness is all that makes God awesome to us as the pure and perfect one who detects evil in the heart no less than in the life and who is resolved to punish evil because he hates it so. When God is called 'the holy one (of Israel)', all these thoughts are brought together.

The New Testament assumes all that the Old Testament teaches of God's character, and adds to it the startling perception that within the unity of the one God there are personal relations. Where the New Testament deals with Jesus Christ it sees him as divine, the Son, the image and fullness of God, to be worshipped alongside his Father; and where the New Testament focuses on the Holy Spirit it presents him also as a divine person. The Old Testament links God's Spirit with creation, providential government, and gifts for prophecy, craftsmanship and devotion. But the thought is simply one of divine power in action.

In the New Testament, however, the Spirit is 'he' rather than 'it', a distinct divine person who speaks, teaches, testifies, hears, leads, searches, comprehends, intercedes, and can be grieved and lied to. In his role as comforter, counsellor, helper, the Spirit has a personal ministry comparable to that of the Lord Jesus Christ himself. Though lacking the technical trinitarian vocabulary which later theology devised, the New Testament unambiguously witnesses to the inner plurality of the one God.

So what is new about God in the New Testament? Not his powers, nor his character—as if he had somehow developed or diminished since Old Testament times. What is new is that a whole fresh stage in his plan has come into effect, bound up with the revelation of God as three-in-one—Father, Son and Holy Spirit in action together to save mankind. This new teaching, essentially, is that:

- Jesus, in becoming man, revealed God's character more deeply;
- God showed his wisdom in reconciling humanity to himself through the death of Jesus Christ;
- God's plan was unfolded for the new international society—the church;
- God was made known as the Father of everyone who is born again in Christ;
- God has promised Christians a glorious destiny with Christ, of which the Spirit gives them a foretaste here and now.

Nature's witness

The biblical writers view the 'natural' order as the work of God's hands, depending on him both for its design and for its continued existence and course. All creation—including mankind—is made for his praise. And as the creation depends on God, so it reveals him. 'The heavens are telling the glory of God,' says the psalmist. 'The whole earth is full of his glory (his manifested presence),' says Isaiah.

Nature proclaims its Maker; the godly person will perceive this, and praise God for nature. Those who fail to see God in creation are blind, because they do not want to see. The apostle Paul writes in his letter to the Romans about God's revelation through nature. He sees God's glory shining so clearly through all created things that anyone who is not led to worship and obedience by what he sees is guilty before God. The whole non-Jewish world is proved guilty because the Creator clearly revealed himself to them in his works, and they refused to respond. They were already in the grip of the anti-God urge

Who among the gods is like you, O Lord? Who is like you—majestic in holiness, awesome in glory, working wonders?

Exodus 15

called sin.

Paul is not saying quite the same as Thomas Aquinas. Thomas claimed that the world could not conceivably be as it is without a First Cause, which is God, and thus God's existence can be proved to thinking people. But Paul is not saying that we can discover the reality of the Creator from the natural order by *argument*. He is saying that the reality of the Creator is immediately known to everyone from the natural order without argument—only people will not acknowledge what they know.

Logically, Thomas's attempted proofs—his famous 'five ways'—are less than conclusive. And if Paul's diagnosis of the real situation is accepted, no one should be surprised to find unbelievers in every age making much of that fact. However, Thomas's kind of argument may well have value in confirming the reasonableness of faith in God to those who already entertain it on other grounds.

COLIN BROWN

Can God be Proved?

People have been trying for thousands of years to prove that God exists. Some of the arguments used can be traced back to Greek philosophy. Over the centuries several types of argument have been put forward:

☐ The **Ontological Argument** from the Greek word *on* (being)—attempts to prove the being of God by reason alone; first put forward by *Anselm* (1033–1109). God is defined as something greater than anything else that can be conceived. Such a being must exist, or if he did not, he would not be the greatest conceivable being.

The argument in its various forms has fascinated philosophers down to the present day. But most philosophers today would regard it as fallacious on the grounds that it is at best a piece of abstract logic. A definition may be logically self-consistent, but does it apply to something that actually exists? Before we can say it does, we need evidence to show that there is something actually corresponding to the definition.

The Cosmological and Teleological Arguments are different from the Ontological Argument in that they are based on reason reflecting on observation. They were put forward by Thomas Aquinas (1225–74), who in turn drew on Aristotle (384–322 BC), and have been restated in various forms ever since.

☐ The **Cosmological Argument**—Greek word *kosmos* (order, world, universe)—argues for a First Cause of everything. Nothing that we see is its own cause. Everything in our experience has causes outside itself and before itself. But such causes cannot go back infinitely. For if there were not a First Cause, which is its own cause and ultimately the cause of everything else, the whole process of causation would never have started. Therefore we presume a First Cause to which we give the name of God.

☐ The **Teleological Argument**—Greek word *telos* (goal, purpose)—is similar. But whereas the Cosmological Argument focuses on causes, the Teleological Argument draws attention to the evidence of design and purpose in the world, not least in inanimate objects which have no intelligence of their own. Just as a watch indicates a watchmaker, so evidence of design and purpose in the world points to a purposeful Creator.

Unanswered questions

The Cosmological and Teleological Arguments are attractive, but they fall short of compelling proof. As they stand, neither of them proves the God of Christian faith or of any other faith. They leave several questions unanswered:

The Mystery of God

No analysis of Christian belief in God is complete without one further point. The God of the Bible is *great*, and his worshippers acknowledge that 'his greatness is unsearchable'. Christians speak of the mystery of God, using 'mystery' to mean, not a puzzle that can be solved, but a reality which surpasses our understanding.

A two-year-old boy whose father has a brain like Einstein's can know his father in a happy parent-child relationship. This is knowledge of the most important kind. Yet the boy could understand very little of what is in his father's mind, however much his father tried to put it into words for him. There are limits to what a two-year-old, however affectionate, can grasp. In our relationship with our Creator we are similarly like very young children before him. We know him in a full and rich sense, for he loves us, he has shown his love in redeeming us, he shows it still in daily mercies, he has opened his hand and his

- ☐ How do we know the First Cause and the great Designer are one and the same as the three-in-one God of Christian faith?
- ☐ Both arguments presuppose an underlying unity in the world, but can we take it for granted that all causes and evidences of design or purpose must be traced back to a single origin?
- ☐ And what about the existence of evil and all the evidence of disharmony in the world? If God is the ultimate cause of everything, is he not therefore the cause of evil?
- ☐ Ever since Charles Darwin's *The Origin of Species* (1859), the question has had to be faced: How far are creatures themselves responsible for their own adaptation to their environment, and thus for the apparent design in their make-up?

To answer such questions takes us beyond the terms of the original argument.

- ☐ Alongside these arguments, there is also the **Moral Argument** which asks: What is the source of our moral values? How do we get our sense of right and wrong? Even atheists and agnostics habitually appeal for justice and fair play. But there is no morality in matter. It is simply there. In a purely materialistic world people may do as they please, and it is those who have the power who decide what is right and wrong. But, for all that, we all regularly try to claim that right is on our side.

The Moral Argument claims that, whether people acknowledge it or not, their sense of moral values points to the existence of a personal, moral Creator, who has built into our moral make-up a sense of justice and obligation to others.

The Moral Argument, like the Cosmological and Teleological Arguments, is not a knock-down proof for the existence of God. But all three arguments draw attention to the same evident fact—our radical lack of self-sufficiency as creatures. Our existence in the world poses questions the world itself cannot answer.

Jesus never tried to prove the existence of God, but his teaching presupposes in his hearers what Calvin later called a *sense of God*. This sense of God is something all human beings have. It provides the point of contact for the preaching of the gospel. The apostle Paul did not try to prove the existence of God from nature. Rather, nature tells us something of what God is like, and that we are not to confuse God with anything in creation. The Christian belief in creation is something we hold by faith.

The Cosmological, Teleological and Moral Arguments fall short of proving the God of Christian faith; this is not ultimately possible by rational argument. But they highlight some of the most fundamental questions posed by our existence in the world. The Christian belief in the Creator answers to our deep-down sense of God. In a way which no other set of beliefs has ever achieved, it enables us to make sense of the world we live in and give meaning to the evidence of cause, purpose and moral values that we find all around us.

JAMES PACKER

God: From the Fathers to the Moderns

Who is God, and what is he like? This question has been answered very differently in different periods of history since New Testament days. The medieval understanding of God, for instance, is light-years away from the modern existential understanding. And these different answers have affected us all. Our opinions are shaped, much more than we think, by ideas dominant in previous centuries. This is just as true of our beliefs about God as of any other area of thought. The pictures of God painted by leading thinkers help, for good or ill, to set the tone for succeeding generations. So we do well to note what these pictures have been.

The God of the Fathers

The early Christian fathers bequeathed to their successors an impressive doctrine of God. The nature of God was central in debate throughout the first five centuries AD. The church had to come to a sound and comprehensive statement of belief about God, both to convince adherents of pagan religions and philosophies, and to exclude heretical opinions.

The constant focal point was the claim, revolutionary if not nonsensical in pagan eyes, that Jesus Christ, the Jew from Galilee, humanity's Saviour from sin and death, is the Son of God. He should be worshipped alongside God the Father, yet on the basis that there is one God only. These long centuries of discussion had both positive and negative results:

- ☐ On the credit side, **the confession of God as Father, Son and Holy Spirit,** 'three in one and one in three', was established as basic to Christianity. The church found standard forms of words both for the trinity (the equal deity of the Son and the Spirit with the Father) and for the incarnation (the full deity and equally full humanity of Jesus Christ).

The Nicene Creed defined the Son as of one 'substance' (or being) with the Father, and the Chalcedonian definition described Jesus Christ as one person in two natures. These became fixed points of reference. With this the writings of certain theologians came to be rated as touchstones of orthodoxy. On the trinity, these theologians were Athanasius and the three Cappadocian fathers (Basil of Caesarea, Gregory of Nyssa and Gregory of Nazianzus) writing in Greek, and Augustine writing in Latin. On the incarnation, they were Cyril of Alexandria (Greek) and Pope Leo (Latin).

- ☐ Another development was more negative: the continuing encounter with Greek philosophies, especially Platonism in its various forms, led theologians to **highlight the contrast between God and his world.** They used terms for God borrowed from philosophy such as eternal being, one in essence, timeless, immaterial, immutable, uncreated, infinite, indivisible and incomprehensible. The more biblical way of describing God, using language closer to human experience, they saw as a potentially misleading concession on God's part to the weakness of man's understanding, and so they played it down. The general effect of this theology was to highlight the truth that God is holy and separate from sinners, and to obscure the equal truth of his personal presence in his people's lives.

In the West, **Augustine** (354–430) was the classic exponent of this account of God as three-in-one and as transcendent. Augustine stressed God's sovereignty. God predestines us according to his own will, and God's grace restores the hearts of those whom he chooses. In recoil from the dualism which he had once accepted, Augustine diagnosed evil as a defect of persons and things that God created good: evil is good gone wrong, which though God overrules and uses, he does not cause.

Augustine also adapted from the neoplatonists their model of the mind's ascent to knowledge. He claimed that understanding of God, who can only be known through the incarnate Son, comes solely as God illumines the willing minds of those who have already taken Christian truth on trust.

'Believe in order to understand' was Augustine's principle here. A good will was, he thought, basic to knowing God. The minds of people unwilling to know God would be left in inward darkness. They would resist the first impulses of God's grace, and by resisting it, they would forfeit that grace altogether.

The God of the medievals

Medieval theology was called 'scholasticism', because it was developed for teaching purposes by professional instructors in monastic schools *(scholae)* and universities. It flourished between the eleventh and sixteenth centuries. **Thomas Aquinas** (1225–74) was its greatest, most creative and most influential figure. (A pope declared his theology to be eternally valid as recently as 1879!)

Thomas's theology, though consciously traditional, as was that of the whole era, was not exclusively so. He took as his basis the orthodox theological heritage, particularly as spelt out by Augustine. But he sought to recast it to fit a different philosophical mould—that provided by the recently rediscovered writings of Aristotle. Aristotle's philosophy prompted Thomas to conceive God not as a static essence, as traditional transcendence-talk might well have led him to do, but as a being whose essence is precisely his constant activity: the dynamism of the one who is the First Cause of everything that is not himself.

Aristotle's method was to analyse everything in terms of causes. This prompted Thomas to develop 'natural theology'—supposedly real and sure knowledge of God gained by reason alone. His method was to note respects in which, as he thought, this world can be shown to be the effect of a First Cause, and then reflect on what the First Cause must be to have produced such effects.

Thomas's natural theology starts with proofs of God's existence. He rejected Anselm's 'ontological' argument (see *Can God be Proved?*), but produced his own famous 'five ways', starting from five observed features of the world around us:

- ☐ motion;
- ☐ cause and effect;
- ☐ the existence of things that are generated and sustained from beyond themselves;
- ☐ degrees of perfection in things;
- ☐ the way each organism strives towards its most perfect state.

Of these famous 'five ways', the first four boil down to the argument from a First Cause, or 'cosmological' argument. The fifth is a form of the argument from design, that the evident nature and purpose of existing things implies an intelligent Designer.

Thomas also tried to exhibit God's oneness, goodness, dominion and perfection as truths of natural theology (knowledge of the God of nature). He claimed that the findings of natural theology are the proper basis on which the truths of supernatural revelation (knowledge of the God of grace) should be received.

Thomas differed from Augustine on the question of knowledge. Both saw all knowledge of God as God's own gift, but they understood this in different ways. Augustine believed that God illumines everyone's mind, yielding an innate awareness of himself which bad people stifle. Thomas held that all knowledge of realities comes as our minds work on what we perceive with our senses. God leads us to know him, therefore, by helping us to think straight about what encounters us from outside. In this Augustine followed a modified form of Plato's thought, Thomas a modified form of Aristotle's.

Is Thomas's natural theology logically and psychologically sound? Did he construct it to show Christians that their faith is rational, or to produce a syllabus for evangelistic instruction? Is his distinction between natural and supernatural realms of being and knowledge good or bad theology? These questions are disputed to this day.

The God of the Reformers

Martin Luther (1483–1546) and his most distinguished admirer, **John Calvin** (1509–1564), the two chief architects of Reformation theology, were Bible men. Their theology, like the New Testament's, revolved round the themes of sin and saving grace, Christ and the church. They avoided commitment to any particular system of philosophy; that was not their interest. And they rejected scholasticism, which they knew well, as unbiblical. Their great aim was to let the Bible, the living word of the living God, speak for itself.

From the Bible they proclaimed the God of the church's faith—transcendent, three-in-one. They set him forth as the holy judge of sin, who graciously gives sinners peace with himself, through faith, on the basis of the death and mediation of Jesus Christ.

Luther and Calvin revived Augustine's sense that true self-knowledge comes only as we listen to God's word in God's presence, and as our conscience learns to echo and apply it, judging our conduct in the light of it. They focused on the crucified and risen Christ as our priest and king (and prophet, Calvin added), who came down from heaven to endure agonies in this world for our salvation.

Faith, they said, is trusting Jesus Christ and his cross to establish us before God as the reconciled and forgiven children of a loving heavenly Father. They focused also on the ministry of the Holy Spirit, who by and with the word enlightens believers, convinces them of their need, evokes their faith, vitally links them with the living Jesus Christ, and sustains them in the struggles of the Christian life. Luther has been called the theologian of justification, and Calvin the theologian of the Holy Spirit, for their epoch-making exposition of these themes.

The medieval picture of the institutional church was as the channel of the grace that strengthens sinners to climb up ladders of merit and devotion to find God, just as Jack climbed the beanstalk to find the giant. This had created the feeling that the transcendent God is also *remote*: 'a doctor who refuses to come into contact with his patients so long as they are ill, but is sufficiently well-disposed toward them to send them medicine through the post (sacramental grace!) with a promise that he will see them when they are recovered' (Philip S. Watson).

Nothing in medieval theology could correct this impression, though there were teachers of mystical prayer who knew better. But the Reformers stressed that the Son of God fully entered the human condition by his incarnation and his suffering; that the Spirit of God now searches, breaks and establishes hearts by means of God's biblical word of law and gospel. Thus they brought back into theology and devotion a biblical awareness that the transcendent God is *close*: a God not far off, but near at hand.

So when the Reformers revived (as they did) Augustine's Bible-based teaching on God's sovereignty in providence and grace, and the decisiveness of his predestination, the sense of God's aliveness and closeness gave their doctrine traumatic impact. In people's religion, it became a matter of first importance to come to terms with predestination, or else to deny it, and so it continued to be for centuries among folk in the Reformation tradition. Puritan religion in Britain and America, with its quest for assurance that God has chosen us, and the Arminian revolt against personal predestination in both its original and later Wesleyan forms, both testify to this.

The God of the Deists

Deism was an English product of the seventeenth century, which, when exported to France and Germany, became the theology of the eighteenth-century Enlightenment. Recoiling from narrow dogmatism and naive superstition, its exponents sought to banish mysteries and miracles and to affirm a 'natural' religion—that is, one rationally based and non-sectarian, that could be demonstrated to everyone without appeal to anything supernatural.

Deists accordingly denied the need for (and sometimes the authenticity of) the biblical revelation. Also, they denied 'particular providence', God's active direction and control of all that comes to pass. They pictured the universe as a complex machine which God, the celestial Mechanic, made, started, and now watches run. Trinity, incarnation and redemption meant nothing to them. Their 'natural' religion was to live uprightly in honour of God the Creator, who after death would reward the good and punish the bad.

The Creator's total remoteness was basic for them: no one meets God in any sense till judgment Day. God's love was thus, at best, reduced to a distant and uninvolved benevolence (God does not love people enough to come to them, or show himself to them, directly), and at worst it was dissolved away entirely. **John Toland** and **Matthew Tindal** in

England, **Benjamin Franklin, Thomas Jefferson** and **Tom Paine** in America, **Voltaire** in France and **Lessing** in Germany were representative Deists.

The God of the Rationalists

Rationalism here means the belief that unaided reason can reach and judge everything, drawing full metaphysical maps of the whole universe and of God too. Reason can judge revelation, if there is such a thing as revelation (and reason can judge that, too). Reason is lord for the Rationalist, and God is what the philosopher declares him to be.

Christians who seek rationality by analysing what has been revealed to us, and those who think Christian belief irrational, are also called rationalists, but (as is obvious) in different senses from the above.

Here are the views of four sample Rationalists:

- ☐ **Benedict Spinoza** (1632–77) was an unorthodox Jew who speculated that the universe is one substance which can be called God or nature. This made him a pantheist, for whom God was an impersonal principle. He was influential, it seems, among eighteenth-century sceptics.
- ☐ **Gottfried Leibniz** (1646–1716) was a Lutheran who wrote defending belief in the trinity. He speculated that the universe consists of an infinite number of 'monads', simple substances without parts which are eternally active. The monads are arranged in an order of importance, with God, the original simple substance, at the top. Leibniz revamped the 'ontological' argument, claiming that an absolutely perfect being must necessarily exist. He also argued that this is the best of all possible worlds, because the evil in it is an integral part of a total picture of maximum good: God could not have made a finite world better. Voltaire the Deist satirized this idea in his novel *Candide*.
- ☐ **Immanuel Kant** (1724–1804) used reason to prohibit metaphysical speculation, arguing that we cannot really think about anything except objects in time and space, and we land ourselves in endless contradictions if we try. He rejected each of the three well-known 'proofs' of God as cases in point. With them he dismissed all notions of revelation and all claims to know God, either intellectually or in relationship. In order to make sense of the morality which reason imposes, he retained a Deist view of God, as the rewarder of virtue and punisher of vice.
- ☐ **Georg Hegel** (1770–1831) worked out a form of what is nowadays called 'panentheism' (see below). He thought this was the truth which Christian doctrine expresses in a primitive and mythical way. All reality is an expression of one thing—Absolute Spirit, for which 'God' is another name. God is the 'world-spirit' at the heart of all that exists. Everything that happens reveals God, and all his life is poured into the world. He does not exist in distinction from the world, but only as its animating force. He is shaping the world into the complex whole through which he will one day perfectly express himself.

God after Kant

Kant's religious philosophy integrated four things:

- ☐ **rationalism:** the view that reason judges everything, including its own limits;
- ☐ **positivism:** we know observed things only;
- ☐ **agnosticism:** God, not being an object in space and time, is unknowable;
- ☐ **morality:** the view that reason's rules of duty are divinely sanctioned.

This philosophy was a watershed. It opened the era of modern Protestantism, in which God is studied without the conviction that he was revealed himself in the Bible, and with a vivid sense that the basic question is always, how can we credibly claim to know God at all?

Conservative Protestants in the Reformation tradition (which includes puritans, pietists and evangelicals) have been unimpressed by Kant. They have gone on believing that God has really revealed himself in the Bible, and that we can understand and know him on this basis. But, Canute-like, they could not stop the Kantian tide coming in. There have been several influential understandings of God in theology since Kant. They have all been put forward in a world where the centre has shifted from God to humankind.

- ☐ **An accent on experience** is associated with **Friedrich Schleiermacher** (1768–1834). Schleiermacher was a child of the Romanticism which dawned as the eighteenth century ended. Romanticism was geared towards feelings, and Schleiermacher based his theology on religious experience. Kant had dismissed revealed truth, and this seemed to leave theologians nothing to rest on or work with. But Schleiermacher maintained that the gap could be filled by the Christian 'God-consciousness', the church's shared sense of dependence on God through the God-filled man Jesus Christ. True theology is God-feelings put into words.

There is an obvious weakness in this approach; how can we tell whether the church's sense of God is adequate? Schleiermacher takes it for granted that God is what he is felt to be, neither less nor more. This weakness becomes glaring when we see that his account of Christian feeling has no place for orthodox belief in the trinity, the incarnation or the atonement. These pioneer eliminations make Schleiermacher a founding father of liberal theology.

- ☐ Liberalism put the **accent on ethics.** Classic liberal theologians were **Albrecht Ritschl** (1822–89) and **Adolf von Harnack** (1851–1930). They saw both the New Testament picture of Christ and the fathers' concept of the trinity as corruptions of the authentic Christian message. That message (they said) is just Jesus' teaching about God and righteousness, as put together by critical historical scholarship.

- ☐ A strong **accent on commitment** came from **Søren Kierkegaard** (1813–55), a Danish Lutheran layman from a pietist background. He became the father-figure of later existentialism by brilliantly expounding the principle that it is only when individuals, fully aware of who they are, take the risk of whole-hearted practical commitment to God in Christ, that they exist as believers. Only then do they know the true God in true faith.

To equate faith with assent to a system, no matter how correct and well argued, is to replace God by an idol. Kierkegaard thought that official Danish Lutheranism, and Hegel expounding God in the historical process, had actually done that. But God is not a passive object, on display for our inspection; he is an active subject, approaching us incognito in Jesus Christ, whom we must follow not fully knowing who he is or where he is leading us.

Kierkegaard's God is the holy, transcendent Creator of whom Luther spoke, who meets people in the wounding word of the law and the healing promise of the gospel, and whose promise is trustworthy however much else about him remains unknown. In this he differs from later existentialists (Rudolf Bultmann, for instance), who take away all specific promises from God's encounter with people. They do this as good Kantians, for the Kantian God is silent. Faith then becomes very much more a leap in the dark than it was for Luther or Kierkegaard.

- ☐ **Karl Barth** put the **accent on transcendence.** Barth (1886–1968), the most distinguished of the group called neo-orthodox, broke with liberalism. Rejecting all natural theology and philosophical speculations about God, he insisted that God speaks to humanity in gracious, sovereign freedom through the Bible alone. We must learn to admit that we are sinners, finite and unable to find God by searching. This means we have to disown our theological fancies, and listen in humble faith to what God says.

The themes of Reformation theology, with the gospel promise, God's 'yes' to sinners, at the centre, were Barth's constant concern. This, he held, is what the Bible proves to be about, when it is allowed to speak. There were, however, some differences. One was that Barth so stressed the discontinuity of the realms of nature and grace that he was never able to affirm in an unambiguous way that Jesus Christ is a totally historical person. But his assertions of the trinity and incarnation, and of God's transcendent freedom, lordship and power are extremely strong.

☐ A twentieth-century tendency has put the **accent on immanence.** Process theologians, mostly American, drawing on the work of A. N. Whitehead, picture a finite God wholly involved in the evolving processes of this world, struggling against evil in a love which permeates everything and strives towards the perfection of all things.

This school of thought has had little to do with the idea of God redeeming what has fallen. The world was never better than it is now; everything is in an ongoing evolutionary process with God at its heart. **Panentheism**, the term applied by process theologians to their view of reality, is a nineteenth-century word meaning that everything exists in God; it stands in contrast to pantheism, which asserts that everything is divine.

Pendulums of reaction and counter-reaction are certain to go on swinging, with no stability anywhere, wherever Kant's rejection of a verbalized word of God in the Bible is maintained.

heart to us, and speaks to us still through the Bible. But intellectually God remains wholly mysterious to us at some points, and more or less mysterious at all points.

With Calvin, Christians recognize that in the biblical revelation God stoops down to our limitations and uses the equivalent of baby-talk in telling us about himself. They recognize too that, although God has told us a great deal in the Bible about himself, there is certainly far more that he has not told us. In this sense God is *incomprehensible*—meaning not that we understand nothing about him at all, but that it is beyond us to understand him fully. This is so both because of our own limitations and also because he has told us only what we need to know in order to grow into spiritual and moral maturity here and now.

So when Christians ask questions about God and the meaning of things, and the Bible does not give specific answers, they will try not to pursue these questions into the realm of speculation, lest their guesses should trip them up. Rather, they will be humbly grateful for all that their heavenly Father has shown them about himself— so grateful that they will be happy to worship him as he is—partly unknown, partly well-known to them. And they will pray for patience to wait for the day when things that are now obscure will be made plain as God reveals more of himself. They will resolutely relate the 'laws' of nature, the ups and downs of history, and all the circumstances and events of each individual's personal life, to the overruling hand of God.

Christians are sure that God, in his sovereignty, ordained what is past, controls what is present and will shape everything that is to come. So for the present they will try to rest content not to know the how and the why of so much of God's work, trusting that all their questions will receive a full answer one day. For, as Paul wrote, 'now we see in a mirror dimly, but then face to face. Now I know in part; then I shall understand fully, even as I have been fully understood.'

For further thinking

QUESTION 1

William Temple said that a person who believes in God but has a false view of his character is in a worse case than an atheist. Why might that be so?

QUESTION 2

Some people today, particularly in the New Age movement, talk about 'Nature' as if it were divine. How is the relationship between God and the world characterized in the Bible?

QUESTION 3

For all that God has revealed himself to humanity, his being is still a mystery—we know only a fraction of what there is to know about him. How can modern scientific people come to terms with the mystery of God?

QUESTION 4

From the information given in the feature article 'God: from the Fathers to the Moderns', which movement in the history of theology laid most stress on God's transcendence—having his existence beyond the universe—and which on his immanence—his involvement with the universe?

BIBLE REFERENCES

God the Father

2 Samuel 7:14–15; Psalms 103:13; Isaiah 9:6; 63:16; 64:8; Jeremiah 3:19; 31:9; Matthew 5:16, 45, 48; 6:4, 9; 11:25–27; Mark 14:36; Luke 11:11–13; 15:11–32; John 1:14; 5:36–37; 10:15, 30; 11:41; 14:2–7; 17:1; Romans 8:15; 1 Corinthians 8:6; 2 Corinthians 1:3; Galatians 4:6; Ephesians 3:14–15; Hebrews 12:7–9; 1 Peter 1:2–3; 1 John 1:2–3

CHAPTER 10

D. A. CARSON

The Personal God

God is, but what is God like? The question is not merely academic, because if what we think about God is basically wrong, we may be worshipping a false God, an idol. And what we worship shapes us. We tend to take on something of the character of what we worship—money, pleasure, success, God, or anything else. So if we will worship God, we must think of him as he is. Otherwise the false image we worship will distort our motives and twist our personalities.

So what is God like? What are his main qualities (which are sometimes called his attributes)? Many of God's characteristics are shared in some degree with human beings. This makes it possible for us to understand what he is like. But the qualities God shares with us are not exactly like ours, for our words are not adequate to express his perfection. God wills, and we will; God loves and we love; God hates, and we hate. But God's will, God's love and God's hate are not exactly like ours. In each case, we must try to detect how God's qualities are like ours, and how they differ.

In addition, God has attributes quite unlike anything else in the universe. They are far harder for us to understand, even when they are described for us. But there are ways of picturing them and glimpsing them, and they are an essential part of what makes God who he is.

Qualities God Shares with People

God is personal. This means he is aware of his own existence, that he reasons, makes free decisions. He is an intelligent moral being, not merely an abstract idea, a 'thing' which somehow exercises fatalistic control over the universe, like a giant robot in a factory. He acts and speaks because he consciously chooses to act and speak, deciding what he will do and what he will say.

All moral virtues belong to God. Jesus has shown us that God is good, loving, forgiving, merciful, gracious, holy, truthful, righteous; that he is a peacemaker, helper, a compassionate provider; that he plans things according to his own perfect will. Because he is perfectly righteous, he is also angry at both sinners and their sin, for light cannot stand darkness, and is jealous of those pledged to be his but who yet turn away and choose some lesser allegiance.

All these qualities belong in some measure to people as well. We, too, can be merciful, truthful, compassionate, angry, jealous. We use our wills and choose our course.

If your conception of God is radically false, then the more devout you are the worse it will be for you. You are opening your soul to be moulded by something base. You had much better be an atheist.

William Temple

God's perfection

What makes these characteristics different in God from in us? It is that in God they are perfect and unqualified, quite untarnished by sin. God is *perfectly* good. Everything he is and everything he does and says is good; he cannot be other than good. God is loving, so much so that the Bible dares say God *is* love. His love, unlike ours, never fails. His forgiveness is far more remarkable than ours. When we forgive we remember that we, too, have sinned; but when God forgives, it is despite the fact he is always the wounded party, and has never sinned.

The Bible tells us that God feels wrath against all sin and all sinners (we are all by nature 'children of wrath'). But, unlike most of our anger, this is not the result of personal pique. It is a necessary part of his justice. He cannot but be angry with sin and with sinners. If he were indifferent he would be denying his own holiness.

This does not mean God's anger is impersonal, merely a symbolic picture of his justice. It is personal enough, but without being

A city bullion broker, I am told, decided to adorn his notepaper with a suitable motto and asked staff for suggestions. The best they came up with was Ingot We Trust.

The Times, London

spiteful, arbitrary, or uncontrolled. His jealousy is justified precisely because he is God, who rightly lays claim to our devotion. Our jealousy, by contrast, is too often (though not always) the result of our desire to hang on to something over which we ought not to make such absolute claims.

More important yet, most of us find we can be loving *or* angry, forgiving *or* jealous, compassionate *or* holy, but not both at once. God is under no such limitations. He cannot be other than both compassionate *and* holy. In what he feels towards a sinful human being, God will invariably be both loving and angry. But to understand better how this can be so, we must think about some other of God's qualities.

Qualities Unique to God

There are some things which can be said of God alone. God alone is self-existing. This means that whereas everything and everyone else depends on him for existence, he is absolutely independent of 'hem. He has life in himself, and he is the source of the life of the universe; but he himself has no source. He alone is utterly self-sufficient. He needs nothing the universe offers him.

It follows that God does not change. His life does not change, his character does not change, his ways do not change, his purposes do not change; even his Son does not change. For this reason, God is supremely reliable and trustworthy.

It is most important to understand God's changelessness correctly. It does not mean he is passionless, that he cannot feel a variety of emotions. The Bible shows us a God who feels very deeply. Nor does it mean that his dealings with a particular person or nation may not change in their experience. Rather, it means God's dealings with us will always be based on the same things—on what God is like.

The unlimited God

Both the glory of God, and the difficulties we have in grappling with what he has revealed of himself, stem from the fact that he transcends the limits we experience. God is essentially unlimited. By contrast, we human beings are limited in time (we are born, live and die at a certain *time* in history); place (if I am in London I am not simultaneously in Montreal or Karachi); power (there are many things I am incapable of doing); knowledge (enough said!). But God is infinite in all these respects.

- He is unlimited in **time**. His realm is eternity. Our very notion of time is bound up with the movement of the stars and planets which he created. We cannot easily think of days or years or any sequence, apart from presuppositions about the movement of planet earth, rotating on its axis and circling the sun. But God is not bound by this system. He made it, and so he is above it.

The problem is that we can scarcely understand what it means to be above time. It certainly does not mean that God is merely static; the God of the Bible stands in active relationship with the universe he created. We are creatures in time, and so if God is to reveal himself to us, it must be in terms of history, of sequence, of 'before' and 'after'. *Before* Paul was converted, *in the days of Pontius Pilate*, Jesus died and rose again, the perfect manifestation of God *within time*, at a specific place in history.

The thought is staggering: the eternal God, the timeless God, has chosen to reveal himself to us in time, because that is the only habitat we understand. And if we find it difficult to understand what it means to say God stands above time, how much more difficult is it for us to understand how this eternal God can reveal himself to us *in* time. There is nothing intrinsically illogical about the idea; but there is much we do not comprehend about it.

- God is unlimited in **place**. He is everywhere; as the theologians say, he is 'omnipresent'. It is impossible to

BRUCE NICHOLLS

Time and Eternity

Throughout human history people have had different pictures of time, especially when they think of eternity or immortality. For many ancient cultures, espe-cially in Africa, Asia and the South Pacific, the rhythmical pattern of the seasons—seed-time and harvest, hot and cold, wet and dry—has given meaning to life itself. The sun, the moon and the stars are the reference points. The goal of living is to harmonize through festivals with the cycle of nature.

There is little thought of the past or the future; the present is all-important. Ancestors are the living dead with whom immediate contact is possible. People from such cultures are offended by impatience, but not by lateness, and this is reflected in the behaviour of students coming from such cultures to study in the West. The apocryphal tombstone inscription, 'Here lies the man who tried to hurry the East', aptly illustrates the tension between different views of time.

Hellenistic culture, which pervaded the world of the New Testament, was dominated by a cyclic view of time. For Plato only eternity as timelessness was real. Time was but a copy of eternity and no event in time had any ultimate meaning. This made the death of Jesus foolishness to the Greeks. The errors of Gnosticism which infiltrated the early church go back to the Greek view of time. The Gnostics saw salvation as deliverance from the wheel of bondage. Hindus also picture time as an endlessly recurring circle. Each life is repeated time and again, in successive reincarnations.

Time is real

The Christian picture of time is quite different, because Christianity has a different view of God as creator and saviour. The Bible speaks of yesterday, today and tomorrow and of God's intervention in history and in individual lives. But time is never viewed as an abstract philosophical concept. God acts in history. Time, like the created world, is real because it is part of God's creative action. It is not illusion. We speak of God's intervention in the world as 'salvation history'.

In the incarnation, cross and resurrection of Jesus Christ we see God's unique and final act that has significance for all time. All those who share in God's eternal life, whether they lived before Christ or after, do so because of this one event in time. Many in the East and West have found this hard to accept. For Mahatma Gandhi no atoning event 2,000 years ago could have eternal meaning now, though he himself wept at the sight of a crucifix. He had a different understanding of the meaning of event and time.

The Bible speaks of time as *chronos*, chronological time of days and hours, and as *kairos*, time of opportunity, promise and fulfilment. We should not exaggerate the difference between these two understandings; both are biblical and should be held together. Christ came in a specific moment of time, and he promised to return visibly in a moment of time. Yet the Bible is rich in expressing times of opportunity and promise. The 'day of the Lord' is seen as the time of fulfilment. At the last day there will be a new creation and time will be caught up into eternity.

Many Christians have pictured time as a straight line, or as a line moving upward, to reflect the idea that biblical time has purpose and is moving towards a goal. Movement along the line is from past to future; God's creation began time, Jesus Christ's coming is the mid-point, and his return will bring time to an end.

Because time is so real to us, we are tempted to think that God is also bound by time and we become involved in unnecessary debates. God is eternal. He is the I AM ('Before Abraham was born I am,' said Jesus); God, who is eternal, created time and surrounds it on all sides. Our future is always present to him. Some have found help in C. S. Lewis's picture of time as a straight line along which we travel and of God as the whole page on which the line is drawn. God from above or outside or all around contains the whole of time and sees it all.

No human analogy or picture can fully explain the mystery of time and eternity. But we can share John's confidence that, when a person responds to Jesus Christ, eternity breaks into time and they experience God's eternal life here and now.

hide from him or to escape from him. He is in everything. But it does not follow that he cannot sometimes appear to people in a localized way. In the Old Testament, God meets with his people personally and at a particular place – in a bright cloud of glory, at the tent in the wilderness, at the temple. When he withdraws from them in wrath, he makes it impossible for them to meet him or experience him; but in one sense even then they cannot escape his presence.

In the New Testament, God meets his people in the most humanly personal way possible—in his Son Jesus. When Jesus is in Galilee, he is not in Jerusalem or Jericho; he is spatially restricted. But God himself is not thereby restricted to any one location, for Jesus continues to pray to him as his 'Father in heaven'.

In other words, just as God is timeless, but meets us in history, so is he omnipresent, but meets us in his Son Jesus. And Jesus lived in a real place, Palestine, and met people in separate encounters on known roads, in boats, in houses. Today, too, he meets with us by his Holy Spirit *where we are*.

■ God is unlimited in **power**. He can do anything: he is 'omnipotent'. But this fact; frequently stressed in the Bible, is often applied wrongly. College lecturers have been known to ask puzzled philosophy undergraduates, 'Is God so powerful that he can make a stone too heavy for him to lift?'—knowing that a 'yes' answer means God cannot lift the stone, and a 'no' answer means God cannot make the stone. Either way there is something he cannot do. In fact, this old chestnut is a trick question: it is asking God to do something self-contradictory, which no one, not even God, can do.

In the same way, God cannot do anything that would violate his own character, or break one of his promises. When Christians say that God is omnipotent, they simply mean that there is no limit to his power, no intrinsic weakness or inability. He can do anything he pleases, but what he pleases will always be in perfect harmony with his character, with all that makes him God.

■ God is unlimited in **knowledge**: he is 'omniscient'. There is nothing that God does not know. This includes not only all brute facts, but also all opinions and thought. He knows the future as well as the past and present—perhaps because he stands above time as we know it, and is not bound by the past-present-future structure which dominates our lives.

Quite clearly, some attributes of God, such as his eternity, are very difficult to understand in their own right. They become that much more difficult when we recognize that this God graciously stoops to meet us where we are—bound by time, place and limitations of power and knowledge. It is hard enough to think deeply about God's timelessness. But it is even more difficult to think about how this timeless God could meet us in history and respond to us in the interplay of real personal relationships.

It is hard enough to understand God's unlimited power, his absolute sovereignty. But it is more difficult to understand how this utterly sovereign God, who does whatever he wants, can have meaningful relationships with us, his creatures, without either reducing us to robots or else sacrificing his own sovereignty.

Yet these very difficulties to our understanding can also prove a help. If we can get them sorted out, they help to explain some of the earlier questions we faced. We said that God is both loving toward sinners and angry with them. We find it hard to imagine how that can be.

The closest analogy might be a good mother or father who both loves and is angry with a disobedient child. But perhaps it is easier to think of God being full of love and wrath 'at the same time' if we remember that he is *above* time. The mystery of God's eternal, timeless being may well help shed light on some other mysteries.

How should we respond?

Our problem with qualities that belong to God alone is that our human experience of what 'persons' and 'personal relationships' are like takes place entirely within the limits of time, space, knowledge and power. But in God we are dealing with a person who is beyond all such limitations. Understandably, we do not know exactly how to resolve these matters. We do not have enough information. But there are several useful things Christians can do when they try to think clearly about God's character.

- We need to **admit ignorance**. We can only know what God discloses of himself. To claim we know more about God than he has revealed is a mark not of knowledge but of arrogance. Indeed, if we knew all there was to know about God, we would have to pass through the very barriers which make us creatures. In short, we would have to be God.
- We must also **worship**. Far from being an excuse for lazy thinking, worship is the only adequate response to the God who made us and who, despite our persistent rebellion and indifference, still delights to make himself known. Such a God will move us to profound adoration, to thinking about God on the large scale and about people on the small scale—precisely the opposite pattern to the predominant attitude in our secular world.
- It is important to **get the problems in perspective**. We may not fully grasp the details of *how* God, above time, reveals himself and interacts with people within time. But, as many scholars have pointed out, there is nothing fundamentally illogical about the idea.
- Above all, we need to **examine how God's qualities work out in practice** in the Bible. This will save us from using our knowledge of them wrongly. Take God's unlimited power. The biblical writers never deduce from this that we are all robots, or that it does not matter what we do because God will have his way in the end. Instead, the Bible uses God's omnipotence to encourage his people and warn his enemies.

Dare a human being fight an omnipotent God? Even if such a God is long-suffering, must he not triumph in the end? Cannot God's people invest great confidence in him precisely because nothing can take place apart from his permission? Even a sparrow cannot drop to the ground without God's permission, so his people need not be prey to anxiety. They can trust their heavenly Father.

Or consider God's limitless presence. The biblical writers never use this idea as if it meant that, because God is everywhere and in everything, an orchid or a daisy is part of God. They recognize that God is also above the universe he has created, and not to be confused with it. The fact that God is everywhere serves as a warning to those who want to escape from him, and as a great comfort and encouragement to those who love him and want to do his will. When Jesus says that he will be with his disciples to the end of the age, he is giving a promise to be savoured and enjoyed, a spur to mission, obedience and worship.

We need to be clear, too, what God's limitless knowledge means in practice. The fact that God knows all things, even the end from the beginning, does not appear in the Bible as some abstruse theory, or to make him into some sort of clairvoyant. But it does have the great value of assuring God's people he is never taken by surprise, he knows what he is doing, he understands our needs and longings. He even knows 'insignificant'

Is God the keystone that supports the structure of our thought? Or is he a personal, warm, attentive presence at the heart of our life? Is he the God postulated by philosophy who gives an ultimate meaning to our world, or is he the living God, in the biblical sense, who touches our hearts?

Leon Joseph Suenens

details, such as when we sit down and when we stand up. With such knowledge, he cannot be tricked or deceived, and his justice will be absolutely fair and impartial.

There are two things that come out very clearly from the Bible's account of God's character. First, his qualities are never described in a way which throws one attribute into conflict with another. In other words, it is wrong to lay such absolute stress on one of God's revealed qualities that others, equally revealed, are neglected.

For instance, it is possible to think so much about God's limitless power that his more personal characteristics—his love, his wrath, his give-and-take with his creatures—fade from view. Equally, some people dwell so much on God as a person that they effectively put aside his omnipotence. Others stress his love, and so conclude that his wrath must be impersonal; or else they decide, against the Bible's teaching, that everyone will ultimately surrender to such magnificent love.

These are dangerous ways of thinking about God. They distort the only evidence we have by suppressing the bits we may not like. And sooner or later we find ourselves worshipping a false god. We must frankly confess that, although we can know God as he is, we cannot, without being God, know all there is to know about him. This means we must take pains to know him as he has revealed himself. It is fatal to speculate about God in such a way that our picture of him is different from the character he has made known.

Second, we need to ask why God has revealed his character to us. It is not to titillate our curiosity but to evoke repentance, faith and worship. Certainly we need to think deeply about God. But God has made himself known to us not primarily to satisfy our intelligence but to meet our many needs. The Bible shows us each of God's qualities first and foremost in the context of the human need that called it forth. God reveals his compassion to people who are lost, his grace to the guilty, his love to the unloving, his eternity to those too preoccupied with what is passing, his wrath to the rebellious.

A God who does not sanctify the everyday is dead, and belief in such a remote God is an intellectual or aesthetic luxury ... it does not lead to the celebration of life. An unemployed God quickly exhausts his capital and becomes a dead God.

Sam Keen

God is greater than the sum of the qualities he has revealed. If all that we can know about God were a jigsaw puzzle, we would be missing many pieces. But the pieces he has graciously given us are magnificent. When we fit these together they form patterns of great beauty and grandeur which stretch our human conceptions to the limit. We must guard against forcing the pieces together in unnatural ways, or throwing some of them away, or introducing new pieces from different puzzles. Otherwise the picture becomes badly distorted and is no longer a picture of God.

God As He Reveals Himself

All we know about God has come to us in *history*. He has revealed himself in historical events and in words spoken by historical people. What he has revealed has affected the history of the nations it has touched.

God has chosen to reveal himself to humanity in a number of remarkable ways. One of these is to use deeply significant names for himself. His 'names' or 'titles' reflect what and who he is. He is 'Yahweh', the personal God of the covenant with his people. (The old word for this was 'Jehovah'; in most Bibles it is given as 'the LORD'.) The name signifies 'I am what I am'. He is 'Yahweh the everlasting God'. He is addressed as 'Yahweh provides', 'Yahweh is our righteousness', 'the Ancient of days', 'the holy One of Israel'.

These names or titles often first called forth in specific contexts, became filled with greater meaning as God revealed himself more and more over successive generations. 'Yahweh is peace', the ancient Israelites gladly affirmed; but when Jesus came and died for our redemption, it could be seen more clearly than ever what that peace was. By the death of his Son, God brought about peace between himself and humanity, and, among God's people, between person and person. Because he himself provided the sacrifice that brought peace about, 'Yahweh is peace' becomes no mere title but a burning summary of what God is like. The same is true of all God's 'names'.

God in Jesus

Perhaps one of the most remarkable features about God's names is that, in one way or another, the New Testament applies them all to Jesus Christ. That the writers of the New Testament do not hesitate to apply divine names and honours to Jesus not only tells us what *Jesus* is like, but equally what *God* is like.

So we gain our clearest view of God's character by studying Jesus. Although God is one, we learn that God is not solitary, but a fellowship of love: the Father loves the Son, and the Son loves the Father, and the Father and the Son make themselves present in believers by the Spirit, and so on.

God the Trinity is treated elsewhere in this book, but what must be stressed here is that God reveals himself as a single God who is a fellowship of love among three 'persons'. And he reveals himself in this way, not to tantalize our minds with deep thoughts, but to draw us into his fellowship of love.

One aim of redemption is that God's people may learn to love God as Jesus loves his Father, and experience the vast dimensions of God's love as Jesus is loved by his Father. The Bible teaching about God as Trinity is thus not only deeply experienced, but also tells us something about what God is like.

The same thing is true about every teaching in the Bible. We study God's providence, for instance –how he mysteriously controls things to bring about his purposes, leaving people responsible for their actions but never relinquishing his own control. And we glimpse something of his wisdom, power, eternity.

We discern how God has progressively revealed himself across the centuries, from the creation, through the call of Abraham, the exodus, the covenant with Moses and the people of Israel, the rise of the prophets, the establishment of David's kingdom, the constant promises which look to one who is to come, and the promises of a new heaven and a new earth. And we see more clearly that God not only forms purposes, he is a God of purpose, a being with goals and will. We see that these purposes include drawing together a people who love him in purity and faith.

This tells us something of what God desires and cherishes. We perceive something of the sweep of his thoughts, and meditate on the amazing love of a sovereign Creator-God who does not reject people who have rebelled against him, but works to draw them back. We read of his concern for justice, and deduce he must be just; of his promises culminating in Jesus, and know him to be faithful; of his frequent judgments on people and nations, and his warning of eternal accountability, and know he is a God to be feared; of his promise of eternal life, and recognize that our basis of hope is as certain as the love of God in Jesus Christ. The entire sweep of the history of redemption reveals what the personal God is like.

Holiness and love

If there are two attributes of God which most completely sum up all that he has revealed of himself, they are holiness and love.

'Holiness' sums up the nature of God. Other persons and things in the Bible are called 'holy', but only because of their relation to God. Holiness is not essentially a question of character: clothes, food and utensils are sometimes called holy. They become holy not because they are good, nor by some magical rite, but because they are peculiarly God's. The *moral* obligation in being called holy lies in this: 'holy people', those who belong to God, must reflect something of God's character. That is part of his mark of ownership. God himself is holy in that he is not bound by creation, not to be compared with anyone or anything: he is completely apart, transcendent, 'holy'. We are holy if we belong to God, if we are set aside for him alone.

The holy God is also the loving God. God's love is not caused by anything in the ones whom he loves, but finds its springs in his own character. We human beings often love because we find the one we love attractive; God loves because it is his nature to love. His love is directed towards the lost world. But the Bible equally declares that God sets his love in a special way on some people, not for any superior value in them, but simply because God has chosen to do so. This love God has towards his people is shown as he works for their good, especially for their eternal well-being. Its greatest demonstration came when he sent his Son to reconcile us to himself.

No description of the character of God can ever be adequate: the subject is too vast. But no other subject so urgently demands our thought. This is God's world, he made us, we will all have to give account to him and in Jesus he has opened up the way for us to know him. Our response must surely be to give our minds to the task of thinking about his character. As we do so, we will become a little more like him.

For further thinking

QUESTION 1

Some people who want to find modern ways of thinking about God have used the analogy of a powerful computer to describe him. Is this a good analogy for God? If not, why not?

QUESTION 2

Are God's holiness and his love ever in conflict?

KLAAS RUNIA

The Trinity

CHAPTER 11

When we speak or write about God the Three-in-one, we are not dealing with a purely theological matter. This belief about God takes us to the very heart of the church's life. You can see this from the central place it commands in the worship of the church. Many of our hymns end with some such doxology as:

Praise God from whom all blessings flow;
Praise him, all creatures here below;
Praise him above, ye heavenly host;
Praise Father, Son and Holy Ghost.

Another well-known hymn begins with the verse:

Holy, holy, holy, Lord God almighty!
Early in the morning our song shall rise to thee;
Holy, holy, holy, merciful and mighty,
God in three persons, blessed Trinity.

When, in a church service, we recite the Creed, we again speak of God the Three-in-one, for we confess him as the One God, who is Father, Son and Holy Spirit: 'I believe in God the Father Almighty, Maker of heaven and earth ... and in Jesus Christ, his only-begotten Son, our Lord ... and in the Holy Spirit.' Our whole life as Christians is surrounded by the Name of God the Trinity. We were baptized into the Name of the Father and the Son and the Holy Spirit. Usually we are married in the same threefold Name. And in many Christian churches we will also be buried in the very same Name.

From all this it is clear that we are not dealing with something that belongs to the periphery of the Christian faith; we are coming to its centre.

And yet, is it really a living doctrine for the average church member? To be honest, I have a suspicion that many church people deviate from it, to one side or the other. Some are virtually 'tri-theists': the Father, the Son and the Holy Spirit are regarded practically as three separate Gods. Others are virtually unitarians: in the practice of their faith the Father alone is God, while Jesus Christ is seen as a special man who reveals the Father, and the Holy Spirit is for them a power rather than a divine Person.

These are both serious deviations. The first amounts to a form of Christian polytheism and, in spite of its Christian colouring, it is not really different from other religions which believe in more than one god. The second means that we have really fallen back into Judaism or a kind of Christian Islam: the Father is God and Jesus is his prophet, while the Holy Spirit is almost completely left out.

The Trinity in the Bible

The first question to ask is, what does the Bible teach about God? For the reason why, throughout the ages, the church has always believed in God as three-in-one is that this belief is based on the Bible.

It may be objected that nowhere in the Bible do we find the doctrine of the trinity clearly formulated. This is always brought out by Jehovah's Witnesses and other sects who reject this doctrine. Their first question always is: Where do you find it in the Bible? People who are using the King James Version might be inclined to point to 1 John 5:7: 'For there are three that bear record in heaven, the Father, the Word and the Holy Ghost.' But it is now generally recognized that this verse does not belong to the original text of the letter; it is a later insertion. The Bible gives us not exposition but evidence. The theological formulation took place later, after the days of the apostles.

The term 'doctrine', as A. W. Wainwright

Without the Spirit it is not possible to hold the Word of God nor without the Son can any draw near to the Father, for the knowledge of the Father is the Son and the knowledge of the Son of God is through the Holy Spirit.

Irenaeus of Lyons

has pointed out, can be taken in a twofold sense. First it can be taken as 'a formal statement of a position'. In this sense the doctrine of the trinity is not found in the Bible: 'There is no formal statement of trinitarian doctrine in the New Testament as there is in the Athanasian Creed or in St Augustine's *De Trinitate.*' But the term 'doctrine' can also mean 'an answer, however fragmentary, to a problem'. In this sense the doctrine does occur in the New Testament, for 'the problem of the trinity was in the minds of certain New Testament writers and . . . they made an attempt to answer it'.

But why was there such a problem? The New Testament writers, together with their fellow believers from Old Testament days, uncompromisingly believed that God is one. Yet at the same time they also believed that Jesus, the Messiah, is the Son of God, and that in a unique sense. Again and again John speaks of the 'only-begotten' Son of the Father. The other three Gospels call him the 'beloved' Son, which means virtually the same. Much later the Nicene Creed was to call Jesus 'God of God, Light of Light, very God of very God'.

In this combination of God who is One and the Messiah who is his Son we find the beginnings of the trinity in the New Testament itself. The biblical roots of this doctrine had nothing to do with philosophical speculation; it was born of the heart of the Christian faith—what was believed about Jesus Christ. It was the coming of Jesus which set in motion the transformation of Jewish monotheism into the Christian doctrine of the trinity.

The same is true of the way this belief developed in history. The church of the first three centuries did not engage in controversies about the trinity because it was fond of speculation (although it cannot be denied that the fathers were fond of it sometimes). This controversy was basically about who Christ is.

The basic issue was: Is Jesus Christ God, is he really and fully God? If so, what does this tell us about the Being of God? At a later stage the same question was asked about the Holy Spirit. But at that time the issue over the nature of Christ had already been settled; the controversy about the divinity and personality of the Spirit was more in the nature of a consequence. The core of the doctrine of the trinity was and is the divinity of Christ.

The Old Testament

Although the main evidence for the doctrine of the trinity is to be found in the New Testament, we need to start with the Old. We must never forget that the New Testament is based on the Old. No statement of belief is complete, unless it is seen within the context of the whole Bible, including the Old Testament.

When we study the Old Testament, one thing immediately stands out: the main emphasis is on the *unity* of God. The word used for 'one' is the ordinary Hebrew numeral. God is all on his own. He has no 'relations'. As far as his Godhead is concerned he is alone, unique. This confession was utterly central for the Jew. It is said of Rabbi Akiba that in the hour of his execution he continued to repeat: 'One, one, one . . .'

The oneness of God, however, is not only Israel's central confession; it is also the central *commandment.* The first of the Ten Commandments, basic to all the other commandments, is: 'You shall have no other gods before me.' To break this commandment is most serious sin, for it offends God in his very essence. Anyone who does have other gods before or as well as God denies by that very fact that God is truly God. He draws the only God into the 'pantheon' and thereby makes him no god.

Israel's religion is monotheistic through and through, from the five 'books of Moses' right through to the last prophets. But are there also indications in the Old Testament of a *plurality* within the one Godhead?

Careful reading of the Old Testament shows no indication of the trinity itself. Yet there are several remarkable aspects which definitely have to be taken into account, if we want to see the full picture of the Old Testament understanding of God. These aspects can be divided into two groups:

- Some passages use **plural forms** for God. One form of the name for God, *Elohim*, is itself plural. This is remarkable in view of the Old Testament emphasis on the unity of God. It cannot be explained as a 'plural of majesty'; this was entirely unknown to the Hebrews. It has been seen as on a level with the words for 'water' and 'heaven', which both also happen to be in the plural in Hebrew. Water can be thought of in individual raindrops or in terms of the mass of water in the ocean. The plural in this case points to 'diversity in unity'. Some believe that the same is true of the plural 'Elohim'.

But there are also passages where God speaks of himself in the plural. We find them in particular in the first chapters of Genesis. 'God said, "Let us make man in *our* image, after *our* likeness…"'; 'The Lord God said, "Now the man has become like one of *us*…"'. But we find it also in Isaiah's vision: 'And I heard the voice of the Lord saying, "Whom shall I send, and who will go for *us*?"'

Jewish commentators have always had much difficulty interpreting these passages. Usually they have interpreted the plural form away, but that is no solution. Christian theologians have also supplied different interpretations. The most satisfactory solution seems to be that within God himself there is some kind of discussion, some interchange of views.

Although these features are important, because they are a faint indication of plurality within the Godhead, we should not overemphasize them. The Old Testament itself does not elaborate on them, nor do these passages play any part in the New Testament. None of the New Testament writers uses them as a starting-point for his reflection on the Being of God.

- Another group of ideas in the Old Testament, however, does play a part in the reflection of the New Testament writers: such concepts as **the word of God, the wisdom of God** and **the spirit of God.** These concepts always occur in connection with God's active dealing with the world in general and with his people in particular.

The Old Testament writers firmly believed that God is the transcendent One, over and above humanity; but they equally firmly believed that he actively intervenes in the world. To express this, the Old Testament often speaks of God in human fashion. It speaks of his hand, his arm, his eyes, his ears, and so on. All these expressions indicate that God is personal and personally active. He himself is present in the world by his hand or arm or eyes or ears. They are, as it were, extensions of his personality, by which he, the transcendent One, is personally involved in the history of this world.

All this is particularly true of the word of God, the wisdom of God and the spirit of God. They are three very powerful extensions of his personality. Take, for instance, God's *word*. God's speaking is not just an empty sound. It is dynamic through and through. God's word is creative. The whole world came into being by his speaking. In Genesis, we read again and again: 'And God said…' The Psalmist wrote: 'By the word of the Lord the heavens were made, and all their host by the breath of his mouth.'

The same is true of the *wisdom* of God. In Proverbs 8, wisdom is represented as a person who is with God, and again it is linked up with God's work of creation. Of course, we should not find a direct indication of the second Person of the Trinity here, as has been done in the past; this is a poetic personification. But it is also a very clear indication of the extension of God's personality.

Finally, the same is true of the *spirit* of God. The Hebrew word sometimes translated 'spirit' originally meant 'movement of air'. Sometimes it means 'wind' or 'storm', but more often it has the meaning of 'breath'—the being that has 'breath' is a living being. Applied to God it means that he is the *living* God, who is constantly in action. In the Old Testament this action is often indicated by the expression 'the spirit of God'. Alan Richardson summed it up: 'God's Spirit is God acting.'

It is therefore not surprising that the Old Testament often speaks of 'the spirit of God' in a personal way. But still it does not go beyond the idea of the extension of God's personality.

Nevertheless, this idea of the extension of God's personality is very important in itself. It shows that there is 'movement' in the living God. His Being is not rigid and motionless, but, as the living God, constantly reaches out towards others. And it is no wonder that later on, in the New Testament, this very same idea serves as a starting-point for further development. Both Paul and John take up the idea of the word and wisdom of God and apply it to Jesus Christ, while the idea of the spirit of God develops into a purely personal understanding of spirit: the Holy Spirit.

So the Old Testament provides possible ground for the growth of belief in God as trinity which was made more explicit in the New Testament. The doctrine was to develop along mainly Greek lines, but the basis for it was already there in Jewish thought.

The New Testament

The New Testament also takes its starting-point in the confession and the commandment that *God is one*. Jesus himself repeats the opening words of the 'Shema'; Paul writes to the Corinthians: 'For us there is one God, from whom are all things and for whom we exist.' James writes: 'You believe that God is one; you do well.' The apostles time and again speak of God the Father *and* our Lord Jesus Christ. In other words, the Father and Jesus are clearly distinguished. Yet the same writers say, with equal emphasis, that *Jesus Christ himself is also God.*

Admittedly, the name 'God' is not often applied to Jesus. We find it in only seven or eight passages, some of which can be translated in a different way. But Christian belief in the deity of Christ does not depend on these passages only. On the contrary, the concept that Jesus is God undergirds the whole New Testament.

- Again and again the name *Kurios* ('Lord', the translation in the Greek Old Testament of the Hebrew name for God) is applied to Jesus. And often it plainly carries its full Old Testament significance.
- Jesus is worshipped.
- Quotations from the Old Testament are transferred from the Lord God to Christ.
- He performs divine functions: creation, forgiveness, judgment.
- Several authors state that Jesus was pre-existent and 'came' from the Father.

Paul sums it all up, when he writes that 'in him [Jesus Christ] the whole fullness of deity dwells bodily'.

All this, naturally, introduced an entirely new element into the doctrine of God. For this is not a matter simply of an extension of divine personality, but in this man, who is at the same time God, we are faced with interaction within the Godhead. No wonder this was *the* stumbling block for the Jews. Judaism knew the idea of extension of God's personality. But the idea of interaction within the extended personality is not Hebrew (nor Hellenistic), but definitely Christian.

As well as the New Testament teaching about Jesus Christ there is also the question of the Holy Spirit. In the New Testament itself this receives less emphasis than belief about Christ. In the Gospels we read comparatively little about the Spirit. John writes: 'As yet the Spirit had not been given, because Jesus was not yet glorified.' But even after

Pentecost, when the Spirit was given to the disciples, the Spirit never comes into the full limelight. This is due to his particular task: to glorify Jesus.

Yet after Pentecost his image does become much clearer. He is much more than a divine power. He is a divine 'person'. Again and again personal names and activities are ascribed to him: leading, allowing, being made sad. Only one conclusion is possible: in the Spirit God himself is with and in the believers.

How then can we describe the New Testament picture of God? On the one hand, God is *one*, truly and absolutely one. On the other hand, this one God exists as *Father, Son and Holy Spirit*. This threefoldness is present throughout the whole New Testament, not as a formal statement, but as a pattern to be seen everywhere. And here and there in the New Testament there are attempts to find an answer to the problem involved in this threefold existence of God:

■ Everywhere in **the first three Gospels** the threefold pattern can be seen. As is to be expected, they show it in particular in the *life* of Jesus. It comes to the fore in his birth: the Father sends Jesus into the world and the Holy Spirit prepares the way. When he is baptized all three persons are present: Jesus in the water, the Father's voice from heaven, the Spirit coming down like a dove.

The same pattern gives the framework for the temptation story. At the end of Matthew's Gospel, as Jesus commissions the disciples, he uses the three names side by side: 'Go therefore and make disciples of all nations, baptizing them in the name of the Father and of the Son and of the Holy Spirit.' Again, this is not a formal statement of doctrine; Jesus is simply bringing out the enormous importance of the new sacrament of Christian baptism. Yet it remains striking that Father, Son and Holy Spirit are mentioned side by side, while at the same time the 'unity' ('the Name', in the singular) is emphasized.

■ In the writings of **Paul**, too, we repeatedly find the three persons linked together. The pattern runs as a golden thread through the texture of all his letters. It is quite evident that he has given much thought to the problems involved. Repeatedly, he comes to grips with the question of the nature of Christ. He writes: 'Christ Jesus . . . always had the nature of God, but he did not think that by force he should try to become equal with God . . . of his own free will he gave up all he had, and took the nature of a servant. He became like man'; 'He is the visible likeness of the invisible God. He is the first-born Son . . . for through him God created everything.'

Paul also wrestled with the nature of the Holy Spirit, as is evident, for example, from a passage in Romans 8, where the Spirit is called both the Spirit of God and the Spirit of Christ. Finally, there are some passages in which Paul sets the three persons side by side.

■ The deepest reflection in the New Testament we find in the writings of **John**. At the very beginning of his Gospel he takes up the Old Testament concept of the word of God and speaks of the 'Word' (*Logos*), who was in the beginning, who was with God, who was God. Two things are set side by side here: the Word is distinguished from God, and yet the Word is at the same time identical with God. In this paradox lies the whole mystery, a mystery, that becomes even greater when John writes: 'And the Word became flesh and dwelt among us, full of grace and truth.' Further on in the Gospel, John moves from the idea of the Word and speaks instead of 'Father' and 'Son', but it is the same mystery. He is 'the only Son . . . at the Father's side'.

John also struggled with the relationship

between Jesus and the Holy Spirit. He clearly distinguished them. He quotes Jesus' words about the Spirit as 'another Counsellor' whom Jesus himself will send to the disciples 'from the Father, even the Spirit of truth who proceeds from the Father'. Yet at the same time Jesus and the Spirit are inseparably related, for the Spirit 'will not speak on his own authority', but 'He will glorify me [Jesus], for he will take what is mine and declare it to you'.

None of this New Testament teaching constitutes a full doctrine of the trinity, but it certainly lays a foundation for such a doctrine. It is sufficient proof that the later doctrine of the trinity, as formulated by the church in its creeds, is not a foreign element imposed upon the New Testament, but rather a natural consequence of the New Testament witness.

The Trinity in the Creeds

This teaching was established in the midst of much controversy. Again and again two heresies raised their heads. One set of views started from the unity of God and said that the Father, the Son and the Holy Spirit are only different ways God has shown himself to mankind in the history of revelation. They are 'modes of revelation', but in the essence of his Being God is simply one. (This is known as **Sabellianism**, or **Modalism**.)

At the other end of the scale was **Arianism**, which also started from God's unity, but then went on to offer quite a different 'solution'. Only the Father is God. Jesus Christ is a created being. Admittedly, he is a very special created being, for his creation was 'before all time', but nevertheless he belongs with the creation rather than with God. As to the Holy Spirit, he was regarded as a power or attribute of God.

The church has rejected both 'solutions' and formulated its own view in the well-known words: **one divine essence (substance or being), existing in three persons**. This view was finally laid down in the so-called Athanasian Creed.

As the church was well aware, this formulation too is inadequate. In the doctrine of the trinity we have to do with a mystery which is beyond all human thought and language. Augustine wrote the famous words: 'When one asks: What three? human speech suffers from a great lack of power. Nevertheless, we say: Three persons, not in order that we should say this, but that we should not be silent.'

Of course, the term 'person' is not adequate either. In fact, in recent years it has been increasingly criticized. Today this term has a meaning different from in the days of the church fathers. In the first centuries it was a rather neutral word, pointing to a personal relationship. Today a 'person' is a self-conscious, autonomous individual. But if you apply this to the Trinity it sounds as if you are speaking of three Gods. For this reason many prefer to speak of three 'modes of existence'. The one God exists in three different ways.

I believe this criticism is correct. What today we mean by the word 'person' applies to the divine Being himself rather than to the divine distinctions within the divine Being. There are not three individual personalities in God. There is only one divine Personality, which contains a threefold distinction.

But at the same time we must make quite clear that the one divine Personality exists in three different *personal* ways. Father, Son and Holy Spirit are not simply three different modes of revelation. (That means 'Modalism', a view which is rather prominent in modern theology, but which the church has always rightly rejected.) God not only *reveals* himself as Father, Son and Holy Spirit; God *is* Father, Son and Holy Spirit. These three names indicate three genuine distinctions within the one personal God, and these three distinctions themselves are fully personal.

The Importance of the Trinity

But why do we as Christians make so much fuss about all this? If we cannot understand it anyway, is it not wiser to drop it as a piece of sterile speculation? Does it really have any theological and religious significance? Is it important for our own personal experience? The answer is Yes. The significance of this doctrine is so great that it is the very foundation of our Christian faith. Why?

- Precisely in this doctrine it becomes clear that God is truly **the living God**, the God who has life in himself, who is literally full of life. Some of the early church fathers used a remarkable expression. They said: 'God is *fertile*. Within the three-in-one God are all the possibilities of person-to-person communication.

God in no way needed the creation. He was not a lonely God, who had to make a projection of himself, so as to have an 'opposite'. The doctrine of the trinity is the end of all pantheism. If, in the depth of his own being, God is three-in-one, he does not need this world in order to come to his full potential. As Emil Brunner put it: 'Only if, in himself, from all eternity, God *is* the loving One, no world is needed for him to be the loving One.'

- The doctrine of the trinity is also of great importance for a proper understanding of the doctrine of **creation**. Brunner again: 'The world as creation is the work of his love.' The idea of God does not need the world to make it complete. Athanasius told us long ago that, because God is 'fertile' and can communicate himself inwardly, he is also able to communicate himself outwardly. But this inward self-communication does not *require* the outward, since there is already communication within the Godhead. Through his Son, God freely reached out to create a world. What he made was something other than himself, but he is its foundation and he is its aim.

- This belief in the trinity is equally essential for the doctrine of **revelation**; in fact it is the basis for all revelation. In the revelation of the Father in the Son through the Spirit, we not only receive some external information about God, but we have the guarantee that God himself is speaking to us and opening his divine heart to us. Revelation is really and fully *self*-revelation.

- But above all the doctrine of the trinity is of importance for our **salvation**. It is the answer to the question whether or not our salvation is really God's work. In the final analysis this is the reason why the church is so vitally interested in the divinity of Jesus Christ and of the Holy Spirit. The vital question to ask about the nature of Jesus Christ is this: In Jesus, do we really meet with God himself?

The same vital question is at stake in the doctrine of the Holy Spirit. Athanasius wrote: 'If the Holy Spirit were a creature, we would have no fellowship with God in him; in that case we would be alien to the divine nature, so that we in no sense would have fellowship with it.'

None of this is bald theory. It is echoed in Christians' personal experience. Believers know by experience that they are children of the Father, that they are redeemed by the Son and that the Holy Spirit is present in their lives. And they also know that in all three relationships they have to do with the one and same God.

It is, as it were, a constant moving to and fro: from the Father through the Son to the Holy Spirit in our lives, and then again from the Holy Spirit in our lives through the Son to the Father. True, we do not always experience this threefoldness as unity. Often the threefoldness in the relationship is more to the fore in our experience than the unity. And yet there is the experience of unity too, especially as the Spirit dwells in us, for in and through the Spirit, Jesus Christ himself is present with us, and in and through Jesus we have fellowship with God the Father.

In spite of this experience, however, it remains a fact that we cannot understand the mystery of the Trinity, let alone take it in. It is far beyond our human thinking. We can only end where we started: by worshipping God the three-in-one. In fact, this was and is the whole reason why the church tries to penetrate this mystery: that we may worship God as he really is; bring him praise, not only for what he has done for us, but above all for what he is in himself. In his worship, the believer will adore God for his incomprehensible greatness and glory.

The Athanasian Creed, the most theological of all ancient creeds, begins with these words: 'And the Catholic faith is this: That we *worship* one God in Trinity, and Trinity in Unity.' And at the end of the first section it repeats it emphatically: 'So that in all things as aforesaid, the Unity in Trinity, and the Trinity in Unity is to be *worshipped*.' This is indeed what the church has done throughout all the centuries of its existence and what it still is doing all over the world. In adoration Christians bow down and sing together:

Holy, holy, holy, Lord God almighty,
All thy works shall praise thy name,
in earth and sky and sea;
Holy, holy, holy, merciful and mighty;
God in three persons, blessed Trinity.

For further thinking

QUESTION 1

Try to put yourself in the position of Jesus' disciples as they experienced him and heard his teaching. What was it in their later reflection on his character and teaching that might have brought them to think that God is three-in-one?

QUESTION 2

How much is lost from Christian faith if we come to agree with those who hold that Jesus of Nazareth is less than divine?

BIBLE REFERENCES

God the Trinity

Isaiah 6:1–8; Matthew 3:13–17; 28:19; John 14:15–23; 15:26; 16:13–15; Acts 2:33–34; 1 Corinthians 12:4–6; 2 Corinthians 13:13; Galatians 4:4–6; Ephesians 2:18; 4:4–6; Philippians 3:3; Hebrews 10:10–17; 1 John 5:1–12

WALTER MOBERLY

The Place of the Bible

CHAPTER 12

The Christian faith teaches that it is possible to know God through Jesus Christ. Because Jesus is risen from the dead and is alive for evermore. Through the Holy Spirit, he is present in the lives of those who trust and follow him. So it is perhaps initially surprising that this faith should attach supreme importance to a book, a book which is a collection of documents all written in the ancient world some 2,000 to 3,000 years ago. If we can know the living God today, why should we bother with ancient documents? Yet the fact is that Christians do attach, and always have attached, central importance to the Bible. Why is this so?

There is, of course, no need to justify the importance of reading the Bible in general terms. The Bible, more than any other single work, has shaped the development of Western civilization over the last 2,000 years. Without a good knowledge of the Bible, an intelligent understanding of this civilization is not possible. But our present concern is to understand the specific role the Bible has within Christian belief. How does the Bible fit within Christian faith and life today?

What Sort of Book is the Bible?

The Bible contains many different writings. At its heart, however, stand the stories which tell how God both spoke and acted in human history.

The early chapters of Genesis set the scene—the world was created by God, but it became twisted and spoiled. The story then tells of how God sought to restore the world by calling the nation of Israel to serve him. The Old Testament recounts the history of Israel from Abraham to Ezra, through its many ups and downs, and shows how God was continually guiding, disciplining and renewing his people.

In the New Testament this whole process reaches a climax—God himself actually becomes a man. When he comes to his people he is rejected and killed by them. Yet he overcomes death and creates a new people to bring a message of forgiveness and new life to all who will receive it.

The importance of this story lies in its being real, historical fact. It is because God has actually done these things that we can know what he is like and receive new life through faith in him. Try setting the Bible history alongside stories such as Superman. However much we might wish to have powers of the kind people have in these stories, we know we never can. The stories are purely imaginary. No one ever has had such powers, and so no one but a child would ever suppose that they could become real for people today.

The new life that the Bible offers is based not on imagination but on fact. It is because certain things happened that the Christian has grounds for belief. Many people misunderstand this. They think that the idea of life after death, for example, is just an attractive idea—something which provides a hopeful perspective for living. But if that is all there is to it, it may ultimately be based upon no more than wishful thinking, a whistling in the dark.

It is because Christ actually did rise from the dead that we can be confident that for others too death will not be the end. But only if it did happen to Christ can we be confident that it can happen again. As the apostle Paul puts it, 'If Christ has not been raised, your faith is futile and you are still in your sins.'

The historical fact provides the basis for belief.

History and interpretation

So then, we know what God is like and we believe in him because of particular things he has done, particular events in which he has acted and made himself known. What do we need to make sense of this knowledge?

- **We need to know what happened**—a reliable historical record, so that we can know what took place, how and when and where. Central to the Bible, therefore, is its historical narrative of how God acted and revealed himself—supremely in the exodus from Egypt and the covenant at Mount Sinai in the Old Testament, and in the life, death and resurrection of Jesus in the New.
- **We need to know what it all means**—an authoritative interpretation of the events. Otherwise the events can sometimes be ambiguous; they do not always carry their own interpretation with them. Had we been present at the crucifixion of Jesus, we might have seen it as just one more public execution among others—perhaps the sad end of a failed revolutionary or idealist.

The moment Christianity loses touch with the inspiration of the New Testament it tends to sink to a sub-Christian level, and its moral witness is weakened or obscured.

F. R. Barry

Even the disciples at the time completely failed to grasp its significance, despite all Jesus had told them. They only saw Jesus suffer and die, and they mourned. They did not see him bearing the sins of the world. It was only later that the full significance of the cross became clear, that 'in Christ God was reconciling the world to himself'.

What we have in the Bible, therefore, is both historical facts and the theological meaning of those facts. The facts alone can be barren or insignificant. The interpretation alone can be arbitrary or ill-founded. Fact and interpretation together provide a true and coherent understanding of God and his dealings with humanity.

Types of writing

There is also much in the Bible other than history and its interpretation. For example:

- **Prayer:** 'Out of the depths I cry to thee, O Lord! Lord, hear my voice!'
- **Joyful praise:** 'Bless the Lord, O my soul; and all that is within me, bless his holy name!'
- **Practical maxims:** 'Go to the ant, you sluggard; consider its ways and be wise!'; 'A cheerful heart has a continual feast'.
- **Prophetic warnings:** 'Turn back, turn back from your evil ways; for why will you die, O house of Israel?'; 'Seek the Lord while he may be found, call upon him while he is near.'
- **Ethical teaching:** 'You shall love your neighbour as yourself'; 'For freedom Christ has set us free. Stand firm, then, and do not let yourselves be burdened again by a yoke of slavery.'

With most of this material the historical question 'Did it happen?' does not apply. The value of the psalms, for instance, lies in the way they embrace the whole range of human emotion; joy and sorrow, hope and disappointment are all there and are brought into relationship with God. The psalms have been used for 3,000 years, because we can so easily identify with them, make them our own and encounter God through them. So history is not the sole channel by which God makes himself known. He reveals himself and speaks to people in many ways.

The Books of the Bible

The Bible has a status and authority greater than that of any other Christian writing. However valuable and important the writings of great Christians, they can never compete with those books which together form the 'canon' of Scripture. For the term 'canon', from the Greek word for 'rule' or 'measure', indicates those writings which are held to make up the authoritative yardstick for belief and practice.

There is a truth to be preserved, and so a canon is necessary to provide the means for distinguishing truth from error. Once a canon exists, the test of whether later beliefs and practices are truly Christian is whether they conform to the canon. Writings included in the canon of the Bible are thereby given a status different from all subsequent Christian writings.

Why this selection?

How and why did these particular writings qualify for inclusion in the biblical canon, and not others? The answer to this is complex and, particularly with regard to the Old Testament, we do not always know as much as we would like.

Sometimes we simply have to accept on faith that the right selection was made, although certainly the experience of reading some of the books rejected from the New Testament canon (such as *Gospel of Peter, Letter of Barnabas*) serves to heighten our appreciation of the vitality and authority of the books that were accepted. Nonetheless, certain principles of selection can be seen:

- Many biblical books are **connected with key figures**: Moses, David, Solomon and the prophets in the Old Testament; the apostles in the New. Not all the writings thus connected were necessarily written by these people. It is highly unlikely that Solomon wrote Ecclesiastes or that Paul wrote Hebrews (though often associated with Paul, Hebrews is in fact anonymous). But the essential point is that these Bible books are historically welded to the key moments in the history of salvation which these people represent.
- **Jesus and the early Christians regarded the Jewish Scriptures as of unique and permanent value.** It is on their authority that the Old Testament is part of the Christian canon of the Bible.
- Initially the only Bible the early church possessed was the Old Testament. But the later parts of the New Testament already refer to the Gospel material and to Paul's letters as authoritative Scripture.
- What set the Bible books apart from other books, and qualified them for the canon, was that they were **recognized as inspired by God**. When the church included books in the canon, it did not think it was giving them some new authority. Rather, it was formally recognizing the inherent authority they already possessed, and which was already experienced in the faith and practice of the church.

The extent of the canon

There has been disagreement among Christians over precisely which books should be included in the canon. There is no problem over the New Testament. All Christians accept all the books of the New Testament, although in the first few centuries after Christ there was a period of hesitation in some areas before certain books, notably Hebrews, James, 2 Peter, 2 and 3 John, Jude and Revelation, were finally recognized.

In the Old Testament the disagreement has arisen over those books known as Deutero-canonical or the Apocrypha. The Jews defined the canon of the Old Testament as excluding the Apocrypha, and this was the Bible used by Jesus. Yet the version of the Old Testament most commonly used in the early church, the Greek translation known as the Septuagint, included the apocryphal books along with the others.

These apocryphal books were generally treated as being of the same standing as the other Old Testament books, although Jerome, the outstanding biblical scholar of the early centuries, did draw a distinction. The Protestant churches have accepted the

Jewish canon of the Old Testament alone as Scripture; the Roman Catholic Church has accepted the Deutero-canonical books as Scripture also.

The Word from God to Us

The Bible is often called the 'word of God'. It is the way, above all others, that he uses to communicate with us—to get *his* thoughts and purposes into *our* minds. But how did books written by many different writers come to be God's 'word'? And can we be sure that we are properly understanding what God has revealed?

Inspiration

The Bible is distinct and special because it is inspired by God. And although the actual word 'inspired' is used only once in the Bible itself, the idea of inspiration is basic to the whole of it. God took the initiative in giving us the Bible. He took the lead in revealing himself in history, in giving his people a right understanding of his revelation, and in providing that a permanent and reliable record of all this should be made. The authority of the Bible is not simply the authority of eminent people, but of God himself.

This means, for example, that the meaning of Jesus Christ as expounded by Paul and others is more than simply the profound and perceptive insights of these people, though it is that. It is the meaning God wanted to be conveyed. God so worked within the thinking of Paul and other writers that their message is at the same time God's message.

All Scripture is inspired by God and is useful for teaching the truth, rebuking error, correcting faults, and giving instruction for right living, so that the person who serves God may be fully qualified and equipped to do every kind of good deed.

Paul, 2 Timothy 3

This divine initiative and overruling make the Bible a unique book. On the one hand it has all the features of any other human book—and can be studied as such. We can examine the different characteristics and emphases of the various writers, investigate how and when their books were written, and in general study them as we would study other ancient writers.

On the other hand we approach the Bible as no other book—to listen to it, to submit to its teaching, to recognize its authority as coming from God, and to be confident that the Holy Spirit will bring it alive for us. The Spirit inspired its writers and he can interpret it afresh to the enquiring reader today.

The Bible, then, is a book which is both human and divine. In the Bible what is said and done is neither simply human nor simply divine, but both together. This is one of the distinctive marks of the way God reveals himself—there are some parallels with the way he made himself known in Jesus Christ.

Many of the difficulties that are made as people try to use and understand the Bible arise from a failure to hold together its human and divine dimensions. Modern scholarly study has emphasized the human aspect of the Bible and the rich diversity of its human authors and emphases. But in so doing it has often lost sight of the divine element and made the Bible a merely human work.

Defenders of the divine dimension, on the other hand, have often misunderstood its implications. They have used it illegitimately to deny or prejudge the examination of the Bible from a human point of view.

One book, many writers

The Bible is one big book made up of many smaller books. As such, it shows both unity ('one') and diversity ('many'). The unity of the Bible flows from its source in God. If God is ultimately responsible for it all, you would expect it to hold together. But the Bible's unity can be seen on other levels too. One story—of creation, fall and redemption—runs throughout.

The chief actor in it all is God. At every point God is making, and remaking, a people who are uniquely his. And although the struggle between good and evil is intense and continuous, there is never any doubt that the supreme power and final victory belong to God.

It is remarkable how frequently biblical writers refer back to, or take for granted, what has gone before. An example is the way the promise to Abraham—that through his descendants all nations will be blessed—is developed and worked out through the centuries. And it is particularly notable how the closing scenes of the final book, Revelation, hark back to the opening scenes in Genesis chapters 1 to 3.

The recognition of the deep unity of the Bible should not be allowed to flatten out the rich diversity of its different writings. The Bible contains many different voices:

- The quiet trust of the 'shepherd' psalm—and Job's overpowering confrontation with God;
- The clear and confident challenge of Moses on the borders of Canaan—and the preacher's cool-headed questioning in Ecclesiastes;
- Paul's mighty exposition of justification by faith alone in his letter to the Romans—and the down-to-earth appeal for practical discipleship in the letter of James.

To hold all this wealth of material together in our minds is no easy thing. Certainly the task of wrestling with the rich spectrum of Bible teaching will satisfy the most questing of minds. But the heart of the matter lies in recognizing that these books are directed to the basic and everyday situations of people's lives. The diversity within the Bible is as rich as life itself.

A helpful picture of biblical unity is that of an orchestra playing a symphony. The orchestra has different instruments, making different sounds, playing different parts. Yet when playing a symphony together they produce a beautiful harmony. And we appreciate the symphony the more if we are aware of the different parts that make it up.

Without error?

Another commonly-drawn consequence of belief in inspiration is the claim that the Bible is 'inerrant' or 'infallible'. If we believe that God overruled and inspired the record of those events upon which faith depends, then it is right to suppose that such an account should be reliable. Clearly an inspired Bible is a reliable Bible. But does this reliability necessarily extend to every single detail?

It is important to keep a sense of proportion here. Some might think that the discovery of one inaccuracy, however small, in any part of the Bible would cast doubt on everything else in the Bible. But this is clearly not the case. Bible truth is rich and strong; it is not fragile like a gas balloon—one prick and the whole thing crashes to the ground.

Many problems also arise through failing to appreciate the variety of writings in the Bible. Much of the Bible is poetry, proverb, challenge, warning—writings that appeal directly to the imagination, the heart, the conscience. Their impact and the way in which they are true will be very different from that of the historical writings in the Bible. And even the historical writings contain poetic and symbolic elements that are not intended to be a straightforward record of events.

So we must make sure that we are interpreting a passage correctly—treating poetry as poetry and symbol as symbol. Otherwise the error may lie with us! God's truth is conveyed by what the Bible writers set down, in the meaning they originally intended. But our understanding of that meaning is fallible.

If you believe what you like in the Gospel, and reject what you like, it is not the Gospel you believe, but yourself.

Augustine

Interpretation

The Bible is trustworthy, then. In it we find God's truth. So this makes it all the more important to understand it correctly. The history of sectarian movements shows that it is possible to justify almost anything from the Bible.

But there are some general things to say here.

- **The Holy Spirit who inspired the Bible also brings it alive to us as we read.** Christians down the ages have testified how God has spoken to them in the pages of the

Bible. Anyone who seeks to know God or to grow in knowledge of him can confidently read and find all he is looking for. There is much more in the Bible that is clear than that is problematic. And sometimes God speaks even through a passage we have not accurately understood.

- **But believing in the Holy Spirit does not guarantee instant understanding of everything.** The Bible comes from a period of history very different from our own. We need to understand what the writers meant in their own time, and only then can we interpret that meaning for our own time. This involves hard thought and study. And the Spirit does not make such work unnecessary, but rather assures us that it will be richly worthwhile in its results.
- **Interpretation is not simply a matter for the individual.** The individual believer is part of the whole body of Christians, and the task of biblical interpretation is carried out within this community as a whole. There is a heritage of 2,000 years of interpreting the Bible. This provides great resources for understanding, both positively in insight into the text, and negatively in showing approaches that are false and should be avoided. And also there is the ongoing work of scholars who work to understand the text in a more accurate way.

Of course they are not always successful, but more and more knowledge is becoming available through their work. The Holy Spirit uses the church's traditions and the researches of scholars to bring the text alive and speak through it. The individual should expect and seek illumination from these sources as well as from his own private reading of the text. There are many books on the Bible, at all levels of understanding, that we can use to help us in this.

Problems Ancient and Modern

We must now consider a few of the objections, both ancient and modern, that may be brought against this understanding of the Bible.

In one sense, of course, the Bible needs no defence. With any great literary or artistic work it is the reader, and not the work, who is on trial. How much more so with the Bible which has proved itself to millions down the centuries. Yet equally we must give full weight to the real difficulties which do exist, particularly those which have arisen through modern knowledge—historical, scientific and philosophical. To turn our backs on such problems does not make them go away.

Our concern is not with those problems which are raised by unbelief. To the person who has made up his mind, say, that miracles are impossible, there is little to be said. We can only point out that the miracles of Jesus are wholly in keeping with his character and his teaching, so that, if a person comes in any way to acknowledge the claims and authority of Jesus, then the whole matter takes on a different complexion. But our concern is with some of the genuine difficulties that may confront the modern seeker for truth as he reads the Bible.

What is the real problem?

It is not always easy to handle problems in the Bible which are posed by modern knowledge. This is particularly so since difficulties usually reflect the larger problem of how to hold together differing attitudes to authority and knowledge. In modern thought we generally work 'from below' and affirm only those things which can be tested within the framework of ordinary human experience. This differs from an approach which accepts knowledge 'from above'—accepting the validity of revelation from God. It is vital to hold these two approaches together. Christians believe in one God who is sovereign over all life. This means that all truth comes from him. And so ultimately truth revealed and truth discovered will not be in conflict. But in practice to hold these approaches in the right tension is not easy.

One position sometimes adopted is to allow that the Bible is true in its moral and religious teaching but unreliable on matters of history and science. This is dangerous since it is precisely in the real world that God's revelation is given. We can remove any possible conflict with the historian or scientist only by discounting what gives the faith its significance—the belief that God has truly and decisively entered into the realm of space and time.

There is no way we can remove all possible conflict. In practice, however, most of the famous conflicts turn out not to be conflicts at all. It is often (though not always) a defective understanding of what the Bible is saying that causes the problems. That is, the issue tends to be less to do with reliability than with interpretation.

Different kinds of story

Most of the areas of conflict lie in the narrative parts of the Bible—Genesis to Esther in the Old Testament, and the Gospels and Acts in the New. How should we read these? Although interpreted history is the central means of biblical revelation it is not the sole means. There are parts of the Bible where history is not an issue—poetry, wisdom, letters and so on. There are also portions of narrative itself which are not, or are not likely to be, intended as history.

There need be no objection in principle to the presence in the Bible of fable, allegory, moral tale, legend and so on—all of which were widely and meaningfully used in the ancient world. The parables of Jesus are an obvious example of the imaginative telling of a story to convey a point. In our modern world, realistic novel writing and some types of drama and film are in some respects parallel.

A difficulty, of course, is that such writing may superficially appear similar to historical writing—so how are we to tell the difference? The short answer is that there is no rule of thumb and there can be legitimate difference of opinion.

The more sensitive the reader is to a wide variety of literature, both ancient and modern, the more he will be sensitive to different types of writing in the Bible. This is the sort of area where the expertise of the scholar can be of particular value to the ordinary reader. Nor need any uncertainty really be a matter of concern. For the issue is not the value of what is written, but simply the means by which its value is conveyed, whether historical, literary and imaginative, or a blend of both.

An interesting example is the famous story of Jonah. How are we to understand it? Many people have assumed that for the book to be true it must be historical. Yet there are many others who think, for literary reasons, that it is not historical, but rather a story making a point. They are not arguing that it is false, but that its value is to be assessed on grounds other than the historical. It would be false only if it were misleading in the picture it gives of what prophecy is, what God is like, and the attitude of God to non-Jews. And nobody suggests this.

Or consider the early chapters of Genesis, which have given rise to much 'science versus religion' conflict. If you read them carefully, you will soon notice that this narrative is quite different from a straightforward historical account, such as the fall of Jerusalem. It is clear too that the writer is simply not interested in the sort of issues that bother modern historians or scientists. This makes it difficult to pinpoint where there is genuine conflict, if at all.

There need be little doubt that the majority of biblical narratives are intended to be historical. Yet, even so, very few are bare historical reporting. Most make use of literary techniques to interest and involve the reader. The history is simplified and interpreted, so that the reader can grasp and remember it more easily. The stories are told in such a way that we can identify with the bold faith of David, feel the depression of Elijah and experience the awful challenge of obedience and trust that confronted Abraham. The stories are historical but they are more than that. They present not only information but also challenge; they are not just a record of facts but an imaginative and evocative portrayal of them.

The writing of the Gospels

In the Gospels people have seen difficulties because the actions of Jesus are presented in different order by different evangelists, and his teachings are sometimes differently worded. But this is because the Gospel writers select and interpret the words and deeds of Jesus to bring out different themes, different emphases, different shades of meaning.

Luke, for example, places the rejection of Jesus at Nazareth at the beginning of the account of his ministry. But Matthew and Mark put this story later. And even in Luke's account Jesus mentions events in Capernaum which must mean that the Nazareth episode is taking place after his ministry has been going on for some time. Luke places the Nazareth episode out of historical sequence because it so well displays the themes that run right through his Gospel and Acts—the fulfilment of the Old Testament; the good news proclaimed to the Jews, rejected by them and offered to the Gentiles.

Or again, Matthew has Jesus saying that God gives 'good things' in answer to prayer, but Luke, in his version, has 'the Holy Spirit'. Is there a real difference? Or does Luke simply mean that the Holy Spirit is the best of the 'good things'? Many difficulties disappear once we appreciate the blend of history and interpretation that the Gospels present. Believing in inspiration does not tell us what literary form inspiration has used, nor remove difficulties of understanding. That can only be done by careful study. Inspiration does mean that such study will not lessen but rather enhance what we can learn from the Bible.

The Bible House bookshop saw incredible scenes... On the day it appeared, word spread like wildfire. A queue rapidly formed, the shop was crammed, and the New Testament sold at a breathtaking rate—one every ten seconds!

Account of the publication of a Polish modern-language translation of the New Testament, 1979

Moral problems

An ancient objection, often raised, concerns the morality—or rather immorality!—of some parts of the Bible, usually certain Old Testament stories. Are they not vicious and ethically primitive? Things to bear in mind when looking at this question are as follows:

- The Old Testament is remarkably frank and honest. It **portrays life as it is**, and shows the failings even of men of God. The great king David commits adultery and murder. Samson, the deliverer of Israel, is a womanizing opportunist. The Bible faithfully describes all these things but it does not thereby condone them.
- Many of the things in the Old Testament that are found objectionable when related to God—earthquakes, famines and so on—are **also present in the world around us**. If these were removed from the Bible, it would not help our faith. They would still confront us in life. We are more likely to come to some understanding, however partial, in this difficult area, if we try to come to grips with the Bible's teaching about it.
- We always do well to pay particular attention to **those passages which do not fit in with our preconceived ideas**. Otherwise we can all too easily use the Bible to confirm our prejudices, rather than to correct and enlarge our understanding. Often it will be precisely the problem passage that will teach the most.
- **The attitude of Jesus to the Old Testament** must be decisive for the Christian. It is clear that Jesus accepted it as a true and faithful revelation of God. The idea that the Old Testament shows a harsh God, different from the loving God of the New Testament, is denied by Jesus.

> We cannot reject his attitude here without undermining his whole moral and spiritual authority.

In fact all the New Testament writers presuppose the validity of the moral and spiritual teaching of the Old. When the apostle John says that God is love, it is the God known from the Old Testament he is talking about. One of the major difficulties many modern readers of the New Testament have is that they are unfamiliar with the Old. The more we see how the New Testament builds on the foundation of the Old, the better we will understand what the Bible is saying.

Fact and challenge

There will always be problems in understanding and applying the Bible. But it is a mistake to think that every problem must be resolved before we can believe the Bible and accept its authority. That would be to deny the reality of God's revelation—a revelation which gives good reasons for faith, but also calls for personal commitment and trust.

The Bible presents both fact and challenge, and confidence about the facts will grow as we respond to the challenges. The truth of the Bible does not depend on our response to it. Good, objective reasons can be given why we should accept it. But it is only as we do in fact respond in trust and commitment to Jesus Christ, and put the Bible to work in everyday life, that we will finally be convinced that here is the true and trustworthy revelation of God—his word to us.

For further thinking

QUESTION 1

There is great diversity in the books of the Bible; they are very different from each other. Yet many people also see an essential unity in the Bible. Do you agree? If so, what are the themes of this unity?

QUESTION 2

It is important to interpret each part of the Bible in a way that fits the type of literature it represents. How would you apply this principle to the book of Job? And how to the first three chapters of Genesis?

QUESTION 3

The Bible was written many centuries ago for people whose culture was very different from our own. Is it possible to apply its teaching to our own lives? If you think it is possible, take one short passage from the Old Testament and one from the New, and work out how their teaching applies to your own situation. How do you read across from their culture to yours?

BIBLE REFERENCES

God's Revelation

Genesis 1:3, 6, 9; 12:1–4; Exodus 3:1–15; Deuteronomy 29:29; 1 Samuel 3:1, 21; Isaiah 22:14; 40:5; 53:1; 56:1; Jeremiah 1:6–8; Daniel 2:19–30; 10:1; Luke 10:21–22; John 12:38; 16:12–15, 25; Romans 1:17–18; 1 Corinthians 2:10; 14:6; Galatians 1:12, 15–16; Hebrews 1:1–3; 1 Peter 1:10–12; Revelation 1:1

■

As the years have passed—and it is now 25 years since I began translating—my conviction has grown that the New Testament is in a quite special sense inspired. It is not magical, nor is it thoughtless: human beings wrote it. But by something which I would not hesitate to describe as a miracle, there is a concentration upon that area of inner truth which is fundamental and ageless.

J. B. Phillips

CHAPTER 13

STEPHEN NEILL

God In Other Religions

There have been many attempts to define religion, none of them entirely satisfactory. Perhaps it is easier to say what religion is not rather than what it is. A useful definition is this: religion is the refusal to believe that the universe can be adequately explained in purely three-dimensional terms. The three dimensions may be taken as the three conditions of our life—space, time and matter; or as the field of the physical sciences which deal with those things that can be counted, measured and weighed. A purely material view of things would naturally exclude the possibility of religion.

Perhaps there are no complete materialists. If there are, they would have to do without many things which are part of ordinary human experience. They would not know what to do with beauty, perhaps regarding it as merely unimportant or insignificant. They would recognize physical passion simply as desire, and would find it hard to understand the value set on persons as persons, which leads to that which alone can be called love in the true sense of the term.

Something beyond

Nearly every human being has some awareness of an aspect of the universe which does not fit into the material categories. For this fourth dimension, the German scholar Rudolf Otto coined the convenient term 'the numinous'. This comes to us, he said, under the dual guise of the terrible and the attractive, awakening the emotions respectively of awe and of delight.

Most of us know what these words mean, and have had what are sometimes called 'peak-experiences'. These experiences are not necessarily religious. To be awed by the magnificence of the Victoria Falls in Africa, or to be delighted by Beethoven's fifth symphony, does not necessarily make a human being religious. But this is the area of human experience in which religion can be born.

When human beings become aware that there is 'something other', a reality hidden within the reality that they know, when they seek after it, try to understand it, give it a name, and enter into some kind of a relationship with it, they are experiencing, though perhaps only in crude ways, the reality of religion.

Christians firmly believe that this other exists. They seek to understand who or what it is, to find the name by which this nameless Other can be called. They want to enter into fellowship and to place themselves at the service of the Other.

What Christians believe is very different from what is believed by the adherents of other religions. But this element of search in the hope of finding is something they have in common with all others who in any way at all share in the same search, and are sincere in their desire and willingness to learn. It is this common element that makes it possible to speak of Christianity among the religions of the world.

The Primal Races

A hundred years ago evolution was much in the air. Everything was thought to be the result of long development. So it was taken that religion also must have developed; and as monotheism—belief in one God only—is the highest form of religion, this must have come very late in the history of humankind. Among the simpler races it was not expected we should find belief in one God; in fact, it was doubted whether there would be found any clear idea of God at all.

This idea was not altogether unreasonable. When a stranger tries to study the religion of an unfamiliar people, he or she becomes aware first of actions and ceremonies, some of which may seem very strange. In quite a number of cases the people themselves cannot give a reason for what they do; that is the way the ancestors said things were to be done, and so they do them. Then the visitor will be told stories, myths. Out of these it may be possible to construct a picture of the way these people think and of what they believe. Next the outsider may be introduced to the world of ancestors and spirits. But there in most cases it stops. These simple people are quite clever enough to keep their secrets and not to tell more than they wish to tell.

The secret God

So it came about that the great Robert Moffat, who lived for forty-nine years among the Tswana people in South Africa, and translated the whole of the Bible into the Tswana language, believed that the Tswana had no word for God, and no idea that only one God exists. He was mistaken.

A scholar named Pater W. Schmidt, of Vienna, set to work to study the simplest people he could find, such as the aboriginal Ainus in Japan and the pygmies of the rain forests in Africa. He wrote twelve big volumes on the *Origin of the Idea of God* (1926 onwards). He found that, in almost every case, the very simplest peoples had a surprisingly clear idea of the one great God. At first scholars were sceptical; but now it is generally agreed that, though many details need further study, the results of Schmidt's work, backed up by that of many others, can be accepted as correct.

What do they know of God?

We are dealing with hundreds of peoples, and millions of human beings. Naturally, among them there are many and great differences. But the following points hold true for a large number of peoples:

- The God they know is **the one who made all things**. Not many of these peoples are like the Hebrews in thinking that God just spoke and it was. They believe that there was something in existence, and that God shaped it and so it took on the form of things as they now are.
- He is **the guardian of the rules and customs** of the tribe or clan. The big eye, the sun, and the small eyes, the stars, are always watching; children are told that, if they do anything wrong, they will not be able to hide it.
- They think that **he gives the rain**. The rain comes down from the sky; that must be because he lives beyond the sky and sends down the rain from where he lives.
- Among many people the idea exists that once **long ago God was very near** to humanity, so close that human beings could reach up and touch the sky. But then someone (in most stories, as in Genesis, a woman) did something by which God was gravely offended; so God went far away; the sky is far beyond our reach, and God is someone whom we cannot see.

Many questions remain unanswered. My ancestors are not your ancestors. Is my God also your God? The Kikuyu in Kenya believe in a great God, whom they call Ngai, and who lives on the top of Mount Kenya. But is he also the God of all the other people living round about? We find the same question being asked in the Old Testament. At one time the Israelites thought that their God, Yahweh, could be worshipped only in the land he had given them. If they were driven out of that land, they would not be able to worship him. Only very gradually did they come to understand that he is the God of the whole earth and of all the people that dwell in it.

Do these simple people worship the great God? Often the answer seems to be no. If they are asked why, the answer may be that little people like us cannot approach a great God like that; so we approach him through the ancestors and spirits, who are nearer to us than he is, and also nearer to him than we are. But among some peoples the great God is worshipped in reverence and fear. A European who accompanied a priest of the Akan people in Ghana, as he climbed a hill for some special ceremony of worship, had a profound feeling of the presence and the reality of God.

Is what they know of God enough?

When we talk to these people of the simpler races about God, they understand who it is of whom we are speaking. If, after they have become Christians, they are asked about their experiences, they are likely to say, 'We knew that God existed and that he was strong; but we did not know . . .' and then will follow a list of the things that they came to know only through Christian teaching—that he is our Father, that he loves us, that he sent his Son to die for us, that he loves the other peoples in the world as much as he loves us.

The heathen in his hunger
Bows down to wood and stone

said the Ghanaian Christian Kwegyir Aggrey.

The apostle Paul said to religious people in Athens, 'What you worship as something unknown I am going to proclaim to you.' This is still the task of the church today.

Judaism

Three great faiths had their origin in the Middle East: Judaism, Christianity and Islam. They are rigidly monotheistic, in that they declare that God is one, that there can be no other object of worship, and that there can be no other basis for the unity of all mankind.

The Jews declare every day, 'Hear, O Israel; the Lord our God is one Lord.'

The Old Testament is not like any other ancient book. About a thousand years were needed for the writing of it, and many hands took part. And so naturally it is a book of marvellous variety. Yet equally marvellous is its unity; it is a book about God, and about his love story with the human race. The picture of God does not come out equally clearly in all parts of the book, but the main lines of it are everywhere present. What kind of a God is this?

- He is **Creator**. This means that nothing whatever can exist apart from his will, and that nothing can escape from his control, although he has given human beings a limited freedom to choose and to act within his over-arching sovereignty.
- He is a **living** God—a rather strange expression. All the life that there is in the universe comes from him: 'In all life thou livest, the true life of all.' He is always active in the world that he has made. This means that he is concerned for his people, and can show himself to them. So the prophets say confidently, 'Thus saith the Lord', being sure that what they say does not come simply from their own imaginations. It has come through living contact with the Spirit of the Lord, who has taken hold of them and compelled them to speak.
- He is a **faithful** God. He has made a reliable universe and he acts reliably in it. If he makes a covenant, he can be relied on to keep it. His people can trust him, because he is trustworthy. This they discover as they try to serve him.
- But he is a **righteous** God, in the sense that he wants his people to be like him. He is not primarily concerned about rituals and forms of worship, though these have their importance. What he is concerned about is plain straightforward integrity in the street and the market-place and the lawcourts. Religion and morality cannot be separated. They belong together, since God is the Lord of all.

- He is a **compassionate** God. Israel knew well that they had not lived up to what God expected of them. Yet through one disaster after another the nation had survived. It was through the wonder of national survival that Israel came to understand the wonder of God's mercy and forgiveness: 'With you there is forgiveness; therefore you are feared.'

God of our fathers

Since they knew that God had drawn near to them, the people of Israel became convinced that this God is not only one who speaks; he is also one who listens: 'Because you answer prayers, people everywhere will come to you.' When we want to learn to pray, we may turn to the book of Psalms, in which almost everything that we could want to say to God is expressed so much better than we could express it ourselves. For a Christian to read through the Jewish book of prayers is a moving experience.

During this century the Jews have been called to endure unimaginable sufferings. And yet they survive. Their faithfulness to the God of their fathers should be an example to the whole world. They believe they have been called to be a 'light to the nations' and that they can fulfil this function best by quiet fidelity to the One who has shown through all the centuries that he can be trusted.

Islam

Islam, like Buddhism and Christianity, has an identifiable historical founder, about whom we know a great deal. Muhammad was born about the year AD 570 in the flourishing commercial city of Mecca. At the age of forty he began his prophetic ministry. In AD 622 he moved to Medina (Yathrib), where he died in AD 632.

The records show him as a man of infinite patience, who preached in Mecca for thirteen years and hardly made a convert. In his later years he showed himself a great leader of men. He gave to the warring Arab tribes unity, a simple creed (the Muslim creed consists only of the two clauses 'I proclaim that there is no God but God, and Muhammad is the apostle of God'), and a sense of destiny. For a thousand years the Christian world was threatened by their armies. Today the followers of Muhammad exercise great influence in the affairs of the world.

But Muhammad never claimed to be the founder of a religion, nor would any of his followers make this claim for him. He affirmed that what he did was to bring back again the ancient faith of Abraham and the older prophets. Other nations had had their prophets. Now God had given to the Arabs the last and greatest of the prophets, to whom he had revealed the fullness of his will in the Qur'an. Muhammad never claimed to have written the Qur'an or any part of it. He received it direct from God (or as some traditions say, through the mediation of the archangel Gabriel).

The Qur'an has existed from all eternity with God in the Arabic language; it is in every particular the utterance of God himself; there is no human element in it at all, Thus Muslims claim for the Qur'an something that Christians have never claimed for the Bible. Even the most conservative admit some human element in the Bible. If that is so, says the Muslim, how can the Bible be the word of God?

The miracle of the Bible is that it has been translated into 1,500 languages, and brings the same message in all. The miracle of the Qur'an is that the Arabic language is so much a part of the revelation that this holy book cannot be translated. It has in fact been translated into many languages, but almost all of these translations have been made by Christians.

No partners

For the Muslim, the Qur'an is the very voice of God himself. We have only to listen, and we shall know exactly who and what God is. We find him to be a very stern and alarming God. Mecca was a city much given to idolatry. Muhammad hated idols, so much of his preaching was controversial: hence the immense emphasis placed on the unity of God, his transcendence, his exaltation far above the world and everything that human beings can understand.

This unity is absolute. The worst of sins, according to the Muslim, is the sin of *Shirk*, saying that God has a partner—not only in the sense in which Christians say this, when they claim that Jesus is the Son of God, but in suggesting that God could in any way relate himself to anything outside himself.

It is said that there are ninety-nine beautiful names of God in the Qur'an, but 'God is love' is not among them. It could not be, since love always implies relatedness, and God is too highly exalted to enter into any kind of relationship. He makes no revelation of himself to humanity; he reveals only his will. Even in paradise people will not know God as he is.

Muslims' favourite description of God is as the compassionate, the merciful. But this mercy is limited to believers. Nothing awaits the unbeliever except to be cast into hell at the day of judgment. In the Qur'an there are fifty per cent more references to hell than to paradise. Unbelief is a grave sin, so the Muslim is entitled to wage holy war against the obstinate unbeliever who will not listen.

God's will is inscrutable; everything is determined by it. But the 'Muslim'—the word means, 'surrendered'—has the proud consciousness of knowing the will of God in the Qur'an and of carrying it out in every detail of life.

Muslims live night and day in an intense awareness of God, from whose gaze they cannot for a moment escape. The name of God is constantly on the lips of the Muslim—*Bismillah*, in the name of God; *Inshallah*, if God wills. Much of this no doubt is conventional; but it does represent also a deep awareness, from which Christians would do well to learn.

Hinduism

Hinduism is a shoreless sea. It has a continuous history of more than 3,000 years. During that time it has gathered into itself so many streams and currents of belief and practice that it is very hard to say just what it is. Hindus say this is a good thing, because it makes Hinduism the most tolerant religion in the world.

Professor Radhakrishnan has distinguished four different levels of religious experience. His analysis takes us to the heart of the Hindu outlook:

- There are **idolaters**—those who cannot worship without some visible form of the divine to help them. We may regret this; we may help them to rise to a higher level of religious consciousness; but we must not blame them. Let them use whatever means of approaching God are most suitable to them.
- Next on the scale are **the religions of incarnation**, among which of course Christianity is to be numbered. Here the worshipper has a mental picture of the one whom he worships, whether it be Christ, or Krishna, or some other. This is a step forward, but it means that the worshipper is still to some extent making God in his own image.
- Then we find those who know that **God cannot be in any way represented**. But they still have an idea of God as one who is personal, one to whom they can talk and who will hear them when they pray. This means that they believe in a limited God.
- Finally we come to the higher wisdom of classical Hinduism. To think of God as person is to set limits to him. But **the true God is the unlimited**, the one who never changes, the one who is always there.

About him we can say nothing positive, because no human words can express what he really is.

The unseen is real

All these forms of approach to God are found in Hinduism. Village Hinduism is a matter of shrines, images and sacrifices. In the great temples hymns are sung to the great gods, to whom the *bhakti*, the loving adoring worship, of the believer is directed. The thinker needs no temple; he lets his thoughts go out to God in devout meditation. The seer tries to realize the great truth *tat tvam asi*—that art thou—the soul in you is identical with Brahman, the great Reality, the One; separate existence is illusion. When a believer is set totally free from illusion, he returns to identity with Brahman. This is deliverance, the highest goal for man..

Hinduism has a profound sense that the great realities are not the visible things; it is the unseen which is real. At best this gives a deeply spiritual view of the world and of human life in it. And Hinduism is basically an optimistic religion. All human beings have the capacity to seek after God. All are on their way towards him. The way may be very long and arduous; it may lead through many successive births into this world. But in the end the way will lead all people to the goal; in the end the soul will be reunited with that one supreme Reality, from which it ought never to have been separated.

Buddhism

Can there be an atheistic religion? If so, is Buddhism that religion?

Unlike Hinduism, which can point to no one founder, and of which the origins are hidden in mystery, Buddhism sprang into being in an identifiable period of history (the sixth century BC), and owes its beginnings to a founder about whom we know a good deal.

The figure of Gautama the Buddha, or 'awakened one', is much encrusted with legend. But we can discern a real person—gentle, compassionate, courteous. At the age of about forty he made a great discovery. He felt a compulsion to pass on his discovery to others, spent the next forty years preaching, and left behind a community which has carried on his work to the present day.

A religion without God?

It is clear that there is nothing in all this about God. Of course the Buddha knew about the gods of Hinduism. But it did not seem to him that they had any power to bring deliverance to mankind. It is not so much that Buddha denied the existence of God as that he simply was not interested—rightly, if his understanding of the meaning of the word 'God' is correct.

In only one passage of the classics does the Buddha seem to hint at the existence of a reality not subject, like all else, to the curse of illusion: 'There is, monks, an unborn, not become, not made, uncompounded, no escape could be shown here for what is born, has become, is made, compounded.' But this other reality is not defined, and there is hardly anything here that corresponds to the idea of God.

What does it all lead to? What is the ultimate, that beyond which there is nothing else? In Christian faith, the clear answer is God—that is what the word God means. If you have reached God, it is impossible to go beyond him. What is the ultimate in Buddhism, that beyond which there is nothing else? The answer is equally clear—it is *Nirvana*.

When Christians, in discussion with Buddhists, talk about God, the result is likely to be complete frustration—the two sides are not on the same wavelength. They should talk about the ultimate.

What then is this Buddhist ultimate, *Nirvana*? The Buddhist will answer that it is so different from everything else that you cannot really talk about it. It is like the flame of a candle after it has been blown out. Clearly it means the end of separate existence, of consciousness, of all those things with which we are familiar in our daily life.

But can this end also be a beginning?

ANDREW KIRK

Christianity and Marxism

Marxism is a set of beliefs, first elaborated by Karl Marx (1818-83), about how modern societies work and how basic oppressions can be eliminated from them. They are sometimes known as 'scientific socialism'. Marx' closest colleague, Friedrich Engels (1820–95), once said that Marxism was derived from a mixture of German philosophy, English economic theory and French socialist politics.

Marx accepted the view of history taught by Georg Hegel (1770–1831), according to which conflicting forces are progressively drawn together until higher values emerge. But he claimed to turn the philosopher's thought upside-down. Marx sought to show that conflict between social groups was due not so much to contradictory ideas as to ways of organizing production.

Under the capitalist mode of production, humanity had reached a peak of personal and social alienation. Capitalism meant that some members of society (the capitalist, wealth-owner or bourgeois class) extracted a profit (technically called 'surplus value') from other members (the workers or proletariat). These latter suffered a double assault on their human dignity: they did not own the fruit of their labour, and they were bought and used by the capitalist like any other commodity.

If working people were to rediscover their true humanity, they must become managers of a production process planned in the interests of all, not objects manipulated by a few. There was only one way this could happen—capitalism must be destroyed. The system could not be patched up. A socialist system, in which the producers of wealth also became the owners, must arise in its place.

Marx believed capitalism was inevitably doomed. Increasing concentration of wealth in the hands of a few would create intolerable social tensions. A revolutionary movement was bound to arise, in favour of a just and equal society. Marx did not predict when this would happen, nor in detail what kind of society would emerge.

During this century some nations have undoubtedly seen material improvement as a result of Marxist revolutions, most notably China. But most Marxist states have evolved into rigid self-perpetuating bureaucracies. This has been more the result of Lenin's (1870–1924) doctrine of the Communist party than Marx' own teachings. Marx himself advocated a democracy, with power exercised at a local level.

'Opium of the people'

Marxism has always been an uncompromising opponent of Christianity. It has accused the church of preaching a message of individual salvation and of a hope after death which, like opium, deadens the pain of oppression but does not cure it. Its traditional atheism is due to several factors:

- It rejects a God who seems to condone exploitation.
- Its rather crude view of nature and evolution excludes God.
- It holds that belief in God obstructs people from shaping their own lives and determining their own destinies.

Certainly Christianity holds no brief for capitalism. But the problem with Marxism is that it is not radical enough. Its basic weakness is its inadequate understanding of human nature. Marx believed that exploitation is primarily the result of the way production is organized. But he ignored the more fundamental cause—our sinfulness, and hence innate self-centredness and aggressive drive for power. He said that, by changing the economic system, the basic antagonism between classes could be done away with. But this meant closing his eyes to people's natural selfishness.

The privilege, the corruption, the loss of motivation which continue to exist in Communist societies are strong evidence for the Christian view of human nature.

A truly free and fair society can dawn only when everyone is liberated from self-seeking. This can happen not through economic and political change—however drastic—nor by moral exhortation, but when men and women voluntarily respond to the gospel of new life in Jesus Christ. And it will only be complete with the coming again of Jesus to 'make all things new'.

From the earthly point of view, this is complete emptiness. But can this emptiness be a way to fullness? Those who have reached what in Zen Buddhism is called the state *sumori* timelessness and the cessation of all thought—will say that this is exactly what it is, bliss with which no other bliss can possibly be compared.

An end to self

This is not an unfamiliar idea to Christians. To draw near to God is to experience a steady process of being emptied. Not that the self is being destroyed, but all those phrases which begin with self—self-pleasing, self-will, self-assertion, self-satisfaction—simply have to go. When they have all gone, what is left? Complete emptiness. But into that emptiness can enter the fullness of God, that fullness which was wholly found in Jesus Christ.

The term which more than any other seems to express the nature of Buddhism is tranquillity. For the Christian, the three great virtues are faith, hope and love. Buddhism does not use these terms, but perhaps they can be translated in a way that Buddhists would understand:

Faith for them means the sure confidence that in the *dharma*, the teaching, they have reached true understanding, and are on the way to deliverance.

Hope is the serene expectation that sometime—it might be today, it might be in some infinitely distant future—they will attain to the state called *Nirvana*.

One great Buddhist virtue is *metta*. This is calm, passionless benevolence, extended in every direction to creatures of every kind.

Christians and Buddhists do not use the same language; but perhaps they should be able to understand one another better than they generally do.

Light of the World

We study other religions not to find fault, but to consider what is admirable in what others have found and to enlarge our own experience. Each of the religions we have covered has a particular genius, something central it has to offer.

- **The primal religions** have a deep sense of the unity of all life. The African has never made the division between the sacred and the secular which those living in the West have made. There is no special sphere of religion. As one African writer has put it, 'The Christian is religious from time to time; the African when he lives in his traditional religion is religious all the time.'
- **Judaism** has a deep continuity of faith and life. Jews have great faithfulness to their calling. There is a danger in this conservatism. It may result in failure to be open to new truth. But to have a firm grounding in the past is the best way to have confidence in the present, and adventurous expectation in relation to the future.
- **Islam** is the faith of surrender. True Muslims are distinguished by an integral sense of the reality and presence of God. This gives a wholeness and unity to their lives.
- **Hindu** spirituality is notable for its inwardness. Hindus have learned to pass from the seen to the unseen, to realize the hidden mystery that is always there.
- **Buddhism** reminds us that seeking deliverance is a very serious business. It demands discipline in meditation, in study, in the ordering of life according to the set principles of the religion. There is no casualness in their approach to matters of religion.

So we may find that all those whom we have studied have seen something important about God. Does this mean there can be revelation of God elsewhere than in Christ and the Bible? Perhaps the clearest way to answer that question is to turn to some words of Jesus: 'God is light and in him is no darkness at all. I am the light of the world.'

When a person recognizes something true about God, it means he is catching a glimpse of Christ, in whose life and teaching the character of God was revealed in full clarity. The difference between Christianity and the other religions is not basically between truth and error, but between total and partial understanding.

For further thinking

QUESTION

In your view, is the God in whom followers of Eastern religions believe the same God that Christians believe in?

Creation: Humanity and the World

PART

CHAPTER 14

JAMES HOUSTON

In the Beginning, God

'In the beginning, God created the heavens and the earth.' These are the opening words of the Bible. To believe that God is the creator of the universe is to see everything very differently from those without such faith. Belief in God's creation brings with it a way of looking at reality that centres on relationship; that sees life in the light of human dependence on God.

There are three distinct levels of study of the created order: the 'facts' of scientific observation; the philosopher's problems about the nature of things and their ultimate origin; and theological understanding of God's revelation. All of these refer to the real world, our world, so it is crucially important not to confuse them, but to understand that they are separate and complementary.

A very popular approach to the world gives the main attention to Nature, with a capital 'N'. This puts the stress on things in themselves, without reference to God. This takes people on a very different path from that of God and relationships. People often confuse God with Nature or leave God out altogether. Nature sees life impersonally, self-sufficiently. Nature is also amoral. In contrast, that God is Creator means that he is personally aware of this world, that reality has a moral as well as a physical dimension, that there are relationships which reach further than materialistic or evolutionary approaches can attain.

Belief about creation forms a necessary and central part of any pattern of Christian belief. And so the way theologians treat this doctrine will reflect their view of other key beliefs. This means that we need to beware of any particular interpretation that distorts the character of God. Creation cannot be treated as an isolated doctrine, any more than a sphere can be sliced into segments without creating distortion.

The Creation of the Universe

We begin by looking at creation from the differing perspectives of the biblical narrative and some other ancient stories. This will help to show the distinctiveness and power of the Bible's account of creation.

Creation in the ancient Near East

The recitation of creation stories in the ancient world bore little resemblance to our detached discussions on creation today. To these ancient peoples it was a matter of worship. Their sagas were not like the telling of fairy tales, but recitations of the annual religious festivals. Recounting these stories had the serious purpose of seeking both to preserve the order of society and to guarantee order and life before the threats of chaotic forces.

Their interest in creation stories was not then the intellectual interest of how-it-all-began, but the desperate desire to continue to triumph over the hostile gods and fates that constantly threatened them with death. Through ritual drama, the primordial events recorded in the myth were brought back into action. These people believed that, when they enacted the creative deeds of the gods at the appropriate season and recited the proper formulae, the renewal and revitalization of nature was assured. These creation myths served to reactivate in a magic way the first acts of creation.

These ancient stories range in time from the myths of the Sumerians, in the fourth millennium BC, to the Canaanite texts found at Ras Shamra, written in about 1400 BC. They concern such subjects as the origin of the gods; the defeat of hostile forces of chaos by heroic gods who then release the forces of life; the upholding of order by kingly figures

TITE TIENOU

Angels and Demons

In recent years there has been a widely-reported resurgence of occultism in the West. This has coincided with a strong movement, in other parts of the world, to return to traditional religious practices. Far more people are now aware of the reality of the spirit world than a generation or two ago. And when we look at the Bible, we find that God has created a universe of which non-material beings form a very real part.

We are not so autonomous as we once supposed. People's experience, in many parts of the world today, goes along with Jesus' teaching to suggest that personal outside forces (angels, demons, spirits) can and do influence the behaviour of human beings.

The spirit world in the Bible

The Bible makes a clear distinction between God and the created universe. The creation of the heavens and the earth refers not only to the material side of the universe but to the spiritual side as well. The thrust of biblical teaching is that the spirit world (the unseen) belongs to the created order. Human beings, of course, are part of both the material and the spiritual creation. This means that, just as we have the capacity for relationship with God, the uncreated Spirit, so we are open to influence by other purely spiritual beings.

This is not to suggest that God created both good and evil spiritual beings. Demonic beings must have taken to evil after their creation. But a proper understanding of the spirit world in the Bible requires that angels and demons be classified as part of creation. Spirits are therefore part of the same realm of experience as human beings. This would explain why, for Jews, for the early Christians and for many peoples of the world today, the activities of spirits in everyday life seem normal and expected.

Angels

God accomplishes his purposes in this world by several means. One of them is through his special messengers, angels. They are spirits at the service of God. Angels proclaim God's will and plan to human beings; they help those in difficulty. In spite of their special role, they are not to be worshipped or given any of the honour due to God alone. They are God's servants for our good and our salvation.

Demons

The existence of demons is linked with that of Satan. Like Satan, demons were once numbered among the good angelic beings. But, as we learn in Jude 6, they 'did not stay within the limits of their proper authority'. The presence of evil in God's good creation will, of course, always be a scandal. Demons are Satan's angels in the world; they accomplish his purpose of working against God's purposes.

The belief in the activities of personal spiritual beings disturbs many in the world today. Some see the New Testament accounts of demon possession entirely as instances of mental illness. But many (if not most) others readily believe in the activities of spirits. Demon possession is quite understandable for them. The mistake this group sometimes makes is to ignore mental illness altogether. To be 'possessed' by a spirit from 'outside' is quite different from nervous or mental disorder.

The New Testament presents us with various accounts of casting out demons in the ministry both of Jesus and of the apostles. They are not to be dismissed lightly. Demon possession is just as real as psychological disorder, and it troubles many today. As the apostle Paul wrote, 'We are not fighting against human beings but against the wicked spiritual forces in the heavenly world, the rulers, authorities and cosmic powers of this dark age.' These 'cosmic powers' do not only attack individual lives; they also infect the structures of nations.

By his death and resurrection, Jesus conquered the power of death and Satan. By his name the apostles healed the sick and cast out demons, for there is no name above that of Jesus. Christians wage an important spiritual war, in which they are called to put into effect the victory Jesus Christ has already won. As they demonstrate his power over evil spirits, they will weaken Satan's rule and strengthen God's kingdom.

in a world ever on the verge of chaos; the emergence of the world as it is from a primordial state in which earth and sky were unseparated.

The Genesis account

There are certain points of resemblance between these ancient near-eastern stories and the Bible's account of creation in the first chapter of Genesis. How far do these stories go back to a common faith—the events of which Genesis tells? It is impossible to know.

The differences, however, far outweigh the resemblances. The primary motive for the creation stories of the ancient pagan world was human preservation in the midst of chaos and uncertainty. Human anxiety was an important ingredient; the basis of these creation stories was how to survive in a threatening world.

■
It is by faith that we understand that the universe was created by God's word.

Letter to the Hebrews

The biblical purpose and narrative of creation is very different. There can be no question of the origin of the gods, for the first words are: 'In the beginning, God.' He has no antecedents, no origin. The power of the word in pagan thought was inherent; it goes forth in its own power. The power of the word in the Bible is according to its source, so that when 'God speaks, it is done'. When God speaks it is not some kind of physical emanation, but the spiritual expression of God's will. Creation then is related to the conscious, moral, personal reality of God himself.

The creation narrative opens with a description of how things were 'in the beginning', when the earth was 'without form' and 'void'. Here, unlike the myths of the ancient world, chaos has no divine power, nor does it represent any threat, even when 'darkness was upon the face of the deep'. For the 'Spirit of God' broods over it all, as the moral governor of the universe, in omnipresence and creative power over all 'the waters'.

This prelude sets the theme for the following two sets of 'creation days', three in each:

God 'forms' in the midst of a world 'without form'

Day 1 Division of light from darkness (verse 4)

Day 2 Division of lower waters from upper waters (verse 7)

Day 3 Division of lower waters from dry land (verse 9); creation of vegetation (verse 11)

God 'fills' in the midst of emptiness (void)

Day 4 Creation of light in the sky (verse 16)

Day 5 Creation of water animals and birds (verse 4)

Day 6 Creation of land animals, man and woman, and the provision of food (verse 29)

The six days of creation focus on the sabbath day, the day by which all the work of creation is over. God reveals the purpose of the sabbath, the day of rest, as a day of celebration and worship of a good God who has made all things 'good'. Unlike the Babylonians who saw the seventh, fourteenth, twenty-first and twenty-eighth days of the month as days of ill omen, when mankind lived in uncertainty of the fates, the Hebrews rejoiced in the sabbath as evidence of the sovereign power and goodness of God. The 'days' of creation begin with the sunset rather than the sunrise, perhaps to indicate that every day begins with God and not by the natural agency of the sun. The practice of Israel was to start the sabbath as a holy day with the sunset of the previous day.

There is no reference to any cause other than God's word. Several points follow this fact:

- **The unargued cause is God.** No proof is given of the Creator. He lives outside all explanation. Indeed, God is not an explanation, as philosophers would like to make him. Rather he is a reality to be confronted and his creation is a fact not a consequence. He will not be bound by human explanations. Likewise in the Bible, creation is assumed and not explained. The Hebrew word for 'to create', which is used of both creation and redemption, is uniquely God's activity.

- The story introduces an indefinable era: **the absolute beginning of all things**. Since space and time are both God's creation, the event includes the creation of time also.
- The Genesis account **does not say whether anything existed before creation**. The prelude tells us how God formed and filled the formlessness and void that came into being in his first act of creation. But it is not revealed what, if anything, he used to create the universe. To safeguard the reality of a God above and beyond all material things, the church fathers developed the notion of God creating 'out of nothing'—uninfluenced, unrestricted, uncaused by anything. It is a form of theological shorthand to indicate that God is sovereign over creation. Thus God's creativity is quite unlike ours. Human beings depend on materials, musical notes, words, for their artistry; God created when nothing was to hand for him to work on.

The Sovereignty of God

The implications then of the opening words of the Bible, 'in the beginning, God created the heavens and the earth', are immense, greater than anything we can conceive. The first words of John's Gospel re-echo the words 'in the beginning'. The beginning of what? The author of Genesis doubtless meant the beginning of the world, or better the beginning of God's creative activity. It is a theme unimaginable to Greek philosophers or contemporary secular science.

Greek understandings of the beginning

Thoughtful Greeks, in the five or six centuries before Christ, had great interest in the question, in what sense did the world have a beginning?

- Some Ionian philosophers thought such a beginning had a **material** basis—water, air, fire, matter.
- A **moral** view was taken by Anaximander who first speculated that it was necessity, 'guilt', or the order of time that led to the infinite becoming finite. But he could not conceive of the universe coming into being through an outside cause; rather it was an ordering process, whereby the infinite came into active existence.
- To the Pythagoreans, it was **number** that was the principle of all things in the world, evidenced in the principles of musical harmony.
- The pre-Socratics, such as Parmenides, were to argue that **mind** is what brought about the beginning and the *logos* (the Word) was the ordering principle of all things.
- Plato thought not of a principle but of an **event**, the world-soul which, as 'the unmoved mover', set the universe in motion.
- Aristotle alone seemed aware of an absolute beginning which so awed him that he made hardly any attempt to determine its meaning. He appears to reject all previous attempts to give a precise philosophical form to the concept. Instead, he confines himself deliberately to the **observable world**, whose 'beginning' must be the supreme cause.

Modern science and the beginning

Modern science is also limited in what it can say about 'the beginning'. This is because of the tentative nature of what it can say about the origin of the universe. There are three major schools of thought on this today:

- There are **the evolutionary theories of the universe**, such as those of Lemaitre and Gamow. They

A. J. MEADOWS

The Christian Origins of Science

Modern science developed in one place only, and over a restricted period of time. The place was Western Europe; the time, from the sixteenth to the seventeenth centuries. It is not immediately obvious why conditions were then particularly favourable. Much of the intellectual background of Western Europe at that time was not original—it was derived from classical antiquity. In technical invention, the Chinese had reached a higher level of sophistication than the Europeans, and at a much earlier stage. Why then was the decisive step to modern science not taken centuries before in Greece or China?

Historians have tried for many years to find an answer to this question. There are many different activities and attitudes which may have played a part. But among the various factors which have been proposed, the Christian faith invariably appears as a major influence. It enters in three ways:

- ☐ As a result of beliefs basic to Christianity as a whole;
- ☐ Through particular developments going on in Christian belief and church structure at the time;
- ☐ Because of the interplay between religious and secular trends.

A predictable universe

One of the basic Christian beliefs underpinning the new scientific enterprise was that when we observe how the material universe works, we are looking at the activity of God. It is therefore an eminently worthwhile study, with a definite spiritual spin-off. What is more, God did not influence the universe in an arbitrary fashion; he chose to operate through laws which applied everywhere and at all times. This emphasis on order, on the predictable, is one without which there can be no science. It was supplemented by the Christian view of history as a line running from point to point, rather than an endlessly repeating cycle of events. For science is an activity which moves on and builds, and only if people see the world doing the same will science come to mean much.

A more specific factor for the origins of science in the sixteenth and seventeenth centuries was that Christians were in dispute over the nature of authority, and where authority came from. This played a significant role in overthrowing traditional views of the universe. Other issues in the Christian thinking of the time had a bearing too. For example, the Protestants were for playing down the pre-Reformation emphasis on contemporary miracles, and this led increasingly to a belief that God normally acts through secondary causes, rather than by direct interference. Science was seen as the best way of describing these secondary causes.

Besides its direct impact, Christianity also set the scene for science through the influence it had on the structure of society in Western Europe. One obvious area in which the Greek and Chinese societies differed from the Western European was in their attitude to manual labour. The former saw this as a fundamentally demeaning activity; the latter did not. This difference, rooted in the Christian basis of society, permitted the growth of a mixture of practical experiment and theory which is an essential feature of modern science.

That Christian ways of thinking had an impact on the origins of science can be seen as we read the comments of the early scientists themselves. Virtually without exception, they saw their investigations of the world around them as a religious activity. Its justification, for them, lay in the better understanding it provided of God's handiwork.

argue for an initial concentration of matter, out of which 'the cosmic egg' was hatched (Lemaitre) or the 'big-bang' explosion took place (Gamow). The former theory is no longer tenable scientifically. The latter can speak only of a relative rather than an absolute beginning.

- Then there are **the steady-state or continuous creation theories** of Hermann Bondi and Fred Hoyle, which see no evidence of a beginning. The universe has always existed and always will exist. Thus it is impossible to speak of an origin of the universe, since no origin is conceived possible.
- **The theory of the pulsating universe** accepts the 'big-bang' hypothesis, but denies that this has happened only once. Instead, it lays open the possibility of cyclical recurrence, of an infinite number of cosmic explosions. This theory echoes James Hutton's pronouncement in 1795 in his book *The Theory of the Earth,* 'it has no vestige of a beginning and no prospect of an end.'

An even more fundamental question is whether science can ever establish that the universe has had an origin in time. Some say this is impossible, because science cannot study an event for which no explanation can be given. Obviously, there could be no physical causes before an absolute beginning, so scientific study could not enter such a field. Science then can never hope to establish an absolute origin for the universe, which means it cannot disprove it either. So, more clearly than Aristotle's conclusion thousands of years earlier, modern science can really say nothing about the origin of the universe. Therefore there is no intrinsic contradiction between science and faith on the matter of the beginning of all things.

Creation in Christian thought

The 'big-bang' versus 'steady-state' controversy is not restricted to the scientists. It has its echoes in Christian ideas of creation. Some theologians think of God primarily as 'immanent', working from within his creation. Others see him much more as 'transcendent', intervening in his creation from outside and beyond it. The first group understand God the Creator as eternally creative; they do not fully distinguish between God as the Creator and as the Sustainer of the universe. But the second group think that God created the universe in a decisive act, and that since then everything has been upheld by his sustaining providence. These different views of God's sovereignty stem, it is worth repeating, from different ideas of the character of God.

Orthodox Christianity firmly links together two pairs of ideas: 'creation from nothing' with God's act of creation, and 'continuous creation' with God's providence. It resists any attempt to merge these two sets of ideas into one. When some modern theologians do confuse creation with providence, they have a reason: they want to show that the ground of our being is God's endless creativity. But the Bible sees no contradiction between God's once-for-all creation and his continuing creativity; in fact it affirms both.

The problem with the immanent view of creation, that God is within the universe to shape it, is that it leaves a gap where God's act of creation should be, and so leaves the believer with an incomplete vision of the universe. Only a God who reaches beyond the universe could ever have created it. Yet all the theological approaches inevitably leave some distortion of the grandeur and mystery of the doctrine of God as Creator. None can cope with all its fullness and range.

The Providence of God

One writer has confessed, 'the longer I live, the more faith I have in Providence, and the less faith I have in my interpretations of Providence.' Providence is the care God takes of all existing things. So its range and depth are immense. The word itself is taken from Abraham's promise to his son Isaac on the way to sacrifice: 'My Son, God will *provide* the lamb for the burnt offering.' 'There is a special providence in the fall of a sparrow,' says Hamlet in Shakespeare's play. This is God's rule as moral governor over all the universe.

There is also God's forgiveness of the sinner. God's great acts of salvation are all part of God's activity in providence: the exodus of the Israelites from Egypt; the death of Jesus Christ for mankind's redemption; the promise of new creation. One important aspect of the idea of providence is as the special exercise of God's creative power, to bring about some beneficial result. This may be the salvation of a people, the provision of manna in the desert, the sending of prophetic teaching, or the simple gift of a humble heart to receive wisdom. It may be a heart open to the gift of the incarnate Christ, as Mary's was, or one receptive to the word of God, as we today may be.

The ways in which we perceive providence will depend on how we understand God:

- It makes a big difference whether we think of God the Creator **personally or impersonally**. If the Creator is not viewed personally, then the focus will be on 'nature', with broad generalizations to do with natural explanations. There will be little scope for providence in history, in miracles, in personal life; it is an approach which follows the tone of this anti-supernatural age. But if the providential God is seen as a personal Creator, then his goodness will be seen in what he does within time—in miracles, in the intimacy of personal experiences, in historical actions.

Such a God will be one who enters into a person's life, who responds to prayers, who suffers and rejoices with human beings. At the same time, since our failures are a wronging of the whole created order, private forgiveness, although a real kind of personal providence, is not enough. So the apostle Paul anticipates that 'the groaning of creation' will cease only when the children of God are fully and finally redeemed.

- Our understanding of **creation** also vitally affects how we see providence. As has been said, if we think of God the Creator as working immanently within his creation, there is less or no distinction between creation and providence. On this basis, God does not work in history and the reality of God's entry into human existence is obscured, if not denied. But the Bible's way of speaking is of 'the Word', Jesus Christ, through whom 'God made all things; not one thing in all creation was made without him'. It speaks of a God who has definite purposes for creation, and of the practical realization of those purposes.

The Bible also expresses a very special relationship between the Creator and his creation: one that is personal and spiritual, rather than impersonal and mechanical. It shows us that there is a link between creation and obedience, since it shows God as a God who reveals himself and creates men and women to respond to that revelation. In spite of humankind's disobedience and the cosmic consequences of sin upon creation, the providence of God in his acts of goodness work not merely for the sustaining of creation, but also for its redemption.

The goodness of God

Providence takes us into ideas of God's glory and holiness. In many religions, worship is the desire for religious harmony in awe of God's holiness, majesty and greatness. His glory and holiness appear to be the focus of worship. But the biblical doctrine of providence goes much further, for it also celebrates the goodness of the Creator. It is the goodness of the Creator that evokes both worship *and* obedience. God's glory may rightly draw wonder and praise from his creatures, and God's holiness may evoke our sense of creatureliness and sin. But it is God's goodness that truly brings forth human obedience.

To the person who believes in God the Creator, this world order is not an impersonal 'nature', whose mechanistic systems mock our deepest needs and aspirations as people. Rather, it is a created order that reflects on the Creator, who is good and who continues to do 'all things well'. Then we can see, as Paul saw, that 'in all things God works for good with those who love him, those whom he has called according to his purpose'.

For further thinking

QUESTION 1

Some people have no belief in a creator. Is it possible for them to see purpose in the universe and in human life?

QUESTION 2

What difference does a belief in God's providence make to how we live our lives?

BIBLE REFERENCES

God the Creator

Genesis 1:1—2:4; 2:5–25; 8:22; 22:8; 45:5–8; 14:18–22; 17:1; 22:13–14; Exodus 3:14; 15:1–18, 26; Deuteronomy 8:7–18; 26:1–11; Judges 6:24; Nehemiah 9:6–25, 32–37; Job 26:5–14; 33:4, 23–30; 38:2–41; Psalms 8:1–9; 19:1–6; 24:1–2; 36:5–9; 90:1–6; 102:25–28; 104:1–30; 115:16; 136:1–9; 139:13–15; 145:15–20; 148:1–10; Proverbs 8:22–31; Ecclesiastes 12:13; Isaiah 40:12–31; 42:5; 44:6, 24; 45:18–19; Jeremiah 10:12–16; 18:5–10; Daniel 4:31; Joel 2:18–23; Amos 4:13; 5:8–9; Matthew 6:28–34; Luke 13:1–5; John 1:1–4; 5:17; Acts 4:24–25; 14:17; 17:23–31; Romans 1:20–23; 8:18–23, 38–39; 1 Corinthians 8:6; 10:26; Colossians 1:15–20; Hebrews 1:1–3; 4:11; 10:6; 11:3

CHAPTER 15

GEORGE CAREY

Made in the Image of God

A school sixth form once agreed in open debate that 'the hope of civilization lies in the pursuit and application of scientific knowledge'. Religion had no place in a utopian society. This life was all, so let us enjoy it. At the end of term, the students asked the headmaster for their job and college references. This was how he phrased one of them:

Biological description John is a living organism. Group: vertebrata. Class: mammalia. Order: primates. Genus: homo. Species: sapiens.
Body structure Organs, tissues, cells—protoplasm. Five organs of sense: sight, taste, touch, sound and smell.
Chemical description A large quantity of carbon. Some gallons of water; various amounts of iron, calcium, magnesium, phosphorus, sulphur, lime, nitrogen, and some mineral salts.
Psychological description A mind, conscious and unconscious; intellectual, emotional and volitional powers; various instincts . IQ 130.
'I hope that John will fit as an admirable unit into the various machines, industrial, commercial and so on, that make up our scientifically-planned society. But regrettably I have serious misgivings about this. There is something in John that refuses to be 'cribbed, cabined and confined' and reaches out to a fulfilment beyond the capacity of a machine-like destiny to supply. In his eager pursuit of scientific knowledge and passionate love of music, as well as in the deep discontent to which he once confessed at his inability to live up to his own ideals, it seems to me that John is on a quest that existence, even in a four-dimensional space-time continuum, can never satisfy.'

Naturally the students had to ask for other more 'real' references. Accurate scientific descriptions were not enough. They left out of their account what it is to be human.

What does the Bible teach about the real nature of humanity?

The Image of God

In some ways we are no different from any other species on earth. We are creatures subject to the usual conditions of space and time. But we know that human beings 'stand out' from other beings in several ways. Some of these are plain enough; they partly explain humankind's superiority over other creatures: our creativity, our intellectual, linguistic and cultural achievements.

But the Bible adds a further and remarkable point. People stand out not by what they *do* but by what they *are*. This is expressed right at the beginning, in the creation story of Genesis 1. God said, 'Let us make man in our image and after our likeness.' It is a theme taken up and developed in other parts of the Bible: we are not like the other creatures; we share God's nature in a special way.

What do we reflect of God?

It is difficult to be very precise about what this sharing of God's nature means, though many theologians have tried.

The main point behind this very important biblical idea of the 'image' is that humanity has been created for a special relationship with God, intended to be personal and eternal. We are above the rest of creation and given 'dominion' over it, not because of the things we can do, but because of the intimate relationship which God wants to share with us. In the Bible 'doing' is always secondary to 'being'. As God intended us, we were called to live life fully in his presence, developing spiritually, mentally and morally as children of God on whom the Creator delights to pour his love.

'Made in God's image' therefore describes us as people who are open to God's call and able to respond to his claims. Yet within this very general picture of humankind's close relationship with God there are particular features which stand out:

- **True knowledge of God and holiness.** We were not created morally neutral. The Bible asserts that we were created as moral beings and that our relationship with him is intended to be one of transparent purity and holiness. The modern assumption is that our moral sense comes through education and group pressure; Christian teaching is that God created us with the knowledge of right and wrong. The coming of sin into human life, however, affected not only our moral state but also, more seriously, our relationship with God.
- **Intellectual power.** We are rational creatures and share in God's rationality which is seen in creation. Humankind's intelligence can be seen in the urge towards creativity—in art, science, religion, play. But, as with every other part of our nature, this creativity has been infected by the blight of sin. None of our achievements has ever come out quite untainted; we have found ways of using all of them for some harmful purpose.
- **Spirituality.** The Bible teaches that we are made for fellowship with God. As the Westminster Confession so beautifully puts it: 'The chief end of man is to glorify God and enjoy him for ever.' We can find true self-expression and deep fulfilment only when we find him.
- **Immortality.** We were made for eternal life with God. This is the clear teaching of the Bible. It is not ours by nature. It is God's gift to his children. Opinions differ about whether humanity was originally created immortal. Some argue that death only came into the world when humankind sinned. Others hold that humanity, according to the Bible, is just as much 'flesh' as the rest of the animal kingdom, and that the 'death' that came with the fall is not physical death, but spiritual separation from God.
- **Dominion.** The Genesis account speaks in the same breath of our creation in the image of God and our dominion over the rest of creation. Our higher position in creation is God-given. He is Lord of all, and in a limited fashion we share in lordship. The whole story sets out in full technicolor the glory and honour with which humanity is crowned and the awesome responsibility that comes with it.

> God created man in order to have someone on whom to shower his love.
>
> *Irenaeus of Lyons*

All this makes it plain that the Bible idea that we were created in the image of God is a crucial tool for a Christian understanding of human nature. The vivid story of the idyllic life in Eden gives expression to a real relationship with God which was meant to endure.

Primal tragedy

Humanity has fallen from its destiny and calling. Adam and Eve were confronted with a choice. They chose sin and independence from God. The image of God in humanity has, by that choice, been spoiled and distorted. As the Genesis account portrays it, Adam and Eve were made for fellowship with God and for sharing in his love and generosity. Their fate, through rejection of God, was to be separate from his life. They 'fell' from grace and it became our fall.

As with the account of our creation, so with our fall: there are different views of how to take the story. Some hold that, unless we believe in a literal, historical fall that actually affected the whole human race, we undermine the central Christian facts of sin and salvation. Others see the Genesis story as plainly figurative, describing poetically the deep alienation between God and humanity. The story is saying that we are sinners and need God. Every person is 'Adam' and every person has 'fallen' from the righteousness God intends for us.

The human condition is tragic. Something wonderful has been lost. And yet, even after our fall and in our sin, we have not completely lost the image of God. It is spoilt, but not destroyed.

The power of man has grown in every sphere except over himself.

Winston Churchill

God's true image

Humanity's fall is not just a theological statement; human history and experience show us that the image has been defaced in us all. As the apostle Paul puts it, 'We have all fallen short of God's standard.' But does this mean that God's image has never been seen in its fullness since the beginning? No, because Jesus Christ is the perfect image of God. That is the New Testament's bold declaration. The task of his mission was to lead us back to God and to restore the image in us.

This is where the New Testament connects the study of Christ with the study of humankind. Because Jesus is both true likeness of God and perfect man, he is the promise of a renewed humanity. To be 'in Christ' is to belong to a 'new humanity', just as to be 'in Adam' is to belong to the old, sinful humanity. The apostle Paul wrote of thc 'new nature which is being renewed in knowledge after the image of its creator'. As the 'image of the invisible God', Jesus is the model of what men and women were created to be.

He [Jesus Christ] reflects the brightness of God's glory and is the exact likeness of God's own being.

Hebrews 1

God's grace in the world

Sin is a reality. It is divisive and tragic. But God is still a loving creator. His ultimate purposes are not thwarted by us. Sin and evil never have the last word in God's creation.

God's love is seen as he acts to care for us and to restrain evil. This is expressed in the word 'grace'. We see it in its full glory in Jesus' death on the cross, which shows us just how much God loves us. But God's grace is also experienced in his personal, day-by-day caring and loving. We can distinguish two aspects of grace: 'special' and 'common'.

- **Special grace** refers specifically to God's grace as it reaches those who want to follow Jesus. It is God's way of blessing his people, the church, as he saves them and gives them his Holy Spirit.
- **Common (or general) grace** applies to everyone alive; it stems from God's universal Fatherhood. His grace is received by us all, whether or not we are Christian, as we share in the many blessings of life. Through our sin we have lost any claim on him, yet he still gives abundant tokens of his generosity and goodness day by day. These gifts are showered on all, regardless of creed, character or colour.

Perhaps the clearest expression of God's common grace is as he preserves truth and morality among people. Christians do not have a monopoly of true and good things and neither is morality the province of the Christian alone. Everyone keeps some sense of what is true, good and beautiful, and this is due to God's grace.

Paul sees a further result of this common grace. It opens people's hearts and minds to the goodness of God, and so prepares them to receive God's special grace in Jesus Christ. When we look around at everything good in the world it speaks to us of a loving God who wants us all to know and experience his love and enter into a deeper relationship with him.

Human Nature

We are 'flesh', made of the 'dust of the earth'. We are part of creation; we eat, excrete, procreate, suffer and die just like the other creatures. The very idea of 'dust' describes our creaturely status. No humanist could speak more definitely of our lowly origins. Far from making us too other-worldly, the Bible cuts us down to size : 'You take away their breath; they die and return to the dust,' says the Psalmist. But if the Bible writers are realistic, they are in no way negative. The Bible affirms life, and joyfully encourages us to enjoy life's pleasures. It tells us that if God has seen fit to create us as physical beings there is nothing in our make-up or anatomy to be ashamed of.

More than animal

But the Bible never stops there. Humankind is mortal, but we are not purely animal. To speak as if we were gives the lie to the idea of the image of God. And so the Bible uses other terms as well: **soul, heart, spirit and body**. Taken together with 'flesh', they give us an account of our nature as being open to the worlds both of flesh and of spirit.

The Bible has an integrated view of human nature. It never sees us as the sum total of different compartments: flesh, soul and spirit. The Bible writers were certainly people of their own time and used their own terms to describe humanity. Yet they believed most firmly in what we today call the 'psychosomatic unity' of the person—the interdependence of body, mind and emotions. Body, soul and spirit are terms the Bible uses to show us as people at home in this world, but with the capacity to reach beyond ourselves to the world of the spirit.

The biggest mistake is to think of ourselves as owning a soul as we would a suitcase or an umbrella. This was the way the ancient Greeks thought. Greek or 'Hellenistic' culture was the background to the first centuries of the church. In Alexandria, for instance, theologians tried to relate their faith to this way of thought. Not surprisingly, this Greek view of 'soul' and 'body' infected the early church, whose catch phrase was *soma sema*, 'the body a tomb'. To their mind, the soul was released from its prison at death and set free.

The same idea is expressed in the song: 'John Brown's body lies a-mouldering in the grave, but his soul goes marching on.' It seems to assume that there are two John Browns: the physical John who went to war, now dead, and the spiritual John, now in heaven. It shows how easy it is to fall into thinking that the real 'me' is somehow different from my physical body.

Humanity and Nature

It is characteristic of people in the West to talk of 'man and creation' as if we were somehow detached from creation. The Bible's teaching questions such an approach. In spite of our special relationship to God, we are still within creation, answerable to the Creator.

Humanity has been set over creation and given 'dominion' over it. We are called to this responsibility of being stewards in God's world. This is true only because we are ourselves creatures and share the same world as other created beings. The history of Western thought has tended to ignore our unity with creation and to exaggerate our independence from it. The education and way of life of modern industrial people tend toward an anti-nature bias, looking on the natural environment as a place to 'use' or 'exploit'.

On the other hand, the tendency in the East (particularly in the religions of the Far East) is to blur the distinction between God, humanity and nature, and this sometimes results in 'Pantheism', the glorification of nature as if it were divine. And even in the West, many television programmes, for instance, speak of 'nature' doing something, as if it were God.

The Bible does not agree with either of these extremes. It neither confuses God with the world nor separates him from it. Its

Man must not be allowed to believe that he is equal either to animals or to angels . . . but he must know both.

Blaise Pascal

approach is that God created all things for his pleasure and he delights in the world he has made. He calls into being the bewildering variety of creatures, animate and inanimate, and he wants them all to be fulfilled in their own way. In the modern world we have been forced by the energy-depleted and increasingly polluted earth to think about the ecology of creation and its conservation. The Bible knew about this long ago.

The Old Testament particularly shows striking insight into the connection between a ruined earth and the attitudes of humankind. Isaiah, for example, dwells on the failure of Israel to obey God's laws; he sees the effect not only in social life but in the poisoning of the world around.

We have to face the fact squarely that we

PAUL CLOWNEY

The Arts

Art has a lot to do with religion. Most of the 'art-works' unearthed by archaeologists link in with some religious practice or other. Until recent times the church was the most important patron of the arts. Contemporary artists regularly discuss their work in 'spiritual' terms.

The reason for this link is that both art and religion are energized by the human need to worship. We naturally call attention to the things we feel important and worthwhile. Our word 'worship' comes from 'worth-ship'. Artists strive to present in a specific way the things they value, whether these are in the spontaneous brushwork of a watercolour or in the distilled language of a love poem. They invariably have a reverence for their art form. Because artistic symbols, like money, can become devalued, artists struggle to express their insights in new ways. They will often consciously reject express-ions which seem worn or easy.

Yet the artist's creation is never really new. Earlier centuries reserved the word 'create' for God alone, as his is the only creation out of nothing. Artists make neither their raw materials nor the hand which manipulates them. Even their minds are not truly their own, but a gift. The artist 'creates' by bringing together existing things, ideas or symbols. He or she is dependent for source material on nature and the culture they live in.

Artists and their times

We cannot understand the arts apart from the culture in which the artist is working. Obviously each age has seen its own art as 'modern'. Work which we deem traditional may once have been experienced as shockingly new, as an assault on the traditions of that time.

As artists express their values they can hardly help but express to some extent the philosophy of their day. Hence the art of the eighteenth-century Enlightenment was sombre, rational and optimistic, reflecting humankind's faith at that period in its own potential. Similarly the diversity and complexity of our own age is apparent in the baffling variety of art produced, much of which seems motivated by disillusionment.

Because new art forms often appear to threaten existing values, many people regard them with suspicion. Christians have been particularly prone to do this. At various times in church history Christian attitudes to the arts have been positively hostile.

Some Christians have argued that our proper priority is our relationship to God, and that the arts are either a superfluous luxury or a dangerous distraction. The Bible's clear injunction against idolatry has been invoked, not only to prohibit pictures of Christ but also against any kind of art. Calvin thought that music contributed to the life of the church, but found drama hazardous because of its power to mislead.

Many artists have been outspoken in their criticism of Christian values and traditions, and this has confirmed some believers in their conviction that no good can come from getting involved in the arts.

This tension between the material world and spiritual obedience is not easily resolved. There is no doubt that the current climate of the arts does pose

are part of nature. Creation is more than our larder, our playground, our sports arena, our theatre of war. It is God's handiwork; we depend on creation more than creation depends on us; it should command our respect.

Our role in nature

'There would be no absolute loss if every human being were to die tomorrow,' said D. H. Lawrence. 'Man is the mistake of creation.' But Lawrence was wrong. The Bible does not view humanity as an accident, nor as an unnecessary appendage to life. We are God's crowning achievement. Without human beings the world would be incomplete and unfinished. In the story of creation, the refrain after each stage is, 'And God saw that it was good.' But not until the climax of the

problems. Present art philosophy leans towards the view that the artist's creative liberty is absolute. Money complicates the issue too. The art market is so dominated by finance that success and value are too narrowly understood.

These factors emphasize the secularization of art, as well as the importance granted it by our society. Because art is increasingly specialized and inaccessible, artists are regularly accused of being elitist. Observers have repeatedly written about the 'crisis' in the arts, claiming that there is no direction for our age.

Creativity: human and divine

Christians noting the state of the arts are often tempted to dismiss this whole area of life. Others argue for a Christian involvement in the arts. The Bible says very little specifically about the arts apart from condemning idolatry—a warning which certainly is relevant to today's art. Yet there is, at the heart of Bible belief, a power-ful encouragement to the artist.

The character of God, as seen both in the Bible and in creation, shows an overwhelming imagination. God's world is full of surprises, not the least of which is humankind's ability to make new things. The variety of the ways God has expressed himself is boundless, which demonstrates how interested he is in material things. It is his character to express himself; the earth shows the work of his hands.

God commands men and women to make use of these things, to explore and utilize creation. Humankind has a role in God's world as manager. This is not a passive role, but requires imagination, sensitivity, action. This means that the purpose of culture is both 'to make the world a better place' and also to return to God with interest the gifts he has given to humanity. That interest is collected as we put God's gifts to work.

The person who feels called to be an artist is privileged. He or she has a vocation in which there is a large element of play. The hard work of artistic expression is a different sort of work from most forms of labour—not superior or inferior to plumbing, but different.

The artist's curiosity can motivate others to discover and explore the significance of the world. Artists can introduce new insights into our regimented and predictable social order; they can make us more aware of the subtleties of life. The artist's responsibility is to feed our imaginations, and so deepen our appreciation of what it is to be human.

The arts today

A recurrent theme of twentieth-century art has been the hopelessness of human affairs. And yet paradoxically another major theme in modern art has been more optimistic: the hope that art itself might provide an escape from the confusion of life.

Neither the pessimist nor the optimist can be wholly right. An art which is obsessed with art itself quickly becomes introspective and loses its driving force. And yet, when artists give their sole attention to the absurdity of the human condition, they fail to account for the wonder and beauty in the world.

The imaginative poetry of the Psalms makes a strong contrast to all this. These poets stress that all creation stands in relationship to its Creator: hills clap their hands, blizzards sing praises. Such wholehearted expressions of praise should typify the Christian artist—who should know the limits of his nature, and the amazing love of God, the source of all gifts.

You have made us for yourself, and our hearts are restless till they find their rest in you.

Augustine

story, the creation of humanity, does the writer say 'God saw everything that he had made and behold it was very good.'

As if to be made in God's image were not privilege enough, humanity's role extends still further. We have been given freedom of choice, and choice implies responsibility. If God calls us to share his nature, it is not surprising that he has given us a distinctive role in the world. We are to be God's agents in the world, representing him and caring for the quality of life: 'Be fruitful and multiply, fill the earth and subdue it and have dominion.' This is not the charter for a despotic tyranny, but it is a summons to be God's co-workers and stewards.

Co-workers

As co-workers with God we are to continue and reflect God's creativity in the world. We do this as we bring to our environment that order, structure and beauty which is our distinctively human contribution. God gains satisfaction and pleasure from his creation; he wants us to take pleasure in it too, as we live in his world and look after it. This shared pleasure opens the door for all kinds of human creativity—in art, music, writing and many other cultural activities.

In the Old Testament, skilled craftsmen were chosen to build the temple—only the best was good enough for God. But some have had a more cramped view of this God-given element. They have overstressed the spiritual side of life and failed to see that one important part of human spirituality is expressed in artistic creativity. Augustine says: 'The beautiful, transmitted through the souls of artists to their hands, comes from that Beauty which is above all souls, for which my soul sighs day and night.'

We cannot but admire Handel's 'Messiah' and Michelangelo's 'The Last Judgment'. They are great works of art in themselves, as well as expressions of praise and adoration to God. Yet great art does not have to be specifically religious in the wider sense. The creative person, as Keats once said, 'carries out a priest-like task for us', because he opens a window for us through which we see afresh the wonder of life. And wonder puts us in our place; it expresses the gulf between our limited existence and the greatness of creation which dwarfs us.

The Bible, however, does not allow us to glory in our artistic accomplishments as if they were ends in themselves. Wonder and awe are our response to the creativity of God expressed in nature; human creativity too draws forth its proper response when it moves us to worship God. Humanity is a worshipping species. It is not just that we have a duty to worship our Maker; worship is part of our nature.

We may think that we have a choice between God or nothing. But in fact we all worship something. As Luther said: 'That to which your heart clings is your god.' Our art, our ambition, even our creativity can be the place where our heart rests, and then the true God is replaced. We need a true consciousness of ourselves; we are created beings who live under the eye of a great God, and this must be the cornerstone of all relationships.

The Ten Commandments make this clear. The first commandment, 'You will have no other gods but me', is the basis for all the rest. If we believe that God is our only Lord, respect for his laws and love for others will follow. Jesus summed up this double focus of the law in the twin command to love: 'You must love the Lord your God with all your heart, mind, soul and strength—and your neighbour as yourself.'

Stewards

God tells humanity in the creation narrative to 'subdue the earth, to till and keep it' as well as having management over it, for which we are answerable to God. In other words humankind has been given a role in this environment, the role of steward. A steward, by definition, is someone who looks after property for someone else. He has no legal claims on it, but he is in charge and answerable to the owner. So it is with humanity. We have no right to act arrogantly or independently. 'All things are put under his feet', as the

Psalmist declares, but this should not encourage a go-it-alone policy.

On the contrary, the Old Testament assumes a 'symbiosis' of all living things: the whole creation working harmoniously together, to the advantage of each component part. In the laws of Israel a foremost human duty was to respect creation and submit to its rhythm and order. Indeed, the attitude to life in this part of the Bible is full of joy, encouraging the people to rejoice in nature's bounty as a token of God's love.

This somewhat idyllic picture is not so easy to recognize today, because of the highly complex industrial societies in which many people live. Our environment is the raw material for our prosperity, but it is not a limitless treasure trove. We are finding to our cost that future generations face the prospect of a bankrupt and exhausted world. A great deal of the blame for this must be placed at the door of our own generation for acting irresponsibly and selfishly towards the world's natural resources.

The problems facing humanity are immense. A Christian contribution is not only possible but necessary. The most relevant biblical concept is our answerability to the Creator. Sin warps our understanding of our role and place in creation and leads us to search for satisfaction in ourselves and our own achievements. So we sink into **relativism** ('there are no absolute standards'), **individualism** ('I matter most') and **agnosticism** ('we doubt that God exists, so we live without him').

There are two modern problems we face as we play out our role in creation:

- **We may overestimate our importance in the world and try to flatter ourselves that we are lords of our environment.** Dr Edmund Leach began a famous course of broadcast lectures: 'Men have become like gods. Isn't it about time that we understood our divinity? Science offers us total mastery over our environment and over our destiny. Yet instead of rejoicing we are secretly afraid.' If men and women are afraid, it may be that our nature informs us such an attitude is wrong. It certainly has practical implications: if we are lords of creation then we can do what we like with our environment. It is ours to use as we wish. When we lose sight of God, we take for ourselves a position that properly belongs to him.

- The glorification of humanity can rebound upon us, so that **the individual no longer matters**. Often, when the dignity and glory of human beings is trumpeted, the personality and worth of the individual is brushed aside.

The classic expression of this is Aldous Huxley's *Brave New World*, in which he explores what a future would be like where our scientific achievements dominate the world. He paints a horrifying picture: genetic engineering gears what kind of people are born to social requirements, and the individual is graded according to his intelligence and usefulness to society. The state comes first and people last.

Christian teaching is bold and uncompromising. Our dignity derives from God alone. If God is, we are. If God is pushed out, we are the losers in the end.

Life in Relationship

So far we have discussed what it means to be human. But the human person can never be treated alone. We cannot survive alone, at least not for very long. Our growth as persons largely depends on the strength of the relationships which connect us with people around. Each of us is born into a family, in itself a unit of society, and we continue in different levels of community. 'People, people who need people, are the luckiest people in the world,' Barbara Streisand's song told us. Most of us are intensely aware of our need for human love and companionship.

But there is an even deeper truth about relationship. What we call 'personhood' comes fully into being only when we are in community with others. 'I', on my own, am an individual. 'I', with others, am a person. This modern insight is not foreign to the Bible, which never treats the individual on his or her own. Humanity was, after all, created male and female. People need fellowship for growth to fulfil the potential within. The Bible's emphasis, especially in the Old Testament, is on 'corporate solidarity': the group is the significant unit, and it is in the network of relationships which make up the group that individuals play their part. The creation narrative says: 'It is not good for man to be alone.'

Husband and wife

The first and most basic of all relationships is the unique pairing of husband and wife for the purpose of sharing, loving and forming new life. In the Bible sexuality is set firmly within this setting. Sex is not a thing in itself, isolated from a continuing relationship.

But Christians have not always had a positive view of sex within marriage. The church has often adopted a grudging and distasteful attitude towards our sexuality—because of the Greek influence on early Christian thought, as we have seen. The body was thought of as something inferior to the soul; it was sinful, sordid. This contrasts with the whole-hearted attitude of the opening chapters of Genesis, which portrays people most emphatically as sexual beings whose sexuality is God-given—to be enjoyed directly and properly. The fulfilment of these desires is rightly found within the unity of husband and wife in an enduring, rich and loving relationship.

What kind of partnership?

Christianity has sometimes encouraged a view of women as second-class citizens—inferior to men before God and socially unequal in the community. Even some of the greatest church fathers were guilty of this. In their eagerness to commend the advantages of chastity for Christian ministry, they accused women of wielding a sinful and seductive influence over men. Women have even been accused of causing humanity's fall! Tertullian made a well-known attack on women: 'You are the Devil's gateway, you are the eater of the forbidden tree. You destroyed, so easily, God's image, man.' It is important to recognize the wrong assumption he makes, that women are excluded from the image of God. Humanity is the image of God, not maleness. The divine charter was: 'God created man in his own image: *male and female* created he them.'

This biblical emphasis rules out all sexist notions. There is no justification for male chauvinism. Women were not created as inferior creatures, but as people of equal standing with men and equal dignity before God. Here is a vital principle to grasp: women are spiritual beings endowed with exactly the same opportunities to find and know God as men are. The Bible never denigrates women spiritually, although not until the ministry of Jesus is the full teaching reached about their spiritual nature.

The modern movement for equality, then, has the Bible on its side. And yet it can lead us astray because of its tendency to blur the physiological and other differences that are there to see. This only makes things more difficult as we try to work out the respective roles of men and women in society. Within the marriage bond there are different roles, duties and responsibilities for each partner to perform.

This is obvious at one level: men cannot give birth nor suckle their young; women cannot give seed. But at other levels, especially in our complex society, the roles are not as clear-cut as they used to be. Modern education and social pressure have given women a freedom undreamed of twenty years ago. This is something to be deeply grateful for, yet in its turn it has its unhealthy side. The breakdown of marriages in industrial society is now a serious social problem and Christian insights into the nature of

JUNE OSBORNE

Male and Female

'God created mankind in his own image: male and female he created them,' says the writer of Genesis. In Greek legend Zeus first created a sexless being. Later, in a fit of divine anger, he split this into man and woman. The division of humankind into two sexes is thus understood to be an imperfect state, a weakening of the power of human beings, because the two sexes pull in different directions. But Genesis speaks out against this idea and says that humankind, male and female, was God's original and creative intention. It was no afterthought that we were created sexual beings, but an essential part of being human, of carrying the image of God.

Christians largely agree that God's nature lies beyond sexuality. God bears neither male nor female sexuality. However, in its attempts to describe God, the Bible frequently uses both masculine images (father, shepherd, king) and feminine images (mother, hen). And so it affirms that both sexes have the task of reflecting the image of God. This insight has sometimes eluded the Christian church and a male-oriented understanding of God has often taken over. But the Bible is quite clear that God's image is not unique to one sex—rather that male and female together bear that responsibility.

Men and women are intended to live in God's world in such a way that we show the stamp of his nature. How does our sexuality help us to do this?

To live as man or woman

Our sexuality expresses that we are people, not animals. Animals share with us the biological differences between male and female; human sexuality penetrates every corner of our being. It affects our instincts, our psyche, our identity. The human sciences tell us that we acquire our sexuality in a complex way, partly through our physical make-up and partly through the roles we expect of our children. Christian teaching agrees with this. In one sense, our sexuality is indelible, given to us. On the other hand, our sexuality is a journey, discovering what it means for us to be God's pattern of a man or woman. It is God's calling to each human being to explore what he has made us. Each person's response to that call will depend on his or her personality and background, society and culture.

It may be, as some Christians believe, that our physical differences are a visible sign of more ultimate psychical and spiritual differences, but the Bible does not explicitly teach that. What is very clear in biblical teaching is that sexuality is good. It is given by God for us to enjoy. The Old Testament Song of Songs is a beautiful expression of erotic love without guilt or shame, and it echoes the creation picture of Adam and Eve who 'were naked, and were not ashamed'.

Some Christians emphasize that the primary purpose of our sexuality is to bear children. But the biblical creation stories do not teach this. The reason they give for sexuality is that it calls us into relationship with one another.

To live in relationship

God himself is personal; he gives himself to us in relationship. And that is how he wants us to live. He did not want Adam to be alone. Without dependency on one another we can never be whole people. Relationship must be founded on self-giving love, complementariness, mutual respect, acceptance and growth. This is seen in a special way in the marriage bond, but is by no means limited to that. However, the Christian believes that the appropriate expression of our sexual nature is always within relationship.

The basis of that relationship is partnership. God commissioned Adam and Eve as partners. Jesus treated male and female alike as his partners in mission. It was men and women together who first spread the news of the gospel.

Where one sex is oppressed by the other it reflects a marred humanity. Conflict between the sexes is the fruit of humankind's separation from God. But in Jesus Christ the male/female relationship has the potential to be restored to God's original ideal. 'There is neither male nor female, for you are all one in Christ Jesus,' wrote Paul, in words which have been called the 'magna carta of humanity'.

marriage are much needed.

The family

The modern family differs very strikingly from families in ancient times. We talk today about the 'nuclear' family—the somewhat isolated unit of mother, father and children. The historical reasons for this are quite well-known.

Before the Industrial Revolution, families were fairly close-knit, with the extended family of grandparents, parents and children, cousins and aunts, all living within a reasonable distance of each other. This is still a common pattern in agricultural societies. But the rise of modern industries gradually brought a change. Men and women went in search of jobs; the industrial cities, big centres of employment, attracted the homeless and jobless; the invention of the railway and the motor car increased mobility.

Today Mr and Mrs Average Family may enjoy four or five moves in a working lifetime. They will build up many important friendships along the way, while at the same time finding a gradual estrangement from their 'home' community and wider family.

It is not just parents who have found themselves adrift from their original moorings; today's children feel cut off or estranged from their parents. We call this 'the generation gap'. Again, the reasons for this are fairly clear. Families rarely seek their relaxation together; teenagers seek their amusements and friendships among their own age-group, and competing interests come into the family.

This division between the generations was not to be found in the Hebrew family. The tribe, the community, was the social context for the individual and his or her family. Great respect was given to the senior members of the family or clan, because they represented the traditions of the tribe. As 'elders' they taught the customs, folklore and religion of the group. Their experience of life and of their God was something they shared with others. Within the family children were definitely 'seen and not heard'. Respect for their seniors was drummed into them from infancy.

Children were expected to 'honour' their parents and parents were exhorted to encourage their children, bringing them up to be responsible citizens and to love God. Yet this did not result in an oppressive society. There was a delightful informality and warmth in the ancient Israelite family which saw in the network of human relationships—grandparents, parents, children, aunts and uncles and cousins—a secure refuge in a threatening and insecure world.

Two special things stand out in the biblical picture of the family:

- The clan structure ensured that **all groups were given a place in the family**. As far as we can tell from the Old Testament, the generations were happily integrated, on the basis of the 'honour' that each had for the others.

The fifth commandment ordered: 'Honour your father and mother, that your days may be long in the land which the Lord your God has given you.' This was the Bible's standard, although like all commandments it was not always obeyed. Jacob deceived his blind father Isaac to cheat Esau of the inheritance; Absalom revolted against his father, King David, and tried to depose him; Joseph's brothers behaved in a most unbrotherly manner by selling him into slavery. But such incidents were seen as aberrations; mutual respect was still the cement of the clan.

- Jewish spirituality **centred on the home.** The synagogue did not develop until quite late in Jewish history, and even when this became an important part of Jewish life it did not displace the family as the focus of religious life. Neither did the Temple and its sacrifices challenge the place of the home as the centre of Israel's faith.

To this day the central religious event in Judaism is the Passover, which is essentially a family event as relatives and friends gather

MICHAEL CASSIDY

The Human Family

The words 'brother' and 'sister' are among the richest in the English language, full of warmth, tenderness, loyalty and mutual care. A schoolboy was seen, in the heat of the day, carrying another boy on his back. 'Isn't he heavy?' asked a passer-by. 'No', said the lad. 'He's my brother.'

The Bible has two distinct ways of understanding the idea of 'the brotherhood of man': firstly the brotherhood of all people everywhere, and secondly the brotherhood of Christians specifically. The first is wide and all-inclusive, and the second is limited and exclusive to Christians.

The unity of all people

In general the idea of brotherhood describes that bond of unity which exists between brothers and sisters, as children of the same parents. The blood tie is, of course, the most obvious, but when related to people generally 'brotherhood' describes that bond which derives from the universal Fatherhood of God. He is our common creator and we are his creatures, so we are linked in a common creaturehood. As the one who has given us life, he is our common Father. So we are his sons and daughters in this wide sense, and this makes us brothers and sisters to one another. Put differently, we would say that because God created everyone in his own image, all are bound together in a unity or family stemming from a common origin.

In South Africa, which is the country I live in, this is a truth of which many people, even Christians, often need reminding. Whites often allow themselves to discriminate against blacks, as if they were not somehow their human brothers and sisters on the basis of common creation and sonship under the general Fatherhood of God.

This sort of common humanity has great ethical implications in all human relationships. It calls people to care for and respect one another for no other reason than that the other person is a fellow human being, created by God in his image. As such we will want to act towards him as we would want him to act towards us.

The other person

An Afrikaner Christian was once driving in a remote country region when his car broke down. After walking many miles he came to a small Indian homestead. The Indian gentleman who came to the door agreed readily to come out and help him. He was not a Christian, but a Hindu. Nor, of course, was he a white man. So perhaps in a country where whites discriminate against blacks, it was quite surprising that he should help so willingly. But he did.

Some hours later, when both men were standing cold and wet beside the repaired car, the Afrikaner said, 'How can I thank you? How can I repay you? Will you accept this money?' The Indian replied, 'No, don't give me your money. You will repay me well if you always keep a place in your heart for the other person.' That Indian did not see a white man, or an Afrikaner man or a Christian man. He just saw a man, a fellow human being, a brother. He had a true concept of the general 'brotherhood of man'.

A certain kind of brotherhood is also experienced when people have something specific in common: as in a club or association or society where common interests are shared; or in an army, when common dangers are faced; or in a nation or city. Napoleon once said of the army he led: 'It has been my privilege to lead a band of brothers.'

Broken relationships

Although we experience different forms and qualities of our family bond, more often than not the human race presents us with a picture, not of unity and care between people, but of hostility and alienation. Much of history is about the general inhumanity of person to person. This suggests that the original brotherhood of love intended by God for humankind has been spoiled. Something has gone wrong. Now this is exactly what the Bible teaches. The Genesis story tells us that, as people sinned and rebelled against God, they broke the relationship between themselves and God. By extension this means they broke fellowship with one another.

Not surprisingly, we find as early as the fourth chapter of Genesis that brother is killing brother. Says God to Cain, 'Where is Abel, your brother?' And it is a question which still comes hauntingly, in a spiritual sense, from God to each of us: 'Where is your brother?—your black brother? your white brother? your non-Christian brother? your blood brother? your different-denomination brother?' Very often, our answer has to be: 'We are distant from our brother and alienated from him.'

God's answer to this breakdown of relationship between humankind and himself and between person and person was to come into the world in Jesus Christ, to die on the cross, and to bring to people the possibility first of forgiveness and then of reconciliation—with their God and with their fellows.

The Christian family

This brings us to the second type of relationship, the more exclusive brotherhood among Christians who have discovered Jesus Christ as Lord and Saviour and Friend. This second form of biblical community speaks of a re-established or restored relationship through the work of God in Christ. Its inner tie is neither physical (as in blood brothers), nor general (as with all human beings), but spiritual (among those whose spirits are in tune with the Spirit of Christ).

As the New Testament sees it, people who accept Jesus as their Lord and Saviour are adopted into God's family. God becomes their Father, not just by making them 'one blood' with all humanity, but by entering into a real family relationship with them. This makes Christians brothers and sisters.

Not surprisingly, therefore, Christians in the New Testament often refer to themselves and to one another as brothers and sisters, and Peter exhorts his readers to 'love the brotherhood'. In fact, Jesus even saw himself as the elder brother of a great Christian family: 'Whoever does the will of my Father who is in heaven is my brother and sister and mother.'

There are distinctive obligations and marks of this Christian family. The first of these is love. Time and again Jesus urged his disciples to love one another. They were to express that love in caring for one another, in repeatedly forgiving one another, in warning and rebuking one another, in showing hospitality to one another, in honouring one another and in serving one another. Indeed, we are to bear one another's burdens, just as that little boy, at the beginning of this article, carried his brother. So special is this love that a special word was taken over from classical Greek to describe it—the word 'philadelphia', from which the great American city took its name. Used five times in the New Testament, this word describes love between Christians as distinct from the love due to all people.

So this wonderful concept calls on us for a twofold response:

- ☐ To care for all people generally, on the basis of our common creation.
- ☐ And to love all Christians specifically, on the basis of our common, restored relationship to God and to each other. We know this brotherhood through Jesus, who died to reconcile us.

A friend of mine even uses the word as a verb. He says, 'We must learn to brother!'

to celebrate Israel's deliverance from Egypt. Father conducts the service with its elaborate symbolism and each member of the family plays a part in it.

The New Testament also places attention on the importance of the family. Although it lays a greater stress on the church as the centre for fellowship, teaching and service, it teaches that the relationship between parents and children is of fundamental importance. Children are to obey their parents. Parents are to be loving and encouraging, rather than repressive. It is their duty to discipline and instruct their children, showing by example the reality of faith.

The Western idea of faith as a private, individual affair is, therefore, quite unknown to Old and New Testament writers. Perhaps modern Christians can learn from the Bible that to be a member of a family is to have spiritual responsibilities towards our relatives. This is especially relevant to parents, because of the clear biblical teaching to bring up one's children to love and fear God.

No man is an island

We saw earlier that in the Bible the group is the basic unit, not the individual. We can now go a little further than that statement. In the Bible God often addresses groups and tribes as if they were individuals: 'Israel, know that I am the Lord'; 'Ephraim, I have redeemed you', and so on. God's blessings and curses on the nation affect the individuals within it. And equally what the individual does has repercussions on the whole community. When an individual sins the whole community shares his or her guilt; it affects and contaminates others. No sin is ever private; it always has a social effect.

When a couple live together without being married, it is not just their own happiness at stake; it causes uncertainty and confusion in the wider family and in the community. Marriage is not just a legal or religious ceremony. It is the public recognition of a new relationship. And God is involved, too. No relationship works as it should when his commandments are broken.

Society and its laws

As soon as communities develop, they require law. Since every community has been penetrated by sin, we need laws to protect both individuals and the group. When we do wrong, the consequences are not only penal but social, so laws are required to safeguard the interests of others.

The earliest law to be found in the Bible is the 'covenant', the agreement God made with Israel after their rescue from Egypt. It gave expression to their promise to live as the people of God—to be a distinctive, holy people. The laws which were given at that time for the life of Israel were called the 'Book of the Covenant'.

The making of the covenant was a recognition that, if a society is to work, it requires a common structure of law to give a framework for living. The absolute centre of the covenant, the Ten Commandments, crystallized the duty of God's people to 'serve God only' and honour others in the community. Jesus was later to make love the heart of the law: 'You must love God with all your heart and your neighbour as yourself.'

The covenant was produced to give a pattern for life. It is as if God says, 'You belong to me; this is how I want you to live. Pattern your life on mine.' And so the covenant reflects the character of God. When we apply this to law in the community, it is clear that we need to have laws, or guidelines, which are going to be standards, allowing us to grow into full dignity as human beings. If the laws are either too restrictive or too lax, they will restrict our development.

Law stands as a model for people when it enshrines good values and fine moral standards. But it will always remain an external standard. It cannot change us inwardly. Its enforcement may send people to prison, but it cannot make us new people with the moral ability to live well.

Paul's understanding of Old Testament law was that although it was good and honourable, in the end it condemned people as sinners. It needed the gospel to make it really effective. Only by trusting in Jesus

MORRIS STUART

One Stock, One People, One City

The central Christian view of race is that there is only one race: the human race! As the apostle Paul said to the Athenians, 'God created every race of men of one stock to inhabit the whole earth's surface.' At the pivotal points where God dealt with humanity—when he created us, when he re-created us in Christ—humankind is presented as indivisible in terms of race or colour.

Race today is not thus understood. Groups of human beings are divided today into superficial 'racial' categories: black, brown, white, red, coloured. The Bible uses other categories: nation, culture, religion and clan. This shows that the important differences in humanity are cultural, not biological. Physical characteristics are simply an—unimportant—fact of life. ('Can the Ethiopian change his colour . . .?') Racial differences are part of the variety and goodness of God's creation.

One people

God's purpose is to bring a new humanity into being. To Abraham was given the promise that through his descendants all the nations of the earth would be blessed. In Jesus, the wall of hostility between peoples was broken down, making them one people.

Reconciliation is the life-style of the new humanity. The church is called to show it. 'Reconciliation' is not the same as 'integration', which usually means making a racial minority conform to the cultural expectations of the dominant racial group.

'God was in Christ reconciling the world to himself . . . and has committed to us the work of reconciliation,' wrote Paul. This is a call to turn belief in reconciliation into daily political, social and economic reconciling. Early Christian communities took this seriously. The leadership of the congregation at Antioch, comprising Africans, Jews and an aristocrat, reflected its multi-racial, multi-cultural and multi-class composition.

Racial injustice and tension have not just happened, they have been generated by the actions and attitudes of people and societies. Racism expresses itself most effectively and disastrously through the structures of society, affecting its entire fabric. Apartheid in South Africa; continuing injustice toward black, brown and red people in the United States of America; the denial of justice to the original peoples of Canada, Australia and parts of South America, are all expressions of sinful structural racism. The Bible teaches that the church is to resist such structures, mainly by living as a reconciled community, but also through speaking out and taking action.

One city

In the Bible, liberation and reconciliation belong together. When the Israelites were liberated from Egypt, they were made into one nation. By his death and resurrection, Jesus freed us from all evil forces that make for division, and reconciled us to God and to each other.

God enters the experience of the racially oppressed, breaks down the hostility of racism and liberates them. At the same time, he comes in judgment on structures of racial oppression and those who benefit from them. If reconciliation between races is ever to happen, those who discriminate need to repent and those discriminated against must be set free. Reconciliation and liberation, love and justice belong together. And reconciliation is costly.

The Christian hope is of one city, the New Jerusalem of justice and peace; of liberated and repentant men and women in reconciled relationships, from every race, tribe, nation and language. Those who share the hope of this city will practise its values now. When they do, their cities may be changed.

Christ and allowing his Spirit to fill us can we experience release from guilt and have the power to live life as it was meant to be, and as the law expressed it.

The Future of Humanity

The Christian view of humanity is strikingly different from secular views, because it brings God into the picture. We are not alone in an indifferent and hostile universe. We are made for a relationship with the Creator of all. This conviction has a powerful effect on the way we live now. But it also has profound implications for our future, as individuals and as a species.

We live at a point in time when many seriously question whether any worthwhile human life will continue into the next century. 'Doom' is the highlight for many pictures of the future.

In the face of this prevailing gloom, the Christian faith says confidently that this is God's world and he will maintain his control over his creation. If we abuse the stewardship we have been given, then one day God will remove it from our grasp. But that does not mean the end of God's plan for the world.

Indeed, Christians declare boldly that God is working his purposes out in creation and one day he is going to restore all things to himself. Humanity's future is but part of a bigger plan, encompassing all things. We must not be so human-centred as to imagine everything pivots on us, but rather remember that all things revolve around God.

If Christians affirm the well-being of our species within the purposes of God for all things, we also affirm the destiny of the individual. We believe it is God's wish that humanity should enjoy his presence for ever. But then what do we make of death? It cuts short our potential; it breaks our relationships; it is one of humankind's most implacable enemies.

We may be told that biological death is an inevitable fact in a changing universe, but this does not mean it comes naturally to us. Quite the reverse in fact. It comes as an invasion of our nature, a sick joke which makes nonsense of our values, ideals and standards. Death is a limitation we cannot accept. The Bible says of God: 'You have set eternity in our hearts.' Our nature protests at something which cuts us off in midstream.

It is on this 'unfinished' aspect of our natures that the Christian faith has a great deal to share with the secular world. We are made for an eternal relationship with God. Our life in this space-time existence is limited, but for those who know God and want to share his life, there is eternity to enjoy his company. Humanity is never finished as far as God is concerned. He has plenty of time for us.

God longs for us to enjoy life of an entirely new quality and dimension. Even our best moments of experiencing God, of spiritual insight, of theological knowledge, ecstasy in prayer and so on, are but faint and fleeting foretastes of a full and lasting joy to come.

We often look at our young children, smile to see them growing up, but know how far they still have to grow before we can really call them mature. Just so God looks at us and shakes his head at the difference between today's reality and what one day will be, when all the potential of the image of God is fulfilled.

Man is incommensurably precious, because God loves him and Jesus died for him and the Spirit can, in the full sense, make a man of him.

F. R. Barry

For further thinking

QUESTION 1

What does it mean to be 'human'? Can the question be answered without reference to the spiritual side of our nature?

QUESTION 2

What is humanity's responsibility as 'steward of creation'? Should the biosphere be simply left as it is, as many aboriginal peoples believe? Or are there responsible ways of exploiting it for the general good?

QUESTION 3

Imagine a person marooned from birth on a desert island, living a completely solitary life. Would such a being be fully a person? Or is relationship with other people a necessary part of being a person? What Christian principles shaped your answer?

QUESTION 4

Does human creativity reflect God's creativity? How does our creativity influence those parts of our life not devoted to work?

BIBLE REFERENCES

The Image of God

Genesis 1:26; 9:6; Romans 8:29; 1 Corinthians 11:7; 15:49; 2 Corinthians 3:18; 4:4; Philippians 2:5–10; Colossians 1:15; 3:10; Hebrews 1:3; James 3:9

Male and Female

Genesis 1:27; 2:7, 18–25; 3:14–20; Joel 2:28–29; Matthew 19:4; Luke 7:36–50; 8:1–3; John 4:5–42; 20:1–18; 1 Corinthians 11:3–16; Galatians 3:28; 1 Peter 3:4

The State

Nehemiah 2:1–8; Isaiah 10:5–6; 45:1–8; Jeremiah 29:7; Daniel 7:23–27; Nahum 3:16–19; Mark 12:13–17; John 19:10–11; Acts 5:27–29; 17:26; 19:35–41; Romans 13:1–7; Philippians 3:20; Colossians 2:15; 1 Timothy 2:1–4; 1 Peter 2:13–17; Revelation 11:15; 18:1–24

DAVID GILLETT

A Flawed Humanity

CHAPTER 16

Men and women have always found it difficult to get to know God. They have felt an inward urge to be at one with him, yet they sense that he is somehow hidden from them. We are often aware of an attraction to be with God and to get back to him. We feel that something in us knows what fellowship with God is like. Many religions are aware of this feeling. There are many different stories of a golden age in our past, where God and humanity lived in harmony together. There is widespread acknowledgement that in some way we have fallen a long way from God.

Throughout history people have suggested many reasons for this human problem. Some have said that it is our physical bodies that hold us back from God. If only we could escape, they say, into some other non-physical, 'transcendental' realm, then we would find God. Others believe that our problem is ignorance. If only we could discover enough about God, they believe, than our problems with him would be over.

The Christian diagnosis

The Bible, on the other hand, declares that the root cause of our problem is sin. We have an inner tendency, even a desire, to go our own way rather than God's. It is this that causes our sense of alienation. As God is holy and completely perfect, human sin erects a barrier between ourselves and God.

The prophet, Jeremiah, wrote: 'Who can understand the human heart? There is nothing else so deceitful; it is too sick to be healed.' Jesus agreed with this diagnosis of our problem. He taught that it is from inside, from our hearts, that come all the evil ideas that lead us to do wrong. This stands in strong contrast to those today who blame 'outside' factors such as the environment or lack of education.

If God is perfect and he made humanity, why are we sinful and cut off from our Creator? This is one of the most basic questions Christianity has to answer. In reply to it, the Bible does not advance a theory or a philosophy of the origin of evil. Instead it tells a story: the story of how Adam and Eve fell from the perfect relationship with God which they originally had. This story, in Genesis 2 and 3, points to an event right at the beginning of our existence on earth. It goes back long before recorded history began.

Humanity's first sin

Adam and Eve represent people as God intended them to be. They had no desire to sin, no experience of disobedience, and lived in full and open fellowship with God, with each other, and with the rest of creation. God did not create them to be like robots, programmed to obey his every word of command. He wanted men and women to obey him by their own free choice, and so he gave them responsibility for making their own decisions.

He told Adam and Eve that they could eat freely from any tree in the garden, except from the tree of knowledge of good and evil. If they ate from that one, then they would die. God gave people the responsibility of being obedient, and he also explained the consequences of disobedience. Clearly, he did not intend to keep humanity perfect by protecting us from every opportunity to sin. Yet he had also created Adam and Eve with the ability to remain completely free from sin and thus live their lives in obedience to him.

In the event, the couple decided to disobey. They listened to the suggestion of the serpent and ate from the forbidden tree. As a result of this 'original sin', they were banished from God's presence. Nothing sinful

Whatever name we call it, [humanity's fall] is a real happening. And ever since, men have continued to sin. The fatal thing about the fall is its continuity; the repetition of that initial decision to be independent by every human being that has come into the world.

D. R. Davies

can co-exist with God's holiness. No longer would they or any other human being experience the perfect freedom of God's creation. Apart from Jesus, no one since Adam and Eve has known complete and open fellowship with God. There are many other consequences of this original act of rebellion, but the heart of the human problem is this separation from God caused by sin.

Inherited sin

Since humanity's fall, everyone inherits an inclination to sin and a desire to go his or her own way rather than to obey God. Human beings are sinful by nature. There is no need to teach a child to do wrong; it comes naturally to everyone.

Jesus talked about us being slaves of sin. He meant that we cannot free ourselves from falling into sin. We can try to do better, and we often succeed, but we cannot altogether escape the bias to sin which affects every one of us. The apostle Paul experienced this inability to live up to the standards which he desired for himself. He was continually aware of being a more sinful person than he wanted to be.

I do not understand what I do; for I don't do what I would like to do, but instead I do what I hate.

Paul's experience of conflict, from Romans 7

Theologians have described our condition since the fall as one of 'total depravity'. They do not mean that everything about us is totally corrupt or that we are as bad as we possibly can be. They mean that every part of human nature is affected by the pull towards sin. There is no area within human life where people can always think purely or act rightly.

There have been Christians who have tried to paint a more pleasant picture of our nature. They have suggested that we can all be sinless and live in perfect fellowship with God if we so choose. But both human experience and the teaching of the Bible deny this, and the church has consistently renounced these falsely optimistic views. If the sickness of human sin is to be dealt with properly, then it is essential to face the full facts of the diagnosis. God's Son had to die to bring humanity back to God. That one fact shows the full seriousness of human sin.

Each person's own sin

Although we are all born with a sinful nature, we each remain responsible for every act of sin and disobedience that we commit. We like to think that, if we had been in Adam's place, we would have obeyed God. But every time we do wrong we confirm our solidarity with the step of disobedience taken by Adam and Eve. We show that we would have done the same.

In fact, the story of Adam and Eve is not just about how it all began; it also describes how temptation leads every human being into sin. The author of the story understood well the psychology of temptation. He was writing as much about himself as about Adam and Eve. He describes the doubt that comes into the mind: 'It won't matter this once, it is not really so bad.' The author knew about that persistent voice in the mind that convinces us to act against our better judgment. Once convinced, we concentrate on the attractions of the particular temptation: 'It would be nice... why not?' Finally, with our conscience suitably silenced, we go our own way. Then, unless we have become very used to a particular sin, we feel pangs of guilt and shame. The experience of Adam and Eve is common to everyone.

There are many ways of describing sin, but the one that the Bible uses most often means 'missing the mark', or falling below the standard God requires. A person can be held to be just as guilty for failing to do what God requires, as for deliberately disobeying his commands. Jesus taught that sins in the imagination are just as sinful as evil actions. Hatred is against God's law as well as murder, and lustful thoughts as well as adultery. But perhaps the most devastating effect of sin is that, when human beings leave God out of the picture, we start playing God ourselves, shaping our lives and our world as we want rather than as God planned.

Although all sin is against God and equally wrong, there is one sin that is described as especially serious. Jesus named this 'sinning against the Holy Spirit'. He was referring to the person who makes a

RUTH ETCHELLS

The Human Dilemma in Modern Literature

'One of the thieves was saved. It's a reasonable percentage, Gogo.'

'What?'

'Suppose we repented.'

'Repented what? . . . Our being born?'

A snatch of dialogue from one of the best known plays of the twentieth century, Samuel Beckett's *Waiting for Godot.* It highlights for us a number of characteristics strongly present in the literature of our time:

- ☐ **A profoundly serious subject matter**, concerned not only with life and death but, inextricably linked with these, salvation and damnation.
- ☐ **A tone that it desperately witty**, comically despairing.
- ☐ **A searching of the nature and limits of human responsibility**—'Suppose we repented.' 'Our being born?'
- ☐ **A frustrated anger** at the seeming ambiguity of the evidence for salvation and the Saviour who might effect it. And bitterness at how arbitrary this so-called 'grace' is, which disposes of some to death and hell and others to life and light, with no apparent reasonable cause. 'One of the thieves was saved. It's a reasonable percentage . . .'

Coming to get you

Whatever else may be said of the literature of the last fifty years, it cannot be described as trivial. It records a consciousness profoundly disturbed, a widespread sense of spiritual dislocation. Franz Kafka perhaps indicates best the direction in which the century's literature was to develop.

In Kafka's *The Trial*, the central figure, a sort of 'Everyman' who embodies the contemporary consciousness, is under arrest. He does not know his crime, nor when it will be judged, nor what the evidence is. He is even uncertain about the nature of the court. He makes sporadic attempts to influence the judgment in his favour, but lapses into furtive and hasty sexual relationships, into incoherence in self-defence, and finally into a loss of will which leads him to self-doubt. A kind of weary fatalism overtakes him. In the penultimate chapter he wanders into the cathedral and meets a priest there who summarizes his position.

The sense of being on trial, of being judged guilty in some sense which the human spirit ambivalently both rejects and accedes to, because to be born may be to be guilty, this is the sickness that modern literature probes. This is also seen in the power of much of Harold Pinter's drama.

Among many other modern dramatists, Pinter disturbs his audiences by exploring the hidden knowledge of guilt that all share. His 'comedies' are menacing because their theme is that of the knock on the door, the interrogation scene, the secret circumstance, relationship or weakness that will expose the individual to those 'who are coming to get you'.

How is the success to be explained of such movements as the Theatre of Cruelty and even the Theatre of the Absurd? It stems from this private and yet corporate knowledge of vulnerability to merciless judgment: we feel guilty on the one hand and doubt whether we are really accountable on the other.

For some writers it is the state of feeling judged which is itself the burden. By contrast, the desperation seems for some to be even greater when the divine judgment throne appears vacated, as in the quotation from Arthur Miller.

Coming of age

This is an ambivalence modern literature records. For some, to be left to the mercy of our own self-judgments is trouble beyond belief. For others, it is making 'good' and 'bad' into gods which is the real sin; this was particularly true of the sixties, when there was violent rejection of revealed or imposed standards. In such a view, human beings must, in 'coming of age', take responsibility ourselves for what we judge to be right or wrong, sin or virtue, and not throw the responsibility on some (man-created) 'god'. John Osborne in drama and Kingsley Amis in poetry and novels fairly reflected this kind of viewpoint. So did, for instance, Stevie Smith, as in her poem, *'Was he married?'*.

This comparatively hopeful mood which saw humanity as capable of forming its own moral laws produced many social and political plays and novels: Arnold Wesker's, for instance. But it found its focus primarily in human relationships.

D. H. Lawrence had established powerfully the potential dignity, integrity, subtlety and richness of the relationship between men and women, and his successors from Iris Murdoch to Susan Hill have with the greatest sensitivity explored it. Human loving in all its varied forms became the main 'good' to be set against gathering uncertainties. But this theme, too, showed itself subject to betrayal and that inexorable sense of guilt, and writers like John Fowles in *The Magus* and *The French Lieutenant's Woman* exposed the manipulation, selfishness and predatoriness of much that passes for love.

A cry for redemption

In such a comparatively dark context three writers stand out, one American, one English and one Russian. The Russian, Alexander Solzhenitsyn, challenges the self-indulgent and introspective West with his account of human integrity and compassion surviving the worst that people could do to each other. Behind his books lies a triumphant Christian faith.

In America Saul Bellow wrote of 'The contract . . . which in his heart each man knows. As we all know, Lord, we know, we know, we know.' He probed what it might mean for human beings to live under divine 'contract', with its requirement of penitence and redemption. Finally, William Golding, after tracing 'the end of innocence' and 'the darkness of man's heart' in his earliest books, accurately diagnosed in *Darkness Visible* the violence and despair of the world in which we live, in which terrorism flourishes.

The secret of the power desired is 'outrage', so one of the main characters discovers. What makes outrage possible is that nothing has any meaning, the world is 'unravelling'.

We are very close here to that absolute evil which Milton long ago made Satan choose: 'Evil be thou my good.' But against it Golding sets a redemptive and sacrificial glory where God intervenes in the human dilemma through his chosen messenger. A man cries out for redemption, and Golding provides a vision of the God who redeems: 'gold as the fire and stern . . . and the smile round the lips was loving and terrible . . .' The sinner cries out, 'The thing they all want without really knowing it—yet that it should be you . . . who really loved me! I tried to throw it away, you know, but it wouldn't go . . . Help me!'

But this is a rare moment of vision in modern literature. More typical is Tom Stoppard's university vice-chancellor in *Jumpers* (one of a number of comically sardonic university anti-heroes of the period). He summarizes that sad half-hope which is all that can be achieved by the twentieth century, with its longing for, and lack of belief in, God's word of saving love: 'Do not despair—many are happy much of the time; more eat than starve, more are healthy than sick, more curable than dying; not so many dying as dead; and one of the thieves was saved.'

deliberate decision to base his life on evil, as though it were good, and who considers the actions of Jesus to be the work of the devil.

Can the devil be blamed?

When people are accused of sin, they have a distinct tendency to make excuses for themselves and, if possible, to blame someone else. This happened in the story of Adam and Eve. Adam blamed Eve and she blamed the serpent! The Bible later identifies the serpent with the devil or Satan, God's arch-enemy in the spiritual realm. But it never allows us to pass all blame for sin to him. We sin because of our own evil desire. Satan merely works on this trait in us.

Satan is portrayed in the Bible as the leader of the spiritual forces that are at war with God. He was himself at one time a good spirit who, because of his own pride, rebelled against God. He personifies all that is evil and opposed to God. His commitment is to hinder the growth of the kingdom of God and generally to advance the cause of evil in the world.

Some Christians feel that we can no longer believe in the existence of Satan as a personal being. They hold that this is merely a primitive way of describing the evil principle at work within the world. But Jesus himself spoke very definitely of Satan as a personal spiritual being. In fact we see the activity of Satan most clearly in the ministry of Jesus.

Satan's influence is certainly considerable, and he often appears to be in control, but his power is limited. The battle between good and evil is not an equally-balanced contest. Satan is part of creation and his operations are limited by God. He works mainly by cunning and obstruction, whereas God is all-powerful. Jesus showed the clear difference between God's power and Satan's intrigues. By a word of command he was always able to overcome the influence of Satan in a person's life. The crucifixion of Jesus is seen as the decisive moment of victory over Satan. Although he is still active in the world, he is already destined to be banished for ever at the end of the age.

Sin will be punished

It is often said that, because God is a God of love, he will forgive everyone in the end. This idea is very attractive, but it gains no support in the teaching of Jesus. He taught that God loves us all and wants us to come back to him, but, if we do not, we will be punished and cut off from him for ever.

God shows his love by extending to us all, through Jesus Christ, the invitation to turn to him in repentance. He also gives people the whole of their lives on earth in which to leave behind their sin and turn to God. But after this life is over everyone must face the judgment of God.

Judgment is also experienced throughout life on this earth. God has so ordered creation that judgment is often a natural consequence of sin. What a man sows he also reaps, said Jesus. Also at times when God himself chooses, he intervenes in direct judgment on individuals or nations. But both of these are temporary and incomplete ways in which the fullness of God's justice is worked out. There is much sin and evil in this world that seemingly goes unpunished. It is not until the final judgment that all will be put right. Then we shall see the total victory of good over evil and their final separation.

Because the judge is God himself, we can be confident that, at that last judgment, everything will be absolutely just. Everyone will be judged on the basis of what they have known of God and his laws. Those who have never heard of God's written law will be judged by what they can see of God and his standards from the evidence of the world around them. Their conscience also will have indicated to them what is right and wrong.

God has provided Jesus Christ as the answer for human sin. This means that everyone will be judged on the basis of his or her relationship to Jesus. If people refuse to accept God's offer of forgiveness through Christ in this life, then they will themselves bear the responsibility for their own judgment.

JACQUES ELLUL

Modern Idolatry

An idol in the Bible is always a representation of something real that people take for God. They may offer it love, worship, prayers, offerings; they may hope for answers to prayer or protection... In other words, idolatry is the tendency in humanity to assign a religious or sacred value and power to something natural.

It is not wrong to make a statue of a person or an animal, any more than it is wrong to have a love for things, or for animals, or for nature. What is evil, the Bible tells us, is to confuse two different realities. Isaiah tells us that an idol is only a piece of wood. But for the one who worships it an idol is not prized for itself. It is the symbol of a religious reality, of a god.

People today are generally of the opinion that these idolatrous, pagan cults have gone from our lives. No longer do we worship animal images, and in the Roman Catholic Church a careful distinction is drawn between what is offered to a saint or to the Virgin and worship given to God.

Yet, without being aware of it, our developed world is filled with idols. They are not the same as those in, say, African religions. We have our own. A text from the Bible may be a pointer to what they are. Paul writes that 'Covetousness is idolatry'. In other words, love of money, the desire to have more and more of it, trust in money—this is idolatry.

Ultimate security

We need to ask some precise questions:

- ☐ In whom, or in what, do we place our trust (our faith)?
- ☐ Where do we look for security and happiness?
- ☐ Whom do we expect to guarantee our future?
- ☐ What do we think can guard our liberty?
- ☐ Whom do we believe on the subject of truth?
- ☐ How do we explain our origins?

If we are honest we will see very quickly that, even if we are Christians, even if we pray, *in reality* we are looking to other certainties and other truths. And this is where our idolatry lies.

- ☐ We believe that **money** is our best guarantee. It is this which gives us confidence for our latter years, or allows us to be happy—money together with insurance.
- ☐ We believe that **the state** is the agent of our security. From it we expect justice, good organization, even truth. This is true of various types of state; there is an idolatry of liberal democracies as well as of communist states. But it must be said that communism is a whole system of idolatry. Many studies have shown how communism is a real religion, with its holy books (Marx); its clergy (the party); its paradise (the promise of world communism coming soon); its criteria for orthodoxy and heresy and its worship, (the cult of personality, as of Stalin, Mao, Tito...). We are looking at a highly effective idolatry—although capitalism makes a strong rival.
- ☐ Again we make an idol of **science**. Here is the road to truth, we believe. And we look to science to resolve all our problems. We expect it to lead us to our destiny, to account for our origins, and to explain everything else. And this idolatry (the attitude of the ordinary non-scientist rather than of most scientists) replaces love for the God of Jesus Christ.

These are, I believe, the three great, modern idolatries: money, the state, science. None of them, of course, is evil in itself, any more than were the bulls and eagles of earlier times. What makes them idols is our idolatrous attitude towards them, which renders them totally opposed to God, radically evil.

Finally we must include some popular modern beliefs; the idolatry of the guru, the prophet, the modern myth-maker, all mushrooming in an amazing way. It has to be clearly stated that all these without exception fall under God's condemnation on all idolatry and false religion. There cannot be room in the human heart both for the God of Jesus Christ and for the love of any of these powers.

Judgment is final

Once God has passed his judgment on an individual, that person's state is fixed for the whole of eternity. There is no retrial. The punishment is eternal. Jesus wanted to offer the clearest possible warning, and so his teaching about hell is very plain. It is the place of eternal punishment that awaits all those who die without Christ. He uses very vivid imagery to describe it: eternal fire; a fire that cannot be extinguished; a furnace where people will cry and grind their teeth; a place of continual decay where God destroys both the soul and the body; a place of deepest darkness.

None of these phrases is to be taken as a literal description. Hell is not a physical place, such as we know the earth to be. Hell is the eternal state of all those who are excluded from God's presence. The strong language emphasizes the dreadful fact of judgment and that, once pronounced, it is final and will never be altered.

Many Christians are undecided about the exact nature of this final state of judgment. Some believe eternal judgment means that those who are excluded from God's presence live eternally conscious of their banishment. Others hold that eternal punishment means complete annihilation. On this view, punishment is eternal, not in the sense that individuals experience its agony for ever, but because, once given, there is no possibility of ever going back on it. Everything is over; individual existence is forfeited for ever.

God wants everyone to escape this future condemnation. He has provided the complete answer to it in Jesus Christ and, consequently, it can be said that God sends no one to hell. We send ourselves when, in this life, we refuse to accept God's offer of free forgiveness.

Judgment and hell are a dark reality, but they do not stand at the centre of Jesus' teaching about human destiny. 'God did not send his Son into the world to be its judge,' said Jesus, 'but to be its saviour.' He holds out to all people the opportunity to accept from him the glorious privilege of knowing God in heaven, of becoming part of a new creation in which sin and darkness are no more.

For further thinking

QUESTION 1

A traditional Christian explanation of where sin comes from brings in 'the world, the flesh and the devil'. Is this explanation still valid and helpful? Are there particular temptations which come from one of the three more than the others?

QUESTION 2

If we inherit a tendency to sinfulness, can we be held responsible for our sin?

QUESTION 3

If you had to focus on one aspect of modern life which leads people into idolatry, which would you select?

BIBLE REFERENCES

Sin

Genesis 3:1–7; 4:7; 6:5–7; Exodus 32:21–30; Leviticus 4:3, 13, 27; 5:1–6; 1 Kings 8:34; 15:30; 2 Chronicles 25:4; 28:10; Nehemiah 1:6; Psalms 32:1–5; 51:5–9; 103:10; Proverbs 10:12; 14:34; Isaiah 1:16–18; 38:17; 53:10–12; Jeremiah 5:23, 25; 17:9–10; Ezekiel 3:20; Daniel 9:16; Micah 1:5; Matthew 1:21; 3:6; 26:28; Mark 1:4; 2:5–7; 7:14–23; John 1:29; 3:16–21; Acts 2:38; Romans 3:23–25; 5:12–13; 6:1–6; 8:2–3; Galatians 1:4; 2:17–21; Titus 3:11; Hebrews 1:3; 7:27; 10:2; 1 Peter 2:22–24; 3:18; 1 John 1:7–10; 3:8

CHAPTER 17

VINAY SAMUEL AND CHRIS SUGDEN

A Spoiled Creation

> In the excitement over the unfolding of his scientific and technical powers, modern man has built a system of production that ravishes nature, and a type of society that mutilates man.
>
> *E. F. Schumacher*

'Mummy, I don't want to die,' says a small three-year-old boy. It does not take long for human beings to learn to protest at the unfairness of life. Why do suffering, sickness and death come uninvited and unexplained? Why do poverty, war and race riots disfigure human society?

The view of the Bible, the source of Christian belief, is that we do not find life on earth in the same condition as when God made it. God did not intend human life to be marked by conflict, suffering and death. A spoiling has taken place on earth as a result of our rebellion against our Maker.

Humanity's fall has corrupted all our relationships:

- It **separated humanity from fellowship with God**. Instead of worshipping a being greater than ourselves, we tend to make idols of what we ourselves have made.
- The fall has **corrupted people's relationships with each other**. Instead of being brothers and sisters to one another, people have become rivals and enemies. Instead of serving each other, people try to enslave one another. Instead of being companions to men, women become their property to be bought and sold, and sex objects to be seduced and discarded.
- The fall has **spoiled our relationship with the good earth** we were commissioned to supervise and develop. Instead of finding nature a willing and co-operative partner, our task of coaxing its fruits is a grim and often painful struggle.

The wholeness, harmony and integration which God intended between each part and member of the created order has been shattered. People are at war with God, with other people, with nature and within themselves. All relationships tend to be self-interested and destructive of wholeness and harmony.

In the midst of the corruption and spoiling of God's good creation, the Christian hope is that both humanity and the world are destined for a glorious future and not for the dustbowls of infinity. In Paul's words: 'In the end the whole created life will be rescued from the tyranny of change and decay, and have its share in that magnificent liberty which can only belong to the children of God.'

God's final purpose is to restore the harmony he intended. He has already addressed the spoiling of this wholeness in the life, death and resurrection of Jesus Christ. In union with him, individuals, societies and nature itself can now taste in anticipation the final wholeness which is their destiny.

The human condition

The suffering, sickness, ageing and death which men and women experience affect their whole being in body, mind and spirit. Besides bringing physical pain, sickness separates people from their fellows through disability or risk of infection. In some societies, people fear contact with those whose sickness marks them as ill-starred or under the anger of the gods. Elsewhere, the mentally ill and the elderly are kept in special homes. Death brings the final separation from the human family.

Death haunts people throughout life. A common human response is to feel that all our effort is finally futile. It pushes some people to seek contact with the dead through mediums. Fear that we are creatures of a malevolent fate drives others to consult astrologers and fortune-tellers. People seek every possible avenue to gain information about their future in the hope that they can control it.

Another tragic indication of humankind's corruption is our possession by evil forces. Instead of being in conscious control of ourselves in the service of our creator, people become the unwilling lair of demonic forces. The depth of human corruption is seen in Satan-worship and contracts with evil spirits, where people willingly worship and cooperate with their destroyer.

People have devised a number of philosophies to cope with death, suffering and evil. Indian religion and Greek philosophy have both seen suffering as a purely material phenomenon from which human beings can hold their real selves separate. Our real self is a spark of the divine within us that is not subject to suffering. Suffering is illusory.

A second view is that suffering is an individual's direct punishment by God, or fate, for their sins in this life or a previous one. Such suffering is sometimes seen as a means of atonement. Secular philosophies, such as Greek Epicureanism or modern materialism, urge that the highest human good is pleasure and happiness, and the worst evil is suffering. Suffering has no merit, value or purpose. It is futile and should be avoided at all costs.

Christian thinking has sometimes been dominated by these views. In one direction it has promoted a life-denying asceticism, a process of self-punishment, and, in the other, the pursuit of happiness.

The general biblical view is that suffering in the world is the result of God's judgment on all human rebellion. This applies to the whole human condition; it does not mean that an individual's suffering is God's judgment on their own personal sin. As a result of the fall, human beings have become frail and perishable creatures, whose final perishable nature will be revealed at the last judgment.

In the Old Testament an entire book, Job, is devoted to the suffering of a righteous person. Suffering is not illusory; it is very real. Job brings his suffering in protest to God. The message of the book is that, if God allows suffering to touch his children, it must be with a purpose. That purpose is not to punish someone directly for personal sin. The suffering of God's people was seen, especially in the Psalms, as part of God's plan to refine faith and restore the wholeness of human life.

Jesus devoted considerable time to addressing human suffering. He healed the sick and raised the dead. His miracles of healing were signs that God was at work to bring in his kingdom, the restoration of his whole creation. Jesus' ministry showed that men and women could experience God's restoration in their very bodies.

Jesus went further and himself experienced great suffering. By accepting that suffering he won a decisive victory over all the forces responsible for disharmony and suffering in all created things. He took on himself God's judgment on human rebellion, and reversed the effects of the fall.

In the light of that victory and on the basis of it, Jesus sent out his disciples to announce the good news that people could be set free from such corruption, and to demonstrate the victory by their ministry of healing. They sought to relieve human suffering and to remove its causes. When suffering would not go away, they looked to use it positively to achieve God's purposes of restoration.

Throughout history, various movements within the church have sought to set limits on the scope of God's restoration in the physical sphere. In the early church, movements strongly influenced by Greek dualism tried to restrict God's restoration to the religious or spiritual realm. The rise of science in the last three centuries has led some within the church to discount the idea that God can ever intervene in miraculous healing. Because all healing comes from God, Christians as a whole have refused to abandon the ministry they inherited from Jesus of healing for the whole person.

Men and women

The harmony of the relationship between

men and women is spoiled by men's domination of 'the fairer sex'. Women are regarded as subordinate and inferior. Their only role is to serve the purposes of men.

- Women are exploited **sexually**. Instead of being the subject of sexual enjoyment, finding their sexual fulfilment together with a man in marriage, they are treated as sex objects designed only to bring men pleasure. Their bodies are used to advertise everything from cigarettes to car tyres.
- Women are exploited **socially**. Men frequently preserve women's chastity on their own terms. A double standard prevails. Women are expected to remain at home chaste, but men may form a number of casual liaisons with impunity. These barriers, meant to preserve women's honour, become prison walls to restrict their freedom. They can only take part in society on terms laid down by men.
- Women are exploited **economically**. According to the Brandt report on world development, women's status very often 'prevents them from having equal access to education, training, jobs, land ownership, credit, business opportunities, and even (as mortality statistics show in some countries) to nutritious food and other necessities for survival'.

In the time of Jesus, the situation was very similar. The major tradition of Jewish teach-

RONALD SIDER

Sin in the System

Two hundred years ago in England, law-abiding, devoutly Christian mine-owners regularly hired ten-year-old children to work in their mines. The children worked for twelve to sixteen hours a day in low, muddy tunnels. The terrible conditions often led to sickness and death within a few years. The Christian mine-owner, meanwhile, made a handsome profit and sent his sons to Oxford or Cambridge. At about the same period, slave ships carried Africans to North America, where they became property to be bred and worked like animals.

Both child labour and slavery were perfectly legal in 1800. But they destroyed people by the thousands, even millions. Does that mean that sin was involved? Did slavery and child labour represent sin in the system?

Legalized oppression

Most Christians think they know what sin is. It is things such as lying, stealing, fornicating. But the Bible links sin not just to consciously-willed individual acts such as these but also to oppression of the poor.

God showed this to the prophet Amos: 'I will not revoke the punishment; because they sell ... the needy for a pair of shoes ... trample the head of the poor into the dust of the earth, and turn aside the way of the afflicted; a man and his father go in to the same maiden, so that my holy name is profaned.' Biblical scholars have shown that some kind of legal fiction underlies the phrase 'sell the needy for a pair of shoes'. This mistreatment of the poor was legal. In one breath God condemns both sexual sins and legalized oppression of the poor.

The prophet Isaiah makes the same kind of link: 'Woe to those who join house to house, who add field to field, until there is no more room, and you are made to dwell alone in the midst of the land ... Woe to those who rise early in the morning, that they may run after strong drink, who tarry late into the evening till wine inflames them.' God condemns the wealthy who amass large landholdings (doubtless at the poor's expense) along with the drunken.

The Bible also clearly teaches that laws themselves are sometimes unjust and therefore an offence against God. Psalm 94 tells us that

ing interpreted the Old Testament as affirming the subordination of women to men. Their fulfilment was to be only through men in the marriage relationship, not in their own persons. Women had few rights in marriage, being regarded as the property of their husbands. They were treated as intellectually inferior beings, were forbidden to learn religious teaching and had no civil rights.

Jesus showed that subjection was not to be the norm for women. Any headship which men exercise is to work only insofar as both men and women are subordinate to Jesus. He taught no form of headship, leadership or power other than the role of the servant who seeks the best interests of others. Jesus broke many of the laws and customs of his day that kept women in seclusion and subjection. He traced the cause of that distorted relationship to the lust of men, and provided the cure for the problem in the new life of the kingdom of God.

In God's kingdom, men's lustful gaze, which had made for women's seclusion, and men's hardness of heart, which had led them to divorce their wives, were to come to an end. In their place was to come an ability to relate to women as sisters in the family of God. A group of women went round with Jesus and, despite all the eagle eyes longing to find fault, he was never accused of immorality.

Paul wrote that 'in Christ there is neither male nor female'. Men and women are not to develop in independence of each other, or in competition, or in a relationship of master and servant. They are complementary as, in mutual subordination to Christ, they use their different roles to seek each other's best interests.

wicked governments sometimes 'make injustice legal'. Sin had penetrated into the duly authorized laws of society.

Society is held together by a complex set of written and unwritten laws, customs and common assumptions. In any society some of these laws and assumptions are good and others are bad because they harm some people and give unjust advantages to others. The powerful can often persuade courts and legislative bodies to pass laws that benefit them (as did slave traders), even though others are harmed (as were slaves). In this way, sin slips into the systems of society.

Sharing the guilt

One of the most devastating results of sin in the system is its subtlety. We tend to accept that what our society says is acceptable.

The wealthy women of Amos' day urged their husbands to earn what they needed for their affluent lifestyle. It did not bother them that their affluence depended on legal oppression of the poor—they may not have realized it very clearly. But God saw the sin in the system and sent his prophet to condemn it: 'Hear this word, you cows of Bashan ... who oppress the poor, who crush the needy, who say to your husbands, "Bring that we may drink." ' According to the Bible, to participate uncritically in unjust systems is displeasing to God.

Unfortunately, it is always easier to see the sin in social systems far removed from us. We all see quite clearly today how sin permeated the systems of child labour and slavery. We were able to discern the sin in South African apartheid or Soviet dictatorship when these things were remote from us personally. But we need to probe the social, economic and political systems nearer home, in time and space, to see if and how racial prejudice or class bias have slipped into the laws and customs of our own communities.

Are housing, education and job opportunities in our area inferior for people not of our own skin colour, for instance? Why do fifty per cent of the children in Central America die of starvation or malnutrition before the age of five at the same time that fifty per cent of the good land in Central America is used to grow export crops for affluent North Americans and Europeans? We need to look at the present plight of minorities and of the poor, and ask to what extent their problems are due to sin in the system.

Christians today need to develop a fully biblical understanding of sin. Consciously-willed individual acts such as lying and adultery are sin. But so is uncritical participation in social systems that are unjust. To resist sin means to resist both.

Throughout history, as members of a still fallen race, Christians have leant towards the Jewish tradition of subordination of women rather than towards Jesus' principles of liberation and equality. Paul illustrates the tension between Jesus' teaching, the culture of his time and the Jewish tradition. 'Hellenistic' or Greek thinking became dominant in the church. In the fifth century, Augustine regarded sexual intercourse as inherently sinful, and women as the source of temptation to such activity. Men were thought to obtain special sanctity by remaining unmarried. The formation of monastic communities was linked with this idea.

Reflecting the world at large, the church has rarely allowed women to exercise significant leadership. Its hierarchy has been exclusively male. The contribution of women has at best been limited to serving women and children. Their contribution to the wider family of the church has been restricted, limiting both their own greater fulfilment and the good of the Christian community. But here and there Jesus' tradition of liberation and equality has been expressed.

In India Christians pioneered the education of women, and trained women to be doctors and nurses. The religious orders and the modern missionary movement have given great scope to single women to bring their service, often in areas where no men would go. Of all missionaries in the world today, seventy-two per cent are women. And in some churches women are now admitted into the ordained ministry.

JOHN GLADWIN

Power and Powerlessness

One of the great problems of our world is the division between the few who possess considerable power over life and property and the many who are almost powerless in both respects. There are millions in our world who experience unending poverty and whose life is dependent on the choices made by others. If we want to change this, we need to understand power.

The Bible provides us with an understanding of power and powerlessness which challenges Christian people to take action:

- In Christian faith **absolute authority and power belong to God alone**. God does not use power in arbitrary and unreliable ways. He always acts in character when he exercises authority. We can trust God to be consistent with all that he has shown himself to be, especially in his Son Jesus Christ. It is people who are unreliable and inconsistent in their use of power and authority.
- Any power and authority which people have is to be understood as **a gift from God**. He made people in his own image, to order and control the life of the world. And he gave them power to carry out this task. This aspect of human nature is not the privilege of the few but the God-given right of the whole of humanity. All people are meant to have a share in this work and to practise responsibility accordingly.
- If power is a gift of God to everyone he has made, then all people who exercise power are to be **accountable to God for its use**. It is God who possesses absolute right. We act as trustees of all that he has given us. Accountability is basic to any Christian understanding of power.

When, as must happen in organized societies, some people take on authority for particular tasks, ways must be found to keep them accountable for their stewardship. This is a reflection of our ultimate accountability to God for all that we do with his gifts. So the law must set limits to power and hold people within those limits. Christians have often been to the fore in movements to ensure this happens. In the Bible no one is above the law and no one possesses absolute rights over anyone else.

- Power and authority are gifts of

In recent years the restriction on women finding their fulfilment only in female pursuits has been all but abandoned. Women's rights movements have sought to provide the means for their total development. The church is slowly becoming aware that the kingdom of God affirms a true interdependence between men and women as the route to their development as whole persons.

People in society

Instead of seeking wholeness and harmony as brothers and sisters, people in society tend to exploit each other wherever possible, even under the cloak of co-operation. This can be seen most graphically on the global scale.

At present two-thirds of the world lives in poverty. The seventy-five per cent of the world population who live in developing countries have access to very limited resources. Meanwhile the wealthy twenty-five per cent protect their wealth with a vast arsenal.

The Brandt report notes: 'More arms do not make mankind safer, only poorer. The world's military spending dwarfs any spending on development. Total military expenditures are approaching 450 billion dollars a year, while annual spending on official development aid is only 20 billion dollars. There is a moral link between the vast spending on arms and the disgracefully low spending on measures to remove hunger and ill-health in the Third World... The cost of a ten-year programme to provide for essential food and health needs in developing

God **to be used in service**. We see the supreme example of this in Jesus Christ. The eternal Son of God came among us as a servant. He did not stand on his position and protect his rights. Jesus offered his service in pursuit of the aim of the kingdom of God. He wanted to save people from death and bondage; to give them life and freedom. He shared our weakness and powerlessness, so that he could transform our experience and destroy the powers which dehumanize us and hold us captive. From Jesus we learn a pattern of service. As he served, so are we to serve.

Authority, then, must be seen as an opportunity for service in the pursuit of clear and good aims. We must ask ourselves, 'For what purpose does this power and authority exist?' If it is a good purpose, then the next question is, 'How are we to use it to serve others and bring the purpose about for them?'

The Bible carries a strong emphasis that those who possess power, position and wealth have an obligation in love to make use of these gifts in the service of the weak, the underprivileged and the poor. The powerful must launch an attack on all that holds the powerless down.

- ☐ Those to whom God gives power must **face up to the necessity of sacrifice**. Jesus accepted the cost of achieving the supreme aim of his service. He went to the cross freely, because there was no other way for salvation to be won. He was prepared to sacrifice everything to fulfil the purpose of love.

Indeed, in Christ we learn the most profound of all Christian insights that through grace the power of God is made perfect in weakness. In his readiness to experience our weakness Christ released the power of God for a weak and powerless humanity.

Those who carry power and position, and are conscious that they carry it on behalf of others and in the face of God, must be ready to yield it if that is the price of reaching the set goal.

Often in this world the powerful want to preserve their power, and they sacrifice others to do so. The gospel introduces the revolutionary thought that true love sometimes involves sacrificing position and power for the sake of others. This would enable the weak and powerless to share in the responsibilities of power and decision-making.

In our world there are unacceptable inequalities in the possession of power and responsibility. So what is most needed? Surely that those who have power should be willing to give it up, so that others may learn how to use it.

countries is less than half of one year's military spending... In East and West a very large proportion of scientists and much of the scientific resources of universities and industry are devoted to armaments.'

Why do people choose self-interest at the expense of another group? Armaments serve to protect the self-interest of a group. Few within the group feel guilty about this. Everyone moves within the same group and it is easy to be blind to its detrimental effect on those outside.

In many cultures people find their identity in and serve the interests of their own tribe, class, racial group, caste or family. Casteism in India, apartheid in South Africa and racism in the West are refined forms of group self-interest. Groups with powerful influence in society such as trades unions and professional associations pursue their own interests under the slogan of justice. But when we look for justice for our own group alone, we are willing injustice for others.

Certain ways of understanding the relationship between the individual and society also shatter the wholeness God intended for persons in community:

- Some see society as only **a collection of individuals** put together as matches in a box. People acknowledge no fundamental interdependence. Such an individualistic view of life underlies modern consumerism. The good life is to build our own corner of the

Only two groups of animals kill members of the same species wholesale—rats and men.

C. S. Lewis

DAVID SECCOMBE

The Responsibility of Wealth

For at least two-thirds of the world poverty is the chief problem. But prosperity too brings its dangers. The Bible's teaching on wealth and poverty is extremely varied. Different insights and attitudes reflect the complexity of human life. To find a balanced viewpoint and an authentic lifestyle we need to take account of it all, even the seemingly contradictory parts:

- **Wealth is a blessing.** The Bible never downgrades the value of our physical life. God created it, it is good, and eventually he will liberate it from the forces which are spoiling it. So the early giants of the faith are seen as people whom God blessed with material wealth—Abraham, Jacob, Job, David, Solomon. When God saved Israel he gave them a prosperous land as well as a relationship with himself. **Without such an affirmation of the rightness of material prosperity there is no motive for physically bettering others.** The Bible never idealizes poverty, though some later Christian movements have done this.

- **Wealth must be worked for.** God's creation does not provide our needs without our labour. We were created to care for God's world, and our fall into sin has added considerably to the burden of doing this. We are expected to work up to six days out of seven to earn our living, but we can increase our yield and decrease our workload by applying our mind to the question.

Poverty is something to be avoided, by diligence and hard work. But to make wealth the aim of our lives is dangerous. The New Testament insists that people should work to the extent of having more than their needs, and thus be able to share. Throughout history Christians have often emphasized the need for hard work. **Unless this duty it accepted, by rich and poor, there can be no hope of eliminating world poverty.** (See the article, *The poor.*)

- **Wealth carries responsibilities.** Israel was warned that if they rebelled against God and disobeyed his commands they could forfeit their material blessings. To obey God includes enjoying his creation in a wholesome way

world and look on it as isolated from the troubles of other people. So, in a world of diminishing resources, the lifeboat ethic urges that those with skills, talents and raw materials should develop them to ensure their own survival; not pour them into the bottomless pit of world poverty.

- Others give **priority to society**. The individual is a mere functionary, a cog in the machine. Technologically advanced societies tend to promote such a view through the processes of the mass media, the production line, impersonal bureaucracies. In theory they proclaim that the individual matters, but in practice they treat a person as a number on a computer print-out.

- Some communist states have tried to practise **the Marxist theory** that once society is organized along lines that are scientifically correct, the happiness of the individual is assured. Such a view denies to the individual any rights over against the state. Many dissidents in the former Soviet Union pointed out the immense suffering that is the price of such an achievement. Marxism also has no answer to the individual's own needs—for a purpose in life, a basis for identity or a hope beyond the grave.

and sharing its blessings with others. This lifestyle is enshrined in the law of Moses in commands such as to lend without interest to someone who has become needy, or to cancel outstanding debts after seven years.

Jesus too insisted that to neglect this kind of 'justice and mercy and faith' brings God's judgment. This concern led, in earlier times, to almsgiving as a Jewish and Christian virtue, and, in recent times, **to concern for development of poor communities**.

- ☐ **Wealth is dangerous.** We fallen human beings easily disregard our responsibilities, especially when wealth makes us feel less dependent on God. The rich are warned to be on their guard. Jesus warns people against greed, which attacks fallen humanity like a disease. Greed comes from the mistaken idea that real life is to be found in possessions; it leads people away from Jesus' kingdom where real life is to be found. Greed also leads to injustice and exploitation, which God hates. **Individuals, communities and societies must guard against greed and injustice if poverty is to be eliminated.**

- ☐ **Jesus' kingdom brings true wealth.** The fall has brought deprivation to humankind at every level. Infertile land, unjust laws, exploitation, laziness, robbery, sickness and accident can all cause material poverty. Jesus saw human poverty as more than a material thing: our need extends to the mental, spiritual and social areas of life.

Jesus spoke about a kingdom where there would be no more poverty of any kind. But this kingdom would only come through his suffering—he had to become poor to make us rich—and he called his followers to share in his work. This could mean suffering, poverty or persecution, but these can be joyfully endured because the outcome is great blessing for ourselves and others, and the final renewal of the whole creation.

In normal times followers of Jesus are called to put all their wealth (possessions, time, abilities, opportunities) to work for the kingdom of Jesus. This means recognizing the things that are of real, eternal value (people reconciled to God and to each other, peace, fellowship, care) and using our money (whose value in itself is temporary) to help create them. We see a practical demonstration of this when the early Jerusalem church generously shared their possessions to abolish poverty in their community. **Those who employ their wealth in the cause of Jesus will enjoy the genuine wealth of his kingdom now and eternally.**

Society: the Bible's teaching

How does the Christian faith analyse and address the spoiling of the creation through economic inequality, war and racism?

The Old Testament vision of a just society includes a just distribution and use of resources. The laws of Moses were framed both to help the Israelite community curb exploitation, and to be a model of political, economic and social justice. The land and resources of Israel were distributed equally.

Many of the laws of Moses were framed to prevent people from becoming hopelessly poor, to preserve their access to the means of making a living, and to avoid their becoming completely dependent on others. The prophets announced God's judgment on systems of land ownership which were inequitable, on rulers who did not protect the poorest, and on a religiosity which did not lead to justice. God punished the Israelites by removing them from their land and by ending their line of kings.

Jesus announced the arrival of the kingdom of God and attacked those forms and forces of evil which prevented the Old Testament vision of justice from being fulfilled. He saw the need to right all wrong relationships. And he traced the cause of these wrong relationships not only to personal sin but also to demonic powers of evil which possess persons, pervade the structures of society and infect the whole created order.

Jesus proclaimed a direct personal relationship with God, with no need for the mediation of a religious hierarchy. He renounced the use of violence for personal or political security. He rejected everything that served to maintain economic inequality, and all forms of social, racial and sexual discrimination. He displayed the bias of the kingdom of God towards those most tragically affected by the harsh effects of the sins of humanity—the powerless, the socially outcast, the sick and the poor.

Jesus gave substance to the vision of a just and whole human society, and this was one reason why he was persecuted by the established order. But in his death and resurrection, Christians believe he won the decisive victory over all evil and made it possible for human society to be liberated from every form of distortion.

In their experience of Jesus Christ through the life of his Holy Spirit, the members of the New Testament churches sought to express the harmony of a restored and just society. They expressed the work of the Spirit as they shared economic resources, as they crossed social barriers and as they used their gifts to serve one another, especially the poor. They claimed that in Christ all the divisions between Jew and Gentile, master and slave, male and female were being broken down. These communities renounced violence. They naturally attracted the weak and the vulnerable, the poor and the non-propertied classes. They gave them a home where they could experience a complete human life.

■ He [William Wilberforce] could not believe that providence, however mysterious his ways, had so constituted the world that the prosperity of one part depended on the depopulation and devastation of another.

John Pollock

Christian views of society

Jesus resisted the powers of the dominant social order, but throughout history the church has found it a difficult task to maintain a faithful witness to his vision. Christianity has been the source of inspiration to those who have undermined and overthrown injustice, but the church has also been a bastion of economic oppression, militarism and racism.

Christians interpret their own ambivalence as a continuing social consequence of the fall, in which they share responsibility and guilt with all humanity. This ambivalence has been a crucial factor subverting the effectiveness of the church's witness, vital enough to justify looking in more detail at the fluctuating Christian approaches to social and economic justice.

- **Early in Christian history**, affluent people began to enter the church without sharing their resources. Thus they undermined the basis for the new equality. Luke and James grappled with this issue to show that the church could only maintain its witness to wholeness when it was able to establish just relationships of sharing.

- Then, in AD 313, the Roman Emperor Constantine was converted and **the dominant social order became officially Christian.** Many Christians gained political power in this order, and the ban against military service was revoked. Such developments ensured that the church would become a bastion of the status quo.

- **The monastic communities**, which arose from the second century onwards, protested against such a compromise. They sought to preserve the biblical demands for equality and justice by practising individual poverty, which of course made everyone equal. They worked to relieve the sufferings of the poor, whom they saw to be victims of an unjust and exploitative system.

The wealthy often supported monasteries with their gifts. The idea behind this was that rich people could obtain salvation by their gifts to the poor. Poverty thus became a mark of God's favour, for poor people could enable rich people to go to heaven. Charity legitimized the unjust status quo. The system which produced inequality was not questioned.

- But **the medieval church** did achieve a measure of interdependence, if not equality, between people within an authoritarian feudal framework. The lords, the church and the poor had their roles in achieving what was seen as a whole, integrated society with each in their allotted station.

- **The Reformation** exposed some of the oppressive aspects of medieval society and rekindled aspects of the biblical vision of a just and equal society. It replaced the idea that we can obtain God's favour by our good works with the idea that God accepts us only on the basis of Jesus' death and resurrection. There was therefore no merit in merely being poor or in giving to the poor. Thus the causes of poverty could be addressed and challenged.

The Reformation also opposed the concept of a hierarchy of sanctity based on merit with the concept of individual equality before God based on God's grace. The legitimization of a social hierarchy was confronted by a vision of a society where all had an equal place.

Calvin in Geneva and the Radical Reformers took some bold initial steps to give reality to this vision of a new society based on God's grace. But events following the Reformation prevented the vision from being fully implemented.

Salvation by faith alone led to a strongly individual understanding of religion and a firm sense of personal responsibility. This became distorted into individualism. The initial attempt to make the vision of the kingdom of Christ a reality in human society faded. The church taught individuals to overcome their own poverty by honesty and hard work, but left the social causes of poverty for the secular authorities to cope with.

This way of thinking found its full expression in Martin Luther's teaching on 'the two kingdoms'. In the world God rules through the 'orders' of society—the rulers and the army. Their commands are given the validity of commands of God. This is the kingdom of the secular ruler, sanctioned by God.

Parallel to this is the kingdom of Christ which extends only over Christians and the church and has authority only over their personal and spiritual lives. In their secular citizenship, they are subject to the kingdom of the world. The kingdom of Christ is not expected to govern the social and political behaviour of Christians.

> Clever men, it has been remarked, are impressed by their difference from their fellows: wise men are conscious of their resemblance to them.
>
> *R. H. Tawney*

Similarly, the secular ruler is not expected to control ecclesiastical matters, but only to give support to the church in the spiritual sphere. So, in effect God has two kingdoms: the church and the world. The end result of this teaching was that many Christians in Germany found it difficult not to obey their secular ruler, even when this was Hitler.

- The growth of industrialization and the colonial expansion of **the eighteenth and nineteenth centuries** put more technology at the service of European nations and brought expanding markets within their reach. These developments further broke up the wholeness of the old agrarian societies by separating the processes of production, distribution and consumption.

The prevailing economic philosophy of laissez-faire capitalism was based on a distorted individualism; each person was free to work for his own advantage, and through the mechanism of the market such unbridled self-interest would develop the common good. The harmony of people's participation in and responsibility to the community was lost.

Large segments of the church had already accepted individualism and divorced the spiritual realm from the social and economic realm. So the church was unable to combat the evils of industrialization and colonization, such as massive exploitation of labour, with any alternative vision of society. Instead it took advantage of the fruits of the new era to increase its own numerical strength and expand its own boundaries.

It stressed one part of the Reformation vision, personal knowledge of Jesus Christ. Then it masked its failure to establish wholeness in society by stressing that in time numerical growth would produce qualitative change. Today such a legacy still influences much Christian theory and practice.

But a number of movements have sought to achieve the biblical vision for a whole, restored society:

- In the nineteenth century, **evangelistic and welfare agencies** produced schools, hospitals and orphanages, and promoted prison reform and social welfare to tackle the symptoms of poverty. William Wilberforce and Lord Shaftesbury attacked the causes of social evil with legislation to prevent exploitation through slavery in the colonies and inhuman working conditions in the factories.
- **Methodist laymen** were influential in the early days of the British Labour movement.
- **Revival movements in America** concentrated on selected social evils such as prostitution, alcoholism, slavery and racism.
- In the late nineteenth century **the social gospel movement** arose to confront the evils of laissez-faire capitalism. Its exponents identified the roots of such a system in a non-Christian view of human nature, which exalted unbridled self-interest and optimistically expected individual selfishness to produce communal benefits. The movement produced the Social Creed of the Christian churches, which was endorsed by the Federal Council of Churches in 1912. It stood for the abolition of child labour, a minimum living wage, reduced hours of labour, and an equitable division of the products of industry.
- The social gospel movement in the West was very optimistic about the possibilities for progress. **The two World Wars** showed the depth and power of human self-interest and destructiveness even in scientific, educated and 'Christian' societies. In a pessimistic reaction, many Christians abandoned hope of changing society. (Though this was

not the whole story, as witness, for example, the Iona community in Scotland, or the Life and Work aspect of the ecumenical movement.)

- In the 1960s **churches in the Third World** emerged out of the shadow of the colonial and missionary umbrella. They made the mission of Jesus Christ their own, and tackled the issues of poverty and injustice in their societies face to face. As they analyse the poverty in their countries from the perspective of the oppressed, they are now drawing on the original vision of the kingdom of God. They join hands with many Christians in Western civil rights, poverty, peace and environmentalist groups.

Their commitment is to the full mission of the church: to establish the vision of a restored humanity. This must include working for social structures which promote equality, economic structures which promote a just distribution of goods, and political structures which enable all members of society to participate in decisions which affect them.

People and nature

Originally human beings were meant to find their true place in nature as the stewards of God's creation. The Bible stresses that humanity's fall has affected the whole creation. The created order is spoilt. Nature is red in tooth and claw. Earthquakes, floods and famines destroy human life. The Bible links these to the fall, though it does not explain exactly how the one has caused the other.

Sometimes men and women treat nature as an enemy to subdue and exploit instead of a trust to nurture and develop. We probe and use its resources with no thought for the effects such depletion might have. Instead of stewarding and husbanding nature, we rape it.

The tools which people use to subdue nature become tools which rob them of their own humanity. In the West, impersonal assembly lines bore people with repetitive work and make co-operative human relationships very difficult. When people are reduced to the level of unreliable machines, they are likely to go on strike. In the sweatshops of the Third World, men, women and children are treated as so many disposable hands to keep the wheels of industry turning.

Yet there are people who refuse to control nature, and instead become its slaves. Sometimes they romanticize nature or even treat it as divine and try to coax its fruits with fertility rites; they may also proclaim a oneness with nature: it must not be altered in any way.

The Old Testament vision of 'shalom', 'peace', is that, in our work as stewards of nature, we human beings should experience unity with God and nature, community with our fellows, and fulfilment for ourselves. Humanity's final destiny will be a home on a renewed earth, at one with God and nature. The New Testament proclaims that this vision was being fulfilled through the death and resurrection of Christ, and looks forward to the renewal of the entire creation when the sons and daughters of God will be restored.

With the rise of technology in the West, the Western church has emphasized our mastery over nature at the expense of our unity with nature. The Eastern church has emphasized our unity with nature at the expense of encouraging a full exercise of our stewardship.

There is a growing awareness that resources are running down, pollution is growing, and technology is escalating out of control. This has given birth to a whole movement and literature calling for a proper and human use of the limited resources on planet earth. It stresses simpler styles of living, less waste, and a closer relationship with and respect for nature. In the biblical view, the coming of the renewed earth depends on the restoration of the children of God. For this reason the church should be vitally concerned with humanity's proper stewardship of nature.

The wholeness of humanity, society and nature under God depends on a correct understanding of the relationship of the world to God. One view sees God as a being totally separate from the world, to whom human beings must do obeisance as servants. This Greek view has heavily influenced Western Christianity. A second view sees God as totally immersed in the world, as a life-force. This view underlies many Eastern religions.

The Bible stresses that God is both transcendent, beyond the world, and immanent, within the world. God is active in the world, not only in the work of men and women subduing nature with their skills, but also in the very forces of nature which are an expression of God's creative power.

God rules the world from outside and energizes it from within. Both the world and the human community find their wholeness when people come to serve God as King, and co-operate with his Spirit who breathes through all creation. By the invasion of his kingdom into the world and the gift of the Spirit to men and women, God has made this a possibility. Its fulfilment will be in a redeemed community of people living on a transformed earth, with the returned Christ as King.

For further thinking

QUESTION 1

One way sin shows itself is in individual acts—sexual lapses, for instance, or dishonesty or cruelty. But is it also correct to speak of sin in the whole way society is structured? In the world economic system, for example?

QUESTION 2

Feminists fight against exploitation of women. What is there in the Bible's teaching to show a right relationship between women and men?

QUESTION 3

Is there a way of exercising power which does not make others powerless? What has the Bible to say on this question?

BIBLE REFERENCES

War and Peace

Exodus 15:3; Deuteronomy 1:41; 1 Samuel 17:33; 2 Samuel 1:27; 22:35; Psalms 85:10; 122:6; 147:14; Ecclesiastes 9:18; Isaiah 2:1–4; 9:6–7; 32:17; 48:22; 57:19; 66:12; Jeremiah 6:4; Ezekiel 34:25; Malachi 2:6; Matthew 24:6–8; Luke 1:79; 2:14; 19:42; Romans 3:17; 15:33; Ephesians 2:14–17; 6:15; Hebrews 7:2; Revelation 6:4

Powers of Evil

Genesis 2:9, 17; 3:5; Deuteronomy 1:39; 1 Samuel 18:10; Job 1:6–12; Matthew 4:1–11; 7:22; 12:22–29; 17:18; Mark 1:23–27; Luke 4:33–35; 8:2, 27–33; 9:1; John 8:44–48; 13:2; 1 Corinthians 5:5; Ephesians 4:27; 6:11–12; Colossians 2:8–15; Hebrews 2:14–15; 1 Peter 5:8; 1 John 3:8–10; Revelation 2:10; 12:9–10; 20:10

STRENGTH IN WEAKNESS

MYRA CHAVE-JONES

Depression

Most people have experienced depression to some degree. It can be just a mood of heaviness lasting for a short time. At the other extreme it can be a paralyzing illness which drags on for months and may need hospital treatment. The universal characteristic of depression is lethargy of body and dreariness of spirit. Everything seems to be too much trouble, and not worth the effort anyway. In severe cases, depression can feel like intense emotional pain which goes on endlessly with no hope of light at the end of the tunnel.

Depression has several possible causes:

- ☐ It can be a **natural reaction after prolonged strain** (which is remedied by rest).
- ☐ It may be a **chemical imbalance** which can be put right by chemotherapy.
- ☐ It is frequently the normal reaction to **the loss** of a loved one, a job, a house, or some significant person or object which represents security.
- ☐ Sometimes there seems to be **no identifiable cause**; it just wells up from a person's deep inner life. This type of depression is the hardest to bear, because it appears irrational. Psychotherapy can often help with the emotional disturbance which is going on below the surface.

Depression is a very strong force. Its presence cannot be denied, although a person may not recognize it for what it is. It affects patterns of eating and sleeping; diminishes interest in sexual and other activities; robs people of the ability to make decisions. One unmistakable characteristic is the sense of failure and worthlessness. Sometimes people are only aware of being bored and not interested in life; they cannot identify underlying depression.

What is wrong?

Like all other pain, depression conveys a message that something needs attention. What that thing is will vary from person to person. Often it can be traced to unexpressed feelings of frustration and anger with another person or situation. For some reason these feelings cannot find an outlet, so they are turned inwards.

The frustration is frequently caused by an unmet need to be dependent. Thus, depression may be telling the sufferer that they need to grow in some way in personality. Certainly, it is giving a clear signal that a change of attitude is called for towards oneself and other people.

Just because people have a Christian faith this does not mean that they may not be depressed from time to time. They still remain human beings! Yet if, at the onset of depression, a person can take a firm grasp on the changeless faithfulness of God, his free forgiveness and his sure promises, this can often halt the slide into a severe episode.

The very nature of depression means that feelings are numbed. Therefore the Christian's normal sources of comfort, their life of prayer and the Bible, may seem to become meaningless.

There is no easy answer to depression, but prevention is better than cure. Prevention lies somewhere in the area of a readily growing knowledge, both intellectually and in experience of the changeless and unconditional love of God. This knowledge will enable us to stand steadily when external events or internal feelings are painful.

E.M. BLAIKLOCK

Grief

Grief is part of the common lot of humanity. The deeper one has loved the more desolate is grief. He who 'bore our griefs and carried our sorrows', became himself 'a man of sorrows and acquainted with grief'. From Jacob, laying his loved Rachel to rest at Bethlehem, on to Job, David, Paul, and the last glittering promises of God, sorrow is shown as a shadow on human life. Even Jesus, who was tried in every human testing, knew grief as human creatures know it. He wept at Lazarus' grave, and the only cause was grief.

Therefore those who suffer grief should first remember that Jesus has trodden their path, but that, if grief is death's companion, Jesus conquered death. They should read much about the resurrection, hold fast to its undoubted truth, and remember that it is because the Lord lives that we 'sorrow not as those who have no hope'.

In that faith is the supreme consolation in bereavement, God has permitted what has happened. In it lies no stroke of retribution, but ultimately a blessed purpose which one day will take shape. To doubt this represents grief's greatest temptation. In such misgiving lies combat, need for prayer and wise counselling.

Walk through the valley

Those who grieve should seek help chiefly from those who tread the same road. Let no one say that grief is sin, or continued grief a spiritual malady. There is no shame in finding the journey hard, but there is peril in not seeking a vision of a goal. Seek hope, whose offspring is faith, but from those who personally speak the words which nourish both. Hope for reunion, some meeting with God to illumine his ways.

Walk strongly in the valley of death's shadow, however painful that walk may be. Work vigorously. Healing is to be found in living to serve for all those who, in their own anguish, seek to alleviate the equal hurt of someone else. Fill what might otherwise be vacant hours of desperation with life's tasks, old and new. Activity is health. To withdraw and close heart and mind is a path to death.

Wounds do not always heal. They always scar. Old hilarity, unclouded happiness, may never return. The younger have years in which life's structure can be rebuilt. They should do so, but in wisdom and never in haste. Age may not find rebirth so easy, but the ageing have fewer years to await a consummation, years which can be rich in refined usefulness.

Memory must not be quenched, but should be purged of self-reproaching. God forgives, if there is something that needs to be forgiven. So do those we have loved and lost. Let eyes, too, be alert for God's tokens on the road, the vast love of caring friends and family, those turns of circumstance too patterned to be chance, and whose lightning stabs the gloom. God cares, God can grieve, God knows, God will guide. Moses went into 'the thick darkness—**where God was**'.

JONI EARECKSON-TADA

Physical Handicap

Looking back on the early months of my injury, it all seems so very long ago and far away. I have coped with my physical disability for over fourteen years now. The initial trauma of all that it means to be paralysed from the neck down has been resolved for many years. Yet once in a while, when I look back on the early adjustments to life in a wheelchair, I readily recall the pain of despair and the pit of depression that I wallowed in during those first few years.

The depression became even more severe as I discovered the permanency of my paralysis. When this realization began to sink in, I discovered a deep and despairing sense of hopelessness: no hope of ever walking again; no hope of ever using my hands again; no hope of enjoying a marriage with children and all those things I had so longed for and dreamed of as a young girl. I wanted to end my life and the frustration I felt at not even being able to do so only intensified my depression. I was so desperate, I even begged one of my friends to help me end it all.

What seemed to make my depression even worse was the fact that I held it in for so long during those weeks in hospital. I experienced a kind of quiet rage. I did not want to drive my family or friends away with bitterness or anger about my situation, so I held it all inside. But slowly, over the months after I went home, I began to share myself with a very small, intimate circle of friends. Once I saw their acceptance and their love, I think that melted a lot of the bitterness and it helped me deal more honestly with my depression.

Hope

First I began to understand that it is OK to be depressed. In fact it was part of the life experience that David and Moses and Solomon went through. Then I began to reconstruct real hope from the word of God, the Bible.

For instance, one thing that really helped me in the middle of my hopelessness and depression was to know that at least one day I would have a body that worked; hands that would hug and feet that would run; not an angel costume, but a glorified body, much like the kind of body Jesus had after his resurrection. He walked with his disciples, ate with them and did very earthly, human things.

It gave me a great deal of comfort to know that I had not been left alone in my hopelessness, that God had provided me the answer by his promise of a new body beyond the grave.

A part of the quiet rage I experienced was anger against God. Inwardly and very quietly I ranted and raved at him in my spirit. Now I think it is better to get angry at God than to walk away from him. It is better honestly to confront our real feelings and let him know this is how we feel—this is awful and my pillow is wet from all my tears, I am sick and tired of this and I cannot stand it one more minute. Far better than pasting on a toothpaste smile and going round gritting your teeth and pretending you are not hurting.

But admittedly I felt some guilt afterwards. I was encouraged by reading examples from the Psalms. In so many, David rants and raves and just cannot understand what God is doing. But by the end there is invariably a ray of hope—'yet will I trust in you.'

The example of Jeremiah was also an encouragement. He was terribly depressed by the horror, the battle, the invasion and the cruelty and mockery that was going on in his day. Yet Jeremiah says that God's loving kindness never ceases, his mercies are new every morning, his compassions never fail, therefore he will trust God.

These examples of people in the Bible who were very real, very honest, very human were a great encouragement. These were people who got angry and upset and depressed. They were not a bunch of plaster saints, but real men and women who hurt and were angry and yet nonetheless held on to what they knew to be true about God.

Coping with a physical disability is never easy. But in the many years that have passed since those early battles with depression, I have come to see that we believe God . . . never because it is easy, but because he is true!

PAT GOODLAND

The Death Experience

If death is 'the last thing we talk about', then we are dismissing from our conversation the most democratic of all human institutions. The only certainty in life is death. The ancient Jews regarded a corpse as unclean and untouchable. Many other cultures perform death rites and customs such as firing arrows or rifle shots over the new grave to ward off evil spirits. Tombstones, slabs and marble chips on top of graves find their origin in a desire to imprison something evil. Death is declared to be fearful, frightening, an unwanted intrusion in life and an increasing problem to humankind.

The dying are moving from a life lived among human companions, and death is thought of as bringing a singularly disturbing aloneness. A major fear is not simply the terrible suffering of a tormented body or the long-drawn-out anguish of failing faculties or even the finality of death, but the experience of aloneness in dying.

In England, for example, fifty per cent of deaths occur in hospitals. These dehumanized institutions with heart machines, drips and monitoring devices make modern death fearful and impersonal, without peace, dignity or control of our own functions. Medicine is so directed towards prevention and cure that the dying patient can sometimes be regarded as a failure.

Coming to terms

Death and decay are a part of the Creator's rhythm of life. Coming to terms with our own death gives meaning and maturity to our lives. In biological terms, death is a necessity. If the living stopped dying, within a short space of time the world would be overpopulated and reproduction would have to cease. Human beings need to die if the human race is to survive. The shortness of life on earth gives urgency to achievement and impetus to reach our goals before human powers diminish.

The tendency to consider death as 'the great unmentionable' is not only short-sighted, it is cruel. The dying reach out for human support, honesty and love. Communication is not only in words. Holding hands, an arm around a weakened body, sitting on the bed all convey a positive message of comfort.

The Christian view of death is one of hope. For the Christian death is a step into life. It leads to a fuller experience of life eternal in heaven. It is not a terminus, but a transition to a richer life. A Christian who has died believing in Jesus Christ has new identity, much as a slow-moving caterpillar leaves its very limited life on a leaf and emerges as a beautiful butterfly.

The evidence for such a faith is based on the resurrection of Jesus Christ. In his continuing life after the first Easter Sunday Jesus was recognizable and capable of normal functions. Yet he was not subject to natural laws, to pain or death. He had risen to life in a new dimension.

The experience of many Christian believers who have skirmished with death, as I did a few years ago, confirms that the death process is not one of terror or ultimate aloneness. God is close at hand enfolding us in sensations of warmth and security. The Christian dies in hope not of reclining on some billowy cloud or playing a harp in timeless eternity, but of entering into the quality of life which God originally made humanity to enjoy. Death is a gracious darkness, alive with the light of God which brings meaning to life on earth and rationality to human death.

SIR NORMAN ANDERSON

The Laws of God

CHAPTER 18

In the Sermon on the Mount, Jesus fully recognized the value of God's law: 'Until heaven and earth disappear, not the smallest letter ... will by any means disappear from the law until everything is accomplished.' But he also claimed to fulfil that law: 'Do not think I have come to abolish the law. I have not come to abolish but to fulfil.' But how, precisely, did he fulfil the law of Moses?

God's law

The ceremonial regulations—largely centred on the temple worship and its animal sacrifices—were so perfectly 'fulfilled' in Jesus Christ's one eternal sacrifice on the cross that the veil of the temple was torn apart when he died. The animal sacrifices, which had pointed on to the divinely planned way of forgiveness and cleansing from sin through Christ's death, had fulfilled their task. Similarly, rules about ceremonial cleanness were replaced by the moral purity they symbolized. In the words of the writer to the Hebrews: 'He set aside the first that he might establish the second.'

The **judicial provisions**, which were designed for the people of Israel as they settled the land and lived in it over the centuries, had also accomplished their purpose when, through the work of Jesus and the mission of the church, the 'people of God' became a worldwide company of the redeemed.

Jesus fulfilled the **moral law** in two ways:

- by keeping it perfectly in his own life, in which he observed its inward intention as well as its outward regulations;
- by dying in place of those who had failed to keep it. He also reinforced its principles for his followers, not as a way of salvation but as a pattern of life. In summary, then, the ceremonial and judicial laws had divine authority, but limited in time until each had been fulfilled by Jesus in the appropriate way. But the moral law (which we find restated in the New Testament) is eternal, based on the character of God himself.

Civil law

Christians now live in many different states, not in one as in the days of the Old Testament. So, while being subject to God's moral law, they are also subject to the civil and criminal laws of the countries in which they live. The New Testament writers make it clear that these human laws have, in principle, divine authority, as setting bounds to the destructive impulses of fallen humanity. Christians are therefore commanded to be obedient to their civil governments.

The apostle Paul wrote: 'There is no authority but by act of God and the existing authorities are instituted by him.' But sometimes civil legislation or government action are clearly contrary to God's moral law, and then the Christian must 'obey God rather than men'. There may well be some circumstances when a government is so evil, and so signally fails to fulfil its God-given functions, that it no longer merits obedience.

In a democracy, of course, almost all citizens have a voice in choosing their government and influencing the laws it enacts, so we should do all in our power to ensure that these are just and beneficial. But Christians should be careful not to try to deprive their fellow-citizens of that liberty to act according to conscience which they would themselves demand. Certainly their aim for society should be not only its public welfare but also God's moral law; but this cannot always be enforced by legal sanctions—nor should it be.

BRUCE KAYE

Finding God's Will

CHAPTER 19

As Christians live their lives and make their choices, they have to try to determine what the will of God is. They draw their understanding of that will both from the Bible and from the whole tradition of Christian ethical thinking.

The Bible

Christian ethical teaching begins with Jesus and his teaching. But as soon as we begin to read the New Testament we are taken a step further back. We notice that Jesus is in constant dialogue with his contemporaries about the Old Testament law. As he faces the questions of who he is, why he has come, and how his followers should live, Jesus does so in the light of the Old Testament heritage.

These Old Testament commandments are set within a specific framework. God made a covenant with Abraham and then with all Israel. That holy nation then in turn came to express its faith in worship at the temple in Jerusalem. This covenant and this temple worship were the focus of Israel's faith and of the morality that flowed from it. There is, of course, a more universal dimension in the stories of the creation of the world and in the picture of human life given to us in such books as the Psalms, Proverbs and Ecclesiastes. But Old Testament morality is still rooted in a particular nation and its history of faith.

Jesus fulfilled the hopes of Israel and made the full knowledge of God a present reality. He announced that the kingdom of God was at hand and called people to repent. With authority he called people to follow him and be his disciples. With that calling he invited people to be like him; just as he took up his cross and followed his calling from God, so his disciples were to take up their cross and follow Jesus.

Jesus sometimes expressed how people were to live by verbal teaching—in parables such as the story of the Good Samaritan, in extreme statements such as 'if your eye offends you pluck it out', and in poetic statements such as 'blessed are the peacemakers, for they shall be called sons of God'. But sometimes it came across in his dealings with individual people, as when he threw money-changers out of the temple, or forgave an adulterous woman.

Law and gospel

Jesus said that he had come not to destroy the law and the prophets but to fulfil them. He was not going to deny the Old Testament by what he did and said. But this did not mean that nothing had changed from the Old Testament with his coming. Rather it meant that there was a clear fulfilment based on a clear foundation. And a fulfilment implies a development, a difference.

The early Christians did not at first fully understand this transition from heritage to fulfilment. They held to their continuity with Israel's heritage, but they were aware that things had changed. What the Old Testament had foreshadowed was now fulfilled in Jesus. In the coming of Jesus, and his death and resurrection, God and his will had received a new dimension.

In the letter to the Hebrews the old covenant is contrasted with the new covenant and Jesus is seen as the fulfilment of, and as superior to, what had gone before. In John's Gospel we learn that the law came through Moses but grace and truth came through Jesus Christ. And Paul tells us that all people are to find peace with God on the same basis, the gospel of Jesus Christ.

There was a new understanding, then, of how we come to know God. And equally there was a new understanding of the behaviour which God called for. The idea of living

Be concerned above everything else with the kingdom of God and with what he requires of you.

Jesus in the Sermon on the Mount, Matthew 6

In the perfect and eternal world the law will vanish, but the results of having lived faithfully under it will not.

C. S. Lewis

for God now extended beyond the life of one nation. Believers, whether Jew or Gentile, were to understand and obey God's will in their everyday lives wherever God placed them. They were no longer members of a holy, covenanted nation with an identifiable territory and a holy city, as Israel had been.

This does not make the Old Testament law entirely a thing of the past. New Testament morality was worked out very much in the light of what had gone before in the Old Testament. The prophets had continually looked to interpret the 'law of Moses' as was appropriate for their own times. Jesus continued this prophetic tradition.

Much of what we find in the New Testament is a continuation of the ethical develop-

BRUCE KAYE

Foundations for Morality

The different ways Christians have approached morality show what variety there is within Christianity. We all bring different aspects of our Christianity into play when we come to ethical decisions.

Redemption and creation

This approach brings together two vital Christian beliefs:

- ☐ **the covenant**, or solemn agreement, which is the basis of the relationship between God and the people he has redeemed;
- ☐ and **creation**, the understanding that the world we live in was made and ordered by God.

In this partnership between covenant and creation, some people think the covenant is more important. This means the teaching of Jesus on the kingdom of God becomes our starting-point for understanding Christian morality.

A Christian looks to the will of God as expressed in Jesus' teaching; he is concerned first and foremost with what Jesus meant when he spoke of life in 'the kingdom'. He looks forward in hope to the day when that kingdom will fully come, as Jesus promised. Such an approach sees the key to morality as the pattern Jesus gave, in his own life and ministry, of the kingdom or rule of God. It means behaviour has a social dimension, because the kingdom is made up of people. And Christian values are relevant for everyone everywhere, just as Jesus' teaching was.

If creation is put first, then what matters most is that this is God's world, designed for our good. The stress falls on the laws God has put into his world from the beginning. Their scope is as wide as the human race. The key belief for this approach is that God has created the world to run in an orderly way. Jesus' life and teaching show us more precisely what God's will is.

Creation and law

According to the approach which makes creation central, the natural order reflects a natural law, which guides us in how we should live. The focus is on the goodness and order of God's creation. This gives a clue to the laws of God, which are inherent in the very way the world is. The natural order points us in the direction of God's will, and these indications are crystallized in the law of God, revealed in the Old Testament and made more explicit in Jesus' teaching. This makes 'the law of God' fundamental to everything. Christian ethics is therefore a matter of obedience to the law of God.

There is another version of this approach to be found in the writings of Thomas Aquinas (1224-74). For Thomas, it is through our reasoning ability that we discern both the character of God and our moral obligations as created by him. Human beings are different from other creatures. They take a share in God's providence, or care for his world, 'by being provident both for self and others'. Because of this, and because of our rational sense, we have access to the natural law. This law has certain fundamental guiding principles which remain the same. But the details of it are subject to change according to changing conditions. It is discovered by right reasoning on the basis of practical experience.

ment already underway in the Old. Yet Jesus' mission brought a decisive change to the place of the law in a believer's life. He did more than take over the Old Testament and restate it. He developed the prophetic tradition of the Old Testament in the light of his own teaching and example. The change from the holy nation of Israel to the universal faith of Christians had a dramatic influence on the shape and understanding of Christian ethics in the New Testament.

Jesus went beyond a morality of commandments. The Sermon on the Mount, particularly the Beatitudes, is a portrait of the ethical character of the kingdom of God. Similarly Paul's lists of virtues and vices suggest what is typical in the kingdom of God. There is a sense of ethical vision; a way

The tradition of natural law has had a considerable impact on the development of legal theory, especially in post-war Europe and in the formation of constitutions for newly independent colonial territories. However, in Protestant theology it is not a widely used notion, though in some circles it has enjoyed something of a revival recently. But it is an important factor in Roman Catholic moral theology. It partly lies behind the disagreement between Protestants and Catholics on such questions as birth control. The Pope's strictures on birth control flow from natural law argument. Contraception is contrary to the 'natural end' of sexual activity.

This tradition of natural law continues to have an important place in Christian ethics. But it needs to be held alongside an understanding of the Bible. The Old Testament and the teaching of Jesus are a clearer statement of that natural law which can be found in the natural order.

This approach gives a ready continuity in moral attitudes from one generation and era to another. The fundamental guiding principles are expressed as laws of a fairly general character, and there is always scope for adapting to changing circumstances.

Freedom and the Spirit

The New Testament tells us that Christian salvation makes us free; not only free from guilt, but also free from legalism and formalism in religion. And to be set free in Jesus Christ is to find a new experience of God's Spirit. This sense of the immediacy of the Holy Spirit, guiding the lives both of individual Christians and of the Christian group, brings a new dimension into Christian living.

Some see this as the most direct way of approach to Christian ethics. If we live to fulfil God's will because we belong to him, then surely God's Spirit will enable us to find what that will is. After all, Jesus said that after him would come the Counsellor, the Holy Spirit, who would guide the disciples into all truth. And in the Acts of the Apostles we find those same disciples being directed by the guidance of the Spirit.

This directly spiritual morality is true to some central elements in Christianity. It stresses the inner experience of God, which is such an important mark of Christian faith. And it keeps us clear of external forms, with the temptations and dangers of legalism. There is, of course, no formal point of continuity from one decision to another in any clear system of values. The continuity comes from the belief that it is the same God who inspires and directs us in every choice we make.

It is quite close to what is called the 'intuitionist' approach. According to the intuitionists individuals are able to receive their values directly, by intuition and immediate awareness. They can act from situation to situation according to that intuitive awareness of what is right.

Example and imitation

One of the most famous books written on this theme is *The Imitation of Christ*, by Thomas à Kempis, written in the fifteenth century. The book begins by quoting Jesus' words from John's Gospel, 'He who follows me shall not walk in darkness.' Thomas saw the imitation of Christ as conforming to the life of Jesus as given to us in the New Testament. He believed that a Christian life means following Jesus, that this is how Jesus taught us to think of it.

The theme of the imitation of Christ can be found elsewhere in the New Testament. Peter, writing to Christians about to endure suffering, appeals to the example of Jesus, who himself suffered unjustly. Paul urges the Corinthians to be imitators of himself as he is of

of setting before people God's ideal of what life should be.

The Christian tradition

Two thousand years of Christian teaching has inevitably had an effect on the way we think of morality. Christian life has to do with God, and so faith, hope and love have had an important part to play. When these three characteristics are held together, they link the religious and ethical aspects of the Christian life together in close relationship.

Sometimes the tradition has been expressed in terms of 'virtues': intellectual and practical virtues; 'cardinal' virtues, of a more generally moral kind; and theological virtues, shaped more speci-

Christ; he calls to the Philippians to follow the example of Jesus' humility. Such an appeal is bound to be very powerful for people who understand their religion as a following of Jesus Christ. It lays great importance on the life and attitudes of Jesus.

In developing this idea, Thomas à Kempis had something broader in mind than simply Christian morality. The path of imitation led to true enlightenment and freedom from all blindness of heart. What he had in mind was akin to what we might call the total piety of a Christian person. This troubled Martin Luther, who thought it could encourage people to believe that simply by following Christ they could find peace with God. That is to say, it led towards justification by works and away from trusting in Jesus' death as the way to find forgiveness.

In the nineteenth century there was great interest in discovering and writing about the life of Jesus. The 'quest of the historical Jesus' certainly had other roots. But it was partly inspired by a desire to discover the simple religion of Jesus and to follow it.

The concept of the imitation of Christ, then, can be ambiguous. Yet, if the dangers are avoided, it can be a powerful way of speaking about Christian ethics. It emphasizes the importance of personal commitment and decision, of motivation in the believer; the example of Jesus gives us social concern; and it makes Christian behaviour something personal rather than formal.

Situation ethics

This too is an approach which highlights the importance of the person in any moral decision, not only the person who is making the decision but also the other person or persons involved. It is sometimes called 'situation ethics', because of the central importance it gives to the situation in which ethical decisions are taken. It has been strongly taught in the twentieth century by Joseph Fletcher. He argued that Christian ethics are founded on six basic principles:

- ☐ The only thing that is intrinsically good is love.
- ☐ What governs any Christian decision is love, nothing else.
- ☐ Love and justice are the same: justice is love distributed.
- ☐ Love wills the neighbour's good, whether we like them or not.
- ☐ Only the end of an action justifies the means, nothing else.
- ☐ Love's decisions are made as the situation dictates, not according to some moral system.

Situation ethics has been criticized for abandoning all general principles. We do still have moral laws to guide us. And yet it is true that every situation is unique to itself and requires its own ethical decision.

This approach consciously avoids both legalism—applying rules and regulations wholesale—and the rejection of any kind of principle, 'anti-nomianism'. Joseph Fletcher offered situation ethics as a half-way between these two extremes. He argued that it is by reason that we make moral judgments; we can be guided by rules, but rules should never dictate our actions. This is not a form of sentimentalism. It requires a considerable degree of hard-headed, practical application to work it out. He is saying that ethical decisions do require justification; any particular decision is justified according to whether it produces and expresses love. Hence there is one single yardstick by which any action is to be judged—love. But there are any number of situations in which love is expressed.

fically by Christian religion. Particularly in the medieval church, the cardinal virtues of prudence, justice, temperance and fortitude were seen as the embodiment in everyday life of the essentially Christian virtues of faith, hope and love.

Some have approached ethical ideas by describing a perfect situation: a vision of the character of the kingdom of God to which Christians should aspire, or a Utopia. The utopian way of dealing with ethics, particularly in the political area, has had a long history, stretching from Plato to modern literature. One of the most famous is the book *Utopia* by the sixteenth-century English Catholic Sir Thomas More. He shows that Utopia is not a concept totally detached from real life, but rather describes an ideal situation with certain obvious points of contact with the realities of the writer's own time.

In these different ways the Bible and the Christian moral tradition combine to give Christians a standpoint and a direction as they make moral decisions. Their understanding of the will of God and their particular life situation—these are two factors which together, in a constantly changing balance, make it possible for Christians to choose rightly.

Making real choices

These moral decisions are not simple for Christians. Christians must be specific in their decision-making, which involves discovering the facts of each question and understanding them rightly. They must learn to face the prospect of compromise with others involved in their decision, and adopt that compromise as a right policy.

The Christian can use the long history of moral teaching, from Christian theologians and also from other moral philosophers. There are some important general points to be aware of:

- What the Christian regards as morally right ought to be capable of being **applied universally**.
- We are ourselves **responsible for our actions** and decisions.
- Christians have always given a foremost place to **compassion, love and humility**.
- Ethical issues, for the Christian, are not simply philosophical questions. They are attempts to **find the will of God**. There is a religious dimension to our morality. We may seek the guidance of the Holy Spirit, not only in our own experience but in the experience of our church.
- Many of the decisions we make do not lend themselves to long debate and thought. We have to **respond to particular circumstances**. In such situations we have to rely heavily on our instincts as Christians. And so forming and developing those instincts is a vital part of ordinary Christian maturing.

This last factor brings us to an important point on which to conclude. Our moral life is not separate from the rest of our Christian living. It both forms and is formed by the whole development of our spirituality in the church and in the world.

The Self discarded comes to life in fellowship with all others, as an infinitesimal element of God's all embracing love—like a particle of sea-spray tossed into the sun's radiance.

Malcolm Muggeridge

For further thinking

QUESTION 1

Christians often point to 'laws of creation': basic principles referred to in the Genesis creation story. An example is monogamy; 'They shall be one flesh.' What other creation laws are there? Are these laws binding on everyone, or just on Christians?

QUESTION 2

Alongside 'laws of creation', other Christians expound 'kingdom ethics': a way of life Jesus taught his disciples. This way is more demanding than laws of creation, or than the ten commandments, because it is a call to those who follow Jesus to live as befits their calling. If a friend were to ask you, 'What is the Christian way of life?' would you begin with laws of creation or with kingdom ethics?

BRUCE KAYE

Good and Evil

For the Christian, moral judgments are not made in the air, but in everyday, practical reality. Christians cannot withdraw from life while they make their decisions. They have to bring their Christian faith to bear on every choice that confronts them. As they do this, they will be influenced by the fact that everyday life is itself a mixture of good and evil. And yet the Christian has a certain detachment from everyday life, because his or her ultimate loyalty is to be the kingdom of heaven.

The choices and decisions that Christians face in life are genuine ones. They are not confronted by a fantasy of good or a fantasy of evil. They actually have the opportunity of choosing, to do good or to do evil. This is because they live in a world that is neither wholly good nor yet wholly evil.

This quality of our human situation comes out in the Genesis accounts of humanity's creation and fall. On any interpretation, these chapters tell us that humanity is socially and physically less than perfect, but not totally catastrophic. Neither good nor evil has the field to itself.

This means that every human situation is morally something of a compound of good and evil. Our motives are never completely good nor completely bad, nor is our judgment, nor are our actions. We may lean in the best circumstances to the good rather than to the ill, but we will never quite escape the influence of our selfishness, the evil within us. Nor will we be perfect in judging the consequences of our actions. And so at the heart of all our moral choices and all our moral behaviour there is an essential ambiguity.

This problem has an added point to it when the Christian has to make choices with a political side to them. There is no longer any such entity as a holy nation, which stands as a whole under the will of God. And it is quite illegitimate, however many Christians may do it, to look on our own religious group as a kind of holy nation, separate from the rest of humanity.

The good that Christians strive for in a secular society will be the highest good that secular society can reach in a fallen world. They must not try to impose on their fellow citizens some mirror copy of the kingdom of God. Yet they must find a good way, and give it practical expression in their secular situation. And all this without losing sight of their own ultimate goals, beyond this world.

War and peace

This dilemma of the impossibility of finding a way of unalloyed perfection for a fallen humanity is constantly with us. It shows itself clearly as Christians discuss the question of violence. Is revolution ever permissible to promote social justice?

- A centre of this controversy is the **World Council of Churches' programme to combat racism**. In 1966 the WCC organized a world conference on church and society in Geneva. That conference came to accept that there are circumstances in which violence is legitimate, when there is no other way to combat oppression. And so, although nonviolence was still recognized as the ideal way, funds were given to help meet the compassionate needs of certain revolutionary groups. This was seen as the lesser of two evils. Pacifism was severely questioned, at this conference and in later Liberation Theology.

- There has been a long tradition of the idea of **a 'just war'**. This concept can be found in the writings of Augustine and particularly in those of Thomas Aquinas. Normally there are seven conditions of a just war. The cause for which the war is conducted must be just; the just purpose must remain during hostilities; the war must have the intention of establishing a good or correcting an evil; it must be waged by acceptable means; war must be only a last resort; victory must be assured; and the war must be aimed at a just peace. How can these

DAVID ATKINSON

Forgiveness

Our Lord taught us to pray, 'Forgive us our sins as we forgive those who sin against us.' What did he mean? What do we mean when we talk about forgiving people and being forgiven?

Forgiveness is concerned with removing barriers which block personal relationships, barriers which are put up when a relationship has been spoiled by one person's consciousness of doing wrong to, or being wronged by, another. It does not mean treating the wrong as unimportant, still less pretending that it never happened. Rather, acknowledging wrong as wrong, the forgiving person acts to prevent the relationship from remaining spoiled either by his own resentment or by the wrongdoer's burden of guilt. Forgiveness flows from 'in spite of' love, not from 'because of' love.

Jesus told the story of a servant who had got into serious debt to his master, and was ordered to forfeit all his possessions in order to pay. In response to the servant's pleading, however, the master in compassion released the debt and reinstated him. When people forgive someone, they respond to wrong by going beyond what strict justice or reason may dictate; they act in sheer grace.

'Forgive us our sins'

In the Bible, many of the references to forgiveness are concerned with God forgiving sinful people their sins. When God forgives and we receive his forgiveness, sin is 'covered' and 'carried away' (two of the Old Testament words translated 'forgive'). Good relationships may then be restored between God and us.

Some of the marks of God's forgiveness, as the Bible understands it, are these:

- ☐ There is **nothing automatic** about forgiveness. It is a mark of the loving, gracious character of God, who is described in one place as 'a God of pardons'. Sin deserves punishment, but forgiveness goes beyond strict justice and God, 'merciful and gracious', shows 'mercy to thousands'.

- ☐ Forgiveness is **received only by the penitent**. God's forgiving spirit is part of his nature, but the experience of being forgiven is open only to those who are willing to change their mind and intention towards God, who desire to get rid of sin and share a restored relationship with him. This is the theme of David's prayer of confession in Psalm 51. He had committed a whole series of wrongs, and in this psalm we find him painfully expressing his humility before God, acknowledging that his wrongs towards others were in fact also sins before God, and then making confession. He longs to receive a 'new heart', and is willing in his future life to praise God and to put him first.

To receive forgiveness costs us our pride, reminds us of our dependence on God, and involves acknowledging that we are in the wrong. When the Old Testament says God 'will by no means clear the guilty', it means that it is only through repentance that we can receive God's gracious forgiveness.

- ☐ Forgiveness is **costly** also to the one who forgives. One of the Old Testament words meaning 'forgive' is related to the idea, central to the Old Testament sacrificial system, of 'making atonement': God's way of bringing himself and his people to be 'at-one'.

conditions be applied to modern wars of liberation, guerilla warfare and terrorism? And do they have any relevance at all to nuclear warfare? These questions are still much debated.

■ Yet on the other side interest in and sympathy for **pacifism** has grown in recent times. Pacifism takes a variety of forms. But basically pacifists want to show that evil is not conquered by evil means and that non-violent policies and actions can be powerful instruments in human

In the New Testament, we are shown how much it cost God to forgive us when we see that for us to be forgiven meant Jesus Christ had to die. Paul, in his letter to the Ephesians, writes that 'we have redemption through his blood, the forgiveness of our trespasses, according to the riches of his grace which he lavished upon us'. We can be forgiven because Christ died in our place to reconcile us to God.

☐ Forgiveness does not only restore a relationship, it **enhances it**. Remember what happened when the prodigal son came home? Jesus' parable shows how forgiveness is not just a legal term looking to the past, but opens the way to a richer life of sonship in the future.

☐ Forgiveness is sometimes **linked to healing**. One of the New Testament words for 'forgive' means 'putting away'; it centres on the removal of barriers to fellowship.

It is the word used in the story of Jesus' encounter with the paralysed man. When Jesus saw the faith of the four friends who had lowered the sick man on his bed into the room where Jesus was preaching, he said to the paralysed man, 'My son, your sins are forgiven you.' And then to underline his divine authority to forgive sins, Jesus healed the man of his paralysis. The barriers, both spiritual and physical in this case, which were preventing the man living freely before God were taken away by the loving action of Christ.

This is not to say that sickness is always linked to particular sin. But sometimes sin produces emotional or physical pain, which is removed when people know themselves to be forgiven by God.

'As we forgive others'

The tragic sequel to the story of the servant with the enormous debt and his forgiving master is that the servant refused to forgive one of his fellows who owed him a trifling few pence. Jesus shows that the man could never have truly understood what it means to be forgiven. Really receiving forgiveness when we are truly penitent for our wrong, must show itself in forgiving others who wrong us.

One of the New Testament words concentrates on this 'forgiving spirit'. 'Be kind to one another, tenderhearted, forgiving one another as God in Christ forgave you.' God's conditions for receiving his forgiveness are that we should repent and be willing to show a forgiving spirit to others.

We need also to remember that forgetting is part of forgiving, and forgiving is not complete until the wrong is 'put away' and eventually forgotten. The tender 'forgiving spirit' of the New Testament writer is so different from the phoney sort of forgiveness we sometimes offer one another. We can too easily miss out the forgetting aspect, and hold on to resentments inwardly, however much we may profess forgiveness outwardly.

It is by experiencing the gracious way God forgives and forgets our wrongs (sometimes helped through our experience of being forgiven by someone else) that we can learn to let go of our resentments. This will have good results for our emotional (and sometimes physical) as well as spiritual health, and for our relationships with others who are relieved of their burden of guilt towards us.

One of the key tasks Christians have is to make known the gospel of forgiveness. One way they do this is by being members of the 'forgiven community'—the church. Another is by seeking to express God's pattern of forgiveness in all their relationships with others. It is part of the meaning of love, the way love is expressed in situations of personal wrong.

We... are citizens of heaven, and we eagerly wait for our Saviour, the Lord Jesus Christ, to come from heaven.

Paul, in Philippians 3

affairs. One of the most striking examples in the modern world of people who have advocated non-violence was Mahatma Gandhi. In turn Gandhi had a very strong influence on the thoughts and actions of Martin Luther King Jr in the United States. But non-violent methods have proved very hard to apply. The civil rights movement in the United States met very violent reactions, and King was killed.

Home is where the heart is

Christians are involved in this world; this is where they are to love their neighbour and seek their neighbour's good. And yet at the same time the Christian has a further loyalty, to 'live in the light of eternity'. Jesus called people to enter the kingdom of God and Paul insisted that the Christian's citizenship is in heaven. Christian living is directed by that hope.

In the New Testament, Christian living is sometimes given particular urgency by the fact that Jesus is soon to return. The world in its present form will come to an end, and the kingdom of God will be established. Some have thought that Jesus' approach to ethics was strongly coloured by this belief; that only when this intense expectation diminished did a more positive appreciation of life

CHRIS SUGDEN

Violence and Non-Violence

A violent action harms or damages persons or property. Some violence expresses frustration or revenge. Any activity which coerces people into adopting certain behaviour against their will, whether it inflicts damage by use of weapons or not, is an act of political violence.

Between 1960 and 1976 over five and a half million people were killed by military violence. Lord Mountbatten said: 'We live in an age of extreme peril because every war today carries the danger that it could spread and involve the superpowers . . . I cannot imagine a situation in which nuclear weapons would be used as battlefield weapons without the conflagration spreading.'

Governments and businesses are also using violence when their economic and social policies cause even indirect harm. In the Bible 'violence' chiefly describes the actions of unjust authorities, such as the king, the priests and the rich, and those who oppress the poor. In the Bible violence is natural to humankind, a characteristic of our rebellion against God. Violence treats people as things. It creates a 'spiral' of violence.

Christians believe that Jesus Christ's way of dealing with violence shows God's solution to humanity's rebellion. In Jesus' time there were revolutionaries who advocated violence to expel the Roman rulers from Palestine. In contrast, he practised non-retaliation and love for enemies. He resisted evil people and evil social practices, but without using violence. He treated people as persons and gave them an opportunity to repent. His death shows that God does not take revenge on rebellious people, but loves his enemies, gives them room to repent and forgives them.

Resistance, revolution and war

In the first centuries of the church, Christians rejected violence and refused to serve in the army. After the Reformation, the Anabaptists and the Quakers revived this tradition. In the 1960s, Martin Luther King Jr used non-violent resistance in the campaigns for civil rights for blacks in the USA.

After Constantine had made Christianity the religion of the Roman Empire, Christians did serve in the army. Augustine developed the 'just war' theory to extend moral standards to the conduct of war.

Christians have held both positions. They disagree on how to interpret Paul's teaching that God gives the officers of the state their authority. Some argue that this means that Christians can serve as 'magistrates', using coercion to prevent some citizens from

in the world emerge.

Through Christian history there have been many different ways of thinking about the future, the return of Christ and the end of the world. One of the finest examples of this theme is to be found in Augustine's book *The City of God*. Augustine wrote at a time of great political instability, in the light of the conquest of the city of Rome in AD 410. His book tries to show how the city of God exists within the world, but yet reaches beyond it and lives in hope. It is an extensive analysis of the actual political conditions of his age, in which Augustine argues powerfully that the Christian is unworldly in the world, in the world but not of it.

How far should the Christian's belief in another reality affect his attitude to the world? Some Christians' morality appears to be world-denying, expecting nothing good here and now. Others are world- or life-affirming. Albert Schweitzer wrote *Civilisation and Ethics*, in which he sees that the European view of the world has tragically failed to discover a secure foundation. He analyses various points of view according to whether they say yes or no to the world, and offers as his own conclusion an ethic based on reverence for life.

harming others, but not to go to war. On the other hand, others deny that Christians can ever use any coercion against people, and so deny that Christians can serve in police forces.

Many Christians have held that the policing role of the civil power, when exercised under strict control of the state, extends to include service in war against other countries. While not minimizing the horrors of war, they contend that, within the limits of a just war, it is a lesser evil to wage war against an abominable tyranny than to allow it to go unchecked. This view was widely adopted by Christians among the allies fighting against Hitler in World War II. The advent of nuclear war seems to me to invalidate the 'lesser evil' idea, since nuclear war has no limits and will end in the greatest possible evil of utter destruction.

Christians have also argued that a violent revolution could be God's way of producing a just society. In common with Calvin, they have drawn on the just war principle to justify armed revolt against a government which continually rewarded evil and punished good. In Latin America recently, some have gone further and justified revolution by the practice of holy war in the Old Testament. Some even combined Marx's dictum that violent acts are the birth-pangs of the revolution with a distortion of the Christian teaching that death is followed by resurrection. Most Christians do not accept these views.

For further thinking

QUESTION 1

Imagine you are given the opportunity to advise the government of your country about one policy change which could improve the moral climate in your society. What would it be? How would you justify it from Jesus' teaching or the Christian moral tradition?

QUESTION 2

Does forgiveness have a necessary link to justice? For example, if one group is being exploited by a more powerful group, should they just forgive their oppressors and accept the situation, or should they fight for justice first?

QUESTION 3

If a person accepts Jesus' teaching, will he or she necessarily take up a pacifist position?

BIBLE REFERENCES

Love

Numbers 14:19; Deuteronomy 7:7–9; 10:18–19; Psalms 86:5; 103:1–18; 107:1–43; 116:1–2; Isaiah 49:16; Hosea 11:1–4; Luke 6:35; 10:25–37; John 3:16; 13:1; 14:21–24; 21:15–17; Romans 5:5, 8; 8:37–39; 1 Corinthians 13:1–13; Galatians 2:20; Ephesians 3:17–19; 5:2; Colossians 3:14; 1 Thessalonians 5:13; James 2:8–13; 1 Peter 1:22; 1 John 3:14–18; 4:7–12

Repentance

2 Kings 17:13; Nehemiah 1:9; Hosea 14:1–2; Matthew 3:2; Mark 1:14–15; Luke 3:8; 15:7; 24:47; Acts 3:19; 17:30; 2 Corinthians 7:8–10; 1 Thessalonians 1:9; Hebrews 6:1–6

CHAPTER 21

SAMUEL ESCOBAR

Work

Work is a fundamental activity for people in every culture. But the way it is understood and the attitudes taken towards it vary greatly, depending on a person's environment, how technically developed their society is and what kind of religious or ideological world-view they hold. A study of history shows us how Christian beliefs have formed attitudes to work and working habits in many societies, changing them significantly.

The focus for such a study is the recovery of a biblical attitude to work brought by the Reformation in the sixteenth century. It contributed to shaping Protestant Europe economically and politically in a way totally different from Catholic Europe, where there still persisted the Greek ideas adopted in the late Middle Ages. The contempt for manual labour in Latin America, for example, which plays an important part in the underdevelopment of that continent, was a result of late medieval attitudes taken there by the Spanish conquest. Work was seen as a curse, an idea quite foreign to the Incas and Aztecs before the Spaniards arrived.

The Creator's mandate

The biblical doctrine of creation presents God as an active working deity, who has made human beings as workers in his image. This teaching runs right through the Old Testament and culminates in Jesus who was a working man before he became an itinerant preacher. Paul, the greatest missionary in the New Testament after Jesus, combined his apostolic work with his tent-making.

Work, then, is in integral part of God's design for humanity. In our working activity, we fulfil God's mandate to 'have dominion' over creation. Only within this framework can we understand the profound spiritual significance of human cultural creativity; likewise God's command to rest one day in seven. We can see the effect of this belief in the first Christian centuries, especially in the contrast it provided to a Graeco-Roman society that was built on the backs of slaves, where a free person would feel demeaned by hands dirtied with work.

In the sixth century, Benedict codified the monastic pattern of life. He insisted on the spiritual value of manual work, forging a lifestyle summarized in the motto *Ore et Labore*, 'pray and work'. But seven centuries later this biblical understanding of work was changed into a purely contemplative monasticism such as that of the Dominicans. Thus Aristotle's view that work should be left to slaves regained a place in the European mind, only to be challenged by the Reformation. The social order codified by Aquinas owed more to Aristotle than to the Bible.

> The provision of Benedict, himself an aristocrat, that his monks should work in fields and shops therefore marks a revolutionary reversal of the traditional attitude towards labour; it is a high peak along the watershed separating the modern from the ancient world.
>
> *Lynn D. White*

Sweat and toil

It was because of the 'fall' of humanity into sin, with its distortion of human life, that toil, idolatry and oppression came to be associated with work. In civilizations ancient and modern, fatigue and suffering surround the work men and women do. This continues to be so despite all the progress made through research and legislation.

The danger and hardship of underground or underwater mining, the risks in dealing with radioactive material in medicine or in energy, the tensions of competition and decision-making at executive level, all are examples of this cost of work; 'by the sweat of your brow you will eat bread.' Equally, the insatiable appetites of the consumer society show us how developed, sophisticated economies, where work is not submitted to God as the real end of life, lead us into a vicious circle of idolatry. They make for hard and productive work, but are ultimately aimless.

Nevertheless, God is not indifferent to the pain of human toil. He heard the cry of the Israelites undergoing forced labour in Egypt and delivered them through the exodus. And the cries of the unpaid labourers, so James tells us, reach the ears of the Lord.

On this basis we can more readily understand the laws in the Bible, many of which have to do with work. The evils that surround work are to be put right: in this way as in others, God requires us to build a better society. These laws also form the foundation for the prophet's message about social justice to the worker, a message of judgment for the oppressor and hope for the oppressed.

Work as a calling

John Calvin grasped this doctrine. It moved him to help in the shaping of European industrial society. He rediscovered work as a calling. The Puritans followed him here, as did Wesley later. And he also had a new vision of capital and credit: not to be confined to the kingdom of darkness, but dedicated to the service of God. In these ideas we see the pattern reappear, so prominent in the book of Proverbs and again in Paul's pastoral writing, of a disciplined and rewarding life based on honest work.

Jesus Christ's victory over evil gave the hope of a new creation, in which working people could find fulfilment. Their work would be consecrated to God and carried out within a framework of justice.

In the light of that vision and hope, what we do on earth takes on a new value. Work is done in and for the Lord, and this gives it a new dimension, whatever the conditions in which it is done. The deep significance of this truth has to be regained in a time like ours.

Some people's concern over ecology, and their ignorance of history, makes them dismiss the Christian understanding of work. And so the full biblical teaching about work needs to be made part of the Christian message today.

Marx attacked nineteenth-century capitalist society for producing an alienated workforce. Some of his strictures were in line with the biblical doctrine of work. But, in the atheistic fury of his criticism, he made the class struggle an end in itself and left out some important aspects of reality. When his theories came to be applied in shaping new societies, they resulted in worse forms of oppression and more totally alienated workers.

The biblical doctrine of work has given some undoubted benefits to Western society. And yet, in today's post-industrial society, market forces and the laws of competition have enslaved humanity afresh. Workers in the developed world know a new alienation and despair. In the developing world they suffer gross injustice. In this situation Christians need to do more than teach the biblical doctrines. We need to reapply them, pointing out their relevance to the real present condition, if these doctrines are to contribute to setting people free in their working lives.

For further thinking

QUESTION

If work is part of God's design for human life, why is it often so tedious? Can anything be done to make it less so?

BIBLE REFERENCES

Work and Rest

Exodus 20:8–11; 23:10–12; 31:1–11; Deuteronomy 16:8; 1 Kings 17:13–14; Ecclesiastes 3:22; 5:18–20; Ephesians 4:28; Colossians 3:23–24; 2 Thessalonians 3:6–13; Hebrews 3:11; 4:3–10

REX GARDNER

Medical Ethics

Medicine sees its task as being to save life, to heal disease, to alleviate pain, to reduce the ill effects of incurable disease, to prevent sickness and to improve the quality of physical life. The Christian, having the example of our Lord's healing ministry and aware that nature has been warped by evil, is prepared to counter pain by the use of artificial means such as drugs, surgery, pain-relieving techniques in childbirth and prophylaxis against common disease.

Rights and responsibilities must be held in balance. The biblical command to replenish the earth has now been more than fully obeyed, and this suggests that couples should take responsibility for the number of their children. What medical techniques are appropriate in helping them to fulfil these responsibilities while continuing that oneness which the Bible puts first in marriage? Is permanent sterilization permissible? On the other hand, have couples any right to produce as many offspring as they wish?

In particular, warned that their foetus is abnormal, have they the right to continue? And if so, who has long-term financial and custodial responsibility for the child's care? More often the woman will feel she has not the physical, spiritual or financial resources to cope with such a baby. Aware of the risk to the continuance of the marriage and the stability of the family if abortion is refused, what is the life-saving decision? Faced with this issue, the doctor will seek wherever possible to conserve life, as God's gift.

Who gets the resources?

Resources are limited. Ethical principles are involved in deciding which patient with chronic disease gets the chance of prolonged life and health by a heart or kidney transplant, or by access to a kidney machine. Where neurosurgical facilities are very scarce, as in developing countries, is it right to divert them to repeated operations on a spina bifida baby, when even a healthy child would have only a fifty per cent chance of survival?

Even where adequate facilities are available, is it right to subject such an infant to a long series of difficult operations, with much time in hospital, when its life expectancy is short? Who decides? If surgery is not to be performed, or is inappropriate, or the baby is rejected by its parents, how is it to be cared for?

In this problem, as at the end of life, Christians in medicine feel that full, loving, tender care should be provided, but that heroic measures to prolong life are not always wise. Yet patients should not be hastened to their Maker by 'euthanasia' before the time God decrees. Again, as death is not the end, the doctor will not struggle to keep alive a body from which the person has departed, and he or she will be alert to the possibility of retrieving organs for transplantation into other patients to afford them new life.

Problems arise when the doctor's conscience disapproves the patient's behaviour. Presented with an acute problem—the pregnant single girl, the injured drunken driver, the wounded bandit—our Lord's example of compassion for sinners must override any judging attitude. It is a different matter when doctors are asked to facilitate behaviour contrary to what they believe to be right; contraception for the unmarried poses an especially difficult problem in this respect.

The Christian in medicine, conscious of the Great Physician, has an ultimate touchstone to apply. What decision should I take in this problem, which I can present to God as work performed on his behalf?

CHAPTER 23

DAVID ATKINSON

Marriage and Divorce

There are a number of different ideas around about the meaning of marriage. Is it just a romantic alliance between a man and a woman, which they can drop when they like? Or is it just a legal and social institution: society's way of regulating sexual behaviour? A more satisfactory approach, which many Christians take, is to see marriage as a 'covenant'—a life-relationship based on a public undertaking involving promises and obligations.

Marriage as a covenant

In the Bible, the way people enter and live within the marriage covenant is compared both with God's covenant with his people and with Jesus' relationship with his church. It is this which gives marriage its meaning and its pattern. We can see how God relates to his people: in self-giving love, by promises, in righteousness, in committed faithfulness, sacrifice, patience, forgiveness, blessing and so on. This is meant to be an ideal, towards which human relationships should grow. And God's covenant also reminds us of God's love and grace as a resource, giving us help in our human relationships to live by his pattern. Because I am forgiven, for example, I can learn to forgive.

Right at the beginning of Genesis we find the great text 'a man shall leave his father and mother, and cleave to his wife, and the two shall become one flesh.' This is used elsewhere in the Bible as a pointer to the meaning of that particular human covenant, man and woman in marriage. It involves:

- A public **leaving** of one family unit to start another;
- The covenanted love-faithfulness indicated by **'cleaving'**;
- Leading to the **'one flesh'**: a complete partnership of man and wife, expressed in and deepened through sexual union.

Marriage is a recognition in society of a new status. The personal partnership of committed love belongs within the framework of a responsibility, a committed obligation. And this is publicly declared and publicly accepted. The partners' relationship with each other affects and is affected by their shared relationship outwards to others. So society is involved in each new marriage and has a proper concern in any decision to break it. Marriage also has a status before God: a vocation to live out in the human covenant something of God's pattern of making relationships.

But the central meaning of marriage is not so much status as relationship. To concentrate on marriage as a covenant relationship is to see it as something more than a social agreement. It is an environment for mutual enrichment, for nurturing, healing and growth: a harvest of the Spirit, alive and constantly adapting rather than a 'still life'. Of course, it needs the dependability which comes from permanence.

Can a marriage be broken?

Some Christians (particularly in the Catholic tradition) speak of marriage as a 'sacrament'. By this they mean among other things that marriages between baptized Christians are 'means of grace' to the partners. Such sacramental marriages, once made, create a new kinship bond 'in the order of nature', so that whatever partners or divorce courts may say, in the eyes of God their union is absolutely indissoluble. You can no more stop being married to a living partner, on this view, than you can cease being related to a brother or sister. (Some dispensation is, however, available to Roman Catholics. In some cases a broken marriage may be declared 'null': never really a marriage.) The churches of the Reformation, on the other hand, including much of the Church of England, believe that 'sacramental' language is unclear. For them, marriages are not absolutely indissoluble in the Catholic sense. These churches, as also the Eastern Orthodox churches, have permitted divorce (and remarriage) in some circumstances.

What breaks a marriage?

For those who understand marriage in covenant terms, the question of divorce is about the possibility of covenant-breaking. Covenants are life-unions, entered into on the basis that they are permanent. They should not be broken. But sometimes they are. This breaking can never happen without damage to the partners involved. A divorce, like an amputation, is the severing of what was once a living union. Indeed, the Old Testament word for divorce is related to cutting down trees, even chopping off heads. This fits in with the way the Old Testament nowhere commands or even encourages divorce. The prophet Malachi says, 'God hates divorce.'

The law of Moses, recorded in Deuteronomy, includes this ruling. Say a man's wife 'finds no favour in his eyes', because of some 'indecency' in her, and he divorces her and gives her a 'certificate of divorce'. She then remarries, but her second husband also divorces her. She cannot then go back to her first husband. This law is referred to in the New Testament, and Jesus explains it as a 'concession', because of men's 'hardness of heart'. Although God's will for marriage is permanence, this Old Testament law does recognize that in a sinful world people do sometimes sinfully abandon their commitments. It provides a way of regulating this to put a curb on husbands' cruelty, and to give some protection to the wife.

This Old Testament law was the basis for a dispute among the rabbis of Jesus' day, and the Pharisees tried to catch Jesus out over it. What about Moses' law? said the Pharisees. Was Jesus going to agree with those who said it meant that a man could divorce his wife for almost any trivial reason, or with the stricter ones who said only if she had committed some sexual sin? (In Jewish law only a man could start divorce proceedings; in cases of adultery he was obliged to divorce his wife.)

In his answer to them, Jesus went back to the creation story: marriage is part of God's plan for the whole human race, intended as a God-given permanent union of one man with one woman. Jesus speaks in very strong terms, which contrast with the comparatively lax views prevailing then and now. He says that if man divorces his wife and marries another, he commits adultery. The seventh commandment, 'Thou shalt not commit adultery', was meant to safeguard the 'one-flesh' relationship, and any unfaithfulness which broke the 'one flesh' came under this commandment. It is the covenant pattern of committed love-faithfulness, with all its creative potential, which is at the heart of a true marriage relationship.

There is a difference of opinion among Christians about the interpretation of some of the New Testament texts. Some believe that Jesus is cancelling Moses' concession—no divorce. Others believe that, while he is certainly saying that the creation pattern is marriage for life, he is also agreeing with the law of Deuteronomy—in a sinful society, some marriages are broken. This may well be supported by the words twice used in Matthew's Gospel, 'except for unfaithfulness'. Jesus is siding with the stricter view, though in a way which recognizes human weakness. But he is going beyond Moses' law to God's purposes in creation for men and women.

'Lesser evil'

The creation idea still holds—and in fact is reinstated in the 'new creation' that Jesus came to bring. But while the world is spoilt and sinful there will always be a tension between this ideal and the 'hardness of heart' which leads to divorce. Christians who acknowledge the tragic reality of divorce often have a difference of opinion about the grounds on which divorce may be allowed:

- Some people think that Matthew's exception means Jesus allows divorce **only on grounds of adultery**;
- Others add the grounds of **desertion by an unbelieving partner**, which the apostle Paul seems to indicate in his letter to the Corinthians;
- Yet others see these, plus 'prevention of cruelty' suggested by Deuteronomy, as indicating the seriousness with which the question of divorce should be approached. They admit that there may sometimes be a sinful abandonment of commitment grave enough to lead to **irreconcilable breakdown**.

The covenant model shows that forgiveness and restoration are the right responses to covenant-breaking—if God repeatedly forgives, so should we. It is only in circumstances where, in human terms, this is no longer possible, that the question of divorce as a lesser evil may be raised. Sometimes sin traps us so that none of the choices open to us are good, and then we can only choose the lesser evil as right in the circumstances. There is always something sinful about divorce, although the responsibility may lie with one partner or with both, or with others involved. Sin as failure to live within God's will is never less than a serious matter. Yet the heart of the Christian gospel is that sins can be forgiven.

Remarriage?

In the Bible, so many Christians believe, when divorce occurs, the right of remarriage

GOTTFRIED OSEI-MENSAH

Polygamy

Polygamy is the marriage of one person with more than one spouse. Normally it takes the form of one man having more than one wife. In some of the world's cultures it is common or normal, particularly in Africa.

Throughout the Old Testament we are introduced to people, both wicked and godly, who were polygamists. Solomon excelled them all with seven hundred wives and three hundred other mistresses.

The practice of polygamy is usually found among societies where survival is a main factor. Such people usually get their livelihood from the land, farmed by age-old methods needing many hands. The death rate is high, especially among children, because of poor hygiene and lack of modern medical treatment. In these societies, every marriageable woman must have a husband and bear as many children as possible. To have many wives and children is a real mark of success for a man, while to be childless or barren is a serious affliction or a curse for a woman.

The New Testament clearly teaches that marriage is a lifelong union between one man and one woman, one flesh'. This is more than a man and a woman agreeing to live together sexually, even with the consent of their society. It is the exclusive commitment of a man and a woman to each other in a lifelong companionship of mutual love and care, until death parts them. Its exclusive nature rules out polygamy as an option for the Christian.

In their teaching on marriage, Jesus and Paul pointed out that this was God's purpose from the beginning. Clearly, God tolerated attitudes to marriage among his ancient people which fell short of his own ideal, because of 'the hardness of their hearts'. Even so, the Old Testament records some bitter experiences of rivalries, jealousies, conspiracies and murders, which were the direct outcome of the polygamous marriages of some of the key personalities in the Old Testament.

is assumed. Whether remarriage is a wise and responsible course is another matter, and there are questions to be asked about psychological factors in the breakdown, as well as the welfare of any children.

Clearly the church should be cautious about solemnizing remarriages, and should never do so lightly. But the church's task goes beyond this. Christians are called to exercise far greater care in marriage preparation, support and reconciliation. They need to find a wise balance between proclaiming God's will for marriage and treating people sensitively at times of tragedy and pain.

For further thinking

QUESTION

According to Jesus' teaching on marriage and divorce, is a divorced person ever free to marry again?

BIBLE REFERENCES

Marriage and the Family

Genesis 1:26–28; 2:18–25; 24:62–67; 29:15–20; Proverbs 19:13–14; 22:6; 23:13–18; 31:10–31; Matthew 1:18–25; 19:3–9; Luke 20:34; John 2:1–2; 19:26–27; 1 Corinthians 7:10–11, 33–34, 38; Ephesians 5:21—6:4; Colossians 3:18–21; Hebrews 13:4

Sexuality

Genesis 2:24; Proverbs 5:18–19; Song of Songs – whole book; Matthew 5:28; 1 Corinthians 6:18–19; 7:3–5; 1 Thessalonians 4:3–6

Not to judge

The New Testament's approach to less-than-ideal marriages is not to judge or condemn when faced with the problem of polygamy. And so, today, the church should offer clear teaching, godly example and patient counselling.

Paul advised young Christians not to divorce their unbelieving spouses on the grounds of their own new-found faith. But if the unbelieving partner deserted because of the difference in faith, Christians were to accept this as their partners' freedom.

The application of this principle to polygamy would seem to be as follows. The converted polygamist and his spouses should serve the Lord in the marital state they are in, provided all the partners involved accept the situation. If any spouse (especially the non-Christian) opts to leave him, then he should not resist but accept it. If the parties involved come to understand the Christian teaching on marriage better, and are convinced that their polygamous situation is wrong, then patient and loving counselling is needed to help them find the Lord's will for everyone concerned.

The church has not the right to exclude a new believer on the ground that his or her spouse is not converted. Neither should the church refuse fellowship to a converted polygamist and his converted spouses. He should not be induced or pressured to divorce or seek divorce. Of course, a Christian is not free to take additional wives!

However in the New Testament certain qualifications are laid down for leaders in the church. Since leaders lead by teaching the truth and guiding God's people who are prone to go astray, they themselves should be worthy 'examples of the flock'. Therefore, whatever other leadership qualities they may have, neither polygamists, nor those married to unbelievers, nor fathers of unruly children, nor people whose homes have broken up may be elected to lead the church! The concern here is not discrimination, but a faithful witness to the word of God in all its purity and transforming power.

We may not use our own or others' culture and traditions to justify polygamous practice in the church. Nor should we take comfort in Old Testament examples of the practice. The clearer light of the New Testament teaching must guide the Christian. The spread of modern medicine and improved hygiene are beginning to relieve the anxieties about survival for increasing numbers of people. Polygamy could die out in a few decades.

A New Creation

PART

CHAPTER 24

DEREK KIDNER

A New Age Dawns

Before we have completed three chapters of the Bible, we read of a world gone wrong. The rest of the Bible is largely about what God has done to put things right. And his solution centres on the calling of a people. First he calls a family, then from the family a nation, and from that nation a Messiah. With the coming of Jesus a new age dawns. God's plan for a new creation is put into effect, with the focus on a new people, the 'community of Jesus'.

The story of God's people begins in Genesis 12. Already of course there had been individual men and women of God, and even some faint family links between them. But with the call of Abram (later to be named Abraham) something new begins. From that point on, God was creating a community.

Called

The call which founded this community set a pattern which God has followed ever since. We are the same kind of human material as they were, and his plans for the world have not changed. Then as now, it was God who took the initiative, not human beings, for Abram's background was pagan.

The call was not just for Abram's private benefit but for the blessing of all the families of the earth. What is more, God had chosen the small and the weak rather than the great and famous, as he still does. With this call he overrode all other loyalties, just as Jesus did in calling his disciples. He set Abram's sights on a better country and, improbable as it might seem, on a multitude of nations that would owe their existence to him.

God looked for one response alone from his people, from which all else would flow: faith in his promise. The New Testament underlines faith as the key response, not only for Abraham in his time but for everyone throughout time.

I will bless those who bless you, But I will curse those who curse you. And through you I will bless all the nations.

God's promise to Abram in Genesis 12

Bound together

But there was more than call and response. There was 'covenant'—the establishing of a bond between God and his people. Instead of settling for a cool and distant relationship, God bound himself to Abraham and his children and dependants in a tie that was permanent and warmly personal. The nearest equivalent to it is marriage, a model which is often used to speak of God's covenant in the Old Testament and the New. The heart of his covenant, like that of human marriage, is the pledge: I will be theirs, and they shall be mine.

Of course, as with any marriage, there were details to spell out if God's covenant was to live up to its name. There was the outward sign, the wedding ring, so to speak, which took the form of circumcision in the Old Testament. There were obligations to accept, summed up in Moses' day by the law and especially by its famous nucleus, the Ten Commandments.

The first four commandments called for undivided loyalty (like the wedding proviso: '... forsaking all other, keep only unto him'). The second group of those commandments emphasized that this was a people for God and for one another, not a bunch of individuals. So another picture of the bond between God and Israel described them not just as husband and wife but as father and family. To God, from this angle, his people were sons and daughters; and to one another, brothers and sisters.

If this sounds a little cosy and inward-looking, two things need saying:

- **Non-Israelite converts were thoroughly welcome.** Once circumcised, said the law, such a foreigner 'shall be as a native of the land' and 'you shall love him as yourself'.

CHRISTOPHER WRIGHT

The Land

Before humanity fell into sin, God dwelt with humankind in the earth, in the garden of Eden. After the fall humanity was alienated from God, barred from Eden and at odds with the earth. The story of redemption begins in Genesis 12 with God's promise to Abraham—a promise which includes a land to live in. Abraham's descendants were to be the nucleus of God's redeemed people; their land the prototype of God's redeemed and recreated earth, where he could once again dwell with men and women.

The fulfilment of this promise of a land is the central theme of the Old Testament's early historical books, running from the exodus, through the conquest of Canaan, to the reign of David. Once the people of Israel were in the land, they had a monumental witness to the power and faithfulness of their redeemer God.

The land was often called Israel's 'inheritance ; it was the proof of their special relationship to God as his children. They knew they were his people because he had given them his land. And it was God's good gift, a place of blessing, to be enjoyed to the full, with festivity and gratitude. And it was to be enjoyed by all. Every individual Israelite and his family had a right to a share in the land, because it was the common inheritance of all God's people. That is why the land was so carefully divided—'by families'.

The earth is the Lord's

However, possession of the land was not 'freehold'. The earth itself, though given into the stewardship of human beings, remains the Lord's. And the land of Israel, though given to Israel to use, was still God's property. He owns the land, he has moral authority over it, and so he has the right to demand that the land should be responsibly and justly used. Several Old Testament laws about how land was to be used reflect this divine concern for economic justice:

- ☐ **In the sabbatical year** (every seventh year) the land was to lie fallow, but 'the poor may eat what grows there'. (See Exodus 23.)
- ☐ **In the Jubilee year** (every fiftieth year) all property was to revert to its original owner or his descendants. This was intended to keep land within families and to keep small household units economically viable. (See Leviticus 25.)

The clear intention was that land use should be distributed as widely as possible. Later on, great royal estates developed, the poor were evicted for debt, and a few oppressors gathered enormous holdings. All this was vehemently condemned by the prophets. Such injustice was a major reason for God's judgment on Israel, which took the form of expulsion from the land and exile in Babylon.

In the New Testament, the promise to Abraham no longer applies only to his physical, national descendants, but to believers in Christ of any nationality. Likewise, the land element of the Old Testament no longer has relevance to the physical territory of Palestine. But it does still have theological significance:

- ☐ It is reflected in the **social dimensions of Christian experience**, especially the believers' love for one another. Like the land in the Old Testament, this fellowship is a 'tangible' proof of relationship with God. It carries very practical responsibilities, including financial equality.
- ☐ It remains the symbol of the **ultimate dwelling-place of God's redeemed people**—not some remote 'heaven', but 'new heavens and a new earth, where righteousness will be at home.'

■ The covenant-people was called to be a **servant nation** to a world which, as God reminded them, was 'all . . . mine'.

So, while much of the Old Testament has to stress the threat that the heathen nations posed to Israel, the thought of them as future converts keeps breaking in. In one of Isaiah's servant songs, the Lord says, 'Through you I will make a covenant with all peoples; through you I will bring light to the nations.'

One point is important at this stage. Israel was, from one angle, a church, but at the same time it was a nation. The two things were not yet separate. So its military set-up, its intricate laws and their enforcement, its structures and customs, were suited to its times and to its citizens.

Their God-given national institutions led them sometimes only a few steps forward, making various concessions to their 'hardness of heart' (as Jesus was to point out), but reminding them at frequent intervals of the love and justice that God expected of them. Not until the New Testament would God's brood be fully fledged, to leave the nest of the parent nation and be truly international.

Redeemed

So far, we have seen this people as called and covenanted. But there was a third strand in their make-up. They were never to forget that they had been called by God's grace. This took on a deeper meaning after the exodus from Egypt. The people were for a long time slaves and captives in that land. They were rescued only by an outstanding act of God at the Passover and the 'Red Sea' (more accurately, the Sea of Reeds).

JIM PUNTON

Shalom

'Shalom' is an exciting Hebrew word. 'Peace' no longer translates it. Shalom is wholeness, completeness, unbrokenness, full health, comprehensive well-being.

For the individual Shalom is soundness of being in every way; between persons it means relationships of trust, openness and caring that enable wholeness; in groups and society it involves social justice so that no sectional interest oppresses or exploits another; for nature it means living interdependently and responsibly, without pollution or destruction.

Shalom encompasses all reality, structural as well as personal. It speaks of the state of affairs where everything works and works together as God originally designed it. It is not a human achievement, but a gift of God.

As God created the world, everything was in shalom with him and with everything else. Then came the fall. Out of right relationship with God, everything lost shalom and became at odds within itself and with others. In his love God has always pursued the restoring of shalom to his universe. His way is through his son, 'the Prince of shalom'.

When Jesus was born, the song over Bethlehem was 'Glory to the highest to God. Shalom on earth among men . . .' The Messiah had come to 'guide our feet into the way of shalom.' He was the man of shalom. His miracles were shalom signs that promised a creation restored to wholeness; to the healed he said, 'Go into shalom.' It was shalom the disciples offered as they went two by two; to reject shalom was to reject salvation.

As the one who came to 'speak shalom to the nations', Jesus rode on the donkey into the City of shalom (Jerusalem). So often he had prayed for its shalom, now he wept for it. At the last supper he said, 'In me you may have shalom; in the world you have oppression.'

Reconciled

It had been predicted that God would make a new 'covenant of shalom' and Jesus knew this would come only through the death of the Messiah, so he spoke of 'the new covenant in my blood'. Isaiah had said, 'The chastisement that brings shalom to us was upon him and by his wounds we are healed.' He gave

This event was, to the Old Testament people of God, something of what the death and resurrection of Jesus are to us. Indeed, Paul called Jesus Christ 'our Passover lamb', and the Israelites' crossing of the sea their baptism. Just as truly as New Testament believers, though in a different way, they were redeemed by blood and set apart by water. They were not simply snatched from Pharaoh's grasp. God set them free from their slavery in Egypt by two specific acts of redemption:

- **The Passover.** When God's judgment fell on the Egyptians in the death of their firstborn, his promise to Israel was not that he would turn a blind eye to them, but that he would accept their 'passover sacrifice' of a lamb for each household. 'When he sees the blood on the lintel and on the two doorposts, the Lord will pass over the door, and will not allow the destroyer to enter your houses.'
- **The crossing of the 'Red Sea'.** This miraculous deliverance set them decisively clear of Egypt and its power. After it they began a new life as a nation under God's authority.

Already, then, the ancient promise to Abraham, 'I will make of you a great nation', was visibly coming true—though there was more to it than anyone had yet suspected. But God had also promised Abraham a land to live in.

Settled

The promised land was a tantalizing pledge. Its immediate effect was to make Abraham and his descendants strangers and pilgrims

his shalom to bring shalom to all. Paul wrote that God was 'pleased through him to reconcile all things to himself, making shalom through the blood of his cross.' Jesus' mission was to bring shalom, and he passed this reconciling ministry on to his disciples: 'Shalom be with you . . . As the Father sent me, so I send you'.

Through trust in the Messiah 'we have shalom with God'. This reconciled relationship brings previously divided people into shalom with one another.' Even Jews and Gentiles can unite in him 'for he himself is our shalom . . . and has broken down the barrier . . . that in himself he might create the two into one new humanity, making shalom.' God's people are freed from discrimination and oppression of race, culture, age, sex—or living in denial of Jesus. We are to 'live in shalom with each other' and 'seek the shalom of all people'. Did Jesus not say 'Blessed are the makers of shalom'? His people are the sign now of the coming kingdom which is 'justice, shalom and joy in the Spirit'.

The powerful among God's people of old failed to make shalom and do justice. So they found themselves deported to Babylon. Through Jeremiah, God says to them (and to us), 'Seek the shalom of the city where I have sent you . . . for in its shalom you will find your own shalom.' Only when we share in God's mission to the world are we open to receive his gift to us.

As we await the Messiah's 'new earth in which justice dwells' we are urged 'to be found by him in shalom'. God's purposes will be fully realized through his Son. All non-shalom will be eradicated and 'the new City of shalom' will come among us. Jesus will bring shalom to all creation: 'the wildest beasts will be in shalom with mankind'. As the prophet said, 'Of his reign and of his shalom, there will be no end.' And through him 'justice and shalom will kiss each other'.

The gospel, then, is 'good news of shalom'. It was God who 'sent out the word, evangelized shalom to those far off and near'. In the words of the prophet Isaiah, 'How beautiful on the mountains are the feet of one who . . . heralds shalom . . . who heralds salvation, who says "Your God reigns".'

Is it surprising that thirteen New Testament letters begin 'To you, grace and shalom from God our Father and the Lord Jesus, the Messiah'? Or that shalom is so often in the prayers of God's people? 'The shalom of God which passes all understanding will keep your hearts and minds in the Messiah Jesus.'

in a land not yet their own. They would have to wait centuries, they were told, until the land's inhabitants had forfeited the right to live there. And even then it took many years for the land to become fully and decisively theirs.

What was the significance of this land that was eventually to be theirs? At a purely practical level it gave Israel its settled place among the nations. But it was more than this. It was the Lord's land. '[The land] belongs to God, and you are like foreigners who are allowed to make use of it.' The sabbath, the firstfruits of the harvest, the temple, Israel itself, were set apart for God, despite the fact that everything belongs to him. And in the same way this land was named as God's although he is 'king of all the earth'. It was a bridgehead for the conquest of a rebel world, a home in which to nurture an adolescent family; but it was also a model of greater things to come.

Aids to obedience

We find in the Old Testament people of God, then, a nation who traced their origin to God's call, and traced that call simply to his love. Their security lay in God's covenant; their liberty stemmed from his acts of redemption; their land was primarily God's;

DAVID ATKINSON

Prophecy

The apostle Paul urged his Christian readers: 'Earnestly desire to prophesy.' What did he mean? What were the Bible prophets? And does prophecy still go on today?

In general terms, the prophet is the man or woman who speaks from God, interpreting God's message to his people, and applying it to their particular situation.

Rich variety

The Old Testament introduces us to a great variety of prophets who seem to have prophesied in many different ways. Among those we meet are:

- Samuel the 'seer', to whom the word of the Lord came in a dream while he was still a child;
- A rather ecstatic 'band of prophets', who influenced King Saul;
- People such as Elijah and Nathan who had very specific messages from God to individuals;
- Writing prophets (such as Amos, Hosea, Isaiah, Jeremiah) whose messages were more often addressed to the people as a whole.

The first great prophet was Moses, whose life and ministry set a pattern for all later prophecy. Like many of his successors, he had a sense of being called by God, an awareness of God's purpose for history, and a strong ethical and social concern. The later prophets frequently called the people back to true obedience to God by reminding them that God had made a covenant with them through Moses after the exodus. That covenant had called the people to obey God. In fact one of the central themes of the prophets is that true worship and a moral way of life always belong together.

There is a variety, too, in the way the prophet was inspired to receive his message, and in the style in which he gave it. Prophetic inspiration sometimes came in moments of ecstasy, sometimes through visions, as when Ezekiel saw the valley of dry bones. More often, though, we simply read that 'the word of the Lord came', perhaps sometimes as a result of study and preparation, sometimes by reflective prayer, sometimes in a symbolic way, as when Jeremiah saw significance in an almond branch, or a pot on the boil.

A common factor is that the prophet receives God's word by direct awareness and senses that he has to proclaim it. The prophet is not, though, an involuntary instrument. He will often give a reason for his message.

The prophet is known as the 'man of God', 'God's servant', 'his messenger', or even his 'watchman'. He enjoys God's

and their role was to be as priests and light-bearers for the blessing of the nations.

Meanwhile they were given throughout their history a variety of aids towards keeping faith with God and with their calling:

- **The law** was designed to make God's will a down-to-earth reality, 'for our good always' (as Moses put it), and 'very near you, in your mouth and in your heart, so that you can do it'. But by its very clarity and rightness it highlighted just how perverse human disobedience is. And so it became a means of convicting people of sin, of their inability to save themselves.
- **The worship**, that is, the whole cult system of priests and sacrifices, feasts and fasts, altar and sanctuary. All these emphasized the holiness of God. They showed that he was separate from people in their sinfulness, yet also that he was concerned to bridge the gulf.

Every one of these institutions was a mere shadow of what it signified. The priests were themselves sinners; the sacrifices, festivals and sanctuary were, so to speak, no more than paper-money, of no value save as

fellowship and speaks from an experience of intimate communion with God. To Amos God 'reveals his secrets'; Jeremiah 'stands in the council of the Lord'.

The prophet is one who 'forthtells' God's word, applying God's truth to the particular circumstances of his time. He also 'foretells' what will come to pass, knowing from his close communion with God what plans God has for the future. He often brings words of warning or judgment, comfort or promise. He is commissioned to proclaim the word he has received from God with urgency and contemporary relevance, calling the people back to the promises and obligations of being God's covenant family.

New Testament prophets

The same word that is used of the Old Testament prophet also describes a continuing function within the New Testament churches. Here also we find a variety of prophetic gifts, from the limited predictions of the travelling prophet Agabus, to the lasting divine authority claimed by the author of Revelation.

Prophets are linked with the apostles as the foundation of the church, and there are some groups of what we may call 'church prophets': men and women who contribute to the worship of the local churches. These groups minister in the following sorts of ways:

- ☐ Proclaiming God's message;
- ☐ Knowing something of the 'divine mysteries';
- ☐ Admonishing and exhorting;
- ☐ Edifying, encouraging and comforting;
- ☐ Bringing secret sins to light;
- ☐ Sometimes, like the 'teacher', interpreting and expounding Scripture.

The New Testament prophets look back to God's revelation in Jesus, and proclaim and apply God's truth revealed in him to the particular needs of the present, looking forward also with warning and hope.

In both Old and New Testaments, the false prophet appears, which is why the people of God are to test the message of every prophet. What are the tests?

- ☐ How closely the message conforms to what God has already revealed;
- ☐ How similar the prophet's character is to Jesus—'By their fruits you shall know them.' Plainly these tests are all the more important to apply today, when we have God's full revelation in Old and New Testaments.

What, then, did Paul mean when he urged his Christian readers, 'Earnestly desire to prophesy'? Seek to have close fellowship with God, with your mind and spirit and character trained by Jesus, that he may use you to proclaim and apply his word revealed in Jesus. Your message will engage with today's situation; it will build others up, and glorify God.

pledges of the reality behind them. That reality is heaven itself, and Jesus Christ is our priest and sacrifice. Both Paul, in Romans 3, and the writer to the Hebrews, in chapters 8–10, go into this matter in some detail.

- **The prophets** were a still livelier voice for God. There is always a risk that law and cult will fossilize, meaning less and less as people use them more and more. So God sent a stream of fearless men to speak out for him as need arose: men such as Samuel, Nathan and Elijah who stood up to kings; men such as Amos, Hosea, Isaiah, and a dozen other 'writing prophets' who warned their generations of God's judgment on their worldliness.

God gave these prophets a new vision also: they foresaw the perfection of a new age to come, when a king would reign in righteousness, when God would dwell among his people, and when the nations would be drawn into his kingdom. This would be God's new day.

A hint of dawn

For about the last 400 years of the old era, Israel was without a prophet, and was sadly conscious of the fact. But it was a pregnant silence, to be ended at the very break of God's new day. **John the Baptist** burst upon Israel as abruptly and urgently as Elijah. And two things gave his message a cutting edge sharper than anything ever known before:

- His **baptism for repentance**. For foreign converts this was nothing new; but for Israelites! It put them on a level with outsiders, and John declared as much: 'Don't start saying among yourselves that Abraham is your ancestor . . . God can take these stones and made descendants for Abraham!' What was more, it made the call to repentance searchingly personal. A person had to repent, not of the nation's sins, but of his own; not with routine apologies or in the privacy of his mind, but decisively and publicly, making his way through the crowd and into the river, confessing his sins.
- His **announcement of the Coming One**. God's King was already among them unrecognized; his baptism would not be just with water, like John's, but with 'Holy Spirit and fire'; his presence would separate the chaff from the wheat. John called him 'The Lamb of God, who takes away the sin of the world.' His role would be to suffer and make atonement, not only for Israel but for the world.

No other prophet had had a message like John's except as fragments of a distant prospect. It could mean only one thing. The new age had now dawned.

Jesus and the kingdom

What John had announced was swiftly confirmed. A voice from heaven was the first to endorse it, hailing Jesus at his baptism as 'my beloved Son'. Afterwards Jesus began his preaching with the words: 'The right time has come and the kingdom of God is near! Turn away from your sins and believe the Good News.'

What did Jesus mean by this 'kingdom', a word so often on his lips? Not just the realm over which God was king, as in our use of the word. Rather, his kingly presence right among them, and his exercise of power.

- **Crisis.** Here was an event that had overtaken them and must be faced; in fact, *the* event of all history.
- **The identity of the King.** Jesus left it to others to draw the conclusion that he was the long-awaited Messiah, though in accepting this royal title he filled it with new meaning.

- And then, to speak in terms of the kingdom was to speak of **the goal of world history**, the everlasting kingdom which would bring all human empires to an end.

The new people of God

'I tell you,' said Jesus to the leaders of Israel, 'the kingdom of God will be taken away from you and given to a people who will produce the proper fruits.' That 'people' would no longer be simply (or even primarily) the earthly nation of Israel. As Paul wrote, 'We are the people (God) called, not only from among the Jews but also from among the Gentiles.' Or as John saw in his Revelation vision, 'They were from every race, tribe, nation and language.' To such, without distinction, would now belong the name 'the Israel of God'.

It took time for this great fact to sink in. Gentile converts, duly circumcised, had long

ANDREW KIRK

The Kingdom of God

The theme of God's kingdom is central to both Old and New Testaments. Some think it is the most important idea of the whole Bible. Jesus said: 'Be concerned above everything else with the kingdom of God.'

In the Old Testament the kingdom expresses God's rule over all things. It tells us that he controls nature, governs Israel and oversees the life of all nations.

God is constantly at work to rule the world. The time will come when he will make everything new.

The kingdom becomes a reality through God's special representative. Sometimes called a king, a prince, a shepherd or a servant, this figure has both human and divine characteristics. He will 'establish justice and peace on the earth'. When this happens an entirely new age will have come.

Jesus began his ministry proclaiming that 'the kingdom of God is near'. Later he said 'it has already come upon you'. A Jewish scholar has written, 'Jesus is the only Jew known from ancient times to have proclaimed that the new age of salvation had already begun.'

Jesus also showed by his actions that God's kingdom was at work through him. He reversed every aspect of life which was hostile to God's new world: disease; demon-possession; guilt; a ritualistic empty religion; a caste system of purity and impurity; the shortage of food (he fed hungry crowds); hostile nature (he calmed a storm); economic exploitation (he drove the money-changers from the temple); even death.

The kingdom marks the end of all that disfigures or destroys what God has created 'very good'. Where the kingdom is, there people are wholly reconciled to God, to one another and to nature; fear, aggression, selfishness, falsehood and suffering are unknown; creation itself is 'set free from its slavery to decay'.

'The kingdom of God' is not used frequently as a term in the New Testament outside the Gospels, but it is very close to the idea of the new creation. God's new order has already begun wherever people recognize and practise his justice and it will not be complete until the end of this world's history. Then God's enemies, such as death and Satan, will be finally destroyed. Everyone and everything 'will openly proclaim that Jesus Christ is Lord'.

The kingdom is open for all people to join. Those who submit themselves to it are likely to be poor, often physically, and always because they recognize their need of God's salvation.

God's kingdom is 'not of this world'; human power, which depends on force, cannot establish it. Men and women cannot own it for themselves. They can only receive it as a gift from God, and surrender themselves unconditionally to its values of self-giving love and justice, compassion, service, non-aggression and readiness to suffer for others.

been welcomed into the Jewish faith, and so they were into what seemed to be the Christian branch of it. But it needed a vision and an act of God to make it dawn on the apostle Peter that there was now no distinction between Jew and Gentile: 'God . . . showed his approval of the Gentiles by giving his Holy Spirit to them, just as he had to us. He made no difference between us and them.' Even after this, Peter himself drew back a little from this revolutionary stance, until Paul corrected him, and the letter to the Galatians shows the battle for this truth still in progress elsewhere. It was a crucial battle.

The issue was not just the relation between Jew and Gentile but between God and his people. Paul could see clearly that the gospel of self-effort through the Jewish law

MARTIN GOLDSMITH

Jews and Christians

Christianity is built on the Jewish foundations of the Old Testament, the Jewish Messiah, and the early church which was largely Jewish. At first the early Christians followed the example of Jesus himself in attending the synagogue and observing Jewish practices. But not long before the destruction of the temple in AD 70, the Jewish leaders declared the Christians a separate movement. Already in the New Testament we have the seeds of the later chasm between Christianity and Judaism. And yet Christians' faith and worship are still firmly rooted in their Jewish background.

Soon after the New Testament era Christians became increasingly hostile to Jews. Bishop Melito of Sardis began the practice of accusing the Jews of deicide—murdering God. Tertullian and others joined the attack against Jews as the enemies of Christ. When Christianity was officially accepted in the Edict of Milan (AD 313), problems multiplied for Jews. Augustine developed a theology which excluded Jews from the people of God, while John Chrysostom and others engaged in passionate polemic against them. Christian witness today constantly faces this sad fact of the church's long history of persecuting Jews. The Crusades, the Inquisition and the Nazi Holocaust stand out in Jewish minds as extreme examples. Even the Reformers, Luther and Calvin, have been described as 'shameful' in what they said about Jews.

Gospel of the Messiah

What then is the Christian attitude to Jews today? Many have felt that with such a history Christians are wrong to evangelize Jews. They say that we should confine ourselves to showing our repentance and love by our kindness and friendship. But this denies the fundamental Christian truth that we can be saved only through faith in Jesus Christ, not through obeying the Law. If Christians truly love their Jewish neighbours, they will want to share with them their most prized possession, the gospel of Jesus the Messiah. They will want to offer this not only to the majority of Jews who are irreligious, but also to the few who stick firmly to their faith.

The Christian believes that the New Testament and the Christian faith are the perfect fulfilment and crown of the Jewish Old Testament faith. But Jewish religion is not pure Old Testament. Centuries of rabbinic traditions have been added. And so Christian witness will not only add the gospel of Jesus Christ to the Old Testament foundation, but will also come into conflict with some aspects of Jewish religious tradition.

Christians in their attitude to the Jew will share Paul's heartfelt wish 'that my own people might be saved'. They will likewise share Paul's sure hope that the Jews will be grafted back into God's church and that finally 'all Israel will be saved'. God will bring multitudes of Jews as well as Gentiles into his kingdom and in his church they shall be one, for our unity in Christ breaks down every barrier.

was no gospel at all. The 'sons of Abraham' were those of any nation who, like Abraham himself, were set right with God through faith, not merit. 'The Israel of God' was marked not by circumcision, nor for that matter by uncircumcision, but by new life through the Spirit.

The people of God were in fact people of the new covenant, long foretold. That covenant sums up the new order which was made possible by the death of Christ and reaffirmed at every Lord's Supper,'the new covenant in my blood'. It transforms the old covenant into an inward reality:

- God's laws written on our hearts, so that, as the Psalmist predicted of Christ himself, 'I love to do your will, my God!'
- God pledged to us, and we to him, just as in the old covenant;
- Direct intimacy with God, for every believer without exception;
- Assured and full forgiveness.

The household of God

Every believer has immediate access to his Lord, but the church is not a collection of individualists, each doing his inspired thing on his own. It is a body and a family with a certain structure and discipline. From the first, the apostles (chosen by Jesus) led and taught and corrected it. Its subsequent officers were picked for their work on the evidence that the Spirit had equipped them for it. In each local group, as the gospel spread, elders were appointed after prayer and fasting—for the choice must be God's.

As the second generation of the church grew up, Paul wrote down guidelines for making such appointments, in his pastoral letters to Timothy and Titus. He had also taken care to make there scattered congregations aware of one another, quick to come to one another's help, as members of God's people as a whole. They were being established as a new international community, 'the whole family in heaven and earth'.

One last word. We have called this people 'the new people of God', and so it is, in the sense that Jesus Christ has made everything new. But Christians are fellow citizens with God's people from the beginning, in direct continuity with all those in the Old Testament whose faith we follow and whose testimony we complete.

For further thinking

QUESTION 1

Jews and Christians share a common scripture and a common revelation of God, yet they differ greatly on how God's promises have been fulfilled. Should Christians relate to Jews as partners in one covenant? Or as non-believers to be evangelized? Or in some other way?

QUESTION 2

Are all the Old Testament laws binding on Christians? Or some of them? Or none?

QUESTION 3

Hans Küng wrote: 'The kingdom is creation healed.' Is this how you understand Jesus' teaching about the kingdom of God? Or does the idea also refer to the community of those who follow Jesus?

CHAPTER 25

GEORGE CAREY

Good News of Freedom

A young man who had been imprisoned on many charges, including arson, burglary, grievous bodily harm and stealing, said to me in prison: 'Christ has changed my whole life. He has made a new person out of me. I know he died to set me free. I may be behind bars now, but I am free in my heart.'

This is the core of Christianity. The good news of the gospel is all about God making people whole and setting them free from prisons of sin, self, fear and death. The simple message of Christianity is that Jesus gave his life for us so that we might live.

But there is little doubt that modern people, even Christians, find the death of Jesus puzzling. His life, teaching and good works are not hard to understand, but the interpretation of his death, other than as a tragedy, is very mysterious. And yet efforts to bypass the death of Jesus, or to minimize its significance, only make Jesus more of an enigma.

■ Only innocence expiates. Crime suffers in quite a different way.

Simone Weil

There are three common ways people understand what Jesus' death meant, all of them false:

- **It was not 'an accident'**. Jesus did not die as a result of an unfortunate accident due to some misunderstanding. He was much more than simply a political pawn. The New Testament writers saw the death of Jesus as the culmination of his life and ministry. Jesus advanced purposefully towards his death.
- **It was not simply 'a martyrdom'**. Other people have suffered worse fates than crucifixion. In Christian history, for example, followers of Jesus have died more painfully than him. Yet, they considered they were dying *for him*, in response to his love. But Jesus' death is seen in the Bible as offered for others, as really achieving something for mankind. In some ultimately unfathomable way his death gave life to men and women: his bondage sets people free, his sufferings give peace and wholeness to the world.
- It was **not just 'a good example'**. Jesus' death is certainly a noble example of someone meeting death with courage and dignity. But the great emphasis of the New Testament is that here is more than a moral lesson: it is the door of God's kingdom.

Indeed his death on a cross is central to Jesus' life and teaching. Far from it being on the edge of his thought, it is at the heart of his whole teaching. His whole career only makes sense when his death is put at the centre.

Who Died?

You cannot understand Jesus' death unless you know who he is. A mere man cannot set people free: free, that is, of those barriers to a fully human life as children of God; free to love and live for God again.

The testimony of the Bible is that he was God's promised Son whose love took him to a lonely cross. The early Christians met a lot of mockery when they preached about Jesus' death. For the Greeks the cross was a stumbling-block, and it was foolishness to the Jews. The idea that God's chosen way of salvation was through the death of a wandering Jewish preacher and healer was outrageous.

The extent of the offence of the cross can be gauged from something that happened in the third century, when the pagans tried to emulate the success of Christianity. They fabricated a pagan redeemer cult based on a first-century wise man called Apollonius of Tyana, for whom they mapped out a career whose main shape was based on the career of Jesus. But they missed out his death. That was too much!

Yet at the centre of Christianity is a dying Saviour who was God himself. It has always been fundamental to the Christian faith that Jesus was the unique and matchless Son of God. Only if it is the work of God himself can the death of Jesus have meaning for the entire human race.

Why Did He Die?

Jesus died to save humanity. The root meaning of the verb 'to save' is 'to rescue from danger'. The danger may be physical peril, national disaster, personal danger, illness of various kinds, as well as anguish of the soul.

But there is a much deeper meaning in the verb 'to save'. In Hebrew it means:

- **'To make room for'**; to rescue from all that constricts and imprisons, and to bring into freedom.
- When people are 'rescued' they move from **captivity to freedom**, from darkness to light and from illness to health.

The noun 'salvation', then, is the state of being saved, and when applied to the Christian faith has a past, present and future application.

- 'Salvation' is located firmly in a **past** event. It has already happened. When Jesus Christ died, once-for-all in history, he saved us, and so we have been set free and made whole.
- This salvation can be experienced in the **present**, through what Jesus has done, and through the presence and power of the Holy Spirit.
- It will be completed in the **future** when God's purposes are fulfilled.

Salvation is a word which means all kinds of wholeness—personal, spiritual, corporate. But the Bible uses it to go to the very heart of the trouble, which is that humanity is separated from God through sin. When people are really conscious of their sinfulness and need, they become aware of the gulf between themselves and God. They long to be 'at one' with him. This longing is met by the Bible doctrine known as **atonement**, 'at-one-ment', the way we are put right with God.

Atonement in the Bible

Throughout the Bible we find a constantly recurring question: how can God and humanity be reconciled?

The Old Testament writers lay the basics for this question. If God is utterly holy, is it possible for sinful people to have any dealings with him? The Old Testament's answer 'yes' is rooted in its firm belief in the love of God for humankind. God has made a covenant with his people. He will not cast them away for ever.

This problem of how a holy God can be reconciled to sinful people is the reason for the God-given system of sacrifices, which were thought to 'propitiate' God and 'expiate' the sins of the people. But not everyone was satisfied that the sacrificial system was effective. The prophets were especially critical.

Only a God who suffers can save us.

Dietrich Bonhoeffer

It was an all-too-easy way of bypassing justice. The question became more and more pressing: can anything we do bridge the gulf between holiness and sin, between God and humanity?

The New Testament answers the question simply and directly: Jesus died a sacrificial death for us all. In other words, reconciliation is central to what it means that Jesus died. All the sacrifices and ritual of the old order were abolished, as the letter to the Hebrews makes clear: 'It is impossible that the blood of bulls and goats could take away sin.' People's sins cannot be borne away by sinless animals. Yet the system did have its value. It kept alive in people's minds the connection between sin and death. Above all it foreshadowed the perfect sacrifice of Jesus.

The perfect sacrifice we could not offer for ourselves, Christ offered for us in his death.

Does this characterize Jesus Christ as some third party, distinct both from God and from people, appeasing God's wrath towards humankind? Not according to the New Testament: 'God was in Christ reconciling the world to himself.' In the work of humanity's salvation the initiative is taken by God himself. The New Testament will not allow any distinction between God and Christ in what happened on the cross. Reconciliation is seen all along as something that begins from God's side.

Now we can begin to see just how radical the Christian gospel of salvation is, and why it was such a 'scandal' in the early days of Christianity. Even today it still offends people who pride themselves on their own good deeds, because it teaches certain things very clearly and simply:

- **We can contribute nothing to our own salvation.** Our nature is so weakened by sin that we cannot rescue ourselves.
- **Salvation is all of 'grace'**—free and undeserved. It is given, never earned.
- **God is personally involved in saving us.** This personal action of God is summed up in Luther's phrase 'the crucified God'. God's only Son, who shares the very nature of God, became a man so that he could die for us.

When we were still helpless, Christ died for the wicked.

Paul in Romans 5

How Did He Die for Us?

The question 'how' introduces us to the theories of the atonement. Exactly what God did in the death of Jesus has been interpreted in different ways in the past. Although the church in the past has arrived at firm definitions of who Jesus was, it has never yet arrived at a fixed understanding of what he did for us. No creed contains an interpretation. Christians have regarded it as self-evident that Jesus' death was utterly decisive for the needs of humanity, but it has been left to each generation to express the truth of this death in its own way.

All these different theories try to explain what it means that Jesus died 'for us'. In his fine book *Miracle on the River Kwai*, E. Gordon tells of a terrible incident in a Second World War Japanese prison camp. The British prisoners were taken back to camp at the end of a hard day's work on the Burma railway. As was customary, the shovels and tools were counted. The Commanding Officer was told that one shovel was missing. The prisoners were lined up and told to produce the missing shovel. No one moved.

The Commanding Officer ordered that a machine gun be trained on the prisoners. 'If the guilty man does not step forward, you will all be shot,' he screamed. Still no one moved. Then, as it looked as if the Commanding Officer was about to give the order to fire, one man stepped forward. He was hustled away and shot. The following day, as the tools were issued, it was found that no shovel was in fact missing; a Japanese soldier had not counted properly.

In a true sense that prisoner died for his friends. Although not guilty, he died as a true substitute; if he had not died, perhaps all of them would have.

Now clearly this can only be a faint picture of what Jesus did for us. God is no prison camp commander and we are far from innocent. Yet it raises for us an important question: How do we understand the idea of Jesus dying for us?

An objective atonement

Apart from 'moral influence' theories like Abelard's, all other theories assume that Jesus Christ's death was an *objective* atonement, through which God and human beings were reconciled as otherwise they could not have been. But theologians are divided over the best way to describe how Jesus rescued us. Did he die as our 'substitute', dying a death we deserved, the innocent for the guilty? Or was he a 'representative' of the new humanity which is re-created in him as the new Adam?

The idea of Jesus as our **'substitute'** has sometimes been rejected as immoral. How can we think of God, some have said, as if he would inflict retributive punishment on the humanity he created and loves? But those who argue for the substitutionary doctrine insist it is far from immoral. The Bible teaches us that God's moral law calls for sin to be punished. 'The wages of sin is death'—the spiritual death of separation from God—but our sin and guilt is expiated as God himself intervenes, through his Son, stepping into our place and dying for sinners.

The idea of Jesus as **'representative'** has difficulties too. Can Jesus really be our representative when he is without sin? As has been said: 'A representative not produced by us but given to us—not chosen by us but the elect of God—is not a representative at all in the first instance, but a substitute.' But, as has been pointed out, the New Testament consistently uses a word meaning 'for, on behalf of' in this context, and avoids one meaning 'instead of'. Yet is it really a question of 'either . . . or' with these two descriptions? Can it not be 'both . . . and'? It is surely possible to see that Jesus' death is *both substitutionary and representative*. Jesus Christ is certainly the representative of a new humanity, but he is also the one who 'becomes sin for us', who dies for the ungodly.

The mystery of the cross

In the end, when faced with the cross of Christ, we are confronted by mystery. The Bible tells us a great deal about the death of Jesus Christ but it makes no attempt at a full and complete explanation of the reason for it. Why should God's love for us compel him to give his only Son? How can it be that Jesus was made sin for us and died in our place? How is it possible for sinful people to be counted as righteous through Jesus Christ's righteousness? How can it be that through his death our destiny is sealed in heaven?

One thing Jesus' death on the cross does make clear is that God personally takes responsibility on himself for the sin, pain, brokenness and suffering of the world, to make it new. He enters into the depths of our human suffering. Jesus takes our question on himself: 'My God, my God, why have you forsaken me?' And we can know in the depths of our need that he is alongside us; he has been there before us. He will help us through to resurrection. Despite the mystery in understanding, God does set us free.

The mystery in the cross is part of the mystery of Christianity; it should not be a stumbling-block to faith. Human life generally is shot through with mysteries. Why do people feel love for each other? It is a mystery. Yet their love is a powerful influence in their lives, affecting everything they think and do. And so it is with the cross. There is power in the cross, claims the New Testament. For those who put their trust in what Jesus did there, it becomes for them 'the power of God for salvation'.

Salvation and New Life

We must never separate the death of Jesus from his life, resurrection and ascension. These are often spoken of together as the 'Christ events'. Although the cross is central to the New Testament, the writers did not talk about a dead saviour but a living saviour who once died. The church is built on the foundation of the cross and resurrection of Jesus. The Christians were only able to preach with such total conviction that Jesus Christ died for sinners because they believed that he was risen, and experienced that fact with intense joy.

What the resurrection means

It is one thing believing the resurrection to be a fact in history; it is quite another thing discovering what it means today. What is the inner meaning of the belief that Jesus was raised from death? The resurrection is not of someone like you or me, but of Jesus Christ who, unlike you or me, lived a special life and claimed a special relationship with God. This makes his resurrection crucial, for our salvation and for our future. The best way to find what it means is to look at four great words the New Testament links with resurrection: power, peace, joy and hope.

■ He [Jesus] was shown with great power to be the Son of God by being raised from death.

Paul in Romans 1

■ **The resurrection shows God's power.** For the first Christians the resurrection proved the claims of the crucified Jesus. He had hung upon the cross in such weakness. But in the resurrection God's power clearly broke through.

This shows us that **Jesus is Lord**. Peter proclaimed to the Jews gathered on the day of Pentecost: 'Listen, fellow Israelites! This Jesus ... God has raised from death ... and is the one God has made Lord and Messiah.' The resurrection proved that Jesus was all he had claimed to be and that he has a right to be called God's Son.

And so **the church was born in power**. The resurrection gave birth to the church. The death of a crucified carpenter could not, by itself, explain why hundreds of his followers were prepared to die for him. But after his resurrection the risen Lord Jesus promised his people that they would know the Spirit's power in a wholly new way. Even today the church is a living witness to the power of the resurrection.

■ **The resurrection brings peace and joy.** If power is the external proof of the resurrection, peace and joy are the internal confirmations of its reality. The New Testament gives Jesus' resurrection a crucial role in our salvation. 'Jesus died for our sins,'

What Kind of Freedom?

Ransomed from the devil

In the early centuries the most commonly accepted theory was that through the death of Jesus mankind was released from the devil's power—his sacrifice was a ransom which paid the price of our release. Although it was never explicitly taught that the ransom was paid to the devil, the theory did border on the idea of a transaction between God and the devil with people as the helpless victims.

The divine Champion

In the medieval period, theologians interpreted what Jesus Christ had achieved according to the images found within their own culture. **Anselm**, in an important book *Cur Deus Homo?* (Why did God become human?), interpreted the death of Jesus along the lines of feudal honour and payment of rights. Because humanity owed God certain dues and could not pay, Jesus Christ, through his exemplary life and sacrificial death, became our champion and paid the dues which separated the 'serfs' (mankind) from the 'baron' (God).

Life-changing love

Abelard taught about 'love which redeems'. This is an almost modern understanding of the power of love. Abelard dispensed with objective theories, that sin was dealt with by some kind of objective payment, and moved across to a subjective understanding that when people see the extent of God's love, generous and undeserved, their hearts are moved to a response.

The defeat of the tyrants

Luther's understanding returned to the early concept of ransom, but he based it more within the teaching of the New Testament. Jesus' death was a once-for-all sacrifice which atoned for sin, and dealt with the 'tyrants' which held mankind in bondage: death, sin and the devil.

The perfect penitent

More modern interpretations have tried to steer a middle course between Abelard's subjective theory and the somewhat harsher interpretations which appear to be saying God's wrath was being placated by an innocent Jesus. So, **McLeod Campbell** (nineteenth century) suggested that Jesus offered a sacrifice of 'vicarious penitence'. That is, Jesus was the perfect penitent and this becomes available for us all.

The eternal cross

H. Bushnell argued that Jesus Christ reveals the cross in the heart

Paul wrote, 'but rose for our justification.' That is, his rising to life gives life to all who follow him. A dead saviour is no good to anyone, but Jesus is alive and through his resurrection evil is defeated. And so peace and joy come to us through what Jesus achieved.

Peace is God's legacy because sin is defeated, and **joy** floods the life of the Christian in the springing up of a new life. In his great chapter on the Christian inheritance, Romans 5, Paul brings these two words together: 'Being justified by faith we have peace with God . . . and we rejoice because of what God has done through our Lord Jesus Christ.'

■ **The resurrection spells hope.** We have the reality of Christ's power, peace and joy now, most certainly. The testimony of millions of Christians through the centuries to this fact makes an impressive story. And Jesus' resurrection has made possible more than the rebirth of the individual. It has given rise to the new community of Jesus, to a whole new humanity.

But we must not forget that our knowledge and our experience are only partial. Salvation is incomplete in this life. We know only too well that all healing is only partial and temporary; physical death is a harsh fact. We live 'in between' Christ's resurrection and the resurrection of all things.

---

of God. The cross was not just something that happened a long time ago, but still today it shows us that God is one with his suffering world. Somehow suffering itself is redemptive. God's sufferings release his love to the world.

The cosmic victory

Gustav Aulen, from Sweden, sees the death of Jesus as a dramatic victory which displays for us the way God deals with human sin and conquers evil.

The crucified God

From Germany, **Jurgen Moltmann** sees the crucifixion as utterly decisive for the Christian faith. In it is revealed the nature of God and the way he works in the world. Jesus was the 'blasphemer' who placed his preaching above the authority of Moses. He was the 'rebel' who broke with the status quo, preaching a kingdom whose values transcended the world's. He was the 'God-forsaken one' who died abandoned on the cross. Moltmann argues that the resurrection of Jesus is an integral part of the cross. It makes sense of the suffering of Jesus. The cross and resurrection together declare to a suffering humanity that God suffered too and has conquered death, as will all Jesus' people.

The political cross

From Latin America in recent years has emerged an understanding of the cross as a model for oppressed people. The appalling social problems in that continent have led Christian leaders of all denominations to realize that the Christian faith cannot be kept out of the political sphere. The church is committed to helping those who are oppressed. The cross is a vital model for Christians working for justice and peace. Jesus suffered in our place, and this has become a model in two different ways:

☐ **Identification with suffering.** Just as Jesus had to accept misunderstanding, pain and death, so his followers are called to bear the sufferings of others.

☐ **Identification with revolutionaries.** Many Christians in South America (and in parts of Africa too) believe that taking up the cross means actual involvement in overthrowing evil regimes.

Christians are divided over these issues, but what liberation theology sees correctly is that the Christian faith has social and political implications. Following the crucified and risen Jesus is not a private affair.

We live in hope. But it is a hope which brightens everything that happens on earth and which gives value to every human achievement. This hope is not just for our future. God has given us a foretaste of it in the resurrection of his Son. It is God's declaration that one day we shall be as he is. So John declares: 'It is not clear what we shall become, but we know that when Christ appears we shall be like him, because we shall see him as he really is.'

Good news indeed

The gospel is good news that we are set free to be the kind of people God wishes us to be. It is good news God offers as a free gift to us who are thoroughly unworthy of his generous self-offering. Jesus' 'once-for-all' offering of himself remains valid to the present day. God will never be content with anything less than that full at-one-ment by which we are made one with God, with our neighbour, with our environment and with our own inner self. Physical health, holiness of life and social well-being make up what the Bible means by 'wholeness of salvation'.

Since good news comes to us freely and with such wonderful benefits, it is for Christian people to show forth this freedom in our lives day by day. Cardinal Suenens once told a journalist why he was so full of hope: 'I am a man of hope, not for human reasons nor from natural optimism. But because I believe the Holy Spirit is at work in the church and in the world, even where his name remains unheard. I am an optimist because I believe the Holy Spirit is the Spirit of creation. To those who welcome him he gives each day fresh freedom and a renewal of joy and hope.'

For further thinking

QUESTION 1

Choose one New Testament picture for what Jesus achieved for us in his death. This list includes some of them: justification, sacrifice, way to God, means of forgiveness, victor over evil, example of suffering, redemption, reconciliation. Why does your chosen picture mean so much to you? How would you explain it to a friend?

QUESTION 2

The greatest example of 'salvation' in the Old Testament was the exodus from Egypt: the people of Israel were led out of slavery and into their 'promised land'. What features of that great story best illustrate the idea of salvation?

QUESTION 3

The first gospel preaching, recorded in the early chapters of the Acts of the Apostles, lays more stress on Jesus' resurrection than on his death. Why might this have been? Can we understand the one apart from the other?

BIBLE REFERENCES

Salvation

Genesis 3:15; 12:1–3; 15:6; Exodus 12:3–7; 14:10–31; 18:10; 24:6–8; Leviticus 16:6–22; Deuteronomy 6:21–23; Isaiah 51:1–6; 52:13—53:12; 55:1–7; 61:1–3; Jeremiah 31:31–36; Ezekiel 36:24–30; Zechariah 9:9; 12:10; 13:1; Matthew 25:31–46; Mark 2:5–11; Luke 4:16–21; 15:4–32; 18:9–14, 35–43; 19:1–10; John 3:1 17; 4:10–14, 42; 5:24; 6:69; 9:35–39; 10:10, 27–29; 17:3; Acts 2:38; 3:13–19; 4:12; 9:3–19; 10:43; 16:22–34; Romans 1:16–17; 3:21–26; 5:1–10; 8:1–4; 10:4–9; 1 Corinthians 1:18–25, 30; 2 Corinthians 6:2; Galatians 2:20; 3:13; 5:1; Ephesians 1:3–14; 2:8–10; Philippians 3:4–11; Colossians 1:3–5, 13–23; 1 Thessalonians 1:10; 1 Timothy 1:15; 2:3–5; 4:10; 2 Timothy 1:9–10; Titus 3:4–7; Hebrews 2:3–4, 9–10; 9:23–28; 1 Peter

1:3–9, 18–23; 2:2–4, 21–25; 3:18–22; 1 John 3:1–8, 16; 4:9–10; Revelation 7:9–11; 12:10–11

The Death of Jesus

Genesis 3:15; Isaiah 52:13—53:12; Jeremiah 31:31–34; Matthew 1:21; 16:21; 26:26–29; 27:27–54; Mark 10:45; 15:21–47; Luke 12:49–50; 22:14–23; John 1:29; 12:24; 19:1–37; Acts 2:22–23; 3:15; 4:10; 8:32–35; 10:38–43; Romans 3:23–25; 5:6–10; 8:1–3; 1 Corinthians 1:22–25; 5:7; 15:3; 2 Corinthians 5:14–21; Galatians 2:20; 3:13; Ephesians 1:7; 2:13; 2:16; Philippians 2:5–10; 3:10; Colossians 1:20; 2:13–15; 3:3; 1 Thessalonians 2:15; 1 Timothy 1:15; 2:5; 2 Timothy 1:10; Titus 3:4–7; Hebrews 2:14–18; 5:7–9; 7:26–27; 9:12–14; 10:11–14, 19–22; 12:2; 1 Peter 1:11, 18–19; 2:21–24; 3:18; 1 John 1:7; Revelation 1:5–7; 5:9–10

Raised from Death

Psalms 16:9–11; Isaiah 26:19; Matthew 22:23–33; 28:1–15; Mark 16:1–8; Luke 24:1–43; John 5:28–29; 6:39–40; 11:25–26; 20:1–28; 21:1–14; Acts 2:29–32; Romans 1:4; 6:4; 8:11; 14:9; 1 Corinthians 15:3–23, 35–58; 2 Corinthians 4:14; Philippians 3:20–21; 1 Thessalonians 4:13 14; Revelation 1:17–18

The New Creation

Isaiah 61:1–3; 65:17–25; Jeremiah 31:33; Ezekiel 37:1–10; Matthew 18:1–4; Luke 4:16–21; John 3:3–5; Acts 3:19–21; Romans 6:4; 8:18–23; 2 Corinthians 5:17; Colossians 3:1–10; Titus 3:4–7; Revelation 21:1–7

CHAPTER 26

GEORGE CAREY

Finding Faith

In our modern secular world the word 'faith' arouses a great deal of scepticism, even derision. 'Faith,' said the schoolboy, 'is believing something you know isn't true.'

But faith is not credulity, believing any half-baked idea that comes along. Even secular life could not operate without faith. Someone in the office asks you for a loan of ten pounds; you lend it, secure in the knowledge that they will pay it back. That is faith. You buy a present for your spouse's birthday, a watch perhaps, believing the maker's guarantee that it is reliable. That is faith.

In the Bible there is scarcely a word which has a more varied and a richer meaning than the word 'faith'. If you have faith in someone, you trust in that person's character. So, in the Bible, faith rests in the character of God. He keeps his promises to men and women; he can be trusted.

In the Old Testament the prophets spoke of the Lord's 'steadfast love', his faithfulness to his people. They may wander away from him but he remains faithful.

The basis of New Testament faith is the life, death and resurrection of Jesus. If people 'believe' in Jesus they trust in the *fact* of what Jesus has done for them. And so even faith is not the most fundamental thing in a person's salvation; what comes first is God's faithfulness, both in promise and in action. Human beings' faith is a response to God's initiative.

Come to me, all of you who are tired from carrying heavy loads, and I will give you rest. Take my yoke and put it on you, and learn from me... and you will find rest.

Jesus, in Matthew 11

Trust and commitment

Especially in Paul's letters and in John's Gospel, we find that faith means trusting our whole life to God. The modern word 'commitment' comes very close to this. The New Testament seldom says merely 'believe...', but rather 'believe in' (literally 'into') God or Jesus. What is required is not just assent to an idea, but humble acceptance of what God has done.

Faith, then, is *trust* in what God has done, which results in a wholehearted commitment, trusting ourselves to him. This affects every area of our life.

The Bible also makes it clear that 'faith' cannot be separated from our life, our behaviour and the world we live in. James writes that 'faith without works is dead'. But he is not contradicting the emphasis in the rest of the New Testament that we are saved by faith alone. His point is that mere intellectual belief is barren. The demons believe in God, he says, but it makes no difference to their conduct. A real faith will always issue in a changed life.

By extension we use the term 'faith' to declare *what* is believed. When Christians in their worship say 'this is the faith of the church', they mean the Christian faith expressed in the Bible and in the creeds of the church. The difference of emphasis between a Protestant and a Catholic understanding of 'faith' comes out here. When a Protestant uses the word 'faith', he or she normally has in mind our personal response to God. The Catholic would most naturally assume that it is the faith of the church that is being discussed, faith expressed in creeds.

In short, to have faith is to accept what God has revealed of himself in Jesus. To have faith is to yield ourselves to Jesus in the light of what he has revealed.

Conversion

The word 'conversion' literally means a 'turning', a 'changeover'. In Britain during the change from coal gas to natural gas, people spoke about being 'converted' to natural gas. When used of the Christian life it is associated with moving from one way of living to another, from ungodliness to holiness, from a life lived without reference to

God to one which puts God at the centre.

Strangely enough, the Greek word for being converted is not used very often in the New Testament, and some have therefore wrongly assumed that the idea of conversion is insignificant. Some important questions are also asked about it:

- Is conversion essential before a person can truly claim to be a Christian?
- Does conversion have to be sudden?
- Can a person be a Christian who has not experienced a black-and-white conversion experience but has grown into a mature acceptance of Jesus Christ?

To give a proper answer to these questions, we must look at some factors which are always present when a person comes to faith in Jesus Christ:

- **Awareness of need.** No one comes to faith in Jesus without a sense that something is missing in life. This can take different forms with different people. One person may be conscious of moral failure, an inability to overcome temptation. Another may be aware of a sense of frustration and futility in life. Another may come to realize that life has no meaning unless God is brought into the picture. All this shows that there are many different kinds of sin, and our longing for God finds expression in very varied ways. In the Bible, Mary Magdalene's problem was different from Paul's, and Peter's was different again. But each of them saw Jesus as the answer.

- **Willingness to turn.** The word for this is 'repentance'. The word for 'repentance' in Greek means to turn round or have a change of heart and attitude. Repentance involves being sincerely sorry for our sin and willing to change direction.

- **Faith in Jesus Christ.** Turning is one thing, but in itself is not enough. Many people like to turn over a new leaf, but this does not make them Christians.

Jesus called people 'to repent *and believe the gospel*'. A person must accept Jesus as who he claimed to be, the Saviour and Lord of our lives. It means taking up his yoke. By a conscious decision, I turn my back on my old life and enter a new life based on Jesus. I become a disciple, a follower of Jesus, who learns to live his way.

In the Acts of the Apostles and the teaching of Paul, the death and resurrection of Jesus are put central in Christian conversion. If Jesus died for sinners and rose to prove it, so the Christian must die to the old nature and begin afresh through the Holy Spirit. This is expressed symbolically in baptism. Indeed, baptism in the New Testament and in the early church was in itself a symbol of conversion, in that it graphically declared a person's rejection of the old life and entry into new life through the Holy Spirit.

Looking back on the questions raised earlier, we may now be able to suggest some answers. It is clear from human experience that 'sudden' conversions are rarely sudden at all. Usually they are the result of thought and exploration which have gone on for a long time. C. S. Lewis told us that he came to belief in God on top of a double-decker bus. But this was the climax of a long, painful search.

For some, conversion is a 'crisis' event. But the experience of many Christians in all traditions of the Christian churches is that this discovery of faith may come through steady growth and teaching in the Christian life, without any crisis of belief or identifiable turning-point.

A distinction has been drawn between 'once-born' and 'twice-born' Christians. Both are valid forms of Christian experience. And yet it remains true that awareness of need, willingness to turn, and belief in Jesus are essential to Christianity itself. A person who

Unless you change and become like children, you will never enter the kingdom of heaven.

Jesus, in Matthew 18

HUGH SILVESTER

Commitment and Openness

Some people shy away from Christian faith-commitment, because they believe it would involve closing their minds to all other truth. Does commitment to Jesus preclude a healthy open-mindedness in our thinking?

While all descriptions of God by people are provisional and partial, Christians are prepared to assert that God is personal. This is not to make him a kind of 'superman'; that would be to make God in humanity's image. But he must contain in himself the highest we know in the created order, that is personhood.

It follows from this that if we are to know God, it will be more like knowing a person than knowing an electron or a mathematical theorem or even an animal. And the key to getting to know a person is trust. As the trust deepens the knowledge grows; and the deepening trust is commitment. There has to be some commitment even in the first tentative stages, a cautious opening of oneself to allow something to communicate.

Getting to know you

This is how we get to know another person:

- ☐ **'Wondering-if'.** Is this person worth knowing? Shall I bother? Shall I take the risk of saying 'Hello'? Does the recommendation of someone else help?
- ☐ **First contact.** A greeting, a sentence, an enquiry. A small promise made, or promise exchanged. 'I'll see you on Thursday.'
- ☐ **Promise and trust.** This is the way the friendship grows. Appointments, letters, shared meals, deeper conversation.
- ☐ **Shared vision.** Exchange of views, adapting our own ways to fit the other person. Doing things together.
- ☐ **Deeper commitment and vows.** These may be informal in a friendship; formal in marriage or partnership.

At each stage there has to be some commitment, some risk. Otherwise there is no opening and no communication.

The movement from being an agnostic (that is, not knowing) to being a Christian can be described along these lines:

1. No personal contact with God. Even doubting his existence. The Bible says that to be like this is to be 'without hope', that is, to have no conviction that life has an ultimate purpose. It is also inevitable that if worship is withheld from the creator it will be given to created things or people.

2. 'Wondering-if', followed by a willingness to listen. Jesus' parable of the sower is followed by 'Take care how you listen'. Some commitment to the Bible and to Christians is vital, even if it is only tentative. A person needs to get the feel of what it is like to believe. The apostle Paul repeatedly emphasizes that it is by faith we get to know God.

3. Conversion or whole-commitment. The believer gives himself to Jesus Christ and Jesus, by his Spirit, gives himself to the believer. There follows a life together, in which the commitment of the believer binds him to the openness of God towards the world and all people. It is also a commitment of love and mutual service to the church.

Being 'open' does not mean being totally open-minded to all possibilities. Just as a scientific view, once adopted, excludes other views, so the Christian view is exclusive of other theologies. But this does not mean that any set of Christian beliefs is exhaustive. They are open-ended to fresh insight and restatement. Being a Christian does not mean being dominated by a form of words, but being submissive to God in Jesus Christ.

has them all is a converted person. The route itself is not the most important thing; what really matters is the destination.

New birth

Conversion from one point of view can be seen as our own effort to do something about our spiritual problem. We are aware, we turn, we believe. This is, of course, oversimplistic, because God too is at work at each point. But there is an element of truth in it. Because the word 'conversion' refers to the human side of becoming a Christian.

'New birth' is the action of God alone. He alone, through his Spirit, gives life to those who turn to him. There cannot therefore be a true conversion without the inner renewal of the individual. My turning is met by God's gracious forgiveness of sin, and the Holy Spirit meets with my inward self.

In the Old Testament, the focus is on national renewal. The prophets realized that the many attempts to reform society had failed. Calls to repent, to turn away from evil to good living and religious observance, had all failed. A more radical way was needed. Instead of imposing the law from outside, the only real way forward was a renewal of the individual.

In the New Testament, the dominant idea is that we are so separated from God through our sin that only a birth from above can make it possible for us to enter the kingdom. Jesus' words to Nicodemus tell us that the way to spiritual life is not through religious knowledge, or through the privileges of human birth. It is the gift of God, through the Holy Spirit.

The means of new birth

A person is born again as a result of the personal activity of God through the Holy Spirit. Jesus told Nicodemus that no one can have eternal life unless they are 'born by water and the spirit'. 'Water' refers to baptism, which will be considered later. For the moment we can say that baptism has always been seen as important in the mystery of regeneration. To be baptized, to enter the church and to be a Christian, all point to the same thing in the New Testament.

We must not fall however into the trap of thinking that baptism automatically gives new birth. Baptism is important for what its graphic symbolism bears witness to: new life in the Spirit and a decisive break with the old nature. It cannot of itself convey life in the Spirit if faith is not present. New birth means:

- **Death to the old life.** New birth means that sin and selfishness are no longer dominant. Only a total, root-and-branch renewal can bring salvation.
- **The start of a new relationship.** The new birth begins an essentially personal happening between God and the individual. It is a wholly new start which results in our membership of God's family.

It is the work of God himself. New birth cannot be earned or bought, only given. As the work of the Holy Spirit it is mysterious. 'The wind blows where it wishes,' said Jesus. 'It is like that with everyone who is born of the Spirit.'

No one can enter the kingdom of God unless he is born of water and the Spirit.

Jesus' words to Nicodemus in John 3

The results of new birth

The New Testament speaks in unmistakable terms about the new life of the believer. He or she now has a new relationship with God as Father, Son and Holy Spirit. People who have God as their Father are taken into the wonder of a secure relationship with their heavenly Creator and Lord. Through the Spirit they are given strength to live as Christians in the world, and this ability to live as Christians will grow with time.

In Christian theology this process of growth is called 'sanctification'. Christians cannot claim to be holy, because they are only too well aware of the power of sin and temptation. What they are confident of claiming is a personal relationship with God. Their desire is to live as those who please God.

The process of growth takes place within the family of God (the church), which is the essential home for all believers. There is no such thing as a 'Robinson Crusoe' Christian; the individual Christian finds his or her life within the Christian community.

The Bible's teaching on new birth points forward to the renewed creation which is prophesied in Scripture. Jesus Christ came to renew not only the individual but also humanity and the whole of creation itself.

This new order in Christ is referred to in the Bible as a 'new creation' and even a 'new man'. These descriptions look beyond the individual and show God's intention to make for himself a new people. The new birth leads to a new hope, therefore, centred on Jesus, which affects individuals, humanity, and even creation itself.

Eternal Life

Someone once wrote on the walls of the British Museum, 'Is there intelligent life on earth?' Someone else scrawled below, 'Yes, but I'm only passing through!' We all want to know what life means and where we are going.

Humanity's most basic questions revolve around the two fundamental issues of *meaning* and *existence*, and they are closely linked together. If this life is all there is, then I may grab what meaning I can from passing moments and events, but in the end it will not amount to much. My life will pass with everything else into everlasting darkness.

To all who received him, to those who believed in his name, [Jesus] gave the right to become children of God.

John 1

The Christian conviction is that Jesus has 'passed through' and made sense of life. He has transformed our existence through his life, death and resurrection, and the new life of the Spirit that he gives to all who come to him.

The Christian has a hope, which breaks the hopelessness of existence. This hope has certain basic ingredients:

- **God's life transforms our existence.** Our natural existence is God-given and is for us to enjoy and use properly. To live fully as human beings we need not only food, clothing and other material things, but also spiritual fulfilment. If life shrinks to enjoyment of material things only, it gives at best passing happiness. The Christian faith proclaims that in Jesus life may be lived at its highest and fullest.
- **Jesus is eternal life.** This life is not our natural right. It is part of God's nature and can only be for us a gift. Jesus said, 'I am the life', and this is a constant New Testament theme, especially in John's Gospel. The life that Jesus gives through a relationship with him is eternal life; it is a relationship, a way of life, that reaches beyond the death of the body.
- **Eternal life begins now.** The Pharisees believed in 'eternal' life, but it was something given to certain fortunate people after death, or at the resurrection of the body. Jesus' teaching is that eternal life begins here and now and is a present reality as well as a future hope. There is thus a continuity between life now and life to come. This life begins when a believer accepts Jesus' offer of salvation and is given the Holy Spirit, and it is deepened as the Christian encounters the risen power of his Lord.

Paul wrote from prison to the Philippian Christians: 'For me to live is Christ and to die is gain.' Death would not introduce him to eternal life, as if for the first time, because he already knew Jesus Christ in the present. But death was a door that would usher him into unbroken fellowship with Jesus.

- **A Christian can be sure of eternal life.** Most of us are apprehensive about the experience of dying. But the Christian hope conquers ultimate fear. The fear of death is a paralysing fear to modern people, who lack a sure knowledge of God, and so are agnostic about life beyond the physical realm.

Tomorrow makes a poor substitute for eternity. The New Testament speaks of the Holy Spirit being given as a 'guarantee' of our inheritance, a sort of down payment of what we will fully receive in heaven.

Through the gift of the Holy Spirit there are foretastes in our experience of our ultimate calling as children of God. These echoes include: the desire to serve God, an awareness of his presence, the overcoming of temptation through his power, the desire to worship. In these and many other ways the Holy Spirit confirms to our hearts that we are children of God. This all gives us firm ground to stand on in the uncertainties and pains of life.

Christian assurance, we must note, is not based on our own subjective experience, but on God's promise that we *are* sons and daughters of God. 'He who comes to me,' said Jesus, 'I will never cast away.' Though we may sometimes feel God is distant, his promise is our guarantee that he will not let us down.

Justification by Faith

In the New Testament many metaphors are used to express the reality of Christian salvation. Descriptions such as new birth, new creation, passing from darkness to light and from prison to freedom, all dramatically express the difference being a Christian makes.

One metaphor, used only by Paul, is 'justification by faith'.

The term is borrowed from the lawcourts of the first century. The judge hears an accusation against a person, and declares the accused 'justified'. 'Not guilty' or 'innocent' are simply not strong enough to express what the judge means. He is really saying, 'You stand before this court as one who is in the right.'

It is important to realize therefore that justification is not primarily a statement of a person's moral worth. It is about a person being legally in the right.

When used in a Christian sense it is a statement about our standing before God. It does not declare that we *are* righteous, but that in God's sight we are in a right relationship with him. It does not tell us *how* we became Christians but that we *are*.

The basis for justification

We need to be justified because we are in a serious position before God. We are incapable of rescuing ourselves. Salvation is only possible if it comes from God.

This is where 'grace' comes in. Grace is God's amazing love for sinners. He came to the rescue through Jesus, 'the righteous for the unrighteous'. Here we have the basis for justification: the death and resurrection of Jesus. Through his death we are released from guilt and blame and through his victory over death we are made children of God.

And so humanity has no cause to boast before God. As the hymn puts it:

Nothing in my hand I bring,
Simply to your cross I cling.

How are we justified?

If grace is the foundation of justification, then surely faith is the means by which justification becomes the Christian's possession. Because of what sin is, we cannot earn salvation from it. This can only be accepted as a *gift*, because it is bought at the price of Jesus' death.

Where then do good deeds come in? Certainly not as a way of justifying ourselves before God. 'I go to church,' says someone, 'and do good to others. Surely these Christian things will be to my credit?' This is a very common belief. But if it were true, it would question the very point of Jesus' death. Why should God go to the extreme length of sending his Son to the cross if people are justified by their own good deeds? This is not to deny the importance of a good life, but good works are the *fruit* not the *root* of justification.

Justification presupposes two things: sin and grace. No sin, no need for justification; no grace, no possibility of it.

Tom Wright

When God justifies me, he does not look at *my* qualities but the qualities of the one who saves me, of Jesus Christ. The Reformers used to talk of the sinner being clothed in the robe of Christ's righteousness. We are made right by his righteousness, not our own. Faith has to be seen as our simple response to an action which is all of God: a response which unites us to Jesus. We can contribute nothing to our salvation except a willingness to respond—to reach out towards the Christian life, to take it and live it in the power of the Spirit.

The result of justification

If you walk out of a court acquitted of a

JERRAM BARRS

Predestination and Human Choice

I have the responsibility to choose whether to seek God and believe or not.

God chooses me to belong to him as part of his plan for the whole of history.

Can we believe that both of these statements are true? Are they not contradictory? If we think they are contradictory which one will we decide is more important and try to hold on to, and which will we explain away? These are questions which concern all Christians, for there are two sets of ideas which seem hard to reconcile.

God
elects (chooses) people (decides their destiny)
is sovereign (has a purpose he is working out in history)

People
have freedom to choose
are responsible for the choices they make
will be judged by God on the basis of their choices

If people are elected by God, how can we have freedom to choose?

If God predestines us, how can he call us to account for the choices we make?

If what we choose to do affects the course of history, how can God at the same time be in control?

☐ **The Bible.** There are many strong statements throughout the Bible about God's plans in history both for nations and for individuals. The apostle Paul writes: 'In Christ we are also chosen, having been predestined according to the plan of him who works out everything in conformity with the purpose of his will.' Some groups in the church have taken such passages and said they mean that God plans everything and therefore people are simply passive, rather like actors playing parts in a play, making their entrances and exits at the author's will.

Yet there are equally strong statements in the Bible about the responsibility of people to choose and about God's response to human choices. John writes: 'Whoever believes in Jesus is not condemned, but whoever does not believe stands condemned already because he has not believed in the name of God's one and only Son.' Some have taken this kind of passage to mean that everything depends on human choice and that therefore God is a passive observer, sitting in heaven, simply confirming what people decide.

The only way that justice can be done to the many passages of both kinds is to hold them together.

☐ **Our experience** also demands that we believe both. Try thinking about prayer. We choose to pray and we believe that our praying makes a difference. Yet at the same time we must believe that God is able to work out his purposes into our own history, otherwise why are we praying to him? And if our prayers are answered through another Christian, do we regard that person simply as a puppet under the total control of God? No, we thank them for their help, and also we thank God for answering our prayer. In practice then, all Christians believe both in the sovereign power of God and in human choice and responsibility.

serious crime, you will be aware as perhaps never before of the value of freedom and the importance of your status in the eyes of everyone as a free person. Yesterday you were the accused. But now you are acquitted and exonerated of blame, free to live normally.

Now imagine your feelings if you were actually guilty of that crime but released because the judge gave you a free pardon. As an analogy it helps us to see what justification means to the Christian. We know that we deserve a guilty verdict, but that in Jesus Christ we are set unreservedly free. We are filled with gratitude for the generosity we have been shown and amazed at such love. A new life now begins—new life made possible

Problems either way

As we have seen, some Christians think it wise to deny either God's sovereignty or human choice in order to defend the other, or because to hold both seems illogical.

What happens if we deny human responsibility? People become puppets or robots pushed around the stage of history. Also biblical statements such as, 'God is not willing that any should perish but wants everyone to come to repentance', have to be ignored or explained away. Further, God is made to be responsible for sin and suffering in the world, even though the Bible explicitly denies this.

What happens if God's sovereignty is denied? People become the only real decision-makers. God becomes an ineffectual figure unable to do what he wishes, frustrated at every turn by people and by Satan. God is not only unable to plan for the future, but may even be taken by surprise by some unexpected twist of history. We would be unable to have any confidence that God could deliver us individually, or that he could bring this age to a close with Jesus Christ's return. It hardly needs to be said that all such ideas are rejected by the Bible. Again we are encouraged to affirm both.

Did Jesus choose to die?

We can see the simultaneous working of human choice and divine sovereignty with particular force and clarity in the account of Jesus' death:

- ☐ It was **planned by God the Father** before the foundation of the world, and foretold in detail in the Old Testament.
- ☐ **Jesus Christ himself freely chose to die** for us. He purposefully went to Jerusalem because he knew he would die there. At the right time he provoked the authorities to even greater rage against him. We see him struggling with the choice in the garden of Gethsemane. He chose to go to the cross in obedience to his Father's purpose.
- ☐ **It was the purpose of Pilate, Caiaphas, Herod and others in authority to kill Jesus.** They were responsible for his death and God judged them for it. Satan also was involved, thinking that Jesus Christ's death would give him victory. Paul even says that if these rulers (human and satanic) had realized what would result from Jesus' death, they would not have crucified him. God took their choices, which were first causes, and used them in his sovereign purpose to bring about our salvation.

Interwoven

The interplay of God's action and people's actions in Christ's death is so close that Peter could say: 'This man was handed over to you (the Jews) by God's set purpose and foreknowledge; and you, with the help of wicked men, put him to death by nailing him to the cross.

From all this we can see that the two threads of predestination and human choice are inextricably interwoven. Christian groups have sometimes tried to make their faith easier to believe by removing one or other of the threads, but we have seen the problems that result. Thankfully we are not forced into this kind of rationalization with its horrifying consequences. Rather we have to accept that, as with the whole of life, our knowledge is limited, and so we may never be able to see *how* the two fit together.

After all, we are not the Creator but creatures, very little persons who do not have total comprehension of reality. We have to be content with affirming that both the Bible and our experience demand that we believe both in the sovereignty of God and in human responsibility.

through the Holy Spirit given to all who follow Jesus. But has our justification actually changed us inwardly?

Here we encounter a real difference of opinion between Roman Catholic and Protestant traditions. The Reformation hardened attitudes so that extreme positions were taken up. The official Roman Catholic position interpreted 'justification' as meaning 'made righteous', which, as we have seen, is not the Bible's teaching.

On the other hand, the Reformers so emphasized the objective declaration of 'not guilty' that they seemed to deny the inner reality of it, and make it a mere 'legal fiction'. This was also a wrong emphasis. Justification is clearly no fiction. It is God's declaration that the Christian *is* a new creation, a child of God and blessed with the presence of God in the Holy Spirit.

Justification is therefore a glorious doctrine. It takes us to the heart of the good news and is at the centre of Christian preaching. Ignore its truth and Christianity stands in danger of confusion at best and heresy at worst. Justification not only honours God's grace but also gives a proper valuation to men and women: without the death of Jesus Christ we would be helpless.

Calling

The idea of people being 'called' by God is a great Bible theme. It is used at a number of levels:

■ Why should one be a Christian?... In order to be truly human.

Hans Küng

- **The name** by which a person is known: so Jesus was called 'Jesus' because the name means 'The Lord saves'.
- **A summons** to a duty or responsibility. So Paul is 'called to be an apostle'; he is aware of the dignity of his office. The word is used today of some professions, and particularly of clergy and missionaries. But in fact it applies to everything God calls us to do: in work, in recreation, in marriage, in singleness—our whole life is a response to God's calling.
- **An invitation** to something important and enjoyable.

When used of God's calling to people to receive his life, these three basic elements combine to a remarkable degree.

'Many are called,' said Jesus, 'but few are chosen.' He meant that God's invitation has to be met by our wholehearted welcome.

God's grace is at the heart of his call. His call flows from his love for humankind. Grace then precedes all that we do, since all we can offer is our acceptance and gratitude. Grace is one of the greatest New Testament words and its root means 'to give pleasure'.

God's call is for everyone

It is a mistake to think that only some are called. The Bible tells us that the good news is for everyone and not for a chosen few; God does not bypass the vast majority of human beings. The nature of God's love is that he is merciful to us. It has been sometimes argued in the church that only the 'elect' are called to salvation (the word 'elect' means 'called'). But we need to be clear that God's love is never less than genuine. If 'God so loved the world' that Jesus died for everyone, then his call is to all people. It is never the will of God that anyone should perish.

Yet although God invites all to open their hearts to his love, he has a special desire for those who respond, that they should enter into the fullness of his call. That call is to please him in the way we live, to enjoy the privilege of Christian fellowship, the openness of his freedom, his peace—the entire inheritance of the children of God.

Our calling reminds us that life itself is impregnated with the presence of God, with his unceasing love and grace. It also reminds us that God awaits our response to his invitation to spend eternity with him. In a word, it tells us that life is a journey which will end before his throne. And then it will be made clear whether we have accepted or rejected the call of God.

Baptism

When the Queen launches a new ship, she says, 'May God bless her and all who sail in her.' Then she smashes a bottle of champagne against the bow.

In the marriage service, the bridegroom says 'I take you to be my wife,' and he slips a ring on the bride's finger.

When a football team score the winning goal in a cup final, the fervent supporters cheer their heads off, throw their caps in the air, jump up and down and yell, 'We've won the Cup!'

In all three, words are combined with actions, speaking with doing. The ritual, or action, gives expression to what is said.

This is what Christians mean when they talk about sacraments. The word 'sacrament' means a sign, pledge or seal. It gives expression to what is said or promised by God. Augustine said long ago about holy communion, 'Add together the word and the loaf and the sacrament is there.' Both baptism and holy communion speak of the same thing, the gospel itself. But the outward sign is different, not bread and wine but water.

Baptism in the ancient world

Our word baptism comes from the Greek word meaning to dip or immerse. Baptism as a religious rite was practised by Jews and other sects long before Christianity appeared. Jews baptized Gentiles who wanted to join the Jewish faith. It signified repentance, a change of direction.

In the Roman mystery religions, it usually meant a departure from the old life or religion and membership of a new company.

The baptism of John

John the Baptist's preaching and baptismal practices rocked the world of Judaism. His call for Jews, who claimed a special relationship with God through Abraham and whose circumcision declared their special status, to repent and be baptized caused an uproar. Especially as this rite was usually offered to the uncircumcised Gentiles.

John saw his baptism as essentially provisional. 'I baptize you with water,' he said, 'but someone is coming who ... will baptize you with the Holy Spirit.' John's baptism spoke only of forgiveness of sins. It looked forward to the coming Messiah, whose baptism would speak also of new life in the Holy Spirit.

Christian baptism

Jesus did not baptize during his ministry. He was himself baptized by John as a sign of his identification with sinners. But after Pentecost the Christian church invited believers in Jesus to be baptized.

Peter made his appeal on the day of Pentecost: 'Each one of you must turn away from his sins and be baptized in the name of Jesus Christ ... and you will receive God's gift, the Holy Spirit.' Most probably people who came forward for baptism were baptized in the name of 'the Father, the Son and the Holy Spirit', perhaps confessing that 'Jesus is Lord'. Some Christians think that baptism always involved 'total immersion' in water; others that we cannot know how much water was used.

The New Testament tells us that baptism declares four complementary truths:

- **Death to the old life.** Water suggests the washing away of sin. Going down into the water expresses dying to the old, sinful way of living. Coming up out of the water suggests a new life with a new Master.
- **The gift of the Spirit.** Through the Spirit, God comes to live among his people. The Spirit joins himself to those who turn to Jesus and becomes the new power for living. A Christian is a new creation.
- **Entry into the church.** Because they belong to Jesus, Christians are members of the church, 'the body of Christ'. And so they join this fellowship of those who love Jesus. They are now committed in love and

PAUL BEASLEY-MURRAY

Should Babies be Baptized?

Baptism is the great New Testament sign of what God does for a person who comes to belong to Jesus Christ. The water declares that our sin is washed away, that we are identified with Jesus who died to evil and rose to new life, that the Spirit is poured out on us. In baptism a person is welcomed into the Christian community.

Throughout the New Testament baptism is always linked with faith. Nowhere in the Bible do we find an explicit reference to babies being baptized. Why? Most churches believe this is because it was too obvious to mention, and so they practise infant baptism. But churches in the Baptist tradition question whether this practice has biblical and theological support sufficient to justify continuing it. Should babies be baptized?

YES

Household baptisms

In ancient society the solidarity of the family was more strongly steessed than in ours. Thus in several New Testament passages we read of so-and-so and his house being baptized. In view of the Old Testament understanding of children as belonging within the covenant, some have believed these households included the man and his family, with children of all ages.

Jesus welcomed children

Jesus welcomed children and gave them his blessing. He said that the kingdom of heaven belongs to such. This makes it seem odd to exclude them from baptism until adulthood.

Proselyte baptism

When a Gentile was converted to Judaism (becoming a proselyte) he was required to be circumcised and baptized, and his family also submitted to initiatory rites; baptism became important since women and girls received it also. It is assumed that the early church applied baptism in the same way to the whole family.

Covenant and circumcision

Under the old covenant children born to Jewish parents were received as of right into the community almost immediately after birth. They belonged to the covenant people, the sign of which was circumcision. Under the new covenant children of Christian parents should be similarly received as of right into the community, and they should receive the sign of this, baptism, which has now replaced circumcision.

NO

'Household' meant servants

In the first century the family extended considerably beyond father, mother and children; it included also relatives and servants. One of the 'household' stories speaks of them all putting their trust in God. Again, *all* the house of Cornelius heard the gospel, received the Spirit, spoke in tongues and were baptized: were babies involved in all this? Another of the stories says a household *believed* and they were baptized.

Childlike trust for adults

The love of Jesus for children and his desire to welcome them is not in doubt. But Jesus declared that they were the models of how mature people should *receive* the kingdom. It is childlike faith which he here holds before us. This is no model for infant baptism.

No clear evidence

There is genuine uncertainty as to whether proselyte baptism was widely known in the time of the early church. John the Baptist provided the model for the baptismal practice which Jesus adopted. Paul writes (in 1 Corinthians 7) of children being 'sanctified' by the faith of a parent—and the unbelieving parent also! This is not evidence that either the children or the unbelieving partner were baptized. Jews used the expression 'sanctified' only of children born after proselyte conversion, and they needed no baptism. There is no clear link between proselyte baptism and Christian baptism in the New Testament.

Christians need no circumcision

There is no evidence that the early church viewed baptism applied to infant children of Christians in the same way as circumcision which marked Jews as children of the covenant. On the contrary Paul puts baptism and faith in opposition to circumcision and the Law. That baptism was not understood as replacing circumcision is seen from the fact that Jewish churches continued to practise the rite of circumcision. For Jews, circumcision was, with the Passover, the greatest of all sacrifices. Christians do not need it, says Paul, since the great sacrifice was offered for them by Jesus, the power of which they know through conversion and baptism.

Some Christians think this biblical evidence does not come down conclusively on either side. And so they argue from pastoral and practical considerations.

Christian parents rightly bring their children up to believe in Jesus, to pray to him and follow him. And so it seems right to give baptism at the beginning of life, rather than wait until some time when we can consider them fully Christian.

To baptize babies, who cannot make their own response to Jesus, seems to undervalue repentance and faith, without which a person cannot be a Christian.

All Christians agree that Jesus died and rose for everyone, from the youngest to the oldest. And children should be brought up as part of the fellowship of faith, should learn about Jesus and grow towards a mature faith.

service to the Christian family.

- **A new covenant made with God.** In the Old Testament God's covenant (or agreement) with the people was sealed in circumcision. In baptism God seals his promise of an unbreakable new covenant, based on Jesus' death for us. It is the sign to us that God's promise has been made.

For further thinking

QUESTION 1

Can a person be fully a Christian without an experience of conversion?

QUESTION 2

If a friend said to you, 'I wish I had your faith', how would you respond? What might be the best way to help another person find faith in Jesus? Try to base your answers on Jesus' teaching.

QUESTION 3

If a person becomes a Christian through repentance and faith, where does baptism come in?

BIBLE REFERENCES

Faith

Genesis 12:1–5; 15:6; Exodus 14:13; 1 Samuel 1:15–18; 1 Kings 17:21–24; 18:41–46; Job 1:9–12, 21; 42:2; Psalms 56:3–4; 106:30–31; Isaiah 7:9; 26:3–4; 43:1–5; Jeremiah 17:7–8; Habakkuk 2:4; Mark 2:5; 6:5–6; 10:52; Luke 7:2–10; John 1:12; 3:15–16; 5:24; 6:68–69; 9:35–38; Acts 2:38–39; 16:31; Romans 1:17; 4:18–22; 5:1; 10:6–13; Galatians 2:20; 3:11–14, 23–29; Ephesians 2:8–9; 1 Timothy 4:1; 6:12; 2 Timothy 1:12; Hebrews 11:1, 6, 8–10; 12:1–2; 1 John 5:1, 4; Revelation 3:19–20

Baptism

Matthew 3:11, 13–17; 28:19; Mark 1:5; 10:38–39; John 3:5; Acts 1:5; 2:38, 41; 8:12–16; 16:33; 19:3–5; Romans 6:1–6; 1 Corinthians 1:13–15; 12:13; Colossians 2:11–15; Titus 3:4–7; 1 Peter 3:21

TOM SMAIL

Life in the Holy Spirit

CHAPTER 27

The Christian life is life lived in the power of the Holy Spirit. For Paul a Christian can be described equally well as 'in Christ' or as 'in the Spirit'. In one place he says quite explicitly that no one can belong to Jesus Christ without having his Spirit at work in him.

The New Testament in general speaks of the Holy Spirit in many different ways, but behind them all is the basic conviction that the Spirit is God personally at work, in the lives of believers and in the fellowship of the church. He unites believers with God, with Jesus Christ and with one another, so that Jesus in all his truth, love and power lives in them, and they live in him.

The word Spirit means wind or breath. Without breath there can be no life; it is itself the chief sign of life. It cannot be seen, but it can be known by its effects and results. The Holy Spirit is like that. He is the basic necessity of the Christian life, so that life becomes dead and unreal without him. But, like the breath or the wind, he is known not in and by himself but through what he does. How can we know for sure that the Spirit is at work in us?

- We will **believe that Jesus is God's Son**, and our Saviour;
- We will **begin to pray** with reality and expectation;
- Our life and character will begin to **bear some resemblance to Jesus**;
- We will begin to **know God's power** in our service for him.

The Spirit does not do his work obtrusively, drawing attention to himself. He does it effectively, bringing us into close relationship with Jesus Christ and with each other, and preparing and empowering us for all that such relationships involve.

The Holy Spirit and New Life

The familiar words of the grace speak of 'the fellowship of the Holy Spirit'. The Greek word translated 'fellowship', *koinonia*, means a having in common, a sharing of life. This is supremely the business of the Holy Spirit, who has been called the 'Go-between God'. He goes between Jesus and us. As he shares Jesus' life, love and power with us, the Spirit enables us to share our lives as Christians with one another in the fellowship of his people.

The Holy Spirit, then, opens up relationships for us both with Jesus and with each other. He brings the exalted life of the risen Jesus Christ to us here on earth, so that Jesus lives in our life and we live in his. And this has the effect that we are united with one another in the worshipping, loving, sharing and serving fellowship which the Spirit is creating in the church.

The Holy Spirit is therefore the creator of the church. His work in the church began on the Day of Pentecost, when the first disciples were filled with the Holy Spirit. This meant that the life of Jesus, which until that time had been something outside and separate from his followers, was now being communicated to them and would be lived within them. From now on they could be shaped into his likeness, could speak with his authority, love with his love and act with his power. They did not need to try by their own efforts to imitate someone who was apart from them, for by the Spirit they were now sharing Jesus' risen life.

Jesus Christ is not merely our example; that would reduce us quickly to despair. Jesus has promised to all believers that,

> To live in the Spirit is to be agonizingly aware of the contrast between what is and what should be.
>
> *John Taylor*

through the Holy Spirit, the life that we see in him will be ours also: a free gift made available to us through his death and resurrection. That promise was kept when the Spirit came at Pentecost, has been kept down all the centuries and is being kept still.

As soon as the disciples received the Spirit at Pentecost they began to draw others into their company and to share their new life in Christ among themselves— even to the extent of sharing their money and their possessions. The Spirit is the missionary Spirit who draws others into fellowship with Jesus. He is also the Spirit of *koinonia*, of sharing, who enables those who belong to Christ to share with each other, in very specific and down-to-earth ways, their prayers, their problems, their gifts, their resources, their love.

In this article we shall be concentrating on how the Spirit shares Jesus with each of us individually. But we need to remember that he never deals with us as isolated individuals. From the very first the Spirit links us in one life with other Christians in the fellowship of the church.

The marks of the Spirit

The first sign that the Holy Spirit has begun to work in a person is not some sudden transformation in that person's character, the appearance of new God-given gifts—although both need to follow in due time. The first mark of the Spirit's activity is when a believer makes two distinctively Christian confessions:

- The Christian will say **'Jesus is Lord'**. Paul tells us that no one can say and mean this without the help of

---

ROBERT BANKS

Faith and Religion

Throughout its history, both adherents and opponents of Christianity have considered it to be a 'religion'. The title of John Calvin's greatest work, for example, *The Institutes of the Christian Religion*, enshrines this attitude. Since the nineteenth century this has also been an integral part of the academic study of Christianity by anthropologists, psychologists and sociologists, as well as experts in comparative religion and the history of religion.

During the last half-century, however, Christianity's status as a religion has come under attack. **Karl Barth** argued that Christian faith was the critique, and end, of all 'religion'. He understood religion as the human attempt to seek and worship God apart from God's revelation of himself. Barth was intensely critical of Christians who sought to understand God's character and will through merely human notions, as happened extensively throughout the liberal theology of the nineteenth century. Yet he could still claim that Christianity, properly conceived, was the absolute and true religion; the religion to end all religions.

Religionless Christianity

Partially influenced by Barth, and partially impelled by the philosopher Nietzsche's severe denunciation of Christendom, **Dietrich Bonhoeffer** went a step further and called for a fully 'religionless Christianity'. But he was using the word 'religion' in a quite specific way. By it he meant the unhealthy alliance between things which should have been kept distinct: Christian faith and speculative philosophical ideas; Christian practice and alien ideas of worship; Christian experience and introspective psychological states.

He correctly saw that this led to a hardening of the living gospel into an abstract doctrinal system, a perverting of the church into a sacred hierarchical institution and a weakening of spirituality into a shallow emotional pietism. Although he would not use the word in relation to Christianity, Bonhoeffer still believed in religion, when rightly understood and practised. Theology was necessary, provided its reflections focused on God's revelation; the church was needed, so long as it served the Holy Spirit. When a person declares that Jesus is the Lord and Master of his life, and is ready to accept the consequences of that declaration as they unfold themselves, they show that the Spirit has been at work in them. On the basis of that confession, a person can be baptized into membership of Christ and his church.

- The Christian will also say, to God, **'Abba, Father'**. The Spirit reveals to us that we have been adopted as children into God's family and so we can address God with the very word that Jesus used, Abba. It is the sign that a person has entered into all the privileges and responsibilities of a child in God's family.

Where people have entered into that personal relationship with Jesus as Lord and with God as Father, there the Spirit has been at work. He has much other work still to do, but the foundation of it all is to relate us to the two other persons of the Trinity, so that we confess the Father and the Son in the Spirit.

Knowing God

When people have come to know God as Father and Jesus as Lord, how have they gained that knowledge? It is not by searching out and weighing evidence or arguments; nor by a long process of experiment or thought. Many learned scholars, historians and philosophers have examined the Bible carefully and long, but have seen in it nothing but ancient stories of a long-ago world. Certainly they have discovered no revelation of God.

Jesus once thanked his Father that the

genuine Christian community; and mature prayer and meditation were still as vital as ever.

A further step in this process was taken by the so-called 'secular theologians'. Some of these, such as **Fritz Buri** and **Paul van Buren**, virtually turned Christianity into a humanism, rejecting all ideas of a spiritual dimension and any recognizable conceptions of worship and prayer.

Bonhoeffer had legitimately sought to prevent people from using Christianity as an intellectual, institutional or psychological crutch, instead of as a force for renewal in thinking, in relationships and in personal development. But these theologians stripped Christianity of its distinctive beliefs, practices and experiences by accommodating it to what they imagined to be the prevailing secular world-view.

It is one thing, like Bonhoeffer, to react against unduly dependent, childish notions of Christianity; it is another to regard humanity as so fully adult that it no longer stands in need of a mature dependence on God. Religionless Christianity is one thing; godless Christianity quite another.

The challenge of the times

Looking back over the centuries shows how much the general cultural climate has affected attitudes in this area. In the early Christian centuries (as in the period of the great prophets), so strong was the need to distinguish genuine faith from the influence of pagan views that accepted 'religious' ideas, practices and terms were commonly held in suspicion. When the threat of such influences was less pressing, from the beginnings of state Christianity up to and beyond the Reformation, presenting Christian faith in 'religious' terms posed no problems.

For nearly two centuries we have been living through another period of challenge. The church has been faced both by competing humanistic world-views and by humanistic infiltration from within. It should come as no surprise, then, to find people such as Barth and Bonhoeffer expressing a prophetic or apostolic reserve about 'religion'.

Even so, people today and modern 'secular' society have an intractably religious character, possessing their own sacred dimension, myths and dogmas. Christianity is inherently supernatural and spiritual. It calls for a paradoxical 'childlike maturity' if it is not just a childish refuge for the immature, or an outgrown stage of human development.

truth about him was concealed from the clever, but revealed to simple people, and when Peter confessed him as Messiah and Son of God, Jesus declared that Peter had not discovered this by himself, but had been shown it by God. It is God himself who opens the eyes and hearts of his people to the truth about himself and his Son. John tells us that it is the work of the Spirit to take what is Christ's and show it to us, and so guide us into all the truth.

In other words, knowledge of God as Father and Jesus Christ as Lord and Saviour does not come by human discovery but by divine revelation. As sinners separated from God we have no mind for his truth, until the moment comes, suddenly or quietly, when we are left saying, 'I see it now'. This is the

The Practice of Prayer

Prayer is right at the heart of the Christian life. To be a Christian is not chiefly to fulfil a series of duties; it is to know a relationship with Jesus Christ. And the most characteristic way this relationship is expressed is through prayer.

When we pray we talk to someone we cannot see, which is not a natural activity. So not surprisingly some people coming fresh to prayer find it hard to get started. Yet this strangeness soon evaporates once a healthy pattern of prayer has been established, and prayer becomes a new and most enriching dimension to life.

Among the questions commonly asked by beginners in prayer are:

☐ **When should I pray?** Most people find a regular pattern most helpful, praying at a set time each day. This of course does not mean that there cannot be other times of prayer as the need arises. It is sensible not to pray for longer than we can readily concentrate, though this time will extend with practice.

☐ **Is there a set posture for prayer?** No. Some find kneeling most helpful; some sitting; some prefer to walk about. Lying down is seldom a good idea!

☐ **Should I use set forms of words?** Many find reassurance and stimulation from using books of prayers, interweaving them with times of prayer in their own words. Sometimes we can progress from set prayers to our own words by means of prayers we compose and write out ourselves. But many people continue to use book prayers from time to time after years.

☐ **Should I pray out loud?** Not necessarily; some just think the words in their heads. But it can be surprisingly helpful actually to utter our prayers, even privately. And the words need not be formal. We can just speak as we would to a respected friend.

☐ **What sbould I pray about?** Everything that is really important to you—yourself and other people, local and worldwide needs. We may feel we need to confess some sin or just to spill out to God some concern which is at present all-absorbing. It is no good pretending we are concerned about things which actually leave us cold. But as our Christian experience grows, we will find the range of our concerns becomes wider.

☐ **How do I sense that God is present?** By starting each time of prayer with a reading from the Bible. It is in the Bible that God has spoken to us, and when we have really taken in a part of what it teaches, we can make our response to God for it—by thanking him for a promise, confessing that we have not kept a command, asking for strength to rise to a challenge, and so on. In this way real two-way conversation gets started, which can readily flow on along whatever lines our deepest concerns may indicate.

This use of the Bible ensures it is the true God we are talking to, not some projection of our hopes and fears. And also, which is vitally important, it means part of our time of prayer is devoted to listening to God as well as talking to him.

work of the Spirit. He opens our eyes and our hearts to the truth that we could not see for ourselves.

This was a point often made at the time of the Reformation. The Reformers asked themselves how we can know that the Bible is not just a collection of ancient documents but the word of God personally addressed to us. John Calvin's answer was that we know that the Bible is the word of God by the 'inner witness of the Holy Spirit'. The same Spirit who first worked in and inspired the Bible writers now works in us as we read them with faith. He brings it home to us that we are not just reading the words of Isaiah or Paul. The living God is addressing a message to us through them, showing us his way, his truth, his life in Christ.

Today, the Bible is surrounded by many scholarly questions which need to be faced and answered: What is it? Who wrote it? Is it true? And yet we can still turn to it with confidence that God will use it to speak to us. Again and again as we read it we come into contact with more than just historical figures of the past. We meet the living Jesus Christ, who speaks just the effective and life-changing word that we need.

This does not come about naturally or automatically, but only through the 'revealing' activity of the Holy Spirit. Without him the words of the Bible are dull, lifeless and full of problems. He opens our ears and our hearts to hear God speaking. Whenever we read the Bible we need to pray, with Charles Wesley, 'Come Holy Ghost, for moved by thee, the prophets wrote and spoke. Unlock the truth, thyself the key, unseal the sacred book.'

In Christian understanding, Holy Bible and Holy Spirit belong together. The one authenticates the other. By the Spirit we recognize and receive the word of God in the Bible. And through the Bible we recognize the Holy Spirit. If anyone claims to be speaking in the power of the Spirit, we shall test that claim. And our yardstick will not be the person's sincerity or conviction, but whether what they say is in agreement with the word of God in the Bible, and compatible with confession of Jesus as the unique Son of God and Saviour of humanity.

This is the test we need to apply to Mormons, Jehovah's Witnesses, Moonies, the promoters of spiritualism and transcendental meditation and so on. Does the truth and the way that they offer really have its source in the Holy Spirit, or does it come from elsewhere? That question is answered by seeing if what they say agrees with the Bible and with its central teaching about the unique place of Jesus. Bible and Spirit belong together; the one interprets the other. And what God has joined together is not for people to tear apart.

Born of the Spirit

All Christians would agree that the making of new Christians is the work of the Holy Spirit; without him no one could ever become a Christian at all. As Jesus put it, 'Unless a man is born again of water and the Spirit, he cannot see or enter the kingdom of God.'

The 'water and Spirit' Jesus spoke of are sometimes thought of as referring to baptism, sometimes to conversion; probably Jesus had both in mind. But however and whenever it happens, becoming a Christian involves such a radical new beginning that it must be described as being born again. And just as we did not bring about out own natural birth, so we cannot bring about our own spiritual rebirth; it is something God does, not we ourselves.

Of course, conversion also involves human activity and human choice. Jesus called people to come to him. He expected them to make their own free response. And we all have come to that moment of decision when we choose to commit ourselves to him. But while all would agree that there is both a work of the Holy Spirit and a human decision involved when a person becomes a Christian, some would put the stress on one side and some on the other.

Some Christians teach that the central turning-point is our human decision for Christ, freely made. It is my choosing Jesus

Christ which opens the door for the Holy Spirit to come and make a new person of me. Until I invite him to come in, the Spirit cannot begin to work in me. The view that our personal decision is the focal point in conversion has both Protestant and Roman Catholic forms. It has been very influential in much modern mass evangelism.

In contrast to this is the view that the key point in conversion is not the human decision, but the work of the Holy Spirit in 'regeneration', or new birth. We are all naturally sinners in rebellion against God. We cannot recognize Jesus, let alone decide for him, unless and until the Holy Spirit comes to help us. He gives us new eyes to see what by ourselves we cannot see, and new hearts and wills to choose what by ourselves we cannot

DONALD ENGLISH

Can We be Perfect?

Can we be perfect? In one sense the answer could hardly be simpler. In the Sermon on the Mount, Jesus said, 'Be perfect, therefore, as your heavenly Father is perfect.' It is when we ask what kind of perfection is intended, and how anyone is likely to achieve it, that the difficulties emerge.

In the Sermon on the Mount Jesus introduces a contrast between inward and outward holiness, between obeying the Law and expressing inner love and purity. Perfection here finds its roots in a person's inner being. It is a matter primarily of attitude, and only secondarily of action. The most relevant question is whether a person's life is dominated by God's love and purity.

The hopelessness of that prospect leads to another way forward. When Jesus told a rich young man to sell all he had, Jesus linked 'being perfect' to following himself. In the epistles this is even more deeply developed; perfection is associated with faith in Christ.

It is easy to be satisfied with half an answer here, as some of the Reformers were inclined to be. We can assert that our perfection is being 'in Christ' by faith. He is perfect; our trust is in him, and so God views us as perfect in Christ. However true that is, it cannot be the whole of the answer, because on its own it could suggest that our moral state does not matter at all. And Paul thought very little of that argument: 'Should we continue to live in sin so that God's grace will increase? Certainly not!'

Perfect in love

There is another side to the story, however. Our moral condition is meant to reflect our standing in Christ. This is why 'presenting everyone perfect in Christ' also involves 'admonishing and teaching everyone in all wisdom... struggling with all (Christ's) energy'. It does not happen automatically. God does accept us because we come to him 'in Christ'. Jesus' perfection does count for us. But we are then called, in Christ, to press on to reflect that perfection in our own daily lives.

How far can we get down that line? One major attempt was by John Wesley, founder of Methodism, in the eighteenth century. The desire for perfection is necessary because it is promised and commanded in the Bible. God promises and commands only what is possible. But it is also necessary because of the purpose of salvation, which is to restore the image of God in humanity, ruined by sin.

'Perfect love' is the experience of God's love dominating our lives. One who is 'perfected in love' may, according to Wesley, make mistakes or have faults because of illness or ignorance. But the fount of his life is love, and this is what matters. He can experience 'moment by moment non-transgression of the known will of God'.

Logically and theologically there are difficulties in such a position. Yet the fact that Methodists in the eighteenth century had perfect love as their aim is undoubtedly a major reason for the quality of their lives and the impact of their mission.

Most Christians would agree that we can never know full perfection until we are finally 'remade' in Christ. But striving towards the goal of complete maturity is one of the chief driving forces of the Christian life.

choose.

When someone hears the gospel, and the Spirit does his deep work of making that person new, then the first act of that new person is freely to decide for Jesus Christ and confess him as Lord. On this view it is not my decision that enables the Spirit to work, but the working of the Spirit that enables me to decide. It means my conversion is not my work but God's work; not something I do but something he does. And all the glory of it belongs not to me but to him.

These two views may not be as irreconcilable as this brief statement makes them appear. We need to test them both, not just by our own experience, but by the teaching of the New Testament, in such a way that God's initiative and the work of the Holy Spirit as well as an individual's free response are fully taken into account.

The Holy Spirit and Growth

Once converted, people are related to Christ and so accepted by God. They have new life, but they have still to be made like Jesus. 'Sanctification' is the process of actually becoming holy, becoming like Christ. Jesus is the new person in the image of God, a human being as God meant him to be, and those who belong to him, who are 'in Christ', have to be changed and reshaped into his likeness. To bring this about is the work of the Holy Spirit, his sanctifying work. Paul summarizes it in this way: 'We are being changed into his likeness from one degree of glory to another. This comes from the Lord who is the Spirit.' His words teach us several important things about the work of sanctification.

Sanctification: a continuous process

'We are being changed . . . from one degree of glory to another.' We never come to a point in the Christian life where we can say that we have arrived and the Spirit's work is complete. Even Paul, at the end of a long and fruitful life in Christ, could look back and say, 'Not that I have . . . already been made perfect, but I press on.' And those whom others have counted the greatest saints have been most conscious of how far short they still fall of the full likeness of Jesus.

Can we reach perfection in this present life? This has been much debated in Christian history. It is important to keep to the balance of New Testament teaching and avoid two extremes:

- We must not fall into a **pessimistic extreme**, which limits our expectation of the real changes that God is able to make at every stage of our life. We can never settle down and say, 'I am as I am; I shall never change now.' That is to deny and close ourselves to the sanctifying power of the Spirit to break old habits and pour the transforming love of God into our hearts.
- We need to avoid an **unrealistic optimism**, which sees perfect sanctification as something easily and quickly within our grasp. The battle against sin is lifelong and unremitting. When we have conquered it on one level, it breaks out again on another. We shall never be done with sin or know final victory over it this side of heaven.

The apostle Paul uses some helpful terms to describe the Christian's present possession of the Holy Spirit. In Romans he tells us that we have the **first-fruits** of the Spirit: the first ripened sheaves of grain, full of promise of the full harvest to come. Then in Ephesians he uses a word meaning **first instalment** or **down payment**; we have now in the Holy Spirit the first instalment of God's new life, which guarantees the full payment still to come.

These careful statements hold the balance between a pessimism about this life, which pushes our being made like Christ entirely into the heavenly future, and an optimism which expects it all to happen the day after

Never had I seen so clearly how true it is that Christian morality is a mountain peak that has been taken but which very few, by and large, can succeed in holding, and whose possession by mankind calls for continued battle.

Teilhard de Chardin

Life-Style Today

P. T. CHANDAPILLA

The life-style of a Christian needs to be simple.

The model for such a life-style, in a country such as India or in any other part of the world, is the grace of our Lord Jesus Christ. Paul's declaration, quoted below, has a very definite bearing on this theme. Paul is pointing the relatively affluent Corinthian church to the example of the Macedonian Christians, who gave generously out of a background of real poverty. In this they were being like Jesus, whose 'grace', although it has to do with more than the physical and material, was still very clearly demonstrated in the simple style of life he adopted.

The setting

I write against the backdrop of the particular economic and social conditions in India, with a population of about 650 million. Of that total at least fifty per cent live below the poverty line, meaning they have less than one simple meal of a bowl of rice and a soup of lentils every twenty-four hours. Their clothing and shelter are of no consequence below this line. When you add to those below the poverty line those who are just poor, they amount to eighty per cent of the present population. This percentage continues to increase, because the explosion in population growth is at its greatest in the lower economic level. Coupled with this is the selfishness of the acquisitive twenty per cent, the 'haves' over against the 'have-nots'.

As I see eight persons out of every ten living in poverty in India, even below the poverty line, the only option I have as a Christian is to choose poverty. This is the only way for me to identify with the majority and to help them. In other words a simple life-style is the logical thing to consider as a follower of the Lord Jesus. How can a Christian in India live in affluence when fifty per cent of Indians live below the poverty line and eighty per cent are poor?

The practice

I want to suggest five different ways this matter of living simply works out in a country like India:

- ☐ A Christian should live **on the level where the majority live**. This means living with the lowest or with the poor, accepting their conditions and limitations. We need to live with what is available to the poor.
- ☐ Christians should limit their own wants and learn to live **just meeting their needs**. This means living on a basic level of life—three ordinary meals in a day, simple clothing for cover and protection and some shelter above our heads from the tropical sun and rain. Anything beyond this is a standard above the average for the Indian population and cannot be considered simple living here.
- ☐ Christians should **give to others** in material need, and to the work of the Christian church, from the savings made by simple living. If Christians live only at the level of needs and not pampering to their wants, they will have plenty to give to others in need. There are many such around them in a country like India.
- ☐ The purpose of a simple life-style is the **spiritual as well as the material enrichment** of these who are last and least. Simple living is not a virtue in itself. It is virtuous only as the Christian contributes to the inner transformation of others who are in poverty. Often, if not always, poverty is a companion of a life without Jesus Christ. It is my observation over many years that people who know Jesus Christ personally do not starve or continue in an existence level below the poverty line.
- ☐ A simple life-style makes it easy to **communicate Jesus of Nazareth**, the only Saviour and Lord of humanity, to those who desperately need him. Jesus was a poor man from birth to death. He freely chose to be so. Christians who live a simple life are identifying themselves with Jesus of Nazareth, and have greater insight to communicate him to the poor.

A simple life-style, then, is not just an option for Christians in India.

Until the basic economic and social conditions rise above the poverty line, Indian Christians cannot afford to think of affluence. Both the model of Jesus and the demands of our poverty-stricken majority call Christians to follow him as true disciples. This necessarily involves a simple life-style. If all the Christians in India were to heed this call, then the minority Christian community (five out of every two hundred Indians) would become a powerful magnet, attracting thousands to follow Jesus Christ.

JOHN MCINNES

A Christian life-style for today will be based primarily on the teaching and example of Jesus.

Jesus gave instruction, not laws, about how to live. He told his disciples not to worry; not to chase after clothes, food, houses and other goods. Do God's will and these necessities will come. Do not hoard money and possessions, but instead give to the poor. Life is more than possessions.

That teaching bites deeply at widespread Western affluence. Most people set their hearts on rooms full of possessions—although there are poor people in the West too. More and more household goods? Bigger and better houses? One car for every two to four people? Can Christians accept such goals?

Instead of avidly accumulating *things* Christians should aim to live simply; to concentrate more and more on caring for *people.* A Christian is to suffer with others, give to those in need, and share the good news of new life to be found by following Jesus. He or she will want other churches to have material goods equal to his or her own, and that will mean both self-restriction and generosity. All this means taking a stand against the prevailing individualist and materialistic aims of Western society.

Salt and light

A Christian life-style will probably be less mobile, more close-knit. The apostle Paul wrote about caring, sharing and loving. But living today is temporary and dispersed. Therefore in such a social climate churches are to be different. They are to be warm, stable understanding groups where deep relationships can be made. And so extended families, open houses, neighbourhood worship clusters, and many other practical expressions of care are beginning to spring up alongside traditional congregational gatherings. This 'being together' provides another benefit: the opportunity to share consumer durables such as washing machines and garden tools. Sharing and caring can be immensely practical.

Another dimension of Christian life-style stems from Jesus' description of his disciples as 'salt' and 'light' in society. This means standing for truth and reform. Take for instance the plunder of the world's resources. Christians will need to stand against that both by example and by speaking out. And this is one reason for not having exclusive use of a car. It guzzles gas. Should we also be using second-hand timber and other recycled building products?

Standing for truth and reform also means refusing to allow life to be ruled by technique and technology. Technology rules today—technology of all sorts, not just the microprocessor. People often do things just because they can, not because they ought to! Christians need to insist that all tools, methods and techniques are to be servants, not masters.

To live Christianity is not to live according to rigid rules. Nor is it to live a primitive life. Some new technology will be of immense service to humanity. What is required is a style of living which puts God and people first.

tomorrow. The beginning, the first-fruits, the down payment of holiness is now. But the completion of it still lies ahead. The process of sanctification must be started now and not postponed, even if it will not be perfected until we see Jesus Christ face to face.

Sanctification: a free gift

Paul insists that we are 'being changed' into Christ's likeness. The verb is passive; the changing is not something that we do, but something that is done to us. Sanctification is a gift rather than a task. The one who gives it to us is the Holy Spirit.

The Christian's experience is of a never-ending battle between the new person the Spirit is creating and the old sinful person still in rebellion against God. Paul calls this a battle between spirit and flesh. 'Spirit' is our human nature as the Spirit of God is renewing and controlling it. 'Flesh' is human nature in its independence of God and disobedience to him.

This battle will not be won by our own striving to subdue the flesh, break sinful habits and follow Jesus. That path leads only to failure and frustration, as Paul himself found. The only way to conquer the flesh is to look away from ourselves and concentrate on Jesus' victory that first Good Friday and Easter Day. As we do, we will find that the Holy Spirit will again and again bring the power of Jesus' victory into our lives.

Christ won the victory over sin, and his Spirit makes that victory effective within us. This is what overcomes our inclinations to resist God's will for us, and puts our sinful nature to death. The same resurrection power strengthens and reinforces everything in us that says yes to God.

This does not eliminate the need for discipline and costly struggle in our quest for holiness. But it means that the strength to endure that discipline and fight these battles does not come from ourselves but from the Holy Spirit. He is both the Spirit of Jesus and the Spirit of holiness. And so it is through what he gives to us and works in us that we are changed more and more into the likeness of our Lord.

It is sometimes said that conduct is supremely important and worship helps it. The truth is that worship is supremely important and conduct tests it.

William Temple

Sanctification is Christ-likeness

To be holy is to be as wholly human as Jesus was. In 1 Corinthians 15 Paul says that 'the last Adam became life-giving Spirit'. We might translate 'last Adam' by 'ultimate man'. Jesus is that ultimate man, a human being as God always designed and meant human beings to be. And that ultimate man pours out his life-giving Spirit on us.

His purpose is not to suppress our humanity and turn us into world-denying ascetics or religious fanatics. He plans to make us into people as whole as he was, rightly related to God and one another in every aspect of our personality, body, thoughts, emotions and actions. He wants us to have a proper concern for and involvement in every aspect of the life of this world that God created and wants to redeem.

Christian holiness is positive and human, not negative and joyless. If it often involves self-denial, that is only a means to the promotion of Jesus' new humanity in us and in others, so that, as Jesus promised, we 'may have life and have it more abundantly'.

What does it mean to be human as Jesus was human? It means to filled, just as he was, with the love and the power of God in perfect balance. To have power without love is dangerous; to have love without power is ineffective. What people noticed about Jesus was a character full of love and actions full of power. The Holy Spirit looks to bring into our lives both the character and the ability of Jesus.

Paul spoke of the 'fruit of the Spirit', meaning those characteristics of love, joy, peace and so on, which the Holy Spirit wants to grow in our lives. When the church has spoken about sanctification it has largely been in terms of this moral transformation of character.

Recently however, under the influence of the Charismatic renewal, there has been a new awareness of what Paul said about the 'gifts of the Spirit', and God-given abilities of speech and action which the Spirit gives to

Christians. These gifts make us able to speak, as in prophecy for instance, and act, as in healing, with something of the power and effectiveness of Jesus. They are a fulfilment of his promise that his people would do the same works that he did, and even greater works too.

It used to be generally taught that these gifts were confined to the first generation of Christians and should not be sought or expected today. But there is no trace of such a withdrawal in the New Testament. If the gifts ceased, it was not because God withdrew them but because people stopped believing in them and expecting them. In recent years, within and beyond the Charismatic renewal, Christians have looked for the Spirit to give them both the love and the power of Jesus, so that they could begin to show something of Jesus' greatness in both word and deed.

Sanctification means renewal in the likeness of Jesus. That means that by his Spirit he shares his risen life with us and gives us *both* his love *and* his power; the fruit that the Spirit grows and the gifts that the Spirit shares. To have fruit without gifts is to be ineffective in service. To have gifts without fruits is to be immature and divisive, as the church was at Corinth. To have both in balance is to begin to be like Jesus.

Witness and Worship

As the New Testament sees it, a life lived in the power of the Holy Spirit will be marked by two key activities: witness and worship.

The missionary Spirit

The Spirit gives us power to be Christ's witnesses. 'You shall receive power when the Holy Spirit comes upon you, and you shall be witnesses to me,' said Jesus just before his ascension. And a little earlier he had committed to his disciples the very same mission to the world that his Father had committed to him, as he breathed on them the Holy Spirit, who alone can enable them to fulfil that mission effectively.

Not all Christians are meant to be evangelists, with a special calling to proclaim the gospel to those who have not yet received it. But all Christians are meant to be witnesses: people whose worship, relationships, attitudes and abilities point beyond themselves to the living Lord who is the source of all their life.

A church in whose preaching there is the authority of the Spirit, in whose worship there is the joy of the Spirit, in whose fellowship there is the love of the Spirit, and in whose service the gifts of the Spirit are in full use—such a church will witness to Christ just by being itself. It will convey to others that Jesus is alive and sharing his life with his people.

We are to be made like Jesus, not for our own sakes only, but in order that through us others may be pointed to him. This is how the Spirit performs his main task of convincing the unbelieving world that Jesus is Lord. A church renewed in the Spirit will be a missionary church, a person renewed in the Spirit will be a missionary person, because the Spirit who renews them is himself the missionary Spirit.

The Spirit and worship

The Spirit brings us into relationship with God, both personally and corporately. And so he has a leading part to play in the worship of God's people. Christian prayer rightly understood is not a do-it-yourself activity, a matter of finding the right techniques to reach God and bring him our requests. Christian prayer is 'in the Spirit', inspired in us and given to us by the Spirit who lives and works within us. Paul tells us both that the ascended Christ prays for us in heaven and that the Spirit prays for us in our hearts. The Spirit prays within us the same effective prayer that Jesus, our High Priest, prays before God. The Spirit shares that prayer with us and gives us a part in it.

The first priority in prayer therefore is not to ask. It is rather to listen to see how the Spirit is going to prompt us to pray, to discover from him for whom and for what we

The moment you wake up each morning, all your wishes and hopes for the day rush at you like wild animals. And the first job each morning consists in shoving it all back; in listening to that other voice, taking that other point of view, letting that other, larger, stronger, quieter life come flowing in.

C. S. Lewis

ought to be asking. The Spirit is God. He knows God's good intentions and purposes for us. And he will lead us into the mind of Christ on the matter that concerns us, both individually and even more as we come together. This gives us confidence that we will pray in accordance with Jesus' will rather than our own, and so our prayers will be effective.

Here is the basis for answered prayer. It is not a question of whether there is something good about us or our prayers, but of whether we are attuned to the Holy Spirit and allow ourselves to be taught by him what and how to pray. Then we shall be caught up into the prayer of Christ himself, and with him in one Spirit will offer our prayers and ourselves to the Father, into whose presence Jesus opens the way.

The Spirit of praise

When Christians pray in the Spirit, their prayer will be full of joy and praise. Paul said, 'Go on being filled with the Spirit, addressing one another in psalms and hymns and songs that the Spirit gives, making melody to the Lord with all your hearts.' A Spirit-filled church or Christian will be a real music centre of praise. It has been said that the church's preaching should be the answer to the questions raised by its praise. Our worship should prompt people to ask why we are so joyful, and we then preach the gospel to give them the answer.

Christian Renewal

John Wesley was the greatest architect of the eighteenth-century revival in England. He travelled prodigiously (over a quarter of a million miles) and preached in churches or in the open air, wherever he had the opportunity. As a result of his long labours the spiritual and moral climate of England was markedly changed.

Revivals (otherwise called 'renewals' or 'awakenings') have been a key feature of Christian history. Without them the church would have become increasingly lifeless and would have lacked what we now see as its essential characteristics. The Christian centuries are far from showing a steady increase in spiritual vitality. They are more a story of alternating renewal and decline. Periods where faith has atrophied and devotion become purely formal have been broken by sudden surges of spiritual life and power. The early days of the monastic movement represented such a surge, and another came when Francis of Assisi burst on the scene. The sixteenth century saw the Reformation, eighteenth-century England the evangelical revival, and in the mid-nineteenth century came an awakening which spread from the United States to Britain. The twentieth century has perhaps been the greatest of all in this respect, with times of Christian renewal in Africa, in East Asia and in Latin America.

Some of these awakenings though by no means all, have been associated with particular charismatic personalities. But we have to look beyond the famous names to find an explanation for what happened. In fact it is a common factor of the revivals that they have been totally unpredictable. They have been expressions of the sovereignty of God, explained only in terms of the power of the Holy Spirit to change people and communities.

Two characteristics of Christian awakenings point to this sovereignty of God:

- ☐ **An increased emphasis on prayer,** as people have grown deeply discontent with the state of their unrevived churches;
- ☐ **Deep repentance,** involving both sorrow for sin and a determination to change.

Many of the renewals in history have given fresh impetus to Christian mission. In particular the nineteenth-century awaking, by giving rise to the greatest expansion of missionary work there has ever been, proved to be the seed of today's worldwide church.

The gift of tongues, which has been the subject of much—sometimes too much—interest in the Charismatic renewal, is simply another way that the Spirit gives some people to express their praise. It is a way of praising God, not in intelligible words formulated by our minds, but in spontaneous utterances of joy that well up from our hearts.

Jesus once said that true worship is in Spirit and in truth. And so the church should worship in the freedom that the Spirit gives, but also in a way that is an ordered reflection of the whole truth of the gospel, as we have received it from Jesus Christ. There is no conflict between freedom and order in Christian worship, since the same Holy Spirit is the author of both.

When people are open to the spirit, the tyranny of the one voice in worship can be broken and many may be led to join in praise, prayer and speaking God's truth. But the same Spirit is also the author of ordered forms of worship, so that worship proceeds not in accordance with our whims or fancies, but in a way that reflects all the aspects of the gospel. The word of God, the Bible, is read and preached systematically, different kinds of prayer are given their rightful place, and the communion is shared in obedience to Jesus' instruction.

It used to be thought that free worship and liturgical worship were mutually exclusive alternatives, with different denominations specializing in the one or the other. But when the Spirit is in charge, he can use both in harmony, so that what is most orderly and faithful to the gospel is also most free and open. Modern liturgy is concerned to provide an ordered framework within which the freedom of the Spirit can most effectively operate, and when that happens Christian worship is at its richest and best.

Holy Spirit and holy communion

The Spirit, as we have seen, makes the word of God effective by enabling us to hear the living Christ speaking to us from the Bible. In the same way the Spirit speaks to us through the bread and wine of the communion table. He uses these material elements to make effective to us the death and resurrection of Jesus. We do not just remember him: we share in him, sharing the forgiveness of sins made possible by his death and the new life made possible by his resurrection.

Modern liturgies have at the centre of the great prayer over the bread and wine a prayer for the Holy Spirit. As the celebrant says, 'Grant that by the power of the Holy Spirit, these gifts of bread and wine may be to us his body and blood.' Our correct forms of words and ardent prayers cannot by themselves make Jesus present. To share Christ's life with us is the prerogative of the Holy Spirit, and this he does at the communion, so that in accordance with Jesus' invitation and promise we 'eat his body and drink his blood'.

When the word of God is read and preached, Jesus comes and speaks to us by the Spirit. In the sacrament he comes in the same Spirit and gives himself to us. We cannot understand the sacrament apart from the word, but the sacrament makes it clear that Jesus wants more for us than just to hear truth spoken about him. He wants actually to share himself with us, and what he has done for us, in his living person, presence and power. When the Spirit is at work in the sacrament, it cannot remain a gloomy memorial service looking back to his sacrifice long ago. It becomes instead a celebration of the presence of the Lord. Once crucified, he is now risen, and comes to share his new life with us and to enable us to share it with one another.

Music is for the soul what the wind is for the ship, blowing her onwards in the direction in which she is steered.

General Booth, founder of the Salvation Army

Receiving the Spirit

We receive the Spirit when we receive Jesus Christ. We are baptized into the realm of the Spirit at precisely the same moment as we are baptized into the realm of Jesus. No one can say 'Jesus is Lord' except by the Holy Spirit.

But just as it takes a whole lifetime and more to see and experience all that there is for

RON DAVIES

Proclaiming His Death

'The Lord Jesus, on the night he was betrayed, took a piece of bread, gave thanks to God, broke it, and said, "This is my body, which is for you. Do this in memory of me." In the same way, after the supper he took the cup and said, "This cup is God's new covenant, sealed with my blood. Whenever you drink it, do so in memory of me." ' So wrote the apostle Paul to the Corinthians. And all sections of the Christian church, with only two notable exceptions, are agreed on the importance of the meal instituted by the Lord Jesus on the night of his betrayal and arrest. Jesus instituted it, and the New Testament understood it, as a means of:

- ☐ **remembering his death for us;**
- ☐ **enjoying and drawing strength from our present communion with him**, in fellowship with other believers;
- ☐ **anticipating the perfect enjoyment of his presence** which will begin when he comes again.

Despite these central points of agreement, however, there has been widespread disagreement about details of meaning and practice. Regrettably these have divided Christians, rather than uniting us in an act which is the focal point of our worship.

One difference is in what different groups call this service, though the significance of the terms comes from their association rather than from their original meaning. Protestants usually speak of the **Lord's table**, the **Lord's supper**, the **holy communion** or the **breaking of bread**. Catholics speak of the **altar**, the **eucharist** (a term the Eastern Orthodox also use) or the **mass**.

'Eucharist' comes from a Greek word meaning 'thanksgiving', and 'the mass' from the Latin words the priest speaks at the end of the service, *missa est*, indicating that the congregation is dismissed. Communion and baptism are usually referred to as sacraments. They are the two services which were instituted by Jesus himself and which specifically proclaim the gospel. The Roman Catholic and Eastern Orthodox Churches also include other rites as sacraments, such as marriage and confirmation.

How is Jesus present?

The main differences, however, are over the meaning of holy communion, or more specifically, what happens in the service—what happens to the bread and wine, and what happens to the worshippers?

Discussion has often concentrated on the words 'do this *in memory of* me' and 'this *is* my body/blood'. But many more factors are involved, including historical development, philosophical, linguistic and cultural background, and other parts of Christian doctrine such as the possibility of Jesus' glorified human nature being present everywhere. Any attempt to summarize the different understandings runs the risk of oversimplification and therefore misrepresentation, but the following is a summary of the main historical differences of interpretation:

- ☐ The Roman Catholic doctrine of **transubstantiation** was officially stated in AD 1215 at the Fourth Lateran Council, affirmed and expounded more fully during the sixteenth-century Council of Trent, and recently reaffirmed in the encyclical *Mysterium Fidei* in 1965 following the Second Vatican Council. It states that, when the priest pronounces the words of Christ, 'This is my body' and 'This is my blood', the elements of bread and wine are miraculously changed into the body and blood of Jesus. These are then offered to God as a propitiatory sacrifice for the sins of the living and the dead: the congregation worships them as the priest lifts them up; and when the congregation partakes of the bread (not the wine), they really receive Jesus Christ's body and blood.
- ☐ The Eastern Orthodox doctrine is similar, although more stress is laid on **the risen, glorified state of Christ**, and on his presence in the whole action of the service rather than only in the bread and wine.
- ☐ The Lutheran view, often referred to as **consubstantiation** (although Martin Luther

himself did not use the term) is that the glorified human nature of Jesus is really present 'in, with and under' the bread and wine.

- ☐ The Zwinglian view (associated with the Swiss Reformer Ulrich Zwingli, but not held in an extreme form by him) stresses that the bread and wine are **symbols only**. It concentrates on the 'remembrance' aspect of the meal.
- ☐ The Calvinist view was formed by John Calvin when he tried to mediate between Luther and Zwingli who disagreed strongly over these matters. He taught that Jesus is really present when the bread is eaten and the wine drunk, but **present in a spiritual way**.

Among English-speaking Christians, the Anglican Reformers adopted the Calvinist view, as did the Puritans, the Nonconformists and the Methodists. Present-day free churches are often Zwinglian, as are some evangelical Anglicans, although others are more Calvinist in their view of communion. Modern Anglo-Catholics hold to a view which has points of similarity with both the Roman Catholic and Lutheran ideas. In today's ecumenical climate, conversations have taken place between various branches of the church attempting to heal the divisions of centuries of theological difference. In Britain the Anglican-Roman Catholic Agreed Statement on the Eucharist (1971) was one result.

Preaching and sharing

To understand this sacrament we need to get back behind the historical differences, to how the Bible describes and interprets it. Paul makes two points which give us clear guidance. In 1 Corinthians 11 he speaks about **proclaiming**, and in 1 Corinthians 10 about **sharing**.

Augustine (AD 354–430) defined a sacrament as 'a visible sign of an invisible reality' and also as 'a visible preaching of the gospel'. This fits well with Paul's teaching. The church's celebration of the holy communion is a visible preaching of the gospel, pointing in particular to Jesus' sacrificial death as the central means of our salvation. When the gospel is proclaimed verbally in the power of the Holy Spirit, Jesus is present and is received by faith. When the church meets in the name of Jesus and celebrates the eucharist, Jesus is present and is received anew by faith.

The 'sharing' is in the body and blood of Christ—Christ spiritually present with us as the one who died for us and who gives us the blessings of 'God's new covenant': forgiveness of sins, fellowship with God, and spiritual strength. These are the blessings that come to a person when they first accept Jesus Christ. They are received anew as our fellowship with Jesus is renewed in the communion service. The sacrifice of Christ is graphically set forth again to our faith, and as we eat and drink we act out our receiving of him who made that sacrifice.

As we eat together from the one loaf, we also declare our fellowship with our fellow believers. This aspect, which has often been missed, is finding renewed emphasis today as Christians offer one another a sign of peace (from a kiss to a handshake!) as part of the service.

The holy communion is rich in significance and should have a position of great importance in the corporate worship of the church. In it we look back to the cross, with grief for our sin and gratitude for our salvation. We look up to an exalted Saviour, present with us by his Spirit, offering again to our faith the rich experience of his fellowship, his forgiveness and his strength. We look around to our brothers and sisters in the family of Christ and rejoice that God has made us his community. We look forward with longing and anticipation to what the book of Revelation calls 'the wedding feast of the Lamb', for we celebrate the feast on earth 'until he comes'.

us in Jesus, so there is no end to our discovery of what the Spirit can do by way of sharing Jesus' life with us. He uses the inner developments as well as the outward circumstances of our lives, in conjunction with the word of the Bible and the fellowship of the church, to open us up more and more to all that he has for us in Christ. As we go on in the Christian life, we are given faith to enter further and further into that holy humanity, that spiritual power, that life of prayer and worship that the Spirit has for us.

To be filled with the Spirit is never a once-for-all experience, on the strength of which we can live for the rest of our lives. We become dry and weary, in our sin we grieve and quench the Spirit, so that we lose some of his power in our lives. We come on times of need and suffering that send us back to God for new resources. We come across promises in God's word that we have not personally made our own.

We need to be reassured, not once but over and over again, that we are God's loved and accepted children and heirs. In all these situations we need to open ourselves to a new filling of the same Holy Spirit, a new sharing in the boundless life of Jesus himself. That is why Paul exhorted the Ephesians to go on being filled with the Spirit. The one who had already come to them must keep on coming, to refresh what he had already done and to lead them into new dimensions of his grace and power.

That coming of the Spirit may be sudden and memorable like his coming at the day of Pentecost, with fire to purify and wind to freshen. The church, and individual Christians in it, needs times of revival and renewal to rediscover the half-forgotten power of the Holy Spirit and to be suddenly transformed to new joy, new victory, new power, new love.

But not all his comings are like that. The Bible speaks of the Spirit as dew as well as wind and fire. The dew falls quietly and almost imperceptibly, but you know it has fallen because everything is made fresh and sweet. So there are quiet and secret comings of the Spirit, evidenced by the new nearness and likeness to Christ that his coming brings to his people, new depth in prayer and new devotion to the sacrament.

Jesus once gave his disciples a promise which may be rightly translated, 'Your heavenly Father goes on being willing to go on giving the Holy Spirit to those who go on asking him'. The heart of all renewal is that we should go on asking the generous Father who through Jesus will go on giving us the Spirit who will go on joining us to Christ in all his overflowing goodness, and to one another in him.

Our prayer for renewal is a prayer for the Spirit who reveals the truth, who inspires the word, who brings us to new birth, who changes our characters and distributes his gifts, who leads our worship and makes real our communion. To him indeed we pray, Come, Holy Spirit.

For further thinking

QUESTION 1

Does the Holy Spirit work only through the church? Or is he active in the whole of humanity?

QUESTION 2

What is it about Christian prayer that distinguishes it from prayer offered in Old Testament times? Do the distinguishing features of Christian prayer help someone who is finding it difficult to pray?

QUESTION 3

A central role of the Holy Spirit is to make us live Christ-like lives. In what ways will such lives be different from good lives lived by people who do not follow Jesus?

QUESTION 4

When Christians celebrate the eucharist or Lord's Supper, are they chiefly remembering something that happened in the past or proclaiming something that is true today? Or is it really not possible to separate the two?

BIBLE REFERENCES

The Holy Spirit

Genesis 1:2; 6:3; Exodus 31:3; Numbers 11:29; Judges 6:34; 15:14; 1 Samuel 10:6; 2 Kings 2:9; Psalms 51:10–11; 139:7; Isaiah 11:2–3; 40:13; 42:1–4; 63:11; Ezekiel 18:31; 36:26; Joel 2:28–29; Zechariah 4:6; Matthew 3:16; 4:1; Luke 1:41; 4:18; 11:13; John 3:6–8; 4:24; 14:17; 15:26; 16:7–15; Acts 2:1–18; 8:29; Romans 8:2–16; 1 Corinthians 2:11–14; 3:16; 6:19; 12:4–13; 2 Corinthians 3:6; 3:17; Galatians 4:6; 5:22–25; Ephesians 1:13; 4:4; 5:18; 6:17; 1 Thessalonians 4:8; 5:19; 2 Timothy 1:7

Prayer

Genesis 18:22–33; 32:9–12; Exodus 17:11–13; 32:11–13; 33:12–16; Judges 16:28; 1 Samuel 1.10–11; 1 Chronicles 29:10–19; Nehemiah 1:5–11; Psalms 57:1–11; Daniel 9:15–19; Jonah 2:1–9; Matthew 6:7–15; 7:7–11; 26:39, 41; Mark 1:35; Luke 9:28–29; 11:9–13; John 14:13; 17:1–26; Acts 4:31; 9:11; 10:9; 12:5; Romans 8:16–17, 26–27; Ephesians 1:15–17; 3:14–21; 6:18; Philippians 1:9–11; Colossians 1:9–10; 4:3; 1 Thessalonians 3:10; 5:17; 1 Timothy 2:1–8; James 5:16; 1 John 5:14–15; Jude 20; Revelation 22:20

Breaking Bread

Exodus 12:15–27, 43–49; Matthew 26:17–30; Mark 14:12–26; Luke 22:7–20; 24:28–31; John 6:53–58; Acts 2:42; 20:11; 1 Corinthians 10:16–22; 11:17–34; Revelation 19:5–9

ANNE LONG

Spirituality through the Ages

Spirituality is not a static, academic concept, but a living, growing relationship between ourselves and God. It concerns our pursuit of him and his of us, a pursuit and encounter in which we, as persons, relate to a Person with whom we can have personal dealings. Spirituality is a feature of all religious traditions, but we limit ourselves here to the Christian tradition.

Spirituality in the New Testament

The New Testament gives us foundations for this personal relationship:

- **The heart of Christian spirituality is Jesus Christ.** The New Testament teaches that he is our way to God, just as God's way to us is through Jesus. We are his followers and he leads us to the Father.
- **Christian spirituality reflects the fact that Jesus became man.** The New Testament emphasizes a positive, world-affirming discipleship. We are not to escape from time, earth and history any more than Jesus did. We must engage with them as the scene of our faith. Christian spirituality affects every area of human experience.
- **In Christian spirituality there is a 'givenness' and a 'working out'.** Our growth as Christians is something God gives, yet we are also to work at it. We cannot save ourselves, yet we are to work out our salvation. We are given new life by God as a free gift, yet we must live it responsibly as stewards of his gifts.
- **Christian spirituality contains a paradox.** As Jesus Christ establishes his rule at the heart of our lives, so self-centredness must gradually give way to him. For the Christian, greatness lies in humility, power is experienced in weakness. It is as we learn through suffering that we are glorified, and as we enter Christ's death that we are filled with his life. The way of the cross becomes the way of the crown.

How have Christians worked out their spirituality through the ages?

The early centuries

Early Christians found themselves defending their faith in different ways. **Ignatius**, Bishop of Antioch, a second-century church father, followed Jesus literally to martyrdom. 'Allow me to be an imitator of the passion of my God,' he wrote. **Irenaeus**, Bishop of Lyons (AD 177), defended Christianity against Gnostic heresy by emphasizing the historic roots of the Christian faith. For him, being a Christian must mean finding our pattern in the historical Jesus. But throughout this period the Greek Platonic tradition behind Gnosticism repeatedly pulled believers away from history and the created world to a spirituality that was world- and flesh-denying, highly intellectualized and deviating from biblical Christianity. Alexandria was the chief centre of this thinking, attracting such teachers as **Origen** and **Clement**.

In the fourth century the Christian church was marked by theological and spiritual divisions, especially about the trinity, and the rapid growth of the institutional church. Both the medieval Latin Church of the West and the Eastern Orthodox Church of the Byzantine Empire had their roots in this era. The Orthodox 'Jesus Prayer' (or prayer of the heart), which has become so extensively used in other Christian traditions, goes back to this early period, finding its way, centuries later, into the Russian Orthodox Church and even more recently into Western Christendom. 'Lord Jesus Christ, Son of God, have mercy on me.' Such a simple prayer, but one that can eventually continue unceasingly within the person using it.

Two Christian writers who contributed richly to spirituality through their writings were **Gregory of Nyssa** (about 330–95) and **Augustine of Hippo** (354–430). Gregory stressed that the true outworking of Christianity is serving God and our neighbour with love and compassion, rather than privately cultivating our own spirit. His was a spirituality strongly linked to social righteousness. And, in contrast to the Eastern tradition which sought to eradicate emotions, Gregory taught that our passions should be controlled and redirected into a more mature and full humanity.

Augustine of Hippo published his *Confessions* in 401. For him, God was home, his place of belonging. 'Our hearts are restless till they find their rest in you.' He wrote of his conversion with great passion and lyricism, for people must be saved with all their humanity and emotions, not despite them. As we dwell on God's utter beauty, so we are led forward to greater wholeness and deeper holiness. But it was not all ecstasy for Augustine. The way to God is always through the cross, and the Christian must accept crucifixion as part of his calling.

In contrast, **the Desert Fathers** (third–fourth centuries) emphasized the theme of conflict. The spiritual life is a battle and 'it is by warfare that the soul makes progress' (Abbot John the Dwarf). Their search for an ascetic spirituality, stressing rigour and discipline, caused them to withdraw from the cities to desert places, often living in the isolation of caves. **Benedict** (who lived about 480–550) was an Italian monk who also saw the Christian life in terms of warfare. His *Rule for Monks* was to have a huge influence on Western monasticism.

The Middle Ages

In the early Middle Ages, two main centres of Christianity emerged, one in Rome and the other in Constantinople. Many political and religious pressures reduced the effectiveness of the church in the West until, in the tenth to the twelfth centuries, spiritual renewal came, largely through the monastic movement.

In England, **Anselm of Canterbury** (about 1033–1109) was part of an intellectual development in Europe, believing that faith was an important foundation for thought and mental speculation about God. In France, **Bernard of Clairvaux** (1090–1153) and **Francis of Assisi** (1181–1226) were also rekindling devotion to God. Bernard loved the Bible. For him it was 'the source of life and my soul knows no other'. Although many biblical scholars today would question his interpretation, he nevertheless gave the Bible, along with the love of God, a central place in his life and teaching.

The late Middle Ages saw a widespread decline in Christian thought and practice, but in the fourteenth and fifteenth centuries there were several spiritual classics written, especially **Thomas à Kempis'** *Imitation of Christ* and **Julian of Norwich's** *Revelations of Divine Love,* in which she graphically describes sixteen visions from God of Christ's death on the cross and love's triumph over sin. She also gives practical advice on prayer for those times when it feels a meaningless activity.

Reformation

The legacy of **Martin Luther** (1483–1546) was a rich one. His own experience of striving to reach God's righteous standards, and despairing, led him to a new discovery of forgiveness, acceptance and love. In the cross God has acted on our behalf, offering us, in Christ, a new relationship with himself. Luther cut through much of the religiosity of his time with his rediscovery of the Bible, his emphasis on the death of Jesus and his new understanding of God's gift of new life for the believer.

Catholic Spain produced three notable writers who were to prove influential in the history of spirituality. **Ignatius of Loyola** (1491–1556) gave up his career as a professional soldier to become a soldier for Jesus. He founded the Jesuit Order in the Roman Catholic Church and wrote the *Spiritual Exercises,* a four-week retreat programme of devotional readings on sin, Christ's kingship, his passion and his risen life. They are still used in retreats today.

John of the Cross (1542–91) and **Teresa of Avila** (1515–82) emphasized the 'negative way', a way of detachment from the world, a costly stripping that would lead a Christian through darkness to reach God's light. They present a tension every Christian must experience between affirmation of the world and detachment from it. John was suspicious of mystical experiences, upholding an obedience that was independent of satisfaction or excitement.

Revival

Of a very different spirituality were **the Wesleys**, John (1703–91) and Charles (1707–88). Both were influential in the Evangelical Revival. Charles wrote over seven thousand sacred songs and poems, and John called the *Methodist Hymn Book* of 1780 'a little body of experimental and practical divinity'. They experienced deeply the renewing power and love of

God—a renewal which was also to contribute to Anglican Evangelicalism through such men as **Charles Simeon** (1759–1836) of Cambridge, with his emphasis on personal experience of Christ and systematic Bible teaching.

A very different kind of revival within the Church of England was the Oxford Movement. **Edward Pusey, John Henry Newman and John Keble** stressed the tradition of the church and Catholicism, especially worship, communion, reverence, reading of devotional books, disciplined prayer and retreats (times of withdrawal and silence). Newman (1801–90) left the Church of England to become a Roman Catholic. He wrote *The Dream of Gerontius*, later to be set to music by Elgar.

Spirituality today

What are the chief influences in twentieth-century spirituality?

The **evangelical movement** has emphasized the saving work of Christ, the centrality of the Bible, personal holiness and evangelism; a significant renewal linked with evangelicalism has been the **East African revival**. Across the different churches, Protestant and Catholic, the **Charismatic renewal** has featured praise, spiritual gifts and colourful worship. **Liberation theology** has underlined a more militant engagement with society and a close identification with world suffering. With similar passion but in a different way, **Mother Teresa** works relentlessly among the poor of Calcutta and maintains that the foundation of her missionary work is to withdraw alone with God to pray. The American monk, **Thomas Merton** (1915-60) adopted a strict, hermit life of prayer. By disengaging from the world, he believed he could become more closely identified with it.

There is widespread spiritual questing today, especially among young people, for transcendence, significance and community. Many search through drugs, cults and experience-centred groups, while others travel Christian paths to discover a Christian spirituality for themselves. Traditional and new-style communities are sought out to give a framework for spiritual growth.

In this climate of widespread soul-searching, the Christian has the riches of centuries to draw upon. The challenge is to see Jesus Christ uniquely as the Way and then, as a pilgrim, to search out the well-trodden paths that many saints have travelled down the years.

HOWARD SNYDER

A Living Community

CHAPTER 28

How to be the church? This was the new, urgent question facing the followers of Jesus after Pentecost. The book of Acts shows how the new believing community responded: 'They devoted themselves to the apostles' teaching and to the fellowship, to the breaking of bread and to prayer.'

These few hundred, and soon several thousand, new Christians found they had been made a living community through Jesus' resurrection and the Holy Spirit's outpouring at Pentecost. Something new and dynamic was happening. Both believers and non-believers sensed the unusual stirring, the feeling of a new movement being born.

Yet, as with all God's work in history, the Spirit's new work was mediated through the old. The new Christian community had roots in the Old Testament and in God's ancient chosen people, Israel. Even Peter on the day of Pentecost made the connection with God's work in the past: 'This is what was spoken by the prophet Joel.' King David himself, he said, was Jesus' forerunner and looked ahead to the New Israel.

Jumping across twenty centuries to today's world is not impossible or strange, for it is the same Spirit of Jesus who works in the church today. As with the believers at Pentecost, so today the church is at root the community of people who confess Jesus as Lord and commit themselves to live for God's kingdom. Jesus spoke for all time when he said, 'Where two or three come together in my name, there am I with them.'

But Christians today, even in new Christian communities, do not exist without connection to the past. Like the first-century believers, the contemporary church is heir to God's work in history—not only in Christ and in the Old Testament, but through two millennia of Christian history as well.

Community and history

The New Testament relates the birth of the Christian community. It gives enough information and insight for believers to understand how the church is to function. The Bible is not an organizational manual or book of discipline, but the church's charter and source of renewed life. Many of our questions about the early Christian community are left unanswered, and this is how God meant it to be. God intends his disciples to live by the spirit and the foundational truths of his written word, not by specific details of form and practice.

Already in the New Testament we find variety in the church. The Jerusalem church, pictured in the early chapters of Acts and briefly elsewhere, was significantly different from the more diverse community at Antioch. It was made up of a different blend of people, and was probably also different in worship and organization. When Paul and his missionary group set out from Antioch, they planted new church communities throughout much of the Mediterranean world. We learn of these new communities in Paul's letters as well as in Acts.

The New Testament writings show that at the basic level of truth, principle, and spiritual dynamic these communities were quite similar. But at the level of custom, culture and specific practice they varied greatly. Also, the New Testament writings reveal a growing understanding that, whatever form it takes, the church is the body of Christ, the New Israel and the community of God's people.

It seems to be by God's design that the limits of the New Testament were set where they were, and that other early Christian

[The church is] a mixed society. It is not a community of saints and dedicated persons, but a society of sinners at every variety of spiritual development.

Max Warren

> Shut in upon itself, the great concern of the Christian community is to preserve its immunity and safeguard its existence.
>
> *Abbé Godin*

writings were not included in the cannon. Writings such as 1 Clement and the Epistles of Ignatius, valuable as they are, already show a hardening of church organization (somewhat different, in fact, from each other). Such emerging patterns need not be taken as hard and fast rules for the church in all times and places. God's plan is that the church should be a *living* community, which means openness and obedience to God's Spirit in each time and place. And this kind of responsiveness to the Spirit means, as history shows, both faithfulness to God's work in the past and openness to new patterns and forms as circumstances change.

Very early in Christian history, however, tensions arose between the church's life and the forms embodying that life. This was inevitable. We could think of it as the tension between the church as an organism and as an organization, or between the charismatic and institutional sides of the church. It is the tension between the new wine of the gospel and the old wineskins which contain it. This tension is always present: the tension between, on the one hand, being the authentic community of the Spirit and, on the other hand, using appropriate means and structures for living as God's community in a particular society and culture.

From one angle this is, in fact, the story of church history. Often the church has grown and prospered, creating or adapting structures to carry its life and witness. Some of these forms have been compatible with the New Testament picture of the church; others less so. Church structures have often provided institutional stability. But they have also often dampened the church's spiritual vigour and hurt its witness.

The church's nearly exclusive reliance on Latin for many centuries, for example, effectively locked up the church's real power. Similarly, the growing split between clergy

'Into all the World'

Christian radio broadcasts take programmes into regions where little is known of the faith. Christian pilots take doctors and evangelists into inaccessible areas. Christian engineers help villagers open up regular water supplies. Bible teachers help new Christians to understand their faith, and study it for themselves. These are just a few of the many ways in which missionary work is done today.

When we receive God's love in our own experience, we are not meant to keep it to ourselves. His love in Jesus is for the whole world, and Christians are 'sent' (the root meaning of 'mission') to take to others what Jesus has brought to them. Jesus was selflessly dedicated to introducing people to the varied richness of his Father. And in this he is a model for those who follow him.

For many Christians this will mean being open with friends and neighbours about why faith is so important. But Christianity will only reach round the world as it is taken across national and cultural boundaries. This is the calling of the true missionary.

The task has been more fully undertaken in the nineteenth and twentieth centuries than ever before, so that the last few generations have been the first to see that worldwide church to which the New Testament looked forward. Christianity had become concentrated in the Western world, and so at first the missionary flow was from North and West to East and South. But this is no longer true. The vitality of Christianity in many countries of Africa, Latin America and East Asia is such that many missionaries are going out from them to other nations where the gospel has made less headway.

Missionary work is often costly. And it requires a real appreciation of the integrity of the other person's culture and life-style. But it is still the church's great commission and calls for all the resources of imagination and compassion that Jesus gives to his people.

and laity ('clericalization'), with all authentic witness and authority pretty well reserved for male clergy, reduced the church's vitality to only a fraction of the New Testament dynamic. At the same time, the growing institutional power and prestige of the church, especially after the conversion of the Emperor Constantine in the fourth century, gave the church the feeling and appearance of success.

From this perspective, the Spirit's vital work in history has been to re-create the church as a living community, calling it back to its biblical life and roots. Church history involves a whole chain of movements of spiritual renewal in the church.

The history of every Christian tradition is dotted with such examples of spiritual resurgence. The various traditions, in fact, themselves generally trace their origin to times of spiritual renewal in the church. When we think of events such as the Protestant Reformation, the twelfth-century evangelical awakening, the revivals in eighteenth-century England and America or twentieth-century Africa—these are but the more visible high peaks in the panorama of God's work throughout history.

At the same time, no single movement or renewal can be taken as fully normative or permanently authentic, because none was perfect in itself. Each was rooted in a particular history and culture. And each in time found its own ways to institutionalize and compromise its own vision. So the constant challenge before the church is to let the Spirit apply the word anew to its present life. We must find ways, in our generation, to be the living community so powerfully sketched in the Bible.

The Community of God's People

The Bible pictures the church in a variety of ways. First and foremost, it is the body of Christ. It is the bride of Christ; the flock of God; the living temple of the Holy Spirit. Virtually all biblical images for the church suggest an essential, living relationship of love between Jesus and the church. This underlines the key role the church plays in God's plan. It emphasizes the fact that 'Christ loved the church and gave himself up for her'. If the church is the *body* of Christ, the means by which Christ the head is able to act in the world, then the church is an indispensable part of the gospel. Salvation inescapably involves believers with the life of the church.

The Bible shows the church surrounded by particular cultures, struggling to be faithful, but sometimes made less effective by unnatural alliances with paganism and Jewish legalism. In the New Testament, the earthly and heavenly sides of the church fit together in one whole. We are not left with one perfect, spiritual church and another compromised, human organization incompatible with it. The church is one; it is the one body of Christ that now exists both on earth and 'in the heavenly realms'.

To understand the church more fully, we need to look at three ways in which the Bible sees the church.

Historical and universal

The church fits into God's overall plan to unite all things in Jesus Christ. The church is the people of God which God has been forming and through which he has been acting down through history. In this sense the church has roots that go back into the Old Testament, back even to the fall of humankind. Its mission stretches forward into all remaining history and into eternity.

Its story is the church's historical dimension. But it has also a universal dimension. This space-time world is really part of a larger, spiritual universe in which God reigns. The church is the body given to Christ, the conquering Saviour. God has chosen to put the church with Christ at the very centre of his plan to reconcile the world to himself.

The church's mission, therefore, is to glorify God by carrying on in the world the works of the kingdom which Jesus began.

Evangelism is just one beggar telling another beggar where to find bread.

D. T. Niles

This gives the church a broader service, continue the ministry Jesus had 'to preach good news to the poor ... to proclaim freedom for the prisoners and recovery of sight for the blind, to release the oppressed, to proclaim the year of the Lord's favour'.

Charismatic rather than institutional

The church is, in a broad sense, an institution. But it is more fundamentally a charismatic community. That is, it exists by the grace (*charis* in Greek) of God and is built up by the gifts of grace (*charismata*) bestowed

Christian Healing

The healing of the sick has received renewed emphasis among Christians in recent years.

Healing was a central part of Jesus' ministry. The name 'Jesus' means 'one who saves', and the word 'to save' includes the idea of 'making well'. When Jesus healed people, it was a sign that the world was to be remade, and suffering and death would be done away with. But Jesus did more than heal sick bodies; he put right the many things that spoil and divide communities, as he changed relationships, lifted up the downtrodden—forgave sins.

When Jesus died he made it possible for all rifts to be healed. On the cross he won the victory over sin and death and the powers that work to destroy our lives, and in his rising again he opened up the way to a new life of wholeness and peace.

Should the healing work of Jesus be taken up by his followers? Certainly he commissioned his followers to heal as well as to preach; certainly the apostles were given powers to heal in the days of the Acts. For a long time it was thought that such gifts had died out with the apostles, but few believe this now. Many churches have a healing ministry today. The details and emphasis vary: some practise laying on of hands as Jesus did; some anoint with oil as in apostolic times. And many people are healed, to their own great joy.

This kind of activity gives a cranky impression to some people. It has received a bad name through so-called 'spiritual healing' or 'faith healing'—depending on the 'faith' or will-power of the individual, not on the power of Christ to heal. This can sometimes be effective. A strong, positive attitude can help healing. But this is different from Christian healing. The signs of a truly Christian approach to healing include:

- ☐ **Seeing the medical profession as an ally.** Modern medicine has its faults, but any approach to healing that ignores it is wrong. At the very least it is part of God's general grace; its origins were much influenced by Christianity; and its practice, especially in the developing world, still involves many Christians. Ideally, doctors and Christian ministers should be involved together in healing.
- ☐ **Working through the Christian community.** There is a healing power in worship and fellowship that is missed in any private ministry. Jesus is present with his church.
- ☐ **Extending the idea of healing beyond the physical.** As with the healing of Jesus, healing is for the whole person; relationships, attitudes and emotions are involved as well as physical ills.
- ☐ **A continuing care for those not healed.** Any approach which suggests that everyone who has faith will be healed is plainly wrong. We cannot fully understanding why sometimes prayer is answered and sometimes not, but a truly Christian ministry will be just as full of love and grace whatever the outcome.
- ☐ **Seeing healing as a 'sign of the kingdom'.** We cannot halt the inevitable results of a sinful world—suffering and death. So even people who have been healed may become ill again, and will eventually die. Healings are a sign here and now that Jesus can and will remake the world so sin, suffering, illness and death will be no more. We see a glimpse now of his power, glory and love.

by the Holy Spirit. As seen biblically, the Christian community is not structured like a business corporation or a university, but like the human body, on the basis of organic life. At its most basic level the church is a community, not an organization.

God's people

Looked at this way, the universal and the charismatic are united, and the church is seen both within the world and reaching beyond the world.

Since the church is the people of God, it comprises all God's people in all nations, including those who have now crossed the space-time boundary and live in the immediate presence of God. But the people of God must have a visible, local expression where people come together in a reconciled and reconciling fellowship. And at this local level the church is the community of the Spirit.

The church finds its identity in this unified, complementary rhythm of being a people and a community, both within a city or culture and within the larger worldwide context. People and community together constitute what the New Testament means by the Greek word *ekklesia*, the called-out and called-together church of God.

The biblical pictures of body of Christ, bride of Christ, household, temple or vineyard of God and so on, reveal the basic idea of the church. These are metaphors, however, and not definitions. While the church is a mystery and escapes adequate definition, the phrase 'the community of God's people' seems to come closest to capturing the reality suggested by the various images the Bible used for the church.

The twin concepts of community and peoplehood emphasize some vital truths:

- **The church is people**, not an institutional structure.
- **The church has a corporate or communal nature** which is absolutely essential to its true being. It is not just a collection of isolated individuals.
- **Being a community and a people is a gift from God** through the work of Jesus Christ and the presence of the Holy Spirit.

The church is not created by human techniques or plans. It is made the people of God through what Jesus Christ has done. This reality opens the door to the possibility of a truer and deeper community than humanity can know in any other way.

The concept of peoplehood is firmly rooted in the Old Testament. It underlines the objective fact that God has been acting throughout history to call and prepare what Peter characterized as 'a chosen people, a royal priesthood, a holy nation, a people belonging to God'. The idea is closely related to the concept of the covenant.

The Greek word for people is *laos*, from which comes the English 'laity'. This means the *whole* church is a laity, a people. Here the emphasis is on the universality of the church—God's people scattered throughout the world in hundreds of specific denominations, movements and other structures.

Seen as the 'people of God', the church is the inclusive, worldwide, corporate reality of the multitude of men and women who, throughout history, have been reconciled to God and to each other through Jesus Christ. God has been moving in history to draw together a pilgrim people. When we look at it from a historical or universal perspective, the church is the people of God.

On the other hand, the church is a *community* or fellowship, a *koinonia*. This is an especially New Testament emphasis and grows directly out of the experience of Pentecost. If peoplehood underlines the continuity of God's plan from Old to New Testament, community calls attention to the 'new covenant', the 'new wine', the 'new thing' God did in the resurrection of Jesus Christ and the gift of the Holy Spirit. This idea focuses on the church as local and visible, on the close personal encounters of its common life. Seen as a charismatic organism, the church is the community of the Holy Spirit.

Steward of God's grace

God has given his people two great resources:

- **The physical world** of space, time, persons, nature and material things;
- **His own Spirit of grace.** The church is charged with the task of being a good steward of these resources. Peter tells us that believers should be 'good stewards of God's varied grace' in using their spiritual gifts. As a charismatic organism, the church is to employ carefully the gifts it has received, to serve and glorify God.

God has graciously saved us through what Jesus has done, applied to us by the Holy Spirit. This provides the basis for the church's community life. The pure light of God's 'varied grace' is then broken down as it shines through the church, as light through a prism, producing the varied, multicoloured *charismata*, or gifts of the Spirit.

The Greek word Peter used for God's 'varied grace' often expresses the idea of 'many coloured', as in the variety of colours

ROBERT SABATH

Christian Communities

From the first flowering of the monastic movement, there have always been Christians living the corporate life. Is this an escape from the rigours of the real world? Or do Christian communities have something essential to teach society and the church? At the heart of God's plan for the world are people in community. Throughout the Bible it is assumed that this is the way it should be.

In the Old Testament, God's strategy was to call out a people for himself. Jesus' first activity, after announcing the arrival of God's kingdom, was to gather together a group of disciples to embody that vision and to pass it on. The coming of the Spirit at Pentecost created the church as a new community. One result was that the disciples were freed from their attachment to the power of possessions.

Throughout the New Testament the church is presented as a community. Paul's central ministry was to form and nurture new communities. In fact, all his writings were originally pastoral letters to small, growing communities of faith. As a theologian of community, Paul summarizes God's ultimate plan as bringing 'all creation together... with Christ as head', transforming a divided creation into a community in Jesus. To bring this about, God would use the church, his reconciled community; it would be like a sign pointing to this plan of universal unity.

The quality of life shared by the early Christian communities was a vital way the church gave substance to the gospel it preached. This new life attracted many to the fellowship of these new people. Throughout the ages, whenever people have rediscovered the Spirit, community has flourished and the power of the secular world has been broken. Every renewal movement in the church has witnessed a recovery of community, from the monastic movement, to John Wesley, to the charismatic renewal today.

The experience of community

More and more people are discovering that they cannot be Christians alone. The renewal of community in the churches is crossing denominational lines and is deeply ecumenical. It is happening within many theological and historical traditions; both inside the institutional structures and outside them; among old and young, families and singles, clergy and lay; within cities, rural areas and suburbs.

This renewal of church as community is taking many different forms. House churches and small groups of people are beginning to meet, not just to study, pray and share, but also to enter a commitment to establish greater discipline and accountability in their

in flowers or clothing. This suggests that the pure, intense but invisible light of God's glorious grace is made colourfully visible in the diversity of spiritual gifts in the Christian community.

This is how the Holy Spirit gives the church its diversity within unity. The church is built up as its members use their spiritual gifts. As Paul puts it, 'The whole body, joined and held together by every supporting ligament, grows and builds itself up in love, as each part does its work.'

The Local Church

Paul tells us again that God has a 'plan' (or 'economy', Greek *oikonomia*) 'to bring all creation together . . . with Christ as head'. The word he uses pictures the whole created order as a house (*oikos*) over which God is sovereign. Within it God is working through Jesus to bring everything into proper relationship. This is, in fact, the biblical version of the kingdom of God.

A central theme of the letter to the Ephesians is that the church plays a key role in this economy of God. The church is God's

relationships. Frequently communities are based on a nucleus of 'households', in which families and single people form a pastoral environment where there can be a greater depth of personal healing and more freedom in ministry. These various communities are experimenting with different forms of pastoral life and new structures of church leadership. Often new economic patterns are created so that local Christians can learn how to support one another and give practical expression to their distinctive life-style.

All of these communities are discovering that conversion to Jesus requires a new pattern of relationships. If every aspect of a person's life is to become truly Christian, that person needs to share life deeply with other Christians. Otherwise a Christian's attitudes and values can be indistinguishable from the society around, as happens so often in today's churches. Without a powerful enough support structure that can form us in the ways of Jesus and break the power of the world in our lives, the world will continue to squeeze us into its mould.

Supporting one another

There is no normative form of community. But there is a Christian life-style, which we fail to find without some deliberate kind of structure and supporting environment. The New Testament speaks of a common life and mind; of bearing one another's burdens; of confronting, correcting, encouraging, exhorting, comforting and edifying one another; of provoking one another to love and good works, of confessing our faults to one another; of weeping with those who weep and rejoicing with those who rejoice; of sharing with one another the same love and unity that Jesus shares with his Father.

The Bible also speaks of breaking free from our attachment to possessions, power and prestige, and of having our hearts softened to the poor and afflicted. It tells us to find our security in God alone, and not in the power of our nation. Too often we simply do not have the kind of structures in our present churches that can support that kind of life. Our communion with one another and with God must be strong enough to enable us to live as the New Testament teaches.

Unfortunately, if most Christians were asked, 'Where is the place on which you feel most dependent for your survival?' few would be able to point to their local churches. Most would name their work place, or some other economic, educational or political institution. It is the social reality in which we feel most rooted that most determines our values and the way we live. We will remain conformed to the values and institutions of our society as long as our security is finally grounded in them.

The need is to create faith communities that gear in to the life of our society, but still are internally strong enough to enable us to survive as Christians. The renewal of church as community will enable us to resist the pressures of our culture and to proclaim something new in the midst of that culture.

oikos, his household, in a special sense. As the body of Christ, the Christian community is joined to Christ and works together with him to fulfil the economy of God. Since the church plays a key role in God's plan, it is important for believers to understand what the church is for, and how God intends it to function.

Based on the idea of God's economy and of the Church as a household *(oikos)*, we may speak of the 'ecology' (*oikologia*) of the Christian community. Ecology means the way living things interact with each other and with their environment. As we have said, the church is more helpfully and accurately understood as a living organism than as an organization. And so it is appropriate to examine the way the different aspects of the church's life fit into an ecological understanding of the church and of God's kingdom-plan generally.

Most of the biblical pictures for the church are ecological images; they picture the church as a living organism of mutually interdependent parts. The primary New Testament image of the church as the body of Christ is certainly ecological. As Christ's body, believers are members of each other, so that when one suffers all suffer. In the New Testament, Christian growth is understood not primarily as individual soul culture, but as the growing health and maturity of the

J. STAFFORD WRIGHT

Deviations from Christianity

All religions which know of him have a respect for Jesus Christ, but Christians alone regard him as the only Son of God in the full sense. This has been the Christian faith, gathered from the Bible, and kept down the ages.

Variant movements use the name of Christian, but maintain that the church has been in error since very early days, especially in worshipping Christ as God. If they are right, God has allowed his people to blaspheme his name down the years, and only now has raised up reformers to correct them. These reformers differ from those at the time of the Reformation, since at that time Protestants, Catholics and Eastern Orthodox were virtually agreed on what the creeds said about the Trinity. In general each of these modern variants claims to be the only true church, so that only its own members will enjoy salvation, or at least salvation of the first rank.

A religion has one or more of the following characteristics:

- ☐ An external authority from God;
- ☐ An inner experience;
- ☐ An intellectual scheme that makes sense;
- ☐ A sense of fellowship;
- ☐ An outline for practical living.

All these find their place in the Christian faith, but if one or two are magnified in isolation, there is a probability of error.

Authority

Jehovah's Witnesses claim the Bible as their sole authority, but their leaders present a strait-jacket of rigid interpretations in their books. Thus there is no serious discussion of other beliefs, as for instance that Jesus Christ is Jehovah, the Lord.

The Worldwide Church of God has its patterns of belief regulated by its founder, Herbert Armstrong.

Mormons (the Church of Jesus Christ of Latter-day Saints) require a second infallible authority to reinterpret and supplement the Bible. This is the *Book of Mormon*, supposedly given to their founder, Joseph Smith, and translated by him miraculously from an ancient language inscribed on golden plates.

Christian Science also has its authoritative revelation which is used to interpret the Bible. This is Mrs Mary Baker Eddy's *Science and Health and Key to the Scriptures*. In places it is highly philosophical with difficult ideas of God and life, but its attraction comes from its advocacy of positive thinking for health and healing.

whole body. Maturity is defined as the Christian community attaining the 'fullness' of Christ. These are ecological ways of looking at the church's life.

Similarly, the common biblical images of the church as a tree or vine, a flock, a household or the bride of Christ are all consistent with an ecological understanding of the Christian community. This ecological approach reinforces our understanding of the church as a community and a people.

Building a model

Such a model for the *oikos* or household of God begins with the fact that the church exists in union with God through Jesus Christ. The purpose of the church is to glorify God and carry out his purposes. The goal of the church is given in Ephesians: To God 'be the glory in the church and in Christ Jesus throughout all generations, for ever and ever!'

An ecological model for the church, then, orients the life of the church towards the glory of God. But how does the church glorify God? What are some of the functions of the life of the church, by which it seeks to fulfil this purpose?

The living community of the church is a fellowship of worship, community and witness.

All its functions are oriented toward the glory of God and each interacts with the

Inner experience

Some individualists seek deeper inner experience beyond conscious thinking. These may allow Jesus as an option, as do **Transcendental Meditation** and some forms of **Yoga**, but, because their methods have been developed by Eastern practitioners or derived from Hinduism, this is not the Jesus Christ of the New Testament—God and Saviour.

New Testament verses may be quoted about God within, but they are taken out of context, since the presence of Christ in our lives by his Holy Spirit comes through the new birth, and is never spoken of as humanity's natural possession. The Spirit reveals God as the personal Father, whereas these seekers look for him as impersonal Spirit, or even as humanity's own inner, divine being. This contrasts with New Testament teaching that it is the Holy Spirit who makes us God's children.

Intellectual schemes

Theosophical (God wisdom) schemes under the influence of Eastern ideas find Christ as one out of many teachers who come between a vague God and humankind. Rudolf Steiner, with his Westernized **Anthroposophy** (Man wisdom) makes Christ central, but holds that the eternal Christ descended on Jesus at his baptism, an old heresy which contradicts the New Testament. **Spiritualism** tries to make sense of the next world, but ignores Bible evidence.

Fellowship

The encouragement of a sense of belonging is important to the authoritarian and practical love groups, but generally less so to the inner experience and intellectual deviations.

Practical love

All the above include good standards, but the idea of practical love as the basis for winning the world is seen in the **Unification Church** (Moonies). Moonies look to Jesus Christ for spiritual salvation, although for them he is not God. They and their founder, the Rev. Sun Myung Moon, look for a second Messiah to bring God's rule to humankind.

The Family of Love (Jesus People, or Children of God) were at first rather more closely intermingled with the Christian churches, but seem now to be taking a more variant line.

We have not included **Christadelphians** (Christ non-existent until his birth at Bethlehem), since they are localized. **Seventh Day Adventists** and **British Israelites** (except the Armstrong version) are orthodox on the Trinity.

Undoubtedly these deviations hold an attraction for many people today. But they lead away from the Christianity of the Bible. The best protection from the harm they sometimes bring is a good understanding of Christian belief.

others in the ecology of the church.

Worship

The primary purpose of the church is to glorify God. When it is faithful to the Bible, the Christian community worships God through all aspects of its life. But praising God becomes the special and highest purpose of the church when it meets together visibly as a worshipping community. For most Christian traditions and throughout most of church history, corporate worship has centred in the reading and proclamation of God's word and the celebration of the Lord's Supper, or holy communion.

Worship consists of both **celebration** and **instruction**. In her worship, through music, liturgy and in other ways, the church

ANDREW KIRK

The Debate about Christian Mission

Among Jesus' last words to his followers were, 'Go and make disciples of all nations.' Christians have a worldwide mission. The last two centuries have seen great missionary activity and considerable success, to the extent that the church is now found in most nations of the world. Yet we still need to ask: what exactly does Christian mission consist of and how should it be fulfilled?

During the twentieth century churches and people of different theological views have come together to consult about and promote Christian mission. The ecumenical (or unity) movement, focused since 1948 in the World Council of Churches, grew out of a great missionary gathering in Edinburgh in 1910. The independence and full participation of the younger, Third World churches have been part of the process of coming to a clearer understanding of what our mission is. The resulting debates about mission have highlighted a number of controversial issues.

At the turn of the century, mission was firmly in the hands of Western churches and agencies. Spurred on by the slogan, 'the evangelization of the world in this generation', Western Christians believed the church was on the threshold of a new expansion. Behind the Edinburgh Conference were the unquestioned assumptions not only that mission was carried out from West to East and from North to South, but also that mission involved introducing the 'benefits' of Western civilization.

After the 1914–18 war this view could no longer be held. By the time of the Jerusalem Conference (1928), planned by the International Missionary Council, a consultative and co-ordinating body formed in 1921, the right of Western churches to assume the lead in, and define, mission was also being questioned.

Younger churches, facing the stark issues of underdevelopment, argued that working for social betterment stood alongside evangelism as an integral part of the church's mission: 'The advancement, by thought and speech and action, of social righteousness is an essential and vital part of the Christian message to mankind' (Report of the Jerusalem Conference).

Another controversial issue, particularly for churches of the East, was the relation between the gospel and non-Christian religions and cultures. Does Christianity fulfil other religions, or totally contradict them? Are other religions real steps on the way to the true God or are they complete perversions, contradicting Christian revelation?

Questions such as these have divided Christians, at least since the Tamboram Conference in 1938. Since then little consensus has been reached. Some have wanted to find a mediating position between superficial acceptance of other religions and dogmatic rejection. Most religions have elements of permanent value. The cultures they represent should most certainly not be despised. And yet Jesus Christ is the Lord and the judge of every expression of life and truth, including the Christian church. (See further the article *The centrality of Christ*.)

Evangelism and social action

Since the 1939–45 war, Christians

celebrates all God is and all he has done. And through the word read, taught, dramatized or whatever, the church hears God speak to her. In worship, celebration works together with instruction, the Spirit with the word.

Community

In the biblical ecology of the church, community is as vitally important as worship. Just as a household is not really a family if it never meets and spends time together, so believers never really experience the church—without Christian community. Just as the human body cannot live without its vital organs, so the church cannot thrive without life in community.

Biblically, community means shared life together based on our new being in Jesus

have tended to polarize further on a number of concerns central to mission.

In Ghana (1958), the International Missionary Council (IMC) voted to become a part of the World Council of Churches (WCC). This was the logical conclusion of a view of mission which stressed that the church, rather than voluntary agencies, was the instrument of mission. But as a result the vision of evangelistic outreach has been dimmed.

Partly in response to this, evangelical Christians, gathered in Berlin in 1966, forcibly restated that evangelism and the planting of new churches were the primary tasks of mission. A new school of mission known as Church Growth grew up in the 1960s to investigate and, if possible, predict mass movements of Christianity. The Church Growth School has felt that certain cultural factors may either advance or hinder a community's openness to the gospel. So, during the 1970s, this school and other Christian organizations have worked to understand what they term 'people groups', cultural groups which may be reached as a unit with the gospel.

In contrast, the successor to IMC (the Commission for World Mission and Evangelism, a department of the WCC) has concentrated on other issues in mission. At Bangkok in 1972, and to a slightly lesser extent at Melbourne in 1980, mission has been interpreted almost exclusively as the active presence of Christians in the struggles of humanity to be free from the social consequences of sin: poverty, powerlessness, racism, sexism and loss of human rights.

It has adopted a largely negative stance towards the aggressive evangelism of evangelical agencies, suggesting that there should be a moratorium on missionaries from the West. The fear is that they may tend to stifle national Christians as they try to develop their own faith and mission strategy. This view has been echoed by some Third World evangelical Christians, who point out that Western missionaries often ignore the social and political implications of evangelism. Today the concept of 'mission in all six continents' is gaining acceptance: the idea that all local mission initiatives should be undertaken as a result of a genuine global partnership among Christians.

Perhaps the single most urgent task of mission today is to relate evangelism to social action. Christians in the ecumenical movement have tended either to ignore or else to redefine evangelism in such a way that the necessity of a new, personal relationship with God through Christ is downgraded. Others have tended to keep the two tasks totally separate, considering only evangelism to be of eternal value.

Christians from many nations are missionaries in today's world—crossing cultural boundaries with the love of God. The work of mission is now more extensive and more international than it has ever been. This work is not prevented by the failure to resolve the issues at present being debated. But undoubtedly Christian missionaries will be better equipped for the task their Lord and Master has given them when a proper balance has been arrived at between the various aspects of mission. In particular:

- ☐ The gospel should be proclaimed both in word and in deed;
- ☐ We need both to identify with the non-Christians in their need and to tell them the Christian 'good news';
- ☐ The church is not only in the business of extending itself, it is also the agent of the mission of God.

Christ. To be born again is to be born into God's family and community. Forms and styles of community vary widely. But any group of believers which fails to experience intimate life together has failed to experience the church as Christ's living body. We must take seriously the fact that believers are members of each other, and take responsibility for the welfare of Christian brothers and sisters in their social, material and spiritual needs.

Two basic elements in the church's community life are:

- **Discipline.** The church is not a chance collection of people, but a community of believers called and united together by the grace of God—a covenant people. Christian believers therefore accept responsibility for each other and agree to exercise such discipline as is necessary to remain faithful to God's covenant. The church takes seriously the Bible's many injunctions to warn, rebuke, exhort, encourage, build one another up in love.
- **The gifts of the spirit.** One way we build each other up is through a practical emphasis on these gifts. Spiritual gifts become vital and practical when they are awakened, recognized and used within the life of a vital Christian community.

The church's task is not to save itself—Christ has already done that. It is rather to give itself in love and service—in fact to die for the world.

Tullio Vinay, founder of the 'Agape' movement in the Waldensian Church

Discipline and the gifts of the Spirit are interdependent. They link together the fruit of the Spirit, and his gifts.

Witness

Witness springs from the church's worship and community life. A church weak in worship has little inclination to witness, nor does it have much to witness about. Similarly, a church with no vital community life has little witness because believers are not growing to maturity and learning to function as healthy disciples. Where community is weak the witness is further compromised, because it becomes too individualistic and degenerates into inviting people to God without involving them in Christian community.

In a healthy Christian community, witness springs not only from Jesus' specific commission, but also from the power of the Holy Spirit and the dynamic of Christian community life. These are the primary springs of the church's impulse to witness in the world. A living Christian community has both the inclination and the power to witness. It witnesses both from concern for human need and for the sake of the coming kingdom of God.

Witness is not the primary purpose of the church, but is the inevitable and necessary fruit of a worshipping, nurturing community and a high priority of the church's life in the world.

The church's witness includes **evangelism** and **service**. Both are basic forms of Christian witness, and in combination each strengthens and reinforces the other. Historically the church has found it difficult to hold evangelism and service together. But where her evangelistic witness has been buttressed by loving service in the spirit of Jesus, and where service has been joined with evangelism, there the church has been at its best and has made its greatest impact for the kingdom.

Evangelism and service may be thought of as representing the church's witness by word and by deed. This is a natural distinction found occasionally in the New Testament. It is witness by word and deed together, not just by individual believers but by the Christian community functioning as a body, which gives the church's life in the world an authentic impact for the kingdom of God.

Combining these several aspects of the life of the believing community yields a more complete model for the church.

As an ecological model, this picture of the church shows that the varied aspects of the church's life are interdependent, and that the glory of God is the focus of that life. The model also provides clues for diagnosing imbalance or maladies in the church's life and for dealing with the question of church structure. Although church forms may vary widely according to culture and circumstance, every vital church must have workable structures for worship, community, and witness.

The Ministry of God's People

The community of God's people exists not merely to be a vital community but to serve God's purpose in the world. It glorifies God not only by worship and community life but by practical ministry beyond itself. To glorify God and to serve his plan, the church must discern God's intention not just for its own life but for all creation.

In the New Testament ministry is understood as the right and responsibility of the whole people of God. The New Testament does not distinguish between 'clergy' and 'laity' but speaks of all believers as constituting the people or laity of God. The word for ministry or service is *diakonia*. It is a great New Testament word which calls the church to a life of servanthood.

Three foundation truths in the New Testament provide the basis for the church's understanding and practice of Christian ministry: the priesthood of believers, the gifts of the Spirit and the example of Jesus Christ.

The priesthood of believers

Peter writes that believers corporately are 'being built into a spiritual house to be a holy priesthood, offering spiritual sacrifices acceptable to God through Jesus Christ'. The church is 'a chosen people, a royal priesthood, a holy nation, a people belonging to God', for the purpose of declaring God's glory.

According to the New Testament, Jesus Christ is the church's great High Priest. The Old Testament priesthood was fulfilled in Jesus Christ, who brought us to God through his sacrifice of himself. But through Christ's priestly work, all believers are made God's priests. We all have a priestly service to bring. This means:

- **All believers have direct access to God.** The Christian believer need not go through a human priest to come to God, for Jesus Christ is the perfect Mediator and High Priest.
- **Christians are priests to each other.** Believers serve and minister to each other as part of the universal priesthood. Not just preachers or pastors, but all believers can and should have a priesthood to each other within the Christian community, drawing one another into close relationship with God.
- **Believers are God's priests in the world.** The church is a missionary priesthood, God's missionary-priests in the world. As priests, believers present God to the world and gather up the world's concerns and present them to God.

The gifts of the Spirit

This is the second foundational truth for the ministry of the church. Paul makes clear that believers have different gifts according to the grace given them. Every believer is to manifest all the 'fruit' of the Spirit. But with the gifts of the Spirit the point is diversity. All believers have gifts, but these gifts vary. The point is that every gift is to be used to serve others and to glorify God.

The priesthood of believers tells us that all Christians are ministers; it does not show how those ministries are to operate or who is responsible for what. Spiritual gifts help here. Christians exercise their priestly ministry in part through the gifts God sovereignly gives.

Spiritual gifts suggest three things about the church's ministry:

- **Every believer has some spiritual gift.** Gifts are not restricted to leaders but are given to

GEORGE CAREY

Priesthood and Ordination

It is a striking fact that the word 'priest', used so frequently today of Christian ministers, is never so used in the New Testament. It is used of Jesus, but never of Christian leaders. The reason is clear—the word 'priest' was used of the Old Testament priesthood, of men offering sacrifices to God on behalf of the people. Now Jesus Christ has died for sin, once and for all, all sacrifices are done away. Jesus is spoken of as a priest: one who brings people to God and God to people. And his church as a whole shares his priesthood. But nowhere in the New Testament do ministers take on a priestly character.

How is it that the Christian ministry is now linked with something it originally rejected?

From missionary movement to institution

The church of Jesus Christ was conceived within the womb of Judaism, but emerged with a new life which affected its organization. Two features of its Jewish origin were at once transformed:

- ☐ **The old distinction between clergy and lay people was destroyed.** There is no clerical caste in the New Testament. All Christians have the Spirit and have been given gifts to use in service.
- ☐ **Differences of function are clearly recognized** and some gifts are regarded as being more prominent than others—teaching, evangelism, healing, prophecy and so on. But all are gifts the Spirit gives to the one body. There is no room for pride or false distinction.

As the church began to settle down, ministers arose as shepherds to the flock. The church grew larger and more complex, and it became necessary to authorize leaders to serve under the apostles. This happened at a every early stage. Also, as churches were established in many centres, the apostles had to appoint leaders for each of them.

'Apostles' were eye-witnesses of the resurrection, and so necessarily restricted in number. So the new leaders were known by two, initially interchangeable, titles: 'presbyter' (the Greek word for 'elder') and 'bishop' (literally overseer' or 'foreman'). 'Deacons' ('assistants') were appointed initially to help with practical matters, but they also had ministries, such as teaching and evangelism.

Opposition has a way of encouraging groups to unite. So it was with false teaching in the church. In the years after the main books of the New Testament were written, the increase of heresies led to congregations clustering around a local ministry of bishops and deacons.

At the beginning of the second century Ignatius, Bishop of Antioch, wrote letters to the bishop of each town he passed through. The letters reveal that in the churches of Asia Minor about that time (AD 110-117) there was a similar pattern of one bishop, several presbyters and a group of deacons. This type of organization is known as the 'threefold order of ministry', and a system of 'ruling' bishops is known as a 'monarchical episcopate'.

In time a sacrificial and sacramental colouring came in which was to affect the nature of Christian ministry. Three factors of importance may be picked out:

- ☐ If it is right to say that the church itself succeeds to Jesus' priestly ministry, by extension it came to be believed that a **special priestly role** fell to those set aside in ministry within the church.
- ☐ **Holy communion began to be seen as a 'sacrifice'.** Although the New Testament does not refer to the sacrament in this way, it was gradually so treated in the early church. The bread and wine were spoken of as 'offerings' and Christian ministers as counterparts of the Old Testament priesthood. Of course, for Christians Jesus' sacrifice is unique and final. But it came to be regarded as a perpetual offering for sin, represented at each eucharist.
- ☐ In time **the holy communion became the primary sign of God's presence and grace**, given when the minister was rightfully ordained.

Priesthood today

As we might expect, there has been a wide difference of opinion on the subject. Most Christian groups believe that an official ministry is essential for leadership, teaching and other specialized gifts. But not all believe that such 'priestly' activities as celebrating holy communion and absolving from sin should receive the prominence given to them in some traditions. Protestant churches from Reformation times have insisted that there is one basic priesthood—the priesthood of all believers. Since Jesus' death cannot be repeated, the holy communion is not a sacrifice and so there is no need for a special priesthood.

So the difference between Catholic and Protestant interpretations may be broadly defined as follows. The Catholic concentrates on priestly and sacramental ministry in which the priest is 'set apart' to represent the flock. The Protestant, however, concentrates on the ministry of the word, in preaching and pastoral care; he has a more functional approach to ordination. In churches which emphasize spiritual gifts, these ministries may not necessarily be concentrated in one person. In principle these understandings should not be irreconcilable, but in practice this difference is at the heart of the problem of disunity.

Ordination

Ordination is the act of the church in marking out those whom it has chosen to exercise authority or to exercise particular ministries such as becoming a missionary. The events leading up to ordination include:

- ☐ **The inward call** of the Holy Spirit which leads candidates to offer themselves;
- ☐ **The external recognition** of the church which accepts the candidates for training. Through some period of assessment they are presented to be ordained by bishops or leaders in the church.

Ordination itself usually takes the form of:

- ☐ **The 'laying on of hands'** which is a way of saying 'this person is set apart for service in this church'. Within the Catholic tradition, great importance is attached to the belief that ordination connects the ordained person to the church in apostolic times, through the bishops who stand in the 'apostolic succession'.
- ☐ **The prayer of the church (or** *epiclesis*) in which the bishop, on behalf of the church, invokes the Spirit to empower the candidate for service.

Should women be ordained?

A revolution has taken place in women's ministry. Twenty years ago women were not acceptable in the ministry of most mainstream denominations. Today they are fully acceptable to many, with only the Roman Catholics, Orthodox and parts of the Anglican Church resisting this development. Some think that:

- ☐ **The gospel requires it.** If Jesus died for all and if equality is the spiritual basis of the Christian community, then women's ordination is a principle which affects the freedom of all.
- ☐ **The New Testament reveals men and women working together** in ministry.
- ☐ **Paul's words** about women staying silent in church derived from social conventions of his day (or simply refers to idle tittle-tattle!). They should not be used as a brake on the use of women's gifts in church.

Others claim that:

- ☐ **Jesus chose twelve men.** If it was his desire for ministers to include women he would have made his will known.
- ☐ **There are texts which exclude women** from teaching offices in the church, such as Paul's 'I do not allow them to teach or to have authority over men.'
- ☐ The Bible teaches that **authority must be exercised by men.**
- ☐ Our present-day concern with the ordination of women is prompted **more by the pressure of our society** than by real gospel insights.
- ☐ Those who believe in a special priesthood of people who represent Jesus at the eucharist and in absolution would often want to add that it is **inappropriate for women to have this priestly function**.

It is certainly difficult to be objective about a subject which arouses fierce emotions. Yet all fair-minded people will agree that women have not been able to use their gifts in the church as they should. Women's ministry is not therefore so much a problem as an opportunity for the church to utilize the talents of gifted women who feel the call of the Spirit to work for Jesus in his church.

all Christians. To be a Christian means to be part of Christ's body, and every part of the body has some function. As Paul wrote: 'The same God gives ability to everyone for their particular service.'

- **Christian ministry operates by and through the grace of God.** Genuine Christian ministry is first and foremost the gracious ministry of God's Spirit through our personalities. It is at root a matter of God's grace, not of human technique, ability or training. Christian ministry is carried out by more than just human efforts, so it produces more than just human results.

- **Spiritual gifts guide the church in using her spiritual priesthood.** While all believers are priests, their priestly ministries vary according to the gifts they receive. One person cannot do all ministry, nor should all believers do the same things. Some people are given leadership ministries for equipping

JULIAN CHARLEY

Governing the Church

Any group of people needs some kind of leadership if it is to hold firmly together, and the church is no exception. The larger the numbers, the greater the need and the more elaborate the structure of government has to become. Jesus Christ is the head of the church and to him has been given 'all authority in heaven and on earth'. The problem is to discover how best we can ensure that Jesus' authority is accepted by the whole church.

Shared leadership

Jesus gave authority to the apostles in the founding of new churches. From the start leadership was meant to be shared. Just as Jesus had sent the apostles out two by two, so they appointed groups of leaders in the churches. They might be called 'elders' (because they were recognized senior members) or 'bishops' (literally, 'those who watch over') or 'deacons' (meaning 'servants'). (See also *Priesthood and Ordination.*)

What mattered was not the title but the task—oversight and service. When Jesus washed the disciples' feet, he showed that Christian leadership was that of a servant, not a boss. Service means being sensitive to what people need. Consequently there was no rigid pattern of church government at the beginning: it was flexible according to the needs of the particular church. Nor was there any sharp distinction between ordained and lay members of the church, even when certain leaders had been given public recognition by some kind of ordination ceremony.

It is a tragedy of church history that this early pattern of ministry has so often been forgotten. By the second century a system of government by bishops had become the norm in East and West and remained unquestioned, at least in the mainstream church if not by radical dissenters, until the Reformation.

Who and how?

In the New Testament leadership is frequently linked with teaching. The church must be kept faithful to the apostolic message and helped to live by Christian standards. It is significant that, in the New Testament, quality of character and spiritual maturity are the most important factors in the choice of the elders. Leadership must be by example as well as by word.

The care and oversight of the members of the fellowship include both encouragement and correction. Good leadership will enable every member of the church to use the gifts he or she has for the benefit of everyone, at the same time harnessing together all the variety the Holy Spirit gives to a lively fellowship. As with the apostles, Christian leaders should spearhead the church's mission in the world.

Church leadership is intended to fit the needs of the church, rather than the church fit the requirements of the ministry. This means that variety is only to be expected. The government of the first churches

and enabling (apostle, prophet, evangelist, pastor, teacher); other believers have other gifts.

The purpose of the leadership gifts is to prepare all God's people for effective ministry through the full diversity of gifts. By discerning which spiritual gifts are present among them, the Christian community can know which ministries should be carried out and who should be involved in which particular ministries.

Servants as Jesus was

It is important not merely that Christians act as priests and use the Spirit's gifts, but especially that such service is done in the spirit of Jesus. Christians are to have the same servant attitude which Jesus showed. Jesus used himself as the example: 'Whoever wants to become great among you must be your servant . . . just as the Son of Man did not come to be served, but to serve, and to give his life as a ransom for many.'

There are three sides to this truth about ministry too:

seems to have reflected the organizations with which most of their members were already familiar, some of them Jewish, some Gentile.

With such diversity, and considerable distances separating the churches, how could they keep in step with one another? Visits and letters from the apostles were one means. When a major problem threatened a split, the apostles called together a representative council in Jerusalem, which then reported back agreed conclusions. It is this combination of local freedom and central direction which pinpoints the difficulty of church government.

Local freedom or central direction?

The Independent, or Congregational, churches believe that by submitting to the Bible and by relying on the Holy Spirit the local church needs no hierarchy or central organization at all. The Christian Brethren have a group of elders but no ordained minister. Other churches 'call' their own minister and take responsibility for his support.

In a Baptist church the minister will be the 'first among equals', with a group of deacons elected by church members. Yet strong as the desire is for liberty at the local level, the Baptists also have a structure of 'Meetings', culminating in the Baptist Union and even beyond in the Baptist World Alliance, to keep the churches in harmony. But the authority of these higher bodies is only a moral force and lacks any practical power to interfere at the local level.

Other churches have sought in differing degrees to exercise much greater central direction. In Methodism, the central body, Conference, has ultimate control in the appointment of ministers to local 'circuits' of churches. Similarly in Presbyterianism there is a well-organized system of government from local church Session to the General Assembly.

The most centralized pattern is clearly that of the Roman Catholic Church. The Second Vatican Council stressed the shared authority of the bishops, of whom the Bishop of Rome is one. Yet the claims made for the Pope include the ability to speak infallibly on special occasions on matters of faith or morals and the authority to intervene in any part of the church where it is felt necessary. Although there are many safeguards, these do not alter the claims themselves, which are unacceptable to other churches. Orthodox Patriarchs or Anglican Primates carry a very different kind of authority, because their churches do not make such exclusive claims for themselves.

All the churches acknowledge the primary authority of the Bible. Some add the early creeds and some of the early councils, as faithfully interpreting the Scriptures. Roman Catholics see a continuing guidance of the church in what it proclaims, which others regard as sometimes adding to or even contradicting the Bible. The concern for lay people to be fairly represented at all levels of church government is increasingly felt in these more centralized churches.

No system of government is perfect. Christian concern must be to guard the truth, inspire the faithful and be adaptable to the needs of each generation.

DAVID GITARI

Church and State

At the time of the beginning of Christianity, the authority of the Roman Empire was not always benevolent. These were the days of despotic emperors such as Claudius, Caligula and Nero. So when the New Testament writers tackle the question of how Christians should relate to the civil power, their answer is relevant to the church in every nation, however pro- or anti-Christian its rulers may be:

☐ The New Testament is written against **an Old Testament background** where this question has already been fully debated. Should the nation have a king or is God their king? What laws are appropriate for the community of God's people? Are prophets authorized to confront kings in the name of God's justice? There is a whole web of relevant passages, which lead up to the Magnificat's 'he has brought down mighty kings . . . and lifted up the lowly', and provide the setting for Pilate's great discussion with Jesus: 'Are you a king then?'

☐ In the writings of both Paul and Peter we find key passages on the subject (Romans 13 and 1 Peter 2), though there is some disagreement on how these should be understood. For Paul, however cruel and arbitrary the state could sometimes be, it was still a God-ordained authority. To resist this authority is to 'resist what God has appointed'. Peter's argument runs along much the same lines. He calls his readers to be 'subject for the Lord's sake' to established authority.

☐ By the time the book of **Revelation** was written, the state had gone beyond its legitimate realm and had usurped powers which belong to God alone. In one of John's visions, the emperor emerges like a 'beast from the sea' who turns completely against God and demands to be worshipped in God's place. When human authority takes this semi-divine status, it is no longer acting in its God-appointed role. The call to Christians to obey no longer applies. They are bound to resist by suffering.

☐ **Jesus said,** 'Render to Caesar the things that are Caesar's, and to God the things that are God's.' This takes us to the heart of the matter of the limits of authority. The state can make rightful demands for taxes, for revenue, for respect—so long as it stays within its proper sphere. But the state should not take what is rightfully God's.

☐ When the demands of God and the state come into conflict, **Christians must obey God**. This is seen right at the beginning, when Peter and John boldly ask the Jewish Sanhedrin (the chief religious council) 'whether it is right in God's sight to obey you rather than God'. But it comes out most crucially in the fundamental Christian confession 'Jesus is Lord'. When the emperor started to go beyond his legitimate authority, the whole empire was called on to declare 'Caesar is Lord'. This presented Christians with an uncompromising clash of loyalties. Who was their Lord, Caesar or Jesus? To choose Jesus was to choose persecution. Many did so.

The implications of this New Testament teaching for us in today's world are very far-reaching.

Church and state in history

In apostolic days the relationship of church with state was largely one of tolerance. Roman governors assumed that the church was a sect of Judaism, which was a tolerated religion within the empire. Once it became clear that the church was a distinct community, the privilege of permitted religion was removed and Christians suffered persecution at the hands of various emperors. In 313, however, Christianity, thanks to Constantine, became the official religion of the Roman Empire. Relations between church and state have never been the same again, though the relationship has taken very different forms in different historical settings.

Three basic forms of church/state relationship have been:

- **The Constantinian form**, according to which the state and the church are separate in principle, but together make one commonwealth. Through the medieval period in Europe, this basic approach was held in a constantly varying balance, as the Popes and the Holy Roman Emperors made rival claims to supremacy.

In Charlemagne's time, the Pope claimed to be superior to emperors. But by the eleventh century the emperor was demanding the right to invest bishops and abbots and to receive homage from them before consecration. After the Reformation, in Lutheran Europe, uniformity of religion was seen as vital to the stability of the state, and each principality took its religious allegiance from its prince (the principle of *cujus regio, ejus religio*).

- **The Augustinian approach** was developed by Augustine of Hippo (354–430) in his *City of God*. It influenced Calvin's model city of Geneva, and, through the Puritan Fathers, had some bearing on the approach to these matters in the USA.

Augustine's thought was also the background for Luther's doctrine of the 'two kingdoms', which holds that the state is competent in matters of administration and justice, and the church in matters of the spirit. These two functions should be kept separate, neither church nor state interfering in the other's province. But the two kingdoms should work together in harmony.

- **The Anabaptist model** arose under the radical reformers, who disliked what they saw as the compromises the Reformation made with civil powers. It is a view still very influential among independent evangelical groups. The Anabaptists believed that the church had nothing to do with the state. It was a community called out of society, and should produce and live by its own Bible-based laws.

Church and state today

The emergence of totalitarian atheistic governments during the twentieth century has clearly shown the dangers of the church being too closely identified with the state. The Orthodox Church in Ethiopia suffered persecution during the Communist revolution for having been so closely identified with Emperor Haile Selassie and his regime.

The great disadvantage of the church getting too hand-in-glove with the state is that the church ceases to be the 'salt of the earth'. If the church is favoured by the state, there is always the temptation to remain silent when it should speak out to remind those in authority of the righteousness which God requires from those to whom he has given authority to rule.

The opposite danger is for the church to withdraw too radically from the world, as the Anabaptists advocated. This again prevents it from becoming the salt of the earth. A Christian community cut off from the rest of society, living an enclosed life of its own, cannot be effective and may become paralyzed or perish altogether. Christians should not be mere obedient spectators, but active participants in the social and political welfare of their nations. Those who have the right to elect leaders, and to influence the welfare of their nation, should take full advantage of their privileges.

In some of the totalitarian states in Europe and Asia, and under some Third World military regimes, this is not always possible. Governments which do not tolerate criticism will be quick to silence the voice of prophets. Christians may be called on to suffer when they stand up for righteousness. But at the same time Christians should be aware that where they do have a strong voice, they need to use it fearlessly. Otherwise they will have only themselves to blame when totalitarian governments take over, such as Idi Amin's regime in Uganda.

Wherever the church exists, it will constantly declare to the people the standards of righteousness and justice which alone exalt a nation. The church should take a lead in giving moral and practical support to the state when it upholds those standards. But when a society accepts as normal such evils as racism, tribalism, corruption, exploitation of man by man, then Christians must speak out like the prophets of old and proclaim the will and the judgment of God. The Christian community must stand as an ever-present reminder to the powers-that-be, telling them that they exist to be servants, of God and of people.

- **Every believer is a servant and minister**, just as each one is a priest and is gifted by the Spirit. Some may be called to exercise their ministry full-time in the service of the church, or may have a ministry of greater prominence. But every believer has a ministry to fulfil, however humble it may seem.
- Success in the Christian priesthood or ministry is to be measured by how far it is **done in the spirit of Jesus**.
- **The ministry of God's people is to continue the work Jesus began**, especially in proclaiming the kingdom of God and good news for the poor. The Christian community is to do the kinds of things Jesus would do if he were physically present on earth today. Jesus' physical, earthly presence now is through the living community, the body of Christ, composed of physical, space-time people. Through the power of the very Spirit of Jesus, Christians are to be his hands and feet on earth today.

Together these three foundational truths all affirm that every believer is called to ministry; that everyone within the body of Christ is a minister, servant and priest. Christians are priests of God and servants of Jesus, gifted by the Holy Spirit. They are therefore commissioned to serve not only each other but the world, for the sake of God's plan and God's kingdom.

While women weep, as they do now, I'll fight; while little children go hungry, I'll fight; while there is a drunkard left, while there is a poor lost girl upon the streets, where there remains one dark soul without the love of God—I'll fight! I'll fight to the very end!

General Booth; the end of his very last speech

The community of the kingdom

Part of the unique character of the Christian community is that it exists to announce the kingdom of God, and begin to give it substance. Sociologically, the community of believers is much like other groups in society. Human social dynamics are at work just as in a club or other social group. The key difference is that God's Spirit produces new spiritual life in believers, which enables the church to live not for herself but for God and his kingdom.

God has formed his people into a community, body and household. The church is called to be in the world yet not of the world. It can only respond to this if it is truly distinct, living as God's counter-culture. Christians do not have the strength to live up to their high kingdom calling except as they share life together in community.

The present world order does not march in step with the coming kingdom. This is why Christians must live within their society as a counter-cultural community. In no other way can they set forth the values of God's kingdom. Yet such a community is precisely the most potent base for transforming all society through the power of the gospel. In this sense, the Christian community is both a witness itself and the basis for the church's witness in the world.

In fact, however, the church through history has frequently failed to embody the reality of the kingdom in its life and witness. To one extent or another, it has at times been subverted or co-opted by the world. Yet precisely at such times God has often renewed his church, calling it back to its New Testament basis and its true purpose. Out of the very weaknesses, failures and disobedience of the church have come the seeds of her renewal, as believers have repented and searched again for the biblical dynamic of the kingdom-community.

Today increasing numbers of Christian believers are becoming sensitive to the biblical ecology of the church. There is still a long way to go, but now as never before believers on all continents appear to be recovering the living dynamic of the church as the community of God's people.

For further thinking

QUESTION 1

Imagine a group of Christians who want to reform their local church or their denomination. Should they expect to find the right forms and patterns directly from the New Testament? Or should they be looking for basic principles from which to work out their practice today? And how much guidance will come from the different traditional patterns in the history of the Church?

QUESTION 2

In many churches worship is led by one minister, often using a set form of worship. Does this restrict the freedom of worship, or ensure an ordered and beautiful liturgy? Which is more important? Can both be true of the same worship services?

QUESTION 3

What role does ordination play in the ministry of the whole church? Does it give primarily an authority to perform certain functions? Or is it more a way of validating in the local church a ministry accepted by the wider church? Can a church's understanding of ordination affect the ministry of the whole body of Christians?

QUESTION 4

Is 'mission' another word for 'evangelism'? Or does it include more?

BIBLE REFERENCES

Worship

Genesis 12:1–9; 28:10–17; Exodus 3:1–6; 4:31; 40:16–33; Deuteronomy 29:25–26; Joshua 5:14; 1 Samuel 1:3; 1 Kings 18:20–39; 1 Chronicles 16:7–42; 29:20; Nehemiah 8:6; Psalms 15:1–5; 48:1–3; 66:4; 95:1–7; Jeremiah 26:2; Zechariah 14:16; Matthew 2:2, 8, 11; 4:9–10; 28:16–17; Mark 5:6; Luke 2:13–14; John 4:20–24; 9:38; 17:1–5; Acts 2:43–47; 16:25; 17:23; Philippians 3:3; Colossians 3:16; Revelation 4:8–11; 22:8–9

Ministry

Exodus 24:13–14; 28:1–4, 35; 1 Samuel 2:11; 3:1–8; Psalms 103:21; Isaiah 6:1–9; Jeremiah 1:6–10; Ezekiel 44:10–14; Mark 3:13–19; 10:42–45; John 13:3–7; Acts 6:1–7; Romans 12:4–8; 13:4–6; 2 Corinthians 3:1–6; 4:1–7; 5:18–20; Ephesians 4:11–13; Colossians 1:7, 23; 1 Timothy 1:12; 3:1–13; 5:17; 2 Timothy 1:3–7; 1 Peter 4:10–11; 5:1–5

Spiritual Gifts

Exodus 31:1–5; Judges 6:34; 14:6; 1 Samuel 16:6; Isaiah 11:2; Joel 2:28; Haggai 1:14; Matthew 25:14–30; Luke 11:13; Acts 2:17; 8:17–21; Romans 12:3–8; 1 Corinthians 12:1–13, 27–30; 14:14–16; Ephesians 1:17; 4:11–12, 30; 2 Timothy 1:7; 1 Peter 4:10–11

Mission

Genesis 1:28; 12:1–3; 17:1–8; Exodus 6:1–8; 19:5–6; Isaiah 11:1–4; 40:1–5; 43:10–13, 21; 58:6–10; 59:16–19; 61:1–4; 66:18; Jeremiah 31:10–12, 31–34; Joel 2:1–2; Jonah – whole book; Micah 4:1–5; Zechariah 9:11–17; Matthew 3:1; 4:23–24; 9:35; 28:18–20; Mark 1:32–34; 3:14–19; 6:34; 10:43–45; Luke 7:22; 10:1–11; 15:3–32; 19:1–10; John 1:9–18; 5:25–27; 6:35–40; 10:7–16; 17:6–26; Acts 1:6–9; 2:37–42; 9:26–30; 10:34–43; 11:18; 13:1–3; 20:18–28; Romans 1:16; 3:21–26; 5:6–11; 10:9–15; 15:15–21; 16:1–16; 1 Corinthians 1:23; 2:1–4; 9:19–23; 2 Corinthians 5:11–21; 8:8–9; Galatians 1:6–9; Ephesians 1:3–10; 2:13–17; 3:7–13; Philippians 2:5–11; Colossians 1:15–20, 29; 1 Thessalonians 1:8–10; 1 Timothy 1:12–17; 2 Timothy 2:1–7; 4:2–5

The Church

Genesis 12:2; 17:7; Exodus 19:4–6; Matthew 16:18; 18:17; Luke 12:32–34; Acts 2:47; 4:32–35; 5:11; 7:38; 20:28; Romans 16:3–5; 1 Corinthians 1:2; 11:18; 12:27; Ephesians 1:22–23; 5:23–32; Colossians 1:18, 24; 1 Timothy 3:15; Hebrews 12:22–24; 1 Peter 2:4–10

CHAPTER 29

ANTHONY THISELTON

Destiny

The Bible writers never discuss human destiny from the standpoint of idle curiosity. When they think about life after death, or about what follows the end of history, the focus is first and foremost on the sovereignty and the love of God. They do not spend time asking whether men and women have the capacity to survive death.

Christian belief about human destiny begins with the question: does it lie within the competence and love of God to grant us a share in a destiny beyond death? Is God's love such that he *wills* such a destiny for us? Is God's sovereignty such that he can *grant* such a destiny to us?

This angle of approach is very different from ideas about human destiny in popular discussion. Popular thought sets the individual at the centre of the stage. And in isolation from broader questions about God and the whole created order, this popular approach stands totally exposed to the well-known criticisms of the sceptic.

How can I know anything about what by definition lies beyond day-to-day human experience? Is the religious believer not simply a victim of his wishful thinking, drawn on by a desire to compensate in some imagined future life for disappointments and sufferings experienced in this life? Questions such as these can only be answered from within the Bible's God-centred framework.

Beginning where the Bible begins

The biblical writers have no illusions about the frailty and mortality of human beings. 'As for man, his days are like grass. He flourishes like a flower of the field; the wind blows over it and it is gone,' says the Psalmist. In the Old Testament there is as yet no full or firm doctrine of life after death. Nevertheless, a longing and then a hope is kindled, not on the basis of some supposed capacity for immortality, but on the basis of the nature of God.

If God has set such value on human beings as to redeem them and show them the favour and joy of his own presence, will all this come to nothing at death? Will God allow this deep and rich relationship to be terminated by mere loss of life, when he is the sovereign and loving God who alone is the source of all life?

A second stream of thought and hope also emerges in the Old Testament. As righteous judge and sovereign king, God has pledged himself to right wrongs. Suffering, injustice and sin are against God's purposes, and these purposes will hold good. Nevertheless, during the Old Testament period, believers accepted the fact that not all wrongs would be put right during their own individual lifespan. There emerged a belief in three great 'last' events:

- **The coming of the Lord** to his people in visitation and vindication;
- **The universal and final righting of wrongs** in an unmistakable and irreversible act of divine judgment;
- **The raising of the dead** to share in this universal manifestation of God's presence and his reign of justice and peace.

However, the focus and central concern in all this is not the individual's desire for compensation or reward, projected into the future as wish-fulfilment. It is the integrity of the character of God, and his sovereignty over both earth and heaven.

Why think about the future?

The emphasis found in the Bible on these last great events has an inevitable effect on our attitude towards the present. If the verdicts and vindication of God will be declared unmistakably only at the end of all things, it follows that we cannot know them finally now.

Therefore, Paul urges, we must resist the temptation to make premature judgments about God, or about other Christians, or even about ourselves, 'before the time'. Our present knowledge is imperfect and our experience is incomplete. 'Now I see in a mirror dimly, but then face to face. Now I know in part; then I shall understand fully.' As long as the present world-order continues, there will inevitably be grey areas, in which the work and ways of God are obscured and intermingled with the human situation. 'We walk by faith, not by sight.'

At the same time, Christians are bidden to look forward *beyond* the ambiguities of the present. It is equally misguided either to pretend that ambiguities and puzzles do not still exist or to live as if they can never be overcome. The future gives the clue to the meaning of the present. No one would judge the competence of an artist, nor the nature and adequacy of his design, while a painting was still in the process of being finished.

Faith, the writer to the Hebrews urges, is 'the assurance of things hoped for'. The evidence of the faith of the Old Testament believers lay in the fact that they based their conduct and view of life on what God had promised to do *in the future*, even though this had not yet come to pass. This writer compares believers to pilgrims, who accept the difficulties and sacrifices of the journey because their eye is on the goal towards which they are travelling. He uses the dynamic image of 'the city' and the contrasting image of 'rest'. Both point to a future goal which makes sense of the dangers and struggles of the present.

The coming of Christ

In one sense, the great 'coming' of God to visit his people took place in the coming of Jesus of Nazareth. Jesus brought a message about God's kingdom: God's active reign was effective in and through his own coming. The words of Jesus confronted the generation who heard them both as judgment and as a promise of life from God. In certain strands of the New Testament, the ministry, death and resurrection of Jesus Christ are seen to usher in a new era and transform our situation in a final and long hoped for way.

Nevertheless, in spite of some claims to the contrary, the early New Testament Christians did not regard these events as totally fulfilling all that was expected of this great final visitation of God. Although God's reign was operative in Jesus, the ways of God had yet to be vindicated publicly, universally and unmistakably—with no trace of hiddenness or ambiguity. Great reversals were still to take place, in which the hidden would be made manifest, the faithful and oppressed would be vindicated, and all wrongs set to right. Jesus is to come again. This time 'every eye will see him'. He will complete the work of re-creation made possible by his first coming. He will usher in 'new heavens and a new earth'.

Mark 13, and its parallel passage Matthew 24, contain Jesus' teaching about this 'second' coming, although their interpretation is complicated by other questions connected with the destruction of Jerusalem by the Romans. He teaches that this coming will be preceded by certain signs. The main emphasis falls on two themes:

- **No one knows the exact time** of this sudden and final coming, not even Jesus himself.
- **Men and women must always be ready** for it, and treat all that it implies with full seriousness and urgency.

At various stages in the history of the church, teaching about Jesus' second coming has suffered discredit through misuse of biblical material. People have tried to produce charts of the signs of the times, according to which some definite moment for this coming could be predicted. Such misunderstandings served merely to produce

It is since Christians have largely ceased to think of the other world that they have become so ineffective in this. Aim at heaven and you will get earth thrown in: aim at earth and you will get neither.

C. S. Lewis

If Christ were coming again tomorrow, I would plant a tree today.

Martin Luther

disillusionment when Jesus did not actually come as predicted.

The sense of expectancy which the New Testament urges on its readers is not a matter of chronological timetables, but of a constant attitude of openness to the coming presence and judgment of God, in the light of which the Christian's attitude to the world is entirely changed. The belief that history is indeed hastening on towards this cosmic climax gives the Christian a sense of urgency and purpose. Yet even the earliest writings of the New Testament warn us that this proper sense of urgency and purpose should never give way to irrational action or to obsession.

In some circles there has been controversy about whether the language describing this final coming is to be taken literally. Does it refer to physical events in space and time? Much of the language quite deliberately draws on well-known standard imagery of the day, which is intended to place it in a given circle of ideas rather than give specific information. Everyday language is being deliberately stretched in order to describe more-than-ordinary events. Yet we must not lose hold of the central point that the final coming of Christ will be public, unmistakable and of cosmic dimensions. It will be no merely inner or spiritual visitation.

■

I don't mind dying. I just don't want to be there when it happens.

Woody Allen

Death and what follows

Many educated Greeks treated death rather lightly. They even looked forward to it as marking the release of the soul from the prison-house of the body. This is not the Christian view. The Bible looks forward hopefully not so much to death as to 'the day when the Lord shall appear'. Indeed death, as such, is regarded as an intrusion which shows there is something tragically wrong in our relation with God, the fact of human sin.

The biblical writers view death not so much as a simple biological fact, but as a symbol of God's pronouncement that the human situation has gone wrong. Death comes as sin's 'wages' and sin gives a 'sting' to death. It is not to be viewed with cavalier detachment as a mere throwing off of physical limitations; nor is the sense of loss and separation in death merely to be shrugged off.

Only when we fully appreciate the tragedy of death can we really grasp the Christian gospel of victory over death. Because Christ has dealt with the problem of sin, what gives death its sting and its horror has now been removed. 'Death is swallowed up in victory.' So now, for the believer in this new and different situation, death is seen in two basic ways:

- In one way, it is simply **'to depart and to be with Christ'**, which Paul describes as 'far better' than our present life.
- But also, death is seen as a **'sleep'** from which the believer 'wakes' into the fresh morning light of heaven.

Each of these ways of describing death makes its own point. But confusion has been caused when people have tried to extract certain time-sequences from these different pictures. Does the Christian at death enter the presence of Jesus at once, or is there a period of waiting in sleep before the final resurrection?

The Bible raises no difficulty. Quite clearly from the point of view of experience, the dead believer is conscious of no interval between dying and entering the fullness of the presence of Christ. Yet equally clearly, the final judgment and resurrection do not take place at one time for one individual and another time for another; they are single events for the whole community. There is no suggestion of a conscious experience of interval from which the dead are then summoned to final judgment and resurrection. It is difficult for us to appreciate events outside time: but this is why the Bible gives us more than one way of picturing this.

The future resurrection

Even some of the very earliest Christians had difficulties over belief in the future resurrection. This has proved to be helpful to later

GRANT OSBORNE

The Millennium

In the book of Revelation (20:1–10) there is a vision of a thousand-year chaining of Satan and reign of those who had not bowed down to the evil 'beast'. The language of Revelation is that of a type of literature known as 'apocalyptic', full of images and Old Testament allusions. So is the 'thousand years', the 'millennium', to be understood as an actual event?

Almost from the beginning, the church has debated whether the 'millennium' will be an actual thousand-year period at the end of this age as a prelude to eternity. In the early church, in fact, this debate was at the heart of questions about the authority of the book of Revelation. It was Augustine (AD 354–430) who was primarily responsible for the view which predominated until the nineteenth century, that the millennium was not literal but symbolic. However, he made no clear distinction between the amillennial or postmillennial views, and both sides have claimed Augustine for their position. Since the nineteenth century three positions have been taken up.

Amillennialism

Often called 'realized millennialism', this position holds that the return of Christ will inaugurate not a reign on earth but rather the judgment and eternal age. The concept of a millennium is based on only one passage, Revelation 20, which is symbolic rather than literal: 'millennium' means a long time or eternity itself. A political and materialistic reference to the millennium is found in some Jewish apocalyptic works, but not in the New Testament. Two principles of interpretation support this view: prophetic passages, particularly in the book of Revelation, often have figurative meaning; and Old Testament passages about the future of Israel are fulfilled in the coming of Jesus and the church. The millennium itself, then, is fulfilled either in this present church age or in eternity. There will not be two resurrections, but one (Revelation 20:4 is a spiritual resurrection) at the end of this age.

Postmillennialism

Although this position does not have as much influence as formerly (its popularity peaked in the early decades of this century), there is renewed interest today. The basic distinction is the belief that a period of Christian growth and prosperity will precede the end of all things. However, Christ will not be present, and it is agreed that Revelation 20 is not set within time. This view is based on God's desire that everyone should be preached to and saved. This implies that the world will be evangelized before the end of the age, and an age of Christian joy and peace will ensue. This view is characterized by a more optimistic view of history than the other two.

Premillennialism

People of this viewpoint believe that Revelation 20 refers to an actual future event. It is believed that, although symbolism is present in the book of Revelation, the symbols (as elsewhere in Jewish apocalyptic) refer to literal events. According to this, Revelation 19 describes the return of Christ accompanied by the 'first resurrection' of the righteous and followed by the thousand-year 'reign' of Christ on earth. This earthly reign will be characterized by peace and righteousness (as prophesied in the Old Testament) and will close with the loosing of Satan, rebellion against Jerusalem, destruction of the Satanic forces, 'second resurrection' of the wicked, and final judgment scenes which Revelation 20 goes on to describe.

generations, since it provoked a detailed discussion of these difficulties by Paul. His response can be found in 1 Corinthians 15.

Paul points out that if resurrection is denied simply as a matter of principle, we can no longer retain the very heart of the Christian message, that Jesus Christ was raised from the dead. But this would contradict the unanimous witness of those who had actually seen Jesus alive, as well as Christian experience of the living Christ.

So far Paul's argument is well-known. The resurrection of Christ is proof that resurrection is possible. But Paul goes on to make points which are far less obvious. He shows that the real focus of doubt or faith is what we believe about God. Has he the competence, the will and the resourcefulness to raise the dead into a transformed mode of existence?

Paul appeals to what we already know of God's creative power in the universe. God is not caught out by lack of range or variety in his creative purposes. He created fish to swim in the sea; birds to fly in the air; stars to float in the heavens. Will his power and wisdom be unequal to the task of giving to human beings an appropriate 'body' (or form of existence) for entering a post-earthly life in God's own immediate presence?

The centre of the doctrine of the resurrection of the body is *not* survival. That concern

TOKUNBOH ADEYEMO

Is Everyone Saved?

In one form or another, nearly all the world's religions and ideologies promise their adherents some form of peace—some way of deliverance from the precarious plight humanity is in. Buddhism and Hinduism promise *nirvana,* blessedness through extinction of individuality and desire. In African traditional religion, a worshipper believes that through divination and prescribed sacrifices he can be delivered from his enemies, real and potential, secure the help of his ancestors and the gods and be prosperous in life. Islam strongly advocates submission to Allah as the pathway to peace. And modern humanism looks forward to a society freed from all forms of violence—social, cultural, economic or political.

The case against pluralism

All these goals can be referred to as 'salvation'. Are they all equally valid? If so, how do all these ways of being saved fit alongside Jesus' words: 'I am the way, the truth, and the life; no man comes to the Father, but by me'? Or Peter's declaration: 'There is no other name (besides Jesus Christ) under heaven given to men by which we must be saved'?

First of all, we must be clear that all truth is of God. God has revealed himself to everyone in nature, history and conscience. Jesus Christ is the light that lights all people. God has never left anyone without a witness. However, the perception and interpretation of divine reality varies from culture to culture.

One key difference is that while non-Christian religions admit the wickedness of humanity and our need of salvation, they do not consider our plight to be so deep as to require a saviour. We can either achieve our own salvation through self-denial (as in Buddhism) or we can co-operate with God through observance of rituals and laws (as in Islam). This amounts to what Christians describe as 'salvation by works'.

In contrast, the Bible demonstrates that human beings are totally lost and cut off from God. Their root problem is their inward nature, which is deceitful above anything imaginable and desperately wicked. Try as we may, by devoutness, morality, philanthropy and legalism, no human being can reach God's standard of perfection and righteousness. In fact the Bible says: 'All are under the power of sin . . . there is no one who is righteous . . . all have turned away from God; they have all gone wrong; no one does what is right, not even one.' The result of sin is alienation from God in time and eternity.

In Jesus Christ, God shows his

belongs to the very different idea of *immortality* (a Greek concept). The heart of resurrection is the transforming power of God, which changes a mode of existence still marked by frailty and sin into a new form of life—one marked by power, glory, and the presence of the Holy Spirit.

Paul uses an analogy from nature to underline several points:

- When we sow a seed, there is **a contrast** between what is actually sown and the flower or fruit that springs up. 'What you sow is not the body which is to be.' Christians are not committed to a crude materialistic view of resurrection according to which the particles of the old body are somehow reassembled into the new. The raised 'body' is not to be understood in the sense of 'physical body'. Resurrection is not a return to life of the kind described in the 'raising' of Lazarus, who presumably died again.
- There is **a change** which is so great and complete that language runs out when we try to describe it. Paul can only remind us that whereas life in the old body was marked by weakness, declining capacities and the humiliation associated with

love for us in a way natural revelation cannot convey. In accordance with God's plan, Jesus paid the price for human sin by his death on the cross, having lived a perfect, sinless life. To anyone who receives Christ by faith God gives the righteousness of Christ. Unlike 'salvation by works' of the other world religions, salvation in Christ is a *gift*. Because of our sinfulness, we are unable to make reparation to God for our failures. God in Christ made the provision for us. And this means there can be no other way of salvation.

The case against universalism

Some theologians agree that Jesus Christ died for the sins of the whole world, but then maintain that this means that everyone will be saved in the end. It is reasoned that since the fall has affected us all, and since God's grace in Jesus is for everyone, it is only logical that everyone will be saved. The idea may seem logical, but it is not biblical. It overlooks the essential biblical conditions for salvation—repentance and faith.

This theory, which is known as 'universalism', denies people the right to make their own choice to reject God's gift. Though God's love has provided a way of forgiveness for every sinner, God's justice makes everyone accountable for his or her own choice. God does not force his will on people, rather he invites them to respond. Each person has an option; if they admit that they need saving, repent and accept God's offer, they will be saved. Those who think they can make it by their own efforts, and refuse God's offer in Christ, are doomed.

We are equally prone to overlooking the Bible's clear teaching about hell. Jesus emphasizes the separation at the end of time between 'sheep' and 'goats'—the former those inheriting God's kingdom and the latter those departing to destruction. Neither do the New Testament writers romanticize heaven and hell. Both of them are as real as palaces and prisons are in this world. The classic story of the rich man and Lazarus with its 'great gulf fixed', vividly illustrates the two eternal destinies for humankind. If everyone is saved automatically as the universalists claim, then the Lord's commission to preach the gospel and make disciples is pointless. And the call to practise holiness is reduced in urgency as well.

One way out of this dilemma has been to suggest that people who have rejected Jesus during their lifetime will have further chances to respond to him after death. But there is no hint of such an idea in Scripture. On the contrary, 'everyone must die once, and after that be judged by God.'

The heart of this argument concerns those who have never heard the gospel and those who die young. To the former, God is a righteous and impartial judge. He will judge everyone according to the light that person received. For those who die in childhood, God's love in Christ is completely effective.

failure and sin, the new mode of existence will be one of glory to which none of these limitations and defeats will apply.

- All the same, the one whose body dies and who is transformed remains **the same individual identity**. Just as in nature it is *this* seed that will become *that* flower, so 'I' will consciously experience the resurrection life. The word 'body' is the nearest we come in the New Testament to our more abstract notions 'identity' and 'manner of existence'; it speaks to the question 'How do we relate to others and to our environment?' The future life really will be 'mine' in a rich and meaningful way. The experience will not be reserved for some thinned-down entity such as a 'soul'.

Once a man is united to God how could he not live for ever? Once a man is separated from God, what can he do but wither and die?

C. S. Lewis

The criticism of a contemporary secular philosopher completely missed this point. He commented that because the 'soul' represents such a remote idea, the gospel of a hereafter was of no more interest to him than the news that his appendix would be eternally preserved in a bottle.

Paul speaks not of souls but of whole people. The resurrection form of life will not be less than physical life; it will certainly be more. Paul asserts that the resurrection body will be like Christ's. But the glory of this, for Paul, lay in the final overcoming of sin and in a full and immediate experience of God, more than in the relatively lesser achievement of leaving behind all physical limitations.

'Totally without hope one cannot live.' To live without hope is to cease to live. Hell is hopelessness. It is no accident that above the entrance to Dante's hell is the inscription: 'Leave behind all hope, you who enter here.'

Fyodor Dostoevsky

The last judgment and heaven

It may appear at first sight as if the two ideas of judgment and of heaven stand in contrast to each other as opposites. Yet the judgment of God means quite simply putting all things finally and irreversibly to rights. And for the Christian believer this is another way of speaking of heaven. The last judgment has little or nothing to do with the idea of a headmaster reading our exam results with 'pass' or 'fail'. It is the public vindication before everyone of the ways of God. It is the caring king setting to rights all that is at variance with his own sovereign and just decrees for the well-being of the realm.

For Christians, the acceptance of God's judgment as the final verdict on their own lives began when they were 'put right' with God, or justified. But this remained a matter of faith. God's verdicts and ways were brought forward into present experience through trust. Now at the last judgment the rightness and truth of God's ways are made public and visible, vindicated beyond all question and contradiction. The in-between time, which had given opportunity for repentance and trust, now gives way to the full light of the day.

That sin is judged and wrong expelled is, then, part of the essential meaning of heaven. Hell can be described as a person's choice to be excluded from the presence of God, because the values which are held are different from theirs. Since God's presence is joy and life, such self-exclusion is loss and pain. The Christian hope is that, since God's presence is joy, 'he will wipe away every tear from their eyes'. Since his presence is life, 'death shall be no more'.

The biblical writers stretch language to its limits to describe the beauty and bliss of that perfect state. But every image and metaphor points even beyond this to the beauty of him who is its source. Heaven, in the Revelation vision, is water to the thirsty; rest to the weary; health to the sick; light to the blind; security to those under threat. But it is all these things only because God himself is all this. 'To the thirsty I will give the fountain of the water of life ... The leaves of the tree were for the healing of the nations.' We are not looking at the static perfection of the frozen shot at the end of a film. God is the *living* God, whose presence holds forth the promise of the ever-new. So the declining capacities and falling opportunities of earthly life are replaced by their opposite: a growing crescendo of glory.

The Bible does not tell us how the perfect

can become yet more perfect. But it has already pointed us to the God whose presence carries us 'from one degree of glory to another'. It is enough that 'There shall no more be anything accursed ... They shall see God's face, and his name shall be on their foreheads. And night shall be no more; they need no light of lamp or sun, for the Lord God will be their light, and they shall reign for ever and ever.' To 'reign' is to be immune from any factor that might threaten or impair this perfect enjoyment of God. Eternity will not exhaust the constantly expanding wonder of exploring God himself.

For further thinking

QUESTION 1

The New Testament writers seem to have expected Jesus to return soon, but so far he has not. Were they mistaken? Should each generation expect the second coming? Or is that expectation bound to get less as the centuries go by?

QUESTION 2

What is it in a person which we expect to survive death?

QUESTION 3

In earlier times the fear of hell and God's judgment was a powerful force in people's minds. Nowadays this is not so, and the church lays less emphasis on these things. Is this gain or loss?

QUESTION 4

If the presence of God in heaven is a Christian's greatest desire, how does that affect all our other desires? Does it make us appreciate this life more or less?

BIBLE REFERENCES

Judgment

Genesis 18:25; Psalms 9:17; Isaiah 3:13–15; Ezekiel 18:1–32; Daniel 12:1–3; Amos 5:14–20; Malachi 2:17—3:5; 4:1–3; Matthew 3:7–12; 11:20–24; 13:37–43; 25:31–46; Luke 16:19–31; John 3:18–21; 5:24–29; Acts 10:42; 17:30–31; Romans 1:18–32; 2:6–11; 14:10–12; 1 Corinthians 3:10–15; 4:3–5; 2 Corinthians 5:10; 2 Thessalonians 1:5–10; 2 Timothy 4:1; Hebrews 2:2–3; 9:27; 10:26–31; 1 Peter 4:5; 2 Peter 3:7–13; 1 John 4:17; Revelation 20:11–15; 22:10–13

The Christian Hope

Isaiah 4:1–6; Jeremiah 32:1–15; Matthew 24:13–14; Romans 5:2; 15:4–6, 13; 1 Corinthians 15:51–58; 2 Corinthians 1:15–22; 4:16–18; Ephesians 1:13–14; 1 Thessalonians 4:13–18; 2 Timothy 1:12; Titus 2:11–13; Hebrews 6:17–20; 11:8–16; 1 Peter 1:3–5; 1 John 3:2–3; Revelation 21:1—22:21

We shall rest and we shall see, we shall see and we shall love, we shall love and we shall pray, in the end which is no end.

Augustine of Hippo

Christian Belief in the Making

PART 6

30 People and Movements Through the Centuries

The Apostolic Fathers
Justin Martyr and the Apologists
The Montanists
Marcion
The Gnostics
Tertullian
Irenaeus
Origen
Athanasius and the Arians
Augustine of Hippo
Roman Catholicism
The Orthodox Churches
Medieval Theology
Anselm
Thomas Aquinas
The Reformation
Martin Luther
Zwingli: first of the Reformed Theologians
Thomas Cranmer
Calvin and the Swiss Reformers
Anabaptists and Baptists
The Puritans
Blaise Pascal
The Enlightenment
Immanuel Kant
Methodism and the Evangelical Revival
Schleiermacher
The Rise of Biblical Criticism
Søren Kierkegaard
Newman and the Tractarians
The Missionary Movement
Liberal Theology
Makers of Christian Belief
The Unity Movement
The Pentecostals
Teilhard de Chardin
Karl Barth
Process Theology
The East African Revival
Rudolf Bultmann
Hans Küng
The Charismatic Movement
Liberation Theology

CHAPTER 30

People and Movements through the Centuries

DONALD HAGNER

The Apostolic Fathers

The earliest Christian writers after the New Testament are known as the 'apostolic fathers', not because they were in any sense apostles themselves, but because their teaching was seen to be in agreement with that of the apostles.

They were not creative or reflective theologians. The content of their writings depends heavily on the Christian tradition they received. Indeed, their writings contain frequent allusion to and even quotation from the New Testament. Nevertheless, the apostolic fathers are important as theologians just because they give us our first opportunity to see how the church utilized the tradition in confronting the problems of the end of the first century and the early decades of the second century. Their orientation is decidedly practical rather than theoretical.

In this group are the following writings, which range from the end of the first to the middle of the second century: two letters (the second, however, is pseudonymous) of Clement of Rome, seven of Ignatius, a letter of Polycarp and an account of his martyrdom, a letter of Barnabas (pseudonymous), an extended account of visions called collectively the Shepherd of Hermas, a letter of Diognetus (whom many, however, categorize as an Apologist), and a manual of early Christian instruction called the *Didache*, the teaching of the twelve apostles.

The Apostles received the Gospel for us from the Lord Jesus Christ, Jesus the Christ was sent from God. The Christ therefore is from God and the Apostles from the Christ.

Clement of Rome

Two major problems confronted these early Christian writers: heresy and division. The answer to both problems was found in the authority of the tradition and of those who were divinely called to carry it on. It is above all the authority of the tradition that preserves the unity of the church. And although several of the apostolic fathers distinguish themselves carefully from the original apostles, they also stress their own importance as perpetuators of the tradition. This leads naturally to a stress upon the hierarchical structure of the leadership of the church.

Clement of Rome, traditionally regarded as bishop of Rome in the last decade of the first century, writing to the strife-torn church of Corinth, calls for repentance, humility and obedience to God. He appeals repeatedly to examples and exhortations drawn from the Old Testament, which he often quotes at length, as well as from the Christian tradition. He calls for the harmony and order of the universe to be reflected in the church. This will be accomplished only by respect for, and proper submission to, bishops and elders (the words remain interchangeable, as in the New Testament) who stand in succession to the apostles and whose authority derives from them.

Ignatius, bishop of Antioch in the first quarter of the second century, also finds the antidote to disorder and heresy in the authority of church leaders, but he exalts the single bishop in each church to a position of supreme authority. Ignatius is the first to articulate a threefold order of ministry consisting of bishop, presbyters, and deacons. All three are important, but Ignatius argues most forcefully for the absolute authority of the bishop. Although the churches to which he writes appear to be doing well, Ignatius stresses the proper recognition of the bishop as a protective measure against error and division. **Polycarp** and the Didache were also concerned with the importance of maintaining proper ecclesiastical order in the subapostolic age.

Although the apostolic fathers saw themselves called to preservation rather than innovation, they inevitably brought a degree of newness by their re-expression of the tradition for their own era. This newness, however, consists solely in extending and applying what was already in the tradition. Against Gnosticism, the humanity of Jesus is stressed; yet at the same time Ignatius readily refers to Jesus as God more than a dozen times. By and large, the Christianity of the apostolic fathers is more Jewish than Hellenistic, and in this connection the Old Testament is understood as a Christian book. If proper conduct rather than theology is stressed, it is because of the immediate situation and not necessarily because the concept of grace had been lost. In many ways the apostolic fathers fulfil the commission of the pastoral epistles to Timothy and Titus to guard the deposit of truth and to uphold proper ethical standards, both being accomplished by a worthy and well-structured order of ministry.

DONALD HAGNER

Justin Martyr and the Apologists

In the second century certain writers turned their energies to the defence of Christianity against the hostile criticisms of those outside the church—both Jews and pagans. These writers are known collectively as the Apologists (or 'Defenders'). With Justin Martyr, the chief representative, names such as **Aristides, Tatian, Athenagoras** and **Theophilus of Antioch** are usually included among the Apologists.

These writers conduct their defence of Christianity in two ways: by directly answering the criticism of their opponents, and by setting out the truth of Christianity generally in the framework of Greek philosophy. The Apologists refute the all-too-common charges that Christianity involved esoteric rites and immorality, necessitated political disloyalty, and was atheistic. They point out that such charges are the result of misunderstanding Christianity, and that, rightly known, this religion is honourable and most worthy of tolerance in the Roman Empire.

But the Apologists are not satisfied only to silence false accusations. Both to the Jew and to the Greek they argue vigorously the truthfulness of Christianity. The argument to the Jew centres on Christ as the fulfilment of Old Testament prophecy and a Christian understanding of the Hebrew Scriptures. Here the Apologists extend considerably the use of the Old Testament begun already in the New Testament and developed further among the apostolic fathers. The argument to the Greek is that Christianity is not only consonant with Greek philosophy but stands in some ways as the culmination of that phil-osophy. It is here above all that the Apologists make their most important contribution to the development of theology in the early church.

Justin Martyr is the finest example of this. Born in Samaria, Justin flourished in the middle of the second century and was martyred in Rome in AD 165. Steeped in philosophy as a young man, after his conversion he began to utilize philosophy in defending Christianity (he is sometimes called 'the Philosopher'). Justin is known for three major works: the *First* and *Second Apology* (which may originally have comprised one work) and the *Dialogue with Trypho the Jew*.

In his *Dialogue* Justin describes Jesus as the fulfiller of the Law and the bearer of the new covenant that brings the old to an end. Virtually the entire gospel is found in detail in the writings of the Old Testament. Justin finds there not only the deity of Christ, but also the cross and resurrection, and the church as the true Israel. On the other hand, Justin regards the gospel as the true philosophy. For Justin, all truth comes finally from God, and this holds true for Greek philosophy and ethics. In a way reminiscent of Philo of Alexandria, Justin argues that Plato was a student of the writings of the Old Testament.

Be zealous to do all things in harmony with God, with the bishop presiding in the place of God and the presbyters in the place of the Council of the Apostles, and the deacons, who are most dear to me, entrusted with the service of Jesus Christ.

Ignatius

I can wish no better thing for you, sirs, than this, that recognizing in this way that intelligence is given to every man, you may be of the same opinion as ourselves, and believe that Jesus is the Christ of God.

Justin Martyr

Although to some extent similar, the gospel exceeds in perfection and truth both Platonic philosophy and Stoic ethics.

The method of Justin and the Apologists is therefore to seek common ground between Christianity and philosophy and to build on that common ground the overwhelming superiority of the Christian faith. The truth of philosophy is thus affirmed and used in the cause of apologetics. Pagan religion, on the other hand, unanimously receives vitriolic condemnation.

The Apologists are important because they show the church in its earliest conversations with its opponents. The truth of the gospel is established with varying degrees of success, but most importantly, on the opponents' turf. Since at bottom the task of the Apologists is the vindication of Christianity, the theology presented is of a special character. It nevertheless remains significant not only as a model for future apologetics, but also because it reveals the considerable potential of philosophy for the elaborations of Christian theology that appear later in the history of the church.

DAVID WRIGHT

The Montanists

Montanus was a recent convert to Christianity in Phrygia in Asia Minor who in about AD 156 began to attract many followers by his 'New Prophecy'. With him were two prophetesses, Maximilla and Prisca (Priscilla). They claimed that the 'Paraclete' (a Greek title for the Holy Spirit) spoke directly through them. Although they were accused of many faults, they were condemned by the early church chiefly because they caused disorder and disturbance. Their teachings were extreme and fanatical rather than heretical.

They taught that Christ would soon return. They made precise predictions which did not come true. This exposed them as false prophets. In preparation for the end, they urged Christians to be strict ascetics, by fasting frequently, eating only dry food and giving up marriage. They called their communities in Phrygia 'Jerusalem', partly in order to attract people. They wanted these communities to be Spirit-filled and closely organized like the first Christian community in Jerusalem.

The Montanists were accused of various errors, including prophesying in 'ecstasy', in a trance. Their opponents argued that true prophets in the Bible and the church always spoke in full control of their senses. This claim was only partly correct. The Montanists were also accused of placing their own prophecies on the same level as or above the teaching of Christ and the apostles, but there is no evidence that the leaders of the 'New Prophecy' intended this to happen. It is interesting that no critic of Montanism argued that prophecy had ceased after the age of the apostles.

One of the most famous converts of Montanism was Tertullian, who adopted the New Prophecy in about AD 207. Montanism appealed to Tertullian for two reasons. It stressed Christian purity and discipline. This fitted in with the strict moral and spiritual demands Tertullian imposed on Christians in his later life. It also stressed the ministry of the Paraclete. Tertullian believed that the new and greater things which would be revealed by the Spirit promised by Jesus were stricter standards for the church and the Christian in pagan society.

Montanism was a challenge to the church at a time when it was heavily concerned with formalizing the traditional pattern of its doctrine and leadership.

DAVID WRIGHT

Marcion

Marcion was the most influential unorthodox theologian in second-century Christianity. He came from the southern shore of the

Black Sea and travelled to Asia Minor and Rome in about AD 140. In both places he was excommunicated as a heretic. He then organized a strong counter-church, which in some eastern regions lasted for centuries.

Marcion's main work was called *Contradictions*. It sharply contrasted Judaism and Christianity. The God of grace was unknown until revealed by Jesus. The God of the Old Testament, who controlled the material world, was a God of strict law and justice, or even of harsh and violent malice. Jesus came to rescue humanity from the power of this inferior God, whom Marcion called the Demiurge, 'maker' of the world.

Marcion believed that only Paul had really understood Jesus' new revelation of the God of love. The other apostles had corrupted it with Jewish ideas. As a basis for his teaching, Marcion recognized as Scripture only ten letters of Paul and Luke's Gospel, behind which stood Paul's authority. Even from these he edited out any statements connecting Jesus with the Old Testament. 'Marcionite' has remained a common label for anyone who exaggerates the difference between the two Testaments.

Paul contrasted not only 'law' and 'gospel' but also 'flesh' and 'spirit'. But Marcion went on to condemn sex and marriage and called for severe asceticism. He also denied that Jesus Christ was truly human. Like the Docetists he regarded Jesus' flesh and blood as only apparent, not real. These views he shared with the Gnostics, but his relationship to Gnosticism has been much debated. He taught no Gnostic myths, and stressed faith rather than knowledge. Yet he obviously squeezed Paul into a Gnostic mould.

Marcion was attacked by numerous writers, especially Irenaeus and Tertullian. His heresy prompted theologians to work out the relation between creation and salvation and the importance of the fall for understanding the problem of evil.

JOHN DRANE

The Gnostics

The Gnostics were not one but many groups of heretics in the second and third centuries. Their thinking was based on the belief that there are two worlds: the world of spirit, where God is, which is holy and pure; and the world of matter, where we are, which is evil and corrupt. If God is holy and pure, they reasoned, then he can have nothing to do with our own world. Salvation cannot be relevant to life in this world: the only hope for men and women is to escape to the spiritual world and find true fulfilment there.

The chance to escape comes at death. But not everyone is qualified to reach the world of spirit. To do so, a person must have a divine 'spark' embedded in their nature, otherwise they will return to the world to start another meaningless round of material existence. Even those with the 'spark' cannot be certain of finding ultimate release, for the evil creators of this world jealously guard every passage to the world of spirit. To outwit them, mere possession of the divine spark is not enough. The spark must be enlightened about its own nature and the nature of true salvation—and for this it requires 'knowledge'. This is not just an intellectual knowledge of theology, but rather a mystical illumination: a direct 'knowing' of the supreme God. This emphasis on 'knowledge' (Greek *gnosis*) is the origin of the term 'Gnostic'.

Many (though not all) Gnostics believed that the secret of this knowledge had originally been imparted to a chosen few by a divine redeemer who descended from the spirit world to this world. Some identified him with the Christian Jesus. But they could not accept what the New Testament says about Jesus.

The earliest Christians undoubtedly believed that Jesus was in some way God himself, even though they did not use the language of the later creeds. But this assumed that God had become a human

> The redemption must therefore be of a spiritual nature; for they affirm that the inner and spiritual man is redeemed by means of knowledge, and that they, having acquired the knowledge of all things, stand henceforth in need of nothing else.
>
> *Irenaeus*

person, and had fully and completely identified himself with our material world. To the Gnostic, this was a contradiction in terms, and many of them agreed with people like Cerinthus, who suggested that the divine influence came to the human Jesus of Nazareth at his baptism, and left him again before the crucifixion. This way, they could accept Jesus as a revealer of divine secrets, while not implying that God either was born or died as a human person. This view of Jesus is called 'Docetism' (from the Greek verb *dokeo*, 'to seem'). On this view, Jesus only 'seemed' to be human as well as divine, but was not really so.

Similar ideas are found in other religions (notably Hinduism). But they contradict the basic teachings of the Bible. The Christian God is not isolated from this world: he is its creator and the material creation is good. God cares for men and women in the affairs of everyday life. Christian salvation is not escaping from this world, but meeting God in it—especially in the life, death and resurrection of Jesus, who is God become man.

GERALD BRAY

Tertullian

Tertullian flourished between about AD 196 and 212. He was the first Latin-speaking Christian writer, a native of Carthage in North Africa. His thought shows the influence of Roman law, and his theology has a more systematic character than that of his Greek-speaking predecessors. His personal position in the church is unknown. According to Jerome, he was a presbyter who broke away into schism after a clash with the Roman clergy, but there is little evidence to substantiate this. He was sympathetic to the Montanists, but their teaching did not seriously affect his own theology.

Like his predecessors, Tertullian was primarily concerned with the proper interpretation of the Bible, 'hermeneutics'. He attacked Gnosticism, rejected allegory and claimed that heretics had no right to use a pagan philosophy as the framework for understanding Scripture. For this reason he is usually called an anti-philosophical writer.

Tertullian was a strong trinitarian. He believed that God had manifested himself with successive highlighting of each of the three persons according to the 'dispensations' or stages of salvation history. Thus the Father corresponds to the Old Testament, the Son to the New Testament and the Holy Spirit to the present age. He believed that the second coming was imminent, and advocated a rigorous asceticism as a preparation for martyrdom, which he regarded as the sign of the spiritual warfare described in the book of Revelation.

Tertullian defended the reality of Christ's manhood and was a firm believer in the resurrection of the body. This he saw as the natural partner of the soul, which was the image of God in humankind and which was responsible for human sin. Baptism was for him a near-magical rite which removed the sin of the flesh and made it holy. Post-baptismal sin was unforgivable, which is why he opposed infant baptism. He believed children might sin without knowing and thus lose their eternal salvation, unless they made up for it by being martyred.

In the history of doctrine, Tertullian is important for his invention of technical terminology. Words such as 'person', 'substance' and 'trinity' acquired their Christian meaning because of the way he used them. He is also an important witness for the Rule of Faith, which was the ancestor of the Apostles' and Nicene Creeds.

GERALD BRAY

Irenaeus

Irenaeus, whose main work was done between about AD 175 and 200, was a Greek-speaking presbyter of Smyrna, a disciple of

Polycarp (see *Apostolic Fathers*). In 177 or 178 he was sent to be bishop of Lyons and is thus an important link-figure between Eastern (Greek) and Western (Latin) theology. Very little of his work survives in the original Greek, and we are dependent for our knowledge of it on Latin and Armenian translations.

Irenaeus was not a systematic theologian, but he tried to give an account of biblical teaching which was designed to combat the various Gnostic heresies. The heart of his teaching was the doctrine of 'recapitulation' by which the redemption of the world in Christ has as its aim the restoration of creation to its original state. Christ was the second Adam, because in him it was possible to return to the relationship with God which human beings had enjoyed in the garden of Eden. The idea follows the apostle Paul up to a point, but Irenaeus worked with a different understanding of future fulfilment. Paul looked *forward* to the second coming of Christ; Irenaeus looked *backward* to the time before the fall.

The idea led Irenaeus to develop Justin's teaching that Mary was the new Eve, the universal mother of the new creation. This was the beginning of the veneration of Mary found today in Roman Catholicism and in the Eastern churches.

Irenaeus believed that human beings were created in the image and likeness of God, but that at the fall they lost the likeness. Salvation consisted of restoring this likeness to the image, which Irenaeus identified with the human soul. He also believed in the resurrection of the body, explaining that this was possible because the body of a Christian was nourished in the Eucharist by the body and blood of Christ.

Irenaeus was the first Christian writer to state explicitly that the writings of the apostles are Scripture on a par with the Old Testament. He recognized most of the books in our New Testament, with the exception of Hebrews, 2 Peter, 2 and 3 John. He was also the first writer to speak of the Rule of Faith, though it is not clear whether he meant Scripture itself, or a confession in the form of a creed, or (as seems likelier) the two viewed as one.

GERALD BRAY

Origen

Origen lived from about AD 185 to 254. A native of Alexandria, the centre of Greek thinking in Egypt, and pupil of Clement, he was the most brilliant theologian among the Greek fathers. Virtually all subsequent developments in theology, whether they are orthodox or heretical, can be traced back to him. His writings were eventually condemned for heresy themselves, but by then (about 400) his reputation and influence were solidly established.

Origen developed the 'allegorical' interpretation of Scripture which he had inherited from Philo and Clement, and made it central to his whole theological method. The Bible could not be taken literally, but had to be understood as a spiritual mystery.

This was particularly important with regard to the fall of humankind which Origen interpreted as a cosmic myth. According to him, every human soul fell away from the Creator at the beginning of time. Growing cold and heavy by this separation, they fell one by one into the world of matter at different moments. There they were imprisoned in bodies, awaiting their freedom. The soul of Jesus, however, did not fall with the others, but clung to the Word who had made it. When the Word took on flesh, the soul of Jesus came with it and brought human life to the womb of Mary. This doctrine would be severely attacked in the fourth and fifth centuries by the School of Antioch, although its influence can be seen quite clearly in the writings of Athanasius.

Origen also contributed to the doctrine of the trinity by insisting that the three Persons were realities from all eternity, and not produced out of one at the moment of creation (as in Irenaeus and Tertullian). At the same time, Platonic influences led Origen to insist that the Son and the Spirit were inferior to the Father, who alone was God in fullness. This teaching later led to the heresy of Arius, who denied the deity of Christ.

Origen's Platonism also accounts for his doctrine of evil and punishment. He taught that evil was non-being, and saw punishment in terms of internal psychological anguish rather than eternal damnation. In the end the universe would return to the beginning and all things would be restored in Christ. This doctrine of universalism was severely criticized by Jerome, and was the immediate cause of Origen's eventual condemnation.

ALASDAIR HERON

Athanasius and the Arians

One of the most important debates in the early church was the Arian controversy, which raged from about 320 to 381. The question was this: is Jesus Christ, as the Son or Word of God, truly and fully God, or is he a being of lower status than God the Father?

Arius came from Alexandria, and the controversy began when he was excommunicated by his bishop, Alexander, for insisting that only the Father was really God. The 'Son' or 'Word' was, strictly speaking, the first of the beings that God the Father had made. So, as Arius put it, 'There was a time when he was not.'

Arius was supported by several other leaders of the church in the East. In 325 the first Christian Roman Emperor, Constantine, called an Ecumenical Council at Nicea in Asia Minor to decide the matter. The Council decisively rejected Arius' teaching and drew up a new creed. This described Jesus Christ as 'the Son of God ...

> **homoousios** *('of the same substance') with the Father, through whom all things were made.'*

The word *homoousios* was intended to make absolutely clear that Arius' teaching was not acceptable. Not only Arius' supporters, however, but many others as well were unhappy with it because it was not a biblical term, and because it could seem to identify the Father and the Son as 'one being', with no distinction of the two persons. Through the next fifty years various other terms were proposed—*homoios* ('like'), *homoiousios* ('of like substance'), and, from the extreme Arian wing, *anomoios* ('unlike'). From about 360, however, a majority consensus began to form around the formula describing the Father and Son (and also the Holy Spirit) as 'one in substance' but acknowledging each as being a distinct *hypostasis* or 'person'.

The great advocate of the Nicene position was **Athanasius** (about 295–373), Alexander's successor as bishop of Alexandria. When Constantine decided that Arius had shifted his ground sufficiently to be restored to communion, Athanasius refused—and was sent into exile. He was exiled four further times by other emperors sympathetic to Arianism. But his refusal to give way—which led to the slogan *Athanasius contra mundum*, 'Athanasius against the world'—eventually bore fruit.

In 381 the Second Ecumenical Council at Constantinople finally excluded all forms of Arianism and approved what is known today as the Nicene Creed. This Council also affirmed that the Holy Spirit is not a created being, but as God's own Spirit 'is worshipped and glorified with the Father and the Son'. Thus Athanasius' stand was vindicated.

The heart of the matter as Athanasius saw it was essentially this: God himself has come among us in Jesus Christ; God himself is present with us in his Spirit. Arius' God by contrast remains eternally remote from us and infinitely distant. So the Arian controversy forced the church to rethink its understanding of God himself in the light of Jesus

Christ as God incarnate 'for us men and for our salvation', and so to reach the distinctively Christian doctrine of the trinity.

GEORGE CAREY

Augustine of Hippo

Augustine of Hippo (354–432) has an unequalled place in Christian history. Without question the greatest theologian since the apostle Paul, he was to command the mind and teaching of the church for the 1,000 years or so after his death.

Yet Augustine had a very curious and unlikely background. The child of Roman parents and brought up in North Africa, he led a worldly and rebellious life until his conversion at the age of thirty-two. His father, Patricius, was an easy-going pagan who had an indulgent regard for his children. Monica, his mother, was an earnest Christian who in spite of her virtues appears to have been rather fussy, over-protective and over-anxious. Augustine increased her anxiety by leaving home at seventeen to study at Carthage University. He drifted away from her faith, and dabbled in many philosophies, searching for meaning and intellectual answers to life. He had a mistress who bore him a son. Monica sought the advice of a bishop who advised her not to pursue Augustine with her maternal anxiety and prayers. 'It is impossible', prophesied the bishop, 'for the son of such tears to be lost.'

And so it was that, after trying many different faiths, Augustine was led to reconsider the faith of his mother. He listened to the arresting sermons of Ambrose, Bishop of Milan, and read the inspiring testimony books of Christians such as Antony of Egypt.

The climax came one day when Augustine was alone in a Milan garden. While thinking about faith he heard a child singing 'take up and read' (a current pop song maybe?). He looked around, saw a Bible, opened it and read Romans 13:14: 'Not in the lusts of the flesh ... but put on the Lord Jesus Christ.' This he did and a new life opened for him. Augustine eventually became Bishop of Hippo (in modern Algeria) where most of his remarkable ministry as a Christian preacher, teacher and theologian took place.

To understand Augustine we must realize that his faith and thinking were influenced greatly by personal experience and controversy. Far from being an ivory-tower theologian, he related his faith to problems and challenges which directly faced him.

He has influenced the church in the following areas.

Humanity's fall and God's grace

It has been said that Augustine 'perfected Christian pessimism'. So it may seem, because Augustine from his conversion taught the absolute inability of humankind to do anything good. Human beings were corrupt and could not please God. His own experience had taught him that salvation was a free gift. It could not be earned.

This teaching brought him into conflict with a British monk called Pelagius, who had no doubt that human beings were free and could please God by their own actions. Adam's sin hurt no one except himself. Augustine won the day in this controversy and Pelagianism (the doctrine that a person's good works are their own contribution to their salvation) was condemned by the church.

Augustine's teaching about grace flowed from his understanding of human nature. Humanity is spiritually depraved and weak; only God can help us. Grace is God's personal activity in rescuing us from sin's hold. However, Augustine appears to treat grace as if it were an impersonal substance which affects what it touches almost mechanically. He distinguished between three types of grace in the Christian life: 'prevenient' grace which first moves the will towards God; 'co-operating' grace that works with those wills God has moved; 'persevering' grace that keeps the Christian secure in salvation.

This teaching was to have a profound

influence on both Catholic and later Protestant theology. Catholic teaching stressed Augustine's idea of grace being given through the sacraments. Protestants expounded his teaching on that grace of God that calls us and saves us. Both lines of thought have their origins in Augustine's thought.

The church and the trinity

Augustine's estimate of the fallenness of humanity was to affect his teaching about the church in two ways.

The importance of the authority of the church. Augustine's own experience taught him that he needed the church's authority not to sink into scepticism again. He could not even rely on his own intellect because that was fallen too. From this he produced the notion of *fides implicita*, 'implicit faith', the idea that the individual shares in the church's faith. The church in a sense believes *for* the Christian.

The 'two churches'. Baptism and church attendance do not by themselves guarantee salvation. Only God knows his 'elect', those who will be saved. Thus Augustine was led to postulate an 'invisible' church known only to God—the elect, the true believers—within the 'visible' church which was the catholic church on earth. This distinction between the visible church and invisible church was to be emphasized by John Calvin and other Protestant theologians.

Taking the Nicene formulation of the trinity as his starting-point, Augustine used personal, human terms as ways of understanding God. From the human experience of love, he saw God as love (God the Father) embracing the beloved (Jesus) with a bond of love uniting them (the Holy Spirit).

A new civilization

Augustine's old age coincided with the old age of the Roman Empire. Many pagans blamed Christianity for the breaking up of the Empire. Augustine met this accusation with his most self-conscious book *The City of God*, which aimed to give a coherent Christian philosophy of history. He contrasted two cities (communities), the city of this world and the city of God, and showed that the community of love based on God will last for ever.

It is one of life's ironies that Augustine died in Hippo just as the Vandals broke through the city walls and occupied the city. But his philosophy and faith were to become the inspiration of a new Christian civilization in later days.

Roman Catholicism

For the first thousand years of its existence the Christian church, though often rocked by controversies, remained essentially one church. It survived the division and fall of the Roman Empire, emerged with renewed strength from the collapse of the state and the ecclesiastical crises of the time, and gained the spiritual and moral dominion of the West, where it also wielded great political power.

A distinctively 'Roman Catholic' tradition developed from two deep divisions which split the church. In 1054, the so-called 'Great Schism' divided the Eastern, Byzantine Church from the Western, Roman Church. Then, in the sixteenth century, Western Christendom was deeply divided as a result of the Protestant Reformation. One response was the Council of Trent (1545–63) called to introduce measures of reform and counter-reform and affirm basic Catholic teaching. The doctrines of Trent were reaffirmed by the First Vatican Council in 1870, which also defined for the first time the doctrine of papal infallibility.

In the twentieth century, two great wars and the inevitable deep social changes which followed them have awoken the Roman Catholic Church from centuries of changelessness. Pope John XXIII was the champion of the new era, the visionary leader who, interpreting the signs of the times, decided that the Roman church must renew itself in order to fulfil its mission.

The Second Vatican Council of 1962–65 was the council of renewal. Since then, Catholicism has undergone drastic changes while at the same time preserving those elements which have characterized it throughout its history.

Unity and distinctiveness

The Roman Catholic Church has proclaimed and defended great doctrines of Christian orthodoxy: biblical theism, the trinity, basic teaching about the person and work of Jesus Christ, his virgin conception, the union in his person of divine and human nature, the objectively sacrificial character of his death, his bodily resurrection, his ascension to the right hand of the Father, and his second coming into this world.

Catholicism today identifies with other Christian communions in its affirmation of human dignity, in its fight for peace and an end to oppression for individuals and peoples, and in its strong opposition to all that runs counter to the moral and spiritual values of the Christian faith.

The strong desire of the church since the Second Vatican Council is that the unity of all Christians should be expressed in word and deed.

What is the special doctrinal position of the Roman Catholic Church? Their belief about **the church** is that it is 'Roman Catholic': they see it as Christ's body here on earth which is centred on Rome. The Roman Catholic believes that Christ gave to Peter special authority to build his church. Peter's successors, the bishops of Rome, are viewed as sharing this unique authority. From this the church has deduced its doctrine of 'infallibility', that as the Pope is the 'vicar' (representative) of Christ on earth, God will not allow his people to drift into error.

The Catholic Church has a high doctrine of **priestly authority**. Because Christ has conferred on Peter the 'power of the keys'—that is, the authority to forgive—only those ordained by the successor of Peter can actually administer the divine graces. (See *Priesthood and Ordination*.)

The sacraments are central to the Roman Catholic Church and to every Catholic believer. The traditional notion of salvation viewed the sacraments as conveying 'grace' for special situations: baptism for the removal of original sin; penance for 'forgiveness'; the mass for feeding on Christ, and so on.

Concerning **the mass**, the central sacrament of the church, the traditional understanding is that through the priestly action of offering the bread to the Father the bread-wafer really becomes the body of Christ. This is known as 'transubstantiation'.

The Virgin Mary has a special place in the faith of the church also. She is seen as the first of the saints and has this high dignity because of her role in bearing Christ, the Lord of Glory. During the last 150 years two important dogmas have emphasized her importance. The first, known as the 'Immaculate Conception' (1854), was formulated to mark her role in bearing the spotless son of God. The second, the 'Bodily Assumption of the Blessed Virgin Mary into heaven' (1950), expressed Catholic belief that she did not die.

These central concerns of the Roman Catholic Church have been, among others, issues of separation from other Christians. Protestants on the whole deny that the true ministry belongs exclusively to the Roman Catholic priesthood. The theory of 'transubstantiation' and the two Marian dogmas are also rejected.

However, the Second Vatican Council introduced a new spirit between Catholic and Protestant Christians. The old bitterness has gone and both traditions desire to overcome the doctrinal difficulties which stop Catholic and Protestant worshipping together. In drawing together since the Council, Protestants and Catholics have discovered that, in spite of the differences, they have more in common than they realized.

It is certainly true that since the Second

Vatican Council it has become difficult to say what the 'faith' of the Catholic Church is on many issues. There is considerable diversity of attitudes and interpretation of official doctrine, ranging from the traditionalist movement, wanting to reinstate conservative practices, to the left-wing beliefs of those who choose violence to change social structures. Between both extremes lies a large selection of views, from the theology of the Dutch bishops to the Latin American theology of liberation, from the Charismatic movement and Opus Dei to the popular piety of the masses in Latin America, where Catholicism has lost its previous megalithic unity.

As always, some feel threatened by the changes. Others welcome them as an opportunity to reaffirm a spiritual, biblical faith, to get back to a gospel of faith in Jesus Christ that gives hope to a needy world. Certainly Roman Catholicism is far from losing its power and influence in the world. The present Pope, John Paul II, is a leader of great impact whose guidance will shape his church's future relationships.

R. A. WHITACRE

The Orthodox Churches

A visitor to a celebration of the liturgy in one of the Eastern Orthodox Churches is usually struck not only by the elaborateness of the ceremony, but also by a feeling of antiquity. This reflects Orthodox theology: it is not only highly developed, it is marked by a deep loyalty to the past. The doctrinal formulations of the Seven Ecumenical Councils held between AD 325 and 787 are still authoritative, and the teachings of the early fathers are considered immediately relevant today.

These past formulations and teachings are authoritative not from mere conservatism but because they reflect the eternal Word of God. By preserving early Christian belief the Orthodox believe they are remaining loyal to the embodiment of the living faith revealed by God. Other Christians question Orthodoxy's claim to be the unique representative of apostolic belief; but even some non-Orthodox are finding in these earlier formulations a way through the impasses which various debates in the West have reached.

Dynamic openness

Another characteristic of Orthodoxy is its attitude towards these formulations of belief. While the faith expressed in the church's tradition is considered a unity, there have been few attempts by Orthodox theologians to write a systematic theology, and none of these attempts are authoritative. The tradition is regarded more as a safeguard against false belief than as an exhaustive expression of correct belief.

Behind such an attitude is the view, central to Orthodoxy, that God has revealed himself to humankind and yet in his essence remains incomprehensible. Our knowledge of such a God can be true but never complete.

In Orthodoxy this open-ended view of God is matched by a dynamic view of humanity. God is free, not ruled by any necessity, and human beings share such freedom because we are in God's image. Thus Orthodoxy, which appears to outsiders as so conservative and static, contains at heart dynamic views of God and humanity which actually imply a continuous growth in our knowledge of God.

Indeed, such seeming contradictions characterize much of Orthodoxy. Otherworldliness is combined with an insistence on the historically concrete, especially the incarnation and the church. A lack of legalism is combined with a strong asceticism. An appeal to reason is combined with distrust of rationalism.

Such antinomies reflect a basic Orthodox view concerning Christian belief. The Orthodox insists that in matters of faith two ideas may appear contradictory and yet both be true. Orthodoxy insists that this approach be applied when formulating all doctrine. The Orthodox criticize any theology which is too rational, too concerned with logical consistency.

Adoring the mystery

Perhaps the most important characteristic of Orthodox theology is its view of the nature of theology itself. It is not speculation about revealed truths, but a personal knowledge of the living God. At the heart of Orthodox theology is not faith seeking understanding, but faith adoring the mystery. The theologian is not primarily one who can discuss the faith because his or her mind has been trained, but one who sees God because his or her heart has been purified. Prayer and love are the marks of a theologian: knowledge that does not produce love and worship is vain.

Great importance is attached to the church's worship, especially the liturgy. In the liturgy God and human beings meet in a special way, and this meeting is at the heart of every Christian doctrine. In the liturgy there is an epic recounting of the history of salvation, with adoration and penitence expressed in the face of so great a salvation. For Orthodoxy the faith is most perfectly presented in the church's worship rather than in any particular systematic theology.

None of these characteristics is unique to Orthodoxy, but they are distinctly characteristic of it. Orthodoxy witnesses by her faith and life to the mystery at the heart of Christianity, the mystery of time and eternity, God and humanity meeting in Jesus and his body, the church.

TONY LANE

Medieval Theology

The Dark Ages (AD 450-1000)

For Western Europe the early part of the Middle Ages was a time of turmoil and anarchy, starting with the collapse of the Roman Empire. There were successive waves of barbarian invasions which did not end until the invaders were eventually converted to Christianity and settled down. The Emperor Charlemagne (died 814) introduced an element of stability and during his reign and those of his immediate successors there was a brief flowering of learning (the 'Carolingian Renaissance') which produced the great philosopher-theologian **John Scotus Erigena** (died 877). But for most of this period there was very little learning and the heritage of the past was in danger of being lost.

Monastic Theology

Theology during this period was largely confined to the monasteries and is thus called monastic theology. It was produced in an atmosphere of commitment and devotion, within the framework of the monastic life as set out in the Rule of **Benedict** (died about 550) and elsewhere. The goal was not the pursuit of knowledge for its own sake, but edification and worship. The approach was one of contemplation and adoration. The theologian was not a detached, academic observer studying his material from outside, but a committed, involved participant. In later times Franciscan devotional writing was to continue this approach.

Scholastic Theology

With greater stability in the eleventh century, Western civilization began to revive. Theologians found themselves faced with the question of the relation between faith (theology) and reason (philosophy). The impact of philosophy led to a new approach to theology: scholastic theology or scholasticism. Theology came to be studied outside the cloister in the university and other 'secular' (non-monastic) settings. The goal was objective intellectual knowledge. The approach was one of questioning, logic, speculation and disputation. It was more important for the theologian to be a trained philosopher than a godly person. Theology had become a detached, objective science. This approach did not eliminate the older monastic approach, but it displaced it from the front line of theology.

Renaissance (AD 1000-1200)

The impact of philosophy on theology began in the eleventh century with the emergence of reason (philosophy) as a tool to be used in theology. **Anselm** used it to demonstrate the rationality of Christian doctrine. Reason had entered theology not (yet) as a means of defining Christian doctrine (which was based on revelation), but as a technique for defending and further understanding this faith.

In the following century the role of reason was further expanded. Lawyers had begun to use philosophical methods to decide or arbitrate between conflicting authorities. Where one law appeared to conflict with another, logic was used to reconcile them and to determine the law. This method was employed by the Italian lawyer **Gratian** in his *Decretum* (about 1150), which became a standard textbook for church or 'canon' law.

Peter Abelard (died 1142), a brilliant but somewhat erratic thinker, proceeded to apply the same methods of theology. He wrote a book called *Sic et Non* (Yes and No), in which he juxtaposed conflicting pronouncements of authority (Scripture, early fathers, councils). His aim was not to ridicule them, but to introduce reason as the arbiter to decide between them, following the lawyer's method. Abelard was not always discreet in his approach and he was condemned for his teaching, due to the intervention of **Bernard of Clairvaux** (died 1153), the last great representative of the older monastic tradition. But Abelard's method was followed (more cautiously) by his disciple **Peter Lombard** (died 1160), who enjoyed Bernard's support. Lombard's *Sentences*, a compilation of sources from the Bible and the fathers, became the standard theological textbook until the time of the Reformation and beyond.

Crisis (AD 1200-1300)

In the thirteenth century theology entered a new and more dangerous phase. Philosophy now appeared not just as a tool for use in theology, but as a rival system of thought. This arose through the translation into Latin of the writings of the ancient Greek philosopher Aristotle (died 322 BC). His writings presented a new way of looking at reality, a whole new world-view or philosophy of life as an alternative to Christianity. Muslim thinkers even claimed that Aristotle supported Islam against Christianity. How was the challenge to be faced?

For a time Aristotle's writings on metaphysics (the nature of being) were banned, but this was only a temporary measure to gain breathing space. Some, particularly the Franciscan theologian **Bonaventure** (died 1274), sought to maintain the older world-view in opposition to the new Aristotelian outlook. But most influential in the long term was the approach of **Thomas Aquinas**, who sought to make a synthesis between faith (theology) and reason (philosophy = Aristotle). He sought to show that Aristotle's philosophy (rightly interpreted and corrected where necessary) could be consistently held in synthesis with Christian theology.

Decay (AD 1300-1500)

Eventually Thomas' approach was to become the official Roman Catholic position. But in his own time it met with limited favour. In the fourteenth and fifteenth centuries his synthesis came under heavy fire and there was increasing scepticism about the possibility of harmonizing faith and reason, theology and philosophy. This process was begun by **John Duns Scotus** (died 1308) and came to a head in the teaching of **William of Occam** (died 1349) and his followers. Philosophy and theology went their separate ways with theology retreating out of the 'natural' realm and relying increasingly on naked faith in God's revelation (the rationality of which could not be shown). Furthermore, scholastic theology and practical spirituality became divorced to the detriment of both. It was out of this unhealthy situation that the Reformation emerged as a summons back to the word of God.

TONY LANE

Anselm

Anselm was born in Italy around AD 1033. As a young man he entered the Benedictine monastery at Bec in Normandy where he eventually became prior and abbot. In 1093 he became Archbishop of Canterbury until his death in 1109, though much of that time was spent out of the country because of disputes with the king over church-state relations. He was the first truly great theologian of the medieval West and is seen by some as the founder of scholasticism.

Anselm pioneered the introduction of philosophy into theology, even if only with a limited role. The content of the Christian faith is given by revelation, not by philosophy. But the theologian who believes can then seek by the use of philosophy to understand more fully what that belief is. Reason can show the rationality or inner coherence of Christian doctrine.

Anselm pursued this method in three major writings. In the *Monologion* (1077), originally called *An Example of Meditation on the Grounds of Faith*, he offered a 'proof' for the existence of God. The fact that we can discern degrees of goodness means that there is an absolute Good by which we measure it. This Good is God. The following year he wrote the *Proslogion*, originally called *Faith Seeking Understanding*, which presented the famous ontological argument for the existence of God: God is defined as 'that than which nothing greater can be conceived'. This being must exist, since were he not to exist he would be inferior to an identical being who did exist. The debate over the validity of this argument began immediately and has continued unabatedly to the present day.

In his most ambitious work, *Cur Deus Homo* (Why God became Man), written in the 1090s, Anselm argued that it was absolutely necessary for God to become man and die to save us. Given that humanity has sinned against him, God can neither abandon the pinnacle of his creation nor simply forgive without some 'satisfaction' to restore his lost honour. But while it is human beings who owe this satisfaction, only God is great enough to be able to pay it. It follows that God had to become human in order, as a human being, to offer this satisfaction by his voluntary death.

Anselm's aim was to show how reasonable faith is, rather than to prove it mathematically. The beauty of the inner harmony of the Christian faith gives joy to the believer who sees the accord of faith and reason. The unbeliever's objections (for example, that it is degrading and unfitting for God to become human) are met and he is pointed to the truth of the Christian faith.

I long to understand in some degree thy truth, which my heart believes and loves. For I do not seek to understand that I may believe, but I believe in order to understand.

TONY LANE

Thomas Aquinas

Thomas Aquinas is the best known and the most influential medieval theologian. He was born in Italy around AD 1225, studied at the University of Naples where he became a Dominican friar, and later at Paris and Cologne under the Dominican theologian Albert the Great who influenced him considerably. In 1252 he returned to Paris as a lecturer. The remainder of his life was spent teaching at Paris and in Italy, where he died in 1274.

Thomas lived during a time of crisis for Christian theology. The writings of Aristotle were becoming known in the West and theologians found themselves faced with a powerful and consistent world-view which stood independently of Christianity (see *Medieval Theology*). How to react to this challenge was the most pressing theological issue of the time. Thomas' approach was the way of synthesis: he sought to integrate the philosophy of Aristotle and Christian theology into one consistent, unified system.

Thomas operated with a two-tier system in which grace (the divine) builds upon nature (the human). Human reason (nature) can discover much that is true about the world, humanity and even God. Divine revelation (grace) perfects this by adding to it. Divine revelation does not stand over against human thought in opposition to it but rather supplements it and brings it to perfection by building upon it. Philosophy (pursued along Aristotelian lines) teaches much that is true: revelation does not reject this but builds upon it and completes it.

For Thomas human reason can establish many truths. 'Natural theology', based on philosophy without appeal to revelation, can demonstrate the existence of God, his eternity, the doctrine of providence and so on. He offered five proofs for the existence of God (see *Can God be Proved?*) although he did not accept the 'ontological argument' put forward by **Anselm**.

Grace does not abolish nature but perfects it.

While reason can establish much about God, major areas lie beyond its grasp. The doctrines of the trinity and the incarnation are examples of truths which cannot be known without divine revelation. These doctrines cannot be established on the basis of reason alone. But while Thomas concedes that these doctrines are *beyond* reason he denies that they are *contrary* to reason.

Thomas did not meet with approval in his own time and some of his teaching was condemned in 1277 and 1284. But it was adopted by his (Dominican) order in 1278 and in 1323 he was canonized. The Reformers rejected his two-tier approach to nature and grace, though this way of thinking entered Protestant theology later. In the Catholic church his influence grew until in 1879 Pope Leo XIII instructed all theological students to study Thomas' works. In recent years, since the Second Vatican Council, his influence has waned.

JAMES ATKINSON

The Reformation

The Reformation developed within a vortex of political, economic, social and intellectual ideas. But essentially it was a religious and spiritual movement carried through by responsible and committed Christian scholars concerned to reform a church which had not only lost the true gospel of the kingdom, but in the process had allowed itself to become a secularized and often corrupted institution. True, the Reformation was not unrelated to contemporary movements such as the Renaissance and the Peasants' War, but one must resist the interpretation that would see it as no more than a political or social protest. There were many who sought to use the Reformation proper for their own political, social or material ends.

The sixteenth century, the century of the Reformation, was a time of great political and social unrest, intellectual questioning and deep discontent. Trade was developing with the discovery of the New World, great and prosperous cities were appearing, money began to rule, the peasants grew discontented. Scholars sought new learning, fresh forms of art. Over the previous two centuries, following the Avignon Captivity and the Great Schism, when Europe had three popes and witnessed a debased and secularized papacy together with an unlearned and ignorant clergy, the church had begun to lose its credibility. There were reforming movements (such as the **Waldensians**), many spiritual movements (such as the **Brethren of the Common Life**), many moral protests (**Savanarola**). All the signs indicated a Reformation was at hand; the question was where, when and by whom it would be initiated.

Its earliest and clearest beginnings may be seen in the fourteenth century with **John Wycliffe**, the Oxford professor of theology. A great critic of medieval scholasticism and a powerful biblical and evangelical scholar, he criticized the secularized papacy; and his theology, especially on the lips of his Poor Preachers, cut at the roots of papal tyranny and popular Catholicism at a deep, human level. **John Huss** expressed similar views in Bohemia. **John Wessel** the Dutch theologian in the fifteenth century and many others are now described as 'reformers before the Reformation'.

Gospel rediscovered

The Reformation proper began when **Martin Luther** posted up his disputation against indulgences in Wittenberg on 31 October 1517. (See *Martin Luther*.) True, this was a protest against the corrupt practice of selling forgiveness. But still more was it a protest on behalf of the biblical evangelical theology which Luther had himself rediscovered. The Reformation was not so much about corrupt practices, as about the pure gospel. Luther is seen to attack indulgences, good works, the papal claims to supremacy, transubstantiation, religious orders; but in all his true concern was to preach Christ, and it was the proclamation of this gospel that called all these practices into question.

At almost the same time the Swiss theologian **Zwingli** carried through anti-papal, anti-hierarchic and anti-monastic reforms in Zurich. This movement, more libertarian, rationalist and socialist, and less theological than Luther's, made great progress in both Switzerland and South-West Germany. It was tragically cut short by the death of Zwingli at the battle of Cappel in 1531, and consequently the leadership passed to the brilliant **John Calvin** in Geneva.

In his *Institutes* Calvin sought to enable people to read and understand the Bible, and also to vindicate Reformation theology against those who attacked it. He based the book on the Apostles' Creed and gave to the world a superb presentation of the Christian faith. His theology of the sovereignty of God made a particular appeal to the changing European society, and after the death of Luther in 1546 and the defeat of the German princes by the Emperor, proved to be the driving force of the Reformation, especially in Northern Germany, Holland, France and later Scotland. Calvinism became involved in the Wars of Religion in France, in the national revolt which freed the Netherlands from Spain, and in the Thirty Years War. In Scotland, too, the Calvinist cause under **John Knox** ousted the French and in so doing safeguarded the English Reformation.

Reform in England

Meanwhile, however, the Reformation in England pursued a peculiar and unique course, complicated by outside political and social forces. Its beginning may be seen as an act of state in 1534 when **Henry VIII** accomplished the overthrow of papal supremacy and the dissolution of the monasteries. His motive was to extend the sovereignty of the central government into all spheres of national life. Henry was a hard Catholic traditionalist and, when he assumed the title of Supreme Head of the Church, it was not from a desire to reform Catholicism and restore biblical and evangelical life. This flame was kept alive by a core of men and women influenced by Lollard ideas and the exciting theologies of Luther and Calvin, strengthened by Christian humanists.

This reform movement surged ahead during the reign of Edward VI, but when the bigoted Catholic Mary succeeded her brother in 1553, everything was restored to what it was before and some 300 scholars and Reformers were burnt at the stake. Yet Mary failed to restore England to the Roman fold; the 'middle way' of the early Reformers was re-established by **Elizabeth I** in 1558–59. Once and for all England was done with Romanism; at that point the country became Protestant though in a peculiarly English, non-confessional fashion. The Elizabethan Settlement produced an Anglicanism which was scriptural, traditional, and national, and which developed its own brilliant spiritual and cultural traditions. The Calvinist Reformation felt itself outside this tradition and finally allied itself with the Puritan Revolution 1640-60. It destroyed the monarch but could not prevail against the Anglican

Church, and eventually resolved itself into sects. The Catholic Counter-Reformation, too, attacked the Anglican Settlement, but by the end of the seventeenth century Anglicanism was secure. Historians consider the Reformation closed by then, but its exponents have always argued that a church once reformed must always submit itself to a continuous process of reformation.

Shock waves

The Radical Reformation (see *Anabaptists and Baptists*) sought not so much the reform as the restitution of the church entirely on New Testament principles. **Anabaptists** and **Radicals** sought to establish local churches of committed believers. They were given a bad name by being identified with bloodshed and fanatical violence, but essentially they were pacifists seeking to separate church from state. They fed a tradition which has developed into the free church Baptist and pietist movements, started Protestant missions and led into many new renewal movements, such as Methodism.

Catholicism was not blind to the truths that Protestantism had rediscovered. In the sixteenth century **Loyola** and **Xavier** were leading lights in the **Counter-Reformation**, and by their establishment of the **Jesuits** sought to purify the church and restore the old Catholic ideals of celibacy, chastity, self-sacrifice and compassionate service to the poor. The movement was powerfully anti-Protestant. The reforming **Council of Trent** (1545–63), the Inquisition, Spanish mysticism and the theology of **Bellarmine** and **Canisius** were all expressions of this growing emphasis on reform, and strictly speaking ought to be called the Roman Reformation rather than the Counter-Reformation. In our own day the Second Vatican Council (1962–65) may be seen as a part of the same reforming process.

The Reformation movement affected every person and every country in Europe, changed the whole face of Western Christendom, renewed the universities, gave democratic government, liberated every individual from the tyranny of church or state, and though at great cost of disunity, wars, nationalism and fanaticism, was yet the cause of incalculable blessing. It is a continuing process, permanently relevant.

JAMES ATKINSON

Martin Luther

Martin Luther was born in Germany in 1483. At the university of Erfurt he gained a brilliant degree in Law, but realized that a career in the civil service was not his vocation, and entered the Augustinian monastery. Here he sought peace with God, but the closer experience with God he expected turned out to be a desperate spiritual struggle. His superiors noted his theological ability and total devotion to the holy life, and he was appointed to a teaching post at the University of Wittenberg. Here for the next few years he studied and lectured on the biblical books of Genesis, Psalms, Romans and Galatians.

History tends to think in terms of dramatic moments; though Luther had shown a concern for reformation for some years, it was not until he nailed up ninety-five Theses against Indulgences on 31 October 1517 that the event proved to be the message. He protested on scriptural and rational grounds that to presume to sell forgiveness for money was a total denial of the gospel. Within a matter of weeks there was hardly a university, monastery or church in Europe which had not heard the reverberations of those hammer blows when this obscure monk-professor nailed his theses on the church door.

At Heidelberg, and later when summoned to a disputation at Leipzig, Luther emerged as the champion of faith alone, grace alone, Scripture alone. He argued his case on the authority of Scripture and ancient Catholic tradition, particularly drawing on Augustine. Book after book issued from the press, three of the most famous, *Address to the German Nobility*, the *Babylonian Captivity* and *The Freedom of a Christian Man*, appearing in 1520. Here he addressed the laity in their own language as well as the clergy in theirs.

Doors flung open

What was the nature of Luther's protest that divided Christendom? It did not arise from a criticism of doctrine, for he was a deeply committed Catholic believer. Nor was it just a protest against religious abuses, for he knew that abuses occur in every human institution. It took its rise from the nature of Luther's religious experience. Luther had pursued with great diligence in the monastery all the ways taught to a monk to find God: the mystic way of prayer, the practical discipline of good works, the intellectual path of reason. Luther went through agonies of stress when he found that the more diligently he pursued the known methods of spiritual growth, the further God seemed distanced from him, so far indeed as to be positively hostile.

It was at this moment of desperate distress and agony of soul that the great foundational truth of Christianity was shown to him: that it was not that God was far off and that men and women had to do everything that was in them to attain his favour, but simply that humankind was far off because of self-centredness and sin, and that God had come all the way in Christ to find us and continues to come to the penitent believing heart. As Luther expressed it, 'the doors of Paradise were flung open to me, and I entered.'

This discovery meant the centrality of Christ, the rediscovery of the original gospel, and the renewal of biblical, evangelical thinking: this was the source of Luther's Reformation theology as he was driven by God to re-form what had been de-formed.

First it showed him the authority of Christ. Luther's life's work was to put the spotlight back onto Jesus Christ, and so to correct the distortions of late medieval theology. To set Christ and his work in the centre, rather than humanity and its works, restored the doctrine of the priesthood of all believers. This theology cut the priest down to size, by taking away his special priestly mediation, and so knocked the bottom out of the Catholic system of worship. Indulgences and purgatory were exposed by the fact of free forgiveness through faith in Christ alone. The mass and transubstantiation were replaced by communion; the cult of Mary and the saints, of pilgrimages and wonder-working images was seen as superstitious and unnecessary. The papal claims to infallibility and universal authority were diagnosed as the claims of a worldly prince, not of a vicar of Christ. It was reformation by demolition.

The doctrine of salvation in Christ alone meant justification by faith alone through the grace of Christ alone. Luther saw this as the central message of the Bible, which to him was the word of God, the sole theological authority.

Attacked on all fronts

Challenged by Rome to recant, Luther refused, and was promptly whisked away into hiding in the Wartburg castle. Here he translated the entire New Testament into superb German in a matter of weeks. Owing to left-wing radical socialist activity Luther had to return to Wittenberg to stabilize university and church life. At this point Luther began to face attacks from the Catholic establishment, from the radical extremists, from the humanist Erasmus (Luther wrote his finest work in reply to Erasmus' attack on his doctrine of the bondage of the will), and worst of all from the peasants, who believed that evangelical freedom meant political freedom, and in spite of Luther's opposition, took up arms to fight for it in 1525, thereby inflicting on the Reformation movement a nearly mortal wound...

Outlawed and excommunicated by Rome, Luther's work was now to inspire and direct the Reformation. In addition to his university lectures and a stream of books (one a fortnight over twenty-five years), he reorganized church life in Saxony, wrote a new liturgy and many

■

I simply say that true Christianity had ceased to exist among those who should have preserved it—the bishops and scholars.

■

My conscience is fast bound to the Word of God. Here I stand. I can no other.

fine hymns, constructed two catechisms, showed his concern for education by fostering schools for girls as well as boys . . . and at the same time completed his translation of the German Bible. In 1546, some thirty years after he had nailed his ninety-five Theses to the door of the Castle Church at Wittenberg, he died and was buried there.

I simply taught, preached, wrote God's Word: I did nothing... The Word did it all.

GABRIEL MÜTZENBERG

Zwingli: First of the Reformed Theologians

Ulrich Zwingli was a man of the mountains, a peasant. He was born in 1484 amid the high mountains at Wildhaus in Switzerland. His strong simplicity was to be expressed in his translation of the Bible into German. In addition he had the voracious thirst for knowledge characteristic of his time.

As a boy he was destined for the priesthood, and studied in the colleges and universities of Basel, Bern and Vienna. Humanism and music fascinated him. He learnt to play the lute, the harp, the horn and many other instruments, and at the same time to read the classical languages which had been purified by the study of philology.

He was ordained priest in 1506, went with the troops to Italy as almoner and returned a declared opponent of foreign service. He loved his country, and wanted to see it strong and virtuous.

The year 1519 marked a turning-point. As preacher at the Grossmünster, the Cathedral of Zurich, he had so far simply preached the Bible. But now he gave himself without stint to pastoring his flock through a fearful epidemic of plague. He nearly died, but recovered more determined than ever to fulfil his vocation, having seen God, like Job, face-to-face. If he was dangerously ill in body, his people were spiritually more so; he put all his strength and all his faith into working for their salvation.

As he preached, gradually the Bible began to open up to him. The church had been in error, he discovered. Worse, it had deceived the faithful. It had taken to itself the divine message as a means of domination. From now on, the Bible was Zurich's book. As was to happen ten years later in Geneva, the people made it their rule. For them, as for Zwingli their pastor, it was the word of God, the gospel, the good news of salvation and of God's power in people and in the world.

The presence of Jesus Christ the Son of God made flesh and made real for the individual and for society, changed everything. In him alone are peace and election to eternal life. The church bore witness to him in its living confession of faith, and by this teaching a true community was forged, both in church and in society. The body of Christ came together at the eucharist to proclaim and to live out its freedom in him, growing stronger as its faith grew deeper.

Zwingli prefigured **Calvin**. His Reformation, carried from Bern, opened the way for Calvin to make Geneva the new Rome. It played a more important role than is often allowed. Through the city of Zurich's foolhardiness, it ended in disaster; a local war broke out, and Zwingli was killed in battle in 1531. Yet the Reformation continued, though it was not to fulfil Zwingli's vision of a totally evangelical Switzerland.

COLIN BUCHANAN

Thomas Cranmer

Cranmer, who lived from 1490 to 1556, was more than anyone else the architect of the English Reformation. He won the favour of Henry VIII, and though he had sympathy with the Protestant stance on the Bible (he secretly married the niece of Osiander, the German reformer) he held a belief in the supremacy of the King above all other causes, and seems to have adjusted his other beliefs on most points during Henry's reign.

In 1532 the Archbishop of Canterbury died, and Henry nominated Cranmer to succeed him. Cranmer made the requisite submission to the Pope (if with reservations) and was consecrated Archbishop. The last links with Rome were broken by Henry, and the Church of England became a nationalized institution. That general framework of belief and worship were to remain the same over the next fourteen years, but the tiny first steps were taken towards new doctrinal standards, a vernacular Bible, reformed preaching, and a vernacular worship-book.

During the reign of Edward VI which followed, Cranmer's theological work triumphed. He exhibited a unique combination of political power, reformed theological conviction and a gift of writing matchless English liturgical prose, expressed in *The Book of Common Prayer* of 1549, and again in the completely revised book of 1552, in which the Protestantism of the reformed Church of England stood out most clearly. His other writings include five books in reply to Stephen Gardiner *On the Lord's Supper* and *The Forty-two Articles of Religion* in 1553.

When Edward died, Cranmer was unwillingly involved in a plot to put Lady Jane Grey, a Protestant, on the throne in place of the nominated successor, Mary. So when Mary obtained the throne Cranmer was doubly certain to suffer—both for his heresies, and for his treasonable opposition to her.

The burnings of Protestants started in Spring 1555, and his own turn came in March 1556. Shortly before he died he signed a paper of recantation, but at his last trial he repudiated it, reaffirmed his Protestantism, stated that his writing on the sacrament would last till the end of the world, and went willingly to be burned outside the north wall of the city of Oxford.

That might have been the end. But Mary herself died in 1558, and the Elizabethan Settlement proved to be very largely a restoration of the work of Archbishop Cranmer. A cautious, gentle man, at the end he yet preferred the truth as he saw it in the Bible to his own principle of obedience to the monarch. Above all others he laid the foundation for reformed religion in the Church of England.

GABRIEL MüTZENBERG

Calvin and the Swiss Reformers

The Reformation was a reawakening. It was not basically an attempt at theoretical speculation and research. It was experience, life. 'Through a sudden conversion,' wrote Calvin, 'God turned and subdued my heart.' The reformer had been captured. He renounced himself to follow Christ. 'I offer my heart as a sacrifice to God.' From then on, he did not achieve his own will but another's. And when Farel begged him to stay in Geneva to establish the Reformation there, he set aside his own inclinations and agreed. 'The glory of God and what belongs to his kingdom must always come first.'

Calvin was born at Noyon, France, in 1509. In Paris, at the College de la Marché, he first acquired a taste for elegant Latin. Then, at the college at Montaigu, he embarked on a regime of excessive asceticism which both Erasmus and Rabelais were to condemn, and which finally ruined his health. He studied law at Orleans, followed the Lutheran Melchior Wolmar to Bourges and demonstrated his mastery of literature in Paris—as well as entering the great debate begun by Luther over reformation. Captured by the living Word of God, he met the humanist and Bible translator Lefèvre d'Étaples, preached the gospel and undertook an exposition of Reformed doctrine. When persecution broke out he fled to Basel where he published in Latin the first edition of his *Institutes of the Christian Religion*.

The book was a masterpiece. He revised it and added to it throughout his life. It was to be the work that set him apart as a leader. **William Farel**, a man of another generation

(1489–1565), converted around 1521 by conscientious reading of the Bible, was in no doubt about Calvin's quality. An evangelist who took no account of blows or catcalls, he preached, became an educationalist, then brought the Reformation to Morat and Neuchatel. After a hard struggle on the part of **Pierre Virel** (1511–71), from Vaud, to bring Geneva over to the Reformers, Farel detained the author of the *Institutes* in the town in 1536.

The three Reformers, bound by deep affection, saw the gospel begin to capture French-speaking Switzerland. Calvin was to stay in Geneva, apart from three happy years in Strasbourg, to his death in 1564. He began as a lecturer in the Scriptures, without pay and virtually anonymous (the secretary of the town council referred to him as 'that Frenchman'). Yet he made of Geneva the Protestant Rome, the model for churchmen and scholars throughout Protestant Europe, the first town to make public education mandatory.

The Reformation was essentially an answer to the question, 'What must I do to be saved?' 'Believe,' said Luther, 'receive God's forgiveness as a free gift.' Justification is a gift of God, received by faith, not earned by merit. The relationship between God and his creatures, marred by sin, is re-established in Christ. This salvation, Calvin insisted, is the sovereign work of God. No one can be restored to God by their own efforts. Everything comes to them as a gift, conveyed by the Word of God as a result of God's mercy and God's choice. Human destiny remains a mystery, hidden in the will of God. Yet the joy of salvation, for whoever tastes the assurance which the Holy Spirit gives, is not an empty phrase.

In the same way the church is one as Christ is one, visible in its institutions, ministry, discipline and witness, but made up of those known only to God.

Calvin applied the gospel to the whole life of society—sexuality, family life, education, welfare—and made it the basis of a new form of civilization.

John Oecolampadius, the reformer from Basel, was strongly committed to the independence of the church from the state. He had some influence over Calvin, but moved more particularly into Zwingli's orbit. Other influential laymen included humanist and doctor **Vadian**, from St Gallen; the painter, writer and statesman **Nicholas Deutsch**, from Bern; and the jurist **Joachim Bifrun**, who translated the New Testament into the Romansch language.

But Calvin surpassed them all. **Theodore Beza**, his disciple and successor, called him 'the greatest light in this world to guide the church of God'.

B. R. WHITE

Anabaptists and Baptists

The Anabaptists were given the name, meaning 're-baptizers', in the 1520s during the early years of the Reformation. They baptized only those who confessed a personal faith (many of whom had already been 'baptized' as infants). Baptists, even today, are often thought of as 'anabaptists' because they do not recognize infant baptism or 'christening' as true Christian baptism and so (in the eyes of other Christians) re-baptize. In the sixteenth century the term 'anabaptist' was also sometimes a more general term of abuse for those whose beliefs in some way conflicted with the beliefs of major churches.

The Anabaptists generally were concerned to base their church order on what they believed to be the one New Testament model authoritative for all time. They held to believer's baptism because they saw it taught in the New Testament; they saw the New Testament form of the church as basically congregational and so stressed the independence of each local gathering. Within these congregations the members helped to hold one another to a high and holy obedience to the Lord Jesus Christ.

They also believed that the New Testament required that the church should be completely separated from any form of state support or control. It was this last belief that caused most other Christians deep uneasiness. Other Christians saw the baptism of each newborn baby into the secular parish community and close links between church and state as the divinely-ordained means of holding society together. Hence many other Christians saw the Anabaptists as subversive of all order.

Consequently, from the earliest days, they were sharply persecuted and their leaders were soon executed. So they never had the opportunity to develop a united policy or one 'denomination' of Anabaptists. Some, in 1534–35, took over the city of Munster in Germany and tried to create the New Jerusalem there by force. Although the Anabaptists at Munster were a small minority of the movement, this confirmed the worst fears of other Christians and persecution immediately became more savage. **Menno Simons** drew many of the persecuted refugees together and the group named after him (the Mennonites) is the most considerable group of direct descendants of the Reformation Anabaptists in the world today.

The modern denomination of Baptists began with an exiled English congregation in Amsterdam, Holland in 1609. It is not clear that they owed a direct debt to the theological thought of the Anabaptists: they probably developed from the Puritan and Separatist traditions. But they viewed the New Testament with very similar assumptions to those of the Anabaptists.

Soon there were two main groups of Baptists: the Arminian or General Baptists who believed that Christ died for all, and the Calvinist or Particular Baptists who believed that Christ died only for the 'elect'. Although most Baptists in the world today are descended more directly from the Calvinists, their Calvinism is generally much less explicit than in the seventeenth century. Until the American Revolution the Baptists in North America were, for all practical purposes, a branch of those in Britain. However, today, the largest number of Baptists in the world is found in the United States. In the United States there are a number of major groups but the largest is the Southern Baptist Convention. Baptists all over the world are linked in the Baptist World Alliance and this includes a considerable number in Eastern Europe. They total some 35 million.

While Baptist churchmanship is basically of a congregationalist type which stresses the independent responsibility of the local congregation, Baptists have, from the earliest days, tended to link together in regional associations and national unions or conventions. In general their theology has been strongly evangelical and they have been in the forefront of Protestant missionary outreach. They have also been rather cautious about ecumenical involvement in schemes for church unions but have been active in co-operation locally with other Christians.

Today, most 'pentecostal' church groups practise believer's baptism and in a number of countries the Baptists have themselves been involved in the charismatic movement. Their patterns of worship, in consequence, vary from the extremes of informality to an emphasis upon formal and choral dignity—sometimes in the same city. Baptists, while willing on occasion to make detailed statements of their faith in the form of quite lengthy Confessions, have always believed that the final authority is the Bible and all credal statements must be judged by that alone.

JAMES PACKER

The Puritans

The Elizabethan Church of England was Calvinistic in doctrine, but its worship and order, after minimal overhauling, were more like what remained in Germany's Lutheran churches. 'Puritans'—'the pure ones—was a contemptuous word coined in the 1560s as a label for Anglicans who wanted their church to adopt various Reformed (Calvinistic) practices, and who sought higher standards of pastoral care, personal piety and national righteousness. They were opposed to wearing surplices, wedding rings, kneeling at communion and crossing babies in baptism (four practices thought to be both superstitious and without biblical authority). They attacked the fixed liturgy of the Elizabethan Prayer Book, and some came to think that bishops were not the best form of church government. Many were ridiculed for conscientiously objecting to sabbath-breaking, trivial amusements, and immoral behaviour. Acting on their biblically-informed consciences cost many Puritan clergy their posts under Archbishops Parker, Whitgift, Bancroft and Laud. Puritan pleas for change were dismissed as disruptive and disloyal, though most sober and godly citizens had puritan sympathies. In the 1620s, despairing of God's cause in old England, Puritans emigrated by the thousand to New England, founding mainly congregational churches there.

Rise and fall

In the years 1640-60 the Puritans came to exercise political control in the British Isles. The Anglican establishment was finally abolished in 1645 when parliament passed an ordinance in favour of establishing a presbyterian church order, though without the means of securing conformity. Cromwell, for his part, was content to accept this lack of uniformity and allowed freedom for each community to follow the church order it preferred: competent Reformed clergy of any party were eligible for appointment as parish ministers so long as they lived godly lives and did not use the Prayer Book.

With the fall of the Commonwealth, the return of the Stuarts, and finally the restoration of the Church of England, some 2,000 Puritan clergy left their parishes rather than conform to the restored church. Many of those who refused to conform, both clerical and lay, were imprisoned over the next twenty-five years for illegally holding non-Anglican services. In 1689 the passing of the Toleration Act, following up earlier temporary dispensations, allowed nonconformity to exist under specified conditions.

After 1662 Puritan theological and spiritual influence in the church, which had grown steadily for a century, faded away, though much of the best work of such authors as **John Owen, Richard Baxter, Thomas Goodwin, John Howe, Stephen Charnock, John Bunyan, Thomas Watson, Thomas Brooks, Matthew Poole** dates from these later years.

Puritan theology

Puritans as a body maintained the divine truth and authority of Scripture, Calvinistic views of sin, grace, faith and the church (for which 'reformed Augustinianism' would be a good name), and the necessity for church, community and individual life to be sanctified by biblical control.

Against Anglican belief that Scripture gives only general guidelines of principle for regulating church life, most Puritans were sure that it gave specific instructions for church order—though Presbyterians, Independents and Baptists, then as since, were at loggerheads as to what the instructions were. In their sense of the unity of all life and knowledge and of the solidarity of communities before God (families, churches, nations), and also in their scholastic mentality, their devotional asceticism and their view of life in this world as preparation for heaven or hell, the Puritans could be called reformed medievals. But more distinctively Calvinistic was their conviction that nothing which is not sanctified by the Bible, whether in thought, conduct or church life, can please God, with its corollary that no individual must do anything which his conscience, taught by the Bible, cannot approve.

Building on the Reformers' understanding of the justification of sinners by faith through grace, and focusing on the pastoral needs and problems of their time, Puritan teachers concentrated on the realities of salvation from sin: regeneration and sanctification; the causes and cure of hypocrisy and 'false peace'; faith and assurance; prayer and communion with God; conscience and casuistry (what we might call 'counselling'); in short, the Holy Spirit's work in the Christian, the life of God in the soul of man. Here their insights are uniquely valuable.

First in this field was **William Perkins** of Cambridge, who borrowed from Beza, Calvin's successor at Geneva, and died at forty-four leaving 2,000 folio pages of popular and technical exposition behind him. For many decades after his death in 1602, Perkins was the best-known and most widely read of English theologians. **John Bunyan's** *Pilgrim's Progress* (in two parts, 1678, 1684) is a marvellous pictorial index to Puritan lore on practical Christianity. *The Westminster Confession and Catechisms* crystallize Puritan views theoretically and for teaching. **John Owen's** expositions of Christ, the Spirit and the life of grace are classic.

The Puritans reintroduced Aquinas' view that the fourth of the ten commandments, about the Sabbath, belongs to the moral law. The Lord's Day—Jesus' resurrection day—should be kept as a sabbath of rest. Most English-speaking Christians have followed the Puritans in this until recently.

MARGUERITE BAUDE

Blaise Pascal

Blaise Pascal (1623–62) was a French mathematician, physicist and religious thinker. His scientific work began when he was not more than eleven years old. His output included treatises or essays in the fields of sound, hydraulics, physics, analytical geometry and algebra. From 1650 to 1660, his researches took him into the higher reaches of mathematics. He also invented the first calculating machine.

Meanwhile, his thoughts were moving in a religious direction, as a result of an initial conversion to Christianity in 1646, followed by a deeper and more heartfelt commitment in 1654. He then met the abbot of Port-Royal-des-Champs and was drawn towards the beliefs of the Jansenists, a group stressing the 'inner life'. He wrote *Les Provinciales (Provincial Letters)* in 1655–56, and from 1657 embarked on the writing of a defence of the Christian religion. This was to be published after his death under the title *Pensées (Thoughts)*; it was his greatest work.

Pascal's scientific genius lay in adopting a new method. From Aristotle to Descartes the field was held by an abstract, deductive approach. Pascal concentrated exclusively on fact, observation and rigorous analysis as the sole tests of truth. His new approach to science, then, was dominated by the idea of objectivity as opposed to philosophical interpretations of nature. When it came to religious thinking, he applied the same principle. The concrete must come before the abstract; in the question of knowing God, experience had the priority. This set him over against traditional religious speculations and metaphysical proofs of God.

From the time of his second conversion, he held without reserve to the truth of Christianity, both intellectually and in experience. It is within this framework that the beliefs of his *Pensées* have to be understood. The penetrating intelligence he applied to religion was tied to his personal discovery of God—the God of the Bible, incarnate in Jesus Christ.

His beliefs focus on three main points; first he had a distinctive understanding of **reason**, seen from the perspective of faith. Pascal took issue both with those who put their whole trust in reason and with those sceptics who despised it. He denounced their presumption in making man 'the measure of all things'. He also confronted those freethinkers who defended liberty of thought and morals, accusing them of being superficial, ignorant of human nature, lovers of pleasure rather than reflection. Faith transcends reason, and faith implies risk. But then faith flows from the heart, which for Pascal stands for sensibility and intuition, and 'the heart has its reasons, which reason knows nothing of'. The heart, for Pascal, is the greatest human faculty, because we use it to love God. God is not to be proved, he is to be experienced.

Second, Pascal also had his own concept of **human nature**. Humanity is full of paradox and contradiction. Majestic and degraded at the same time, we contain both the abyss and the infinite. Without God we are nothing, destined for death. We cannot know God by our own efforts; we can only be saved by him. Humanity is a paradox, but God too is a mystery; he has made himself known, yet still remains the hidden God, incomprehensible in his fullness, known only through faith. Christianity carries credence only because it makes sense of human contradictions, making us known to ourselves.

Finally, he had a characteristic view of **human existence**. Without God, we are drawn by our controlling passions to destruction and condemnation. Pleasure corrupts us and egoism ruins us. Without God life is absurdity and nothingness. We are made for eternity and the infinite, as we are aware whenever we consciously reflect on the matter.

Faith, which expresses a personal decision to say yes to God, leads to reconciliation and peace. But there is also born out of faith a transformed life and a total consecration to God. That is why Pascal was so opposed to the relativism of the Jesuits; his beliefs were rigorous and his morality uncompromising.

Pascal's thinking can be summed up in this affirmation: 'Nothing which is not God can ever bring me fulfilment.'

COLIN BROWN

The Enlightenment

Enlightenment, wrote Immanuel Kant, is mankind's emergence from immaturity. It is humanity's coming of age. It is our determination not to be bound by the dogmas and customs of bygone ages. It is our refusal to accept any authority outside ourselves. Enlightenment is mankind's endeavour to be guided by his own reason.

The eighteenth century was not yet, for the German philosopher Kant, an enlightened age. There were many vestiges of the superstitions of the past and much servile acquiescence to the authority of the church and state. But the eighteenth century was an age of enlightenment, in which people were in process of casting off external authority and bringing everything to the bar of reason.

Kant's own writings sum up this attitude to enlightenment. He undertook a thorough reappraisal of the main areas of philosophy, seeking to explore the scope and limits of reason, to work out a scheme of ethics based on rational principles, and to restate religion in terms of moral instruction. Kant himself embodied the culmination of the German Enlightenment, but the Age of Enlightenment had its roots in the seventeenth century and it extended through Western Europe, especially Britain, France and Germany, to the new world.

Hand-in-hand with enlightened philosophy went a belief that natural science, which had made impressive strides in the seventeenth century, could answer every question. Men were becoming increasingly aware of the possibility of explaining the mysteries of the universe in terms of all-embracing natural laws. Coupled with this was a growing scepticism about the church and state which joined forces in suppressing free inquiry and political liberty. Three words sum up the ideals of Enlightenment: Reason, Nature and Progress. But all three words require careful definition, and none of them means quite the same thing every time it is used.

In philosophy great stress was laid on reason. But eighteenth-century philosophy became increasingly critical of the Rationalism of the previous century. Whereas the Rationalists sought to discover the rational structure of reality by the right use of reason, eighteenth-century philosophers were more and more influenced by Empiricism with its stress on the role of the senses in acquiring knowledge. In this they followed **John Locke** (1632–1704) who believed that the mind was like a blank sheet and all its knowledge came via the senses which left impressions on it. The role of reason was to interpret these impressions. The greatest philosophical minds of the eighteenth century, **David Hume** (1711–76) and **Immanuel Kant** (1724–1804), laid great stress on reason, but were sceptical about its powers. In their different ways, both believed that we must be guided by reason. But both believed that the human mind was not equipped to speculate beyond the immediate testimony of the senses.

In politics Enlightened thought found typical expression in the idea of the social contract which also had its origins in the seventeenth century, but which found its most eloquent spokesman in **Jean-Jacques Rousseau** (1717–78). Rejecting the idea that kings were divinely appointed and their rule inviolable, Rousseau argued that the ordering of society presupposes a social contract. For the sake of public order and common good, individuals surrender part of their individual liberty. The state depends upon the general will of the people, and its laws should be framed for their common good. No law is sacrosanct. All may be changed to meet the needs of society. The government itself may be overthrown in order to create a better society. Enlightened ideas contributed to the political theorizing behind the Declaration of Independence of the United States of America (1776) and the French Revolution (1789).

Rousseau himself believed that society and religion were corrupting influences on humanity. People were born free, but everywhere they find themselves enchained by civilization. Like the Deists, Rousseau believed in the religion of nature and that Christianity was a perverted version of an original lofty, altruistic worship of the supreme being. For Rousseau progress lay in a return to nature, not least in the realm of education. Children, he believed, had a natural goodness and curiosity which should be fostered naturally rather than repressed by being made to conform to rules and learn things in which the child was not interested. For **Voltaire** (1694–1778), progress was to be obtained by stamping out the infamous one, the church, and by returning to the dictates of reason.

There was both an optimistic and a pessimistic side to the Enlightenment. Its greatest philosophers believed in reason, but were sceptical about its powers. In its most optimistic mood, the Enlightenment sought a secularized version of the heavenly city. It was to be established by rational people, setting aside ignorance and prejudice, and appealing to the naturally good and wise element in all. In its pessimistic mood, it realized that this was an impossible dream. Even the Enlightened philosophers themselves fell lamentably short of the necessary nobility of nature, and the masses did not care. Rousseau's famous phrase, 'It may be necessary to compel a man to be free', found poignant echo in the comment made of the French Revolution, 'Liberty, what crimes are committed in thy name!'

The Age of Enlightenment was also the age of many other things, not least the Evangelical Revival. In some ways the two movements might seem like polar opposites. But there were those like the preacher, theologian and philosopher **Jonathan Edwards** (1703–58) who combined the philosophical thinking of his day with the theology cherished down the centuries. The Age of Enlightenment died with the French Revolution. In philosophy and literature it gave way to Idealism and Romanticism. People felt that there must be more to reality than enlightened reasonableness. The dogmas of the Enlightenment began to look naive, hollow and artificial. But, duly adapted, its ideas passed into the bloodstream of the nineteenth and twentieth centuries.

PAUL HELM

Immanuel Kant

Immanuel Kant (1724–1804) was born of Pietist parents in Königsberg, Germany, where he lived throughout his life, becoming Professor of Logic and Metaphysics at the University in 1770. He is one of the most important, complex and difficult philosophers. He was 'awakened from his dogmatic slumbers' by reading the Scottish philosopher David Hume. His desire to combat Hume's scepticism led to his self-proclaimed 'Copernican revolution' in philosophy, expounded in *The Critique of Pure Reason*, according to which the mind is to be regarded as the organizer of sensory experience.

Kant spurned natural theology for two main reasons. He thought that some of the proofs of God's existence were invalid, but more basically he held that all attempts to think systematically about God led to contradictions in thought. But though God could not be thought, yet he could be 'postulated'. His existence is rationally required by morality, since only God can establish the highest virtue which morality requires. Kant denied the possibility of knowing God, either through reason or revelation, but upheld morality's need for God.

The moral law has its source in reason, and Kant gave central importance to the individual's duty of observing it for its own sake, and not because of pleasure or reward. Pure religious faith lies in recognizing such moral duties as the commands of God. Such religious faith is to be distinguished from the various 'ecclesiastical faiths', for though pure religious faith might arise out of them it does not depend upon any of them, but only upon reason. Hence religious faith does not depend for its validity on anything that may have happened in history, such as the death and resurrection of Jesus, much less on our knowledge of such events.

Kant's moral religion allowed for a radical approach to the Bible, since Christian faith does not depend upon it. Although Kant did not initiate the critical treatment of the biblical text his work gave impetus to it.

Kant's work in religion has provided the unquestioned starting-point for a series of influential Protestant theologians from Schleiermacher and Albrecht Ritschl to Paul Tillich and Karl Barth.

DONALD ENGLISH

Methodism and the Evangelical Revival

Methodism originated in eighteenth-century England. The present World Methodist Council has constituent churches from sixty-two countries, with a membership of 20 million and 40 million adherents.

John and Charles Wesley, ministers in the Church of England, were its founders. John (1703–91) was predominant as preacher, organizer, apologist. Charles (1707–88) wrote the hymns through which the Methodists learned their theology and celebrated their experience.

John Wesley's life was a fascinating meeting-point of many varied Christian traditions. His father was a devout, scholarly, somewhat impractical, 'high church' clergyman in the parish of Epworth, Lincolnshire. His mother raised her large family with a mixture of high-church theology, Puritan devotion and sturdy independence. Her influence on his life was an abiding one.

At Oxford University, John led a group of students dubbed the 'Holy Club'. They met for Bible study, prayer, discussion, reading and social caring, and were committed to disciplined living and study, together with faithful attendance at sacraments. Here John realized the essential 'inwardness' of Christian experience, as he deepened his knowledge of early Christian, Roman Catholic and Church of England, mystical and neo-platonist, Puritan and other writings.

In 1725, after much heart-searching, he offered himself for ordination, seeking to give himself wholly to God, a decision which marked the following years with enormous zeal and dedication.

In 1735 John and Charles Wesley went to Georgia as missionaries. It was a disastrous experience for both of them, but brought them into close contact with an influence that was to be decisive— Reformation teaching as understood and experienced by a Pietist group called the Moravians. They had a simple faith in Christ, a strong emphasis on the death of Jesus on the cross, an intimate though disciplined fellowship and powerful missionary zeal. On returning to England in 1738 John and Charles met the Moravian Peter Bo..hler. He convinced them that conversion as an immediate experience of justification by grace through faith was biblical, contemporary, and what they were needing.

The experience came to John after the reading of words by Martin Luther. His account of it is memorable. 'About a quarter before nine, while he was describing the change which God works in the heart through faith in Christ, I felt my heart strangely warmed. I felt I did trust in Christ alone for salvation and an assurance was given me that he had taken away *my* sins, even *mine*, and saved *me* from the law of sin and death.'

This experience was the turning-point for the Wesleys' ministry. John travelled, on horseback or coach, some quarter of a million miles, preaching 40,000 times, though banned from many pulpits, often physically assaulted, and constantly criticized by religious leaders who suspected or resented the success of his preaching. The message has been summed up as: 'All men need to be saved, all men can be saved, all men can know themselves saved, and all men may be saved to the uttermost.' The source and authority for his entire message was the Bible, though tradition, reason and experience were not neglected.

The Methodists were organized in Societies for mutual fellowship and growth. They practised social righteousness in concern for their neighbours and their nation. Wesley protested that they would not leave the Church of England—they received the sacraments and attended Anglican worship. Yet steadily they became independent—only partly because the Church of England seemed incapable of containing them. When Wesley died there were 77,000 Methodists in England, and 470 preaching houses, the most famous of which are the first, Wesley's New Room in Bristol, and the eventual headquarters, Wesley's Chapel in City Road, London.

Methodism was not the only element in the eighteenth-century Revival. **George Whitefield**, who also belonged to the Holy Club, was a notable evangelist, and was supported in a much more Calvinistic theological position by Selina, Countess of Huntingdon. Other Church of England clergy were also prominent, including **Samuel Walker, William Grimshaw, Henry Venn, and John Berridge.** Some of them worked with Wesley, but many would not join him because of his use of lay preachers, his 'Arminian' theology in stressing human response to divine grace, and his habit of preaching in other men's parishes. A little later came **Charles Simeon**, who did much to consolidate an Evangelical party within the Church of England which is a powerful influence to this day.

Another branch of the Revival was among those Christians known as **Dissenters**. Organized as Independents, Presbyterians or Baptists, they had lost some of their early zeal, but the Evangelical Revival influenced them also, and the hymns of the great hymn-writers **Isaac Watts** and **Philip Doddridge** were used by the Methodists.

After the wars of the seventeenth century, in the face of rationalist philosophy, the degraded lifestyle of the many poorer people and the possibility of a revolution like the one which was to tear France apart, the eighteenth-century Revival was a notable example of God's work at a time when the nation desperately needed it.

JOHN DRANE

Schleiermacher

Friedrich Schleiermacher was born into a pious German family in 1768, and by the time he died in 1834 he was one of the most influential theologians in Europe. He dabbled in politics and the church, but his first love was always the study of philosophy and its relevance to the Christian faith.

Christians had traditionally taken their beliefs about God from two sources: the natural world and the Bible. When human reason had reached its limits, the Bible was appealed to for certainty about God's dealings with men and women. But things changed with the Enlightenment. The Bible began to be looked on as an ordinary book, containing not revelations about God but a mixture of history, ancient philosophy and mythology. And none of that seemed as if it would stand up to critical scrutiny.

So Schleiermacher felt that religious belief would remain credible only if it was removed from the realm of rational investigation altogether. He therefore argued that the essence of religious belief is quite different from the essence of things such as behaviour or science that can be analysed rationally. Faith, he said, is pure feeling—the feeling shared by all religious people, that they are totally dependent on someone or something other than themselves.

This certainly rescued Christianity from the onslaughts of the rationalists. But what was left was a very vague, subjective belief. God, for example, could be defined only as 'whatever people felt dependent on'. Sin was nothing more than our natural self-assertiveness and desire for independence. Jesus too was regarded as the supreme example of a dependent person, but nothing more.

Schleiermacher's distinction between the world of reason and the world of religion has been so widely accepted by more recent theologians that he has rightly been dubbed 'the father of modern theology'. Despite that, many people, Christians and non-Christians alike, would question the wisdom of trying to separate religious faith from facts that are open to rational investigation. Most people would regard a religion that is based solely on the feelings of committed believers as not only irrational and subjective, but also worthless.

ANTHONY THISELTON

The Rise of Biblical Criticism

The term 'biblical criticism' is used of a variety of approaches and methods used in the scholarly study of the Bible. It stresses the importance of historical, linguistic and literary questions. Serious biblical criticism began in the seventeenth century, when the intellectual climate of the day demanded that every belief be submitted to critical questioning, and nothing could be accepted simply on the basis of tradition.

The philosopher **Baruch Spinoza** (1632–77) urged the importance of asking about the authorship, date, occasion and purpose of the biblical writings. **Richard Simon**, a French Roman Catholic priest, carried this approach further, and concluded, for example, that Moses could not have written the whole of the first five books of the Bible, the Pentateuch.

One major question emerged in the eighteenth century which is still with us. **J. S. Semler** (1725–88) attacked what he called the 'pietistical sanctimoniousness' with which the Bible is often used. He argued, instead, for a purely historical, non-doctrinal, approach to the Bible. But can biblical criticism be independent of Christian theology? Today many scholars try to adopt some kind of middle position.

A second major issue concerned the identification of 'sources' within the Bible. **J. G. Eichhorn** (1752–1827) proposed the existence of sources within the Old Testament on the basis of such phenomena as differences in style and vocabulary and duplication of material. **Julius Wellhausen** (1844–1918) developed a theory of sources of the Pentateuch which turned traditional understanding of biblical chronology upside-down, arguing that the prophetic writings were earlier than the Law. Critics of Wellhausen saw that his scheme fitted in all too readily with the evolutionary philosophies of the day, but others claimed that it made better sense of the data.

Source criticism was also applied to the first three Gospels. **J. J. Griesbach** (1745–1812) was the first to produce a 'synopsis', which set out the similarities and differences between them in parallel columns. This ushered in a succession of different theories about the sources of these Gospels and which draws from which—a question still debated.

A third fundamental issue raised by biblical criticism stems from the attempt to identify different theological outlooks within the Bible itself. **F. C. Baur** (1792–1860) argued that within the New Testament there was a 'Pauline' type of Christianity which was very different from that of Peter and the Jerusalem Church. He also argued that only four of Paul's letters were genuine. The debate about different 'theologies' continues today.

A further set of questions was raised around 1890-1920 by the so-called 'history of religions' approach. Scholars such as **Gunkel** and **Bousset** attempted to view biblical faith against the background of other cults and religions. This inevitably raised questions about parallels, similarities and possible borrowings.

Between 1920 and 1950 form criticism of the Gospels emerged. This enquired into the shaping of the material in a period of oral transmission before it was committed to writing. **Rudolf Bultmann** (1884–1976) contributed to this movement, arguing that very little could be traced back to Jesus himself. Since 1950 attention has shifted to redaction criticism, which focuses on the distinctive theological concerns and literary methods of the Gospel-writers themselves.

Other important approaches include textual criticism (the evaluation of manuscripts) and critical assessment of how archaeological discoveries bear on biblical history.

ANTHONY THISELTON

Søren Kierkegaard

Søren Kierkegaard (1813–55) insisted that Christian faith is more than a matter of having 'correct' beliefs. Faith involves personal commitment and practical obedience. If faith is thought of simply as having the right ideas, then there is always the danger that it can be secondhand and so superficial or false.

Kierkegaard came to hold this view for a number of good reasons. First, there was a strong element of formalism in the Lutheran Danish State Church of his day. He attacked what he called 'nominal' Christianity, the idea that 'we are all Christians'. He wrote with irony: 'Christianity has been abolished by expansion.' The human race wanted to 'sneak out of being a Christian by the help of this shoal of name-Christians.' Society treated even an atheist as a Christian as long as he could afford the fee for a church funeral!

Second, as a young man Kierkegaard had always held his father in great respect, and even began to train for ordination to the Christian ministry mainly to meet his father's wishes ('He believes that Canaan itself lies on the other side of a theological degree.') But then he discovered things in his father's life that surprised and shocked him, and which seemed to belie his father's seemingly strict and rigid Christian faith. At that moment Kierkegaard decided to think and to do not what others expected of him, but only what seemed true or worthwhile in his own experience.

Kierkegaard went through a period of crisis and even of moral decline. But through his anguish and despair he eventually found

> The books of the New Testament are to be read as human books and examined as human books... The more exact the criticism and the more rigorous the judgment, the better.

faith. He remained an individualist, and for this reason he was never entirely successful in throwing off doubt and uncertainty. Yet for him, this aspect was precisely what gave faith an authentic stamp. Faith, he insisted, must always be a moment-by-moment experience. He urged that faith must never rest on some false security such as formal church membership or a supposed improvement in moral conduct, or even on a past once-for-all experience. In his own life, however, this seemed also to mean the anguish that sprang from an almost daily struggle with doubt.

Third, Kierkegaard despised the armchair ease with which philosophers of the day claimed to have access to the thoughts of God. No one, he urged, can see the whole of reality, and even a glimpse into a little of the truth is always a costly matter. Knowledge of God is never a matter of theory; still less, of trying to prove his existence. 'To prove the existence of one who is present is a shameless affront since it is an attempt to make him ridiculous... One proves God's existence by worship.' True knowledge of God will transform the one who knows him and will involve him in a costly discipleship. For truth concerns life no less than it concerns thought.

ALISTAIR MASON

Newman and the Tractarians

England had a religious revival in the early nineteenth century. From it came, among other things, Victorian respectability, and Tractarianism, the rediscovery by Protestants of the Catholic tradition.

The other name for Tractarianism is the Oxford Movement. One Oxford college, Oriel, had led the way in reviving academic standards in the university. Its Fellows also led the way in suggesting practical reforms in the Church of England. In 1832 a reforming Whig government came into power, and under it (and the Tory government that followed it) the church had its finances and administration put in order. The Tractarians emerged as a group of younger Fellows at Oriel opposed to these useful, and inevitable, reforms. They saw any change as a political intrusion in the church's affairs and stirred up Tory feeling against the spokesmen of reform. Their leaders were **John Henry Newman**, who was Vicar of the University Church, **Hurrell Froude**, and (ex-Oriel) **John Keble**, already famous for his religious poetry in *The Christian Year*.

In 1833 these men began to publish the *Tracts for the Times*. Newman wrote several of them, in a lively quotable style, urging clergymen to think what their ordination meant. 'Magnify your office,' he wrote. Perhaps tidy-minded reforms were reducing the church to a branch of the civil service. Perhaps, as Froude said, 'the gentleman heresy' was turning Anglican clergy into nothing but gentlemen. Certainly the Church of England, like many other churches in the nineteenth century, had to find its own voice apart from the state.

The Tractarians rediscovered this in the Catholic tradition. Like other Romantics, they discovered a sense of history. How different English Protestantism was from the Middle Ages, and from the early church! Some wonderful things had been lost. They discovered the (Roman Catholic) churches of the Continent. French Catholicism, winning back ground after the French Revolution, seemed much more adapted to facing the modern world.

By talking in this vein, the Tractarians aroused the ever-present English fears of popery. Froude had said tactless things about the English Reformation. In *Tract 90*, Newman tried to prove a Roman Catholic could sign the Anglican 39 Articles. He and his younger followers dropped his earlier argument that Anglicanism as the 'middle way' had the best of both Catholic and Protestant worlds, and spoke instead of 'our stepmother, the Church of England'. After a long agony of indecision, Newman submitted to Rome in 1845. Under the staider **Edward Pusey**, the movement developed into modern Anglo-Catholicism, less academic, more interested in ceremonial, often just as provocative.

Newman was greater than Tractarianism. His sermons search our hearts with a deep moral insight. Both in Newman and Keble there is an absence of claptrap, a sense of thinking what words mean and when to be silent. His pioneer historical thinking about the development of doctrine brought him nothing but trouble in his lifetime, but lies behind much modern Roman Catholic theology. He himself developed, and yet throughout remained true to his deepest insights, as he showed in his great spiritual autobiography, *Apologia pro Vita Sua*. He died a cardinal in 1890.

PETER COTTERELL

The Missionary Movement

The missionary movement can be said to have begun at Pentecost. Jesus had promised his followers that they would receive power and so become his witnesses. Pentecost's three thousand or so converts are a reminder that mission is about salvation from sin, making disciples and building churches.

The American historian K. S. Latourette divides the history of the missionary movement into four periods. The first five centuries saw the good news of the gospel taken as far as Britain in the West and out to China in the East, to Ethiopia in Africa and northwards beyond the Danube. Then the 'thousand years of uncertainty' (AD 500 to 1500) were years in which the church lost its Bible and forgot its mission. Even so, mission was not entirely absent: Francis of Assisi (1181–1226) made three missionary journeys to the Muslim world.

The third period is that of the 'three centuries of advance' (AD 1500 to 1800). They are signposted at one end by the Protestant Reformation and the rediscovery of salvation by faith and the restoration of the Bible in the language of the people, and at the other end by William Carey and the establishing of the 'Particular Baptist Society for propagating the Gospel among the heathen' (1792).

The fourth period, the 'great century', spans the vast enterprise of the missionary societies since that time. Missions multiplied: denominational societies such as Carey's; interdenominational societies such as the China Inland Mission, founded by Hudson Taylor in 1865; specialist missions for Bible translation such as the Bible Societies, and distribution organizations for radio and publishing. There was student work, medical and educational work, relief work through such agencies as World Vision, Christian Aid and Tear Fund. The first World Missionary Conference was held in Edinburgh in 1910. Influential in recent years has been the Lausanne Movement, an international congress in 1974 which has led to major congresses on evangelism in Africa, Asia and Latin America.

Contrary to popular opinion the missionary movement has not collapsed in the twentieth century. On the contrary, the astonishing and explosive growth of the worldwide church at the present time has led to the description of the period 1945–69 as 'the twenty-five unbelievable years', and the worldwide growth has continued into the eighties.

As the church has been planted worldwide, so the younger churches have developed their own mission outreach. A fundamental change in world mission has taken place: 'uniflow' mission (in which the West did all the sending) has ended and 'multi-flow' mission has begun.

The missionary movement today has to operate in four distinct worlds: the developed world, the communist world, the developing (or 'third') world and the Muslim world. Exciting new developments in mission are occurring (see *The Debate about Christian*

Mission). Multi-flow mission has brought Japanese missionaries to Africa, Latin Americans to Portugal, Nigerians to the Sudan. Missionaries released from their work in other lands have been redeployed amongst immigrants in Britain, France, Italy. Mission societies are co-operating rather than competing and short-term missionaries are making vital contributions to world mission. The missionary with a secular job is opening up countries otherwise closed to mission. And there is now available better training than there has ever been.

In Russia and China the church has demonstrated its power to outlast the attacks of atheism. The worldwide church is proving to be the major new factor in the missionary movement, the major vehicle for world mission.

S. W. SYKES

Liberal Theology

Liberal theology is the name given to a type of theology which has flourished in western Europe, particularly since the eighteenth century. Liberalism as a whole is the name given to a much broader movement dating from the same period, emphasizing the principle of freedom in political, economic and social matters. With reference to theology, liberalism took the form of a demand for freedom from intellectual constraints and the right to question alleged authorities, and to enquire into their credentials.

Liberal theological movements can be identified in Protestantism (where liberal theology began), in Roman Catholicism and in Judaism. In each of these contexts liberal theology takes a number of forms and passes through a number of stages. Many of its forms were strenuously resisted in the eighteenth and nineteenth centuries, and in the twentieth century there was a strong conservative counter-attack in Protestantism (associated with Karl Barth and Emil Brunner). However, liberal theology is now present in most major denominations, and provides an important stimulus for theological discussion.

The basic principle of liberalism is that all alleged authorities in human affairs ought to be subject to critical enquiry. In theology this obviously raises the question whether the sources and norms of theology are purely human. Does not the inspiration of the Bible and the promised guidance of the Holy Spirit in the church mean that authority in theology is no merely human matter? Liberal theologians argue that all theology demands human judgment, and that Christian obedience can never be blind submission to a mere assertion. Christians have a moral duty not to be naive or credulous. Many people claim to speak with divine authority; it is unavoidable that we discriminate between such claims.

Liberal theologians also have argued that Christians must respond intellectually to new discoveries (for example, concerning the age of the earth) and to scientific hypotheses about human origins. It is undoubtedly true that new discoveries cause people to change the way in which they understand human life. Sometimes these changes are not easy to reconcile with traditional Christian views, and prolonged and uncomfortable argument is necessary in order to clarify the situation. Liberal theologians have sometimes failed to be sufficiently critical of the status of the new hypotheses, and have been over-hasty in abandoning traditional views. At the same time, however, liberal theology has served to stimulate intellectual enquiry and keep theological thought in touch with contemporary culture.

STEPHEN NEILL

The Unity Movement

From the time of the New Testament the church of Jesus Christ has always experienced divisions; but there have always been Christians who have been deeply concerned for unity. 'Work very hard to keep the unity of the Spirit,' wrote the apostle Paul.

Particularly in the twentieth century the churches have begun to take the problem of unity seriously to heart. A fresh call to the churches to seek unity came from the third world, where missionaries found their work hindered by their divisions, and from this the whole movement took its rise.

The first World Missionary Conference (Edinburgh, 1910) is taken as the starting-point of the modern movement for unity. Out of that conference grew the movement called Faith and Order, which called Christians together to face honestly their differences of belief and church organization and to seek the way out from them into unity (Lausanne, 1927). Just about the same time (Stockholm, 1925), Life and Work called the churches to make common cause in their response to the social and international problems of the world.

In 1938 these three movements decided to create a World Council of Churches, to be a fellowship of churches which confess Jesus Christ our Lord as God and Saviour. The first assembly, at which more than a hundred churches were represented, was dominated by Western churches. But gradually the fellowship has extended itself to every continent and to almost every country. Apart from the Roman Catholic Church, which still feels unable to join, all the main divisions of the church are found within the fellowship. The aim of the World Council is unaltered—to work for the unity and renewal of the church.

Many other movements are developing at the present time. Some are regional (especially in Asia and Africa); some are confessional (such as the Lutheran World Federation); some have a doctrinal basis (fellowships of evangelicals). Some believe only in a spiritual unity, but most hold that there should be a visible unity so that the world may see and believe.

Every year (18–25 January) Christians meet to pray that God will give to the church that unity which Jesus Christ intended for it. There is still a long way to go, but there are also many signs that these prayers are being heard. At least today, for the first time for centuries, many Christians are as concerned for the welfare of the whole worldwide church as they are for their narrower denominational concerns.

I pray that they may all be one. Father! May they be in us, just as you are in me and I am in you. May they be one, so that the world will believe that you sent me.

Part of Jesus' great prayer recorded in John 17

JULIAN WARD

The Pentecostals

During the late nineteenth and early twentieth centuries there developed among Christians influenced by various revivals and spiritual awakenings a desire for a closer experience of God. Some 'holiness groups' taught the possibility of an experience of entire sanctification, sometimes called, at that time, the baptism of the Holy Spirit; others spoke of a 'second blessing'. Some leaders and evangelists taught that the baptism of the Holy Spirit was an enduement of power for Christian service given by Christ to the believer after his conversion. There were those who taught that the power of God could miraculously heal the sick. Some also taught that after the Second Coming of Christ he will set up his millenial kingdom on earth (premillenialism) and Christians should live in expectation of his imminent return.

It was out of this background that Pentecostalism was born in America at the turn of the century. One of the key events occurred at the Bethel Bible College, Kansas, on New Year's Day, 1901, when one of the students received a vivid spiritual experience, and spoke in tongues. Other students then shared in this experience. Since then, for most Pentecostals, the supreme sign of being baptized in the Spirit is the gift of speaking in tongues (also called 'glossolalia'). The baptism in the Spirit is regarded as an enduement of power to enable Christians to witness effectively to their faith. It is received by faith and, as

But you shall receive power when the Holy Spirit has come upon you; and you shall be my witnesses in Jerusalem and in all Judea and Samaria and to the end of the earth.

Acts 1

Pentecostals understand it, is a sign that God has raised his Son from the dead and exalted him to universal lordship.

Pentecostal experience

From 1905 to 1909 the Apostolic Faith Gospel Mission in Azusa Street, Los Angeles, became a famous Pentecostal centre. People from all over the world visited it, received a Pentecostal experience and took home the message of Christ as Saviour, Healer, Baptizer in the Holy Spirit and coming King. This message was received gladly by some and provoked strong hostility amongst others. In the course of time numerous Pentecostal denominations were formed all over the world. Today, through the Charismatic movement, many Christians in the historic denominations have had a Pentecostal experience and manifest the gifts of the Spirit described by Paul, particularly in 1 Corinthians 12.

Pentecostal services are characterized by lively and enthusiastic worship with the freedom for believers to exercise the gifts of the Spirit. But disorder and undue emotionalism are usually avoided, and Paul's guidance in 1 Corinthians 14 for the right use of tongues and prophecy in public worship is generally applied. Warmth of fellowship attracts outsiders and a sense of belonging to a wider community is enhanced through regular national and international conventions.

Dynamic spiritual experience generates a natural desire to share one's faith, and evangelistic crusades are often led by healing evangelists. Converts are encouraged to study the Bible, to pray, to seek the baptism in the Holy Spirit and to join in the life of the local church. Believers are taught that they should seek to be continuously filled with the Spirit in order to manifest the fruit of the Spirit. Many Pentecostal churches adhere to forms of self-government while others belong to centrally-governed denominations.

Although neglected in earlier years, Pentecostals have a developing concern for Christian education and involvement in social and political issues. They have seen very rapid church growth in many parts of the world since their beginnings, and in Latin America Pentecostal churches are generally acknowledged to be the fastest growing churches in the world. Pentecostalism stands as a challenge to purely intellectual forms of Christianity that seem to lack a vivid experience of the presence of God. In a day when many churches are declining in numbers, Pentecostalism is a witness to the power of the gospel to transform many lives today.

HENRI BLOCHER

Teilhard de Chardin

Pierre Teilhard de Chardin (1881–1955) was a French Jesuit palaeontologist and thinker. A self-confessed 'son of the earth', Teilhard practised geology and palaeontology and won recognition for his scientific achievements. Yet Teilhard said he was equally a 'child of heaven', owing to education and to the influence of his mother whose devotion to the Sacred Heart affected him deeply. Religious fervour and passionate interest in science at first collided: God and the world vied for his heart like two 'rival stars'. Teilhard reconciled them in traditional Jesuit fashion: through worldly asceticism and militant mysticism.

Teilhardism emerged as a new worldview and a new interpretation of Christianity fused in one. Biological Evolution (all-embracing, from electrons to modern cultures) and Redemptive Incarnation stood for the same universal process, transmuting Multitude into Unity, Matter into Spirit, into God. The clue to the meaning of all life is found by taking into account the whole 'phenomenon', the total picture, not leaving out human thought and its fruits ('noosphere'), and seeing the world as evolving ('cosmogenesis') rather than static.

Evolution is moving ever upwards towards a peak: the Omega point. Omega,

Teilhard shows, must be personal *and* absolute, eternal: Omega is Christ. Optimistically, he saw evil as only a by-product of evolution, something which in turn will contribute to universal progress: redemptive evolution.

Teilhard composed some two hundred essays expounding his 'Hyper-Physics' and 'Neo-Christianity'. These include *The Divine Milieu*, a mystical tract (1926–27) and his major synthesis, *The Phenomenon of Man* (1938–40).

As guardians of orthodoxy his Catholic superiors prevented the spread of Teilhard's vision; he lost his professorial post, was sent away from Paris and was forbidden to publish his works except for technical papers. They were printed only after his death. The Holy Office warned against them (1962), but they exerted immediate influence, not least on the Second Vatican Council. Teilhardism has since been compared with 'process theology'; although foreign to dialectical thinking, it has opened the way for (or been combined with) Neo-Marxist views in theologies of 'hope' and 'liberation'.

JAMES B. TORRANCE

Karl Barth

Karl Barth (1886–1968) was born in a Swiss Protestant home. He studied in Switzerland and Germany before the First World War under some of the leading liberal theologians of the day, but during his first pastorates in Geneva and Safenwil came to see the bankruptcy of much Protestant humanistic thinking in a war-torn world. In his early *Commentary on Romans* (1919) he sought to call the church back to the living God of the Bible who has spoken to us once and for all in Jesus Christ the living Word, and who meets us as the transcendent Lord in the present moment in the crisis of decision and encounter. The theology of this earlier period of his life has been called the 'theology of crisis' or 'dialectical theology' because of its stress on the cross of Christ as God's 'yes' and 'no' to the world—his word of both grace and judgment.

In 1932 he began writing his massive *Church Dogmatics*, which was to occupy his mind for the rest of his life, where his concern was to unfold the implications of the Christian doctrines of the trinity and the incarnation in every area of Christian life and doctrine.

Two things produced the shift to this more Christ-centred approach. The first was the recognition that the existentialism of his earlier period, with its one-sided emphasis on the present moment of divine-human encounter and decision, could weaken the central stress of the Bible on what God has done for mankind in reconciling the world to himself in Christ. The second was the rise to power of Hitler, with the persecution of the Jews and the 'natural theology' of the 'German Christians', who sought to justify National Socialism and racist policies by appealing to a doctrine of the natural 'orders of creation'. This Barth felt betrayed the Christian understanding of grace by appealing to sources of revelation other than Jesus Christ: he was the Jew in whom God has broken down the barriers between the Jews and all other ethnic groups (the 'Gentiles'); he is head over church and state; to him alone we owe supreme loyalty. This found explicit formulation in the *Barmen Declaration* of 1934, which was largely Barth's work. Barth was deprived of his Chair by the Nazis in 1934 and became Professor of Theology in Basel in his native Switzerland.

Barth's unique and lasting contribution was to unpack with great consistency the Christian doctrine that the Son of God, by whom and for whom all things and all people were created, himself became man to fulfil his purpose of binding God and humanity together in covenant love. Barth saw himself standing in the tradition of the ancient fathers of the church and the Protestant Reformers, engaging in lifelong dialogue with liberal Protestantism on the left and Roman Catholicism on the right—both of which he felt weakened the emphasis of the Bible that God accepts us by grace alone in Jesus Christ.

GEORGE CAREY

Process Theology

Process Theology in its origin was closely associated with the great mathematician and philosopher **A. N. Whitehead.** It offers itself as a modern restatement of the Christian faith which has its basis in what Whitehead and others saw as two failures: the failure of Christianity to show how God is at work in an evolving and expanding universe; and the failure of science to detect purpose in the universe whilst allowing it in the affairs of men.

The Process theologian starts with four assumptions: that the universe is not static but evolving; that purpose is to be discerned in creation; that beauty and order, ugliness and disorder, mind and matter belong together; and that God is actively involved in creation and is personally affected by events.

The word 'process' should therefore be taken very seriously. Because God is in active relationship with the universe, even he cannot be outside the process. Although Lord of all, as Creator of the ever-changing process he must include all the possibilities of change in himself. God is therefore viewed as being 'dipolar' in nature—'primordial' and 'consequent'.

Both God and the world are affected by their 'meeting' which is called the 'creative nexus'. For God there are failures as well as successes: things go wrong as well as right. The Christian must take the things that fail as seriously as the successes of creation.

By working from the reality of evolution, Process Theology deals more seriously than most philosophies with the age-old problem of evil and pain. These are seen as inevitable consequences of creation in process of 'becoming'. But such is God's personal involvement in the universe that nothing is lost, because he ceaselessly works to draw all things to himself.

Criticism of Process Theology has been extensive and includes the following: that its doctrine of God implies pantheism (that is, confusing God with the world, making God as temporal as the world and the world as eternal as God); that it has an over-optimistic view of the value of evil; that it underestimates the seriousness of sin; that Christ is not central to its thought; and that it suggests that everyone will be saved.

More recent Process theologians include: **Norman Pittenger, Charles Hartshorne** and **John Cobb**. The writings of Teilhard de Chardin tie in very closely with it. Process Theology appeals to the self-consciousness of twentieth-century people who are not satisfied with a simple 'God-out-there' religion.

Glossary of terms used in Process Theology

Primordial aspect. That aspect which God had from the beginning of containing in himself all the potentialities of life.

Consequent aspect. That aspect of God which comes into contact with what is not himself, which is changed through the encounter.

Dipolar nature. That the two aspects belong together and God works through creation to bring about his purposes.

BISHOP DAVID GITARI

The East African Revival

The East African Revival is described here as typical of many different movements in different parts of the world, though it has its own distinctive East African emphasis. It is a spiritual reawakening movement which began in Rwanda in 1936. The movement spread to Uganda, Kenya and Tanzania and has continued to influence the life of the church in Eastern Africa to the present day.

The movement has consistently preached the need for every person to accept Jesus Christ as a personal Saviour. Baptism and confirmation are in themselves inadequate for salvation. When people give their testimony that they have accepted Jesus Christ as a personal Saviour, they are received into the revival fellowship by the singing of the chorus popularly known as *Tukutendereza*, a Luganda word meaning 'Praise the Lord'.

The new 'brothers and sisters in the Lord' are expected to live lives of daily fellowship with the Lord and constant self-examination. They are expected to attend the weekly fellowship meetings where they have to 'walk in light'. To walk in light means giving a testimony of how one has been spiritually since the previous meeting. If someone has fallen into any temptations, these are to be revealed as an indication of a person's commitment to live a life of constant self-examination and repentance.

The message of East African Revival is to a large extent biblical and evangelical. The Revival Brethren are keen and dedicated Christians and are pillars of the local congregations. The movement has, however, tended to be legalistic in that stress has been put on external things in determining whether a person is genuinely saved or not. The fact that the majority of leaders in the movement have not been theologically trained has made the movement fall into a number of controversial heretical teachings from time to time which have caused schism. These controversies have generally been short-lived and have not caused much damage to the movement.

More seriously, the *Kufufuka* (raised from the dead) controversy has split the movement for about twenty years. The *Kufufuka* brethren have a testimony of not merely being saved but also having been 'raised from spiritual slumber', which they interpret in purely legalistic terms. They preach against taking bank loans, paying dowry, keeping dogs and keeping their daughters in their homes if they have illegitimate children. This schismatic movement is now much weaker than it was a decade ago.

Despite its weaknesses, the Revival movement has had a great impact in the life of the church in East Africa. One great advantage is that the movement has remained within the church rather than trying to form a separatist church. It has therefore helped to revive the church and challenge nominal Christianity. It was the Revival brethren who, in the early fifties, were able to bear witness courageously during the Mau Mau uprising in Kenya. Many died as martyrs as they were not prepared to deny the name of Jesus. The same can be said of Revival brethren in Uganda during the time of Idi Amin.

Some of the leading East African Revival brethren have been able to share the message of Revival in other parts of the world. These include **William Nagenda** of Uganda and **Bishop Festo Kivengere**. The basic message of personal salvation and daily fellowship with the Lord is necessary to all Christians everywhere. The East African Revival has remained an East African phenomenon primarily because it has embraced a kind of East African culture which is difficult to export elsewhere.

JOH. HEINRICH SCHMID

Rudolf Bultmann

Coming from a background of liberal theology, Rudolf Bultmann (1884–1976) at an early stage embraced the dialectical theology of Karl Barth, but passed beyond it. With Martin Dibelius (1883–1947) he was founder of the school of 'form criticism', as applied to the study of the Gospels. Bultmann's system of 'demythologizing' the New Testament has aroused both worldwide support and fierce debate within the churches.

In contrast to traditional Christian belief, Bultmann distinguishes between historical reality and non-historical 'truth as received by faith'. The only exceptions are the life and crucifixion of Jesus which must be historical, though his resurrection is not. The 'how?' and 'why?' of Jesus' life and death are however unimportant for the Christian. History and faith lead in different directions. Historical certainty as a basis of faith is just as improper as Catholic justification by works.

Unlike Kierkegaard, Bultmann does not see the key salvation event as the life of Jesus, but his death. He does not see in the death of Jesus a sacrifice or atonement, but the liberating judgment of God on all human selfishness. To believe in the cross means to surrender to its security and to live from then on by God's grace and forgiveness. This means dying to oneself and to the world and so appropriating the cross of Christ for oneself. This is personal resurrection.

Bultmann is most famous for his article on 'Demythologization' which appeared in 1941. He maintains that the story of salvation as presented in the New Testament is myth. Today it must be reinterpreted. ('Myth' is a way in which the 'other-worldly-divine' is expressed in 'this-worldly-human' terms.) He denies (as does all liberal theology stemming from Kant) that God can reveal himself in actual history.

Bultmann's use of the term 'myth' is derived from the study of the history of religions in which all 'other-worldly-divine' falls into the same category. It is certainly not based on what the Bible claims for itself or for God.

How should the gospel be reinterpreted today? Bultmann adopted the existentialist ideas of the philosopher Martin Heidegger (1889–1976). Certain basic awarenesses, so-called 'existentials', are part of human existence; humankind is aware of its own existence, its responsibility and threats. We all make decisions. We experience trouble, anxiety and death. People can lose themselves or save themselves. The gospel must be expounded in terms of these 'existentials' in such a way that we learn from Christ to understand our situation in new terms.

In trying to reinterpret the gospel, Bultmann has aimed to make it relevant to the world of today. But rather than taking the gospel as it stands in the New Testament and applying it afresh, he has tried to fit it into a completely different mould, that of existentialist philosophy, so producing a different message.

ROBERT ENGLAND

Hans Küng

Hans Küng, a Swiss (born 1928), is a Catholic theologian who first achieved fame with the publication of a doctoral thesis on 'justification'; he maintained that, properly understood, there was no essential difference on the nature of justification between the teaching of the reformed theologian Barth and that of the Catholic Church.

Similar success attended other less technical works such as *The Council and Reunion* (1961), which sought to prepare Catholics for the Second Vatican Council. Here, and in his later more sustained treatments on the theme of the church, Küng presented the Catholic position in a forward-looking way. He stressed the place of the Holy Spirit in the church and replaced the emphasis on the clergy, bishops and papacy with one on the whole people of God. The papacy was seen as a ministry of service in succession to Peter rather than a monarchy with temporal power or supremacy of rule over the whole church. This stance has been applied practically in the many acute and penetrating criticisms of the church's life voiced in Küng's shorter works. Church unity, and Catholic renewal and reform, have been his constant interests.

Throughout, Küng's work has been marked by the application of the historical method to biblical texts, church traditions and especially church formulations of the faith. This enabled him to avoid mere repetition of past teaching and where necessary to sit lightly to traditional positions.

The publication in 1970 of the book *Infallible* took the previous criticisms of the papacy to their logical conclusion. Küng called in question the historical basis of the papal claims and challenged the implied infallibility of certain papal declarations concerning birth control. He contradicted the central papal assertion that under certain defined conditions the church could speak infallibly through the person of the Pope, and that such statements were inherently free from error. Küng preferred to speak of the church 'remaining in the Truth'. This suggestion provoked a still unfinished debate and brought Küng into renewed conflict with the church authorities, who ultimately withdrew recognition of him as an accredited teacher of the Roman Catholic faith.

The controversy highlighted Küng's exceptional gift of identifying issues which trouble the mind of the church and writing about them in depth. Thus the immense success of Küng's magisterial work *On Being a Christian* (1974) is due in large measure to its ability to speak of Christ out of an astonishing empathy with the mood, concerns and dilemmas of secularized, industrial people.

TOM SMAIL

The Charismatic Movement

The Charismatic movement has been very influential among both Protestants and Catholics from the 1960s on. The word 'charismatic' refers to the *Charismata*, the gifts of grace, such as tongues, prophecy and healing, which in the New Testament the Holy Spirit gives to believers to build up the church and empower it for its mission. Against traditional teaching that these gifts were for the early church only, charismatics claim to have rediscovered them and to be exercising them today. The movement is sometimes called neo-Pentecostalism, because it represents the overflow of the distinctive insights and experiences of the Pentecostal denominations into the historic churches.

The movement rose in reaction to the secular Christianity of the sixties which had little room for experience of God, and also to an evangelical religion which overemphasized correctness of belief and behaviour and left little scope for immediate spiritual experience. For the charismatics, God is not dead or distant but living and working among his people, bestowing gifts and power.

Following the Pentecostals, charismatics testify to a personal experience usually described as being baptized in the Spirit. In answer to prayer, often accompanied by the laying on of hands, the Holy Spirit is consciously received in a fresh and immediate way which leads to new contact with God in Christ, new fellowship with others, and new ability to witness effectively. Those baptized in the Spirit begin to exercise spiritual gifts, the first of which is often—some would say always—speaking in tongues. This is prayer in phrases which the speaker does not understand but which express his praise and joy in the Spirit. The appropriateness of the phrase 'baptism in the Spirit' and its relationship to water baptism and conversion are debated among charismatics. All would insist that the experience itself is more important than the explanation of it, so that in charismatic literature, testimony has priority over teaching.

Charismatic renewal is marked by spontaneity in worship. Many share in services by exercising their spiritual gifts, and warmth and freedom are more important than formality and liturgy. The movement has majored on healing ministries both to bodies and minds. It has drawn people together in prayer groups and communities, covenanted to pray with and for one another and to share gifts, problems and tasks—sometimes even houses and possessions as well. It has made a significant contribution to Christian unity at grass-roots level, creating acceptance and affection between different kinds of Christians and notably between Catholics and Protestants.

The movement has been accused of divisiveness in making distinctions between 'first-class Christians', who have been renewed in the Spirit, and 'second-class Christians', who have not. Although its main effect has been to unite, it has also given rise to new church groupings making exclusive and sectarian claims for themselves. It has tended to overemphasize experience and underplay the need for good thinking and has been called 'a movement in search of a theology'. It has tended to look for painless, instant and miraculous solutions to all problems and failed to recognize the place of discipline, suffering and sharing Christ's cross in the Christian life. It has been largely, although not by any means entirely, unconcerned and uncreative about social issues.

Only the future will show whether this movement can outgrow these immaturities. To avoid one-sidedness, charismatics who believe in the renewal of the church need to look beyond their own limited company and concerns to all that the Spirit is doing and saying among God's people. Nevertheless, those who are sensitive to the Spirit will agree that he is excitingly and creatively at work at the heart of the charismatic renewal. From it all Christians can learn that it is only through personal and corporate experience of the Spirit that the church can convincingly and powerfully proclaim that Jesus is Lord.

ANDREW KIRK

Liberation Theology

Liberation Theology is a movement which originated in Latin America in the mid-1960s. It has since been adopted by various sections of the worldwide church, particularly where oppressive regimes exist or where there is much poverty. Taking social and political reality seriously, it seeks to discover the nature of Christian obedience in concrete situations. It has been described as a 'critical reflection on Christian praxis [action] in the light of the Word'.

It has been critical of European theology: first, for separating the meaning of the gospel from engagement in political and social struggle; second, for allowing modern secular culture to restrict faith to the private life of individuals; third, for being concerned mainly with intellectual rather than practical questions. The challenge it has faced is not that of the self-sufficiency and scepticism of a scientific age leading to dwindling interest in Christian commitment, but that of the loss of basic human rights for millions of people.

In serving the church with a continuous, relevant programme of study Liberation Theology has set itself three basic goals.

First, it aims to show why many Christians in recent years understand the task of the church differently. Liberation Theology has grown out of personal contact with acute human deprivation. From this vantage-point it interprets the Bible afresh. This has been described as doing theology from 'the edge of history', from the position of those without power to shape their future. For many centuries theology has only been done by the privileged classes.

Experience of poverty and a new reading of the Bible has led the church to see its mission primarily in terms of helping the poor to throw off oppression and become free to share equally in the wealth of their nations. It is a Christian imperative to struggle beside the poor to attain these ends. The God of the Bible specially identified himself with those who suffer from the modern idolatries of power-seeking and the personal accumulation of wealth. He demands the end of all exploitation and corruption. My humanity can be affirmed only by fully accepting that of my neighbour.

The second aim of Liberation Theology is to review constantly the church's attitudes and activities. It criticizes the church, for example, for having limited its pastoral work to the spiritual and moral needs of individuals; for creating, through a powerful educational and sacramental system, a largely passive and unthinking laity; for issuing decrees on social issues based on theoretical principles, isolated from an experience of real conditions, and for hesitating to make categorical pronouncements on grave social abuses.

Third, it aims to make theology serve a process of total human liberation. It is more concerned with Christian obedience in concrete situations than with correct belief. The latter must be judged by its ability to clarify the meaning of God's liberating activity today. This will be measured by the meaning of the kingdom as displayed in Jesus Christ, the model of a new humanity and a new age. Christian obedience will be discovered today in an experience of poverty. It will be illuminated by the Marxist class analysis of society and corrected by listening to God's Word made flesh.

Liberation Theology has provided Christians with a theological basis for a new kind of commitment. No longer defending present political and economic systems, the church in many places is now speaking officially against oppressive regimes. Meanwhile groups of Christians have become directly involved in socialist and populist governments and in grass-roots communities dedicated to achieving justice and freedom. Liberation Theology has challenged every section of the worldwide church to reconsider its understanding of its mission.

Negatively, it may be accused of blurring the distinction between God's special history of salvation and world history, and between the church and the poor in general. Sometimes it equates God's kingdom with a free and fair society in the future. It can be simplistic in its analysis of complex social systems. It may neglect the universal meaning of the cross as God's answer to idolatry, guilt and injustice, whoever may commit it.

It has raised inescapable questions. Does the church understand the gospel as good news of total liberation, as much from unjust laws and institutions as from personal guilt? Is the church's life a true reflection of God's new creation brought into being by the Holy Spirit?

Glossary

This glossary is for ready reference. To find out about a belief in more detail, it would be best to go through the index to the pages where it is dealt with in the main text.

A

Abba In Aramaic (the language Jesus used) this means 'dear father'. Jesus used it in prayer to God, and taught his followers to do the same.

Adoption Christians are 'adopted' as sons and daughters in the family of God.

Adoptionist One who believes that Jesus was adopted as *Son of God* when the Spirit descended on him at his baptism, rather than that, as the Bible indicates, he always was Son of God.

Advent (literally 'coming') Refers to Jesus' first coming, in his *incarnation*, and to his *second coming*, at the end of the age.

Agnostic One who believes that spiritual questions cannot be settled one way or the other because of the limitations of human knowledge.

Alienation (literally 'estrangement'). Used by Karl Marx to describe how repetitive work estranges people from their creativity. Christians also sometimes use it of humanity's separation from the life of God.

Allegory Speech or writing where the literal meaning takes second place to the symbolic meaning. Some Bible *interpretation*, especially in the *early church*, saw more allegory in the Bible than is really there.

Almighty Describes God's ability to do anything which is not against his character and laws.

Altar Place where *sacrifices* are made. Frequently used in the Old Testament, but altars are no longer needed since the final sacrifice of the *death of Jesus*. However, the word has come to be used of the *holy table* in the *eucharist.*

Amen The word Christians commonly use at the close of each prayer. It means 'let it be so'.

Anabaptist (literally 'one who re-baptizes') Radicals at the time of the *Reformation*, who believed that the Reformers did not go far enough in restoring *church order* to the New Testament pattern.

Analogy The method of description which compares like with like. In religious matters, we often express ourselves through 'the language of analogy', as when we say 'God is Father', meaning that God's relationship to humanity has some likeness to our own parenting.

Angel (literally 'messenger') Spiritual being who serves God. According to the Bible, angels' chief role is *worship*, but they also undertake tasks which bring them into contact with human life.

Anglican Member of the Church of England, or of a member-church of the 'Anglican Communion', the worldwide fellowship of churches in special relationship with the Church of England.

Anglo-Catholic Member of the Anglican Communion whose beliefs and practices are in some ways close to those of *Roman Catholics*, Modern Anglo-Catholics are successors of the *Tractarians.*

Antinomian One who holds that the *Law of God* in the Bible has no place in Christian life. Many believe this is not the New Testament view.

Apocalyptic A type of writing which uses images and symbols, as in the book of Revelation and some of the prophets.

Apocrypha See *Deuterocanonical writings.*

Apologetics (from the Latin *apologia*, a legal speech for the defence) The study of how to justify Christianity in face of ideas or cultures that oppose it. The *Apologists* were second-century defenders of the faith against both Judaism and polytheism.

Apostle (literally 'one who is sent') One of the twelve men appointed by Jesus to 'be with him and be sent out to preach'. After Jesus' *ascension*, as eye-witnesses of the resurrection, the apostles (less Judas Iscariot) spread the gospel and founded the church. (Paul was made an apostle through meeting the risen Jesus).

Apostolic fathers Christian writers and leaders in the time directly after the apostles.

Apostolic succession In Catholic belief, the unbroken line of *bishops* from the *apostles* to the present, such that each new bishop has been consecrated by other bishops in the succession. Some hold that the early part of this line is not demonstrable.

Arianism The belief that the *Son of God* is neither eternal nor divine; it thus undermines belief in the *Trinity*. Arius was condemned at the *Council* of Nicea (325), but Arianism continued for some time after that.

Arminian One who holds that people are free to choose for or against faith in Jesus Christ, and that Christians can fall away from such faith. These beliefs, which derive from sixteenth-century Dutchman Jacobus Arminius, stand in opposition to some emphases within *Calvinism.*

Ascension Jesus' return to his Father's glory and his exaltation as King. It took place in his disciples' presence forty days after his *resurrection* and ten days before the giving of the Spirit at *Pentecost.*

Asceticism (literally 'training') Self-denial and self-discipline, sometimes used by Christians to avoid being mastered by the world. Often a feature of *monasticism.*

Assumption (sometimes called 'Bodily Assumption') The belief, not found in the New Testament but held by Roman Catholics, that the Virgin Mary was taken up body and soul into heaven at the end of her life.

Atheist One who believes there is no god. This is not a very common belief, since many people without faith in God are in fact *agnostics.*

Atonement (literally 'at-one-ment') The bringing of people back into relationship with God. In the Old Testament this was achieved through animal *sacrifices*, but the *death of Jesus* made full and final atonement for everyone who believes in him.

Authority That which can rightfully command our total acceptance and obedience. For Christians, authority lies in God through Jesus Christ. One great issue at the *Reformation* was whether God's authority comes to us through the church (as Catholics believe) or through the *Bible* (the Reformers' teaching). More recently, *reason* and spiritual intuition have become alternative authorities.

B

Baptism The washing or immersion of a person in water in the Name of the *Trinity*, as a sign of all God promises to people who are *in Christ* such as *forgiveness, new birth*, membership of the *church*. Baptism is firmly linked in the New Testament to *faith* and *repentance*. (See also *sacrament*.)

Baptism in the Holy Spirit Where John the Baptist baptized in water, to signify *repentance* and *forgiveness*, Jesus' baptism is in 'water *and Spirit*', to signify the greater gift of *new birth*. There is disagreement today as to whether this term refers simply to Christian *baptism* as such, or also to a stage of coming alive to the *Holy Spirit* subsequent to *conversion*, as some *Pentecostals* and *Charismatics* teach.

Baptist Member of the worldwide fellowship of churches which teach that only people old enough to make a personal step of *repentance* and *faith* should receive *baptism*. These churches are basically *Congregational* in *church order*.

Bible, The (sometimes also called 'the *Scriptures*') A collection of books written over a period of many centuries, which are recognized by the church as having God's *authority*. It is accepted, particularly by *Protestants*, that the Bible contains everything we need to know for *salvation*, and that beliefs not to be found in the Bible should not be made articles of faith.

Biblical criticism The scholarly study of the Bible, especially its historical background, language and literary styles.

Bishop (literally 'overseer') In the New Testament, means the same as *presbyter*, but by the second century bishops began to be in sole charge of *congregations* or of Christians in a town or area. In Catholic belief, bishops have a vital role in ensuring the continuity of *church* and *faith*.

Blessing The giving of spiritual benefits, especially through the *gospel*; sometimes it refers to the form of words used. Some Christians also use this word instead of *consecration*.

Bodily assumption See *Assumption*.

Body of Christ The most characteristic picture of the *church* used by the apostle Paul. The picture conveys that each member of the church has a role and that Christians depend on each other. Some also take it to suggest that through the church *Christ* is present in the world.

C

Calling (also known as *election*) An invitation or summons God issues to people, initially to follow him but then also to perform specific tasks in the world or the church. God's calling of people is an expression of his *grace*. Not everyone who receives God's call obeys it.

Calvary The hill on which Jesus was crucified. Sometimes used as shorthand for the *death of Jesus*.

Calvinist One who draws his beliefs particularly from John Calvin's *Institutes of the Christian Religion*. The term has come to be used particularly of those who stress God's sovereignty, and hold that God's *predestination* is more important in a person's *salvation* than human *free will*. Calvinists are thus opposed to *Arminianism*.

Canon, The The list of books regarded as rightly belonging within the *Bible*, because they possess God's *authority*. This list was finalized by the *church* in the fourth century. Before that time there was some uncertainty as to whether a few books in the final list should be excluded or a few others included.

Canon law Laws made by some churches, such as the Roman Catholic church or the Church of England, covering many matters of faith, discipline and morality.

Cardinal virtues Practical, moral virtues, especially prudence, justice, temperance and fortitude. These can be ways of expressing in everyday life the so-called 'theological virtues' of faith, hope and love.

Catechism Body of basic teaching used to instruct new believers in the Christian faith, often in preparation for *baptism* and/or *confirmation*.

Catholic Member of that tradition among the three great Christian traditions which gives first importance to the *church*, its *priests* and *sacraments*, which are seen as the chief means through which God's *grace* comes to the believer. Catholics also particularly value the continuity of the present church with the church of previous ages. The term includes *Roman Catholics* but reaches wider. See also *Western church*.

Cause Person, force or event as a result of which other events take place. Christians speak of God as the *First Cause*, through whom everything else came into being. They also accept *secondary causes*, bringing results which, while not outside God's *providence*, are not directly caused by him.

Charismatic One who particularly stresses the importance of the *Holy Spirit* in Christian life, *worship* and *witness*. The *gifts of the Spirit (charismata)* also receive great emphasis. Charismatics have much in common with *Pentecostals*, but also some differences. Some are *separatists*, but many remain firmly rooted in the main *denominations*.

Christ The Greek word for *Messiah*, so that 'Jesus Christ' means 'Jesus the Messiah'.

Christ, In A phrase frequently used by the apostle Paul. Those 'in Christ' are identified with Jesus in his *death* and *resurrection*, through which they have received *forgiveness* and *new birth*. *Baptism* is the sign of coming in Christ.

Christian One who follows Jesus Christ. The word was first used in Antioch a few years after Jesus' *resurrection* and *ascension*.

Christian Brethren (sometimes called 'Plymouth Brethren' or 'The Brethren') Members of independent *congregations* in continuity with a nineteenth-century movement to return to New Testament patterns of church life. The Brethren are not a *denomination*, and the term includes a range of congregations from the highly exclusive to those much more open.

Christening Sometimes used of the *baptism* of infants, particularly by those who do not believe infant baptism is true baptism. It refers to the giving of a name to the one baptized.

Christmas The celebration of the birth of Jesus. Christians took over an existing pagan festival, and some features date back to pre-Christian times. (See also *incarnation*.)

Christology The study of the nature of Jesus Christ, and in particular the relation between the divine and human in him.

Church The worldwide community of all those who follow Jesus Christ. It includes the 'church militant'—all Christians now living and the 'church triumphant'—all Christians who have died. Membership of the church is a vital part of what it means to be a Christian. Some distinguish the 'visible church'—a structured organization and the 'invisible church'—those within the visible church who are truly *regenerate*. The word is also sometimes used of a *congregation*, of a *denomination* or of a building in which Christians gather.

Church fathers (sometimes called *Early fathers*) Writers and thinkers in the first few Christian centuries who played a part in the formation of Christian belief.

Church order Matters to do with the government, structuring, *ministry* and *discipline* of *congregations* and *denominations*.

Circumcision The removal of the foreskin as a sign of membership in the *covenant* people of Israel. This was done to Israelite males on the eighth day after birth and to non-Israelites on conversion to Judaism. There was dispute in New Testament times as to whether Gentile converts to

Christianity should be circumcised.

Common grace See *grace*.

Communion of saints The *fellowship* of all Christians, which extends beyond death.

Confession The acknowledging of *sin*, either individually or corporately. Fundamentally, we admit sin and ask *forgiveness* from God. But the New Testament also encourages Christians to confess to each other in some circumstances. Catholics believe sin should be confessed to a *priest*, who is authorized to absolve the penitent or exact *penance*. The word is also used for a statement of faith.

Confirmation The service (Catholics would say *sacrament*) in which people already baptized are received into full membership of their *church* and are admitted to *holy communion*. It is a feature of churches which have *bishops*. Those confirmed repeat their baptismal vows and receive the *laying on of hands* from the bishop. In Catholic belief, confirmation is the sign of receiving the *Holy Spirit*. Others see baptism as the sign of this, and associate confirmation with strengthening in the Holy Spirit.

Congregation Local community of Christians who come together regularly for *worship* and co-operate in Christian *service* and *witness*.

Congregationalist One who holds that the local *congregation* should be independent of central denominational control, governing its own life as guided by the *Bible* (hence the alternative name *Independent*).

Consecration The setting apart of people or things for God's use. The word most normally refers to a believer devoting himself or herself to a holy life, but it is also used of setting apart bread and wine for use in the *eucharist* or water for *baptism*.

Conversion Turning to Christianity from some other faith or world-view or from none. It involves *repentance* and *faith*, but in all other respects each person's conversion is unique to him or her; no fixed sequence of events is required. (See also *new birth*.)

Cosmology The study of the structure, origin and development of the universe. It is of great interest to Christians because it bears on God's *creation* of all things. Each culture has its own understanding of cosmology.

Council A gathering of bishops or representatives of the whole church, to take decisions on matters of belief or practice. Important councils have been:—the *Ecumenical (or General) Councils*, held between the fourth and ninth centuries, whose decisions have held great authority in the worldwide church ever since. They are particularly highly valued by the *Orthodox churches*. The *First and Second Vatican Councils* (1870 and 1962–65) were meetings of all the cardinals and bishops of the *Roman Catholic* church.

Counter-Reformation (or 'Catholic Reformation') A movement for reform and expansion in the *Roman Catholic* church of the sixteenth and seventeenth centuries, partly in response to the *Reformation*. Among its key features were the Council of Trent (1545–63) and the beginnings of the *Jesuit* movement.

Covenant A solemn agreement made by God with his people, with the aim of securing a lasting relationship between them. The 'old covenant' (or *testament*) included the giving of God's *Law* and eventually failed through the people's inability to keep it. The prophesied 'new covenant', made through the *death of Jesus*, overcomes this drawback by ensuring *forgiveness* and *new birth*.

Covetousness A strong desire for things it is not right for us to have. The last of the Ten Commandments tells us to avoid it. Many think it the most prevalent of modern sins.

Creation God's action in bringing into being the universe and everything in it. Humanity is the crown of creation. Belief in God as Creator brings the conviction that the universe and life in it are ultimately purposeful. The question how God created has been widely debated since Darwin proposed the theory of *evolution*.

Creed Formal statements of belief made in the early Christian centuries. The central creeds (especially the *Nicene* and *Apostles'* creeds) are accepted by all Christians and are used regularly in baptismal and other *liturgies*.

Cross The wooden gallows on which Jesus was nailed to die (crucified). Sometimes used as a shorthand for the *death of Jesus*. The cross has become the central emblem of Christianity. (See also *Calvary*.)

Cults Deviations from Christianity, often incorporating some ancient *heresy*. Their members are often marked by single-minded commitment. It is characteristic of cults to concentrate on some aspect of faith to such an extent as to make the whole structure unbalanced.

D

Deacon (literally 'servant') In the New Testament, appointed initially to help in practical matters, but soon developed wider ministries. Since then, 'deacon' has become a specific office in the church, though interpreted differently in different traditions.

Death of Jesus The New Testament sees Jesus' crucifixion as the central part of God's plan for our *salvation*. Jesus died in our place, as our *representative* and *substitute*, so that we could receive God's *forgiveness* rather than *judgment*. Jesus' death is the basic act of God's *grace*. (See also *atonement*.)

Deist One who believes in God, but not that God has revealed himself to mankind directly. A Deist believes in a this-wordly religion providing the basis for an upright life. This seventeenth-century philosophy was the basis for the eighteenth-century *Enlightenment*.

Demon Evil spirit working for the *Devil* against God and goodness. Jesus saw demons invading people's personalities and frequently he cast them out. Belief in demons is common in primitive cultures, but has only recently been re-emphasized in the West.

Denomination Organized grouping of *congregations* with similar beliefs, *church order*, and/or *liturgy*. These groupings are commonly international, and it is through them that Christians relate to other denominations, to civic structures and to governments.

Deutero-canonical writings Books whose qualifications to be included in the *canon* of *Scripture* are disputed. Catholics include these writings as part of the Bible, but Protestants consider them to be of lesser authority and leave them out or bind them separately. (Sometimes called *Apocrypha*.)

Devil, The (also called *Satan*) A personalized power of evil, leader of spiritual forces opposed to God. His authority strictly subordinate to God's as Christian belief does not allow *dualism*. It is widely believed the Devil is a fallen *angel*, not created evil by God. The *death of Jesus* and his *resurrection* have ensured Satan's eventual defeat.

Disciple One who follows Jesus in order to learn from him and to grow to spiritual maturity. God's plan is not just that people should become adherents of Christianity but that they should go on to be full disciples.

Discipline The application of certain rules of life to keep Christians, individually and corporately, within a spiritually and morally healthy way of life. In church life, the exercise of discipline is reckoned one of the marks of a true church. Its ultimate sanction is *excommunication*.

Dispensation A distinct period during the history of salvation. Some Christians speak of the 'dispensation of the Law' (from Moses to Christ) or the 'dispensation of grace' (from Christ's first coming to his second). *Dispensationalists* (often to be found among the *Christian Brethren*) believe that in each period God acts towards people in a way typical of that dispensation.

Dissenter See *Nonconformist.*

Divinty The being of God. Christians believe that Jesus Christ shares God's divinity.

Divorce The official breaking of a *marriage* covenant. Many Christians, especially Catholics, believe that marriage is indissoluble and that no civil divorce can affect the continuance of a marriage in God's eyes. Others believe that, although God's intention is lifelong marriage, divorce is allowable in certain circumstances.

Docetist (from a Greek word meaning 'to seem') One who believed that the *Son of God* only *seemed* to live and die in the flesh. This early *heresy* would have fatally undermined Christianity as faith in the *incarnation.*

Doctrine A belief carefully formulated. 'Christian doctrine' can be used for the whole body of belief.

Dogma Close to *doctrine*, but can carry overtones of a fixed and inflexible system of belief. *Dogmatics* is the study of Christian doctrine, often in a way which centres on its philosophical implications.

Dualism The belief that there are equal and opposite forces of good and evil at work in the universe. This is an old *heresy* which it is all too easy to fall into when speaking of the *Devil* and the presence of evil. It was taught in an extreme form by the Manichaeans who spread widely from the third century.

E

Early church The church in the first few centuries, after the days of the *primitive church.*

Early fathers See *church fathers.*

Easter The period when Christians remember the *death of Jesus* and his *resurrection.*

Eastern church The churches at the eastern end of the Mediterranean, originally based on Constantinople (Byzantium), which sought to be independent of Rome. These churches were largely Greek-speaking. This division became absolute after the *Great Schism* and the *Orthodox churches* are heirs to the Eastern tradition.

Ecclesiastical To do with the church. (The Greek word for church is *ecclesia*, 'assembly'.)

Ecumenical To do with the unity of all Christians. The ecumenical movement looks to draw all Christians into one *fellowship*, as a witness to a divided world of God's *reconciliation.*

Ecumenical council See *council.*

Elder See *presbyter.*

Election See *calling.*

Enlightenment, The An eighteenth-century movement believing that humanity should be guided by human reason and not by external *authority, dogma* or *revelation.* This movement has had great influence on the development of modern thought.

Episcopacy Form of church government which treats *bishops* as an integral part of the system.

Epistemology The philosophy of knowledge, particularly enquiring in to how we know and what the sources of our knowledge are.

Epistle The old term for the letters, mainly written by *apostles,* included in the New Testament.

Eschatology The study of the 'last things', what will happen at the end of the age, and in particular at the *second coming* of Jesus Christ.

Essene Member of a strict Jewish community based at Qumran on the Dead Sea. Their characteristic beliefs were kept secret, but some are now known from the Dead Sea Scrolls. They were the third main division of Judaism in Jesus' time, along with the *Pharisees* and *Sadducees.*

Eternity The state of being beyond and uninfluenced by time. Eternity is seen as the dimension where only God is at home, though believers will join him hereafter. In the New Testament, 'eternal life' is available as soon as a person turns to Jesus, giving foretastes of eternity within our temporal existence.

Ethics The study of morality and moral choices. Christian ethics seek to relate the teaching of the *Bible*, and the long tradition of interpretation of the Bible's moral teaching, to contemporary thinking and decision-making.

Eucharist See *holy communion.*

Evangelical One in whose Christian faith great importance is given to the teachings of the *Bible* as the basis for belief and to personal *conversion* as a necessity for true Christianity. Evangelicalism is in continuity with the *Reformation*, but traces more direct lines of descent to the *revivals* of the eighteenth and nineteenth centuries. Many evangelicals are in *independent* congregations, but many also are within main *denominations.*

Evangelism (the 'evangel' means the *gospel*) Telling other people of the *gospel* of *salvation* through Jesus, with the aim that they might *repent*, believe and find new life in him. The means used to spread the gospel are many and various; all need to be relevant to the particular culture of the people being approached. Evangelism is not the whole of Christian *mission,* but many believe mission to be inadequate without it.

Evil Harm which comes to human beings, turning us away from God and from goodness. Often divided into—*moral evil*, harm which comes through other people's actions or our own, as in war, oppression, avoidable accident;—*natural evil*, which comes through events in the natural order such as disease or natural disaster. The origins of evil are a mystery, though there are hints that it is connected with humanity's *fall.*

Evolution The theory that the development of all forms of life takes place through a series of modifications, the direction of which is governed by environmental factors. This theory, put forward by Charles Darwin in the mid-nineteenth century, has come under strong attack, but is still accepted by the majority of scientists. Some of its proponents use it as a philosophy, explaining many aspects of life and society in a way which excludes God. But while many Christians hold *creation* and evolution to be mutually exclusive concepts, others believe God might have created life as we know it by a process in which evolution has played a part.

Excommunication The exclusion, by due authority, of a church member from participation in services of *holy communion* for reasons of *discipline.*

Existentialist One who rejects externally imposed values and codes, in the belief that a person has to make his or her own choices in terms that make sense of his or her own existence. It is a modern philosophy, sometimes leading to despair, though often also to real human courage. Many existentialists are *atheists*, though some have sought to integrate existentialism with Christian faith.

Exodus, The The escape of the Israelites under Moses from slavery in Egypt, resulting eventually in their establishment in their own land. The Old Testament and Judaism look back to it as God's greatest deliverance, when Israel became a nation. New Testament teaching about *salvation* sometimes makes use of exodus imagery.

Exorcism Casting *demons* out of people in Jesus' name. Many believe this should only be done rarely, and only by people set apart for this ministry within the church.

Expiation Making an offering or taking action that atones for *sin.* Some believe this is the right word to describe the effect of the *death of Jesus*, but others feel it is too objective a term and prefer the more personal *propitiation.*

F

Faith Personal belief and trust in a person or an idea, such that loss will be inevitable if the object of faith proves untrustworthy. Christian faith in Jesus Christ is therefore more than intellectual assent to beliefs: it is personal commitment to Jesus. Faith is regularly linked in the New Testament to *repentance*.

Fall, The Humanity's choice to be independent of God and his will, a choice in which we are all involved and which has resulted in the deflection of humanity from the path God intended, the distortion of the *image of God* in mankind and the spoiling of the creation itself. There is a disagreement as to whether the fall was an actual historical event or expresses a truth about humanity's character and relationship to God.

Fasting Going without food or other things so as to focus concentration and devotion on *prayer*.

Fatalist One who believes his destiny is shaped by impersonal spiritual forces not taking individual welfare into consideration. Often, but not always, this belief leads to an attitude of resignation. It cannot co-exist with faith in the personal God.

Fatherhood of God The quality in God which relates to humanity in a parental way, caring and guiding. It was Jesus' characteristic way of referring to God. Christians commonly speak of the first *person* of the *trinity* as 'God the Father'.

Fathers See *church fathers* and *apostolic fathers*.

Fellowship Doing things and having things in common within the Christian community. The emphasis is on shared participation rather than simply common membership or meeting together. Its New Testament usage makes clear that we are not intended to live isolated Christian lives, but to find encouragement and support among other Christians.

Filled with the Spirit Having our personalities and wills so open to the *Holy Spirit* that we put no obstacle in the way of his enriching our lives and using us in God's service. The apostle Paul teaches that it is to be a continual rather than a once-for-all filling.

First Cause See *cause*.

Flesh Our lives and personalities when they are directed in a way that leaves God out of account and acts as if there were no spiritual dimension. The apostle Paul sets flesh in total opposition to *spirit*.

Forgiveness One of the great blessings made available through the *death of Jesus* is that people can know themselves to be forgiven by God, free of the guilt which would otherwise hold them apart from him. Just as forgiveness is a central feature of the relationship between God and humanity, so it is to characterize relationships between people: we are to forgive as we have been forgiven.

Free will The quality in humanity which is able to make choices, not totally governed by outside factors. Christians disagree on how to relate our free-will decision whether or not to follow Jesus to our understanding of *predestination*.

Fruit of the Spirit Qualities in a Christian's life which result from the work of the *Holy Spirit in sanctification*. First place among them is given to *love*, joy and peace.

G

Gentile Term used by Jews of one who is not a Jew.

Gifts of the Spirit Abilities given to believers by the *Holy Spirit*, to be used for the good of the whole Christian body. The emphasis is on the gifts coming from God directly rather than just natural abilities. Also, the Spirit gives a rich variety of gifts, so that each person has a distinct part to play.

Glory A quality of the eternal God in his majesty, which he promises to share with believers hereafter. God's glory was seen in terms men and women can understand in the character of Jesus.

Gnostic Member of one of a group of movements holding that *salvation* is attained through a secret knowledge *(gnosis)*. Many early Christian writers opposed the Gnostics, certainly in the second century, perhaps also in the New Testament. Gnosticism was subversive of true Christianity, because it taught *dualism*, and had no place for Jesus Christ as the only *Mediator* between God and humanity.

God Christians believe, not vaguely in a god, but specifically in God whom Jesus called Father. The Bible's teaching about God is that he is *holy*, perfect and *transcendent*, but also that in his grace and goodness he is close to us in our everyday lives, and relates to us in a personal way. He is *Creator* of the universe. He sent Jesus the *Son of God* to fulfil his eternal plan for humanity's *salvation*.

Gospel (written with a small 'g') The good news of what God has done through Jesus, and especially his *death* and *resurrection*. He has made available to us *forgiveness* and *new birth* in the *Holy Spirit*. It is through hearing the gospel that people can come to receive Jesus and find his new life.

Gospel (with a capital 'G') One of the four accounts of the life, death and resurrection of Jesus found in the New Testament. The Gospels are more than just biographies; they interpret the meaning of Jesus in a way that calls forth a response of *faith*.

Grace The quality in God which gives freely; its root meaning is 'giving pleasure'. Grace is always given, never earned. It is a relationship word; not a 'force'. It is often divided into

—*special grace: forgiveness* and other blessings which come specifically through the *death of Jesus*.

—*common grace:* goodness in life and society which comes from God's *creating* and *sustaining* the world.

Great Schism The final separation in the eleventh century between the *Western* and *Eastern* churches.

H

Healing An important part of Jesus' *ministry* was to *heal* people, as a sign that the *kingdom of God* had come. Christians since have been involved in healing in Jesus' name, using both medical means and *prayer*. Many churches today hold services of healing. 'Christian healing' is to be distinguished from 'spiritual healing', which is usually carried out by *spiritualists*.

Heaven The presence of God, where believers will find the final fulfilment of the *love*, joy and peace they have begun to experience on earth. As well as representing the presence of God and his goodness, heaven also stands for the absence of sin and all the disharmony that has resulted from the *fall*.

Hell The word translates two New Testaments concepts: *Hades*, the place of the departed, an idea close to the Old Testament *Sheol*; and *Gehenna*, a place of torment. The concept of hell in the latter sense holds before us the fact that to reject Jesus Christ brings eternal *judgment*. There is disagreement as to whether hell actually goes on for ever or is an experience of instantaneous destruction.

Hellenism The predominantly Greek culture that began with Alexander the Great and continued for centuries alongside Roman culture. It was thus a very influential aspect of the cultural background to the New Testament.

Heresy This originally meant simply a party or school of thought, but Christians came to use it of a teaching that split off from and contradicted orthodox Christianity. Today it is confined to teaching that subverts a central Christian belief, such as the *trinity*, the *divinity of Christ* or the *atonement*, and thus results in something not truly Christian.

Hermeneutics The study of how to interpret the Bible, in such a way as to be true to its original meaning and also relevant to today's questions.

Hierarchy System of government which employs officials of graded status. By extension it has come to refer to a group of top church leaders, such as *bishops* and archdeacons, or *pope*, cardinals and bishops.

High priest In the Old Testament, he was the *priest* specially appointed for certain duties connected with the *sacrifices*, especially those on the Day of Atonement. The writer to the Hebrews applies the term to Jesus, the one who presents his own sacrifice of Himself and has fully opened the way to God.

Holy A quality initially of God, denoting his separation from anything that is not wholly pure. The Bible also applies it to objects, religious officials and so on who are set apart for use in God's service. But ordinary believers are also called to be holy, to live lives that reflect the character of God as seen in Jesus. (See also *sanctification*.)

Holy communion The service in which the *congregation* take a piece of bread and a sip of wine as a token that they owe their spiritual life to the *death of Jesus*. It was instituted by Jesus at the Last Supper, when he took bread and wine saying 'This is my body', 'This is my blood'. The service is also known as the *eucharist* (meaning 'thanksgiving', the *mass* (the Roman Catholic term) and the *Lord's supper*. (See also *real presence, sacrament*.)

Holy Spirit The personal presence of God, active in the *church* and in the world. He is the third person of the Trinity, not to be thought of as a force or influence but fully personal. In the Old Testament, the Spirit was given to particular individuals for special tasks. But at *Pentecost* Jesus Christ gave the Holy Spirit to every believer, and Jesus has been present with his people by the Holy Spirit ever since.

Holy table A special table in most churches from which *holy communion* is administered. (Some call it the *altar*.)

Hope A Christian virtue only equalled in importance by *faith* and *love*. It means the conviction that our life and our relationship with Jesus do not end at our physical death, and that therefore the spiritual dimension of believers' lives cannot be destroyed by any temporal forces. Hope is thus able to sustain Christians even in great adversity.

Humanist One who sets great store by the capacity of human nature, by the aesthetic and moral senses, and by education. Today most humanists believe in humanism rather than in God, but there has been a long tradition of Christian humanism which started at the time of the *Renaissance*.

I

Icon An image, usually of Jesus or the *Virgin Mary*, used in the worship of the *Orthodox churches*. They are not mere religious decorations but are seen as windows into a spiritual world.

Idol Something physical or natural that people take for God and worship. Many tribal cultures have used idols, but there are a number of features of modern life which have become objects of worship, such as money, the state, science.

Image of God That in the nature of human beings which reflects the nature of God. Some believe this takes the form of a combination of qualities in humanity, such as reason or the religious, moral or aesthetic sense. Others hold that the 'image' means the special relationship humanity has with God, from which these qualities stem. All the goodness in humanity comes from this aspect of our *creation*, but the image of God has been spoilt in us by the *fall*.

Immaculate Conception In Catholic belief, the idea that the *Virgin Mary* was from the time of her conception free from *original sin*. This is not a New Testament belief, but it was made an article of faith for Roman Catholics in the nineteenth century.

Immanence The quality in God which causes him to be involved in the life of humanity and the world, and not stay remote from it. The chief evidence for God's immanence is the *incarnation* of the *Son of God*. Christians try to hold belief in God's immanence in balance with belief in his *transcendence*.

Incarnation (literally 'taking flesh') The action of God in becoming a wholly human person in Jesus of Nazareth, subject to place, time and all other human attributes. What made Jesus' humanity unique was his freedom from *sin*. In his full humanity can be seen everything about the character of God which can be conveyed in human terms. (See also *Christology*.)

'In Christ' See *Christ, In*.

Independent See *Congregationalist*.

Indissoluble A quality which some Christians believe to be a necessary part of *marriage*. It means a marriage cannot be broken, and that no civil *divorce* can make a couple not married who have been duly joined in a church ceremony. This view is held by Roman Catholics and some others.

Indulgence In Catholic belief, remission of the debt owed to God for *sin* after the guilt has been forgiven. This is thought possible due to the 'treasury of merit' believed to have been built up by Jesus, the *Virgin Mary* and the *saints*. It was the sale of indulgences for money which provoked Martin Luther to issue the theses which launched the *Reformation*.

Inerrant The quality of being without any mistakes of fact or interpretation which some Christians attribute to the *Bible*. The word is used to defend the Bible's *authority* in face of those who are thought to take too low a view of its *inspiration*.

Infallible A term very close in meaning to *inerrant* when used of the Bible. It is also applied by Roman Catholics to the *Pope* when pronouncing on a matter of doctrine.

Inspiration (literally 'in-breathing') The means by which the *Bible*, a collection of books written by human writers, became also the *word of God*. The *Holy Spirit* is believed so to have inspired the writers that their books carry the meaning God intended, but without lessening the individuality of the writers.

Intercession The aspect of prayer in which believers make specific petitions to God on behalf of themselves, other people or groups. The word is also applied in the New Testament to an activity of Jesus since his *ascension*: that he intercedes with God on behalf of humanity as humanity's representative.

Intermediate state The condition some Christians think believers are in between their physical death and the *second coming* of Jesus Christ. It is seen as a state of waiting, sometimes described as 'sleep', for the full *salvation* which is to come. Belief in this state does not take away from the hope that a believer's next experience after death will be the presence of Jesus Christ.

Interpretation The attempt to understand the *Bible* in a way true to its original meaning and apply it to present-day concerns. (See also *hermeneutics*.)

J

Jesuit Member of the Society of Jesus, a religious order founded in the sixteenth century by Ignatius Loyola.

Jesus (literally 'one who saves') The man born in Bethlehem and brought up in Nazareth who became an itinerant teacher and healer, was crucified and rose again. His followers came to believe he was the *Messiah (Christ)* and the *Son of God*.

Jubilee Year In Israel every fiftieth year all land reverted to its original owner from whoever had bought it. The intention was to keep land in family units and prevent vast estates being built up. Some believe that the Jubilee law is reflected in Jesus' understanding of the freedom and justice he came to bring.

Judgment The activity of God in calling people to account for what they have made of their lives. Believers and unbelievers alike will face judgment, but there will be no condemnation for those *'in Christ'*. Jesus claimed that God had given to him the authority to judge, and this assures us that judgment will be fair and perceptive. It will take place at Jesus' *second coming*. (See also *hell*.)

Justification God's reckoning of a person to be righteous before him, in standing rather than in quality of life, though the second naturally flows from the first. It is an image from the law-courts, meaning 'acquittal'. The means of justification have been thought to be:

—*justification by faith*, in that all that we need to be made right with God has been achieved in the *death of Jesus*, and believers simply receive it by *faith* (this was a key *Reformation* belief);

—*justification by works*, according to which we are made right with God through our own righteous acts. This is widely seen as unbiblical today, though many attempt a fusion of the two ideas.

Just war The idea that war can sometimes be morally justified, but only as a last resort, and under strictly defined conditions. This teaching was put forward in medieval times, but attempts have been made to apply it through to the modern period though some hold it is not relevant to nuclear warfare.

K

Kenosis (literally 'he emptied himself') A theory about the *incarnation* which holds that, in becoming Jesus of Nazareth, the *Son of God* put aside all distinctively divine attributes and revealed God simply and solely through his humanity.

Kingdom of God (or *Kingdom of heaven*) The rule and authority of God and every person and community in whom that rule is accepted. The Jews had hoped for the kingdom of David to be re-established, but Jesus brought a kingdom with a different kind of power, the quality of which was largely unrecognized. The kingdom of God is entered through adopting Jesus' way of living in the power of the Spirit; its chief concerns are with the poor and oppressed. Though hidden now, the kingdom of God will finally overturn all earthly power at the *second coming* of Jesus.

L

Laity The whole people (Greek, *laos*) of God, whether clergy or not. It has often been used for the people of God excluding the clergy, with the result that a contrast has arisen between active, *ordained* Christians and passive ones. This has harmed the *mission* of the *church*.

Lamb of God A title for Jesus used by John the Baptist and by the writer of Revelation, which highlights his *sacrifice* for our *sins* and the victory he won in his *death*.

Law, The A set of God-given commandments, centred on the Ten Commandments, but often thought of as including the first five books of the Bible. Law is God's fatherly instruction to his people, outlining the pattern of behaviour through which they can best love him and their neighbours. We can never find salvation by keeping the Law, because we all fail to keep it fully. So the attempt to establish our righteousness by legal means is doomed and leads away from the gospel of Jesus.

Laying on of hands The identification of a person before God as the object of special *prayer* by placing hands on him or her. This was done in the Bible for *healing*, for *ordination* and for receiving the *Holy Spirit*. It is also used today by a *bishop* in *confirmation*.

Legalism The approach to religion which sees its centre in keeping rules and regulations. While keeping God's *law* is important, the legalistic approach is deadening and undermines *faith* in the *gospel*.

Lent The period of forty days leading up to *Easter*, during which Christians are encouraged to exercise special *self-discipline* to prepare to celebrate Easter. The forty days are associated with the time of Jesus' temptation in the wilderness.

Lesser evil The approach to *ethics* which holds that, because this is a *fallen* world, a perfect moral path is not always open to us and we must sometimes choose the lesser of two evils, as for instance in circumstances of war or of marriage breakdown.

Liberal theology A type of theology which asserts the freedom to question alleged authorities and to avoid intellectual constrains. It is thus often critical of orthodox Christianity. It has flourished from the eighteenth century, though more dominant in some periods than in others.

Liberation theology A movement which has arisen in Latin America in the last fifteen years, which looks to apply Christian belief in concrete action (*praxis*), especially in the face of situations of oppression and political injustice.

Liturgy A set form of *worship*, usually published in a book. Liturgy is sometimes followed word for word, and sometimes provides a framework within which there some freedom of expression. It is characteristic of *Catholic, Orthodox* and *Anglican* worship, but not of the *nonconformist* (or 'free') churches, though this distinction is not absolute.

Lord, The A title for God in the Old Testament, generally written 'the LORD', used because God's name, Yahweh, was too *holy* to be spoken. It was used in the New Testament of Jesus Christ and has become a key term in Christian *worship* of him.

Lord's supper See *holy communion*.

Love The chief and most characteristic Christian virtue, so distinctive that the New Testament coined a new word for it, *agape*. Christian love is more than an emotion: it is an active caring for other people whether or not they do anything to provoke it. It is a central quality of God and is seen at its most essential in Jesus.

Lutheran Member of a worldwide fellowship of churches that follow the teaching of Martin Luther and base their beliefs on the Augsburg Confession.

M

Marcionite One who followed the teaching of Marcion in the second century, in particular that the God of the Old Testament is not the Father of Jesus Christ.

Marriage A covenant publicly made between one man and one woman that they will form a lifelong partnership of love and sexual exclusiveness, and are happy to be considered by society as a partnership.

Martyr One who dies for his *faith*, refusing to turn from it despite persecution. Christians are often martyred when the state takes to itself god-like powers. The word also means *witness*.

Marxist One who follows the teaching of Karl Marx, in which communism had its origin. In particular Marxists believe that human nature is characterized by the need to work productively, that society is shaped by people's relationships to the means of production and that capitalism will be swept away by an inevitable historical process. Marxism is vastly influential in today's world and is usually, though not always, anti-Christian.

Mary See *Virgin Mary.*

Mass See *holy communion.*

Materialist One who gives highest value to the physical and observable in life, and does not accept the reality of anything that cannot be seen, touched and measured.

Mediator A title given to Jesus Christ, describing his function in bringing together God and humanity. He is uniquely qualified to do this, because he is both human and divine.

Medieval Pertaining to the time of the Middle Ages. In Christian thought this period was characterized by an appeal to *natural theology* and an attempt to harmonize Bible teaching with the philosophy of Aristotle.

Meditation A form of *prayer* using silent concentration, sometimes focusing on particular phrases or objects in order to approach God without being distracted by the everyday.

Messiah (literally 'anointed one') The one whose coming was prophesied in the Old Testament, who would set his people free and bring in a new age. Christians believe this Messiah is Jesus though he seldom openly claimed as much, because the Jews of his day expected a different kind of fulfilment. (See also *Christ.*)

Metaphysics The study of what is fundamental to being. It has often taken the form of studying what is beyond scientific proof.

Methodist Member of a worldwide fellowship of churches based on the teaching of John and Charles Wesley and tracing their descent to the eighteenth-century *revival* in Britain.

Millennium, The A thousand-year period prophesied in the book of Revelation when the righteous will rule on earth. This has been interpreted in three basic ways

—*Amillennialists* hold that the thousand-year period is symbolic and that Jesus' *second coming* will bring, not a reign on earth, but the eternal age;

—*Postmillennialists* believe that Jesus will come again after the millennium, which will be a period of spiritual prosperity;

—*Premillennialists* maintain that Jesus' return will happen before the millennium and that he will reign with his people on earth.

Ministry (literally 'service') The whole range of service all members of the *church* offer to one another and to society as a whole. It is made up of many and varied particular ministries, according to the diversity of the *gifts of the Spirit.* That ministry for which *ordination* is appropriate forms an important part of the whole of the church's ministry, but everyone is involved. The model for all Christian service is the ministry of Jesus.

Miracle A mighty work, beyond the normal functioning of human beings, which evokes wonder and in which we hear God speaking of his personal involvement with and care for people.

Mission (from a root word meaning 'sent') The whole range of what Jesus has sent the *church* into the world to do: to bring the love of God to people in all their need. Jesus said, 'As my Father has sent me, so I send you.' This means that the church must seek to fulfil all that Jesus did for people. This includes *evangelism* as central, but also service and care of the needy, together with what is now called 'humanization': the helping of people to overcome political and other circumstances which reduce their humanity.

Missionary At one level this means anyone who works to fulfil the church's *mission.* But more usually it is confined to those who cross cultural boundaries with the *gospel*, preaching and interpreting it in a way that is sensitive and relevant to the new context.

Modalism (also called 'Sabellianism') The view that the three *persons* of the *Trinity* are simply different manifestations of the one Godhead. This preserves God's unity at the expense of the distinctiveness of the *Son of God* and the *Holy Spirit.* This was a third-century theology.

Monasticism The practice of withdrawing from full involvement in the world to form communities of monks or nuns. This practice began in the early centuries, has taken many forms and continues today. Much medieval Christian scholarship was carried on in monasteries.

Monism The belief that all things, material and immaterial, personal and impersonal, are essentially one stuff. It is the underlying philosophy of Hinduism.

Monophysite One who held that Christ had one nature not two. Often this resulted in undervaluing Jesus' humanity through the strength of his divinity. It was a very influential view from the fourth and fifth centuries.

Monotheist One who believes that there is only one God. This belief is totally basic to Christianity, Judaism and Islam. Christian belief in the *Trinity* in no way lessens Christian monotheism.

Montanist Member of a second-century group who looked to bring back enthusiasm into Christianity that had become rather arid and theoretical.

Mystery Something that we can know but never fully understand, as particularly the mystery of God himself. All religion contains mystery, which can present a problem to the tidier type of mind. But the fact that we cannot understand everything need not prevent us understanding as much as we can.

Mystic One who pursues the interior life of the spirit, using any of a vast number of spiritual methods in the effort to know and experience the divine at the deepest possible level. Though mysticism is not restricted to Christianity, there is a long Christian mystical tradition that continues today.

Myth A story through which people seek to encapsulate a religious idea. Some myths are powerful means of conveying spiritual truths. There is disagreement among Christians about whether there are any myths in the Bible. In particular, is the story of the garden of Eden a factual account or a myth?

N

Natural theology Knowledge of God reached through reason alone, without resort to *revelation.* It is often thought of as complementary to revealed religion. This method was a feature of *medieval* theology, especially that of Thomas Aquinas, and has remained influential particularly in *Catholic* circles.

Neo-orthodoxy The type of twentieth-century theology associated with Karl Barth which provided a critical reaction to *liberal theology* and stressed the importance of God's *revelation* through the *Word of God.*

New birth (also called *regeneration*) Jesus said, 'Unless a person is born again he cannot see the kingdom of God.' Where *conversion* describes a person's response to God, new birth describes God's work in a person through the *Holy Spirit,* to give him a fresh start and a life in a new dimension. A Christian is not simply forgiven and called to try again in his own strength; he receives a new life of relationship with God.

New creation The realm opened up through the *death of Jesus,* his resurrection and the giving of the *Holy Spirit.* It contains possibilities otherwise closed to us through the *fall,* particularly relationship with God and the whole spiritual life. Central to the new creation are the new community of the *church* and a restored hope of eternal life.

Nonconformist (in some places called 'free churchman') One who does not accept the established church of his nation and joins instead a *denomination* or *congregation* that is free of ties with the state.

Numinous That which we sense to be other than and beyond our everyday, material lives. The term was first used by Rudolf Otto in his book *The Idea of the Holy*, to describe what is basic to all religions.

O

Occultism Involvement with secret supernatural forces, often including magic. There has been a resurgence of interest in the occult in the West recently. Occult practices are strongly warned against in the Bible.

Omnipotent See *almighty*.

Omnipresent Present everywhere, describing the fact that God is not localized and can be known simultaneously by people all over the world.

Omniscient Knowing everything, describing the fact that there are no limits to God's knowledge.

Ontological To do with the essential nature of things. Thus the 'Ontological argument' for the existence of God maintains that, in the nature of things, a being must exist who is greater than everything else or there would not be a supreme being.

Ordination A commissioning of people to a particular *ministry* within the whole ministry of the church, normally involving teaching pastoral care, ministry of the *sacraments* and leadership. It is performed by *laying on of hands* by leaders of a denomination, with prayer for the enabling of the *Holy Spirit*. Many, particularly Catholics, believe that orders are indelible: once ordained, always ordained.

Original sin The predisposition towards sin which is part of all humanity, believed to stem from humanity's *fall*. This belief does not take away from individual responsibility, but it does highlight the inbuilt factors within environment and heredity which push us towards disobedience, and it corresponds to observable facts about universal human nature. (See also *image of God* and *the fall*.)

Orthodox churches One of the three great Christian traditions in continuity with the *Eastern church* and made more distinct from the time of the *Great Schism*. Orthodoxy includes the Greek Orthodox, Russian Orthodox, Armenian, Coptic (Egyptian) and Ethiopian Orthodox churches. Its central characteristics are a prizing of *tradition*, a beautiful *liturgy* and a deep continuity with the doctrine of the *ecumenical councils*.

P

Pacifist One who believes that war is never justified and so refuses to bear arms. The majority of Christians in the *early church* were pacifists, as were some *Anabaptists*, who were persecuted by the state for it. A continuing pacifist tradition has run through the history of Christianity, and is probably stronger today than ever before.

Pagan One who is thought to be unenlightened as to true religion. It is often used of adherents of primitive religions, but is sometimes now extended to those who have no faith.

Panentheist One who holds that everything exists in God, a view which is rather different from *pantheism*. It is an understanding popular in twentieth-century theology, with its accent on God as *immanent*, and especially in *Process Theology*.

Pantheist One who holds that everything is divine, so that many pantheists worship nature. A tendency of pantheism is to be morally neutral, since everything is an aspect of the divine being. The idea is close to *monism*.

Parable A story which conveys spiritual truth. It is a characteristic of Jesus' teaching method. He often used parables to bring home the unexpectedness of the *kingdom of God* and the urgency of responding to himself.

Paraclete (literally 'one who is called alongside') A term used in John's Gospel for the *Holy Spirit*. It has been variously translated, but in the context of John's teaching it seems to mean 'the one who is to us what Jesus was to his *disciples*'.

Paradise A term used infrequently in the Bible meaning 'the blessed state hereafter'.

Passion The Passion of Jesus is his suffering as his death approached, including his *temptation* in Gethsemane, his humiliation by Roman soldiers and his suffering on the *cross*.

Passover God's action in preparation for the *exodus* of Israel from Egypt, when he 'passed over' the Israelite families while afflicting the Egyptians. The term is also used of the great Jewish festival which recalls this incident, and in particular the Passover meal in Jewish homes. It is thought that, at the Last Supper, Jesus used Passover symbolism in instituting the *holy communion*.

Pastor (literally 'shepherd') One who cares for people in spiritual, emotional and practical need. It is a *ministry* which closely reflects that of Jesus, the 'Good Shepherd'.

Penance In Catholic and Orthodox belief, the performance of an assigned duty in restitution for *sin*. It is held to be a *sacrament*, and absolution of guilt may be made dependent on it.

Pentecost The Jewish festival during which the *Holy Spirit* was first given to the *church*. It is thus one of the three great Christian festivals, along with *Christmas* and *Easter*. Sometimes the Christian festival is called *Whitsun*.

Pentecostal Member of the worldwide fellowship of churches which stress the *gifts of the Spirit* and personal experience of the *Holy Spirit* in a Christian's life. Their *worship* is usually informal and vigorous. Dating only from the beginning of the twentieth century, Pentecostalism has spread at an astonishing rate, and some would now call it the fourth great Christian tradition alongside *Catholicism, Orthodoxy* and *Protestantism*, although in many respects it is a branch of the third.

Person A technical term used in defining belief in the *trinity*, to describe the Father, Son and Holy Spirit severally.

Person of Christ Everything to do with who Jesus Christ is, his identity and nature. (See also *Christology*.)

Pharisee Member of a sect of Judaism, strict in observance of the *Law*. Unlike the *Sadducees*, they taught the importance of the whole Law, not only the worship in the *Temple*.

Philosophy (literally 'love of wisdom') The age-old study of the reality of things, trying to make sense of the world and of life through clear thinking and observation. It involves the accurate use of language and logic.

Pietist Member of a movement in the seventeenth and eighteenth centuries that sought to bring back devotion and holy living into a Protestantism which had become rigid and theoretical. Without ever becoming a structured *denomination*, the Pietists contributed much to the development of Protestantism.

Pluralism The existence of many religions side by side in the same community—a frequent occurrence in the modern world. It is sometimes used of the view that all religions are equally valid.

Polygamy One man having more than one wife. It is particularly common in Africa, where the introduction of Christian marriage in a polygamous context has to be tactfully and sensitively carried through.

Polytheist One who believes in more than one god. Polytheism was the normal religion in the Near Eastern, Greek and Roman cultures which redominated at the time of the beginnings of Christianity.

Pope The Bishop of Rome and leader of worldwide Roman Catholicism. Roman Catholics see him as the successor of Peter and vicar (representative) of Christ on earth. (See also *infallible*.)

Praxis The practical application of Christian beliefs in concrete situations, often of political and economic oppression. It is a key belief of *Liberation Theology* that theoretical doctrine does not constitute true theology, but needs to be given effect in action.

Prayer The believer's conscious practice of relationship with God, sometimes taking the form of *worship*, sometimes of *meditation*, sometimes of *intercession*. Words are often used, though some people pray in thought only. All prayer is a two-way relationship. It is the central activity of the Christian life.

Predestination God's deciding of a person's destiny in advance. Christians have always found it hard to reconcile this with human *free will*, and our responsibility to choose *repentance* and *faith*.

Pre-existent Being in existence before the universe was created. This is plainly true of God the Creator, but Christians also teach that the *Son of God* is pre-existent—that he has always been. This was an area of conflict between orthodox Christianity and the *Arians*.

Presbyter (literally *elder*) One appointed to lead a *congregation*, sometimes on his own, sometimes with others. Presbyters were appointed in all the New Testament churches, to ensure continuity of leadership once the *apostles* had moved on. It is now an order of *ministry*. There is some dispute about whether this is what *Anglicans* mean when they use the word *priest*.

Presbyterian Member of a worldwide fellowship of churches that are led by *presbyters*, though important decisions are taken by the whole *congregation*. Presbyterianism is a structured *denomination*, relating from congregation to session to presbytery to synod.

Preserver See *Sustainer*.

Priest One who represents God to people and people to God. The term is also used of one who offers *sacrifices*. The Old Testament priests were a central part of Israel's faith, but since the *death of Jesus* has opened the way for every believer to come to God, many hold that we no longer need a special priestly caste. On this understanding, every believer is a priest. But Catholics see a continuing role for special priests, as those who offer God's *grace* to the people at the *sacrifice* of the *mass*.

Primitive church A term sometimes used of the church in the time of the *apostles*.

Principalities and powers Authorities in the world that possess something of the *demonic*, so that the apostle Paul can write of them as forces against which the Christians must struggle, using spiritual weapons. Some hold that the term indicates political authority when it is godless.

Process theology A modern form of theology teaching that God is involved in the whole process of *evolution*, holding good and evil together on the way to a resolution of the suffering in the world.

Prophet One who prophesies, declares the word of God as it bears on particular national, communal, or personal circumstances. Prophecy also contains elements of prediction, though they are not its centre. Prophets were very important in Old Testament religion, bringing God's *revelation*. They reappear in the New, but stand in a different relationship to the completed revelation.

Propitiation The making of an offering that brings a person back into relationship with another who has been offended. Some believe this is the right word to describe the achievement of the *death of Jesus* in *reconciling* humanity with God, though others prefer the more objective *expiation*.

Proselyte A non-Jew who is brought to faith in Judaism and allowed to worship in the synagogue. The proselytes were often impressed by the early preaching of the Christian *gospel*, which began in the synagogues.

Protestant Member of one of the three great Christian traditions, beside *Catholics* and the *Orthodox*. It is a general title given to the successors of those who separated from the Church of Rome at the *Reformation*. Its particular features have been an emphasis on the authority of the *Bible* above that of the *church*, and a rejection of any priestly caste. The latter has sometimes made Protestantism highly individualistic. Protestantism has also shown a tendency to subdivide into many different *denominations*.

Providence The care God takes of all existing things. His acts of *salvation*, as in the *death of Jesus*, are part of his providence, but so is his care for us in *common grace*. God is able to care far everything because of his universal *sovereignty*.

Purgatory In Catholic belief, this is where the spirit goes after death, to be 'purged' and prepared for heaven.

Puritan Member of a group of biblically-based Christians who wanted to bring the church back to a pure faith and practice. They were often scorned for undue solemnity, but their achievements were great, especially at the time of Oliver Cromwell in England, and in the settlements made by the Pilgrim Fathers.

R

Rabbi Jewish teacher who, in Jesus' time, would gather round him a group of *disciples*. Jesus was called 'Rabbi', though his methods were often highly distinctive.

Ransom Payment offered to secure someone's release. It is therefore sometimes used to describe what was achieved by the *death of Jesus*, being close in meaning to *redemption*.

Rationalist One who believes that everything can be judged by unaided reason, and that reason is superior to *revelation* (if any has been made). Rationalism was an important school of philosophy in the seventeenth and eighteenth centuries, and its influence is still felt.

Real presence Jesus' presence as Christians take the bread and wine at *holy communion*. There are different views as to whether he is present in a miraculous, bodily way (*transubstantiation*) or in a spiritual way.

Reconciliation The bringing of two estranged parties back into relationship. It is one of the central images for what was achieved in the *death of Jesus*, bringing God and humanity into harmony and taking away the barrier due to *sin*. Once reconciled to God, Christians are equipped to bring reconciliation across the divisions in the world.

Redemption The buying someone back from slavery to secure their freedom. It is a concept used frequently in the Bible, in the Old Testament to describe what God did for Israel at the *exodus*, and in the New as an image carrying the meaning of the *death of Jesus*.

Reformation, The The great sixteenth-century movement to reform the Church of Rome, which resulted, against the wishes of many of its leaders, in the division of the Catholic church. The key beliefs of the Reformers were *justification by faith* and the priesthood of all believers (see *priest*). The division caused by the Reformation has remained deep ever since, though there are some signs that bridges are being built across it today.

Reformed churches A worldwide fellowship of churches, sometimes but not always forming distinct denominations, which are in line of descent from John Calvin. They base their teaching on his *Institutes of the Christian Religion*.

Regeneration See *new birth*.

Reincarnation The belief that we live a series of succeeding lives, sometimes at different levels of being. This is not a Christian belief. It is important in Hinduism.

Renaissance, The (literally 'rebirth') A group of movements in the fourteenth, fifteenth and sixteenth centuries, which marked the transition from the *medieval* period. It was marked by a great interest in the works of classical times and in classical forms in art. Another important feature was its deep *humanism*. The bearing of the Renaissance on the *Reformation* is much debated.

Renewal A return to a deeper Christian faith and life on the part of a person or a community. Renewal is generally preceded by *prayer* and a sense of something wrong, and results in increased *sanctification*. The term is also used in a way close to *revival* or *awakening*.

Repentance (literally 'change of mind') A compete turning round, from any way other than Jesus' way to following Jesus. Repentance may be accompanied by feelings of remorse, but the key is the actual change of heart and life. Without repentance there is no real *conversion*. It is often linked in the New Testament to *faith*.

Representative A term used to describe the position Jesus held in his *death*. Being fully human and yet without sin, he became the representative person, who died for us, representing the whole of humanity in its guilt for sin. (See also *substitute*.)

Resurrection The action of God in raising Jesus to life from the grave. As the risen Lord, Jesus is eternally living and can still be known today. His resurrection also confirmed that he is the unique *Son of God*. In his victory over death, Jesus has given us confidence that death is not the end of all life.

Resurrection of the body The belief that at the *second coming* of Jesus Christians will be raised from death to life with God, not in their physical bodies but in their essential selves.

Revelation God's action in making known to humanity his character, his will and his ways. This revelation has been made in history, through specific acts of revelation, supremely in the life, death and resurrection of Jesus. The record and interpretation of these historical acts is in the *Bible*, which Christians believe God has so inspired as to ensure that his revelation is fully accessible to us. (See also *word of God*.)

Revival A turning of many in a community back to God, through an unusually powerful working of the *Holy Spirit*. There have been many revivals in recent centuries, including several in different parts of the world in this generation.

Ritual A symbolic action, usually in the context of worship, that points to a spiritual truth.

Roman Catholic A member of the Church of Rome, acknowledging allegiance to the *Pope*. The Roman Catholic church is the largest Christian denomination. For many centuries, especially since the *Reformation*, it was deeply conservative, but since the *Second Vatican Council* (see *councils*) it has begun to be more open to renewal.

S

Sabbath The day in the week when people are called to rest from labour and reflect on God, as God rested on the 'seventh day' of *creation*. This practice ensures a rhythm of activity and recreation in life. Jews observe Saturday as the sabbath (as do Seventh Day Adventists). Christians keep Sunday in a similar, though less rigorous way.

Sacrament Augustine called this, 'an outward and visible sign of an inward and spiritual grace'. It is a sign, or dramatization, giving an effect more powerful than words. The two sacraments of the *gospel*, ordained by Jesus, are *baptism* and *holy communion*. Catholics also count other ceremonies as sacraments: *confirmation, marriage, ordination, penance* and extreme unction.

Sacrifice In the Old Testament, animal sacrifice provided the means by which *sin* might be atoned for and relationship with God preserved. The sacrifice of Jesus in his *death* was a full and final means of *atonement*. From that time there has been no need of further sacrifices, though Catholics see a representation of Jesus' sacrifice in the *mass*.

Sadducee Member of a Jewish sect, powerful at the time of Jesus, who set great store by regular worship in the *Temple*.

Saint (literally 'holy person') In New Testament usage, anyone who is '*in Christ*' so that the word is interchangeable with *Christian*. But Catholics reserve it for people of special holiness who are 'canonized'—authorized to be called saints. In Catholic belief, the saints can be called on to intercede with God for us.

Salvation The rescuing of someone from danger. In the Bible it means bringing some one from captivity (to *sin*) into the fullness and freedom of God. Salvation has a past reference: a believer has been saved through the *death of Jesus* once-for-all; a present application: we can know God's freedom today through the power of the *Holy Spirit*; and a future hope: believers will be rescued from all the effects of the *fall* at Jesus' *second coming*.

Sanctification (literally 'being made holy') The progressive conforming of a believer's life and character to that of Jesus, through the inward work of the *Holy Spirit*. Where *justification* is what begins a person's Christian life, sanctification is intended to mark its continuance. It will never be complete until the end.

Satan See *the Devil*.

Saviour One who brings *salvation*. The name Jesus means 'Saviour'.

Schism A separation between two groups of Christians. The most important have been the *Great Schism* (between *Western* and *Eastern churches*) and the *Reformation*. But there have been many others before and since.

Scholasticism An approach to theology in *medieval* times, of those who worked outside the monasteries, often in universities. The approach was detached and objective, using logic, debate find speculation.

Scribe A Jewish teacher of the *Law*. They often opposed Jesus' teaching.

Scripture See *the Bible*.

Second Adam A title sometimes given to Jesus, indicating that he stands at the beginning of a *new creation*, just as Adam stood at the beginning of the old, fallen creation.

Second coming The belief that Jesus Christ will come again, publicly as Lord of all, to end the present age and introduce the eternal age. It will be the Day of *Judgment*, but also the day when *salvation* is fully realized. Jesus frequently spoke of this, but warned that we can never know in advance when it will be.

Secondary cause See *cause*.

Sect Can refer to a *cult*, but is also used of Christian groups that tend to become exclusive through overvaluing secondary beliefs.

Secular Concerned exclusively with this world, taking no account of a spiritual dimension. Secularism is the most characteristic feature of the modern Western world.

Self-existent Looking to no one or nothing else as the source of existence. It therefore only describes God, as everything else comes into being through him.

Separatist One who is ready to divide off from other Christians, often on grounds which do not involve centrally important beliefs.

Septuagint A translation of the Hebrew Old Testament into Greek.

Servant of the Lord A character who

appears in four poems in the prophecy of Isaiah. In the New Testament, this concept, of a person who would suffer for many, is applied to Jesus.

Shalom (Hebrew for 'peace') The state of being in harmony with God, with the world, with others and within oneself. It is the richest of blessings and close to the New Testament idea of *reconciliation*.

Sin Carries a range of meanings, including breaking God's *Law* falling short of God's intention for human life. Sin includes both specific wrong actions and a condition, a fatal flaw in everything human beings do, even their best endeavours. It is because of our sinfulness, for which we deserve God's *judgment*, that we stand in need of the *salvation* that Jesus has made available. (See *the fall, original sin, total depravity*.)

Situation ethics An approach to *ethics* which gives greatest importance to the situation in which an ethical decision has to be made, rather than to any moral system. It is founded on the belief that the only intrinsically good thing is *love*. It is a healthy corrective against *legalism*, but has an inadequate understanding of God's *Law* as a guide to loving.

Son of God A title given to Jesus Christ, designating him as one who is *pre-existent* and shares the being of God. It is as the Son of God that Christ is spoken of as the second person of the *Trinity*.

Son of man The title Jesus most frequently used of himself. It seems to refer to a prophecy in Daniel about a divine figure who would break in from heaven. This one was widely expected in Jesus' time. The term highlights both Jesus' divinity and his humanity.

Soul In the Bible, this term is used for the whole self or person, body and mind. It does not mean some separate entity which separates from the rest at death. Christian immortality is an aspect of the whole person.

Sovereignty A quality of God denoting his freedom from any kind of outward restraint. He is free to act as he wills, without limitation. But he will only act in accordance with his character, which means that his actions are not arbitrary but reliable and always for the good of his people.

Speaking in tongues (sometimes called 'glossolalia') Using languages unknown to the speaker, usually in praise to God, though sometimes carrying a message to others. When this *gift of the Spirit* is used publicly, there should always be someone who can interpret the meaning. When used privately, its great value seems to be that it can give expression to emotions that are beyond words.

Special grace See *grace*.

Spirit That aspect of a person which can recognize the God-ward dimension and is open to relationship with God. It is therefore the most important part of us and the apostle Paul often contrasts it to *flesh*. (See also *Holy Spirit*.)

Spiritualism The practice of seeking dealings with the spirits of people who have died. It is clearly condemned in the Bible.

Stewardship The relationship in which people stand both to God's *creation* and to their own abilities and possessions. We do not own these things; they remain God's, but we have the responsibility of using and managing them to the best of our ability as stewards.

Substance A technical term used in defining the doctrine of the *trinity*. It means 'being', so that the *Son of God* is 'one in being with the Father'.

Substitute A way of describing the role Jesus fulfilled in his *death*. He died instead of us, who deserved to be separated from God as a result of our *sin*. Because he died, believers can be free of guilt. (See also *representative*.)

Sustainer God as the one who holds the creation in continued being, providing and maintaining all the conditions necessary for life to carry on. This is an important belief, which contrasts with the view that God started the universe off and has left it to its own devices.

Syncretism The combining of different faiths in such a way as to blur their distinctiveness. This is fatal to Christianity, which maintains the centrality of Jesus Christ.

T

Temple The building in Jerusalem which was set apart as the centre of Israel's *worship* and *sacrifices*. First built by Solomon but destroyed when Jerusalem fell to the Babylonians, it was replaced after the Jews returned from exile. In Jesus' time Herod's Temple had been completed, but soon after this too was destroyed by the Romans and no Temple has since been built.

Temptation The pull towards *sin* which all humanity, including Jesus experiences in different ways. To be tempted is not in itself sinful, just human. Sin only comes when a temptation is welcomed and yielded to.

Testament (literally 'covenant') The two testaments together form the *Bible*. The Old Testament covers the period of the *creation* and the first *covenant*, made first with Abraham, renewed with Moses, and struggled with throughout the history of Israel. The New Testament deals with the new covenant, made by Jesus. It describes his life, *death* and *resurrection*, and also covers the life and growth of the *church* in the time of the *apostles*.

Testimony A believer's description of his or her personal experience of the impact of Jesus and the new life he brings. Sensitively used, testimony is an important part of *evangelism*.

Theism Belief in God. Christianity starts with theism and builds from there, giving specific content to theism through God's *revelation* and particularly through the character and teaching of Jesus.

Theodicy A justification of the ways of God, particularly in the face of suffering and other things that make it hard to believe that he is both *omnipotent* and all-loving.

Theology The study of God. Christian theology is not based on speculation about him, but sets itself the task of understanding and interpreting the *revelation* he has made of himself.

Total depravity A technical term, meaning the condition of humanity since the *fall*. It does not mean that everything about us is totally corrupt, but rather that all our qualities and all our endeavours contain a fatal flaw that spoils them and makes them fall short of the best.

Tractarian One of a group of members of the Church of England in the nineteenth century who tried to take that church back beyond the *Reformation* to its *Catholic* heritage. (See *Anglo-catholic*.)

Tradition What is passed on of the faith from generation to generation. Tradition gives Christianity its continuity, but its *authority* is always secondary to the *Bible*.

Transcendent Extending beyond human and earthly limitations and concerns. God is transcendent and always stretches beyond our understanding. But he is also *immanent*, so that his 'otherness' does not make him remote.

Transfiguration The occasion when Jesus appeared to Peter, James and John in his full glory.

Transubstantiation In Catholic belief, the view that the bread and wine in the *mass* miraculously become the actual body and blood of Jesus.

Trinity The threefoldness of God, Father, *Son* and *Holy Spirit*. Within the unity of God, the three *persons* are distinct and function in distinctive ways. This key Christian belief is required by the New Testament evidence that Jesus was the *incarnation* of the eternal God, and that the *Holy Spirit* is divine and personal.

U

Unitarian One who believes that only the Father is God, and that Jesus and the *Holy Spirit* are not divine. It is not a Christian belief.

Universalist One who believes that all humanity will eventually receive *salvation*, even if many have no *faith* in Jesus. This view is based on New Testament teaching that all things will finally be summed up in Jesus Christ, but many believe this does not include those who have rejected him.

V

Virgin birth The belief that Mary conceived and gave birth to Jesus while still a virgin, through the miraculous intervention of the *Holy Spirit*.

Virgin Mary The mother of Jesus. A lady worthy of great honour. In Catholic belief, she has been elevated to a high position and is called upon to intercede with God for believers. (See also *Assumption* and *Immaculate conception*.)

Vocation See *calling*.

W

Western church The church in the western half of the Mediterranean, based on Rome, Latin-speaking. It developed its own form of life under the papacy and its successors are those in the *Catholic* tradition, and the churches of the *Reformation*.

Whitsun See *Pentecost*.

Witness The act of declaring all a believer knows about Jesus Christ and the *gospel*. Although only some Christians have the *ministry* of *evangelism*, all are called to bear witness when opportunity arises.

Word of God (with a capital 'W') A title given to Jesus which points to him as the *revelation* of God, the communication of God to mankind. The idea has an extensive background, both in Jewish and Greek thought. Its Greek form is *logos*.

Word of God (with a small 'w') The *revelation* of God to be found in the *Bible*. Some Christians hold that the Bible *is* the word of God; others that it contains the word of God. (See also *inspiration, revelation*.)

Work of Christ Everything Christ has achieved for humanity, especially in his *death* and *resurrection*.

Worship Bringing praise, thanksgiving and adoration to God as the central part of our service to him. Worship can be individual, but its focus is corporate, when a Christian community comes together. Music, prayer, preaching, the reading of the Bible and sharing in *holy communion* are key aspects of Christian worship. (See also *liturgy*.)

Y

Yahweh (rendered 'Jehovah' in some Bibles) The Hebrew name for God, thought too holy to be spoken in Old Testament times. (See *the Lord*.)

Z

Zealot Member of a Jewish sect in Jesus' time, which tried to overthrow the occupying Romans by force.

Index

This index has been designed to be useful to the reader rather than to be completely exhaustive. A number of themes appear very frequently in the book and these have been indexed only where they are the chief point at issue or where representative treatment is given.

A

B

C

D

E

F

G

Q

R

S

T

U

V

W

Z